THE NOTEBOOKS OF
ROBERT FROST

THE NOTEBOOKS OF
ROBERT FROST

EDITED BY
ROBERT FAGGEN

THE BELKNAP PRESS OF HARVARD UNIVERSITY PRESS
Cambridge, Massachusetts
London, England
2006

Library of Congress Cataloging-in-Publication Data

Frost, Robert, 1874–1963.
    The notebooks of Robert Frost / edited by Robert Faggen.
      p. cm.
    First scholarly edition of notebooks kept by Frost, transcribed and annotated.
    Includes bibliographical references and index.
    ISBN-13: 978-0-674-02311-6 (alk. paper)
    ISBN-10: 0-674-02311-0 (alk. paper)
     1. Frost, Robert, 1874–1963—Notebooks, sketchbooks, etc.
    2. Frost, Robert, 1874–1963—Manuscripts.   I. Faggen, Robert.   II. Title.
    PS3511.R94A6   2006
  818′5203—dc22   2006042992

Contents

Introduction

Robert Frost's poetry has long compelled readers with its clarity, dramatic tension, and vocal presence. Its pleasure arises from the promise of cognitive order—what Frost called "a momentary stay against confusion." His poetry has become to many an alternative to the complexity and despair of modernity.

Yet Frost himself emphasized the ephemeral quality of moral order and often took pleasure in uncertainty and chaos. When Frost spoke of his poetry and of poetics in general, he delighted in being challenging, threatening, and mischievous—as he was in a 1927 letter to his friend Sidney Cox: "My poems—I should suppose everybody's poems—are all set to trip the reader head and foremost into the boundless. Ever since infancy I have had the habit of leaving my blocks carts chairs and such like ordinaries where people would be pretty sure to fall forward over them in the dark. Forward, you understand, *and* in the dark. I may leave my toys in the wrong place and so in vain. It is my intentions we are speaking of—my innate mischievousness."

The analogy between poetry and a child's "ordinaries" shows the delight Frost took in appearing casual and unassuming to the unsuspecting reader. But the extraordinary use of "ordinary" as a noun also resonates with older meanings of the word. "Ordinaries" were ecclesiastical figures of authority and guidance, as well as devotional texts and manuals containing instructions and *sententiae* for the conduct of life. Those of us raised reading "The Road Not Taken," "Stopping by Woods on a Snowy Evening," and "Birches" know how readily Frost's poems can become guidebooks for the spirit of individualism, at least until one encounters the quirkiness of the guide-narrator of the poem "Directive," "who only has at heart your getting lost."

The more than forty notebooks Frost left behind are in all of these senses "ordinaries," unassuming dime-store spiral pads and school theme books, teeming with terse thoughts about life, literature, philosophy, religion, politics, and science. The mixture of phrases, sayings, meditations, stories, topical lists, dialogues, teaching notes, and drafts of poems provides a rich if chaotic map of Frost's fields of mental play. The reader of the notebooks confronts a combination of candor and cryptic evasion, the same kind of paradox we find Frost expressing when he told a friend, "I have written to keep the curious out of the secret places of my mind both in my verse and in my letters to such as you." Frost's notebooks do not reveal the "secret places" of his mind, if by that one means personal, confessional, and, perhaps, lurid psychological agonies and revelations. Neither journal nor diary would be an appropriate term to describe the notebook writing that began long before he became famous. The energy and immediacy of Frost's style of thought tumble over each other in a manner that seems impatient of narrative.

The notebooks allow us to see is Frost at work in all aspects of his role as writer—as teacher, lecturer, essayist, and poet. They often reveal the larger scope of preoccupations only mentioned or obliquely suggested in the poems, and they survive as the remains of a chaotic laboratory in which many of his inventions went through constant experimentation and trial.

Though the notebooks embrace a wide variety of forms, fragmentary notations and suggestively epigrammatic meditations predominate. The notebooks have some of the quality of the highly compressed and resonant fragments of Heraclitus, in addition to the proverbial power of the "Sayings of the Spartans." Aristotle and Quintilian's view that enthymeme and figurative sayings were strategic instruments for instruction and learning impressed the classically trained and rhetorically astute Frost. The notebooks might also give additional weight to Kenneth Burke's question, "Could the most complex and sophisticated works of art legitimately be considered somewhat as 'proverbs writ large'?" In keeping with modern revivals of the aphoristic philosophical tradition, Frost's notebooks have the probing qualities of Pascal's *Pensées* and the wit of Lichtenberg's "Waste Books." Frost's notebooks, like Pascal's and Lichtenberg's, refuse easy editorial arrangement as extended, logical arguments, but that does little to diminish their inspired intensity or the focus of their thought. Lichtenberg called his notebooks "The Waste Books," a term used by English business houses to designate ledgers in which transactions were entered as they occurred before they were recorded in more formal account books. (It is worth noting that Isaac Newton also called his notebooks "Waste Books.")

Lichtenberg's waste metaphor may also be appropriate for Frost's notebooks, where we see the poet trying out thoughts and ideas, poems, and essays without the ordering and framing demanded by publication. But "waste" was something in which Frost rejoiced as a necessary expense of creation, its glory rather than its detritus; for, as he wrote in "A Pod of the Milkweed," "waste was of the essence of the scheme." Frost found the epigrammatic and proverbial utterance emerging from fragile and flawed observations more likely to inspire a movement from belief to action than extended forms of logic: "Carry the world by storm of belief. Get the belief stated just enough (and not too much) for acting on. A kind of built up narrative answers purpose best. It stays alive longest and has to be blundered into shape out of all sorts of picked up human fragments and mistakes observations. Nothing matters if what it figures is right to live by" (24.22r). Readers may find the lack of punctuation in the phrase "human fragments and mistakes observations" either confusing or provocative, and no attempt in this edition has been made at silent corrections for the sake of an artificial clarity. Frost penned thousands of observations in his notebooks that do not deserve the violence of an arbitrary arrangement or system, no matter how much the entries drive toward truth. The notebooks reveal Frost's interest in the freshness and renewal of thought and language rather than in finalities:

> So I have found that for my own survival I had to have phrases of salvation if I was to keep anything worth keeping.
> Truth what is truth? said Pilate and we know not and no search can make us know, said someone else. But I said can't we know? We can know well enough to go on with being tried every day in our courage to tell it. What is truth? Truth is that that takes fresh courage to tell it. It takes all our best skill too. (31.40r)

The entries should be taken less as notes toward a supreme fiction than as notes about the nature of supreme fictions, and ways to resist them. They are Frost's scraps of palliative reason to get on with in a world of broken knowledge.

Robert Frost kept notebooks for more than six decades, from the 1890s to the 1960s; that so many of them survive is, in itself, evidence that he wanted them to survive. He was usually careful, if not eager, to destroy manuscripts he did not want published. For example, his Norton Lectures at Harvard, which were invited with the intention of later publication, remain unpublished because the only known transcript disappeared in Frost's possession. Yet within these notebooks there are numerous references to the titles and reported themes of those lectures. Though Frost would make holograph copies of some of his more notable lyrics to give to friends, relatively few drafts of his major published poetry remain. Evidence suggests that Frost drafted the poems in the same or similar notebooks to the ones presented here, tore out the pages he wanted transcribed, and then destroyed early drafts. But trial lines and early drafts of a number of poems can be found in the surviving notebooks.

In spite of or because of his self-consciousness, Frost not only kept a number of notebooks over the years, he occasionally donated them to libraries and endorsed their preservation. Frost clearly preserved notebooks and note-

[original dimensions 7-¾ x 10 inches]
"Nature is a chaos . . ." Notebook 4, p. 25r.
Rauner Special Collections Library, Dartmouth College.

book pages that he had drafted years, if not decades, earlier, and these reveal that Frost continued to draw on the thinking in them throughout a lifetime of writing. One of the notebook leaves in the Barrett collection at the University of Virginia contains Frost's own headnote: "This is as old as the Derry Days You can see from it where one idea started R.F. 1951." Two notebooks circa 1912 and earlier were given by Frost to Robert Newdick, his first biographer, with the teasing inscription "For R.N. to Keep and get what he can out of by ingenious inference. R.F. 1935." Frost donated several other notebooks from the turn of the century to the University of Virginia Library. Other notebooks remained in his possession. Kathleen Morrison, his secretary for the last two decades of his life, donated them to the Dartmouth College Library after his death, with some idea that they would be mined by scholars and eventually published.

Morrison herself observed the way Frost worked in the notebooks. "A visitor to Frost during his later years, either in his study on Brewster Street, in Cambridge, or at the cabin on the Homer Noble Farm in Ripton, Vermont, might find him stretched out in his armchair, homemade lapboard on his knee, his feet surrounded by a clutter of notebooks. Nearby on the floor would lie a small, well-worn, brown leather satchel half-opened, showing more notebooks and many sheets of paper covered by handwriting." She also observed that "They [the notebooks] were his constant companions such that he took one with him wherever he traveled."* As physical presences, they take a variety of forms including five-cent spiral flip pads and date books (with few appointments recorded) small enough to fit in a shirt pocket. Some are ruled school theme books, others are spiral bound loose-leaf books. And then there are simply solitary sheets of paper, some of them torn out from the notepads and the loose-leaf books.

The notebooks reveal much about the style as well as the substance of Frost's thinking. In this edition, they are arranged in chronological order. But this arrangement is slightly misleading, and most of the assigned dates are approximate. Though it is possible to date a number of notebooks based on calendars or dates printed inside the covers, or from Frost's infrequent historical allusions, it is not clear that the entries, even if begun in a particular year, follow each other in sequence. Frost's thoughts often flowed with no discernable logic, and the silences, interstices, and leaps make reading the notebooks an imaginative challenge. In a notebook of about 1913, he paid such a compliment to Bergson's style of thought: "Bergson's is a literary philosophy because it uses for everything the idea of every sentence being a fresh start not a mere logical derivation from the last sentence" (9.4r). Though the content indicates that a cluster of entries were made in close sequence, changes and addition in different color inks or pencil as well as alteration in handwriting sometimes imply long intervals. One of Frost's largest surviving

---

* Kathleen Johnston Morrison, "Introduction" to *Prose Jottings of Robert Frost*, edited by Edward Connery Lathem and Hyde Cox (Northeast Kingdom Publishers: Vermont, 1982), ix–x.

notebooks contains an end page with a small fern still pressed onto it. Next to the fern, Frost appears to have written the place and date of the first entries in the notebook, and then continued to mark the dates of his writing in the notebook over several decades. Evidence from the style of handwriting suggests that certain notebooks were completed from beginning to end within a short span of time, but often Frost seemed continually to weave back and forth among entries and thoughts over considerable stretches of time (53r):

> Lake Willoughby 1909
>> Been in it ever since
>
> 1949
> 1938

Frost's mind ranges widely in the notebooks. Little in them can be characterized as quotidian or banal. The parallels in Frost's thinking about aesthetics, politics, religion, science, and poetry are evident. Passages, for example, of his 1959 "Future of Man" essay on science and culture appear as verse in one notebook among verse trials for the thematically related poem "Pod of the Milkweed." Numerous dialogues and sketches for plays reveal the extent of Frost's love of drama and its importance in his imagination and development as a lyric poet. Paragraph-long meditations, drafts of unpublished essays, and notes related to talks and lectures intermingle with lists of stories, topics, phrases, and epigrams, and among aphorisms and proverbs often in seeming isolation but with subtle connections to each other.

Little in the way of commentary on historical events is to be found, but World War I, the New Deal, and the Cold War receive more specific attention. The notebooks from the late 1920s on reveal Frost's increasing political preoccupations. There are numerous comments about Eleanor and Franklin Roosevelt and, in reaction to the New Deal, comments on poverty, virtue, utopia, and democracy. Several notebooks take on a thematic unity, as in the case of one theme book bearing the inscription "Democracy" on the cover, with the intriguing subtitle "Disappointed in the Ocean." In other notebooks, among the many meditations, are notes for a poem or talk entitled "History of the United States," and the entry after that phrase is "the land was ours before we were the lands," which became the first line of "The Gift Outright." Trial lines for the poems "Does No One Ever Feel This Way in the Least" and "America Is Hard to See" mingle with thoughts on the relations of justice and mercy, and notes for a talk and an essay entitled "What became of New England." Many notebooks over the years contain short or extended meditations on the United States, the Puritans, and democracy, including a compressed observation on the founding: "Jefferson and others painted the Constitution. Washington sat for it" (29.10r).

Frost's notebooks may be more true to his thinking than his public lectures; the notebooks became a preferred venue because they provided a more fluid forum in which he could work. "I'm terrible about my lectures," he wrote to a friend, "In my anxiety to keep them from becoming part of my literary life, I leave them rolling around in my head like clouds rolling around in the sky." Frost resisted having his talks become definitive "lectures," just as he always would insist on "saying" a poem rather than "reading" it: the possibilities of meaning were always left to fresh development, if only in tone. The image of poems and thoughts developing as forms out of "rolling clouds" underlies his vision of individual creation in his "Letter to *The Amherst Student,*" which was itself developed and drafted in the notebooks:

> We people are thrust forward out of the suggestions of form in the rolling clouds of nature. In us nature reaches its height of form and exceeds itself. When in doubt there is always form to go on with. Anyone who has achieved the least form to be sure of it, is lost to the larger excruciations. I think it must stroke faith the right way. The artist, the poet might be expected to be the most aware of such assurance. But it is really everybody's sanity to feel it and live by it. Fortunately, too, no forms are more engrossing, gratifying, comforting, staying than those lesser ones we throw off, like vortex rings of smoke, all our individual enterprise needing nobody's cooperation; a basket, a letter, a garden, a room, an idea, a picture, a poem.

For Frost poetry was "the will braving alien entanglements" and creating modest stays against annihilating chaos. In the same letter to *The Amherst Student* he underscored the terror of creating amidst a grand chaos: the "background is hugeness and confusion shading away from where we stand into black and utter chaos; and against the background any small man-made figure of order and concentration. What pleasanter than that this should be so?" Clearly he took delight in the terror. It is precisely that grim "hugeness" that gives satisfaction to the relative smallness of our creations: "Anything I lay upon it is as velvet, as the saying goes." The notebooks give an even better representation of this mythology than do Frost's poems.

Frost's vision of the small utterance against the chaos looks forward to Czeslaw Milosz's resolution, stated in one prose poem, to express himself in single sentence: "To find my home in one sentence, concise as if hammered in metal . . . An unnamed need for order, for rhythm, for form, which three words are opposed to chaos and nothingness." Frost was hardly the first

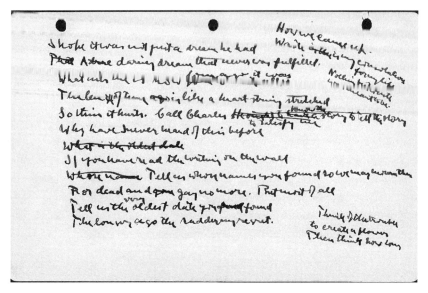

[original dimensions 6-½ x 9 inches]
"I hope it was not just a dream he had . . ." Notebook 5, p. 12r.
Rauner Special Collections Library, Dartmouth College.

champion of the aphorism, and he knew well how brilliantly thinkers as different as Bacon, Pascal, and Nietzsche used the aphorism or fragment as the most appropriate instrument in a world of broken knowledge. Of course, he was also deep in Emerson, who had mastered its use in the essay. Both Frost and Milosz seem to point backward to Herman Melville's praise of Solomon's aphoristic wisdom as "the fine-hammered steel of woe." For Melville, the author of the encyclopedic *Moby-Dick,* and Milosz, the author of such expansive collage-like poems as "The Separate Notebooks" or "The Rising of the Sun," the concision of the solitary, wise sentence ultimately became an elusive goal. Frost championed the epigrammatic phrase but also recognized, as his notebooks suggest, that "poetry is that which defies organization." Taken as a whole, Frost's notebooks resemble more the modernist collages of T. S. Eliot or of Ezra Pound than his own published poetry.

At one point in *A Masque of Reason,* Frost's imagined "forty-third chapter" to the Book of Job centuries later, Job proclaims that although "we don't where we are, or who we are," there is still a recognition that "we know well enough to go ahead with. / I mean we seem to know enough to act on." And what *do* we act on? Perhaps we have only what Job's wife calls "lots of unsystematic stray scraps of palliative reason." This has precedent in the kind of fragmented, uncertain knowledge that Francis Bacon wrote of in the beginning of *The Advancement of Learning,* warning that "the contemplation of God's creatures and works produceth (having regard to the works and creatures themselves) knowledge, but having regard to God, no perfect knowledge, but wonder which is broken knowledge" (I.1.3). Bacon's sense of "broken knowledge" has something in common with Frost's aphoristic "scraps of palliative reason." For Bacon, "aphorisms, representing a knowledge broken, do invite men to inquire further; whereas methods, carrying the show of the total, do secure men, as if they were farthest"(II.17.7). Frost, even more than Bacon, seems to take great pleasure in the further inquiry and the pleasantness of tackling the surrounding hugeness and confusion.

The aphoristic style of writing in the notebooks can be seen as an outgrowth of Frost's lifelong work as a teacher. Though Frost lectured to large university audiences in his later years, his teaching began in small secondary schools at the turn of the last century, more than a decade before the publication of his first book, and a great deal of the material in the notebooks appears to grow out of his classroom experiences. From 1906 to 1911 Frost taught English at Pinkerton Academy in Derry, and then psychology at Plymouth Normal School, before moving his family to England in 1912. A notebook he kept the year he taught at Plymouth provides a list of 190 numbered topics suggesting his engagement with the philosophical and psychological work of Charles Darwin, Henri Bergson, Hugo Munsterberg, Herbert Spencer, and William James. Notebooks from the 1920s, 1930s, and 1940s reveal yet more about the intersection of his teaching and poetry as he occupied positions at Amherst, the University of Michigan, Harvard, and Dartmouth. In a 1924 letter to Louis Untermeyer, Frost described teaching two courses at Amherst while wrestling with progressive attitudes toward education and the psychology of thinking. His comments display some of Frost's characteristic drift between playful amusement and seriousness:

> They [the students] fancied themselves as thinkers. At Amherst you *thought,* while at other colleges you merely *learned* . . . I found that by thinking they meant stocking up with radical ideas, by learning they meant stocking up with conservative ideas—a harmless distinction, bless their simple hearts. I really liked them . . . They had picked up the idea somewhere that the time was past for the teacher to teach the pupil. From now on it was the thing for the pupil to teach himself using, as he saw fit, the teacher for instrument. The understanding was that my leg was always on

the table for anyone to seize me by that thought he could swing me as an instrument to teach himself with. So we had an amusing year I should have had my picture taken just as I sat there patiently waiting, waiting for the youth to take education into their own hands and start the new world. Sometimes I laughed and sometimes I cried a little internally, I gave one course in reading and one course in philosophy, but they both came to the same thing. I was determined to have it out with my youngsters and betters as to what thinking really was. We reached an agreement that most of what they regarded as thinking, their own and other peoples, was nothing but voting—taking sides on an issue they had nothing to do with laying down. But not on that account did we despair. We went bravely to work to discover, not only if we couldn't have ideas, but if we hadn't had them, a few of them, at least, without knowing it.

Frost kept a notebook of the questions he posed to students and the books read in class. It also maps the way he continued to think about what constitutes originality in ideas and the relationships between thought and action. Many of these topics were informed, no doubt, by his years as a special student at Harvard, studying under or reading the works of Josiah Royce, George Santayana, and William James. From the entries, one detects that words and deeds were inextricably connected in Frost's mind, and that the only truths were those which were ratified as deeds. There are numerous meditations on the circularity of thought, and on the relationship between the will, representation, and truth. One entry about Schopenhauer suggests that Frost's method of considering a philosophical position was to brood extensively on its fundamental metaphors: "At least a year on the book's name on the spine before reading the book. The World as Will" (4.15r).

Frost used *think* as a noun. The process of creating an aphorism was a "think," underscoring the relationship between thought and the process of thinking. In "A Lover's Quarrel," a documentary film of 1957 about the poet's life, Frost recounts to a group of Sarah Lawrence students a discussion he had earlier in the day while touring the U.S. Navy ship *Essex:*

> They were with me today on the Essex—the old carrier. Old subject, peace and war. I had to have another think at it. That always means another way to say it. I said to him, "Peace you only have through war or threat of war," and he nodded grimly. Anything like that bothers me all the time, I say a new one to it. The occasion had given me a fresh think. There's usually an occasion meeting somebody, reading something in the paper, hear-

ing something about the world. It's all just this one thing, a *think,* and the excitement you get of having a think that you want to pass to other people.*

This particular "think" on peace and war has some of the qualities of pithiness, wit, and paradox, characteristic of both proverb and aphorism. It could almost be a variation on an epigram he wrote in a letter to F. S. Flint in 1916: "Have I let myself be too nasty to some of my contemporaries. War is war and sometimes I think peace is too. Damn there goes an epigramn [*sic*]." Frost's humorous recognition of his own aphoristic tendencies is more than confirmed in the notebooks. He filled them with such "thinks," renewals of language in an ongoing dialogue with himself and imaginary others.

From some of the earliest surviving notebook pages, circa 1900 at the Derry Farm in New Hampshire, we see Frost's preoccupation with the relationship of metaphor, poetry, and thought. Frost was concerned about the role of metaphor in all thinking, about the cultural presence of metaphor, and about the transformation of metaphors into ideas in poetry:

Metaphor May not be far but it is our farthest forth.
Only accumulations of ages. (3.1r)

Half a century later, in the early 1950s, Frost penned the entry: "Poetry is the dawning of an idea" (38.5r). Frost was clearly concerned with how one thinks in poetry, and whether or not it is appropriate to speak of ideas in poetry. In an early notebook, one entry provides a teacher's skeptical challenge to his students, if not to himself: "What is an idea? How many on the page? Put your finger on the ideas on the page. On one page in your own writing. An idea that you can call your own" (8.21r). In another notebook, however, he gives a far less skeptical, though complex, assertion of the relationship of poetry and ideas: "A poem is the act of having an idea and how it feels to have an idea" (4.36r). Frost's meditations on thought, metaphor, and poetry would produce over the course of decades a grand fugue without resolution.

The notebooks are replete with memorable figurative sayings, and these provide an interpretive temptation similar to that of the poems. They are both a delight and a hazard as readers excerpt and quote them as endpoints rather than momentary stays in Frost's ever-shifting Frost's thinking. Of course, that kind of plucking is a risk a reader takes in the interpretation of

---

* I am very grateful to John Ridland for calling my attention to this remarkable statement.

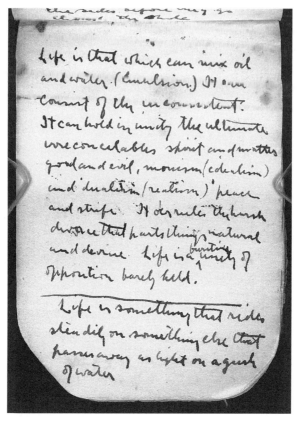

[original dimensions 4-⅛ x 2-¾ inches]
"Life is that which can mix oil and water . . ." Notebook 8, p. 58r.
Clifton Waller Barrett Library of American Literature, University of Virginia.

almost any rhetorically skilled writer. But in Frost's case, the power and lure of his aphorisms has made him both one of the most remembered and yet widely misapprehended of modern poets. Frost found the aphoristic and proverbial style a compelling tradition of wisdom literature. Often in his notebooks, as in some of his talks, he would raise the question of the relationship of wisdom to literature with such questions or comments as "Does Wisdom Matter" (which became a favorite topic for his public lectures, talks, and conversations), or "I would rather be wise than artistic." One extended meditation in the notebooks bears the title "Religion, Science, and Gossip." While there is little of what one would ordinarily call gossip in any of the notebooks, "gossip" in Frost's mind turns out to be another word for wisdom. As he considers the difference between philosophy and wisdom, Frost also wonders whether the "wise sayings" of a culture should or should not be widely disseminated. Impressed by Plato's account in the *Protagoras* of the way Spartans expelled strangers when their wise men spoke, Frost perhaps perceived an analogy to Jesus' justification for speaking in parables: "How like Marks saying Christians in their exclusiveness must talk in parable so the wrong people wont understand them and so get saved" (43.4r). Readers will, no doubt, note the connection here to the notorious passage in Frost's "Directive":

> I have kept hidden in the instep arch
> Of an old cedar at the waterside
> A broken drinking goblet like the Grail
> Under a spell so the wrong ones can't find it,
> So can't get saved, as Saint Mark says they mustn't.

It may not be easy to square Frost's somewhat detached observation of Mark with the tone of the narrator of "Directive," though the notebooks reveal the extent of his preoccupation with the genesis and nature of secrecy, and with the persuasive power of proverbial sayings.

As Frost pursues his meditation on "gossip," he makes casual reference to another ancient wise saying, "Good fences make good neighbors." This line in "Mending Wall" is usually quoted as Frost's invention, although in these notebooks he says otherwise. The poem's famous competing maxim, "Something there is that doesn't love a wall" is usually quoted without reference to the other line. Both those sayings play off of a remarkable proverb in an earlier poem "The Tuft of Flowers": Men work together I tell him from the heart / Whether they work together or apart. And, of course, this couplet should be considered in the light of a variation earlier in the poem "'As all must be [alone],' I said within my heart / 'Whether they work together or apart.'" Every aphorism in Frost needs to be seen in light of many others. What the notebooks show is that his elaborate counterpoint among aphorisms was an essential quality of his mind. For example, Frost's poetic "thinks" about labor must also include "The fact is the sweetest dream that labor knows," from "Mowing," as well as "Three foggy mornings and one rainy day / Will rot the best birch fence a man can build," spoken by the husband in "Home Burial."

For Frost, aphorisms and sayings define boundaries and havens. "The Death of the Hired Man" contains aphorisms in dialogue as the poem's characters Mary and Warren debate the meaning of home:

'Home is the place where, when you have to go there,
They have to take you in.'
                              'I should have called it
Something you somehow haven't to deserve.'

From its etymology, an aphorism is a definition of boundary or horizon, and Frost's aphorisms seem to be preoccupied with defining thresholds and limits. "All life is cellular physically and socially," he wrote in one notebook (21.2r) and echoed with significant variations in many others.

This preoccupation haunts the notebooks. In two solitary entries in separate notebooks (24.46v, 25.1r) the phrase "Oh please let me flourish" appears, perhaps as a trial line, perhaps as an invocation to an unknown muse. But the entry takes on greater meaning when read in light of two other solitary entries from two different earlier notebooks: "To flourish is to play" (24.46v) and "To flourish is to become dangerous" (12.11r). These lines taken together may seem contradictory and paradoxical, and taken as an evolution of his thinking may seem demanding and enigmatic. But they are not entirely obscure.

In a 1961 reading at Yale, Frost spoke contemptuously of obscurity, but upheld the power of "dark sayings": "Some people don't know the difference between obscurity and what are called in ancient times 'dark sayings,' that you go deeper, darker in your life. But obscurity isn't that. Obscurity is a cover for nothing. You go looking for it and it comes out 'A stitch in time saves nine.' But there are dark sayings." A "dark saying," as Frost well knew, was the ancient Hebraic phrase for a proverb, and it appears in both Proverbs and Psalms. The Hebrew word for proverb was *mashal,* which meant "coupling"—in other words an association of ideas demanding considerable thought and interpretation. Frost reminded his audience that the power and validity of "dark sayings" was neither their inherent gloominess nor their opacity, but their power to inspire continued thought. In this sense, he was well in line with Nietzsche's defense of the aphoristic style of *Thus Spoke Zarathustra:* "An aphorism, properly stamped and molded, has not been 'deciphered' when it has simply been read; rather, one has then to begin in *exegesis,* for which is required an art of exegesis."

The pairing of thoughts is inherent to both metaphor and proverb. It can also produce meaning through paradox and contradiction, and Frost's notebooks reveal how much he enjoyed going by contraries. One notebook (4) contains several variations on a proverb about courage: "Greatest of all virtues is courage. Saddest thing that this should be so." A version of this appears as a crucial line in "A Masque of Mercy": "The saddest thing in life / Is

[original dimensions 4-⅛ x 6 inches]
"The philosopher says dismiss the idea of purpose . . ." Notebook 21, p. 4r.
Rauner Special Collections Library, Dartmouth College.

that the best thing in it should be courage." Numerous notebook entries address the conflict and paradox of justice and mercy, and the paradoxes of virtue receive epigrammatic treatment in fragments on Milton, written during the Derry years: "The only free man is the abject slave of virtue" (3.1r). Frost came to see the couplet as "the pleasant symbol of coupling," a formal metaphor for the yoking of thematic contradictions. But these "couplings" were often more tense than pleasant, as in the poem "From Iron": "Nature within her inmost self divides / To trouble men with having to take sides."

Frost's observations suggest that contradiction and conflict are the conditions of existence. A notebook kept largely during his few years in England, 1912–1914, contains a number of notable entries about opposites:

> Life is that which can mix oil and water (Emulsion). It can consist of the inconsistent. It can hold in unity the ultimate irreconcilables spirit and matter good and evil, monism (idealism) and dualism (realism) peace and strife. It over rules the harsh divorce that parts things natural and divine. Life is a bursting unity of opposition barely held. (8.58r)

This rich entry can help interpret and be interpreted in light of another entry occurring on a subsequent page in the same notebook:

> All a man's art is a bursting unity of opposites. Christs message almost
> tears itself apart with its great contradictions. (8.58v)

Christianity and the Sermon on the Mount, in particular, receive considerable
thought in a number of notebooks, including extensive entries for a series of
talks he gave on religion and Christianity gathered under the heading "Our
Darkest Concern." His sense of the fundamental importance of contradiction extends from art and religion to politics:

> A nation should be just as full of conflict as it can contain, physically, men-
> tally, financially. But of course it must contain. The strain must be short of
> the bursting point—just short. The citizen must love his enemy within
> more than he loves his enemy without . . . (29.23r)

In all three entries, the potential violence suggested by "bursting" reveals an
important aspect of Frost's thinking: Wisdom literature, particularly of the
Hebrew Bible, was a rebuke to the Deuteronomic world of law and national
covenant. Frost's love of the proverb became symbolic of his particular approach to the contradictions of individual freedom within the constraints of
social and national identity.

Contradiction in Frost rarely yields resolution, and Frost's notebooks reveal his generally skeptical attitude toward dialectics:

> Opposite of Civilization{Barbarism
>   Utopia
> Hegel taught doctrine of opposites, but said nothing about everything's
> having more than one opposite. (4.42r)

"Coupling" for Frost may be at best a euphemism for the precarious and po-
tentially vertiginous movement in his thinking. The following lines emerge in
the midst of a prose entry, giving form to his consideration of the balance of
internal and external forces in the human psyche (24.4r):

> Outward in space to Beyondness
> Backward in time to Beyondness
> How much does such Beyondness
> Come inward to affect our lives?

A similar rhythm describing thought occurs in "To a Thinker," and we can
see that cryptic utterances in the notebooks may become less so as we read
them in the context of each other, and of the poems:

From form to content and back to form,
From norm to crazy and back to norm.
From bound to free and back to bound,
From sound to sense and back to sound.
So back and forth. It almost scares
A man the way things come in pairs.

One of the "pairs" Frost revisits most frequently in the notebooks is that of "sound and sense." Most of Frost's theory about the "sound of sense" has been quoted from his published letters, but the notebooks provide his most extensive and trenchant comments on this elusive and controversial subject. Entries on this topic include short phrases such as "Writing down the voice" or "Realism of the voice," as well as remarkable meditations of several pages' length in which he develops his views. Frost connected vocal intonation to questions of artistic originality and reproduction, transcendence and spiritual incarnation, subject matter and form. A few entries from several different notebooks reveal just how complex and possibly contradictory Frost's thoughts about these subjects could become:

> The sound is everything. The best means of achieving it our vowels consonants accent meter but the best of all for variety is meaning. Great thoughts are of value as they supply profound tones. (24.28v)

But one may well wonder whether this comment is confirmed, modified or contradicted by another entry:

> Form is only the last refinement of subject matter. (29.3r)

Or by another:

> A poem must be a statement susceptible of being reduced to an argument as the old fashioned word is. But it may not be a dogged statement. (4.28r)

Or by this comment at the beginning of an entry of several pages on sound in poetry:

> Last refinement of subject matter vocal imagination Vocal Imagination as Subject Matter (44.1r)

The nuanced variations on a theme make Frost's notebooks a fine example of Walter Pater's view that "it is only the roughness of the eye that makes any two persons, things, situations, seem alike." These writings demand the

The old Latin Greek philosophy history
was really vocational for a large part of
the students, they who were to be preachers and
teachers.

. Latin Poetry
Worldly not scholarly
Number of words left natural in accent
Indifferently Latin of any period. Purity
    no consideration   (I have just learned
(January 31 1950) that the earlier Latin poetry
was not quantitative but accentual like our
    Intent concentration on the intention dims
and distorts everything not in the center of vision
Deliberate distortion is an attempt to treat
the not central as central.   You can only be
strictly true to one thing at a time.

    All art begins in pleasure and whatever
wisdom it may or may not wind up in. The
wisdom may be left to your keepers, your friends
and relatives to provide. You can trust them to
keep you from falling off a roof or getting in jail.
Art is the last of your childhood and may be followed
somewhat irresponsibly. An artist will say
a lot of wise things anyway without trying to
be wise.

28

[original dimensions 6 x 9-½ inches]
"The old Latin Greek philosophy history . . ." Notebook 22, p. 28v.
Rauner Special Collections Library, Dartmouth College.

reader circulate among them, giving permission to allow many different thoughts to modify any preconceived order. We find Frost in the notebooks developing his own philosophy of circulation:

> No logic runs away into nothingness. The mind of man is an unvicious circle that no desperation can break through. Knowledge is the same. We get a slight hold on our first poem the better to understand our second, the better to understand our third and so on until we are back with all our experience of poetry on a day the better to understand our first poem. (22.17)

But even such a portrayal of the pleasures of merely circulating needs to be read in terms of additional variations on the theme, including this one about "vicious circles" of learning:

> Space is circular? In vain produced all rays return? Time is circular. The furthest now is on the opposite side of the circle of time to that on which we stand. I believe if space looks circular and time too it is because thought is circular. There is no reasoning so straight that it is not ultimately when followed out a vicious circle. Learning is a vicious circle certainly forever returning on itself. We learn A by which to learn B by which to learn D by which to learn A again and so on round and round. (22.17r)

This passage alludes to Frost's interests in Aristotle, Zeno, Emerson, Darwin, and Einstein and illuminates in many aspects other passages in his writing. Often one finds less circularity than centrifugal force in the movement from notebook entry to entry.

Because the notebooks, for the most part, do not provide drafts of his published poems, we have only a few demonstrations of his method of composition. He would claim that his poems came to him rather quickly, and that he tended to work over details only once the poem was on the page. The notebooks do, however, provide insight into the metaphors and the poetic ideas that became poems. Entries from a notebook written in 1915–1917 are particularly striking when considered with one of his great georgics, "The Grindstone": "Nothing but a grindstone—puts the universe in its place" (19.5r). A few entries later on the same page we find: "When we face the universe confronts itself. We are like the two ends of a straight line that in infinity is a circle. We are its extremes meeting" (19.5r). If Frost's pastoral and georgic poems seem unassuming and muted in their cosmological preoccupations, the notebooks allows us to see their intent and scope with greater clarity. In the same notebook, we find another aphoristic vision: "Life is something that rides steadily on something else that passes away as light on a gush of water"

(8.58r). Written at least a decade before the publication of "West-Running Brook," the metaphors suggest the development of that poem's governing metaphor.

Many of the entries, though terse, are far less cryptic and at times stunningly frank about language, class, and race. The notebook entries reveal the boldness of Frost's thought and his particularly irreverent attitude toward European literary and intellectual traditions. One entry from the early 1920s demonstrates the intensity of Frost's contempt for an American literary language too attached to its European roots:

> I must have registered the pious wish I wished in 1915 when the Germans were being execrated for having destroyed Reims Cathedral. I wished they could with one shell blow Shakespeare out of the English language. The past overawes us too much in art. If America has any advantage of Europe it is in being less clogged with the productions of art. We aren't in the same danger of seeing anywhere around us already done the thing we were just about to do. That's why I think America was invented not discovered to give us a chance to extricate ourselves from what we had materialized out of our minds and natures. Our most precious heritage is what we haven't in our possession—what we haven't made and so have still to make. (13.3r–3v)

One could comment on many remarkable aspects of this entry, including its assertion of the importance of art in establishing a unique national identity. Its language also provides a greater understanding of the origins and meaning of "The Gift Outright," which Frost would write almost two decades later.

Still, the reader needs to remain on guard against the seductive and authoritative finality of certain entries. One notebook begins with what could be a useful warning description of much of Frost's writing: "These are not monologues but my part in a conversation in which the other part of an ongoing drama is more or less implied." An entry may be Frost's momentary dramatizing of a particular position, just one voice among an array of conflicting voices. The hundreds of entries Frost made in his notebooks over the decades leave plenty of room to speculate on what kinds of internal and external dialogues produced them. Such speculation no doubt will alter the way we think about many of the poems. Consider one little poem Frost published, entitled "Pertinax":

> Let chaos storm!
> Let cloud shapes swarm!
> I wait for form.

This could (and has) been taken as a rather straightforward representation of Frost's faith in order triumphing over chaos. Indeed the title has usually been taken as the Latin word *pertinax,* which means persistent or stubborn. The notebooks reveal, however, that Frost had a strong interest in the historical figure of Pertinax, which would suggest something considerably more complex about both the poem and Frost's sense of the relationship of order and chaos. One notebook contains a dialogue of a dozen pages between Pertinax, who rose to become Roman emperor only to be murdered 87 days later, and his consul Didius Julianus, who followed him as Roman emperor and also lasted only a few months, as they debate politics, economics, and the fragility of order. The opening lines establish the conflict between the characters:

> Do you believe in signs
> The only signs I believe in are the first steps taken in carrying out an idea.
> (35.IV)

The notebooks are the first steps taken, and they show the extent not only of Frost's more than passing interest in such fleeting tragic figures as Pertinax, but also just how many steps the poet himself would in time take in carrying out his ideas and his search for order and form.

Editorial Procedures

This edition provides a modified facsimile transcription of all the known notebooks of Robert Frost. The existence of a significant number of loose pages, none of which appear to fit in the intact notebooks (and not all of which are sheets from notebooks), suggests, of course, that Frost kept more notebooks than those we have. Transcriptions of those loose pages, no less substantial in content than those found in the notebooks, are also provided here. In addition to bound notebooks, I have included transcriptions of several sets of unbound notes, including several sheets from the Derry Farm era, and three sets of notes on such topics as "religion, science, and gossip," "the monotony of sentence sounds," and "the Puritans." Within the notebooks, one often finds Frost working up talks and short essays. No typescripts or drafts of essays in preparation for publication have been included.

Nothing in Frost's hand has been excluded or deleted from the notebooks. No modifications have been made to Frost's spelling or to his punctuation. His strikethroughs have been preserved and indications have been made in footnotes about whether phrases were written above or, in some instances, below the line. Frost himself is famous for saying "Poetry is what is lost in translation." Of course, something is lost in transcription. Though I have indicated when Frost changed from blue to black ink or from ink to pencil, there are degrees of darkness, relative size of words and phrases, and various other nuances that would be nearly impossible to convey without very cumbersome apparatus. The major feature of the original notebooks that it has not been practical to preserve is the line breaks of Frost's entries, because there are often only a few words per line. Line breaks have been retained, however, as have other spatial arrangements on the page when they are clearly part of Frost's emphasis and meaning or when he is writing verse.

Textual and formatting matters have been confined to footnotes. Endnotes are explanatory and attempt to identify Frost's references but do not engage in interpretive debates. A number of phrases and words which resonate throughout the notebooks and also in Frost's poetry and some of his essays and letters are cross-referenced for the reader's convenience.

The notebooks are arranged as best as possible in chronological order from the earliest entry. This creates some anomalies. The first notebook, for example, is filled with drafts of poems likely to have been written in the 1950s. However, it also contains the draft of a poem Frost wrote in the 1890s, the oldest entry in any of the notebooks. Because of that single entry, the notebook earns its place as first in this volume. Frost himself indicates in Notebook 4 that he first started making entries in the book in 1909; however, it appears that the majority of the entries may be from the late 1930s on. So, the notebook appears early in the chronology but its content belongs mostly to material found in later notebooks. There are several other instances, in addition to Notebook 4, such as the Derry Note Leaves and the notebooks Frost sent to his first biographer Robert Newdick, in which Frost himself indicates when he may have made the first entries in the notebook. Otherwise, I have relied on biographical evidence (farming, teaching, and lecturing) implied by the notes or references to historical events. There are also noticeable differences between Frost's early and late handwriting. Precise dating of particular entries, as I explain in the introduction, is nearly impossible.

The title given to each notebook in the table of contents is the first entry of that notebook and is no way intended to characterize the notebook. The library call numbers of the notebooks have been retained for the convenience of those who wish to examine them.

Symbols:
{ } word or phrase written above the line
[illegible] illegible word or phrase
[?] an uncertain reading
~~word or phrase struck through~~
[r] recto
[v] verso

THE NOTEBOOKS OF
ROBERT FROST

"Hunter James"

MS. 001981. *Green canvas stitched diary book with beige spine, 6″ × 9¼″ unruled white woven pages with ragged ends. All entries are in blue ink unless otherwise noted. The notebook contains a draft of one of Frost's earliest known poems, "The reason of my perfect ease," as well as drafts of much later work, including "Pod of the Milkweed."*

[*1r*]   Hunter James* [1]

[*2r*]   [blank]

[*3r*]   Old   old   nineties

The reason of my perfect ease† [2]
In the society of trees
Is that their cold struggles pass
Too far below my social class
~~To notice~~ {For me} to be ~~by them~~ mask
~~For what~~ I am and love afraid

~~To notice~~ [~~illegible~~] afraid
~~For~~
To notice or be by them made
For what ~~I think I am~~ am and love afraid

[*3v*]   [blank]

[*4r*]   [blank]

[*4v*]   He was poet and‡

---

* Sixteen pages torn out after 1r.
† Entry written in pencil.
‡ Entry written in pencil.

[5r]   Once in a while I was very blue
        Nothing I took or did for it would do
        I wrote of Henry Hudson his crew
        That left

[6r–20r]   [blank]

[20v]*   The fact that must be faced that must be braved
        Is that we always come to the abyss
        Something remains for reason to dismiss
        And you will never hear the last of this

[21r]   [blank]

[21v]   From countless florets {the} one lone carapace
        Yet toward the immortality of race
        He figures as no {No unimportant} negligible ace
        Because his mind {is full} his body plump
        With a design of sowing earth with seed
        That shall ensure whatever he may fail
        Pasture and garden shall {should} not lack for weed
        And to his equinoxical trump
        Shall {blow} [illegible phrase] a gale
        That can sound up in a case
        [three illegible lines]
        And when O [illegible phrase]
        Bede even case of too creed up as ace
        Should {To} open it nature and unseen
        He should not be the last of them that teem
        There could be a worse genetics than to claim
        He had a mighty monarch for his sire
        Nothing less generous or less untame
        Or less unafraid of passion and desire
        Or less

[22r]   [blank]

----

* Entries in 20v–27r written upside-down horizontally on the page, right to left.

[22v]   From many florets one lone carapace
~~And if he~~ feels no negligible ace
It that his mind is full his body [illegible]
For sowing such a*

From many florets one lone carapace
~~And~~ {he} ~~feels~~ yet no negligible ace
Because his mind is full his body plums
For sowing earth with such [illegible] seed
As shall insure what [illegible] all fail
Pasture and garden shall not lack for weed
But let {not} [illegible] anyone mislead
Alas what bots it yes what does it boot
That every sequin is in undersuit

When autumn blows in equinoctical gale
And sounds [illegible]

[23r]   [blank]

[23v]   To pour a libation on the ground
~~Should be to God~~ {you [?understand]} acceptable enough
But when into yourself the stuff is downed
Both you are wasted and the precious stuff[3]
The rites become a double sacrifice
The God of Waste is celebrated twice
Some offerings are only heaved and would
{Then} ~~And~~ by the {thrift and} sophistry of ~~thrifty~~ priests
Are [illegible] {from the fire on the altar saved}
For hypocreation ~~to gorge~~ in their feasts
~~The gift of heaven must be thrown away~~
~~As in religious the Sabbath Day~~
~~A tenth of wealth of~~ one day in seven
Of {feasts one} [illegible] tenth of time one day in seven
Must be {entirely sacrificed} [illegible] to Heaven
If only as a tribute to

---

* Two diagonal lines are drawn through this stanza.

[24r] One must be very righteous to set up
As To be the power of the {passion} [?poison] Cup
[illegible]
Or soldier set ~~up for the bole~~
~~To keep another~~ [illegible]

The fact that meant to faced that must be braved
That may his will be taken and embraced

[24v] The pod {may be an Egrets} [~~illegible~~] carapace
From many flowers one [illegible]
But yet so bursting full of fertile seed[4]
[?Found] Then {sound for} the stackling sake
The moon [illegible] talking is the worse the late
It should make sure whatever she may fail
Pasture and garden should not fact [illegible]
Alas what boots it though, what don't boot
The [illegible] seeds sequein {seple or flake} ~~has a parachute~~
Has packed without a silken parachute
With a capacity of sustained drift
And ven at times an amp— lift
To carry it off in light and airy drift
To a choice of its own for taking root
~~But all in vain~~
In vain in vain From   a lucky germ
Of all empodered in our pachyderm
To grace him with another human brain
That is not gathered to abidale
And is not to us {human} beyond dispute

[25r] To pour out {a} [~~illegible~~] libation on the ground
So must and {should be} sacrifice enough
But when into your self this is suff is –
Both you are wanted the precious stuff
The [illegible] becomes a soule sacrifice
[~~two illegible lines~~]
the god of Waste is celebrated twice
Some [illegible] wrestle but

The offering is the only haves
A t god by the offending
And there is permanently sat
[~~illegible line~~]
For hypocrite to gorge on at a feast

[25v]   The pod looks nothing but a curio[5]
Of curiosity but even so   Of curiosity but even so
{He is not so upside down} ~~upside down~~ as not to know
The difference between expense and waste
Waste is where only God can see the sense
Where man can see {it shall be called} [~~illegible~~] expense
~~Where there [illegible remainder of line]~~
My theory may not be to his taste
[~~illegible~~] with dissembled haste
But everything with dissembled haste
~~If I am any judge is on the~~ go
From the beginnings been on the go
That's been [illegible] nothing coming in
Expect the [illegible]
Waste is the expense we cannot explain
In which God only sees the sense

Expense is when when we invest
We see a little bit of grain
~~Expense is~~ And {stay} ~~check~~ the well dissembled haste
Waste the expense we cannot explain
In which God only sees the sense
It is religious to assume

[26r]   [blank]

[26v]   In my book of books
I see his figure as the God of waste
We pour [~~illegible~~] {out} on the ground in sacrifice
We pour it down our throats and that is twice*

---

* Many pages are torn out after 26v.

[27r]ᵇ The pod seems nothing but a curio
Of curiosity but even so
He's no so upside down as not to know
The difference between expense and waste
~~Expense is what man sees the purpose of~~
Waste's what God⁷ only sees the purpose of
All is but spending fuel in a sense
Once ~~it got~~ {the blaze} started farewell all was go
~~But what man~~ And if {our observation} was not mistaken no thing can?
[~~illegible phrase~~]
Got started
Or call what man sees the meaning of
Waste is where only God can see the sense
~~But all is spending all is on the go~~
~~Everything is~~
The universe ~~as a whole~~ {really is} spending thing
Every thing we can see is on the go

[27v] He's dead he must after two such nights.
I wasn't fooled by his farm {of} refuge talk
As someone else was evidently fooled.
~~Not so long after~~ [illegible]
This is the place all right. ~~His deception was~~

        ~~This is the place~~
~~There is no house. The barn is quite a barn~~

        ~~It is so~~ [illegible] ~~where near~~
~~Answer to his description. Where he said~~ was
~~The house is not~~

[28r]★ That's what he was when he was young and handsome
His ~~own~~ ideal but he had ideals were his [glass]
Of ~~his~~ sincerity. He struck at trifles of sincerity.
He got afraid of ~~what~~ things he had to say
As our professing Christ to congregation
He wasn't sure he meant. He went back

★ Page written in black ink and upside-down horizontally on the page, right to left.

To his apprenticeship as a man of [?humor]
Got out the tools of the trade for comfort
Ostracization for the disappointment
He had to be to everybody but himself.
He's a sad case of scrupulosity
But [illegible] talk saying too much in his presence
But you don't resist say talking do you Enoch
We're baseball friends old pitcher catcher friends
He says the only catcher that [illegible] could hold me.
So much for what he was. Another thing

[28v]   He's dead he must be after two such nights
Its nowhere near univer [illegible phrase] Its pretty nearly
Its near enough
There is the place all
Answers to the description he gave me.
The house is not much but the barn is standing
That not quite accurate exactly it. There is no house
It happens but the bars is quite a barn

This is the place all right by his decription.
The house is not much the barn is standing
The only out is that there is not house
But the barns standing and its quite a barn

    It is only religious to believe that those who lose bravely in peace or war
are never lost to the great purpose. I made this sentiment personal in the
with thoughts mostly aloud.*

[29r]   I preached a sermon on him once He didn't come

Don't preach it now

               He says don't preach it now.
Her listening to us—every word we say
//Im
Im feeling better since I had my spell.

                    •   •   •

---

* This entry and 20r written in black ink and upside-down horizontally on the page, right
to left.

That's probably his son. He's state police.

He said we were as good as under arrest

Not my son I ddint mean by him
Didn't I tell you it would be like this.
Misjudgment nothing can be done about
His son's as wise and [?thoughtful] as a judge
And has to be keep from hasty judgment
In And closing in on his sin [illegible] {before} [illegible]
Yes that's the son. He's coming after him.
I{ll get us} m getting us coffee

My sermon would explain a lot [illegible] {it's a dismal night}
If he is not [illegible] man you've captured
I didn't capture him. He captured me
He rose up from the ditch and captured me
He made a sort of fling latched on me
[illegible]
He runs away from second childishness
He isn't responsible. He [illegible]
[illegible line]
His wife thought he was married to a preacher

[30r–36r]   [blank]

[37r]*   When was it? Where should we suppose it was
{But} Right in the middle of the Perfect Field
Beside the stone he hadn't burred
Such wishes My wish is it to be buried
Besi

[38r]   [blank]

[38v]   The cloud was like a heavy lifted lid
The cloud looked like like a heavy lifted lid
The sun looked down beneath on what we did
From ninety million miles or more away

---

* 37r–42v written in black ink.

And it was

Twas late upon an Armagedden day

He knows how to consider the expense
Where to let them ruse our expense
Or shut them up in jail at our expense
It all depends

[39r]   A   For the Lands sakeyou in captive Enoch Lincoln[8]
He runs away from second childishness all man's craziness

C   I didn't capture him he captured me
He rose up form the ditch beside the road—
And made a sort of What id he make a f lying Lachle on you me?

A   He's torn the very patches off his knees
He runs away from second second childishness second childishness

A   Mrs Deforest has a child like that
She has to keep when she
She has to keep tied with a halter rope
With play of wing with row wing free to play
She goes with his with him on a leash
Him one of those [illegible] you all
Who either want is
Some to set fire and some to run away
Who simply light out with every chance they get

Or
[illegible]
But That am old fashioned [illegible] with children
That was
[?Psychologists] {are} said supposed to favor
For fear of what it might do them later
Ive called [illegible] Police
Became for him
Didn't I tell it would be like this

[39v]   Don't get them [illegible] mixed up I'm not the first
[illegible phrase]

I didn't say you were. We all are [illegible]
Im felling better sure I had
I take a better view than yesterday [illegible]
[illegible] will misunderstand if they can

[40r]   That's no way to describe him to a stranger
He It's He's Enoch Lincoln named for Enoch Lincoln
The Governor of Maine who wrote the poem
About the {our} village when he sojourned there
In Fryberg to recast his energy
He tangled in our academy I think
The new [view] of the boundary fight with
Yet that [illegible] you never heard of him.
Lincoln Nebraska was named after him
His book on exhibition
And he was your captain He was no relation.
Don't get me {Did I say you were} all mixed up Im no relation
The feeling better since I had my spell
I like a better view of who I am young
You're literary. But you never heard
Of the American {New England} poet Enoch Lincoln
His books a rarity. I have a copy
I think {ought} only wait a moment
Yes new of or so you can say you had
And treasure it with [illegible] feeling
You promised it to me.
                    Scarlet yours
And you shall take it home with you tonight
We know who you are if you don't throw
I come from succession of successes
Im showing the leap of village life

[40v]⁹   The very latest creed thing that has to be believed
For you {us} to in your calculation
Is that its all a concept self conceived
Which lands you clear way back on Pantheism

And nothing very new in which to rejoice
Nothing so far from

Nothing so very   to rejoice in
It has the ~~reassurance~~ of a good remark
And has the [~~illegible~~] of you alone in
~~Juging~~ our saying All is God or God is All

Not so   what if
No   it your
At least there has the mind to rejoice in
If the assurance of an apt recall
And
Nothing so very moral to rejoic in
It has But reassurance of ~~the~~ {a} good recall

Nothing so very moral to rejoice in
[~~illegible line~~]
The reassurance of a great [illegible]

[*41r*]   Im with you there. You cant go down {to} deep
For me [illegible] Nurse. History that coming
I [~~illegible~~] {old} leave with us slumming
What we don't know about the depths of Fryberg
It beat the words of the Old Testament

I [~~illegible~~] could tell just as bad {low ~~down~~}case stores
Above high [illegible] in the highest penthouse
Abou the high life on the highest roofs
On the penthouses of ~~the~~ {our} greatest city

I never said you couldn't. Life is awful
Yes full of awe as is all Gods Creation
{The poet's} [~~illegible~~] a soothsayer soothingsayer
It some time since I read it. You haven't read it.

[~~illegible line~~]
Sooth doesn't come from soothing father

I didn't tell you it wouldn't be like this.

Enoch's himself a tumble down dick preacher

•   •   •

Now now my [illegible] {dear} you're not to talk about

The unhappy is their pressure—is my pressure
Enoch I preached a sermon you once

[41v]   Oh even keep the jail at our expense

And

Of who should keep
Or even kept in jail at my expense
And
Of who should keep them down at our expense
And [illegible] even kept [illegible] at our expense
Kept [illegible] up in jail at our expense
It is an [illegible] at our expense later {any} case
The question

Lefty cannot [?withdraw] and say good night
Will you [?a minute] [?shows] something for you

He calls our
Lefty because because
Left because I used to pitch left handed
And preach he says a little to the left
What made him shy was he had a poem for me
He brings me poems and I wrote him poems
We [illegible] was a Poetry
Between us were were the Poetry
We "coestablished" the Poetry Society
Of Fryburg. Were each others [?mystic]

[42r]   You did come
                    Are right don't preach it now
For I'm a pilgrim can [illegible] with you long
[illegible line]
                He has a singing voice
Yes that his song. [illegible] To attend his another hour
Wasn't

The Enoch in the Bible walks with God
I'll tell you more about him when he's gone

Yes why he's called the Gold for Christmas Man

I'll tell you why I call his son the Judge

This is Judge Lincoln of the State Police

He knows sadly where to draw the line
Between the good for nothing and the bad
He's ~~there were kept at their expense~~
[~~illegible line~~]
Better that good for nothing kept them
~~At your expense than that we had to keep them~~
[~~two illegible lines~~]

A tumble down dick minister himself
That all he is parinian. But never mind
He seems to have a mind. My husband checks

[42v]   Why the old rascal headed all the time
[~~Illegible line~~]
For you folks and yet letting on to me
[~~Six illegible lines~~]

[43r–82v]   [blank]

[1r]*   Ways Forward

1 He hated Christmas as a child because he saw many {children} looking in the store windows with longing for the finest toys they were too poor to have.

2 There were Sore Heads Sap Heads and Hard Heads[10] The Sore Heads were the hungry radicals who [?disguised] To conceal their anger at not having enough. The Sap Heads could hardly bear it that others were not as well

---

* Entries beginning here are written from the back of the notebook toward the front.

off as they were. The Hard Heads feared the Sore Heads as enemies of the social contract that we had a right to our luck and our ability but rather respected the Sore Heads for their frank reason and their threat. They too despised the Sap Heads for sentiments they (the Sapheads) didn't quite know what to do about. The Sap Heads were sort of socialist verging on unreasonable communists. By the time he got old enough (twenty-one) to see all this he guessed he was a Hard Head. His decision to say Arnoldian[11] as Mounts and that hardly even to eternal life the Sap Head rested his case on the dark prayer Thy Kingdom Come on Earth[12]

2 Pacifism[13] could end mens hurting each other

[1v]   [blank]

[2r]   Amer condu

      Fulfillment in full

[2v]   [blank]

[3r]   He may be nothing but a curio
      Of curiously but even so
      He's not so upside down as not to know
      That all we everything Farewell all go
      The difference is between expense and waste

[3v]   [blank]

[4r]   in War. Marxism would end men's hurting each other in peace. Christ was a Christian pacifist[14] Jew. Marx was an atheist pacifist Jew—sociologist

      Here will or regret one see
      Ranks [illegible] and degrees

      3 Graduated scare of loyalties top of
      which is loyalty above friendship kinship college
      [illegible] and even country
      Highest is yourself which sociologists say
      is to humanity as a whole (hole)

Rise on stepping stones of your dead friends
to chief commenced
    Eeny meaney
    Miney moe
    Mussolini
    Hitler
    Joe
    Whats the difference how know
    <u>We</u>-<u>are</u>-<u>out!</u>

[4v]   [blank]

[5r]   1838 Born

1865–1872	Teach	1872[15]
1873	Marry	
1874	RF B	
1875	J.F. B	
1885	WPF D[16]	

[5v]   [blank]

NOTEBOOK 2

"The Hermits"

MS. 001879. *Brown soft paper cover flip pad, 3⅞″ × 6¼″ with black cloth strip binding at the top, stitched pages. Ruled paper. Many pages torn out. Entries are in pencil unless otherwise noted. Frost's notes about poultry farming and references to stories and articles he published on the subject indicate that entries in this notebook may date from as early as 1903.*

[1r]   Book I

    1 The Hermits
    2 The Enervating Touch
    3 The Thankless crime
    4. An Unconscious Channel
    5 Ace & the Pigs
    6 The Last Night in P House
    7 A Penny Saved[1]
    8 Desolation
    9 The <u>One</u> Woman
    10 The <u>Nights</u> Lodging
    11 Old Home Week

[2r]   1 Ginseng
    2 ~~A Very Young Thing. The Ruthless Idealist~~
    3 ~~Polly Formerly Annette-Hawk Farm~~
    4 ~~Capon Strain~~[2]
    5 ~~The Prenatal Influence of Incubators~~
    6 ~~Early Eggs~~
    7 The Victor-Victim (Cecil Rhodes)[3]
    8 ~~An Old Home One Who Staid.~~
    9 Imaginary Encounters Cl. & Br on the beach
    10 ~~The Arm of the Lord~~
    11 ~~The Flight of the Lady Play~~

[*2v*]   No 1

Grandser Probity

The Land Agent Only Sale

[illegible] Moderation M̶o̶ Let me see what stuff they put in gingerbread
Well never mind Oh ginger! "If you'll find my wife mispronounce a bad
word!" These Algerines—Excuse m̶y̶ me!" Old fashioned drinking. He
opened his mouth a hundred dollars too soon on a lot of cows. Dozy wood.
Never buy a critter that you cant easily turn. He's got about as much foresight as if his eye were all in the back of his head.*

Sleet is local rain or snow

The mild winter is God taking part in the coal strike (Its important enough
for that)

Heap of living in a cow.

[*3r*]   12 S̶u̶m̶m̶a̶r̶y̶ ̶o̶f̶ ̶t̶h̶e̶ ̶W̶e̶e̶k̶s̶ ̶N̶e̶w̶s̶ ̶f̶r̶o̶m̶ ̶B̶a̶r̶n̶h̶a̶m̶ (Sun has it)
13 Fairy Tales of Farming I̶n̶t̶e̶r̶s̶p̶e̶r̶s̶e̶d̶ ̶w̶i̶t̶h̶ With I̶n̶t̶e̶r̶l̶u̶d̶e̶s̶ ̶o̶n̶ ̶S̶c̶i̶e̶n̶c̶e̶

(a̶)̶{W}ith Scientific Interludes
(a) Keeping ahead of the Cow
(b) Muck. Fathers and Sons {Ingredients}
(c) 50,000 Acre in Ginseng.
(d) Figuring on the Wall
(e) Run Out. Spanish Rum
(f) Hawk Farm
(g) The Freaks of Lightening
(h) Speed of an electric vehicle (if the machinery can be made last and the
strain the limit will truly be the shed of the spark itself.
(i) A Week of Weather
(j) Damably Ackly. How to load hay
(k) The Proud Agent.
(l) Been Here a Long Time
(m) Seed Potatoes.

---

* This sentence written in black ink.

[*3v*] No II

Song—The Fourteen Perfect Children. I thought you would have my future at the least.

The artists   The grocer*   Cert (in Kitchen)   The lawyer[†]

(Whats this young man yet to do with it)

Father (sent Paul)   Caponsach[4]   Going with anybody?

~~Those w~~

The roads were so muddy here last week that a piece of one was turned over and it was found that a horse could travel it just as well head downwards because in extricating any one foot he got some other stuck so fast that he was perfectly safe until he got another still stuck in extricating that.

[*4r*] 13 (cont)

(m) A Hay Farm   Paisleys Meadow
(o) The Philosophy of Potato Bugs
(p) A Run of Luck in Trapping
(q) Pedometer and 1 cyclometer.
(r) A lot of thermometers to steady the temperature.
(s) Snow the poor mans fertilizer[‡]

[*4v*] 12

(You all come from Barnham you or your fathers or your fathers father and to Barnham you look back in wonder at what you have become. Yet the wonder is not so great for there flourish[5] and always have the simple virtues that make a man—~~and the rest is but added into you~~) to ~~which all that is added is as nothing~~) having which the rest may at any time be added unto him

 Half way back where the incapable go: way back whence the capable come.

---

* Line drawn from "(in kitchen)" to "The grocer."
[†] Line drawn from "(whats this young man yet to to do with it)" to "The Lawyer."
[‡] Last item on list written in black ink.

[5r] 14 A Telephone on the Farm

15 ~~Short Sleeves too Soon. He had bought himself out of neighbors~~

16 Slab City

17 ~~Paisley Meadow Lake~~

18 Paddy's Rescue

19 Over-educated

20 ~~A Ruthless Idealist (Shelley) The friend killer~~

21 The ~~few~~ ~~Junk Man~~ {Syrian Pedler}   ~~Poland good country~~ {I dont like Syrian Gothic?}

22 The Abstruse Laureate

23 ~~How [?Ethlane] Call Came to Jesus.~~[6]

[5v] 13(g) I don knows I believe what Im a going to tell you tonight but its most likely true

[6r] 24 The Rural Electrics (Mr. Cl.)

25 To Carry On

26 Opening the Amazon (Mr. Cl)

27 A Survivor from the Winter of our Discontent[7] A Survival.

28 How to Pay.

29 ~~The Obligation play~~

30 Superintendant of School's Report.

31 ~~The Disinterested One has to take his own side in a quarrel~~   ~~A Play~~

32 "Alleged"

33 ~~The Enfeebling Touch~~   ~~The Tram figuring Touch~~

[6v] 34 Their spread. Conflict with the railroads What they can offer compared with the railroads What they will do for New England. Abandoned farms in the hill country. What been done and what remains to do. Pleasure grounds. The further north is not always the further into the wilderness. It is the further east or west within certain limits.

[7r]* 34 ~~The Sanitorium~~[(23)]

35 The Arch-Roycrofter.[8] Vitality covers a multitude of sins. The books. The kind of free lover. His profits from what never profited Shelley Thoreau Emerson Whitman and Ruskin. ~~Said some funny things about~~ [illegible] Been

---

* With the exception of the first entry, which is in pencil, page written in black ink.

amusing about people that deserved it. Looking for a charity {not detrimental not to both sides}
36 Without Benefit of Sleep   The Limit of Demonstration. The Strain of
Resistance
37 The Diagnostician Concensus Sentium
38 The Murder Thought & Others. Whats in a Name. Malpractice. Mental as-
sault etc.
39 Mysterious Claims and the Sceptre.
40 Consolation for a Love. (The devil take her.)

[7v] "I give hope to the hopeless" And the price?
Depends on the furnishing of the room I give it in.

The best philosophy is that which accounts for the most realities. Of course
experience has taught us that the realities of today may prove the unreality of
tomorrow. But good we come to believe is no illusion and by the same process of thought neither is evil. Both must be accounted for and denying is not
accounting.

Has hypnotism received recognition in the courts?

Hypnotic sleep sufferer.

[illegible]

Kimball Book⁹

Book of Texts

[8r]* 41 To Restore the Sound to Health. Rebuilding Jerusalem. 'Sal I can make you
sick and well again without your {knowing it.}
42 a) The Testimony of Babes
42 b) The Indelicacy of Children Crux of the Matter
43 Terminology. I know what you are going to say to me.
45 Behold Anew Heaven and a new Earth. (Name for Whole) Heavenly Concord (N.H.)
46 To Bolster Authority.

---

* Page written in black ink.

47 The Reality of Evil (Comparatively unreal)
48 (a) An Excuse for M<u>arriage</u>
48 (b) The ~~Kind of Marriage~~
49 The Fear of Miracle
50 The Moral Struggles of My Home Neighbors.
51 Last Chapter of Last Historical Novel
(Labelers)

[*8v*]*   Claims:
Mortal Mind Family.
Nothing lost in Sod
Impersonal Error.
The Woodbury Thought
Hypnotism-Malpractice
Divine Mind
Deny a Claim
Source of Supply.
Mental Assasination
The Murder Thought.
Treat General Situation
Divine moral and mortal mind

[*9r*]†   52 lives for a Poet in Business
53 Why Not   The Wrong Temperament
54
54 It is necessary to enquire of every politician what it is he has in view by
which he justifies himself for his innumerable ~~perv~~ minor perversions of
right and truth
55 Causerie in Democracy
~~56 Two Pennies~~
58 The Artistic Conscience—The Enfeebling Touch. The Scientific Conscience—The Fear of Miracles.
58 The Dogs in the Frith
59 A Weather Book
60 Confessions of a Graduate

---

* Page written in black ink.
† Page written in black ink.

[9v] Never open your mouth on anything   dollar too soon

Heard at the Aquarium

He (in admiration) Oh come see the coloring of this Queen Trigger Fish
She (sweeping by indifferently) Oh {Humph} no wonder, {no wonder—}
she's a queen—no wonder*

A passenger who had his eyes tied to the page of a book had them
A passenger on the—train had his eyes glued to the page of a book when a
sudden lurch of the car jerked them completely out of the socket onto his
cheeks. The were replaced by an energetic modest young physician who was
so ready with his card that we have decided to furnish his name to reliable
parties upon application

[10r] 61 [Illegible]
62 Lo conducter (Sawyer)
63 The N.Y.C. Foot Bridge
64 Drifting Girls.
65 The Correspondence [illegible] Peril
66 Variable Sun
67 The Information Bureau
68 Mother & Babe Sentiment
69 The Unselfish Love of Yoke Fellow Oxen
70 The Diminishing Family
71 Professor Loeb-Prenatal Influence and Heredity[10]

[10v]†   The Discriminating Clerk

Do you see that fellow there said the faithful clerk. Well he's a stray. He
doesn't belong in here. How do I know Cant you see. To be sure he's well
dressed. But waite till I show you. We can't afford to have such people buy
here and the way we with our select trade and the way we prevent them is
this: He stepped up to the customer with inquired his wants with crushing
politeness served him and was back Then he continued Did you notice the
lost look on his face—not the real thing. You may have noticed {too} that he

---

* This line and the two above it written in black ink.
† Page written in black ink.

did not ask the price. Well he didn't. So I charged him treble actually th treble and he never murmured. I knew he wouldnt He wasn't going to give himself away; but that was just where he did give himself away. But he's learned his lesson. We'll never see him again. We don't have to refuse to ~~deal~~ {sell} ~~with~~ to such people.

[11r]*   72 Nigger & Bacon

73 Wide Open Town

74 Growing Old Fast So as to be Ready.

75 Take it out of Politics

76 I remember how funny I used to think it was to ask the Station agent, etc. He has been relieved of all those questions.

77 The Flat Builder

78 ~~The Corner Dancer~~

79 ~~Number or Teeth~~

80 Weather Copy

81 Barometric Chart of New York for Slumming Parties[11]

[11v]†   If it is a good thing to be dead it must be half as good to be half dead

This train is just in from St. Louis. You dont look it.

Old Crovell Place

Stone Library

Tenney Place

[12r]‡   82 How Bryan[12] may get back. Symposium

83 Go down in ~~the morning~~ afternoon come back in the morning.

84 City Men and Old Homer.

85 Lumber in the City

86 ~~[illegible]~~ {Common Sense}

87 The Upper End of the Island Fort Washington too

88 Hens on the Island

89 Health of Wild Animals in Captivity

90 French in the Park.

---

* Page written in black ink.

† Page written in black ink.

‡ With the exception entires 87 and 91, which are in pencil, page written in black ink.

91 The First Mannish Woman. He's a girl
92 The New Advertising.

[12v]   Side Hill Poultry Farm Readers

It is easy enough for you and your friends to find {it} out ~~whether~~ {if} {we}
~~we sell~~ sell more eggs than are laid on our own place. We suggest that you take
this course. Club together and order from widely separate localities in large
and small quantities more eggs than by your own admission we can possibly
have to sell within a given time and see if you got them. As we acknowledge
to no more than100 hens {~~and it filled out that?~~} we can fill no more than 360
egg machines on any given day unless we send out eggs more than two
weeks old which find ourselves not to do.
    Our whole business on the farm where it can be seen of ever all men at all
hours ~~that~~ {the above} is your proof. ~~You~~ If you come to see us when you
leave you can be sure you <u>have</u> seen us and all there is to us. We have nothing
else where better or worse. And as for the trap nests if you drop in on us unexpectedly which you are cordially invited to do you can satisfy yourself that
they are in operation. And if that is not enough you can have {a transcript}
any leaf in our ~~ree~~ egg record book sworn to before a justice of the peace

[13r] Everything is open and above board. [Sidehill is not a collective noun denot-
ing a number of hen farmers with headquarters at Sidehill.]*

93 The South American Countries and the U.S. Their political & trade relations with us and how much they are Americanized.
94 Crows & Potatoes
95 Experiment Station Bulletins
96 High Tensions Farming. Ginseng
97 ~~Letter to the [R illegible]~~
98 The Breeder (Mag.)
99 Card Case on Wealth Land Condition of Indians, South America, At Expense of C.S. New York Boasting
~~100 Moon Sun & Wind Worshippers~~
101 Anchor Ice
102 An Auction Plot

---

* Frost's brackets.

[*13v*]   Poultry series

\ Trap nests[13]
\ Incubation. Prenatal influence
Capon Strain Called on to Investigate advertisers
o Poor Mother (and the fate of her brood & tail (Broody hen) {lost more than she had.}*
\ Molly & the Hawk Conflict of emotions
Cock Tails. Not a follower. An Innovator
o Abandoned Hen Farm. Handwriting on the wall Ginseng
o The Worst Possible Hen farm {There's a kind of fellow that always wants to know your secret. Heats what hatches em}
\ A just judge. Ive seen that bird before.
\ Old Welch Goes to the Show[14] {Fair enough to groom 'em and tame a little. groom 'em well that's a good one}†
\ The Courage of His Convictions. Investment
 \Hawk preventatives
 \An Artists Scare Crow.
o All that Was Coming to Him.
Died on the Place. Died of Old Age
Plasticity of the Hen
How long eggs may remain cool
Come and See Original & Only Divested
\A Revelation   28 Hour Hen
Fire Bug   A Seeker for Truth
A Neighborhood of Poultrymen
The Worst [?d] Chicken
\The Question of A Feather

[*14r*]   103 Where your [illegible] country produce comes from.   Consul Groan & Marketmen
104. Misplaced Stark Tablet
105 Witch hazel & the other [illegible] decoction
106 Yankee Rennaisance
107 Trap Nest Department. & Measly [illegible] Interesting Things {Curio Column} Cancelled With Poultry

---

* This phrase written slightly below the line.
† "Fair enough to groom . . . that's a gone one." written in margin.

108 Side. I lill Poultry Farm Reader
109 The Tramps Short Cut
110 The Hen's Out put
111 Some Hen Houses
112 The Extra Yard.
113. Twenty Eight Hour Hen

[14v] Someone saw a fox at his hen house door and said, You wont find any hens there. We've gone out of the hen business. There's no living in hens.

Look a here, stranger, said the fox, what you say may be true but do you know its a damn dangerous doctrine you're spreading. If everybody came to believe that I don't know what should become of foxes.

And foxes arent the only ones said the stranger.

"No theres hawks too."

And the people that sell poultry appliances said the stranger with the bitterness of experience.*

As I understand it Roosevelt only got in as a sort of rider to the main proposition which was McKinley.[15]

Yes Rough Rider

The Wood Chicken

A Seeker for Truth

[15r] 114. The Law & The Outlaw. The One Officer and his Criminal
115. The Inherited [illegible] {[illegible]} Plot
116 A District School Teacher Favorites
117 Bricaults[16] Adv.   Trap Nest Club
118 Long Love
119 To a Scare Crow in Winter
120 Choice of Motives (High School)
121 Distinction & the Student Business Man
122 Glad to be Anything Acceptable
123 The Contemplative Criminal
97? [series of 8 numbers struck-through]

124 Fly Time   Mud Time   [illegible] 130

---

* Short line drawn here.

[*15v*]   I suggested to the miracle worker that she might have been mistaken as to—

115 I was when I was courting etc.

139. Before Thermometers, A Year Ago Today, Almanac Days, Weather Lore the First Nature Poetry, Philosophy of March Weather. The Tree Tend & What He Knows about It. Old Almanacs. When to Wean a Calf Mud Time Mad Fever
(Talked more because of the uncertainty.)
"Acts like a [?Dron].—I bet had been any of this time it would have rained with the signs favorable Last night. All signs fail etc. He's as if it thought it <u>had</u> rained.
Question when Spring begins.

[*16r*]*   125 Axolotl[17]
While not mentioned by Wood {or Kingsley} Probably larva or tadpole stage {(Not)} Mexico
126 ~~The Ice Plant~~
127 Why We Say 'Guess First'
128 The Validity of Darwin[18] in the Courts Law of the Survival of the Fittest. Is there any such law.
129 All that Were Entitled (in the parish)
130 ~~The Astrologer and My Weakness for Impossibles.~~
131 My Faults Regarded as My Misfortunes. How the G S. Knew?
132 The Weather   Published Monthly the Weather permitting in N.C. where as Mark says there is more weather accordingly than in any other part of the country.
134 The One Book (Not Bible)
135 Mr. Browns Test   Paganism in N.H.

[*16v*]   [blank]

[*17r*]   136 ~~The Soap Girl~~†
137 ~~In An Old Cellar~~
138 Bargain Hunter for Am Exp

----

* First three lines of this page written in black ink.
† Entry written in black ink.

18r]–[*19r*]   [blank]

[*19v*]*   Gonzales Pizarre's general officer Oreillane first down the river in 1540 Don
Pedro de Texeira left Para up the river in 1637.
Acuña sent by the King to investigate Things best fitted in his opinion to enrich owners of country wood sugar tobacco & tobacco. Climate equable under the equator. Salubriouals Named from tribe of women on Canaris river
(about 7 degrees west of Mouth.)
1899 U.S.S. Wilmington 348 feet fall in 2300 miles {less than Yosemite falls}. To
Iguito Peru Manaor capital of Amazonas (30,000) Fevers in forest. Navigation
something like that of Miss. [Disappointment?]† Rubber not inexhaustible.
Natives Industrious Nothing to eat. Santaren 70 Southerners after war enterprise ascended 20 years before Herndon descended in '53 Every ton of rubber
cost two lives.

[*20r*]   [blank]

[*20v*]‡   Edition with feature articles
Times Sat Review   worth ? crit.
McClures Mag[19]
Newspaper syndicate

---

* Page written in black ink.
† Frost's brackets.
‡ Page written in black ink.

"All these different psycological experiments"

MS. "Derry." These pages are in the Barrett Collection of the University of Virginia library (6261 B2). 6¾" × 8½" blue ruled notebook paper. All entries are in blue ink unless otherwise noted.

[1r]   [illegible]

All these different psycological experiments

Poetry as measure
Sight and Insight. Sense and Insense
Stretching the Idea of ~~Belief~~ Imagination
    Accused of talking as if to an audience when I have none
          Believes in telephone
Believing the Future in [1]   (How soon you foresee what
  you are going to say.   I thought of that poem as I
  No surprise to author none to reader[2]
The Parties to Poetry
    What You Have to Have Been   Lousy?
The Ultimate Essay (Attempt)
    Metaphor May not be far but it is our farthest forth.
We Can Communicate: We Cant Communicate
    Aristotle Imitation
        The great word is Verification
~~The~~ Learning a   Need not be sound if it is
Means for Conveying Sound a sound
Seized Leisure and the Artists Revolt from the Middle Class
Greater
Balance expected missed and compensated for

Science Pointed toward Domesticity[3] and Robot a domestic

•   •   •

High School Boys Disillusionment—Finds we are joke of Europe
Over

[1v]   Give them the right to be Courteous [?Peasant]
Tradesman Grasping
Greatest ~~Middle~~ Upper Middle Class the World Has Known

[1r]*   This is old as Derry days
You can see from it where one idea started R. F. 1951[†]

'Milton'

I hate most the fellow who makes common stories
of the ~~a~~ flight of man.
He came out of the heavy mist and contemplated
the terms and accepted them. They were then
as they are now: A little more pleasure than pain,
pain greater in length and breadth but exceeded
by pleasure in height, one more pleasure than pain
~~when all~~ by actual count, ~~in~~ the pleasure of being
alive.
The Fan. (Baseball)
The Tramp Worshipper (A Boy at the Roadside

Milton spoke in terms of the studies o his youth ~~of the~~ about the great events
that were drawing had drawn him away from those studies.[4] In Comus "Love
Virtue, she alone is free."[5] The only free man is the abject slave of virtue. Not
so says—.[‡] The freeman will use virtue as he will use vice to the ends of his
own free spirit.

The three unities are of Reality {Decorative Form} Design and Signficance.

Architecture may be pure Design—Design only in stone.

•   •   •

Thought advances like spilled water along dry ground. Stopping gathering breaking out and running again.

"Don't write unless you have something to say." <u>Until</u> you have something to say. Go and get something to say.

[*1v*] We approve of people to their faces to gain their approval. We disapprove them ~~when they are absent~~ behind their backs to gain our own approval. But we are the two-faced devils.

A Tentative Farm. He thought he would; then he thought he wouldn't.
The Store in the Evening
Toffile Berry

The Outlook thinks Curtis will be the great aviator in history because he ~~was the first~~ sailed down the Hudson[6] like Fulton[7] Egan thinks Perry's exploit was equal to Columbus[8] because it was possibly as hard. Wellman thinks to get into history by crossing the Atlantic in an airship because Columbus crossed the Atlantic.[9] They are all like imitators of the great. Their intention is good, but they don't know what the great really did for them to imitate. Columbus for instance didn't cross the Atlantic. He didn't suffer hardships and privations. At least not for these thing is he Columbus. Why is he immortal then? Can't you tell? Well because he had the faith that so few are capable of the faith in an idea. Not for him to feel his way round Africa to Ind. He launched out into space with ~~confidence~~ the supreme confidence of reason. Great in his confidence, great in his justification. The nearest him among the aviators and the only ones near him are the Wright brothers.[10]

"If I prayed every day what you pray I don't see
how I could help calling myself a Utopian."

MS. 001714. *Black buckram binding with red trim along the spine and red triangle trim on the corners of the front cover, 7 ¾" × 10". Stitched pages. Ruled pages with page numbers stamped in black in the upper right hand corner of each page. Entries are in blue ink unless otherwise noted. Frost indicates at the end of the notebook that he started making entries in it in 1909, and entries appear to continue into the 1950's.*

[First seven pages torn out]

[*1r*] 7

   If I prayed every day what you pray I do{nt}* see how I could help calling myself a Utopian.
   What do I pray?
   Thy kingdom come[1] on earth as it is in heaven.[2]

   I suspect this is just another phase of the same after-the-war conscien{tiousness} as gave us pacifism:[3] 'We can get along without hurting each other"
              Marx says even in business.

Dainty sorrows (only for everybody.)[4]

I start to run as fast as ~~seem~~ {possible} from as far back ~~as~~ in history as possible to see if the momentum I get up ~~whose~~ wont land me when I jump from now at least six months into the future. Defaulting debtor a slave—a prisoner—a bankrupt. Now if we can afford it the failure will have his person and something besides. Never down too quick. Life for everybody is

---

* "nt" written below line.

meant to be a trajectory from less to more.[5] Less of everything you please to more of it.

Isnt it too bad Freud made ~~such a~~ {the} great mistake of assuming Freud was wrong: our ruling passion is to mind each others business[6]
To teach, reform, interfere in the business of others, is mans strongest passion.

[2r]   17
Story of the carefree Finses bower lady
Story of Joseph Albany's[7] singing daughter.

What will ~~we~~ make everybody rich poor or middling?
The best you could hope for would be middling*
But I though middle class was the worst character you could have.
Story of the cigar box and the counter-revolutionary
How much a bomb costs. Me in Amherst
Story of the crutch farm in South Shaftesbury.[8]
Story of the unhappy child at the amateur theatricals.
Story of not being chosen by the eagle for Jove's cup bearer.[9]
Story of Darwinian[10] suicides and Marxian murderers.
The Boston cod[†] [11] and the pater mater frater complex.[12]
Neither or Both
Story of the very poor man on fifteen a week for forty years.
Story of the very rich man in the Pullman car.
Story of the man who wouldn't let himself be lost by one fatal mistake. Blood poison, tetanus syphilis.
Story of the equalitarian who thought it would be all right to use your literary reputation to get the better of an officious official.
    Story of the campaign speech in favor of slavery

[3r]   19
Story of planned economy on Easter Island where the population was limited to nine hundred by killing either the newborn at one end or an old person at the other.[13]
Story of the book of the Golden Peasant and the strike on the pyramid
    Story of the one armed teacher who became first citizen of <u>Glastonbury</u>.[14]

---

* This line written in black ink.
† There is a line-arrow written from "cod" up to "suicides" in the previous line.

Story of the encounter with the man who thought too well of humanity to despair of its becoming utopian. Not just our faults, but our virtues stand in the way of the perfect state.

Story of Tristan da Cunha and the Circumnavigators. {tourists}[15]

I can separate from all these betterments in mind the one betterment we are going to see in practice. Man to have his body and a little property besides to go with it. Youd call the logic bad that let a man out with the poor debtors oath. If a man is so improvident as to incur a debt he can't pay what does he deserve but prison?

We have come a long way from {through} the Gracchi[16] John Bull[17] and the Albigenses[18] John Milton the Levellers[19] and the French Revolution. It cant be the story ends there though. Cautiously now to keep what we have and reach for a little more. The intense competitive effort must be kept while we release

[4v]   20

a little of the gain to the others. Difusion is all there is to Democracy.[20] Difusion of what.

[5r]   21

If the trajectory is from less to more, it will be hard to arrange it so that some wont start with too little and so go to too much. Exact termini.

Most beautiful thing in the world is conflicting interests where both are good. Our best hope for the persistance of life on earth. What's become of the dangerous tendency to—Why it ran into the dangerous tendency to—Any principle to the full would is frightening to contemplate and is what we get our scare editorials out of

We are betrayed by what is false within.[21] Meredith Rather say we are engaged by what is strong within and determined we shall try each others strength.

[6r]   23

Story of the hard drinkers disbelief in disinterestedness[22]

•   •   •

Dont talk to me about getting rid of poverty. All principles are bad except as they are checked ~~about~~ in <u>about</u> mid career by contrary principles.
"For Christ's sake forget the poor some of the time."[23]
There are many beautiful things in the world besides poverty.
Of course poverty has its bad side just the same as war has

It was {as} if a botanist went out to find ~~plants~~ {flowers} and got interested in picking berries.

You wont let men have war to be heroic in. That was all your excitement for one while. And now you are going to ~~take a~~ deny them poverty as a field of heroic action. Arent you hasty?

What Became of New England?[24]

Plato and the Executive. The Poet As Executive[25]

Who told You You could Write?

[7r]   25
The Poem must have as good a point as a anecdote or a joke. It is the more effective if it has something analogous to the practical joke—an action—a "put up job" such as being carried out as a serenade or valentine or requiem or memorial address

Regional in source but not in market

A regionalist is one who picked out a region (such as the abdomen fundament or elbow and has a pain it.*

Story of the man who invented Confusion to Bugs (or Bug Confusion).[26]
How to play Confusion

Story of the man who originated the slogan No rivers to the sea.† [27]

Brandeis' slogan Let there be no great men but politicians.[28]

•   •   •

---

* Entry written in pencil.
† This entry and the one above it written in pencil.

Civilization is what the {a great} state {in its greatness} can indulge when in {time of} prosperity. Our privacy[29] is permitted us even unto {the point} [of] secrecy and deception; Our individuality even unto the point of eccentricity {sophistication} and perversion.

See 39*

[8v] 26

This is the radiance of civilization.[30]

We are permitted risk speculation and gambling.

[9r] 27

Our indolence to the point of worthlessness self ruin and the ruin of our families. our risk to the point of speculation and gambling. speech to the point of prose literature and poetry
We are indulged in a room a piece with a door we can lock. We are indulged in the most irregular hours of sleeping and eating. We are even encouraged to cut each others throats in the picturesque conflicts of trading horses and jack knives. A great nation in its greatness can afford much.[31] It can let many go to great lengths of sin

Utopia versus Civilization.
"War will wipe out civilization." Any distress will wipe out or tend to wipe out civilization. Civilization is the variousness and vagariousness we are indulged in by the state in its prosperity. A great nation in it greatness can afford much. A morbid irridescence is not beyond its purse. We are permitted privacy secrecy and even deceit before there is any misgiving.† So in our domestic lives and also in business and on the stock exchange. We are permitted individuality excentricity {sophistication} and even perversity before the evil days draw nigh. All these are our properties in prosperity. But we hold them only by indulgence of the commune and like our land property

[10r] 29

they may be called in and expropriated by right of eminent domain. Kismet. Let the will of the tribe be done. All Always waiting there like the skeleton in

---

* This is Frost's note.
† There is a line arrow from "permitted" up to the "Civilization" in "Utopia versus Civilization."

the closet of flesh in the hard and firm framework of our lives {namely} our universal brotherhood The least emaciation of the state and we begin to weaken toward each other and make up to each other and creep next to each other and talk affectionately about how much more we are for each other than against each other. We get out the old utopian comforter for cuddling warmth. Surely out mothers didnt pour us out on the world to crowd and hurt each other. Our panic doting is terrible {murderous}. All who will not join in our whine of mutual dependence must ~~be~~ perish without ruth. The reality of our dependence on each other is there and will be invoked in emergency.   So innocent ~~an~~ a privilege {even} as privacy may have to be given up in the hour of regimentation. The enemy is in the gates; [illegible] perhaps it will be a nervous relief if I am compelled to stop thinking of myself. Cultivation that had reached the point of sophistication may ~~as~~ well be dispensed with at least for awhile.

[10v]   30
Civilization is the opposite of Utopia[32]

as it was when Pericles[33] Socrates Alcibiades[34] and Critias[35] were spending Athens

[11r]   31
There is health in the communal uncivilization of the barbarians Esquimaux[36] and Navahoe.[37] Many have mistaken their nearness to Utopia for a higher civilization than the multifarious originality ~~and~~ of our great powers. A Utopian civilization is the last contradiction in terms. Utopia is a recourse of the tribe in emaciation. Civilization is an exuberance of peace and plenty. It is beautifully dangerous in its capacity for self destruction* It easily runs to traits of disease It is ephemeral flowers that may have to be forgotten for ~~the~~ the necessary leaves and branches.

The brilliance of a whole skeleton as an ornament in the living rooms of the brave.†

What do you tell them?—I tell them not to be so crude.—Crude yourself—What do you tell them?—I tell them what at least [illegible] cant insult their origin;—But [illegible] I remind them always that I like crudity in them and they mustnt hate it in themselves. Crude is raw and raw is raw material

---

* There is an arrow drawn to the second line of text on 10v.

† There is an arrow drawn to the first line of text on 10v.

to work with, for which we must thank God,[38] Their home villages are better
material because rawer

[12r]   33

than their Greenwich Village.[39] Greenwich Village is not properly grist for
any refinery. Neither is Europe as good grist as America. It is too far refined
already. Refinement on refinement runs out to vanishment

Every form of life creates pitiful situations. The poor Goose Girl throwing
herself at the feet of mercy for the single goose she has lost from her flock.[40]

The pacifist[41] is sure we need not hurt each other in war. The Marxist goes
further: he is sure we need not hurt each other in peace. The Marxist's is the
profounder pacifism.

Down here is ~~thers~~ a small shack of a hut but in it just now I heard the
most remarkable talker with the noblest voice uttering the largest ideas and
sentiments since Socrates in Athens. I wish you could have heard it. I left
before it ended. (Then he tells ~~of the~~ the story of the book of the Golden
Peasant in Egypt) I should have written some of it down. But it was getting
dark. Who could

[13r]   37

the speaker be in such a wretched neighborhood. Great thoughts grave
thoughts

Great is Harvard and the greatest of her greatness is simply in asking
greatness of her graduates. let them find out for themselves what in the various walks that is.

Story of God the seducer.[42] Story of God the {Lavish} Waster[43]

The news {every morning} disorders [illegible] {your mind} just as sleeping in a bed disorders ~~it~~ {the bed}. You have to make your mind up fresh every day just as {you} do your bed.~~room~~. Make up the bed—make up your
mind.

•   •   •

Inefficient	good for nothing—	self ruinous
Privacy	secrecy	deceit
Individuality	excentricity	perversion

Tyranny is an excess of individuality that wipes out individuality equally ~~with~~ as communism wipes it out.

[14v]   38

The most God like of attributes is to give us all a good stiff trial and then when we are worsted gather us all to the bosom of mercy. How God like the great men who give us a good run for our money, get our money all away from us and then {most} Godlike in the conclusion treat us all to the mercy of free libraries hospitals, museums and universities.

You might think it was men in office, but men who had {become} at the end of the ages at last all sweet like artists and women. And there were no men left of the old fashioned rough and sissy-scorning kind

[15r]   39

Thrifty Well-to-do. Rich	This Is the Radiance of
Distinguished Exquisite Precious	Civilization[44] These Its Rays

Individuality Eccentricity ~~Sophistication~~* Perversion

Privacy secrecy deceit

Inefficient worthless self ruinous ~~family ruinous~~
~~Indolence~~
Indolent
~~risk~~ {Investment} Speculation gambling Wizard of Odds
Talk   prose   poetry
Late hours for study of society—wee small hours, Sit up all night sleep all day

There will always be the martyr to new thought and there will always be the soldier to take up the cause of the martyr
under title some things that will always be.

---

* "Sophistication" is written above the line.

Always be matter and force—force and fraud—fist and mouth

At least a year on the book's name {on the spine} before reading the book. The World as Will[45]

Ɵ Ambulance and army— New Deal and Eyedcal.[46] We have had an ambulance interval between battles. Now for business again.

New Deal a {Patriotism-Matriotism} wifely administration. The Great American Wife of song and story is permitted by her business man husband to spend all his money while deprecating him as no æsthete and a mere moneymaker It has had {shown} every effeminate attribute [illegible phrase or sentence] Plus Mrs R's help.[47]

[15v]   40

on having it come over you in imagination just as if someone had said it to you on [illegible] interrupting your talk as he entered the room: What do you know about it.

[16r]   41

Class in 1939 R.W. Em[48]

Course in reminiscences

—in learning how to have something to say
—in watching your own effectiveness in company
—in transferring that to paper at a gain rather than loss.
—in writing down what you have said rather than what you are going to say.
—in how scholars differ from {the} literary chiefly in the ways their knowledge is come by.
    What's become of Waring?[49] Yale Younger Poets[50]

—recollecting the epithets {phrases} you may have scored with
—   "   "   metaphors and analogies you have
used with effect—persuasion or charm {How to tell when you are thinking}
—in thinking about the book. All of us some of the time just think the book—nearly all of us all the time.
    What is more hateful than the thought of the few rhymes there are the few verse forms and meters. The one question is how shall the mind be kept off them.

—in repressing exclamations {and stock words} by harnessing emotion strictly to the wit-mill.

—in worrying. To the sick in mind we say don't worry—work. To the healthy boys I say where I leave them dont work worry.

[*17r*] 43

5 Letter to Seniors in a College

3 Preface to Robinson[50]   Grief and Grievance[51]

2 Education by Poetry[52]   ~~Education in Metaphor~~

4 ~~Sounds~~ as Subject-matter.   Sounds as Subject Matter[53]

5 The Shape a Poem Takes[54]

Crudity Efficiency and the Rate {Speed} of Poetry

Rewards.

Dark Darker Darkest[55]

An Equalizer Once in So Often for the Public ~~Health~~ {Health}[56]

[*17v*] 44

The special tone the big ones in Washington came to use in speaking of ~~rest of us~~ any of the rest of us as A littel man.

[*18r*] 45

School of the Total Book.

School Book.

"A farmer too an excellent knave in grain

Mad cause he was hindered transportation {Duch. of Malfi}[57]

"Wee folk good folk*

Trooping all together"[58]—the populace

Acquitted (Play)[59]

Rubbering in Oaxaca[60]

The Woodpecker—The Old Sequester

---

* There is an arrow pointing from here to "44" on the previous page.

⌊ 19r ⌋ 47

A nation is as many people as without too much straining can settle their dif
ferences amicably. We hate ~~those~~ our own at least less than we hate the foreigner. The Bible says Love your enemies⌐ We can at least love those at
home better than those in other countries.⁶²

Brandeis' love of little businesses. Let there be no great men but politicians*

Rhyme word to be regarded as the last syllable of a long word like ing or ly

Has he a good appetite	Most important thing
No appetite is good	to learn is bravery. Saddest
	thing is that this should be so†⁶³

All questions are merely academic to the academic mind.

Sympathy with the young in the pains of initiation. Rouse them to the responsibilities of mind. Discipline: that they should be tightly shut in and left
free to get at one chosen point only.

[20r] 49

Scene: he arrives just in time to snatch an {unread} letter from her [~~illegible~~]
that he should never have sent

Nothing more social than to work alone⁶⁴

Life catches on something to resist itself⁶⁵

To put love in its place so it will hold a while. The fallacious think poetry
must be on the side of love's not being put in its social place. Poetry is on
both sides.

[20v] 50

When the ruling class thought they needed variety to [~~illegible~~] keep their
hold on first place they invented democracy as a {just one more} form of

---

* See 8r above.

† There is a vertical line drawn between these two sets of sentences.

government in which they {thought they} could pretty safely risk their position and yet look willing to give it up. They were making shift to hold on The imperceptibility of the gains to that is arguable there has been none in emancipation.

Women going into business has taken marriage out of business

In the story of debt and the poor debtor. My grandmother escape from the kitchen and the indication women may do everything but {hunting war and sports and art}Having to fight by the millions—like it or not

Not realized number two: to stay out of the wash of opinion. All for Lindburg[66] all against

Not as great an achievement as they cheered.

Last fight in Madison Square Garden[67]

Crudity of ordering a poem of me.

[*21r*] 51

1 All men created free and equally funny[68]

2 Extension of the right to pride of ancestry[69]

4 Poor not to be persuaded their sorrows are no worse than those of the rich. Anyway the rich have daintier sorrows.[70] Well then, all this complaining literature of the democracy of the last fifty years has been {of} the common man's coming at last into the dainty sorrow of finding life a vanity of vanities.[71] Solomon—Chirstina Rosetti.[72] Kings—then fine ladies {finely}—and now the proletariat[73] {grossly}. The discovery is my forgiveness of the Lewis-Dreiser sort[74]

3 Confidence reposed in them as locomotive engineers. Who would have predicted {in 1895} {say} that anything so universally individual as ~~would~~ millions driving {a} tons of steel {apiece} on trackless roads and responsibly taking each others lives in the name of dangerous pleasure?

5 Least realized of rights that of not crowding, though of the crowd.[75] He that has power to hurt. Not to seek his own advantage. Cartoons of Milquetoast justifying the rude and unscrupulous.

[22r]   53

A Resolution to Refrain

Our democracy[76] with a written constitution to keep power from taking its natural course toward centralization and monarchy may be like the sad attempts {of a woman} to keep young {or keep a pup young with whisky} and keep thought from generalization. {Generalization is to be defined as observation ageing-or thought ageing.} Our democracy may be against nature. The reverse of the seal of the United States expresses the arrest the founders had in mind. It is a cone truncated into a table where they wanted the human to leave off. It is finished at the point where the apex should be with the divine eye.[77] The New Deal's[78] impatience with the idea of power refraining and breaking off.

[22v]   54

Don't tell the poem in other and worse English of your own to show you understand it. But say something of your own based on the poem (not an opinion of it though.)

School boy one who tells over what he has read in the order in which he read it. Habit grows into an eagerness to tell right away what he has read as if it were as much news as the days [illegible] Get ready to stand cross-questioning by a lawyer* Learn to put add your weight to that of the thing itself in pushing it down into your memory

New England schooling designed to establish two habits: taking thought to add your own weight to deepen the impression anything gives you, and taking another look to see if your first look was right. It cultivated [illegible fears] the fear of forgetting and the fear of mistake. (It is important to exhaust in a moments survey, the possibilities of error—all the places you could go wrong.) (A circle of all the things it isnt round the things it is.)

[23r]   55

Negro Biblicals

David Took a Census[79]
Abraham Said She Was His Sister[80] [?bis]

---

* This sentence from "Get ready . . ." written in left margin.

Joshua and Daylight Saving Time
Jonah and New York (The Final Traffic Jam)
The Forty-fourth Chapter of Job[81]
For Christs Sake Forget the Poor Some of the Time[82]

The sentences must spring from each other and talk to each other even when there is only one character speaking   Self repartee

Learn* in school to quote your teachers correctly so that all your life long ~~you will quote~~ as gossip or reporter you will quote everybody correctly except when from malice or mischief you [illegible] misquote people on purpose. Formula for examination questions: What do you think I (the Teacher) think was the date of the battle of Hastings?[83] of Yorktown†[84]

Let me press you a little further to answer for your position. You say you never would have written about the poor if

[24r]   57

you had known ~~anything was~~ {it was} going to make people do anything about them. You say you wouldnt dare to get rid of poverty ~~so much~~ for fear of losing the good that has always come from it. You say poetry has always to look to Want ~~of~~ {for} various kinds for tragedy. Is poverty one of the kinds poetry depends on for subject matter and if so musnt I suspect that poetry has a vested interest in [illegible] seeing the poor kept poor. The answer is yes: and my counter question is Do you always use the term vested interest as evil? A poet certainly makes his living directly or indirectly from poetry (if that is evil) and his poetry certainly depends as much on the sorrows of poverty as on the sorrows of plenty (if that is an evil.)[85]

All the best people pulled out, we are told, and went to live in Canada.[86] There was nothing left in the United States but the revolutionary rabble. But all that is intellectual artistic scientific industrial and political has occurred in the United States; Practically nothing in Canada. It proves ~~one or both of two things~~ either that nothing {good} comes of the best people or that nothing important can happen in a colonial state.

[24v]   58

They are untroubled with the suspicion that someone else is getting more out of {the} proceedings {structure} than they are.

---

* There is an arrow drawn from this word to text at the bottom of 20v.
† "Yorktown" written in blue ink.

[25r]   59

Nature is a chaos. Humanity is a ruck. The ruck is the medium of kings
They assert themselves on it to give it some semblance of order. They build it
into gradations of power narrowing upward to the throne. There are periods
of felicity when the state stands {lasts} for a reign and even two or three
reigns or a dynasty. The people are persuaded to {accept} their subordina-
tions. But the ruck is a discouraging medium to work in. Form is only
roughly achieved there and at best leaves in the mind a dissatisfaction ~~and~~ a
fear {of} impermanence ~~contemplation~~ and {a} relative confusion. It is always as transitional as rolling clouds where a figure never quite takes shape
before it begins to be another figure. Contemplation turns from in it mental
distress to the physicians. The true revolt from it is not into madness or into a
<u>re</u>form. It is onward in the line projected by nature to human nature {and so
on to individual nature.} It is the one man working in a medium of paint
words or notes—or wood or iron. Nothing composes the mind like composing {composition}.[87] Let a {mere} man attempt no more than he is meant for.
Other men are too much for him to count on organizing. Let him compose
words into a poem.

[25v]   60

Some are interested in incomes some in outcomes.

[26r]   61

Outcomes.*

You are confused about that then. You have it to hold onto that all nature
taken together and including human nature in peace and war must be just a
little more in favor ~~than~~ of man than against him say a fraction of one percent at <u>least</u> or else our hold on the planet wouldnt have so increased. Have I
not said so in a poem.[88] And again you are reading a novel. You are awaiting
its outcome. You are awaiting the outcome of the baseball or football season.
You may be predicting it or betting on it. You are awaiting the outcome of an
investment, or the enterprise or ambition of one of your children. There is
your own ambition to attend. There is a war [~~illegible~~] to watch with as much
patience as you can command. Greatest of all your interests if you are of a
philosophical turn will be the outcome of the struggle for their shares in life

---

* There is an arrow drawn from this word to the entry on 25v.

between employer and employee. There is the possibility that there will be no employers in future but politicians elect. Nothing is clearer than that you would like to ~~be~~ stay in the watch stands till it was surer Very orderly I should say your minds needs were

[26v]   62

Take my word

For it Sammy[89]

[27r]   63

The New Deal has ~~worked~~ so dealt as to demonstrate incontrovertably that the rich are all bad. I have lived with the poor and know that they are greedy and dishonest—in a word bad* So much for the upper and the lower end. Both the upper and lower class are bad. There is left the middle class to consider. But the middle class is the bourgeoisie {our ~~the~~ favorite black beast of} that ~~it~~ has been tried and found ~~evil~~ {out} by all the literature of the last fifty years. Communists and all the intelligentsia are agreed that the middle class is bad. Both ends {then} and the middle—they are all bad. We are arrived at a conclusion that means nothing When all is bad it makes no difference whether it is called good or bad. Be it all called good and lets start over[90]

Nothing for composure so good as composition.[91]

Statistics[92] are the way I {have to} look at everybody but myself. I have less need of them in handling the few I am thrown with than a president in handling his millions of people.

[27v]   64

And <u>glut</u> thyself with what thy womb devours[93]

  all to be slighted except the word <u>glut</u>

but I used to read womb devours as ~~of~~ e its equal in accent

Left on base—so many a poem

* ~~The~~ {One} sentence must speak to another till the accents begin to single out particular words for notice without italics. ~~They are~~ Sentences are

---

* There is an arrow drawn here pointing to lines on 26v.

only literature as they affect each others intonations. Good writing is self repartee

[28r] 65

A poem is a triumph of association

July 1949

A poem is a run of lucky recalls[94]

A poem must be a statement susceptible of being reduced to an argument as the old fashioned word is. But it may not be a dogged statement. It must have a wild way with it. Those who [~~illegible~~] oppose the poem as statement are found the most [~~illegible sentence~~] ~~give to~~ {guilty of} [the] sentence as statement and nothing but statement. They seem never to have been troubled in the ear by the doggedness of what they were writing. Statement yes but it is only as the poem and the sentence within the poem ~~transcend~~ {exceed} statement (not fall short of it) that poetry arises. *All beauty may come from the way context is woven to make stress certain on one particular word. As in the following:

~~Philosophy~~ I write it now "God is the everready one" and with the certainty that the reader will speak me wrong till he has heard me longer. {The} Philosopher sets boldly forth ~~to on~~ {in} in uncharted ~~places~~ {space} to find anew the unity we need for sanity. He fares far and fearless without God or prejudice for or against ~~him~~ {God}. The philosopher is braver than most of us in the dark confusion. He seeks unity. He trusts he will

[29r] 67

find {come on} it. {But he is determined to do without it till he can find it in his own course of experience}. He may only have come somewhere near it before he dies. At his greatest he may have said ~~Thought~~ {Reason} or Will. We hope his One has satisfied him. He has dared to cut loose in infinity like Lucretius' master Epicurus.[95] {He has suffered privation-deprivation. So} His adventure may move us ~~to action~~ stay at homes to admiration. [~~illegible phrase~~] {But it somehow leaves us loveless} {Fortunately} for us in our lives there is ~~provided provision~~ merciful provision of an easier one in the church among our houses ~~For us God is an everready One. We too must have one [illegible] a simple one for our simplicity.~~ God have him any time from childhood on. {whom} there had to {He We can} be an everyday One for our simplicity.

[*30r*]   69

{Half} One scene Plays

The Wife-beater (with a straw hat) (His tie deranged)
The Blindman's Plunge | into the ditch
The Irrevocable Letter.
The Letter Revoked

[*31r*]   71

"To be furious is to be frightened out of fear"[96] Shakespeare said for Stephen Crane[97]

I must have taken it as a truth accepted that a thing of beauty[98] will never cease to be beautiful. Its beauty will in fact increase. Which is the opposite doctrine to Emersons in Verily know when half gods go the gods arrive[99]: the poets and poems we have loved and ceased to love are to be regarded as stepping stones of our dead selves to higher things. Growth is a distressful change of taste for the better. Taste improving is on ~~its~~ {the} way upward to creation. Nay-nay. It is more likely on the way to dissatisfaction and ineffectuality. A person who has found out young from Aldous Huxley[100] how really bad Poe is will hardly from the superiority of the position this gives him be ~~likely to find himself~~ able to go far with anything he himself attempts. The fastidious are apt to be stuck in complaints. Taste isnt exactly fear but it is at best the caution with which we must be bold. Creation is the boldness. ({How to} Be with caution bold is the problem)[101]

[*31v*]   72

A course in which you assigned marks for the year early in the year and put it on the class to show cause by personal appearance and appeal why the mark should be changed for later work.

A course in which you ~~told the class~~ predicted early what number of the class would probably never be able to ~~get~~ use more than three punctuation marks well.

Aristocratic to scorn the fear of drink vandalism

The one who makes the law has always been above the law. The common man makes our law. So if we seem lawless it is small wonder

[*32r*]*   [illegible] —Poet [   ]†
Divine right   Consent
Justice   Mercy[102]
Liberty   Equality

Practice will be found to move back and forward on a keyboard between them.

Current   Classic   Not stuck in the {golden mean.}
Talking   Intoning

Property is anything you fear to lose ~~for fear~~ lest you wont have more is good where ~~that~~ {it} came from. It may be knowledge ~~you have~~ acquired It may be a phrase you ~~already~~ pride yourself on having had. Some property is inevitable Too much property clogs the flow of life. Life finally thickens and comes to rest and death in self-choked in its own properties‡

Life is ~~that in~~ a stream that parts around islands great and small[103]

Signs of life { hoop   Deaden what is so soon to die? Fire for form:[104]
           Cat and spool or block

Response. Something to respond to

Rather have you right than lively. New radicalism conservative already {Progressive} School {infected with ~~the~~

Any thinking is protective. It will be said in education Hard to contaminate a living source. [illegible]

[*32v*]   [illegible phrase] between President and Congress on one side and Supreme court on the other.

Offsetting arrogances.

•   •   •

---

* 32r and 32v are both unruled pages that have been inserted into the notebook. There are five cartoon drawings in the upper right corner of 32r of a head of a man with a hat.
†Frost's brackets.
‡ Passage written slant upward from left to right across the page.

Present came flooding ~~in the shape of~~ {as current} science
"   "   "   "   literature
"   comes   "   "   politics.
Science had no choice but to be current

There was no ancient science ~~for~~ for a students background. Literature in school once entirely classic has become perilously current Politics has become perilously current Religion stays pretty well classic. Have to [illegible] act

Our darkest concern[105]—We might give way to thoughts like these. Presented us in every lesson.

Grasp with them is no more than hanging on desperately to a beam end bobbing in the dark.

Great times contracted into now. Tendency ~~to gather~~ in draw ourselves up in to the present as to draw ourselves into the nation.

Im terribly tired aren't you. Wake me up in twenty years from now This noticeable [page torn]

[33r]   73

A course (half course) in finding subjects to write on that are neither pro nor con.

Originality is of the Devil*.[106] {God always was God. The only new thing is the Devil} It is ~~the only~~ {all there} is to ambition that last infirmity of noble minds[107] by which sin fell the angels.[108] Heaven was truth and Lucifer originated Hell. Christ was truth and should have sufficed But he was up his own sleeve from which original thinkers have been drawing surprise ever since

Self discipline may be likened unto as much form as the idea gives itself in prose. Discipline as we get it from the drill sergeant and the enemy is more like the form imposed on us by prosody. One is individual the other tribal.

Our lawlessness and lack of discipline have been under criticism from the Kiplings of England[109] ever since we were born a nation. Now they are under severer criticism from our enemy the German Nazi The English oddly enough have been lumped with us as all undisciplined democrats together.

What has been been the matter with us we are forced by arms to consider. Some say bad educators. Too much freedom. We agree that we must give up some freedom for the purposes of war. But we love our freedom and mean to come back to it as soon as the war is over. We merely Nazify for the to deal with the Natzi in war. {To the Nazis I will show myself nasty.} It is disturbing to think about but as a matter of fact the Natzi only Nazified for the purposes of war.

[33v] 74

Some way to measure the reluctance you feel to learn an attachment for an attraction[110]

[34r] 75

[illegible] In lovers quarrels[111] we are fighting {fighting to deny} {to keep from} not to seeing or admitting each others faults. When the fights die down it means we have acceptance of {given in and} and the faults have been accepted. Why you fool do I have to tell you what I want to keep you from being.

This is a very country is a very broad pan to be only human nature deep. [illegible] Try to move it and opinion rushes all to one side and slops over. I sometimes wish it were regional enoug to be cut up as by the [illegible] separator in an icepan.

The separateness of the parts is as important as the connection {of the parts}.[112] True in a poem and true in [illegible] society.

Our commitments are not calculated. {For them to be} at all fateful we must be seduced into them. Pleasure leads.

A man is known by the boldness of his commitments—his attachments. (Also per contra by the boldness of his detachments, but of these elsewhere) Commitments to the life the material the form and then the grace the resourcefulness with which the compromises and or adjustments are made. Suppose you are

[34v] 76

Story of the editorial lamenting the good old days when there was nothing but firelight and the family had to gather in around it and entertain each other. Kerosene lamps were [illegible] breaking up the family to "sit sullenly" each by himself and read to himself.

[35r]   77

recklessness enough to seek your pleasure in depicting a hunting scene by weaving cloth. How much can you get out of having to give in?

Mercy seems first to appear in the story of Jonah.[113] Jonah ran away [illegible sentence] {for} fear Gods mercy would let him down and not carry out the prophesy {he had} assigned him.

Mercy comes into its own in the New Testament where it is the whole thing. The whole scheme there is framed up to insure our failure to live up to the Sermon on the Mount and so leave us nothing for it but to throw ourselves on Mercy. I wonder who or wi in heaven or hell or what in the nature of things is at the back of it. I can see in the nature of things the certain bafflement of reason. The only way reason can be made to seem prevalent is by recession as by constant {re} amputation of an offending limb or member.[114] Growth and increase are irrational

[35v]   78

Research-boy chronicler historian are all worth being in an ascending scale. It is for me to decide how far up I want to go. I sometimes wish there were more strict chroniclers for me to read. Though historians are my favorites they can disturb me greatly with a tendency to be novelists. They can overindulge the dramatic and storified till I lose my confidence that there is such a thing as fact. Maybe there isnt any such thing. For many a fact of history I have put faith in I have lived to see a low down appear to the effect that it was a barefaced lie. But examine a first class history like Burys Greece[115] for the irreducible reality and there's really a considerable mass to rest in. Dubieties are frankly marked. For instance we might like to think but do not positively know that Asia (the Phoenicians for Persia) was beaten by Greeks at Salamis[116] and away off out of communication. by Greeks at Humera Asia (the Phoenicians of Carthage) was beaten by Greeks at Humera on exactly the same day.[117] It shapes up poetically that way. Ancients liked to tell it that way. But is it enough to tell it that way let it go at that? Am I content to call it history when it leaves me as insecure as that? Fiction has its realm to be true to and history has another. I like the boundaries between the two well defined. I have been told they cant be kept so

[*36r*]   79

The danger of the age is that too many kinds of people will fail to realize that the separateness of the parts is as important as the connection of the parts.[118] The parts must not possibly be derived from each other, but must be made to look like a good set. This is equally true of the parts of a poem and the parts of society.

The Money. People in the Money Hervey's friends and Hervey[119]

An idealist is one who has been given something to want that he can never have.

A poem is the act of having an idea and how it feels to have an idea

Opinions doctrines causes only as I can use them like love death and ~~religion~~ sorrow as the building parts of a poem or story.

We say tastes differ and then proceed to quarrel with other tastes and particularly not to allow for the preference to be absolutely good-for-nothing.

[*37r*]   81

No lack of purpose when at war. The aim then is to win. But after the war what? The same as before the war and during the war—to win. To win position, promotion credit respect honor money fame—victory or victories little and big.

Repression and expression (Extraction)

Smatter Pop. They have so smattered that no matter what you tell them they think they have heard it before yet if you stop half way in the recitation and ask them to tell the rest they can do nothing. Also any inaccuracy is near enough or is even better than that it is poetry.

Power divided against itself gives our other traits {than power} a chance.

We have had years enough to satisfy ourselves pretty surely that all men are mortal and that nobody practically has hopes of a longer life than a hundred years. But we lack data for determining the life span of a nation. Says it shall wave a thousand years

[*37v*]   82

whose flag has braved a thousand years the battle and the breeze. ~~Campbell wrote that~~ [~~illegible~~] More than a hundred years have been added to the age of the British flag since Campbell[120] wrote that and the prophets have been proved wrong {by the World War} who thought the British Empire's time was up. Rome got about a thousand good years out of it. We havent the facts to base an opinion on.

To keep the world from becoming a harder place to save the soul[121] in we have to keep getting on into new sets of circumstances; because the greatest danger we meet with is a [i̶l̶l̶e̶g̶i̶b̶l̶e̶] situation we are too familiar with and so arent roused to attack with our truest spirit.

[*38r*]   83

Is Bulfinch's <u>Age of Fable</u>[122] what is meant by the Humanities.

Subjects to Use

What it's smart to wear. What its smart to like. What its smart to think.

The history of a reputation

Expectation of meaning and deduction

A Better word than communication (correspondence

ABC and 123[123] is the poem of education as distinguished from apprentice-ship.

How many books to read per year

Confidence based on what the other fellow may be assumed to have missed

The length of time it takes to learn the weight that should be given a word (Democracy

Against the Vocabularians.

I thought I was an {acromatic} lense. I'm afraid I am a prism.

"My stomach is not good—but I do think"

·   ·   ·

As good as his word but no better or worse than his word

Bancroft and Fletcher.[124]
Keats on Art[125]

And think that I may never live to trace
Their shadows <u>with the magic hand of chance</u>[126]

[38v]   84
I have been all throug Palgrave[127] looking for a poem idealistic in this sense
and found few or none

Think of the happiness of having said right out that sometimes you feel
sure of bad sometimes of good. You dont care who minds. The heart asks
pleasure first[128]

But sure with patience I can bear
A loss I never knew Cibber[129]

Great merit in some eyes to lose patience over a loss one never knew Idealists

Between the breasts*

deep settling in or between armrests

[39r]   85
Sometimes I Feel That Way a title for a book of verse that varies ~~all the
way~~ {from} faith to unfaith and back again uncensored. Is this the justice that
on earth we find. A Happiness Beyond Ideals An ideal being something very
very high that ~~you~~ {we} ~~cant~~ we cant possibly live up to but cant possibly
keep from trying to live up {Cant possibly both live} Example the Sermon on
the Mount. Abolition of Poverty ~~High as~~ Utopia. Peace. Only the Sermon on
the Mount is a perfect example. The others are easily disposed of so that
we can go about our business. They need not trouble us long. ~~High but not
high enough~~ {The Sermon on the Mount does forever.} But {there is} ~~better
than high aspiration~~ better than high aspiration is deep in dwelling. (Poetry is

---

* Line written slanted upward from left to right.

deep indwelling.) It gets in [illegible] {deep down under} the fear that we will be ~~punished~~ {bombed or struck by lightening} for saying recklessly exactly what we feel. It is abandon~~ded~~{ment} to the truth. Look back over any anthology such as Palgraves Couches or Untermeyer's[130] for cry {in them} for betterment. ~~Poetry~~ {A poem} is not to be looked on as something that can be improved on. The flaws out of it would make no difference in its poeticality. That is of about the same for a poet all his life in his earliest poems equally with his later poems

[*40r*]   103

> ~~When you~~
> ~~You cant be put in prison for original sin When I hear you talk too much about~~ it

No one can touch you or imprision you for original sin. So it a safe thing to confess to and it may relieve {you} ~~your conscience~~ of the real wickedness you have on our conscience if you keep saying mea culpa in the vague religious way of the saints.
His only sin was original sin
It was it was
He confessed with a sanctimonious grin
He

Must* learn to enjoy people I dont like and ~~do~~ {don't}† approve of.

If‡ that star is as big as astronomers say [~~it is~~] it must be as far away as they say or it wouldnt shine so small.

A people who have to have too much done for them are done for.

Suppose we agree that every loss by sickness {death} fire {accident} failure in business ~~can~~ should be insured against. There then must be a lot of success to carry all the unsuccess. Success

[*41r*]   105
must be allowed to succeed [illegible] without any limit but the police. Suc-

---

* "I don't" written in blue ink.

† "Must learn . . . shine so small" written in pencil.

‡ This entry is written vertically along the left-hand margin of the page from bottom to top.

cess must be allowed to succeed because as the saying is nothing succeeds like it. Health grows healthier strength stronger and wealth wealthier The insurance plan would be to use this fact of nature for the benefit of all, and spread the success of the greatest even to the least of their brethren. But it always remember the greatest must be allowed to succeed greatly. The only reservation is that ~~they should be able~~ success should not be allowed to usurp the functions of government and do {to much of} the law making and law enforcing for their employees. That way slavery lies. It is a constant threat. The government must not consent to be outgoverned by big business. It must rise in its arrogance to beat down any arrogance of its subjects. Of course. It {Govt} may have to reach a distance into business to hold it where it wont do more harm than its very necessary good. Nothing is pure. Business must do some law making and law enforcing to be effective. [illegible] Government must do some business to hurt big business when it needs anyway to curb it.

[42r]   107

One opposite of Individualism would be Hero-worship like
Carlyles.[131]
Opposite of Civilization {Barbarism
                                          {Eutopia[132]
Hegel taught a doctrine of opposites, but said nothing about ~~there~~ everything's having more than one opposite.[133]
The Constant Symbol[134] in poetry is of confluence without compromise.

A liberal[135] is one who would give everyone time to unflold his story—times not just time.

* K. Bowen[136] at {Bread Loaf} said John Adams made politics and politics made him—they were [illegible] one growth. Aug 1949

* Perish the word compromise. Poetry forgive me for ~~let~~ having it pass the barrier of my teeth. Except as the two enter into each other neither exists. No intention is so definitely in mind that it has anything to lose by going into effect. Compromises would mean half defeat: which is a thing no proud spirit need admit. There is nothing more non existent and so silly to think and talk about as what might have been.

•   •   •

Of a man who cant get over having once been important: He has been deflated but wont go down

[43r]   109

Some of the new poetry shows the same lesions there must be in the brains of the poets.

Great are the Greeks we keep saying. They have taught us everything. But they didn't set us the example of imitating anybody. It was Rome that imposed on us the imitation of the Greeks and the imitation of Christ. They were never better than imitators. We will [illegible] {never} be [illegible] till we break from under the spell of [illegible] Rome.

"God rest you merry gentlemen
Let nothing you." amaze[137]

Mrs Eleanor Roosevelt says every girl should learn to carry her liquor.[138] The idea should be extended to greater things. Every girl every boy is necessarily somewhat crazed with the confusion of the times. Every human being must learn to carry his own craziness and confusion and not bother shi his friends about it. He will have clarifications but they will be momentary {flashes} like this—little shapes like poems vortex smoke rings

[44r]   111

you can give off within the general unshapeability.

Nobility—what is it? It is to be above the four considerations common {man} lives {by} [illegible] the fear of jail, of the poor house of the insane asylum and of Hell.[139] These are the basic four the state is founded on. Nobility rises above such low fears to such lofty fears as the fear of the enemy

Clinic

The cure is not something for you to love and so take your mind off yourself. The doctor may have said so. But shallow shallow. The cure is something an idea a child an enterprise a faith (such as Christianity or Communism) you have set your heart on to make it prevail. You must have taken both sword and shield for it. For it you must learn the meaning of what it is to be with caution bold.[140]

[45r]   113

This spreading every word out into all its denotations and connotations as you read along is as if [illegible] it had been written on blotting paper. The stronger the writing the sharper the definition in the place. The direction of the piles combs the word into the one single one of its meanings intended like a hair. Some would have it that the words are cowlicks that wont be combed straight in a direction.

To August 1949

You have to be pretty secret in your thinking if you are going to secrete anything.

Not to get stuck in the golden mean. Life ranges on a scale between the two extremes.

Difficulties beyond help from science
How much friendship is feigning.
How much false friendship you can use
How much friendship you are justified in feigning for the institution's sake
At what point will you feel safe in breaking off a false friendship.

[46r]   115

Difficulties beyond the help of Science
Deciding when to leave an attachment for an attraction.[141] Remember that the definition of loyalty is merely that for the lack of which your gang will shoot you with or without a fair trial.[142] Is it a virtue to have risen easily on stepping stones of your dead friends and admirations to higher things?

Infantilism is reckoned a disease. Primitivism if genuine and not merely affected is pretty much the same disease. If affected for purposes of art it may be disgusting but a least it is [illegible] negligible. We turn our minds away from adolescents who to pass the time away are always asking if it wouldn't be possible to take this or that position. The answer is Do you really take it. We have no patience with artists who pose a form of insanity to see what God or man can do about it. Give us the crazy who are clearly crazy in their own right. To the concentration camp[143] all those who would get into a dark corner and gnaw their fingernails in imitation of the bonefide crazy.

The Preamble[144]

It should have gone thus: life liberty and the pursuit of pleasure. Happiness is too much to talkabout. But pleasure now. Such as for instance wine women and song. Something you honestly find you cant help giving way to.

Pay the Piper[145]

The piper must of course be paid. But never in all the ages till lately has any one given {much of} any thought to the money man who has ~~pai~~ paid him. The piper his tune and the dancers to it were all our theme [~~illegible~~] and history. It will be the same again. Trust the spirit of man to be high spirited. Trust the soul to rise above considerations of expense. It has gone a good way back to its own superiority. [~~illegible~~] The day {is} not long past when Dwight Morrow[146] could begin an address to the meat packers of Chicago, the Swifts and {the} Cudahys.[147] ~~We that were once despised~~ You that were once despised as butchers we that were once despised as usurers[148] have been made the lords of the new world. Look at us here assembled to eat in glory. But fate overlooks them both to start to put them back if not into oblivion at least into slight regard. The usurer has been reduced to an interest of 2% All history from having been economical will now return to the adventurous.

Somebody put up the money for the Puritans, but we forget their names in the story.*

"Open covenants openly arrived at"[149]
Open atoms openly arrived at
Open weapons openly arrived at.
Open poems openly arrived at.
Why should anyone resent having the heart plucked out of his secret? (mystery)
It is necessary to be very secret in order to secret anything that will take ~~the~~ friends or enemies by surprise.†

---

* This entry is written vertically along the left-hand margin of the page from bottom to top.
† There is a line running from "surprise" across the paragraph to the entry that begins "The game is to surprise . . ."

To surprise is one great effect in war and art.
Of course there is also the effectiveness
of threatening with the overt but inevitable.
The bride could tell a tale of what hung over her
all day long her wedding day till bed time*
The game is to surprise our enemies in war our friends in peace

When Peattie[150] says he puts humanity before his country he thinks hastily. Or so I suspected. We reach up from self to humanity through the nation. He may mean that what brings on rebellions and revolutions is something in us we might call supernational something larger than the nation. But it should distrust itself and should be distrusted (Leave attachment for attraction)[151]

[47v] 118

No rivers to the sea (except they go[152] underground

Confusion to bugs[153] (by spraying them with each others juice)

The short way to solve the race problem is to make a law that beginning today no one {for fifty years} shall marry his own color. That would be fairer as it would [illegible] bring out a fairer [illegible] blend than the present laissez faire method. The pure black source would be [illegible] destroyed at once

Don't forget how the Christian world hated Darwin for threatening their beliefs and the how {the} Darwin[illegible]ians hated Lamark[154] to the point of destroying {him} by discrediting him for threatening their belief.

The fault of {the} modern state is that it wants to bestow blessings on its people too directly {by dole} {and subsidy}† as if they were beggars instead of indirectly as if they were friends. The older state was a development of provision so favorable to its people that they were almost unaware of it.

[48r] 119

The question rises is our restless discontent the thing in us nature can best use for her purposes (if she has any)

·   ·   ·

---

* This section, from "Of course" to "bed time," is bracketed off.
† Phrase located above paragraph and inserted via line.

~~The account of creation~~ The story to account for the creation by attributing to it a creator ~~is~~, but that isn't what we mean. {It is on the way there but} It is more than that. The story to bring the creator down from the dangerously near abstract and impersonal into a human being with an {earthly} mother if not an earthly father, but neither is that what we mean. From polytheism to monotheism and back to ameliorated polytheism is a good story and is on the way no doubt but still seems far short of the goal. The churches are no more than roadside camping places. Does it never strike us that the journeys end is behind us and {by a merciful} provision ~~is merciful that~~ we are probably travelling in a wide circle however straight our aim.[155] We want to know if there isn't a Something and our wanting to know is probably all there is.

You cant tell me the rays haven't always acted on us a little if they are so terribly effective in concentrated uranium radium barridium and plutonium.[156]

[*48v*]   120

Between Learning & Creation. What we make is off the vital into the accumulated.

To Rest in a Process. What can't be rounded out neednt be an unhappiness if we simply enter it as unfinished business. No—unfinishable.

Greek for "Whatever else may be numerically stated" (Thucid)[157]

There cant help being a difference to the arts under a college president with a conscientious concern for them and a college president with a weakness for them.
Science ~~pokes~~ {sticks a poker} into nature as into {the} a dark hole of an unknown wild animal that now and then gave a vicious bite to the end of the poker.[158]

[*49r*]   121

True humility is a kind of carelessness that stays none too sure the mind is worth educating beyond the next idea the body worth providing for beyond the next meal and the soul worth saving beyond the momentary magnanimity.[159] There is no humility at all in this ~~anxiety~~ religious anxiety for salvation here or hereafter. And whats the use of all this talk about it? We must come in with enough greed for punishment to give an opponent a solid satisfaction in the genuineness of the game We may be irresistable or immovable as the case requires. We may be ambitious (but not too ambitious) to get something achieved clear away outside of us in the objective world such as an elastic irridescence that floats a moment before bursting us into spray.

[49v]   122

"I see by {be} the papers"—Mr. Dooley[160]

Out of Brookings Institute[161] comes word to reassure the world that there will be 300 000 000 of us in fifty or a hundred years more and we will be eight times as well off as now. To Have ready for me by tomorrow a sentence of not more than three hundred words telling what eight times as well off would mean.

Title of Lecture

Absent thee from felicity a while

Insipid and Vapid.

The three insipidities the world will owe to America and remember it for are the Movies comic strips the Comics and {the} Cokes. Mind you none of them are vicious evils. They are not bad enough for the magnificence of Hell. All they have is size and vapidity.

How Hard it Is to Avoid Being a King or Escape from Being a King.[162] Take the case of George Washington as an example and the case of the King that abdicated and the son who refused to succeed him.

[50r]   123

Eliots Cocktailian Episcopalians[163]

~~You have to stay around with a person after he has said a thing~~

After a person has said a thing you have to stay around with him a long time and perhaps hear him put it in different ways at different times if you are going to understand him* The teacher has the advantage that he has his hear-

---

* "From a long . . ." to the end of this sentence crossed-out with downward, diagonal lines slanted from right to left.

ers where they have to stay around with him long enough to to get ⌊illegible⌋ {how} he means what he says.

Mens animi—the thoughts of my emotion.[164]

Eloquence and exuberance in the still small voice. Such is poetry.

On what {which most} the enterprise and your part in it go forward, knowledge and or belief

I Beg Leave to Differ

I make bold to say

[*51r*] 125
    The radical said to the conservative
If eventually why not now.

    The conservative said to the radical You are going to die eventually! so why not now. And he slew the radical.

    By the law of diminishing returns civilization must some day arrive at so-cialism but why anticipate the day.

    The human race ha as an enterprise has reached a point of vastness when by the law of diminishing returns we get socialism.

    Thales of Miletus[165] first guessed that [illegible] all was one element. He guessed it might be water. We have come a long way to where we think we almost know what it may be. Tomorrow we may know. Anyway this much be said of it in advance. It will be no different from the multiplicity we see all round us except that the multiety will be hidden in it. Every detail will be there as in natural life only we cant see it any better than if we had deliber-ately bandaged our eyes. We [illegible] have driven variety into concealment into occlusion.[166]

[*52r*] 127
    [four lines crossed out and illegible]

•   •   •

He: The greatest thing to learn is bravery.
She: The saddest thing is that this has to be.[167]

[53r]*   139

> From
> Willoughby Cliff [168]
> September 1909
> Been in this book
> ever since.
> (till [illegible] 1949)
> till 1938

[149–157 blank]

---

* A small fern is pressed on the page to the left of the text.

"Submission to the law of the machine"

MS. 001979. *Three ring binder leaves with no binding, 6½″ × 9″. All entries are in blue ink unless otherwise noted. Included with the notebook is a note by Frost's secretary, Kathleen Johnston Morrison, on a white piece of 3″ × 5″ notepaper that reads, "'Waste' theme again—all through the note books—This is a an early book (internal evidence—e.g. Tramp sleeping in barn poem—I remember R.F. telling the story) KM."*

[1r] Submission to the law of the machine
The mighty copper wound magnetic spool
The atomic vortex in the molecule
The tiniest ~~electric~~ {excited} {erratic} smithereens
Even those familiar with it haven't seen
~~Submission to the nature of the tool~~
Submission to the thing you want to rule
So it wont ~~cut~~ {blast} or crush you for a fool
~~Thats~~ {[illegible]} what I take humility[1] to mean.

And much more [illegible] the ~~instrument is~~ {parts {two} ~~I act between~~}*

~~Are men and women~~
Are me {myself} and people me ~~and God or [illegible]~~
The danger is that I shall overrun
And not serve time in study. ~~Havent I~~
                              ~~And he low~~
                              And {to} decice

~~Have I not been to apt to overrun~~

~~I have been all to~~

                    •   •   •

---

* This bracketed phrase written beneath the line. Within the bracketed phrase, "two" is written beneath the word "parts".

I have been all too apt to overrun

And much more when the problem is believers
Before I speak in argument or prayer
What pressure god and man are like to bear

[2r]   [illegible]

I did not care
I cared not what proportions of my time {all the} day
Was
Was being spent used well spent thrown away
Or what propriety was being wronged
I wanted what it was to be prolonged

Not only was I truly not concerned
Not only that {so} but I was not concerned
If the occasion so intensely burned
It [illegible]

[2v]   [illegible line]

Moments there are I willingly prolong
No And never [illegible]
Regardless of [?hi]
Now matter how I seem to waste[2] or spend
The present

Much as to travelers of the past I owed

[3r]   Sing Muse of Epic {Heroic} now
About the Trojan row
And And [illegible] when it ended, how
The Trojan Fall and how
Aeneas fled from Troy
And brought along his boy
And aged father too
Who claimed he Venus knew

~~But~~ {But} left his wife behind
~~And how her fate was kind~~
~~Tis said she wasnt murdered~~
B
Among the womankind
That by the Greeks were herded
Together to be murdered
[?Neither] they had good looks
~~Or were~~
Or ~~could~~ qualify as cooks
In which case they were saved
And married or enslaved.
~~The boy survived the war~~
~~To be the ancestor of~~
~~The little boy Julus~~
~~Survived it all to fool us~~
~~By being incestor~~
But more than her Julus?
Creusa lived to foolus[3]

[*4r*]   you sail without a light

My name is Christopher Columbus
I cant be moved by ~~all this~~ {?threat} and rumpus
Put up your knives and go below
We're members of the O. {HO Hi Ho}   O. Hi.O*
A stock exchange affiliate
I ~~know~~ {see} who you are!
~~Lets hear some more~~!   Vociferate!
For such a husky ~~lot~~ {herd} of boys ghostly noise
You make a ~~very husky~~ {very [illegible]} noise
~~It does you fools us good to strike~~ {you strike and strike and strike and strike}
I end by sailing where I like.
What's that? a shot across our bow?
(I cant be bothered with you now.)†
You pirate dont you hear me shout

---

* Phrase written in black ink.

† There is an arrow from this parenthetical line to the space above the line before it.

I tell you bring your ship about
Who are you

We're the Saint Marie

More than four hundred years {[illegible]} at sea
Bound for the riches of Cathay
But that you {brute} at [illegible] in the {our} way. {[illegible]} {desert {sea-
coast} bars our way}*

Curse on it for at desert land waste
But never mind {it}† and whats the haste‡

Stand by for me {us} to come aboard
[illegible]
We'll welcome you with fire {shot} and sword
Don't put on airs, you're in distress
We've heard your psychic S.O.S.

Colundres! Christophes! No less!
What no one left alive but you

He boards again
Columbus boards in I [illegible]
Till someone comes up over [side]§

The meekly [?vaunt] single file
Columbus brooch alone awhile**

[4v]

They've named it for Americas
Instead of me for all the fus and what is worse
It seems to me imperious
It baffles everything I do

---

* This bracketed phrase below the line. Additionally, within this bracketed phrase, the word "{seacoast}" is below the phrase itself.
† Inserted above the line.
‡ This line and the one above it written in the left hand margin.
§ These three lines written diagonally from top to bottom, in the left-hand margin.
** Written vertically from top to bottom, halfway up the left-hand margin.

To find a shorter passage through
To Asia than Da Gama

[5r]*   America is hard to see[4]
Your lookout says and I agree
Many can't see it from without
And blind with ~~cowardice~~ {an imported} doubt
Many can't see it from within
And[†] Well my experience has been
It cant be taught as a doctrine
~~Failure to see it is not a sin~~ {Failure to see its not a sin}
{And anyway much less a punishable crime}
~~Failure [illegible] to see~~ its not a crime
~~I mean to~~ {you will be} punish{ed}[‡] ~~you~~ for this time.
~~But for your sake and peace of mind~~
Which would you feel more badly tricked
If I declared you derelict
The shipping was in danger from
And sank you with a mercy bomb
Or claimed you as my lawful prize

A great big girl comes down the deck
From the direction of the bow
~~Is this~~ Whats all the academic row
Between the living and the dead
Im not your wooden figure head
~~Excuse me if [illegible]~~
And nobody need think I am[§]
You must be Ira bella. Damn!
No let me tell you who I am
I am the Goddess Liberty
My pleasure {mission}** is to set men free
From what they think they know or see

---

* Except where noted, this page written in black ink.
† Written in left-hand margin.
‡ Written below the line.
§ This line written in blue ink.
** This word written in blue ink.

[*6r*]   At eve the rain blurred the windows
And the rain dimmed mountains throng them
The rainy rainy mountains
As the left* to linger knew them,

The [illegible] forest roaring
The last leaf sky-high blowing
And all the keeps it autumn
Is it raining isnt snowing

The excess and waste of water
And of {when} it ever comes?
The outing to the river
To watch the rocky fluces

To be the ghost of summer
With whom a house is haunted
The waiting to be summoned
{The too}† unsurely [illegible] wanted
The waiting to be [?wanted/wasted]

[*7r*]‡   You know what <u>we</u> do when we fear
The snow spreads all too clear a sheet
Too long a season of the year
To stay unreassured by skulking feet?

We run and rumple up the snow
By playing games of fox and geese
So that we neednt have to know
If any prowl against our peace

T
So clean a sheet so clean a sheet
All around the house of snow on snow
Fills me with the fear prowling feet

---

* "As the left" written in black ink.
† Written in left-hand margin.
‡ First two stanzas written in black ink.

O
With such a clean unbroken sheet
All round the house of snow on snow
My fears increase of prowling feet
That simply could not help but show

The snow
It simply cannot help but show
~~If any came with prowling feet~~
On such a white unbroken sheet
My dear I would want to know
If any came with prowling feet
And

[8r]*   What are you back here for
                          My name's adult
I went to school when young without result.[5]

The thing for you to do is join a cult.

I know a married woman out in Lennox
Who took some summer courses in eugenics[6]
~~Much good I hope it did her~~ children {After she'd had a mess of}

~~I got a notion from~~ {And I've been reading that} the ancient Mayas[7] {Ah yes!}
~~That if you~~ {Believed} ~~went and~~ {that if} you got your head trephined
Twould let a sort of skylight in your mind.

I did think some of going in for Shinto[8]
The bullet has come back from where its been to
With the belief that if could enter into
The gun again and be shot forth again
With better aim by better trigger men.†

---

* Page written in black ink.
† This stanza has a line with an arrow drawn from it to below the line "The thing for you
. . . is join a cult."

[9r]* They heard the click of coincidence
As if it were a trap that had them both.

[10r] The built themselves a tawdry pleasure house
If one might judge the ruins. Pleasure house
Not dwelling house nor lumber camp nor iron nor factory mill Not vast
Not vast but vast enough
But vast enough to mark its inch of boards
Seem paper thin. There though partly down partly

Though partly fallen like a dead fall trap.
It hung there caught on its own insides of scantling
There was admission to it still at risk
By evening we might see it fall the the rest some more
Stepped on and crushed flat by {the} weight of winter
But this was summer when it had its season
Of dance if dance it was or roller skating

[11r] The one who built it did not spare his lumber
The who had the idea and took the loss
We hoped he had the pleasure and had it over
Before the idea was proven valueless a mistake
Perhaps Perhaps he was not one who lived for pleasure
Or even planned to ask if he was happy
So long as he was working at the trade
Of giving others pleasure. The kind of man He was one
That might build a pavillion on the moon
With someone elses money. Well hes gone He is gone
Nothing of {but} good of one so gone as he.
Impossible to say of some how far
They will have got since any given time.
Look for him by some water {ocean} in the world
Before you try some mare {on the} moon

[12r] I hope it was not just a dream he had
That A dare daring dream that never was fulfilled.

·   ·   ·

---

* Pages beginning here and continuing through 16r are written vertically, from the bottom of the page to the top.

How we came up
Waste ~~is the~~ is my consolation for my life
Nothing but waste was meant to be*

What ails me is how ~~gone to Waste all is~~ {long ago it was}
The length of time ~~ago~~ is like a heart string stretched
So thin it hurts. Call Charles He ~~ought to have~~ {to satisfy me}† ~~a story to tell~~
{know the} story
Why have I never heard of this before
~~What is the oldest date~~
If you have read the writing on the wall
~~Whose name~~ Tell us whose name you found so we may mourn them
For dead and ~~gone~~ say no more. But most of all
Tell us the {very} oldest date you [~~illegible~~] found
The longer ago the sadder my regret.

Think of the troubles to create a flower
Then think how long‡

[13r]   Perhaps they live as long as we but somewhere else
The oldest dates were of the early nineties
When you were young, that's all, ~~and~~ {but} like the mill hands
Were living somewhere else.

Tell Charles he'll ~~have the whole [roo] thing down on~~ us {shoot the whole thing down}
~~It wants to quench its~~ He at first to quench its gable in the lake
Its aimed to shoot itself ~~front forward~~ head first into the lake
~~As if to~~ {And} quench its gable in the ~~lake~~ muddy lake
As would become a very thirsty place
If such it was We dont know what it was
Glass bottles

I stand here lost in wonder how the throng
Were turned ~~to~~ from ~~city~~ {city} streets to revelry

---

* These three lines written to the right of the previous two diagonally from top left to bottom right.
† Written below the line.
‡ These two lines written to the right of the line "The longer ago the sadder my regret."

In so forced in violence upon   wilderness
Assuming the place prospered and they came

[14r]   And speed and noise {might} and risk and wealth and travel.
My watch aid after midnight. By his gait
He should be going home from

[15r]   One of those towns that {we} flash crash past with loud {their} switches
And flash past with str their street lights leaving me
Unsatisfied about them I picked out
To come back to and live in for a while.
I failed to catch its name on the dark station
But by on my schedule railroad schedule and {by} my watch
Assuming that we weren't behind {we were running and on} the time
Troy it would be another town of Troy.[9]
Memento of {the} irrevocable loss.

Reminder
A namesake
In memory*

But that was not the reason of my choice
I look {chose} it for a solitary name
My eye caught going home along its street   He responsibly was
Past houses everyone of which was dark.   over
He did not turn to watch our whirl of cinders
Or meet my look {for me} along our row of window row
His back was turned indifferent to might noise

[16r]   He had become a talker to himself
From age or sorrow an oblivious talker,
{One} He was {And long} past caring what we heard him say
But if we cared, the roaring of the train
Was [there] {always} something to take refuge in
We need not listen too coherently He musnt speak ever so coherently
We and not [illegible] and we need not look

---

* These three lines written to the right of "Memento of {the} irrevocable loss."

Nor need we more than glance at his rehearsal
He had one gesture of the head thrown back
As if he plowed a field of sunken reefs
And since he had no hands to spare for ruins

He had one gesture of the head thrown back
He might have got from plowing rocky land
Whose since the work took all the hands he had
To ~~that~~ right the plowshare losing out of furrow
He drove with buckled reins behind the head
And had to use his head to hold his horses.

[*16v*]*   Or was it that he threw his head far back
To save someone by absent influence
He could not reach in time to save by hand
From ~~death from an imaginary~~ {falling from a visionary} brink
He sighed his body limply and despaired.
A station of the train {once} caught him out [~~illegible~~]
When he was saying Let it not have been!
He wanted to avert the already done.

Form of grief
Mechanically passionate
His grief exceeded being felt as grief.†

[*17r*]‡   {And}§ The danger is you will over do
Your praise when {its} wholly left to you.
{But}** When no one else will [{illegible}] be your friend
You{'re} ~~have to be your~~ {driven}†† {[illegible] to be your} own in the end.[10]
And

•   •   •

---

* This page written lengthwise, top to bottom.
† These three lines written in the right margin diagonally from bottom left to top right.
‡ This page to 25r written lengthwise, bottom to top.
§ Written above sentence in left-hand margin.
** Written above sentence in left-hand margin.
†† Written beneath the line.

How {you're} sadly ~~your~~ apt to over do*

I overdid it last night he said
Before I climbed the ladder to bed

Im not as good as I made it out
That anyone ~~is~~ is I rather doubt

[*18r*]¹¹ ~~A vagabond came one night to the farm~~
~~who hated to cause undue alarm~~

To make him safe to sleep in the hay
He said we could take his pipe away

And here were his matches. Tramp polite
He said he ~~wanted~~ {used} {wanted}† to do things right.
Which started him off on a rigmarole
Of self respect to shame the soul—

Much too noble a hard luck yarn
To pay for ~~a~~ {an unmade} bed ~~of hay~~ in the barn.

{We} {I} thought how lucky the one who stays
Where other people can tell his praise—

Such as it is, however brief
As that ~~at least~~, he isnt {a thug or} thief

~~There was a lot [illegible] said‡~~
~~Last night before I~~ {went up} ~~sent to bed~~§

~~4 prided himself on doing things right~~

Im not as good as I made it out
{That}** ~~Not~~ if any one is I really doubt

---

* This line and those that follow it on the page written in the right margin.
† Written beneath the line and in black ink.
‡ This line and the rest on the page written in right margin.
§ These two lines written in black ink.
** Written beneath the line.

Next day he was almost someone else
In the dignity of our [?pureness]

I mean that he isnt considered
Such as that he isnt a thug
A cattle thief or firebug
That he isnt a firebug or thief

[19v]   The Holdens came to get him after church
On a misunderstanding of the morning sermon
The preacher hadnt necessarily ~~in mind~~ had
Such human waste as Marion in mind
He ~~was just~~ {had been} talking about waste in general
Attempting a just reconciliation with it
~~How much waste~~ To save the ~~young~~ ideal young from turning better
Great nations as their greatness could afford
~~The greatest waste especially in war~~
~~As writers~~ Incalulable waste in peace and war
   ~~Witness the price of [illegible]~~ {weapons and} ~~ammunition~~
   ~~Left over from war now on the market.~~
   ~~As witness the great loss of [illegible] for speed~~
   And the low price of war goods on the market
   At any ~~time~~ {in any} year} ~~line and the low~~ {and the great} ~~price of~~ goods
   Left

[20r]   As witness the great loss of lives in the war
As witness the great loss of lives for speed
In peace and war as witness the low price
Of things left over from the war no~~w on the market~~
~~What was it all about.~~
~~If not at such a dismal case~~ as
Something about if not at such a case
As ~~Marion.~~ {Arlo Bates.} The pious would like to know.
Several ~~came at~~ {attacked} him in the vestibule
Where as the custom was he laid in wait
For any compliments they ~~might be~~ {might} have for him
To cheer him over his ~~descent~~ {let down} from preaching
Not least of those who has a lot to say
Was Jane his roving daughter just come home

To ~~stay~~ rest a week or so from social work
In some slum settlement. She thought in terms
Of wretchedness and how to ~~make things go over~~ reconstruct the state
~~So as not to~~ So as to save the good for little or nothing

[21r] From the embarrassment of being ~~poor~~ wretched
No compliments from her today for father.
Dad was for {waste she said—} ~~Dad~~ was praising waste
On the assumption God was a seducer[12]
Who betrayed ~~us by spring and youth and love and~~ love
~~Into~~   people into it with spring
And youth and love. Her father hung her head
~~But w an~~
~~An awkward [illegible]~~
Merely because he thought she was too public
With what they had been ~~over~~ often over at home.
~~Home was where Jane was at her righteous worst.~~
~~The Holdens listened hard but they took no part~~
The Holdens took no part in any of this
But ~~listen [illegible]~~ but cocked an ear for any ~~confirmation~~{mention}
~~[illegible] their suspicion Eldridge was~~

[22r]* To make him safe to sleep in the hay
He said I could take his pipe away.

And here were his matches. Tramp-polite
He said he wanted to do things right.

Which started him on a rigmarole
Of selfrespect to shame the soul—

Much too noble a hard luck yarn
To pay for an unmaid bed in the barn.

Next day he ~~was~~ {hoped} hoping I {had} understood
He didnt mean to claim he was good

                    .   .   .

----

* Entries from this page to the end of the notebook are written on lined, three-ring loose-leaf paper.

~~There were a lot of things~~ I said
Before I climbed the ladder to bed

Make [?dim] Allowance

Next day he was almost someone else⋆
In the off hand manner of his farewells

In all that so   he said
Before I climbed the ladder to bed

I guess you must have understood
I didnt mean to claim I was good

[23r] He cleared this field of all the stones but one
He sank them where they lay too big to stir to
He digged each stone its pit ~~or grave~~ {so close} beside it
With his own shovel all he had to do
As he would tell {[illegible]} you was to save ~~them~~ {[illegible]} in
He sunk them in the ~~low~~ subsoil down ~~down~~ below {low {low} low.}†
~~The depth of plowing~~

With his own shovel he digged each one into its pit
So close beside it all he had to do was
Was ease it in

[24r] At his time or at any time of night
At this time or any time of year.
On foot I mean on this back road ~~[illegible] a man alone~~ {alone}
It could be no one else. ~~I stopped the pump~~ What is he after?
                ~~What we stood and tried~~
~~To stare each other~~ I hope I [?stand] him out of [?conciliance]
If you are sure it was your wayward brother
He{'s}‡ ~~wants~~ {here} to see how we are making out
Two women on a farm without a man.

                •   •   •

⋆ This line and the rest on the page written in right margin.
† "low [~~illegible~~] {low} low" written beneath the line.
‡ Written beneath the line.

It suddenly raised hatred to ~~hatred~~
To [illegible] his looking like a town policeman*

~~It suddenly [?seemed] harder than it had~~
~~As if to start him on~~ about his business
~~More likely to what see what there is~~
Or to see if here was anything more
He hadnt taken from us that we might take
~~I hoped [illegible].~~
At least he saw we have a cow to milk
I was just watering Lesbia at the pump.

[25r]   ~~And~~ {He} could have learned form her a whole lot more
About [illegible] {the} milking hours bad farmers keep
And from her ~~having~~ being pastured on a tether
Something about our [illegible phrase] fence unfavorable about our fences.[13]
About ~~the~~ fences. [illegible] ~~defenses~~ [illegible] {of} defenseless woman
I hope he saw enough to ~~satisfy~~ {gratify} him
~~Theres nothing left of us~~
Or satisfy him anymore wise [illegible] {poor} {This isnt all}†
~~He may be out ther~~

[26r]‡   March Makers

The bees and I are go between
And as from this to that we go
"Remember me to so and so"
(With pollen dust the flower means.[14]

I couple things in [illegible] space and time
Distant with near and old with new
By saying "May be likened to."
And Locking {the} couplet with a rhyme
I lock the couplet with a rhyme

                    •   •   •

---

* These three lines written to the right of the previous three lines (From "If you are sure . . ." to ". . . without a man").

† Written beneath the line.

‡ 26r and 27r written across the page, along the ruled lines.

My coupling in is in Space and time
Of near with far and old with new
By saying "May be likened to."
I lock the couplet with a rhyme

I couple things in space and time
By saying "May be likened to"
And as a sign of what I do
I like a pair of likes that rhyme

[27r]   The Great Misgiving

In prose this time. And how two peoples look at the Eastern and the
Western. Both had it greatly. And I am tired of not seeing it through to further if not ultimate understanding. of leaving* it as it is and not seeing it
through to further if not ultimate understanding.

I can't be sweepingly general in history more than in anything else if I am
going to be stuck in trifles otherwise known as scruples so permit me the
largeness of dividing the world westward from about the land of moab and
eastward from about the land of moab. Westward from there we have the
Aryan Semite. Eastward European. West Eastward they have been mainly
Asiatic.[15]

---

* There is an arrow to "of leaving" from the word "tired."

"Bring all under the influence of the great books as under a spell"

MS. RN935566. Box 1428, Boston University, Richards Collection. Brown soft-paper-covered notebook, 7″ × 8½″, with canvas binding. Ruled white paper. Entries are in black ink unless otherwise noted. Notebook is in an envelope postmarked October 6th, 1935 and addressed in Frost's hand to "Professor Robert Newdick/English Department/Ohio State University/Columbus Ohio." The upper right corner reads "From Robert Frost Amherst MASS."

[*cover*] Bring all under the influence of the <u>great</u> books as under a <u>spell</u>.[1]

Teach all the <u>satisfactions</u> of successful speech.

1912

(Most of this goes back to earlier than the above date. R. F. 1935)

[*1r*] For R.N.[2] to Keep and get what he can out of by ingenious inference R.F. 1935

[*1v*] [blank]

[*2r*] [blank]

[*2v*] [blank]

[*2v*] [insert on a cut page, after p. 15]:

Winging
Wherein is a teacher like a fireman
Wherein not

If you grant me the friendly letter as end and aim it is all I ask: you grant me everything

We wont assume that they are all going to be writers. [illegible] Silly to teach as if we did.

Suppose they show a little vein of humor a vein mocking as <u>vein</u> of homily truth.

[3r]   Against inquisitorial and exegetical reading
For   devotional reading.

Part of literature in the education of the emotions
    Superior to music here because better balanced.

Danger of taking away the pleasure of finding beauty for ourselves.

Danger of exhausting interest by overusing in youth.
Leave reading to the self-imposed labor.

In literature we come into the enjoyment of what we have gained in other things subjects. Fruitional.

Not prepared to labor hard in it till the fire of joy burns a steady and unquenchable flame

[3v]   The Waiting Spirit[3]

    The spirit wont stand waiting for years till the mechanics of learning are mastered. It must be enlisted from the first or it will fly away to other things

    There are all sorts of zests to depend on—the zest even of spelling {* A good deal {Most} of the zest in everything comes from seeing what it is for— in [illegible] {having} the end in view. too much to ask children to go years without knowing what their studies are all about.

[4r]   Like two circles one looks at with a partition between the eyes and the circles. They float together
        Eclipsing circles of books they can enjoy and books they ought to enjoy.
        Convergence of the eyes to prevent image being double[4]

                    •   •   •

─────────────
* Frost's open bracket.

Education depends on the number of times you have stirred to a right feeling. Number of times the fine thrill has [illegible] {run your fiber}. [illegible].
On correcting anyone
{Not a question of arguing anyone into their reading of good books. The will should not be aroused for or against till late in education.

How many books are available for the teacher's library?

To be remembered that the thrill in is launched nowhere else as in simple poetry.*

After the mechanical part of reading has been acquired (and haste is everything here) nothing counts but the spell I speak of.

[4v]   This rain is as dry as a sand storm

[5r]   (I seem not to have hated the word thrill as much as I do now in 1935)[†]

They are all sorts bad cheap good

Aim is not <u>any thrill</u>[‡] but only response to the fine [illegible] impulsions.

The writing and reading converge on the point of conscious use of words sentence forms intonations and figures in (marks of personality) [illegible] in both [illegible] pupil and authors. The pupil has to learn at last to equal himself in a way with great ones. Put himself in their place. This is the culmination of both reading and writing and where The education should possibly [leave] those who done well in [illegible] English.

Figures of speech sentence forms etc should be discriminated first and first named in their accidental appearance in ones own writing. They are taken in [illegible] from the vernacular rather than from literature.

[5v]   (This must be some after-notes on a talk I called "A Literary Moment. A Good Teacher Know One When He Sees It R.F. 1935)

·   ·   ·

---

* Line drawn from the end of this entry back up to the phrase "The Waiting Spirit," diagonally from bottom right to top left.
[†] Frost's entry.
[‡] Arrow from the word "thrill" to the word "all" in the phrase above.

Recurrence of the Moment
Hanging round for the moment

To know a moment when you see it—that is to be a teacher. "There there you are—you've said it" is the most influencing thing you can say to a person. Or I know exactly—you get it just as I have felt it. Fellow feeling and common experience.

Question of what the teacher shall address himself to in these readings—hand writing spelling grammar punctuation paraphrasing ideas imagination reality tones ideas

You may say that what you can wait for is the idea but if you never address yourself in comment to anything but the mechanics who will believe you?

[6r]   It is healthy and normal for things and objects to keep a childs mind off words (spoken or written) till he is well along in years.

He is in no more {little more} need of being corrected in his early writing than in his early speech. Why spread the day of self-consciousness?

Probably he first notices his speech with satisfaction when he thinks he has given an antagonist his answer "good and plenty."

The He will be aware of having acquitted himself well in speech before even he is in writing.
~~Urgently in the writing~~

[illegible] In the writing it will probably be a letter he is proud of as giving his enemy what he deserves.

[6v]   [blank]

[7r]   The problem will be to show him that such moments are literary and they must be repeated. They must be extended to other feelings and brought into his writing.

He must be taught that the fun of being epigrammatic is the {a} legitimate fun of literature.

•   •   •

Will he ever feel the satisfaction of being epigrammatic in an examination in history. The question is crucial.   Has he time?

Poverty and inertness are the result of our teaching thus far.

The mind must be induced to flow: to see that there is a plenty to say on a thousand subjects.
Let the teacher threaten to use up all his ideas on

[7v]   [blank]

[8r]   a given subject and see how the child will beg for a chance {to talk or write} before it is too late.

All quality From quantity quality by selection. Many random movements are ap more apt than a few to contain the right movement.

Care not to divert a mind from a thought on which it is running free by much talk about the way it is running.

Intonation possibilities of what they read and what they write should be noticed as early as anything.

Cultivate shame but don't try to before the instinct for it makes itself apparent.

Here we may be all touch the artistic soonest and most directly.

[8v]   "Aim low enough: As much as we can expect is to get them to write a good business letter." All right aim low enough but why not make it a good friendly letter?—And that lets in everything.

Recognition

[9r]   Something of the artistic experience for all.

Make conscious of sentence form the wrong way by present method.*

·   ·   ·

---

* This entry and the one above it written in pencil.

The subject you know for yours assembles the scattering experience of years. [Is a gatherer]*

~~Many times~~ You be able to say "I am forced to notice," "I am forced to think."

Things happen to you and things occur to you, the latter with as little help from you as the former.

It is the thing "given" from without that has substance. This is the age of the given. We look to see if we find patriotism given in our natures. We look to seek if we find any

[9v]   [blank]

[10r]   modifying passion along with it.

What occurs to you must be given from without.

We'll say ten happenings make an occurrence.

What we call creation is at most the modifying influence of one actual thing on another in the mind.

We are on safest ground with things remembered.

Every thing that is a thing is out there and there it stands waiting under your eye till some day you notice it.

⟩┤[31r]   [blank]

[31v]   Pursuit of the Spirit to its Source

[32r]   Assigned subjects

Incentives to the spirit. The

·   ·   ·

---

* Frost's brackets. Beginning with this entry the rest of the page is written in black ink.

The right kind of subject as an example solely,

The moment

[32v]

Division of Nature.

[33r] Reading for pleasure reading for [illegible] improvement
Families where the word improvement is never heard.
Movies in the name of improvement.

[33v]   your Doubts and Docility

[34r] [blank]

[34v]   The Better Part of
Imagination

[35r] Efficiency [illegible] in reading

[35v] Composing in Things.

[36r] Recognition. Now tell us something we dont know. Tell us something we
know but haven't been told before. (heard before
Material you didnt know you had before

The Log Keepers

Rulers must Rule

The Wreck of the Raft

The Four Boys

[36v]

The Moment

[*37r*] Care not to turn their nature all to seeking your approval. A little scorn of that wont hurt them.

Not to have children [illegible] remember you as having taught them anything in particular. May they remember you as an old friend. That is what it is to have been right with them in their good moments.

[*37v*] The Waiting Spirit

How long will the spirit be put off.

Evidence that the spirit is there in the first place in the bubbling of children.

All Quantity copiousness is something given in the childs nature. Something to keep.
   Manipulate it into something.
   From quantity quality

   Practical help in what to address yourself to in theme reading. "I'd keep that if I were you." Let me have a copy of that

{First} Taste the satisfactions of successful speech. When.

[*38r*] They like a game because it gets somewhere.

The spirit is deedal. Ends real and false. Success with teachers. Success with the work in completion

The Jumping Frog[5] {Not what I can load you up with
                  It is what do you say

          inappreciation helps
Privation that the spirit may come
Cheering the spirit on
Inappreciation. Near is dear. Someone far
The [illegible] enough away to chastise

⌈ 38v ⌉   (Somebody angered me by saying About as much as we can expect from them is a correct business letter. RF. 1935)

A Business Letter

Assuming a good deal to assume that writing can be taught—that anything can be taught.

Any writing that is to [illegible] some one else is speech. To not for The less make believe the better. The best make believe is play.

As to the saying Don't write till you have something to say

[Back
cover]*

"She's . . . writer I guess you'd call it Wants to go on the stage"

MS. 002337. *Brown soft paper cover flip pad, 5¾" × 3½", with canvas strip binding at top. Pages stitched. Ruled paper. Entries in pencil unless otherwise noted.*

[1r]*   She's [illegible] writer I guess you'd call it Wants to go on the stage

> Can always get angry in a prizefight
> Dont want to know your friends
> Thats not it at all
> Let off for first offense hushed up. Not just mischief
> You are tolerant enough but you havent the courage of

1 Scene   Fall River Boat ~~Theo~~ {Bro}. Spider Ames {Scar}
~~Porter~~   Mrs [illegible] Bru {Porter} The hold-up.
2 Scene   ~~The Barn Studio~~ {Apartment} Bro and Sister
~~Showing the Clay Model~~ {The explanation}
3 Scene   The Barn Studio Brother Sister
Tony Artirdge The disfiguration
4 {5} {4} Scene Squared Circle (Smoke) {Apartment Bro and Wife. Give it up.} Spider [illegible] Bro etc   Spider's debut   ({I dont know you} Tell with you.)
6.   Village Home The impenitent wretch {mentions spider}
7.   Village Home   Heroic measures
8   Football Field (Togs) Bro. Spider etc.
9   Corridor Bro Wife Sister Spider {After the game}

After the reception.

> Cant go as near wrong without going wrong.
> Why do you want to see a prizefight.

---

* 1r and 1v written in black ink.

I'd like to be larger than I am.
Toss up whether Id go on the stage,
I can tell you whats the matter with you.
Don't go on our account
Are you that dubb?
We can do this as well as you if we try
Splendid influence on the boys

The Strong-Arm Man

[*1v*] Doesn't believe he struck attacked him but wouldnt care if he did—that is etc.

[*2r*] Effeminized yellow and white Civilization Meet in Congress to Arbitrate Inheritance of the Earth.

Senior Boys.

[*3r-20r*] [blank]

[*21r*] 1 What you expect to find for a teacher in Psychology[1]
2 Your education and mine
3. Insight that makes the novelist also makes the psychologist
4. Character sketches that also show insight.
5. Frequency in experience provokes generalization
6. Why we don't always see a trait in ourselves until we see it in someone else
7 Sentiment for unalterable faith
8 We recall but what we have once recalled
9 Fatigue and inspiration
10 Literary imagination
11 Climax of mandatory attention

[*21v*]   [Gotch][2]

12. {Danger of loss of} immediacy in writing. Immediacy of psychic accommodation in social intercourse
13. In falling in love. In loving children (which is teaching)
14 Good nature, kindness is surplus energy
15 Learn to psychologize rather than learn [to] psychology
16 Response more inchoate when the idea is more remote.
17 There is probably an emotion in everything

18. Test time sense with metronome

19. Mountain distances

20. Imitate different kinds of education

21 Consecration {the woman

the task

the [?mask]

22 Appropriativeness*

[22r]   23 Evolution[3]

24 Age of accent on "and"[†]

25 Grasping from first to last

26 Generous and giving and altruistic from love

27 When giving is taking

28 "No psychosis without neurons" (Topic)

29 The thought thinks

30 Books: Plato's Republic[4]

Rousseau's Emile

Montaigne's Education of Children[5]

Pestalozzi's Leonard and Gertrude[6]

31 Pedagogy of Moving Pictures

32 Lessons in Tables of Contents

33 Pedagogy of running down predecessor

34 Which is most valuable observation of psychology or clarification?

over

[22v]   31. As to the presence or absence of our subjects in their curriculum

32. As to breadth of curriculum

33. As to result of education. What shall be the test?

34 As to relation of education to life of people

35 As to school practice

36 As to inclination to develop caste

37 As to discipline knowledge use

38 As to the cultivation of our nature in its fullness

39 Ramification due to scene of faculties: due to multiplicity of life.

⸱   ⸱   ⸱

* Items 21 and 22 written in black ink.

† Items 23 and 24 written in black ink.

40 Taking   Rejecting   Selecting

Giving   Giving is taking

Taking   {Grasping Rejecting   ⎧ Dodging
                Mouthing   ⎨ Lieing

Selecting   ⎛ Memory
                ⎨ Imagination
                ⎝ Judgment Reason

[23r]   Taking   is Self   Self-Seeking
            Giving   {Love
            Friendship
            Doubt
            Task

Giving is for value received; higher at price of lower.

---

41 As to individual or [et] mass work.
42 Mind probably receptive as long as the brain continues to grow
43 Put off what you know in English on entering class in anything else.
44 Kind of facts that will give every biography a different form
45 Keeping unspoiled the natural
46 Random movements like branches of unformed tree
47 Intellect is only selective nature come into the walls of the self
48 We <u>laugh</u> at our desire {in order} to save some part of self from the reckless giving of love.*

[23v]   49 Speaks with authority as one of the highly educated; speaks with authority as a professional educator†
50 Why discourage radicalism in youth any more than mathematics in one who has a natural gift for it.
51. Teaching a little too scientific mothering a little too unscientific?
52. Facts must be well apart when first learned

---

* Items 47 and 48 written in black ink with the exception of the phrase "in order," which is written in pencil.

† Item 49 written in black ink.

53. We speak from the impulse that has found vent in empirically learned language

The science of language cannot strengthen that impulse at all.

Our psychologising must go on a long time before we can reduce it to a science and then the science furnishes no new impulse.

54 Fill that backward abyss with something. Nothing for the

[*24r*]   forward abyss   History

55 Dramatic teaching advances by ~~situat~~ creating situation like {that} of Aggasiz in the fish story[7]

56 Abstraction of Froebels gifts.[8]

57 The older we grow the more we appreciate any ground on which we can meet without being too personal

58 Never abandon a prejudice till reason has shown it to be absolutely not sacred. The validity of a prejudice is established by its stubbornness

59 Education for failure not included in Spencers[9] plan

60 Cultivate the feeling that "they" could have done it and then regret that they werent allowed to.

61 If the task should be self ~~set~~ mastered why not also self-set.

62 Lesson on experimental and accidental variation

[*24v*]   63 Lesson on the way all mental states tend to go off in action.

64 Will says how soon and to what end they shall go off.

65 Lesson in defining

66 No right to give any [~~illegible~~] lecture ~~that~~ the form of which is not visible.

67 Mixed motives

68 Fear of Being Bad

69 Impulse and Attention

70 Resuming the image

71 Reaction from repeated stimulation

72 Memory nothing but gains from repetition

73 Consciousness of and attention to are not very different in meaning

74 Ideas of education valuable as they depart from things and approach last things. (Include first things)

[*25r*]   75 Religion ~~always~~ prescribed forms and for its own satisfaction found the reason why.

76 Kipling on duty; Wordsworth too[10]

77 Our nature is like a bucket to be filled

Our nature is like a seed to be watered and tended and unfolded

Our nature is like a conflagration ready to run in any direction where it finds fuel. Appetites and impulses

78 As for experience of other teachers who have gone out from the normal

79 How many times {Sat Oct 28} and how in what way in what connection to what purpose (use) way has psychology come into your thought or conversations.

80 You possess thoughts you have had

81 The sacredness of three. Intuitional numbers

[26v] 82 Fringe in vision etc.

83 Largest group of dots by direct perception. Intuitive addition

Largest group of groups

Intuitive multiplication

Does nearness of spots help?

Does one out of symmetry hinder?

Does the mind try to make groups where none are obvious.

Why so grateful for groups of three in thought.

Composition of pictures satisfies instinct for group?

Science is asking questions. Psychology is asking questions of inner processes

Group of heterogeneous groups harder

84 Observation and explanation of inner processes.

85 Devotional reading of the classic

[27r] 86. Not to learn ideal conditions without which they cannot work but ideal conditions they must work but ideal conditions they must try to bring about.

87 Danger of the doctrine We learn to do right by doing wrong

88 Give an account of your sensations when you see anyone whipped

89 Study the brain outside of school for exam.

90 Test in observing and explaining mental processes. Experiments as check.

91 May one remember a memory.

92 School virtues

Hasty judgement of character

Deliberate speed?

Kind you intend to have (of order)

Every discipline and method has its poison

Forward looking thoughts

93 Image of the intonation that fades as you try to bring to the lips. Writing by ear.

94 Aphasia a lesson[11]

95 Great American joke; shifting ~~to som~~ your responsibility to keep yourself good onto someone else and then trying to [?comfort] yourself and be as bad as you can.

96 I know my sense is mocked in everything.

97. Distinguishing between what is remembered ~~and~~ of reality and what is ~~imagined~~ remembered only as imagined

98 Amount of pastimes attacking

99 Japanese Ladder. "We fail." Ten leaf clover.

100 Jump first and recog pin next

101 Flow of saliva automatic?

102. How you see a face in imagination

103. Adjustment a lesson

104 Gangliated states of consciousness

105 Defend your sacred prejudice even if it is only in favor of some family pronunciation.

106 Sustaining power of ground all round

107 To attend to anything is inevitably to <u>act</u> in such a way as to attend to it more or else as to attend to it less.

108 Rythm in all

109 I do not mean those other [?lands]

   When I mourn what we are you

110 Blindfolded bull among terrors: such is the soul.

111 Can we tell beforehand what we are going to remember and what forget?

112 Flatter ourselves in the worst folly of all namely that we can ~~be~~ take a middle ground

113 Study of the changes in a lifelong desire

114 Pupils must find something to philosophize about

115 Will is attention when it is chooses what to take in volition when it decides what shall {go out}

116 ~~Will to~~ Pleasure is life: pain is death

117 Perception cuts out surfaces to act upon. Bergson[12]

118 No thought without action. Complete action is useful action.

119 Every image is an impulse. Ideo motor.

120 When will the will release the impulse. When it is for it's own selfish interest.

121 The self is the flowing state of consciousness.

122 Genesis of functions

123 Every function comes both before and after every other function. Circle in the ~~live~~ action if not in the reason

124 Genesis of the will from the impulse of the idea.

[29r] 125 Involuntary attention to preferred interests

126 Selective in action because we single out [~~illegible~~] best movements

127 Movements are given

128 How the wish to live if it sleeps still purrs in states of consciousness

129 Creative after images.

130 We were given reason to turn nature against herself.

131 Temptation to give credit for thought however erroneous just because it is thought.

132 Philosophers treatment of the Poets.

133 Low tone of grammar school literature

134 Composition in the grades

135 Follow the lines ~~you~~ of thing as you use them follow the lines you like the curves of.

136. Can too small pains be added together to make a large pain?

[29v] 137 Lay out a course of reading and study for someone who hasnt had Hist of Ed

138 Make plans for carrying your own work further.

139 In unicellular life what is the difference between eating each other and marrying[13]

140 I cant doubt that the apperceptive basis is from the first moment of life enormous in comparison with the sensational element it takes to itself.

141 How to Tell a Person from a Thing

142 Moat.

143 The things present to sense are never equal to the things contributed to the mental state by previous experience

144 Change

145 An Alma Mater Boy

146 Commentate

147 Ability of First Children

[*30r*] 148 Every mood o'erleaps itself

149 How many pains make an agony?

150 Subliminal people.

151 Not marry because she wasn't good enough—because she was too good

152 Pedagogy can only help teaching as criticism helps literature How is that?

153 Such ignorance amounts to innocence and should be preserved like a virtue.

154 A New Theory of Success So many friends {gone over.}

155 Like some creature in a broken shell he lived on in ~~his~~ {a} broken heart*

156 Saying new things and saying new things others are eager to say with you.

157 Seen through the mind and vanishing†

    Like dragons of the giant fern

    Vague forms that launched the thunderbolt

158 Mislaid Doorkey   Asking for Roses

The Road to India   Ghost House   The Visit

A Ghostly Progress   The that Be for Me

According to Bergson   A Hole in the Grave

159 What I only am to outsider angers me. Love take my side

[*30v*]‡ 160 Pensiveness and reaction time

161 Treetop Cradle

162 Whited Tragedy

163 The Independent requires of us the Lords song.

164 Whenever I doubt if my letters {to a friend} are numerous or long enough I am sustained by the thought that it was not at a friend of anybody that Luther threw ink by the bottlefull.

165 One feels like a Mothers Superior in this nunnery.

166 To sink to bad grammar is vulgar; to rise to bad grammar is a figure of speech.

167 The thing remembered must have to start itself or how ~~it~~ what would determine the {solider} associations ~~that~~ by which ~~it~~ or on which it lifts itself to consciousness?

                •   •   •

---

* Items 153–155 written in black ink.

† This entry written in black ink.

‡ Page written in black ink except items 160 and 166, which are written in pencil.

[31r]

167 What more is needed to measure the changes of an indefinite thing than an indefinite instrument

168 Plainly enough figurativeness is only coyness*

169 Girlery of gals or gallery of girls

170 M We get truth like a man trying to drink out of {at} a hydrant

171 Personality is character iridescent with the emotional.

172 Tell how it resembles what it is like and how it differs from what it is like

173 We must be sure you mean it doubtful as we maybe as to how you mean it.

174 My modesty is for other people I havent much of an opinion of what they are the opinion they are capable of entertaining of me.

175 I cant help suspecting that the smallest thing we mention is perhaps very large.

176 Noticeable that after the earliest observation the child works not from nature but his copy of nature

[31v]

177 From consciousness of effective expression [illegible] in retort

178 A president chosen by the psychologist

179 Expression Suffrager

180 Fumble with the rudimentary impulses

181 {Complete act} Complete field of vision. Etc

182 The Cross Roads Ghost {& lucky snap.}†

183 No self activity even in school paper

184 I am weary of the light that bathes us all

185 Incredible that once she loved {mother}.

186 Dont worry about the sins of labor.

187 That a land should become uninhabitable before it becomes uninhabitable.‡

188 Abandonded [?Farm] School. How Leonard Teaches Your Children

189 Second wife to finish rearing children is like second authors to f {Quilller Couch to finish Stevenson}[14]

Edward E. Weaver Ph.D.
Bedford, N. H.§

---

* Items 167 and 168 written in black ink.

† Item 182 written in blue ink.

‡ Items 185–187 written in blue ink.

§ Not in Frost's hand. Written upside down, at bottom of the page.

[*32r*] 190 The teacher mistakes: he hasnt the honor of having to make people better. His privilege to boast of is that of being occupied with the idealizing part of people's nature.

[*1r*]* Miss Gurgle: She whiffles. She puts it in the form of a question that expects the answer yes, but readily falls in with a no Don't you just love books? Could hug five or six. Don't you just love style? When a book has no style [illegible] of course I read it for the plot. Don't you think characters ought to grow? I think the words in it are too long or some of them are. Yes and on the other hand some of them are too short. I agree with you entirely. Don't you feel different at different times. He's got a Bartlett's Quotations and he can tell you exactly who wrote anything after he's looked in that. He used to read five or six books a day.—She praises Mr. Some of the time She pronounces the éd.

[*2r*] Miss Pains. She's reading at something. Marius the Epicurean.[15] She doesn't want to miss anything. She takes notes. Etymologies. She aims to be systematic. She passes her hand over forehead and complains of an oppressed-feeling. Gets so much good out of the womans club. They keep setting her book mark back. Likes wholesome books. Agrees with Miss Gurgle in admiring Roget[13] (Trouble with this is it cannot give you different concepts for same thing only different words for same concepts, and really there are only a few of those that are presentable.) She goes to sleep reading

[*3r*] Mr. Degree. Has to read for relaxation. After teaching Milton all day turns naturally to what is least like him. No prig: reads for pleasure—finds he has to. Reads for the story.

[*4r*] We like a comparison because it keeps balance in thinking of one thing to think of another. We like laughter in tears and tears in laughter.

[*5r*] Mr. Reverse. Knows about books but never reads them. Literary gossip. Money out of books Talks about big editions

[*6r*] Mr. Atkins. Kipling quotations and citations He likes strong writers.

[*7r*] Mr. Bethan. Perennial wonder that the new newest seeming things are old. No one believes in his sincerity. Plot is to make him read a certain book and

---

* Entries begin other side of pad.

(popular best-seller-describe) and satisfy themselves of his app pleasure in it. Simplicity? It not offending anybody {people} by letting it leak out that you have more words or ideas than they have.

[8r] [blank]

[9r] [blank]

[33r] 1 Colored spot or cross in closed eyes.
2. Bradley Color [illegible]

[33v] Your gravity becomes your perished soul As [illegible] does rotten fruit

Not worth a breakfast in the cheapest country under the [illegible]

The nearer the church the further from God

Alert {To keep consistency
    To see an opening.

[34r]
Milk	65.
Butter	30.
Potatoes	15.
Eggs	25.
Poultry	10.
[illegible]	
Vegetables (Winter)	20.
" (Summer)	20

"A Place Apart"

Notebook is in the Barrett Collection of the University of Virginia library (6261 B2). Black leather pocket flip pad, 4⅛″ × 2¾″. Unruled white paper. Calendar printed inside the front cover. "Printers and Stationers/Ludgate Hill E.C." printed inside the back cover. All entries written in black ink unless otherwise noted.

[1r]*   A Place Apart

    A Record Self Kept

[?Demurrer]

    Deliberate

        O Raymond Drey[1]
        Wellington House
        Wellington
        Manchester

[1v]†   Mag was deaf as [?Delsabrag]
    Down among the dead men
    In [?Tober] Morey Bay
    In Thrales Entire
    Rocks stand grey to the sun
    Dove that perched upon the mast
    All night I heard a singing bird
    Upon the topmost tree
    Distant heights of glaring
    Like a dreary dawn
    Her face toward the Hinkey

---

* Page written in pencil.
† Page written in pencil.

No end to any [?row]
The footpath way
Pavements fanged with
A reeking deck on a nothing sea
Robin robin redbreast
A crooked stile
Milk comes frozen home in pail

[side of page]:

        Day when it first thunders in March
[?Such cape] Ways be foul   I never saw a moor
Little revenge herself   I am in love with the sea
[?King rils trees of love]   A garden is lovesome

[2r]   Great names boosted in literature* by patriots
An Hundred Collars[2]
Nocturnes for Atlantic
Tariff Reform and cost of living
Other Lives (Villagers)
Any difference is a fault
He refused to be hurried by life as by a bad teacher
In Public Places Acquaintances[†]
Rough breathing on English
In the Que
St. George and the Blonde Beast
The Refluent Wave
Superior youths
Settting out Vegetables Oct. 20[‡]
    I will vote with you. I will send my children to school with you. But I will
not sleep with you.

[2v][§]   Ale does more than Milton can
To justify Gods ways to man[3]
In winter I stand up to tend the quail

---

* Words to "by patriots" written in pencil.
[†] Entry written in pencil.
[‡] This entry and "Superior youths" written in pencil.
[§] Page written lengthwise from center to left and, with the exception of the last entry, in pencil.

A jeweled pheasant
Come if brave and meek—on thirty bob a week
His breeches cost him but a crown
Joy for a penny (Penny bus)[4]
Smooth sheets of water
[?were and been]
No traveling at all (Luck boys and the king
New books—Mr. Mudies Librarie[5]

The swinke of hedges

[*3r*]   On Being Mistaken for Someone else.
Venus and Adonis[6]—Meaning
The Dervish and the Strike
Road sunken deep
Sin burdening the Negro Heart.
Departure from the word laid down must be under stress and impromptu
If imitative it makes the set poetic language
Youth is afraid he isn't wanted. all age knows is that he wants.
Hedges the man on horseback can see over. Good roads for the man on horseback no pavements for the man on foot.
Que sais je[7]
What they are afraid of here cant be done to equalize men is so much greater than over there that I am encouraged to believe all fears are baseless.

[*3v*]   Father Uncle Son on Marriage
Becoming a Pest
Effect of Circuit Lib on Private Lib
Who slew the blonde beast?
Not Lord Burnham[8]
Stay at the point of love   Don't just stay together.
Eagle on the mast.
Story of the hen that changed nests.
Bite the lip to do it.
The way to teach women to vote is to let them vote
The neighbor laughs you out of yourself Some couldn't hate you out of yourself. You hedge yourself about, you wall yourself about with love to save yourself. You mustn't think your differences shall be allowed. You will fight for them if they are attacked at night. Patriotism.

Advertisement in Times for someone to see nothing but my good qualities.

[1ʳ] Englishman and Amer. meet as they understand each other from newspa
per.

We know nothing about any <u>whole</u> improvement in stock brought about
by breeding.

War represents what faith we wont be laughed or reasoned out of.

Time has moved the fixed stars

The Summoner of Populations

Grasson your lawn my lord

Why I Buckle My Shoe

My Patrons

When business can boast of heroic failure then may business become a
profession

Literature is most original when it picks up crumbs of whatever is going

Poet and patron King

Love has no way or posture*

[4ᵛ] Truant Teacher

The Never Thought of It—Rank.

Heaven without Hell were a house without a cellar under it.

Professor on the Mountain

Professor in Bed[9]

Dont write so much as to fix any stage as a habit

It becomes a duty to entertain one of the class as a servant in you family.
You lose class if you evade it.

Spelling may express feelings

We come into the meaning of all forms and words as Chesterton

[5ʳ] says he came into the orthodoxy [10] So we end by not being original

Post impressionist and the incoherent talker

Hole in the wood that breaks into next hole to it.

The Chinese Princess {Doll}—

The Parthenogenesis[11] old style Secret

{New style}

---

* Entry written in pencil.

It irks me to think that charity is a thing like washing hand and dishes that must be forever done over I long to find a way to do it so it will stay done.

[*5v*]   Reality is a relationship
Old knowledges know the new fact
Monism of <u>active</u> idea
"Know backwards: live forwards"[12]
Tendency; pointing

[*6r*]*   Professorial mind and originality
What's new it says is not true
What is is true is not new.
The Set Screw
The Maternity Front
As a bird that flys[13] before you and thinks it is pursued
Top of Saint Paul's on a level with the key hole
A berry for every leaf
The idea of the disease is the last touch
Short on the guide rope
Reproductiveness is not a part of us: we are a part of it.

[*6v*]   [blank]

[*7r*]   We are either feeding our own children or our parent's child.
The girl—the president had courted for her college.
The hefty farmer who took a notion to come to college at 25
A dream of Jawn D.† [14]
The Planchette Type-writer[15]
We see so many strange words never heard in speech when we read an English book we come to think that

[*7v*]   all book language should be a thing by itself. We don't know that these words are still vernacular in England
The Student Business Man‡
Hands clenched to make the most of his opportunities

---

* Page, except for the last entry, written in pencil.

† Entries from "The girl" on written in pencil.

‡ This entry and the rest below it on the page written in pencil.

The painter is lucky he can entertain no illusions as to where he gets his lines. He may imagine them but he knows in just what sense he may do that. He never fools himself with the notion that he creates them out of nothing-ness.

[8r]   Tense2 thy2 strings2 and1 break4 the1 third 2 ½.*

You must feel that the thing happened that way not for the purposes of the author. Why it should happen you don't know but it did. It is the didness of it that makes it taste strong

[8v]   As to War, as to anything you have become too conscious of doing: you love your ability to judge the occasions for it. You are afraid you do it for less and less reason each successive time

[9r]   There are a lot of things you allow to come into your mind illicit.†
We all like to be the only one.
~~The Am~~ Modern
Douglas Larder The
Macbeth Villa

[9v]   [blank]

[10r]   Once I knew a beautiful woman
and we were safe for a long time
There was a strangeness about her eyes and about her forehead and about her upper lips that I never found till an ill day for her and me (for both of us) I met it in a shrunken and fearful face prepared by oiling and drying in the sun by savages for their worship. And ~~this was~~ her face was beautiful and this not and this made hers not so ~~It slowly~~ drawing it to itself. I could not come near enough to her in the dark at night to forget it.

[10v]   When it rains up it fills the river Ledlin[16] sooner than when it rains down
The Two Women (Brazil)
The Man who discouraged martyrdom‡

---

* Entry written in pencil lengthwise from center to right margin.
† Entry written in pencil.
‡ First three entries written in pencil.

This rain is as dry as a sand storm

He might not be bad in this particular case But if he is capable of being
and I know it I have the right to accuse him

[*11r*]   That a man had eyes and a nose and lips and a lower face and spaced somehow this stone is able to tell without much cutting It is left flat. Shoulders
arms legs—these are suggested . The piece stands erect—there is the statement that it is a man without help of headgear or garment

It is {made} man ~~distinguished from woman~~ by the essential sign without
help ~~from~~ of headgear or dress.

[*11v*]   [blank]

[*12r*]   Play.

No! ~~He neednt think because~~
I'll roll the wheel over arrow points with Old Swallow or Heavy Head
when I get ready
I'll roll the wheel to blow smoke on my Dream
It is a bad day

Not with [?Apinokquesistai]

[*12v*]   [blank]

[*13r*]   The first stone sang   The buffalo is my medicine

White Calf Bull

[*13v*]   [blank]

[*14r*]   Take any characterless sentence: The gates will be open between 2 {two}
and five P.M. Now underline any word in it and see how the stress you give it
in the sentence suggests another sentence to follow.

The <u>gates</u> will be open between two and five P.M. You can come into the
yard and wait for the door to open.

[*14v*]   The danger is that the second time you will be too ready. The third time
afraid of being too ready.

[15r]   I have seen people here who frankly sent their husbands to be rid of them. One kind of sending.

A sentence carries a certain number of words and those have their sound indeed but the sentence has [illegible] a sound of its own apart from the words which is the sentence proper. It was before words were. It still has existence without the embodiment of words in the cries of our nature

The mind or spirit is not really active unless it is finding constantly new tones of voice.[17]

Fetching just far enough.[18]

[15v]   [blank.]

[16r]   Your feeling is less important than what you are going to do about it.

You can always tell a realist from a romantic in this way. The realist will marry some girl he has has alwa grown up with and always been around: the romantic wants a girl from off somewhere—someone that he knew not of.

[16v]   [blank]

[17r]   What a see Shakespeare among them all. They were all smut, but he was to various to miss everything in life but smut; or they were all bloody but he was too various to miss everything in life but the blood. And they were all one swilling tone of verse but he was as various as the tones of speech.

It is never safe to write down anything that has not come to you definitely as an experience previous to this time of writing. The preexistent in experience.

[17v]   [blank]

[18r]   Tools: turned the edge o the razor. Broke the handle of the file.

One story of mononcle told to please one another to give me pain.

Half our conversation is no more than voting—signifying our adherence to some well known idea in the field. Whats the good of it?

[18v]   The Oh's and O's of Poetry[19]
           Metaphor and Synechdoche[20]
           The School and the Poet

[*19r*]   They come to me with stories I may hear
And welcome

Metaphor is not only in thought it is in the sentence sounds as well. We are playing at other sounds than the ones you would expect in the place. Metaphor is make believe. Metaphor is ~~this~~ everything out of its place. It is the whole of poetry in one sense
Synechdoche as in another.

[*19v*]   [blank]

[*20r*]   The Calf I was to market.
Exalting God till you make him everything and then blaming him for the evil you cant help seeing
Thank the poor for [keeping/kicking] up a kind of living very useful to those who have to get along on little to do great deeds Alfred* [21]

[*20v*]   The individual is both better and worse than society. Society punishes the individual when he is worse and the individual society when he is better.†

[*21r*]‡   What is an idea? How many to the page? Put your finger on the ideas on one page. On one page in your own writing. An idea and idea that you can call your own.
Is poetry off somewhere {where you look for it out of hours}
or is it where you can take it as you go along.
The books ought to suggest each its own way of being reported on characters scene, plot, what all of them have

[*21v*]   A business letter
A friendly letter

---

* Entry written in pencil.
† Entry written from center to left margin.
‡ 21r, 21v, and 22r written in pencil.

[22r]   Was it out of his poor love of anything but himself that he had won his
way

> Less and less he thought it mattered if no one found him out
> Out of my light! Ye fool yourselves
> The Ice-breakers. The bubble blowers The Pith Lady The Soul Hole. Who

lives here.

[22v]   Progress is like walking on a rolling barrel. The interest is not in where
you are going but in keeping up with and on top of the barrel. Adjustment is
the exciting game of life.

> I can't look forward picking a way for a life unlived—except with dread.
> When people praise you give them their satisfaction in the matter. Con-

sider where they come in.

[23r]   Lavish teaching on the girl when she is never going to use it?

> He never knew that the pretensions of the unintellectual lords of creation

were not absurd—because he was brought up in the New England proffessor
aristocracy.

> The Bible. Pictures of Eve. The Latest Life of Christ. The Interlinear

Translator

[23v]   [blank]

[24r]   After I have poured out words I am left foolish and inclined to talk though
I say nothing unless someone ~~some wi~~ will speak and save me.*

> I am not sorry but rather enlarged that through me life must stab some-

one. That I must

[24v]   [blank]

[25r]   Yearning across the barrier

> Let man not bring together what God has put asunder.
> ~~Everything simply everything just when it seems on the point of yielding~~
> ~~itself to knowledge~~

---

* Entry written in pencil.

We have mastered a ~~thought~~ realm of thought or all but mastered it. There is one almost negligible part that refuses to be brought into knowledge. That is because that little irreducible part

[*25v*]   part of a real adjacent that we haven't touched at all and didn't expect the existence of.

> The Basis of Fact
> Good Relief (for a teacher: got to Hell as G.G. said)

[*26–31*]   [blank]

[*32r*]   The essential sentence is some tone of voice some one of the tones belonging to a man as its set of songs belongs to a kind of bird

That the first function of voice ~~is to~~ in writing is to pin these tones to the page definitely enough for recognition.

There has been insistance enough of clear images of sight. More important are the clear images of sound.

Good writing deals with things present to the eye of the mind in tones of voice present to the ear of the mind.[22]

[*32v*]   Mystery of the Sea   Conrad[23]
Williams ~~on~~
Tarn of Tranquility Galsworthy[24]
Father & Son Goose[25]
Selections from Shaw[26]
When I Was a Child Mankind
Salve Moore[27]
Poems Rosamond Watson[28]
Oscar Wilde—Hopkins[29]
What A Woman Wants of A Man
(No one knows after all these years.)
G.K believes in unicorns[30]
Wentz believes in fairies
Hewlett[31] believes in gods
Sharp and the farm
How belief is there in your knowledge
The business man goes on belief—he can't know

[*33r*]   Culture that goes on belief not allowed tolerated.

You must know what you know by passing examination.

Aristocracy of examinees.

No sooner is systematic knowledge established in the schools than we begin to advocate using unsystematics (zeros not as conjugative, multiplication not in tables) The fact that there is more vitality in an unsystematized fact than a systematized. More available.

The poems stand in some such loose relation as a ring of flushed girls who have just stopped dancing and let go hands.

[*33v*]   We excape blame for so many sins we have committed we can afford to accept blame for a few we haven't.

We lovers are in the net of the stars to our sorrow as inexorably as the Olympian pair were to their shame[32]

Belief is the devil. Belief is fortune telling.

Six times in succession I cut the trump I was bidden.

The best mind asks and answers his own questions not questions asked by others.

The Ring You Could Pick Diamonds Out Of

To a Saxon Boy

[*34r*]   Business and belief. More faith in business than in college

When you are in England do as the Romans did.

The generation fixes on somebody it may or any body to justify neglecting everybody else. Mansfield.[33] Tennyson.

Ninetenths of a mans poetry makes him and then he makes the other tenth.

It is the artificiality of the hunt as it is of school that makes it an unpleasant copy of life.

If I refuse to slay

Rather than, let live in error

[*34v*]   Chesteron makes the most of the fact that the bad old times were not all bad. (Beer and Chas II) [34]

He thinks because the last regime is going out the one before the last is coming back.

He asks where are we going?

He says we do not know. It is toward greater freedom in the movement of the spirit, that is to say greater sincerity or truth of feeling. To be quite free to choose one must be free to refuse. That is as true in religion and love as it is in life itself. The old maid the atheist and the artist are types of those who refuse. Science and industrialism are one. Both have

[35r]   set free men from the land men and women from each other. When women went into business they took marriage out of business. Marriage and love have approximated. We are leaving behind a representative form of government as not giving freedom enough of choice. The unit of representative government was a minute representative govt. the family, which retained patriarchal tendencies too marked. It was only representative ~~on~~ in the best instances. The new and more direct form of govt is not resigned to give greater individual freedom though it will give that too but by giving everyone a part in the franchise to release new feelings and aspirations of the people taken as a whole.

Sincerity is an organic compound {spiritual elements} the formula for which is different for every generation.

[35v]

Seldom a new element enters the compound. The differences are due to varying proportions of extravagance doubt speech silence sentiment ruthlessness passion reflection, etc. Once a generation finds the balance. It holds it by phrases and art for a little while and then goodby.

She would have felt as sad for any omission in the creed as the child who remembers in bed that he has forgotten to kiss his mother good night.[35]
Doggerel
People who smoke all day through
Chimney factory at Loudvater
Bugs go traveling for food and a friend.
The Circus on the Road

[36r]   The Private Mad House*

---

* Entry written in pencil.

Peace and Uncle Jebuel. Beaming with a paper in his hand. How we take the lead.

Babies right

The university

The Big Aggie {The University}[36]
Too broad in shoulders*
She was a Townie

Between you and I
Experimental Psychologist {Between you and I}
She Writes for the Magazines
He Reads Aloud the Story Of the Near Sighted Lover in the N. Archives of Mating

[36v]   Conferring Retroactive Degrees on the Immortal Dead
(In Honoring them we shall honor {or submit} ourselves.)
The I can't wait a minute man
I cant wait for recognition man
Declaration of Babies' arms.
University invites the high school in conference
High School invites district school.†
He had so many more children than a mere mother. Sense of time: who can estimate a minute.

[37r]   Civilization moves like advances like the fire in the soot at the back of the fire place.[37]
As every food carries its poison so every form of discipline
We'll all be no one left alive or at work who can't answer direct questions
Selectiveness is that which forgets.
Hedonism and Democracy[38]
Is that what we are to you a trial? Or are we merely to be thought of as fighting for place as charter members of aristocracy‡

---

* Entry written in pencil.
† This entry and the one above it written in pencil.
‡ This entry and the one above it written in pencil.

[*37v*]*   Can I do it Everyone said of course he could and must. He would find the money—and—well perhaps he could get in without examinations.

    What would Marcus Aurelius say to aggressiveness?[39] His is the philosophy of a man who has nothing to gain and everything to lose. He has simply to hold himself up to holding on. He is born to a position beyond any incentives but the highest. He has to make the most of those to keep from lapsing. He could not make incentives of the pleasures and as pleasures alone he would have none of them. Commodus[40] was otherwise

[*38r*]   Suppose we write poetry as we make a dynamo without ornament—well only the great poetry can be written that way.†

    Time is near when all ~~but~~ Americans but a few millions in Pittsburg will be graduates of college.
    "Suggestion" to explain everything
    Pedagogy. Hypnotism
    Old Lady quotes Thoreau on never too late to be improving yourself.‡ [41]
    Till somebody runs ahead of professors:
    Saved to culture.
    Poetry but is it truth?

[*38v*]§   Uncle Sam has been telling Russia that she mustn't massacre Jews[42]
    Where James boarded
    Hopeful atmosphere
    He quoted Thoreau and the daily paper to him
    Baccalaureate sermon to the primary school grads
    Husband of the landlady—where was he educated? Most natural thing to ask
    Practical poetry.
    Conflict between high school and college

---

* Page written in pencil.
† Entry written in pencil.
‡ This entry and those below it on the page written in pencil.
§ 38v, 39r, 39v, 40r written in pencil.

[39r]   Men have nothing but vague theory why they are as they are Idlers in Argentina assigned as reason for Idleness Day was too long. They were too poor to work.

One of them has come to us. Where is he going?

Th Hollis said I could have all the brushwood I wanted to [illegible] bank my peas.

[39v]   One good thing about Hardy[43]—He has planted himself on the wrongs that can't be righted.

Sexual disparity of sexes

Once you get enough inspiration for a time or two you can finish your poems by logic. But you don't want to certainly some things you can't do without plenty of slaves and subjects

Society as symbolical. King of peas

[40r]   and stood for this or that.

How may words be made to hold their sounds. Spelling is approximate. They only hold the sounds for those who have heard them:

Sentences only hold their sounds for those who have heard them. The real intonations of Homer's verse are long since lost. That is why we drop into scansion.

The complete reactionary cant exist you can still have under a where you have a kings however enfeebled

[40v]   Just as the letters of a word cant communicate the sound of the word to one who hasn't previously heard it so the words of sentence cant communicate an intonation that to one who hasn't previously heard it. That is to say the best part of a language must soon die.

Would it be a good idea to write without any intonation of idiom so as to prepare nothing but that could

[41r]   be read by the eye—like math.

No doubt in my mind but that the determining event in the thinking of the past forty years was the Franco Prussian War.[44]   It made the Frenchman think internationally because nationalism had been whipped out of him. He couldn't think nationalism and think well of himself. He became altruistic to transcend defeat. And like a Frenchman he drew the world along with him. We all became international and altruistic. But the physical fact of the German became too much for the Frenchman. He could not get rid of him with a thought

[41v]   Nothing can originate with a physical fact but action. So now the Frenchman has set about goes with action—direct action. And the world thinks that
kind of thought too.

One cant get outside of his country nor outside of the style of thought of
his time—any more than a woman can get outside of the style of dress of the
time.

Sacrifice: The Christian sacrifices himself: the man his enemy

The danger of being cruel because you see life is tragic I must spare you
(as instrument of God)

[42r]*   Jigging spoon doll among the M-day

Poetry we are agreed is some sound

Manufactured men from schools rather than men who have grown in ap-
prenticeships

Verily we progress

So true is it that we lose the meaning of form that we cant enter into the
spirit of an unformulted poem Sufficiently to complete it.

Poetry cannot be written from a thought It is a feeling that when emotion
may pick it for its use [illegible] left by my sound [?antecedent] thinking

[42v]   There is nothing we can really think of except what happens to us

Words exist in the mouth not in books. Books cant arrest their change

Sentences exist in the mouth.   A sentence {is} a sound apart from the
sound of the words.

The census takers[45]—Looking down main street.

Poets of the utilitarian (Homer

Seeing things in non utilitarian lines.

Don't you hate or love anyone enough to make fun of him.

[43r]   ~~Civilization is like a bad bed~~ We lie as uncomfortably in society as in a bad
old bed that rolls us together in the middle

He thought they might be good poems because he was afraid they were

Do you believe the soul is inhabited?

That's a new one to me I haven't thought of it

I believe in the reversibility of soul and body

Do you believe in the—exteriority of the body

---

* 43r, 43v, 44r, 44v written in pencil.

[43ᵛ]   I would increase everyman's chance not anybody's certainty

Only a few fairies believe in people I find

My one fear is that I shall not be enough here   Does Yeats believe in fairies?¹⁶

While I am here

This is for you

Help me

What will you do

The Character of Life

The Yankee likes to play with the old trapping of aristocracy I the secret societies

Whether our slight class feeling is the remains of an old thing

[44ʳ]   or the beginning of a new.

> The Scalp (Interpreter)

Knew their people on the hoof*

Im not a realist but an actualist. A realist is satisfied if what he writes seems as if it must have happened. I set down nothing that hasn't ~~actually~~ to my knowledge actually happened in words and tones I have actually heard. No book words

Every extra thing you do in the house makes you feel as if you would soon get where you would never work again.

[44ᵛ]   Is poetry ornament laid on or even is it even special beauty set apart and segregated

How the sentence sounds are enough and held apart—

How long will they stay on paper.

Poetry lives in the tenor of the sentence.†

The poetry in ~~that lies~~ adjectives is more likely to be laid on than that in nouns and verbs and prepositions.

Word that m denotes next to nothing but connotes all the dim poetry you ever read it in. Meaning nothing associates everything.

[45ʳ]   They have an air of thinking

Anything you may say you will have heard before

---

* First three entries written in pencil.

† First four entries written in pencil.

The Weather Wine and the Watch Charm Uncle

One son takes business as an adventure and goes to market. One goes to school and becomes infallible.

$$\left\{ \begin{array}{l} \text{Suggestion and Approach} \\ \text{On Winning Approval} \end{array} \right\}$$

I heard the loathsome R Grant[47] say on how much a year one can support a soul. I like facts faced But now we dream dreams.

[45v]   Trees in the village street

In mid afternoon in summer time

The Clear sound images

Clear sight images have been attended to.

Exponents to denote stress.*

Sentence sounds haven't been noticed any more than perspective once.

$$\left\{ \begin{array}{l} \text{(This is your sort of thing} \\ \text{This is my sort of thing)} \end{array} \right\}$$

Four years and one

Hundred and Four.

[46r]   <u>The Brood Nigger,</u>

It is the common way to think of the sentence as saying something. It must do something as well.†

I'm not particular about what the actors are going to do. If there's something doing in their lives (as well as saying). What do we mean by action

Tooth pick march

In the bedroom (falling apart.

[46v]‡   All his days: tale of the invention he wouldn't push

You have to stick the knife home then give it a turn

No one does anything except by force of someone else

Fatigue likes forgetting as an advantage. Theres as much hate as love in all getting on.

"Tempest" in daily use for thunderstorm

Master and the master

---

* Entry and those below it on the page written in pencil.

† Entry and one above it written in pencil.

‡ Pages 46v through 48v written in pencil.

[47r]   How can you tell whether a person's use of a word is individual conscious
literary bookish or natural

The Verifier

Letter to Judith

Critical ideas

Today is word day: we shall judge everybody by his choice of ideas

This book deserves this much space. Excuse us if we leave it blank We happen to know this fellow and what he looks

[47v]   Clear thought clear image (clear figure)

Image of things seen that is as far as most carry it.

Recognizable image.

Curl most significant thing in nature. Things return upon themselves.

Bliss is "let up"

Heaven must be too

There must be some work somewhere like ones dream

Apple raising

[48r]   Last of the birth process at twenty flushes the mind with ideals and ~~assimilates~~ closes the nature separately or conjointly with another

As worm may be divided and live in two parts. Some unborn inhibition must be broken down.

When a thing begins to taste like the sum of its parts it's a sure sign you have too much of it.

[48v]   The white facets on the [?privet] hedges.

Before the baby's ~~eyes~~ {iris} changed to blue.

If the same thing happens to you ten times something is sure to ~~happen~~ occur to you. Just as in a counting machine a certain number of changes in the units place end thus comes a change in the tensplace.

Reproductive imagination and transcendent imagination (?)

[49r]   It is possible to be just as speculative ~~in the~~ about people as about God and animals.

A is speculative I am introspective. W. is intuitive.

The question of how any intonations are made fast to the paper. By the context partly: partly by idomatic signs.

Accident and design

Shop

[49v]   The poet is himself creative in something that is a resultant of these two, the intonation (sound of sense[48]) and the ~~rhythm~~ metre.

No indelicacy to appear in public with the children you have begotten. At the same time you don't care to be seen begetting them.

A teacher taught world is a world saved

[50r]   Why will we be looking for the bottom of things that haven't got a bottom

We are so ambitious to be away off somewhere or away up somewhere that we can't wait to start from where we are.

Evil clings so in all acts the even when we not only mean but achieve our prettiest bravest noblest best we are often a scourge even to those we do not hate. Our sincerest prayers are no more than groans that this should be so.

[50v]   Suspicion that these tales of magic and the miraculous are some last remains of what some other age was as great in as ~~we are~~ ours is in science and mechanics.

[51r]   Throw on more dollars (R.R. story[49]
Eat too much and grow thin. Analogy.
Borrowed daughter. Social service story.   Mrs. Russells
Kill him before he has the time to change his will.
The Homestead plan man.

[51v]   We look upward in prayer when upward is only outward as now we know?

I am here who have been there. Time, time! It is almost as mysterious that I can be in different places at different times as that I could be in different places at the same time.

[52r]   Walls of books with here and there a window in them. The books are part of what we perceive with in looking out the windows.

Roosevelt couldn't put Humpty-dumpty together again.[50]

He "snapped the whip" He swung the line one way but when he tried to swing it back before it stopped going the way it was going why of course he snapped it off

[52v]   Unless words aren't pretty well stuck where they have no tendency to pull back {they have no savor of where they came from} when they are moved as by emotion

Every poet has his regular characteristic displacement—that is to say distance of moving words phrases and things from their place

[53r]   So much of this over national American stuff errs in including the criticism of which it is with what it is {the poem with the poem} It is too conscious

Poetry comes half way: the world comes half way.

Words that have been mouthed like a common tin cup

[53v]   The difference is more in the way we need it said to feel it. Billy Sunday[51] satisfies some: old poeticisms satisfy some.

I begin to see that all is not from within outward any more than all is from without inward. In everything we work from both directions at once.

[54r]   Ideas are there; thoughts are there always the same you don't think them out you perceive them. You are known by the degrees you have risen to perceive. (There may be something to this).

Children can't enjoy the joke of an animal standing on its head in a picture because they can't see why they shouldn't turn the picture round and bring the animal right side up (though they should make the trees stand on their head.

[54v]   They get the most out of life who take most naturally to whats taken for granted.
I've been as
If I have been inadequately sad over sorrow its because I have been afraid of not being cheerful enough to beat the cause of sorrow. I have been as sad as I dared to be—as sad.

[55r]   as I could be without coming to a standstill.
The strangeness is all in thinking two things at once, in being in two places at once. This is all there is to metaphor.

From the outside in.
Do we go out of ourselves and {look in to} see whether we are coming out where we should

[55v]   A poem would be no good that hadn't doors I wouldn't leave them open though.

Shall we bring up children to the idea that love bonds are indisoluable and let them find out that they are not always or bring them up to the idea that they are disoluable and let them find out that they are not always so.

[56r]   Synechdochist[52]
I love best to cite instances that will bother you to bring in any formula. I like instances that just miss coming in under a formula; or that suggest but don't quite state some new formula. I like the instances of instinct that bother the evolutionist.[53]

[56v]   When [?Hernle] died he asked me to go on with what he had been. We had a long talk about it. All his ideas of art—had I grasped them.
Persuading the Am Indian to give up the continent. Explaining our greater need to him. Explaining him into—Indian Territory. Explaining him off the earth. Employ a force of lawyers.

[57r]   John Eliot[54] lived with the Indians for many years and enjoyed the friendship of a great chief. He kept a diary chiefly of the things he found he could say with acceptance to his friend the chief.
The English Teacher.

What pleasure he took in his old age was in what didn't please him.

[57v]   You will have a hard time in looking back into history to find anything very wrong done by the victorious. The victorious write the history.

Chasing a drop of quicksilver around a plate with pinches.

Ball and funnel. Some balls make a noise running round the sides before they go through the hole.

[58r]   Life is that which can mix oil and water (Emulsion) It can consist of the inconsistent. It can hold in unity the ultimate irreconilables spirit and matter good and evil, monism (idealism) and dualism (realism) peace and strife.[55] It over rules the harsh divorce that parts things natural and divine Life is a {bursting[56]} unity of opposition barely held.

•   •   •

Life is something that rides steadily on something else that passes away as light on a gush of water.

[58v]   ~~Are? not~~ He rides them   the opposites.

All a man's art is a bursting unity of opposites. Christs message almost tears itself apart with its {great} contradictions.

Ever since man was man he has known the generous thrill of owning a better. There is a better man than I am. How does he bring himself to it? Christ is one he taken to do it with.

[59r–v]   [blank]

[60r]*   Trow? Will he come, think?
What is he—sick of it?
All is.
Cosset⎫
Cattering⎬
Chirk up
A well constructed novel or epic with the chapters named conjunctional
"When" "If" "But"—"Though" "Yet"

[60v]   Flower Guidance

As I went from flower to flower
(I have told you how)
I have told you what I found
Dead not growing on the ground
Look upon me now

If you would not find yourself
In an evil hour
Too far on a fatal track
Clasp your hands behind your back
Never pick a flower.

[61r]   [blank]

·   ·   ·

---

* Page written in pencil.

[*61v*]   [blank]

[*62r*]   Inside the Horse-shoe
           Turning Back
           Long Jump
           High jump
           Three Chairs
           The Narrowz

[*63–64*]   [blank]

"Beggars in England"

MS. 001725. *Black clothbound notebook with outer corners slant cut by machine, 3″ × 4″ unruled pages. Entries are in black ink unless otherwise noted. "Calendar for 1910" stamped inside the front cover. Though the date of the calendar is 1910, material within the notebook suggests that entries might correlate with later dates. Entries on 2r suggest experiences in England in 1913. Entries on 7r, 7v, and 10v suggest that Frost may be noting thoughts for use in teaching at Amherst College, which he began in 1917.*

[1r]   Beggars in England
Pursuit of G.B.S.[1]
Failure of Puritanism of Milton
No stir at the stations
[?r]inderwoods {Holly
Play: Failure of Puritanism
American News in the Times.
Bundles of Toothpicks for kindling
Joy for a Penny[2]
Something of doing everything for its own sake*
Library in Beaconsfield school[3]
More foreign news in English papers?
Our seeming contempt for foreigners
As deep as spirit may go—as one may go with spirit
The popping of little lighting flame

[1v]   Subjects for Lesley[4]
Best things in life
Absent-mindedness of elders.
She must furnish set of subjects first

---

* This entry to the end of the page written in pencil.

Killing things
Pleasure of writing verse—what is it*

Glad to see a future for us as long as it is future

[2r]   Hadn't heard of Montessori.[5] <u>Had</u> read SK and GB[6]
Schools here are like the streets of Boston; schools with us likes streets of Washington.
We see out and out English men so little that we are [illegible] likely to forget that the English still consider us predominately English. Article in Times
Mrs. Tynan Hinkson[7] couldnt let her English country friends know that she wrote poetry. Strange they weren't readers enough to know it themselves. The secret sin of writing verse.
Things I was looking For. (Among [illegible] others love of liter.
Too physical a nature to see ~~two~~ {both} sides to the question
His nature is to vigorous too physical—
If Emerson Had Written a Play
My First English School Room
Marrying was important because need for children. Let it be.
Brilliance of thy locks shows more intellect and less dignity than in real life. Conflict here.

[2v]   The Bagpipes. A boatload of the Scotch
It does you good to hear that somethings are the same as at home

Melanism[8]

Self wronged   Peace of the World
3 pts of <u>Gin</u> a day
Wood keep s better out of doors.   No sewer

[3r]   The Man With a Week to Live: Insurance
All—I try to deny myself every virtue.

___

The Dentist Criminal.

___

•   •   •

___
* Page to this point written in pencil.

The colleges. Honorary degrees to the dead.

Figuring about profits or the wall

He had written something for the magazines. The earliest mating records in the world at Cold Harbor [illegible] U.S.A. Kissing the drawer in the card case.

[3v]   [blank]

[4r]   They think monogamous thought is sentimental.*
Criticism is where we say behind In back things to each others' faces.
Corners one has been in. Cruxes one has found.

In looking up train time you have to be on your guard (consciously) against certain things viz getting wrong direction getting Sunday trains. Not so in writing poetry.

Bergsons[9] is a literary philosophy because it uses for everything the idea of every sentence being a fresh start not a mere logical derivation from the last sentence.

[4v]   [blank]

[5r]   On Seeing Shakespeare's Rhythm Done in Musical Notation by Harriet.[10]— all I can say is it's a damned poor tune.

Musical notes are taken because they can express so much.   [He] And they express nothing.

Terrible god   devoted men[†]
Fear of the incalculable in your best friend.   Night fear.

---
* First three entries written in pencil.
[†] This entry and the one below it written in pencil.

[6r]   Children in arms not admitted. How can you blame children for being in arms when the whole nation is in arms?

Fellow feeling between Carnegie and the Kaiser because they have both been in the steel business.[11]

In Isolation.

No right prevails of itself or except as human being espouse it.

There is no evil but that was at some time indistinguishable from good. God himself did not know [illegible] the devil from his good angels.

Extrication.

Not as a woman weeps: but as a man—against his nature and against his will.

Rub your finger on a smooth surface so as to make it "catch" and vibrate enough for a "note": just so the speech rhythm on the verse rhythm.

[6v]   [blank]

[7r]   Offhand judgement is the only kind in human affairs. You may be as conversant as you will with all knowledge in the world the final act of judgement is always a jump.

You must remember that no sentence is quite on the page any way. The sentence concept that holds the words together is supplied by the voice.★

In America where even the lower classes treat the lower classes with respect and politeness.

‖ Prize for the best plan for hiding something—was to make sure of its remaining hidden
‖ for 10000 years and yet found at the end of that time.

[7v]   The smoke flowed down the roof and in the open window and up the chimney again.

[8r]   Closeness of style and intensity of style.

·   ·   ·

★ This entry and the one above it written in pencil.

Something in the sentence that is more effective than any chosen word.*

My first conquest of a superstition Pis-en-lit.

Spit apat upo!

Certain cadences belong to us by birth as certain runs of voice belong to a kind of bird.[12]

The Volunteer—U.S. Grant.[13]

You don't know whether to offer pay. You dont know whether to ask if a thing is for sale. You dont know whether to speak love. You are afraid

[8v]   of assuming too much in another person.

Prescott and Mabel.

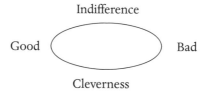

Indifference

Good   Bad

Cleverness

[9r]   "But What They Fought Eachother For."[14]

"We." As Americans us it in this war.

Losses at Chevy Chase[15]

English winter day is always at morn. White sky black castle.

Getting letters   { Advertisement
                    { Sunshine Society[16]

Then Children One had some and come back. The other was going.†

[?Extrication] as [illegible] [illegible] initiative in every sentence

[9v]   Sometimes the donkey pulls the cart sometimes the cart pushes the donkey
Speech rhythm [illegible] is the donkey

•   •   •

---

* Entry written in pencil.

† Beginning of page through this entry written in pencil.

I should expect to see connection between any two things in existence

I can show connection*

"Seem to bear rather than rejoice"

[*10r*]   A ninth wave gathering half the deep
And full of voices slowly rose and plunged
Roaring and all the wave was as a flame
And down the wave and in the flames was borne[†]

Only too glad to be sorry when its too late.

I doubt if any thing is more related to another thing than it is to any third thing except as we make it (and bid our will avouch it.)

[*10v*]   [blank]

[*11r*]   The sentence form almost seems the soul of a certain set of words. We see inspiration as it takes liberties with the words and yet saves the word.

Nothing counts but the increment.

I took his body on my back ~~and whiles I‡~~
And whiles I gaed and whiter I sat

[*11v*]   All we are saying against War is only the measure of the goodness of our resolution never to fight again. It is worth just as much as a drunkard reasons for really believing that ~~now~~ things are {now} going to be different—he will never get drunk again.

[*12r*]   113 acres till. Unpainted 2 miles out sugar orchard and 900 trees. 3000 wood Babcock 25 acres flat 2 miles no road Stowe.

•   •   •

---

* A pencil line with an arrow tip runs across the page from this phrase to the entry that starts "I doubt if anything . . ." in 10r. This entry and the one below it written in pencil.
† First four lines written in pencil.
‡ This line and the one below it written in pencil.

Money test* I don't blame him for wanting to get it as cheap as he could.
Pretty cheap sort of person told him what he wanted etc.

What do you think of a man that always brings his own books to read in
the train instead of buying magazines of†

A person who is able to think well of himself for what he cant understand.
He says: My mind doesnt work that way, implying it works some other way
when

[12v]   it doesnt work at all

[13r]   The difficulty with church is the mixture it is of spiritual and social doctrine and human ideal and real God and our neighbor. We forget that the
people arent God and cant be expected to be or we go to the other extreme
and forget that mere brotherliness isnt spiritual exaltation.

There is more upkeep than uplift in all our getting together in halls‡

[14r]   Affectation and Business

When I can't get justice, I say there are better men than these who refuse it
me: I will go over their heads to the better men, and to the better still and so
on up to the best man of all. He shall be my king.

We are sick of our triumph in the Civil War. There is a revolution of feeling a disillusionment in which we see ourselves without glory, in which we
love our hold on our reasons for fighting till we can believe we scarcely had
any in which we see ourselves as the hulking bully able to have

[14v]   The Man with Springs to Sell

The Spring that Roiled Itself. Little dog bath§
Mrs Lynch and the Destroyers of Property[17]

---

* Written up the left margin next to the following two sentences.
† "I don't blame him" to "buying magazines of" written in pencil.
‡ Entry written in pencil.
§ These three words written in pencil.

The Homestead Idea Man*

The Socialist who asked me to give him books he could sell to raise money to help him help the cause of poetry. He thinks priests are in religion for what they can get out of it.

[15r]   our way by main strength, whether right or wrong.

Resentment against being taught.
"The O's in Hamlet."[18]
Hang it all! No let Georgia do it.
Oh what is and what is not poetry in a poem of Stevenson's—Christmas morning.[19]
The something fierce that rises in my nature at the sight of someone else trying to get the better of me.
Equality is as difficult to attain

[15v]†   Its sure that the trade basis for society and the state is worse than this territorial basis or ever the tribal basis because it would leave the best ~~tribes~~ {states} weakest in number—the poetry state the mechanical state the

[16r]   even for a moment as the exact meeting of sharp points. We slide off above or below each other.

Flesh will pale.
Flesh will burn[20]

[16v]   Sog Magog Mempleremagog[21]

God and crime are two ends of the same thing. For you can see God slipping off into virtue, virtue into beauty beauty into property and property into crime. All but the last are manifest in the Catholic Church.

[17r]   Book of Records.[22] Every single thing on earth is the best for exactly what it

---

* This entry and the one below it written in pencil.
† Page written vertically up the left side, top to bottom.

is Someone is easily the [?lasiest/lamest] man in the world with one eye and a poor memory for names.

Ten poems as NBs to throw away
 The Spooner Farm is the coldest place in the U.S.[23]
 In her dancing she thinks only of other dancing. Yet I suppose she knows a little of life—[illegible] not enough to manage with a man in love for more than a few weeks. On a bus in N.Y.

[17v] [blank]

[18r] The image to the eye and the image to the ear are two equal peaks like the letter M

[18v] 1st Boundaries: where what goes out fromi us meets what goes out from them throwing up a ridge. Adversity.

2nd What I will die for but wont argue.

3rd Responsibility

[19r] A deed is the only perfect judgement

   A. B. C. and 1 2 3[24]

A deed being the only judgement. So much is this so that the simplest decision acted on lifts a man above higher than the most beautiful and complex decision not acted on.

Better men often common men because more of their decisions are acted on.*

[19v] [blank]

---

* Written up the right hand margin, bottom to top.

[20r]   Woe be unto a land where the office has to seek the man. The ruler must love rule and aspire to rule. The great ruler is one in whom the general [illegible] trust in law and order becomes a delight in law and order.

The Waiting Spirit.[25] How Long will it wait?

Why does even a parrot learn

[20v]   swearing before any other form of speech. Because it is more spiritual than any other.

[21r]   Which would you rather: think you were right when you were wrong or and not know why you were defeated or be defeated when you were really right.

[21v–32r]   [blank]

[32v]   One-two-three-go! No good   Come back, come back.

Let me not to the marriage   of true minds

[46v]   Not how much you can think but how much you can think that will act. Thought is controlled by action. What we have to do may be terrible but it is required of us to keep us from thinking nonsense Wars are not sent to make us better or nobler but to make keep nations from thinking nonsense.

[2r]*   It is important to know where I got this vers libre
I don't want you to think that I got this vers libre from Whitman
Or from the French writers who got theirs from Whitman
I dont wh want you to know where I got it
Forbear you man not {think I am} as original as I am.
Surely I got it form somewhere
I dont pretend to say I invented it?
Mrs Ro[illegible] Adam[illegible]
    Peel Terrace

---

* At this point, Frost begins writing from the other end of the notebook toward the middle, with several pages left blank in between.

[3r]   You know I many have quite [illegible]

Well let me give you the beat
I never read Whitman
   Not ours to know it
I have no French
So I am cleared of that suspicion on my own testimony
I may owe something to a little thing I must have read in the nineties.
It was by Steve Crane[26] of failed memory. (Too bad)

It went like this

The impact of the dollar on the human heart—
But I don't owe much.
I am very much my own teacher
Now that we have settled that for the [illegible] light of society
A word about my rhythm

[4r]   I knew history would want to know
I make it go this way
For the same reason that soldiers fall out of step in crossing a bridge
So the structure of the universe wont get to vibrating too much and break down

William Sharp[27] has written some vers libre I am told
Never read him—or her

[5r]   The Strong Creed

It would be a poor sort of man that would refuse power that was rightly his.
   No man can know what power he can call rightly his unless he presses a little.

                     Laboratory Psychology

Knows just a little ~~more~~ {less} than than the truth and in that little (Scientific

[6r]   To be supposed that
   An older person would read ~~more~~ (to himself) than a younger as reading through thicker stuff being retarded by the sense of many side issues

Any one would read silently poetry slower than prose

Anyone would read poetry or prose the slower for having been accustomed by having it read aloud to give it the line of spoken sentences.

[*7r*]   Amherst

Make your mark with me and you will make your mark in the world. Make your mark with me and you will get a mark. Bryant[28] made his mark in the world early and nothing he failed to do afterward could unmake it.

The mere man who has "done something" may not be a good critic. He may not be able to teach criticism. He may still be of worth as

[*7v*]   a teacher for his attitude of mind toward what he has done and toward what there is to do.

The Capital M   Two peaks
The Bridge (Rhythm
Nodding Yes

[*8r*]   The Carrot
Doors (Synecdoche)[29]
A Bent Pin
[illegible]
Bookcase and Window
Cart and Horse (Two rhythms)
My Pasture (Logic-Material)
Restarting by rereading what you have already written down
The Snow Plow
Larruping an Emotion
The Clothes Line
Donkey and Cart

[*9r*]   Mind becomes like the attick of an ~~old~~ a house you have long lived in. It is ~~full~~ so full of everything you cant fail to find costume in it for carrying out plays of any period.
    Maple sugar
What has villany to do with tragedy
    Pratt of Shutesbury swunga scythe one hundred years and one.
    Still Corners[30]

[9v]   Loose she words any one can get an emotion out of.

Multiplication when conditions favor. Wild horses in S. America[31]

Responsibility of "being out in front " No one to ask advice of.

The Overtaker. Self consciousness comes up

[10r]   with you and laughs

There is waste[32] there is what we leave behind there is what we shed every day. Is it time that we must concern ourselves with that equally with what we keep and go forward to? No. We may glance back and down but we look principally the way we are going.

[10v]   Some sort of rigors of the class. Not the rigor of argument. Capping ideas. Like word building word and - making and taking.

[11r]   Money O!

Litter's [illegible] Midnight Caller
Gold at € for Christmas Pay
Two Pensions.
To pay a debt I didnt owe with borrowed money.
Boughten Votes.
When Did He Get It (Rag Picker)
Bequest of Lost Money.

"All my thoughts of every thing"

MS. 001334. *Brown soft paper cover bound notebook, 6¾" × 8¼." Canvas strip binding on left side. Pages stitched. Paper ruled. "ACFAD Boston/01084" stamped inside back cover. All entries in black ink unless otherwise noted.*

[*1r*] ~~All my thoughts of every thing~~

I thought you wanted to show me a flower
On its stem as it stood growing.

[*1v*]   Barrel Whang   Poplin   Bungey

Little Town   Still Corners[1]   Muddy Boo   Lost Nation
Springs   The Haunted Sprng.
The Soap Girl
Two Pensions   A Deep Water Penny
Acquitted[2]
Toffile ~~Berry~~ L Lajway[3]
The Faithful fish (Fish of Faith How faithfully they try to climb the fall
The Otter Skin (fifty dollars)
Lull in assertion of behive diving sichification for sincerity. Don care period
Brave denial. Braver concession {I have only the} first
The Sap Yoke
New Y London Laughs at New York. New York laughs at Boston (tries to think it does) Boston laughs at Portland, Portland laughs at Littleton Littleton at Franconia[4] Franconia at Easton Easton at Bungay[5] ~~Bungay at~~ the last an almost mythical fake named place ~~for~~ invented for Easton to relieve itself on. myth
'There goes a million!" You think you have given her up. Any woman can marry any man she wants to. The girl that will decide to marry you is

[2r] The Man Who Couldn't Lose His Temper
Bartlett[6]

The Woman Who Couldn't Lose Her Temper
Mrs Fisher[7]

The Time I Didn't Lose My Temper

The Seven Sheds
   Both his father and his mother were his step parents*
How to Take a Hero. You musnt assume you can ever learn from him what it
is to have gone to war[†]
There a Threat in It (Mosher and Suffrage[8]

The Poet The Inventor and The Reformer
An art of the work and an art of getting pay for the work

John Fisher's Case and My Mother's[9]

The Artists Colony Paolo and Francesca[10] Shoot the Baby. How Ethlane
Came to Jesus.[11] Way thy talk about the native's Haygreed character

The Scalp-dancer—who could sit motionless as to everything else and move
his scalp in time forward and sideways shake his hair stand on end and swirl
in cowlicks scalp snapping electricity

[2v] The biologist has to grasp more desperately at altruism be than the Christian
because he asks the individual to do many things that for the race that will
cause to interest the individual at death

It has been found that no one can get back into life on earth except in
descendents that somewhat resemble him no knows yet just how much but
probably a great deal. His only hope then is in the perpetuation of his race.

[illegible paragraph]

---

* Entry written in blue ink.
† From "You musnt" to "war" written in blue ink.

[*3r*]   Once I had a little ~~flying~~ gig
That every pebble in the road at night
Flung sky high with me and from side to side
And when

Oh once I had a little racing gig
~~That every pebble in the road at night~~
That didn't weigh a quarter of its load
~~That every little pebble in the load~~
That every ~~frozen~~ rut ~~or~~ {and} pebble in the road
Flung sky high with me and to left and right

Oh once I had an airy gig
That gave a leap at every stone
And tossed me lightly in my seat

Oh once I had a little airy gig
Not more than half as heavy as its load

[*3v*]   when there was society to be made the most of. In – she was failing right
there when she died. She probably died of the failure. And a good thing she
did it in time before she involved her husband in it and undid in no time at all
what she had undeniably done for him in half a life time of patient sacrifice.

Plymouth—This was the port of entry of our freedom
No slip of all that under sail or steam
Has gathered people to us
But Pilgrim manned the Mayflower in a dream[12]
Has been their anxious envoy to this shore.

Come in a Second Coming to the West
Come in a second coming to this land
Where once you left the print of feet impressed
As deep in rock as other have in sand

"Two Poets"

MS. 001732. *Brown soft cover notebook, 6⅝″ × 8⅜″ with black strip binding on left side. Stitched pages. Ruled paper. Entries written in blue ink unless otherwise noted.*

[*Cover*] Two Poets.
A Poetical Boss
If Art Came to America

[*1r*] {First scene} ~~Stage~~ is a bookstore window display of two poets' books {(enlarged)} and their photographs. The actors are all life size except ~~w~~ one a giant who{se} ~~limbs~~ {arms and head reach} in and out of the scene now and then for ~~to~~ a book {or to rearrange the books} without taking any part in the play, [He] {and who} seems not see what is going on.

Mr. Poise {Poesie} is about {thinking} writing.   Poetry starter
Poetry office Take out every other line.   Started half the poets
in America
Creating Cannell

What's ~~W~~ Vest doing in that gallery?

Exercises in reducing each others ~~poet~~ poems.

Oh Bertran de Bornagain[1]
Your sword is mightier than your pen
Next time attack me with your sword
I'd rather bar be cut than bored.
You'd rather I'd be cut than bored.

The duel. Abercrombie[2]

·   ·   ·

The Senator who was asked to do something for the arts. His story of the Dianner on Madison Square Garden[3] The Poet or Something. I cant control you Too late now for anyone to control you.*

Features no more, but what is between the features. Scrapings of the brain pan.

[1v]   Publisher's <u>contract</u> <u>iniquitous.</u>†

Do you give lessons

Read us your poem about what the minister said when he ruined the furnace door with a shovelful of coal.

Read us a poem about the fishes heaven.

Woman beating backs of crowd Whats in there

Amos Poise wrote that—not I

Amos Poise crosses stage with one follower who introduces his hero Ethelred on one ~~we~~ [illegible] whose work we hold second only to the Bible.

Small group invidiously asks for Poises autograph right before Vest‡ Woman [illegible] mistakes Poise for Vest. Rushes in a asks for your poem about what he minister etc

[2r]§   Bookstore window (as herein before) Book fair day Ethelred Vest {at desk} autographing ~~for~~ for throng

Second Scene Poetical Headquarters.

2v–26r]   [blank]

---

* This paragraph written in blue ink.
† Entry written in blue ink.
‡ Line drawn in left margin from this word to the entry "Read us your poem. . . ."
§ Page written in blue ink.

[27r]   At certain point   I leave these ladies to you
(Two or three men.)   Poise is coming
        Salon   How in the name did you get him
                (Enters Poise

Would you mind telling us Mr. Nematode how a poem comes to you? I suppose its a foolish question to ask. Do you just have an inspiration.

Nematode makes a comical gesture of putting ~~on~~ a forefinger {meditatively} to his ~~forehead~~ {brow} like a pistol ~~with his~~ {the} thumb raised like the hammer of it.

Its a fair question Nem You neednt start to search yourself for a funny answer that turneth away the ~~th~~ the rank outsider. Mrs Osbert means do you [illegible] start a poem idea first—something like that dont you Mrs Osbert—or sound first. Do you hear it coming before you see it?

I just want to know how poems are made that all I suppose. I hope theres no harm in that Not so I can write them myself—you neednt be jealous. Just ~~so~~ out of curiosity. Its not a secret is it

Are you sure you dont mean how reputations in poetry are made.

No I wanted to know how poems were made. But I

[27v]   ~~suppose I shall~~ how reputations ~~are~~ in poetry are made will be better than nothing. I dont want to miss ~~the~~ {any legitimate} opportunity ~~altogether~~ {of} to improve myself.

What have I got that you got you all together if I am ~~not~~ to get ~~anything~~ {nothing} out of you. {We dont have Mr. Wests} with us everyday.

West here probably knows his processes better than any of us because he wrote more. You make a regular business of it [illegible] dont you At least you dont mind who says you make a regular business out of it. The word business cant scare you harsh? You appear simultaneously {every day} in how many newspapers is it ~~from~~ {between} {from}* Boston to Los Angeles {inclusive}? You're syndicated arent you. You {must} write your poem a day I understand

I do. And I'm always twenty one poems or three weeks of poetry ahead of the game.

So you wont feel the editors right after you.

And if I did today my [?light] would still keep

---

* Inserted below the line.

[28r] coming to the world for three weeks after I was dead.

You must have poetry on your mind {pretty much} all the time.

You dont know Alfred. No one could be less bedeviled by his art than he is. Twenty three hours of the twenty four your wouldnt know he was an artists at all

If an idea for a poem comes to me when I am playing [illegible] golf at the club for instance I just tell it to trot along {for the present} and come round to my office tomorrow morning You come round to my office at eleven oclock tomorrow morning and I'll write you down you little rudiment so you'll think you were always written down. Call on a man of business in business {his} hours of business.

You're so human Mr. West. No wonder you are beloved loved. How good natured of you not make fun of us.

At least I speak the human language.

But do you mean you have a poetry office too. Mr. Like Ezekiel Poise's that he has just opened in Boise city. Mr. Ame has was telling about it

[28v] before you came in

Ame) Wonderful manufactory There I saw poems and poets made at one and the same stroke while I sat and waited.

2 How did you get in there Ame. Werent you a little out of your element there.

By {Through} the mistaken kindness of a friend . He {who} wanted me to see Ezekiel[illegible] {for comparison with Alfred} bodyguard gang. There are the {you have the} truly great

All the ladies) Tell us about it {him}. Did you see a little mouse run under his chair.

A young fellow named Ryowith knocked at Ezekiels door. Come in. Mr. Poise I come to you in an emergency I have beem {have} wanted time in the studios of Paris till my family who are rich and southern have threatened to cut me off {penniless} if I dont turn to [illegible] and make good at once in some one of the arts. I have come all the way from Paris for help.

[29r] Stand up Eddie and make that little speech about how you make poetry & what your methods are.

H How much money is involved. What do you stand to lose if cut off.

Modesty forbid that I should talk in millions. But it is a large sum.

It must {shall} not be lost. Which of the arts do you choose to make good in?

It may as well be poetry seeing it is to you I have come.

Set right down and write it then.

Between them they worked out in talk and writing a half dozen free verse snippets in what was left of the afternoon. I staid to see it through. Poems like

> *Few know*
> *That the clear day*
> *Had a moment of mist*
> *To start with*
> *When the sun steamed {up} the dew*

I could ~~write~~ [illegible] {reel them off} with one ~~lobe~~ brain tied behind me till this [illegible] came home to roost.

[29v]   Introduction in Greenwich Village[4]

By supper time they were [illegible] tired and slipped off in three batches to the three editors that were to publish anything Ezekiel sends them. [illegible]

So thats the way its done.

Ames ~~came off an embittered man~~ {has never been the same since}.

{It embittered him.} Nothing can come of such machinations.

You wait and see. The poems I ~~saw~~ [illegible] {almost helped write} helped write that {fateful} day will go ringing down the anthologies forever.

For the simple reason that nobody has the courage of his likes and dislikes. They'll all admire anything they're {told to}

Ezekiel says there are only ~~two people~~ three people in the world that know a poem from a corporals guard {anyway} ~~William Butler Yeats and Bernarnd Shaw~~ {H.G. Wells and Arnold Bennett.}[5]

No! Surely not Wells and Bennett

Maybe one of them was Yeats

That sounds more likely.

Is that the way Yeats pronounces it himself to rhyme ~~it~~ with Keats because if it is ~~I can use it~~ {can do}

[30r]   ~~with great effect~~ {some execution with it} at the club next week. ~~He's the poet~~ {English}

We're on Tagore[6] and Yeats ~~is the English poet~~ comes in as the English poet who advised him to resort to costume if he was going to lecture in America.

So thats the way reputations are made

Yes and poems written.

I find the trend of conversation very depressing.

Takes the romance all out of it doesn't it Mrs Bleach

One would almost rather not hear such things.

And yet there is no denying they ~~give one an they~~ come in terribly handy—give one a great advantage in intellectual society.

Theyre very sophisticating

Yes highly.

They let you into the know.

And your story of the way Poise does it is nothing to what you can see happening any day in Greewich Village. I knock at any door a perfect stranger and introduce myself to the first comer as Mr. Clade

[*30v*] the Poet Leonidas W. Clade. We bow. Euthenia come here a moment {(She's in the kitchenette)} This is M. Clade the poet. I want you to meet him and so does he. We are {the Misses} Eugenia and Euthenia. Prospect the painters. ~~And~~ The introduction is complete. Everybodys reputation is made and that without the exchange of a simple credential. The poet has written nothing the painters have painted nothing but thenceforth they will be received a their own valuation. The beauty of it is that it obviates the need of achievement and saves years of hard work.

Let the children play Roscoe. ~~Where does the shoe pinch you.~~   Why see evil ~~What~~

everywhere. Whats get out of the stories you tell about Poise in ~~the~~ an admiration for the generosity of the man. Let you tell it he has given their start to more than half the recent poets of America and

[*31r*] England.

He has but ~~it~~ not to reward their merit so much as to show his own power.

There you go again. And I understand some of his poets have stood up very well under criticism.

You're a good man Alfred. You make us all love you.

I take off my hat to those that pass with the critics. I don't you know.

All you get is countless readers.

And the love of the human race.

.But I'm not cultured {cultivated}. I'm just an ordinary fellow {with a natural gift for singsong}

Its a safe bet Alfred hasnt read a single one of Poises poets to know whether he[s] worth reading or not. Alfred's education has been neglected.

Don't pretend to tell y us you despise yourself [illegible] utterly Alfred.

Oh I get what I want out of life. I just dont want you to think I dont know there are other standards than

[31v]   We dont get you such

than those my friends judge me by.

Mrs Bleach has been called out of the room during the forgoing. She returns with a telegram for Alfred West.

For you Mr. West.

He goes to apart in the room to open it. While he is gone one of the ladies speaks for the first time.

Who is Ezekiel Poise Why have I never heard of him.

Thank God we dont all have

Dont let it embarrass you Mr Trail. Thank God we were not all bound to know all the poets that could come up.

Speaking of the Devil. [illegible] West turns to the group holding out the form a little tremulously as if it would speak for itself. — He must have left to do this.

No bad news I hope.

Listen. (He reads it again himself dazed) Listen to this: Stupidity carried beyond a certain point becomes {she} a public offence against the public. I hereby assume the public quarrel is your case. My

[32r]   seconds will wait on you. Signed Ezekiel Poise Boise City Do you pronounce B-o-I-s-e Boys like boys as in boys and girls.

Whats it all about?

(He reads it again)

How delightful

It's a challenge

How delightful

Mrs Bleach means delightfully ridiculous. We ought to be grateful to anyone who is willing to play the fool as this world {for us} because it saves us the trouble. {of doing it ourselves}

Just as we ought to [illegible] anyone who is willing to play the thief {criminal} because it saves us the shame of play it ourselves[.]

Do you care Alfred.

It hurts me to be treated so. I feel the impact. (He sets down and reads the telegram again) What have I done to write his notice.   I like little   His stuff is so warm

And if he dont see me hed do me no harm

(Ame takes the telegram) Nonsense. You cant fight duels any more.   Not in this country

Thats so

[32v]   One lady sits silent all throughout very flustered and edified by the [illegible] but obviously not entertained.

Do you suppose its my sense of humor or failing me worn out fro by {my} having run been a columnist so many years.

Youre tired old man.

Its evident that Poise doesnt like me.

You cant expect everybody to like you

Why cant I. I dont see why they shouldnt like me I dont ask them to admire me. Im the friendly sort you know.

I believe you are Alfred and I believe that the whole story {with you.} You are protesting the truth when you {You are not ambitious to be great and} you're no hypocrite when you say your not {so}.

The ladies have gotten in motion to leave. They say the conventional compliments in shaking hands with the guest of the evening and are followed into the hall by their hostess. {Men rise} There is a silence that of suppressed curiosity. Our lady goes out looking backward.

Tomanyrot Alfred. You leave it to me to deal with

[33r]   Lecture to Country audience on How to Like poetry How important it is to poets that you should like poetry. Max Berbohms[7] picture.

I to blame for having drawn his attention to us

this. I know Ezekiel now. We got to be pretty good friends. At bottom he's just another fellow like you and me. You watch me bring him down off his airs with a joke.

What'll you say to him?

I'll answer him by telegram at once. Just as you assume the publics quarrel with Alfred West, I beg to assume his quarrel with you. My seconds will notify you of {my choice of} weapons. Signed Hal Ame. Then if it ever gets as far as that Ill name unsold copies of his own books at twenty yards paces.

You mean you'll read that the you'll read them at each other a l'outrance

Now you are coming to. No throw them at each other as missles or missives. But it wont get that far. I'll make him feel too foolish.

I'd like to see you hurling books with your best foot forward hurling books at someone {It would be safer with the covers off—just the sheet the way the publishers trade in them}

You can be one of my seconds. No I dont mean a word I'm saying. Forget the whole thing

[33v]   How will I know I didnt refuse to fight from cowardice
Because I'll tell
By my telling you every time you are in doubt. You are not going to fight because the law doesnt let you fight

No real man invokes the protection of the law.

Where did you quote that sentiment from? Not your from your own works, thou man of peace. The biggest reason for your not fighting is be-cause we cant have your spell broken. We cant have your poetry interrupted. What we ask of you Alfred is poetry. I dont believe you realize—

That's enough Hal. You've said it before. Where do you suppose Mrs Bleach is

Staying out of the way.

Lets call her.

One moment.

What (They look at each other)

You're way down.

[34r]   One sleep will cure me
It will take a sleep will it?
I'm afraid so Hal.—What is it
Im angry at you because I cant think of what to say to you.

[34v–51r]   [blank]

[51v]   Doesnt that result in their being pretty much all alike—all you.

•   •   •

They are more different than you would think. I supply everything but their differences. I depend on them for their differences. I throw myself into their personalities.

O Bertran de Bornagain[8]
Your sword is mightier than your pen

Aspasia[9]   aphasia.[10]

[52r]   MS in clip on the wall—very large   Poets Office. One flight up.
          Tentative trial sheets.
              He didn't come he was brought. Puts Bath tub against wall
              Dont lift those skirts   Branch office in London

Yes he came to me a day or two ago
Wasnt he afraid he'd compromise himself.
He was unhappy and had to come
Could you make him out?
I should think he was hopeless   ~~The poor devil~~
Did you tell him so
How could I the poor devil and after all look at what I did to Selma. {She came to her writing nothing but amiable sonnets} She went home of the opinion she was born writing free verse. It shows it can be done.
Mass production of poets

[52v]   my wife'd tell you.
          Youre a good man to say so.
          You've done a lot for me
          Don't go
          Yes I must. You're tired out. Good night.
          Wallace sits dazed
          After a little while ~~Wallace~~ {he} says Plaudits plaudits
          After another while he throws off his coat.

[53r]   My cup is full then if you are safe. Tell no more tonight. {You were neither of you hurt.} I can imagine it was a farce. It was meant to be. ~~Never mind~~ Not quite. what. Well never mind tonight. I'm in no mood. I can bear to have broken in on. As long as you are all right dear man. Its been a day with [?her] beyond [?his] stars. Yes. Yes. Goodnight

Choke and be damned.

(After reciting it) Be good t the kiddies. I put it up to you. It's up to you re member.

It's up to us.

Don't throw them to the cars by the hundred. Don't. Take me away from here. You've had enough.

Exit all but two night clerks at the desk. One tries to exchange a smile with the other but gets snubbed with a mutter and a toss of the head sideways. Shut up your god damn silly face.

~~Alone~~ In the dim vastness of the Bridal Suite.—Want anything you dont see. ~~Just wh~~ Everything OK. This gives me my chance to tell you: If theres anything of yours I havent read its because you haven't written it. [illegible] I dont know which Id be in if it wasnt for you ~~the~~ {the} jail {the asylum} the almshouse or the morgue.[11] Thats the kind of debtor you see in yours truly. Im yours. I guess

[53v]   Remember I said he was greater than I

Good scout. We dont believe you. Not for us.

Promise to read him.

(Not very enthusiastic): We promise

All right then. What shall I say for a good night poem before you put me to bed [illegible]?

—In the Bridal Suite. You for the Bridal Suite the Bridegroom of the Muses.

That sounds pretty plural. What do you take me for a Mormon. {Who are you marring with now?} I've got one wife ~~as it is~~ {already}. Well ~~any~~ What? name your poem and show your familiarity with my works.

That one about what the minister said when he missed the furnace door with a shovel full of coal.

I'll bet I know what he said without asking. He said hed ~~get an~~ sell the {damned} furnace and get a kelvinator or a frigidaire.

Something quiet and sad for good night ~~Jimmie~~ {Wallie}

How about the ~~one about the~~ Child in the Traffic.

You want to choke us Hard.

[54r]   A few words of policy now and then A stroke of policy now and then.

let me write it right. Hold on to him a minute longer while I think. Don't drop him I have it. What the parson said introducing him on Mothers Day in

Chicago. There have three great poets of the people David the Psalmist Bobbie Burns[12] and now all together—chorus— ~~Loisis~~Wallie Myers. We'll write all that underscoring the cast. Now one more poem Loisis to pay the score. No. Yes. Men I feel as if I ought to remind you that in the opinion of some a peoples poet is nothing in comparison with a poets poet.

Whats that

One who writes to the approbation of his fellow artists

Where is there one

In New York—Elihu Means. I just got this letter from him.

Never heard of him Cut it out. This is your day. {We don't ~~know~~ {care} what Elihu means.} We mean you. One more poem to please the governor of the State of Colorado, Wallie.

I want you to remember the name of Elihu Means to please me I want you to buy him and read him

What is it about him

I'm going to read what he says I can stand you better than I can all the little futile lies that twiddle rhymes in unread solitude*

[54v]   Is that the way poetry is written

~~Scenes~~ Sit back in your chair. You are taken on.

I know whats the matter with me and I know what to do about it.

Oh well if hes satisfied to go on as he is.

You can deny that you have ever been to me. You naturally will and I can't blame you. Our conference has come to nothing. It was a moment of weakness on your part thats all. You ~~are a~~ stand on your own

I haven't much on you†

legs . You are an authentic poet in your own right. You should never have come to me or anyone else. Forget that you have.

Maker of poets.   Maker of makers {A poet is a maker well I am a maker of makers.}

•   •   •

---

* This entry written up the right margin, vertically, from top to bottom.

† Entry is circled.

Dont you see the fun in it. I confess I think it is shameful. And you a ~~writer~~ of columnist.

Dont let them come down to earth. Let it not be said he has touch it today. Ill sign the clerks register {for him} Where shall I say from {If he wrote his own signature the register would be torn piece partial to get it out.} Now speak your little piece. What shall I say? Keeping away from the earth. What you wrote about Lindburgh. He saw what a crow does away in the midst of the sea {by starlight} when it doesnt know anyone is watching it. Where shall we say from. From Arcady Sam No no no none of that for him. Say from the heart then. I'll bet you haven't got the name right. You

"A time when nothing, neither religion nor patriotism comes to an apex"

MS. 001723. *Pocket flip notepad with brown cover, 3″ × 5″ ruled pages. Entries are in black ink unless otherwise noted.*

[*1r*]   A time when nothing, neither religion nor patriotism comes to an apex.*

Just as we make a reservoir of clay or something that will hold water we are right in taking for our storage class people who will {naturally} hold money.

*We find the parts of religion in everyone, the idea of sacrifice, of submission.

Reasons for wanting to produce at home all we reasonably can: there is safety in peace as well as war in variety of industry-in peace it is from business disaster and famine; there is increase in

[*1v*]   population and so in strength for ~~both~~ the undertakings both of war and of peace-the greater the population the greater the levy of men and of money. Great deeds, great works !

A great many more than half the industrial class are where by a wise stroke of concession they can be detached from the party of dissatisfaction that threatens the state. We are of little faith not to see the simple way to save ourselves from the Russian contagion.

You can't favor the industrial class as against the ~~agricultural~~ capitalist without doing it as against the agricultural, and so turning the agricultural industrial

[2r]   Realism of the voice.[1]

The king is mostly the first over both ~~genius and~~ creative genius and philoso-pher because he has command of that most worldly part of the world, the deeded part, the first part {in importance} whose name is that it can be some-times steered forward by the creative genius and sometimes {wisely} right by the philosopher, but forward or backward {wisely} right or {unwisely} wrong, it keeps going always and must be ridden somehow by {anyone} the one who has the special power for keeping in the saddle of it.

America the Lummox of Nations.

[3r]   Wilson really scorns those whose patriotism he is best able to fight the war with.[2]

The greatest charity is to give way to an occasional inconsistency.

Authority, which is out of ourselves, does hate liberty which is in ourselves and viceversa. No one with us cares to personify the authority outright on ac-count of the enmity he would incur.

How authority which is really no more a projection of our own natures ~~got~~ [illegible] appears first as an actual person of war and tyranny quite separate

[4r]   from ourselves. It was an age of personification (actual) of most of our proj-ections. Something.

Why the Proletariat must rule[3]
   Because they can take thought for and encourage more human traits.
   Because our new needs have given them the power [illegible] over us.
   Because all is vanity and of all our ranks conditions and degrees not one matters.
   (We talk as if society could be saved by this or that [illegible] govt. policy. But every society is short-lived

[5r]   The Lost Cellar.[4]

I can see that a pacifist[5] must be absolutely sure of his own bravery, so sure that he assumes bravery of everyone-and makes no account of it.

·   ·   ·

Wealth is just one of the most important ways of getting your self importance.

I met a pacifist who exalted cowardice as the only real hope of ending war.

[5v]* Whether we win or whether we lose we have still the chance to win or loose ~~by~~ by either loss or gain, and so on a gain to win or loose by

[6r] Subjects for next years lectures
　　　Simplicity
　　　That we have nothing to do with books except to write them.

Say whose your candidate for king to em.†

Seeking out your own advantage is something to rise to.

"Nothing permanent achieved by force."

Suicide for spite against the argufier.

What's On.

[6v]‡ This little pig turned prophet and told {on} the whole game. He saw the end of it all in the crash of civilization.

He that has power to hurt and will do none.[6]

A sad self-knowledge. Ignorance is as good as knowledge. When we lose one part of our ignorance we sigh and say, Oh my lost innocence.

Shaw thinks better knowledge[7] as between nations will bring them together in peace, and yet he thinks families from knowing to much of

[7r]§ themselves are nests of hate and must be broken up.[8]

·　·　·

---

* Page written in pencil.
† This and following entries on the page written in pencil.
‡ Page written in pencil.
§ Page written in pencil.

A connoisseur of brave deaths.

Abolishing the capitalist would mean abolishing the farmer included.

~~you~~ The socialist means to abolish the farmer by driving him to work in the cities, and [illegible] when he has left the farms vacant he will send squads of city industrials on weekly wage into the country for spells to cultivate the land. The president is up to this.[9]

[7v]* You say you can endure the wading through the waste and rubbish[10] for the little really interesting in a hard subject. But the real professor {tells} that, to one who knows, there is no waste or rubbish and all is interesting.

We always talk as if the states must go on when we argue against socialism. But what's to prevent it being that the states and all are doomed and that ~~their death a~~ socialism is only their last illness.

An Intelligencer-one who by travel and current

[8r]† reading and by meeting interesting people calculates to keep posted.

Must have interesting people and pleasant surroundings! Oh but these are rewards for those who fear thought that they must have work.

People that can take any side of a question. I think they like to try on other people's ideas as girls try on each other's dresses to see how they seem in them.

[8v] Max E.[11] is like a man beside a cannon who makes a throwing motion with his arm every time it goes off and tries to think he is hurling its death {and} destruction. Or like a person who dips his hand in a terrible flood of water.‡

Emerson's Mistake about Nature.[12]

• • •

---

* Page written in pencil.
† Page written in pencil.
‡ Entry written in pencil.

The Adoptive American like O'Reilly.[13]

Living Abroad

[*9r*]   European Opinion.

Dont go near anyone till you are strong-selfed enough not to be too much influenced.

Is American literature merely colonial?

Does our literature merely reflect what happens to be going on in English literature?

Poe made the modern short story.

Mach.[14]

[*9v*]   Interstices. How the ineffable gets in between the bronze, beads, or language you work in and the thing you try to represent: and {again} between the thing you represent and the thing you liken it to to represent it.

[*10r*]*   Education of information.
      "   of criticism. "
      "   rapture.
           participation.
Education by joining in with what is done and no questions asked.

The rich have waited to be asked to come and live humbly and meanly with the poor. They have waited to be asked.

The weakness of unity is what it is. Its effect is to break it into competitive parts that again strengthen toward unity.

To flourish is to become dangerous.[15]

------

* Entry written in pencil.

[10v] Asked your reasons to suddenly you always give a bad one first. Why didnt you go to jail for your conscientious objections? Death and jail are the only defeat. It would be to loose the fight. We have to compromise at some point to save ourselves and I compromised there. Because I'm a coward and believe in cowardice. Fear is our greatest hope of ending wars and competition. Third and real reason: because though I believe in martyrdom and going the whole length for a cause. I wont have the my country for my cause (the state is an ugly thing). I choose to make my last stand on something else.

[11r]* The flow of talk goes forward. words or no words, we must make a sound of voices to each other and we will; but it will be better if we can launch a thought now and then on the stream of words.

Culture is to know things in the first instance {at first hand} (at the source).

Special Privilege {in} Chief: to be out of the Illusion of Life.

Who are the dragged: the disillusioned few or the many illusioned.

[11v]† Abnegation. The spoiled daughter as social worker. She will not be better than the worst. Her man and his crimes. Murder.

[12] Got the idea too young that it was not for him to find out and study what others thought but for others to find out and study what he thought.

The teacher said to his writing class, All I am is a straw to catch at. But re- member I am that if it seems to you you are drowning. I think most of you are.

Why is it any more sincere and less hypocritical to sink give up and sink back into what we came out of than to strain forward to what we are going to be- come?

[13r] Tell a well educated college boy the best thought right out of your own thinking and he accepts it with a <u>Do</u> they say so? He is disappointed when you have to admit No <u>I</u> say so but they will say so after I show them.

• • •

---

* Entries on this page written horizontally and upside-down, from right to left.
† Page written in pencil.

There is this about outside: nothing is so outside that it ~~illegible~~ isnt still inside. Absolute outsideness forever eludes us. But it is there and no one can doubt that from it some virtue proceeds inward to the very center. It may even be more governing than what radiates from the center. Kings have ruled in the name of it calling it their

[14r]   divine right. Every elected ruler governs by it who consults his conscience instead of his electorate. He governs from without inward as an idealist, from within outward as a realist.

It is best to be flattered when your thought is taken for what everybody has thought, just as it is when your simile passes for a folk saying from a locality.

(*Message of May 21, 1919*)
Pres Wilson says we must be on our guard against our rivals in commerce[16]: in other words we must live in a wholesome fear of them. At the same time he is afraid they are too crippled

[15r]   by the war to be very dangerous. In other words the unctuous man is afraid they are nothing to be afraid of. Ain't that too bad for them or us or which is it?

Only one way to come into this vast hollow with no surrounding walls.

The Real Estate Agent's Inn (Contoocook)[17]

Sets and Sequences.

If a Christian should go on [?receding] with self-abnegation and humility never taking his pay for it forever, where would he come out in the end?

[15v]   Take the Os and Oh's of a play of Shakespeare.[18] Notice the tones of them and the meaning of the tones. How are the tones indicated unless by the sentences the O's and Oh's are in? The sentences are a notation then for indicating the tones of the Oh's. Omit the O's and the sentences still indicate the tones. All good sentences idicate tones that might be said in Ohs alone or in the Ohs with the {same} sentences.

[16r]   ~~Saying the unsayable~~

You can always get a little more litterature if you are willing to go a little closer into what has been considered left unsaid as unspeakable, just as you can always get a little more melon by going a little closer to the rind or a little more dinner by scraping the plate with a table knife.

Derivative and Original Poetry. Originality depends on the faculty of noticing. Strange things happen in us and things not so strange. Cultivate the faculty of noticing[19] or you will notice ~~no more~~ only what has been noticed and called to your attention before.

[16v]   Enterprise of Undergraduates. Undergraduates neglect their studies for various enterprises of their own, athletics, society, business administration. (They neglect them for nothing at all, but that is another matter) The thing is they almost never neglect them for anything more enterprising intellectually, such as the creative in art or scholarship. Modus vivendi found by teachers and those who want to neglect studies more or less for games society and administration. Confessed

[17r]   there is something to be said for them.

The Witch at Holts.[20]

Immortality. The Inspector of Mummies. The Spoilers.[21] Our loss not their gain.
A Book of the Dead.[22]

Off for the South Seas. His wife may not go with him. I may go. Who am I? I'll tell you who I am: I'm the original of the picture on the cover of Magazine just out. Have you seen it? | | Five children to dispose of. Well if you wont take two of them—if you won't accept a fair offer. I'll clear out first and leave you the lot. She cleaned out first—went to France to help in war. Staid in away till the children would come on her. | | Heaven is let up.[23]

[17v]   Explanation of the failure of some people to get on with others. They use the right words and phrases. But they cant get the tones of voice unselfconscious intimate and inoffensive. Their tones {are} offish uncomfortable constrained unconfident uningratiating. They cant ring true even when they arent playing

a part ~~wh~~ and when it ought to be easy to ring true. They are the opposite from the great actors who can ring true even when they are playing a part and when it ought to be hard to ring true.

[*18r*] The Latest People.

Couldn't miss the movies in his own town. Would ~~nt be in the talk~~ be left out of the talk of the town.

Aknahton Walks the World[24]

It seems to Harpers that Howells deserves to be made a classic.[25] They have made an appropriation to give him the necessary publicity.

All the accents of meter are alike at least there is nothing in them to show difference. The accents I speak of are all different. My chief interest is in what we have to indicate this difference.

[*18v*]* [The Kaa of Bee Fiaggi]

He thought he was prevailing by ~~free of~~ sheer worldly <u>force</u> and shrewdness, the traits that as a poet he wasn't supposed to have. His wife listened to his ruthless talk and for a long time ~~believed~~ half believed him. Reckless of losing her he still talked on. But all the time he was really a good poet and got ~~not~~ [illegible] no inch further than his poetry made way for him. [illegible] {So much} for his thinking he could beat the world at its own game. Who was the biggest fool at last.

[*19v*] $60000 if she would stay true to the boy who died.

[*20v*]† Humboldt[26]
Henry Adams[27]
Prioresses Tale[28]
Nunne Priest's Tale[29]
Teodore & Honoria[30]

. . .

---

* Page written in pencil with the exception of the entry that begins 'Culture is to know,' which is in black ink.
† Page written in pencil.

To make a spiritual parade before the company.

We get on because we have this in common that both of us are indifferent to money. He doesn't care how large an amount of it he has and I don t care how small an amount I have.

[*21r*] The Buffalo papers said I made an attack on ambiguity. The Syracuse papers said I was suffering from hasty recognition. (false recognition. I had tried hard to show how unavoidably ambiguous we are most of the time in word, phrase, sentence and tone, {deed} and even situation. (The position I found myself in on that platform was ambiguous.) I surrendered to ambiguity. | | I had tried to show how the educated suffer from false recognition-from recognizing too hastily a new thing for something known of

Range of playfulness proof of real culture.

[*21v*] Christmas 1921
Give to the poor to make them happy but not to purchase happiness for yourself that night Do not forget to be wretched with them, your giving cannot reach to touch.

Why give at all?

Life is that which beguiles us into taking sides in the conflict of pressure and resistance, force and control. Art is that which disengages us to concern ourselves with the tremor of the universal deadlock.[31]

[*22r*] The Census Taker[32]-Ill ask you in the train some day.

I Met Columbus out in the Pacific beyond the Isthmus.[33]

The New Picture and how to seem interested in it.

The Whippoorwill wasn't saying much-though present.

The mind is given its speed of more miles an hour than even the stream of time so that it can go choose. absolutely how fast it will go with the stream or whether it will stand still on it or go against it. The great thing is that it can stay in one place

[*22v*]   for a while and it is probably the only thing that can.[34]

Displacement Due to Poetry. Poetic Displacement.

Poetry brings pollen of one flower ~~from~~ to another flower.[35]

He threw the whole machine out of his shop and out of mind for ~~a~~ one fault, and recreated it entire from a fresh conception of what it was intended to do.

The slight lovely hope-what chance has it by itself, unhelped and unfavored from without?

[*23r*]   Its not long life that anyone would ever object to but long death.

Writing Down the Voice.

In tracing back an idea institution or species to its origin it is as as it were to consider a larkspur,[36] and descending ~~to~~ from more flower to less go right past the stem and come to an end with the spur. It looks as if the pale point of the spur were what the flower had derived from instead of from the stem, which is not flowerlike at all.

[line drawing of larkspur with stem]

[*23v*]   We look for the line between good and evil and see it only imperfectly for the reason that we are the line ourselves.

A good share of hypocrisy is Let's not say till we see.[37]

Regular fellow said all the faculty wanted a literary magazine for was to ~~put~~ publish any good themes in they got in their classes.

Reality and unreality in pronunciation. Lesley[38] persists in saying a dog. the dog.

[*24r*]   Is Poetry Highbrow or Lowbrow.[39]
     The ballads are one and Comus[40] is the other. The distinction in Poetry
     has no significance. ~~Poetry is neither the one nor the other and it~~ Poetry

may be either but it doesnt matter which it is so long* as it is spirited. Nor ought it to matter of anything which it is so long as it is spirited.

A Prayer before Going Abroad. God not help us not to take the English as the English take us

[1r]† The Bottle Imp
The Isle of Voices
Mr. Higgenbothams Catastrophe
The Jumping Frog⁴¹

[1v] On Being Funny (like Mark Twain and wanting to assume the dignity of the masterful. The Clown's Wife.⁴² Live to right the impression.

The Idyl of No Choice

[2r]‡ The Humanist Exhumed. In re Mat Arnold.⁴³
Mat's prose says, It makes me mad that people don't see the complete thought involved in their half thoughts. Starting where they do they have got to come out thus and so. They have got to think this. Then his ~~prose~~ poetry says, After all I dont think it myself What am I pretending? Their opposition has ~~talked me into a rage~~ made me talk myself into a [illegible] rage of certainty where there can be no certainty. Who am I but a foiled circuitous wanderer to take dejectedly my seat upon the intellectual

[2v] throne.⁴⁴

[3r]§ Remember how we gave to time
The lovely bell we cast
~~Too [illegible] stately and~~ {stately and   of}
~~A bell of [illegible]~~ prolonged ~~a note~~ {a note} ~~reverberance~~
For striking fast

.   .   .

---

* Page written in pencil.
† Frost reverses the order of the writing here, beginning entries from the rear toward the center of the book.
‡ Page written in pencil.
§ Page written vertically on the page.

~~Time~~
~~Not once~~
So   And how

[4r]* Time struck it like an oldster {adept} at the bells
And

[5r] But once an hour and then a few

[5v]† Something that you unexpectedly see a person thinking of himself often makes ~~me~~ you dislike him as nothing else in looks or words or actions can make me.

The adjectives {words} pushed from behind unhelped from the side or from in front.

Digging out what your reason really is for an act already done.

They don't conjoin any more properly than verbs and adjectives.

[6r] You must expect to be happy because you are good: but you must contrive your goodness in some way out of your happiness.

Rather a sensualist any day than a sensibilitist[45] one who makes of himself as a nature framed to enjoy greatly and needing interesting [~~illegible~~] friends and pleasant surroundings but destined also to suffer greatly in a terrible world from the want of these essentials—

[6v]‡ {There are} The clever who consider themselves clever because they deal with urban subjects. ~~There are~~ The free who consider themselves free because they deal with sexual subjects. The radical ~~because~~ who consider themselves radical because they deal with anti-government subjects. The artistic who consider themselves artistic because they deal with rosy and moonlight

---

* Page written vertically on the page.
† Page written in pencil.
‡ Page written in pencil.

subjects. But of course there cant be particular subject matter that makes people artistic clever free or radical.
Heroic in patriotism in religion.

[7r] Governments chief end is to propagate small farmers

We went to the oak wood
to cut the oak wood.

The present is more derived from the future than from the past.

No one has really tasted discipline who is only self disciplined.

Four Layers. The Fobses[46] have servants who live under the same roof with them and a farmer and his wife who have a home on the place to themselves. And [illegible] The farmer

[7v] and his wife have to make a stand with the servants lest they {servants} should fail to see the difference in their condition and try to drag them down to [illegible] their level. Now we are farmers too but on our own hook and would you believe it but. [Illegible] when Fobses' farmer's wife sees us with the Fobses as equals she rather resents it, and I am afraid if we had to [illegible] {be} much {with} her we might have to insist on our slight superiority to her if inferiority to the Fobses who are so of course the top of the stratification because they are so rich.

[8r] The Protean Pro German and his Refuge in Pacifism.

The Rich Reformer and the Poor Man's Daughter.

Speculation in Blue Shore Lake Front.

When birding one morning at sunrise, I asked a bird if he knew what kind I didn't know if he knew what kind of bird he was himself, and he said he didn't but he could always tell another bird of the same kind when he saw one.

[8v] Some people neglect their studies for business, [illegible] society and government so wholly that they not only stay away from classes, they stay away

from college. Everyone has heard of them. I want you to hear of the few who stay away from college and even the intellectual part of college to pursue intellectuality. So very enterprising are they in scholarship or the arts.

[9r]   The Wherewithal* Where They Got Their Money.
                Revolutionary Funds
                Buying Blue Lake ~~for~~ as Agent
                Two Pensions
                Mortgage Fire Telescope[47]
                I'm a Duk for Water

[9v]†   ~~W~~ A Poem containing metaphors or a poem that is a metaphor. The latter may be spread thin so that the canvas almost shows through.

[10r]   In Fulfillment. A tale of ~~the~~ a lady ~~lady~~ {spy} on the liberty trail on the Kaiser's business living

There is some {living} principle in Longfellow like what is cooked out of milk when it is Pasteurized.

AMERICA

How was it nurtured to such bursting[48] forth?
    It stole into existence ~~when~~
    It stole its growth unregarded by nations, to great to see realities.
    It saved itself whole under the very nose of halfsuspicious England.
    And now God discloses it Lo I uncover the West

[10v]   He discloses it as a power. Shall it be only as a
                power and not as an Idea too?

Riches and Thought are remote. Poverty ~~als~~ and Toil alone are realizing.

Eating is the primal aggression. Benificent interference is the ultimate ~~inter-ference~~ aggression.

                        •   •   •

---

* Phrase written at the bottom of the page with a line indicating insertion at the top.
† Page written in pencil.

If it is sweet to Englishmen that England though a little island north away should half the lands and all the seas and make them better for her righteousness, why should not Germans wish such

[11r]   glory for their country in their turn. Wish it? Yes. But And ask England for it if she dares. But why should not England deny her her request?

What Social reform has nothing to do with the war between nations except in every nation to use it the predicament to extort from rulers some of its desiderata. The hope of the social revolutionist that the war may mean the end of nations is vain. Nationalism is one thing and socialism another. One does not take the place of the other.

[11v]   Mechanism or Idealism what's the difference? By any name all monisms come to the same thing. It all is a question of good and bad. If all is good or all bad we were still secure in monism. But we find in experience that there is a division between good and bad. We get both permanently so far as we have gone.

Reason has to be slurred over in every moment of action. Action and reason are two different sequences or lineages that keep pretty well along together, reason just a little behind, catching up by skipping a space at

[12r]   moments of action.

English Dept. ought to be dedicated to the exquisiteness of language which is attainable and appreciable {can be experienced} only in a mother tongue.

War is the last expression of what we will bear for belief. It is the chastisement that none but the most distant can give us. Near is dear. There must be someone far enough away to chastise you more than the near and dear can be expected to.

Machine-made proletariat.[49] Out of the machines as much as the cloth they wove.

[12v]   Efficiency in reading. Efficient reading is taken to be the kind that gets the most information out of a book in a given the shortest time. But mightn't it be the kind that gets the fullest flavor of the book. The eye reader might have

the advantage in skimming for salient facts. The ear reader would have the advantage in getting into the subtler facts that lie in tone implication and style. The ear reader (who is of course ~~partly~~ an eye reader also) alone has any chance of attaining distinction in knowledge and expression.

[*13r*]   The soft surface of the earth is no more than the thickness of a tarnish on a metal ball.*

A Book of Kings.

~~In teaching give success and then failure~~ The first state in which a pupil can get a lot done is one of innocence. Keep the pupil there in the long wait for his first accidental success. Make the most of that to make it memorable because the memory is what he has got to live on through succeeding failure.[†]

[*13v*]   See how some people always steer the conversation where they have done some thinking of their own. No teacher of course could steer them there by any questioning or set examination.

[*14r*]   Sally Cleghorn[50]
Madison Bates[51] Manchester.
   valley Timmouth Pond[52]
Timmouth—Clarendon Springs-
Middletown Springs-

Stratton VT (deserted)

Tyson Lakes Tyson Furnace

[*14v*]   Paul never would go to work for more than $14 a week because he knew he wouldn't get it.

Sweet Revenge on the Bar
Paul was Part Human.

•   •   •

* Entry written in pencil.
† Entry written in pencil.

Oh boys its Saturday night
Hooray hooray hooray
Five meals out of the boss
And two nights in the hay
Do lumberjack eat hay? No they're part human.

[15r]   Waste Wood   Slash
            A Good Burn
            Shoulder High.

Moving a Brick Chimney across a River.

Three Stolen Apples.

A Dead Orchard.

Sling Shots at Bellows Falls.

On the Town. The Witch of Warren.

Our Troubles. Poor beclouded minds.

Prophetic dreams.

[15v]   The Word Image
          Vocal Reality   Style
          The Making Touch
          The Time for Discipline
          Cultivating a Difference or
          Derivative and Original Poetry
          Eliminating the Not-You

[16r]   His Sister Went Primative (Indian Guide).

You have to be attractive enough to get people within striking distance.

Our best hopes are our fears according to Sal Kleg. The only thing that will
end war is cowardice.

·   ·   ·

Suppose you came constantly to a class and waited in silence day after day for someone in it to find something to say resolved not to help it one bit. Could {they feel} embarrassment,] they {might} get something out of [?them/this]

[16v]   Man in the first seat in room did all the reciting in German class. All you had to do if you didn't want to recite was keep out of the first seat. Notice the cunning smile on the face of any American boy you tell that to. Easy to infer from it that his idea is to get as little {as possible} of what is the teachers idea to give him.

I came to live in the house of a professor who was off in Europe having what a professor would call a good time. He had left [illegible] all his books for me to have a good time with but had taken good care that I shouldn't have too good

[17r]   a time with them. He had marked them all up with a pencil wherever he had found a mistake of any kind just as if they were written exercises by pupils. And he had used the pencil on them for nothing but mistakes. He had never praised anything (I should have loathed his praise), but he had never contributed an idea or interesting commentary.

But not all professors are the same. One who came to the rescue for day w in a course on the French Revolution when the regular professor was absent finding that the class had been kept all the time on politics economics
    over

[17v]   and the mental diseases of the great and hadn't heard of the Guillotine, said, What, haven't heard about the Guillotine. Why the Guillotine is a very interesting thing, and then went at it with pictures and story to make a perfectly good Revolution exciting.

[25r]   Is poetry highbrow[53]

"The Copperhead"

MS. 001722. *Brown paper cover flip pad with black binding strip, 3" × 5." Pages stitched. White ruled paper. Entries are in blue ink unless otherwise noted.*

[1r]   The Copperhead[1]

The Carding Room[2]

History of the Town of Bungay*[3]

The {Gentle} Chief Who Held His Own in a Savage Tribe. The Unpromising Child Who Was Allowed to Grow Up.

Mallice Hoose

One half English Colonist
One half Scotch Emigrant.[4]

[1v]   Egotistical to think the universe run for us or something related to us? Just as egotistical that we live entirely for ourselves individually

The malicious talker commits himself to an enmity.

The blind old man indulged in gardening. Ability to let things go to smash for an idea.

The resemblance to the shrunken face in the museum
Downward looking similes[5]

---

* Preceding three phrases written in pencil. Remaining page written in black ink.

[*2r*]* Purposeful lifelike concrete {metaphoric} practical voluntary heroic—such must school work be if it is to engage the spirit.

To make [illegible] the personality more frequent.

Clearness must be crystal clearness to amount to a literary quality. Obscurity if it is carried far enough may be valued above it. "Clearness force beauty"!

Disabuse in education.

Fetched and Far-fetched. Everything out of its place—out of its well estab-lished place[6]

[*2v*] [blank]

[*3r*]† Almost Stories

     The Man Who was almost able to trust us for seventy five cents.

I must have registered the pious wish I wished in 1915 when the Germans were being execrated for having destroyed Reims Cathedral.[7] I wished they could with one shell blow Shakespeare out of the English language. The past overawes us too much in art. If America has any advantage of Europe it is in being less clogged with the products of art. We arent in the same danger of seeing anywhere around us already done the thing we were just about to do. That's why I think America was invented not discovered to give us a chance

[*3v*]‡ to extricate ourselves from what we had materialized out of our minds and natures. Our most precious heritage is what we haven't in {our} possession - what we havent made and so have still to make.[8]

Wo
The artist wouldnt hate the village he came out of so much if it had nothing on him. What could he care for its contempt if he had made such a noise in the world that it was sure to have seen his picture in the Sunday papers

---

* Page written in black ink.
† Page written in black ink.
‡ Page written in black ink.

[4r]*   Every object in the field of vision except the one in the exact center is double to our eyes. On a flat canvas allowance should be made for this—seriously
now!
I am not sure that the present is not quite as much derived from the future as
from the past.

May what I do come to form without mental interferance as perfectly as the
nest the bird builds or the shell the shellfish may what I am as perfectly as the
shell the shellfish [illegible] grows.

Do we mean to say that it would be nothing to our sense of form if the
sentences of a paragraph just made

[4v]   [blank]

[5r]†   a set?

What is sacred, the natural thing, [illegible] the artificial thing the natural
man or the civilized man.

The positive part of the man maybe the more valuable, but the negative is

The negative or restraining part of me is no worse than my anticipation of
the check the positive part of another man will put on my positive. It is that
that [illegible] halts my positive well this side of conflict with other peoples
positive.

[5v]‡   Loving is not choosing. A choice word in writing is never equal to a beloved
word—a word at that point fallen in love with.

[6r]§   Caught fire from earth [illegible]
At my window in the darkness looking for me.

This is a fire I caught from the earth[9]

·   ·   ·

---

* Page written in pencil.
† Page written in pencil.
‡ Page written in pencil.
§ First three lines in pencil. Remaining lines on this page in black ink.

If you make too much of Nancy Hanks[10] you make her too much of an exception among the lowly and the lowly are left where they are unhelped by
having her for one of them.

This {life} is a necessary part of something better. that we shall have a personal interest in when we [illegible]

I have forgotten why I left the world.

[*7v*]   [blank]

[*7r*]*   What is the most transcendental thing a boy can do? Marry a woman twice
his age.

Interesting people and pleasant surroundings. It is not what you are nor what
you have. But a chance to succeed or fail in doing something. There's where
philosophy comes in and religion come in. You'll need both {to keep
uspoiled}† in both success and failure.

Bridgeman[11] bade his class multiply everything in nature by three! Jack 'em
up! Heighten!

[*8r*]   What looks like wasted lives in nature is overlapping lives. Everything lives
the death of something else.[12]
                Removes
God made the Chair as Creator from which artificers copy their chair[13] What
then is the artist who copies the artificers chairs and the person who
moveyizes the artists picture and the movy magazine that reproduces the
moveyized chair?

The three interests in Ballads.‡

[*8v*]   [blank]

[*9r*]§   [Four illegible lines]

     • • •

---

* Page written in black ink.
† Written below the line.
‡ This line written in pencil.
§ Page written in black ink unless otherwise noted.

First we're skin and then we're scale.
Even success itself must fail.

Literary quality of Shakespear*

What is a School Boy

1 He remembers everything in the order in which he learned it. He has yet to lose his knowledge in order to find it.

2. He hasnt acquired or has somehow lost the pride that hates to be told what to do when he ought to have thought of it himself.

[9v]†   Taught {(schooled rather)} to think he is better than anyone he can pick a flaw in Stone knife handkerchief[14]

3 He hasn't got on the right side of his discipline.

[illegible] Danger of staying too long on the wrong side of your discipline: you might get so you would like discipline for its own sake both for yourself and for others.

Reality of the subject
"   "   " voice[15]
Reality of the symbol

[10r]   The Puritan will be hated but that will only fix him in history

Roger Casement[16] and the Wrong He Hated. The Traitor.

I saw a witch well-hidden in her wiles. (Wealth)‡ I could ask and she would tell me.

·   ·   ·

---

* This line written in pencil.
† Page written in pencil unless otherwise noted.
‡ Preceding written in blue ink. Remaining in pencil.

Locality gives art. Nationality is a shell locality puts on ~~as~~ to hold its warmth and perfume.

Hatred of the overgrown nation like the hatred of mankind. Misanthropy.

[*10v*]* Stringing you with sentences that string along as if they were all one string

Originality or effect of it from saying no to every yes. Why bother to ~~deny~~ dispute what someone else has affirmed If you wait a little you will find something to affirm yourself and so wont be left out of the game or conversations. Breaking with parents comes from too great haste to be at life It is like crude contradiction.

Wait for your chance for affirmation, ~~till~~

Race Prejudice Stories
~~The first to speak has the floor for tit the idea he speaks.~~

[*11r*]† Crude contradiction for the sake of taking part.

The first to speak his idea has the floor for it for the occasion so far as I am concerned. I wont utter anything in conflict ~~till I~~ till such time as I can do so [illegible] without conflict.

Staid too long under correction.
School ought to be a place where correctness predominates and crowds out incorrectness.

Mere correctness has been attacked by modern schools of art. As much as to say correctness is no matter where there is significance

[*11v*]‡ Sorry but I don't like [illegible] {these} trees
With stones plugged in their cavities

.   .   .

---

* First sentence written in pencil. Remaining in blue ink.
† Page written in black ink.
‡ Page written in black ink.

Better have some trees coming on
So when the older ones must be gone

Inflect Oh.   Naked Oh

Damp from cellar aging the new metal door at Bryn Athyn.[17]
Appointment with <u>Crain</u>[18] to hear how architecture renews itself from nature What its origins are in nature Day coach architecture carried over into
house architecture

[12r]   Note on back of manuscript poems of Burns: He must get in love for experience before he tries to write another.[19]

On Rewards. [illegible] Interesting people and pleasant surroundings. Diligent in his work, he shall stand before kings. Greenwich Village[20] invented for
those who want their rewards before they are ripe.

On Experience. How shall I get experience? By getting into trouble. How
shall I get into trouble? By getting married or by sitting still till your hat blows
off or by sleeping till you miss your train.

[12v]*   Flays Ambiguity

Buffalo paper said I made an attack on ambiguity.

Who took this loss? Persepolis Nineveh, Ctesiphon[21]

Get experience and we'll give you a job. Burns saying on getting in love.
Never saw a moor. Not to write about murder until you have murdered or
been murdered. Incomplete experience. Several crimes and as many in
decenies I expect not to commit. At least for the sake of experience.

[13r]†   The way to draw off from the colleges the people who have not business
there is to pay more wages to conductors brakemen and people that dont
need an education thanks to professors preachers editors and authors. Let the
educated be glad to see the others bought off. and let them look to be taken

---

* Page written in black ink.
† Page written in pencil.

care of by their fellow intellectuals who go in for the executive jobs of governing and creating nations. They are their cousins,

[13v]* Look for shadows where theres light

[14r]† Three ways to tell a poem.
First find out by diagnosis whether the man who wrote it is a poet.
Second find out if he wrote it in the right way.
Third see if it passes the critical tests for a poem.

The fewer royalties they get the more necessary it is that they should behave like royalty.

I've been splashed into so often by sudden teachers questions and had my wits scattered that I can never give the real reason for any thing I have done the first time I am asked for it.

[14v] [blank]

[15r] ~~Cor~~ Abducted to Fight a Duel. The ~~Ab~~ abductor killed on the way.‡ Gun carrying after the war.

Cheap Evolutions[22]

Evolution of marriage—from promiscuity to group marriage to polygamy to monogamy.
Evolution of government from {Absolute} Monarchy to {Limited Monarchy} to Oligarchy to Democracy.[23]

The English Novel goes on the safe assumption that real ladies and gentlemen will commonly be formed in the best ~~English~~ society bred to manners, but now and then to prove the rule it will be found sporadically in America.

[15v] [blank]

---

* Page written in pencil.
† Page written in pencil.
‡ This sentence and the one before it written in pencil.

[16r]* The Woodpecker. The old man who made money in back timber lots and spoiled his children with it. A Contiguity of Shade. (You got it—I've got the money)

After Pertenax.   The Sale of an Empire. The frugal meal.[24]

The New Englander hates the Puritan in himself.

In youth I looked for flowers
Where now I look for trees.

How to tell a breeze from a wind. - At least at night. By the dew. The breeze may blow and there may still be dew. But if the wind blows there will be none.

[16v]† You may walk dry shod under the stars in the open meadows as in the day-time. No need of keeping to bare ground and {or} under trees.

When a mere child gets you going as in her contempt for the moving pictures which it happens your husband is the town exibitor of and you so far forget your superiority as to throw a picture she keeps on her table into her waste basket and when she rescues it throw it away again and then again. Like a dispute on art.

No blueberries any more.

[17r]   The Impuritanly Puritan.

[18–23r]   [blank]

[23v]‡ DH Fletcher
548 Park Ave

---

* Page written in black ink.
† Page written in blue ink.
‡ Page written in pencil.

"The furthest two things can be away from each other"

MS. 001690. *Brown paper cover flip pad, 4⅜" × 2⅞", canvas strip binding at top. "Standard Memorandum Book"/Made in U.S.A." stamped inside front cover. Stitched pages. Ruled paper. Entries are in blue ink unless otherwise noted.*

[1r]   The furthest two things can be away from each other {in time or space} is on opposite sides of a circle large or small.

What is the opposite of the present time? One half the time from now till it shall be now again*

Make a straight line. Make four lines parallel with it exactly above and below on each side of it. ~~Two~~ The first line will make a circle if carried out indefinitely. Two of the ~~circles~~ lines will make a circle exactly equal to the first circle. Which two? One of the lines will make a circle larger than the first circle. Which line? One smaller than the first circle Which line? Some {infinite} straight lines {are longer than others} What becomes of a parabola carried out? How can any circle be

[2r]   made except by a straight line carried out. Whats the difference between a straight line and a segment of a finite circle. Does that quality of space by ~~which~~ virtue of which straight lines are all bent do nothing to bent lines. I should think it would make a finite circle an infinite coil.[1]

New alternative: you are either good or sick—don't argue with me.—I still keep the old choices between good and bad, well and sick. I know I am sometimes well and bad sometimes sick and bad and sometimes I'm good and sick as the say.

Another new alternative: manly—aesthetic.

---

* This entry and the one above it written in pencil.

[3r]   The Chiropractor. No opposition from level he belongs to.

If sex is all why do sex marriers part on their differences in other things.
Conflict of other interests

   Like a ball hung in a front of a jet. Repulsed.*

How many have gone in a class that mind saying I don't know and Not prepared.

   It becomes a joke how under the two party system we forever go through
the motions of conflicting whether we disagree or not. Some actually complain of the†

[4r]‡   emptiness of our fights. They do seem false. But after all theres comfort in
the thought that even in a country as large and among as many people it
seems impossible to find anything to fight about at times.

Kin neighbor fellow citizen fellow man. That is the order of consideration
and preferance. Not all are susceptible of the same treatment. But let my the
fellowman console himself with the thought that far as he is from the center
of my favor my fellow animal is further. Beyond Saturn Neptune and Uranus

[5r]   There are things I would do {I would do things} to my fellow animal that I
never except in extremely strict siege as in Death and Polar exploration would
do to my fellow man. That ought to be something. Only a fool would blunt
this gradation. Only a sentimentalist would reverse them and prefer an Armenian (such as Michael Arlen) to an Chicagoan (such as Ben Hecht)[2] or a
lap dog to a baby. Some day there may be no more nations no more races and
everywhere perhaps be home (we'll grant it for the sake of argument but till
that time lets not resent having to distinguish near from far.

[6r]   We detect the days when words flourished and this world flourished on a
logic they were put together into.[3] Scholasticism looks empty from this dis-

---

* "Repulsed" written in black ink.
† Entry written in black ink.
‡ 3v—4v written in black ink.

tance. Now we are in an age of logic things can be put together into. Science is that logic. How soon will it seem expose itself as empty of meaning for life and love.

The way the line stood still four years like the line were two streams hold each other show perfect the Balance of power in Europe really was—miraculously perfect.

Eugenicists want legislation to go to bed.

[*5r*]   His sons permission to get out—the Rosenwassers[4]

The writing takes all this room—the words born of words—the development—the connection—the transition.

    Refraction Makes Color {Irridescent}*
Metaphor (the saying of one thing when you mean another) is the one way permitted by God for going crooked or at least not straight.[†][5]

    Why the teacher's given question It is about something he has had ideas on himself and he wants to see what ideas you can get up on it in a pinch. What chance have you?

[*6r*]   The slight querulousness in the English voice. It complains because it is sorry other people (races) are so inferior to the English and do things so badly. The so called English hypocricy lies in complaining as if it were sorry other races were inferior when really it is glad.

Frobenius[6]
Presidents of U.S. in verse.

Spitting on the Shield[7]

Faults that don't belong to me or rather lapses that aren't faults. Our horse that interfered.

---

* "Irridescent" written in black ink.

† Entry starting with "Metaphor" written in pencil.

[7r]   In earnest. How manage to be and convince others you are. Responsibility
stakes. (Question is what it sounds as if you were ready to do about it. Actions
must must must sound deep in the words. Boy that who assured me he was sincere
in his poem. Boy who said wouldn't it be possible to maintain etc? Do you
maintain it?
Topics for debate in art. Is America a fit country to live in? Puritanism versus
Paganism.
The Volstead Act.[8]
What the young know versus what the old know*
What you are versus what you have.

[8r]   Her Maiden Name

The clerk desk clerk and the wife who kept her own name maiden name in
the lobby {summons}

To Do Over The sophisticated radical college boy clerk.

Mrs. Taylor's Marriage Ring or Teasing Taylor

The father was hanged for killing the mother. Years afterward the son was
hanged for killing a police officer. On the gallows he gave the address of two
illegitimate sons of his own to the priest saying it would be interesting to follow them—their lives and see if hanging ran in families. Then he told the
sheriff not to be so opposed to capital punishment as he heard he was (read it
in newspapers)

[9r]   She was so jilted that she simply couldn't stay in the same town with
him—if she could find a good job elsewhere. She wouldn't want to drop too
much salary. The wonder of Barrie[9] is how he ever persuades the actor to
make such fools of themselves on the stage for him. Maybe its because its because he always sounds as if he were forgiving the world for what he has suffered in some way.

The tone of {plain} statement is one tone and not to be despised. All the
same it has been my great object in poetry to avoid the use of it.

Im bound away.[10]

---

* Arrow written to the next line.

[*10r*]* Some people get the idea that ordinary things ~~will do in poetry because th~~ of poetry will do because the ordinary things of poetry are the extraordinary things of every day life. The mortality from this one mistake is ~~appalling~~ frightful There must be ~~no common~~ no ordinary things poetical or un-poetical in poetry. I had to choose I should want to err on the side of the unpoetical. By ordinary things I mean metaphor (however high) already made and in use.

Man will go down to the sea again—that's what all this {sea} hanker of po-etry of means. The last state of life will be got of pure protoplasm and gobs of pure ectoplasm matter

[*10v*] perpetuation—immortal segmentation. In breathless quiet after all their ills. Riprarian existence ~~rocked~~ round and covered in wave and tide. No fish in the sea no men on land. Shrivels flesh by Omega rays Poison of poisons. Poi-son—principal apotheorized. ~~Blast~~ Blasting to touch or approach. Ray con-scious Bubbles and froths a little with cosmic rays But grown consciousness of coarser rays of light and heat that prompted to science art and civilization. Traces of convolution that seemed to shift bowel like in the waves. Simple salt epoch. Cycle rounded.

[*11r*] and mind almost indistinguishable ~~one from the other~~ {from each other} on the wet flat beach when the tide is out one thinking and one feeling both hungry for the salt and thirsting for the water of the primordial brine. That will be the meeting of the extremes the close of the circle—when they touch and collide in the surf.[11] Danger of their crossing and so starting the old mis-ery of humanity all over again. Happiest†

Is it possible to conceive of anything that doesn't rest on something else? Does ~~that prove~~ {your} no prove the circularity of thought? Or the infinity?[12]

Loathe to see any one so glad of ~~this~~ being sad as Leonard in Two Lives.[13] I should think any honest person so unsure of his motives for writing as he must be would shut up and write nothing

---

* Page written in black ink.

† "all over again. Happiest" written up left side of page, bottom to top.

[11v]   Story of the man that was first straightened out and then kicked out of the army.

What the new youth said: Dont you dogmatize to me about dates and facts. I regard everything as a matter of opinion.

{Beginning}* I am going to tell you this very saddest thing in the universe so be prepared. It is a fact that the only reason for love is to keep people within striking and arresting distance of us.

{Beginning} What put that member of {the comparison} into your head?
    I assure you absolutely nothing but similarity

[12r]   Isnt something you had just been reading about lately.
    No
    Isnt it something you are always read up on—something always on the car-
pet with you.
    No
    Unscrambling your Motives—to find out what you are punishing anyone
for for instance. Why do we kill dogs that bite. So as to make sure they wont
be too well represented by offspring. [illegible letter]

    You strike out the form (length tone sentence structure) and in a few
strokes set the quality the first time you write a poem. After that all there is
to do is to keep the form and fire up to the quality in finishing.[14]

[13r]   The only thing taste and judgement approve is a {thing} we are accustomed
to. No combination no idea is enjoyable unless we have come across it in this
or another existence before.
    Nothing however scientific but is partly empirical.
    You say But the action of the electrons that looks capricious and free will-
ful only look so from our present imperfect knowledge. Presently they will be
brought under and reduced to law. I answer that when that happens some
thing else in nature just beyond them will look capricious and unreducable to
law. It is the beyondness that always has in it the suggestion of free will and
creative choice†

---

* Written on line above with arrow to the beginning of this sentence.
† Entry written in black ink.

[*14r*]   Bookend Poem is one with a stanza at each end that can be set any distance apart for filler stanzas

Hitching along—by metaphor such is change if not progress

There can be a lot of us whose morals do not matter—lot of us whose sins can be regarded as amiable. Prayer of the wastrel: may it be my luck to fall in with the irresponsibles.

Here we sit on the dead mans chest jovially pretending ~~with~~ the moral's sake that drink and the devil had shortened appreciably the lives of the rest

[*15r*]   The first generosity: not to spare in giving birth. The others follow.

Life is that which parts to meet itself a stranger—surprised.[15] All of life is to make the touch justly. There are no helps except the race helps to the individual.

Held to Hit

Dont strike him too hard or youll knock him out of your other hand.

Sleep is the surest provision that our continuoussnes and logic shall be broken at least on the surface.[15] [~~Illegible letter~~] It assures that our thought shant become one hardball of hair in the stomach of an Angora cat.*

[*16r*]†   How to be democratic ~~throuh~~ though choice. Never dare say where you may not find virtue.

How to be generous through prudent. Loan as Franklin loaned with the stipulation that the loan should be repaid to another borrower.

Do you mean that the vowels and consonants of a particular word sound like its meaning or only seem to from long association? Do you mean that the vowels and consonants of a sentence can be manipulated to ~~mean~~ sound like its meaning?

•   •   •

---

* Entry written in black ink.
† Page written in black ink.

On Me

On High $\Big\{$ He made the hill
            He prayed to God

[17r]*   If this be error and upon me proved the pillared firmament is rottenness and all our yesterdays have lighted fools.[17]

I should be democratic if or from a profound skepticism as to our worldly judgements and ranks.

One way to go—Carter Goodrich[18]
Another way—Gorham[19]

Ev Like produces like in the old machine idea: Evolution[20] is the doctrine that like produces unlike.

[24r]   Australian Writers[21]

Prose	Poetry
Marcus Clark[22]	AL Gordon[23]
Rolf Boldrewood[24]	Henry Lawson[25]
Mrs Aneas Gunn[26]	Henry Kendall[27]
Henry Larson[28]	A.B. Paterson[29]
Roy Bridges[30]	C.J. Dennis[31]
Ethel Turner[32]	Bernard O'Dowd[33]

Tom Collins' Such is Life[34]
For the Clarks For the Term of His Natural Life[35]
Robbery Under Arms—Boldrewood[36]
Geoffrey Hamlyn—Henry Kingsley[37]
While the Billy Boils Henry Lawson[38]
We of the Never Never   Mrs. Gunn[39]
The Bush—Bernard O'Dowd[40]

---

* Page written in black ink.

[*24v*]   How do you get exact attention?

How taught not to miss details

Do you draw

Anything happen or occur to you last {week}

J. H. Holmes great man[41]

[*25–40*]   Blank

[*41v*]   Fitchburg Savings Bank
Gardner Cathos

"Learn lives of poet"

MS. 001734. *Brown soft paper cover notebook, 3" × 4⅞", black canvas strip binding on the left side. Pages stitched. White ruled paper. Entries are in pencil unless otherwise noted.*

[*1r–1v*] [Names of Amherst students from the classes of 1923 and 1924. See note 1]

[*2r*] Learn lives of poet

Show why you read it by tones—revealing or interpreting tones

[*1v*] Read for tones that save comment

Read for comment.

Say what you want to learn to do with books—sell them talk condescendingly toward them, read them aloud. quote from them go them one

[*2v*] You can be almost as much of a reformer as you like if you dont insist too much on being the advertiser you have a right to be at the same time

Introspection versus observation To be able to say you must have felt this way or that from the way you behaved. Shall you get at the truth about yourself from the inside or the outside?

[*3r*] better, reduce them to essentials. get put yourself in the authors place behind them.

How the speaker acts about what he is saying.

•   •   •

---

* Bracket encloses entry on narrative criticism on opposite page.

Narrative criticism. Adventure with a book. Something that reflected on a book. Something done with or by a book

How he acts about what he is saying.

[*3v*] 1) Formal philosophy has added not one philosophy to the natural philoso-phers already existing in the world as attitudes toward life or living.
2) Philosophies adverbially represented in connection with the word true. Ab-solutely essentially practically relatively (Relatively means reasoning in a circle[2]—stone knife handker.[3]
[illegible] 3) Violence to logic and reason is the soul of action. In harmony

[*4r*] What philosophers to take up? What books to read at the source

What do you find yourself asking as if your belief or philosophy was

Violence and logic

Exchanging brains for knowledge.

History Its theory and Practice Croce[4] (Harcourt Science of History Froude[5](Ariel

[*4v*] We allow that God can do evil that good may come of it (evil will bless)[6] but the minute a man tries it saying the good end justifies the bad means we call him a Catholic and a Jesuit.

[*5r*]   All thoughts are possible ways {for me} to go no one of which I shall go. Thinking is aberrant. It is the beginning of in the insanities. Most of it I can tell for fear of encouraging it and carrying it further off the track of deeds.

As everything is connected with everything else it is plain that from any one thing as sex or alimentation or ambition all other things may be made to look as if they were derived.

[*5v*] 1 yes or no answers
2 Name {One word} answers
3 One sentence answers

4 Idea answers (Anything you would put forward as an idea about the book read

5 Answers that involve having the book with you

Did you think you were being psychoanalyzed by a teacher.

Have you noticed attending for college examinations to become intelligence tests?

Do you assume any responsibility for the direction of your own education

[6r]   Questions Oct 10 based on questions by 10 in class

May Tolstoy have written Ivan Ilyitch[7] to make the well sympathize with the sick?

I

Does Tolstoy ask us to believe the poor are more virtuous than the rich.

2

Was Polikushka[8] a man of weak character?

3

Is there any reason for the stories in the book being arranged in their particular order

4

[6v]   He means right.

Yes or No

Sept 1924

Are there any books you were intending to read when you got round to them?

Is there anything interesting you have lacked time for since you were in college.

.   .   .

Are you good at memorizing?

Do you object on principle to having to memorize?

~~Do you object~~ Has praise of anything ever made you hate it?

back 2)

[7r]   Affecting color

Did the mistress see the money again after Polikushka lost it?

5

On whom ~~did~~ in illness did Ivan Ilyitch depend most for comfort?

6

What did he die of.

7

What kind of beauty {if any} may these stories be said to have

8

What kind of house ~~did~~ would the one Polyiskar lived in be called?

9

[7v]   15

What should you judge was the Russian soul from this book

18 Is this story morbid

Whats your supposition about Julia Pastrana[9] on page 124 ~~Danilov~~[10] on page 136 Valdai bells[11] on page 136.

Or anything you would put to forward as a real idea about the book neither for nor against it.

[8r] How many of the stories use a love {or sex} interest?

10

Give de one detail that you would call morbid

11

One that you would call realistic but not morbid.

12

~~What is by~~ Define by having

13

Compare the mood of Ivan Ilyitch with the ladies in the third death.

14

Give any idea you have on Tolstoys [illegible] belief that one mans gain is another mans loss

[8v] Talk on translators English and translations

See some alone

Let them tell me about a book not assigned. Book news week.

Hand in commentary {or notes} on what has been read or talked about in class. What for example would be [illegible] would notes or a commentary be? Only hand in if credible.*

Another book news week

[9r] Look up notes in general to see ~~of~~ what kinds there are of them and be prepared to annotate selected pages

Make me think of a girl talking baseball. Such words? Make a home strike. The field man pitched the ball in. The referee called the hit unfair. The

---

* Entry written in black ink.

Bostons[12] have more points. {The way their} picked up school words dont make good graft on sentences.

Suggest a set method for dealing with a book to introduce it*

[*9v*]   Like the trunk of a small tree that has been trimmed of many branches {my} life has a straight crookedness.[13] The foot in the air always threatens aberrancy.

A fellow with enough sense of all the possible ways of going wrong to make a good teacher.

There are a few things such as Owl Crater where the mile through meteorite embedded that I had soon hear of as have an {original} idea.

[*10r*]   And truly it was not too much to say
Had we but in us to assume in {March}
Such white luxuriance of latter May

All these little inconsistencies are nothing but <u>the</u> inconsistency spirit and matter unknown and known. Knowledge is the inroad of matter into spirit.[14]

[*10v*]   using book†

[*11r*]‡   ~~Date of~~

ı Define epithet[15]
2 Define hypocrite
3 "   morbid
4 "   ~~epic~~
4 "   moral
5 What is the Odyssey—moral immoral or unmoral?
6 What is Ivan Ilyitch
7 What is Dowsons ~~verse~~ {Cynara}?[16]

---

* Entry written in black ink.
† Written up bottom right of page referring to ıır.
‡ Page written in black ink.

8 What is Kipling's verse?

9 What is Davidsons Ballad of Hell[17]

10 How much of Odysseus ten year wanderings ~~does~~ after Troy does Homer tell ~~and~~

11 within how near the end does he begin the story. 12 As you make it out what was the fault of the suitors. 13 What conduct would have been correct for them

[11v]* in the circumstances?

14 How did Odysseus draw the dead around him in Hades?

15 What is the great difference between Odysseus and Ivan Ilyitch as sufferers.

16 Give five epithets somewhat regularly applied in the Odyssey†

17 Five consecutive lines of Dowson

18 Five consecutive lines of Kipling.

19 Five more "   "   "   "

20 Name the book and another you bring me as news.

21 Date of Odyssey Date of Davids Psalms

22 10 Stock lines.

with name of those they are applied to

[12r] Whittemore suggests ten names be given to anything anyone wants to read

There's a kind of person who thinks you cant keep from falling off {on} the one side without falling off on the other.

Bear right as you can before you have to go ahead.

Safe kind of lecture: list of Shakespeare on the stage and his book in the hand of the audience.

[12v] Either

·   ·   ·

---

* Page written in black ink.

† There is a line drawn from the end of this line to the last line of this leaf: "with name of those they are applied to."

All you know is all that exists or what you dont know has no relation to what you do know. What we dont know may not concern us We fight outward from what we know. I left college and went into the mill to refrain.[18] He that hath power to hurt (assert)

The women wounded themselves imitations of the wounds ~~that~~ by which their husbands had died. Our defects are wounds She was resolved to be

[*13r*]   When the details dont seem close enough together maynt it be that not all the kinds of details are recognized, as for instance the tones of voice Some words are in only for ~~the indi~~ helping indicate tones of voice.[19] Borrow[20] gives some space to flavoring

Is there a shame that belongs to thought ~~th~~ and keeps young people from speaking out their ideas too publicly.

[*13v*]   Only ask that you mix past and present as if time was all one and leave novels for some other course

[*14r*]   Must learn {drolling from Borrow} to enjoy just telling what others say or think without showing yourself for or against it

Just as within a man is divided against himself part good and part bad and getting the sense of pleasurable sin out of the opposition so without is society divided and some are set aside to furnish the resistance to evil that makes sin a delight.*
Bitter and sweet.†

[*14v*]   Object of No 1 {To see how tell tale
                        how amusing
                    the titles
                    How distributed
                    your ~~re~~ selections

To try you on the {recent} lingo of criticism with an everyday distinction

•   •   •

---

* Entry written in black ink.
† Entry written in black ink.

To give you a chance to outdo Borrow. Give you a chance to show some positive merit in wisdom

To find out strictly {honestly} you hold a book {and the world}* to account morally.

[15r]† 1 Give good names to five stories in Lavengro
2 Give five good double names to five good stories in Lavengro
3 Who are the two {the five} most striking people in the book
4 Would you call the style in the book literary or unliterary? Whats the difference‡
5 What is the meaning of Lavengro, Sapengro {Petulengro?
6 What personal contact have you had with Gipsies
7 What should you say [illegible] for [illegible] or against forbidding them the roads

[15v] To try with you with the old fashioned lingo of criticism

To find out if any of you had looked into Romany Rye

To see if you would notice without having if pointed out to you that this was a forerunner of all the art that has gone primitive The first of the moderns both to use sympathise with savages and barbarians—not just from the poor.

[16r]§ 8 Name some of Borrow's languages and tell {briefly} how he came by them.
9 What Give [illegible] three things or people Borrow apostrophizes
10 Why didnt Isobel? and Borrow marry
11 Who do you gather were was Borrows favorite author in English
12 Tell how Lavengro resembles any other books you have read or heard of.
13 Explain Mrs. Hernes dislike for Borrow
14 Borrow dislike for America.
15 Do you know of in
   Name any other literary man who

---

* This bracketed phrase written below the line.
† Page written in black ink except where noted.
‡ Phrase "Whats the difference" written in pencil.
§ Page written in black ink.

[*16v*]   had Borrows interest in prizefighting

Suppose you were contemplating a life as free as Borrows what obstacles would you see in your way?

Curse of including the question in the answer—or even the title.

[*17r*]   Notice anything lately you haven't had pointed out to you. Outside of books. Inside. ~~Either~~ Notice something about Coriolanus[21] ~~or~~ {and} learn ~~exact~~ with exactness twenty-five lines of it.

Primitive folkways childlike irresponsible happy go lucky daredevil

Huxley[22]
Anderson[23]

[*17v*]   You are supposed never to make a good phrase or metaphor* because you are under pressure and compulsion even when ~~not~~ not under special examination. I try everyway that I can think of to give you the freedom to show something more than the merely negative virtues of writing

*nor command your ideas

[*18r*]   Rule of thumb Grasp

Soundness

Think it will rain etc—forms of speech in which we spoke as if we thought

The cure for Intellectual Turbulence—all this craziness over newly come by ideas is {~~of everybody~~}to develop an ambition to get up a few ideas ~~for yourself~~ {of our own} yes and no are amost never ideas by themselves They ~~may~~ are merely salt or sugar <u>in</u> ideas.

When do children get old enough to be expected to challenge us. When to be expected to be expected to ~~distinguish~~ give credit and claim credit for ideas?

[18v] Extremes memorizing poetry—noticing something all your own about the poetry

Our originality is often present us in things and events. Adventures go seeking their originality in places and events. The The {imaginative} philosophical scorn the pursuit of originality in outward experience.

The same idea differently arrived at is not the same. Something of its different origin clings to it. Parmenides and Einstein spherical universe.[24]

[19r]   Mores plural of more

Latin tag, or sociological cant.

Not {expressing *or} applying but summoning by free pleasure. This is freedom   Proof: variety of sources[†]

Not to apply like and dislike and test too soon.

Th That shuts you up and makes you harsh and illiberal.

Liberal arts   polite

Literature.

Two liberal thieves were shot

Liberal shepherds call a grosser name.

Schoolboy is one who is eager to tell you what he learned overnight and tell it in the order in which he learned it.[25]

[19v] stray materialism tin scraping beauty latitude prism shoon organism disinterestedness[26] o're Which of these words would you expect never to see in serious verse which never in serious prose

•   •   •

---

* "Expressing" written in black ink.

† Phrase written on the right side of the page, bottom to top, in black ink.

Tell anything you noticed about Mark T.'s[27] way of being funny
Tell anything that has happened to you in connection with any of our books
Tell anything that has occurred to you in connections with anything

sheen apple dost

[20r]   ~~Define moral morbid hypocrite literary language~~ {Tell {in one sentence each} me you mean by an} original idea. illustrate from any of our books.

In a hundred-word article characterize {[illegible]} Table Talk[28] {Typee}[29] or Lavengro without using either praise or blame.

Dramatis personae of Coriolanus

~~Which of these words would you never expect to see in serious poetry, moon objective~~

Ten lines of Dowson

Moon emotional ~~prince~~ objective sex paradise thine hypothetical rationalist subjective

[20v]   Examples as general as your generalization.

Deeds and Things

Dont be afraid of possessions for fear they will possess you.

Burrs and Porcupine Quills—details that stick to you without any effort on your part to hold them.[30]

Some side reading in connection with what book

[21r]   How Ideas Occupy Place

Territoriality of Ideas

Even in yourself there are things antagonistic to yourself that you forget in dealing with things more antagonistic still outside yourself. If there were

none antagonistic outside consciousness ~~would~~ of oppositions would break
out inside. That would be war
At the point of breaking there would be a new boundary, beyond which—

   Easiest thing to remember you ever came across.

[21v]   Story of Your Relations with a Book.
Your Earliest Book or Magazine Reading
The Oldest Book in Your Possession.
do you know personally about*
What's the Interest in First Editions
Classify Notes in Some Annotated Book. Give Examples†
Who Will Act Faustus?[31]
Wholl give dramatic reading.
of anything.‡

[22r]   ABC and 123[32]

A little staked in {over} books

Dont be afraid of having a few possessions.

   Thoreau wouldnt own a house for fear it would
own him[33]

   Memories are the least material of possessions.§

   Paints cost more than ink

   An idea comes as near to something for nothing as you can get.**

We say poor scholar because the appreciation of letterature can develop on
less money than the appreciation of music or painting. Literature takes less
capital than

---

* Entry written in black ink.
† "Give examples" written in black ink.
‡ Entry written in black ink.
§ Page from "Memories are the least . . ." to the end written in black ink.
** There is a box drawn around this sentence.

[*22v*]* ~~Grasp is what doesn't let go of o~~>

Are radical ideas you stock up with any less property than conservative ideas?

Something you get up ("how is this for an idea?" is better than anything you stock up with.

Has experiment ever caught as thinking or feeling anything we hadnt caught ourselves thinking or feeling by merely looking in.

[*23r*] "The style is the man": rather style is the way the speaker or writer acts about what he is saying. Name some ways of acting. ~~Difference~~ {Distinguish} between Tenneson's and Browning's ways.
Read in tones that save comment.

Narrative criticism. Tell something about yourself in connection with a book that shows how you must have felt about it. To make criticism more objective and less introspective. Observe yourself in action. Behaviorism.[34]

[*23v*] Trying mind by overt acts—mind by things rather than things by mind.

~~Avoid~~ {Spare me} flubdub English-such as a girl talks at a baseball game.

Show me the slang or cant of economics sociology ~~or~~ philosophy etc.

Difference between thinking the book and thinking about and over and above it. What are some of the kinds of commentary possible?

Non chronological. Only ask that you mix past and

[*24r*] present as if time was all one and leave novels for some other course. Inconsistency of asking for narrative criticism and barring novels which are narrative criticism of life.

Notice anything lately ~~inside or outside of books~~ that you havent had pointed out to you inside or outside of books?

•   •   •

---

* 22v–25r written in black ink.

Distortion of sentence due to trying to include the question in the answer.

Dont be in a hurry to close—in on a book with [illegible]

[24v]   {A liberal doesn't dislike} A liberal[35] seldom hates at sight likes or you {your}
dislikes. He* Describe without too obvious like or dislike. Spare me the
words like and dislike. This is

Crude description: "a five hundred page 1000 dollar prize story. I like it."
There must be better inside stuff to say about jewelry even—pearls and diamonds.

It is said that you cant be forced to have ideas. Neither can you be forced to
enjoy ideas. If you cant enjoy them you cant fully understand them. The why
school?

[25r]   can stand a lot of things you'd think he couldnt.

Our originality is often presented in things and events. Adventurers go seeking their originality in things and events: but philosophers scorn the pursuit
of originality in outward experience. By originality I mean that which shall
distinguish them and make them interesting. What

What you stick to counts less than what sticks to you like burrs and porcupine quills.[36] Small dog that had wandering porcupine

[25v]†   quills in him. He howled when they were passing through his vital spots.
Easiest things on va to remember on various planes you ever came across.

Non-habit forming course

Danger

Liberal is a man who though not conservative himself is perfectly willing
others should be conservative. Never hates at first sight. Willing to present v
the other side with strong arguments.

---

* Sentence continues on to 25r: "can stand a lot of things you'd think he couldnt."
† First three entries written in pencil. "Liberal is a man . . ." written in black ink.

[*26r*]   Wont hide the weaknesses of his own

The intolerant are people who are afraid it is up to them to accept any idea that presents itself because they have always been accepting not getting up.

Rousseau is on one who wants to go back to principles from which society came and start society over

A liberal is a man not afraid of other peoples ideas because he has had ideas of his own.*

An illiberal is a man afraid of other peoples ideas because he knows will have to accept them.

[*26v*]   How do we get the way {Cather's} Paul[37] was. Diamond Necklace.[38] How do you get against life and taking part in life.

You think you are running your class just because you dont let the good boys do what they please with it. But no. You are letting the bad boys run it: The same as jail birds run a jail. To whom can you tell whole stories. How long a story in company? On what about it depend what experience have you had

[*27r*]   What is philosophy.

Education as inuring.

Tom-tom in poetry.

That poetry is the root of the matter whether you find you can write it better in prose free verse or poetry.

Getting jumped on to reduce your waste line.

How to be loose without disaster.

[*27v*]   After all is said beauty may belong to youth and song.

· · ·

---

* Sentence written in black ink.

The road that lost its reason.
     The widows pasture

Canabalism a perversion. Lady into Meat. Youd say we had nobody as sophisticated in America. To hallow the unhallowed.

The world has a lot of strange motions.★ [39]

Advice to a person about to tell a short story orally.

[*28r*]   Education

Snapping on their heads—{Think!}

So girls wont get better marks than boys

~~Humor & cowardice in ideals~~†

Humor an idealists cowardice[40]

A humorist is a cowardly idealist.

Humor is ~~opposed~~ {a let down} to passion and belief

1 Belief 2 Humor 3 Reason

Humor occupies a middle place between Belief and Reason

[*28v*]‡   The professional feeler gets so he cant feel except professionally Thats why poets and such seem so lacking in general sensibility moral commercial and political.

     One danger of changing materially is that the final form may depend for its meaning on your ~~remem~~ having seen and remembered the first form.

                    •   •   •

★ Entry written in black ink.
† This and following entries on the page written in black ink.
‡ 28v–32v written in black ink, except where noted.

The separation is as important as the connection[41]

By a {prepared} scale show your

[*29r*]   range in the appreciation of beauty (how far {down} to the apparently un-
beautiful can you go) {honestly say you go}. Your range in the appreciation
of ideas (how far up to the super intellectual can you honestly say you go.

A poem you can repose in. Maybe you dont ask to feel secure.

Most of our wrangling puts us in the false position of sounding nearer
right than we really think we are.

[*30v*]   Adventurous is not W̶ experimental. Experimental belongs to the laboratory,
Adventure to life. Much of recent art has been merely experimental. It tries
poetry with first one element then another omitted. It leaves out the head
Then it is too emotional. It leaves out the heart Then it is too intellectual It
leaves out the feet Then it is free verse. Adventure ends in the poorhouse Experiment in the madhouse Water spout theory of learning from above down
from below up till it meets

[*31r*]   Begin at the beginning both of your subject and of yourself. I suppose the
earliest beginning of yourself is when you wake from sleep. Picking up the
subject is like picking up the thread with the eye of the needle: it is necessary
to being further back w̶i̶t̶h̶ than with the thread itself and gather in the fiber
or filament the projects beyond the thread.

[*31v*]   Can you imitate flow a̶n̶d̶ with inlaid pieces? Is flow of any aesthetic value.
Some would say make the pieces beautiful and fit them in as flowingly as possible.

Interview me.

Emily Dickinson's Life the way colleges make boys overestimate the reputation of people connected with them. T. Hardy G A S Hardy [side of page]:
Johnsoniana and the Wife[42]

[*32r*]   Santayana. Behavior is a belief.[43]

· · ·

On having goes at things instead of taking courses*

Sprees

$\left\{\begin{array}{l}\text{Knife lost blade-lost handle}^\dagger\\\text{Step constitution}\\\text{Her Stepfathers Wife}\end{array}\right.$

Evil-merodach[44]

Whom's you little friend He's an unknown singer who records the meadowlark. Take me up to him and introduce us.// I don't know whether to or not. Hes anybody that I chanced upon

[*32v*]   In composing poetry I am packing up to go a long way on wings.

I am making as compact as possible to smuggle out. Dodge the death tax[45] which want to take everything. Fool the waylayers who lie in wait to strip you of yourself.

He is in the soul-careful still-small-voice age. Dont ask him to speak out full and strong.

[*33r*]‡   In his similes the two terms come together like a collision

I like a mystery that cant be solved and best of all mysteries a deed the mo-tive of which remains a mystery.

A pointed event is just as good luck as a good idea§

I am aware of its details sticking into me in different places like ten or twenty claws

[*33v*]   He shuts you into a basket and then sticks his sword first from one side then another the short way then from one end then the other the longway.

---

* This line written in pencil.

† These bracketed lines written in pencil but the bracket itself is written in black ink.

‡ 33r, 33v and 34r written in pencil except where noted.

§ Entry written in black ink.

Then he takes you out alive and whole instead of full of holes but having had an experience.

The simple way*

Men as bacteria that cause growth to take strange forms of science and civilization.[46] Like oak gills and willow gills.

[*34r*] Protoplasm the amoeba is immortal except when real life uses it and kills it.

Immoralist without being immoral.

$\left\{\begin{array}{l}\text{The bat flew out of my mouth}\\\text{I nearly died in my sleep}\end{array}\right.$

If color values can be done in black and white what can color itself add to form?

[*34v*]† Recovering the conception by rereading what you have already written is a fo impossible.

No one book must bear too much of the burden of study—looking up words or looking into meanings.

Repetition analyzes.

Let us speak about our reading when we are pleased with ourselves—out of the pride of discernment.

[*35r*] The Magnificent—and the takers down—Come you down from off your throne or perch.

This disposition to trust the medicine from Brazil Mexico or Thibet is identical with the craving for the exotic in art.

· · ·

---

* Entry written in black ink.

† 34v, 35r and 35v written in black ink.

Not Ready. The boy that expected at every step to be rejected for hernia and ~~bro~~ fallen arches.

[35v]   A cultivation that would bring you back to simple broad effects in art. That would be democratic because it would make extremes meet.

On Them. On Me.

You dont know who I am I dont know who you are. Which of us has most ancestry to doubt of

[36r]   What book were you ever to read by what other?*

Half your thinking is spent just coming out on the same views that all the world has always had. Very terms in us surprise you when you emerge with their internal evidence much thought behind them

[36v]   Sultan of the Mountain
Rita Forbes[47]
Madagascar
   Chase Osborn[48]
Journal of His First Voyage
   Columbus[49]
Social Life among the Insects[50]
   Warner
American Revolution
   McIlwain[51]
Anthropology
   Kroeber[52]
Tale of Brittany
   Lote[53]
Seven Lively Arts[†]
   Seldes[54]

Pearls and Savages[55]
   Hurley

---

* Entry written in black ink.
† This and the remainder of the page written in black ink.

[*37r*]   Greenland[56]
             Rasmussen[57]
             Police Dogs

[*37v*]   Its hard to get anywhere either by travel or travail

             Make it as hard as you can for the old (aged)—that is progress.

             Till he invented automobiles Man never had the speed ~~before~~ to feel the
             body-sway of the curves he put into his roads.

             The Dark Entry

[*38r*]*   Gibbon Auto[58] 6
             Emile[59] 5
             Conquest of Mexico[60] 2
             All for Love[61] 3
             ~~Eng T~~ Rep Men[62] 4
             Walden[63] 1

             Ways of handling these Business for All for Love

             Prescotts comparison of old chief with Solomon: of society with feudalism
             Art

             [~~illegible~~] Faustus

[*38v*]   Lack of Roaring Camp[64]
             Pop Edition 1.⁰⁰ Houghton Mifflin

             Palmer's Odyssey   [~~illegible~~] 8[65]
             Riverside Literature Series[66]

             Golden Legend[67] 56

[*39r*]   Palamas
             Immovable Life[68]

                              •   •   •

---

* Page written in black ink.

Ernst Boershmann[69]
Picturesque China *
Brentano[70]
Scribner[71]

I.A. MacCrae
Chelmsford
Mass.

S.P. Crawford[†]
49 High St N

L Crooks 28 Pomery Terrace
1073M Northampton

[39v]   Shelleys Philosophical View of Reform[72]   B) 8

De Tocqueville[73]
Doctrine of Degrees[74]   B) 96
Schools of Gaul[75]   B)97
Rites of the Twice-born[76]   B)109
The Samklya System[77]   B) 109
Hist Evidence of Virgin Birth[78]   115
Moral and Social Significance of Concept of Personality[79]   C)3

Jacob 13 Spring St.

Address—1601 University Ave

[?Home-] Bingham 0290
Authority[‡]

[40r]   Petrie Egyptian Stories[80]
Ancient Gems[81]   73
Barus Poems   77

---

* This entry and the remainder of the page written in black ink.
† This address written in black ink.
‡ This word written in black ink.

Collins Poems[82]		77
John Clare[83]		77
Shelleys Prose		78
Trelawneys Last Days of Shelley & Byron[84]	78	
Mary Wollstonecraft[85]		80
Tosa Diary[86]		80
Taylor's Thug[87]		83
Lucretius[88]		75
Piraki Log[89]	229	
Letters of Trelawny[90]		
English Madrigals[91]		B)5
Donnes Sermons[92]		6

[40v]   Oxford University Press

Aurbeys Brief Lives[93]		
John Donne's Poems[94]		
Spencers Poems[95]	28	
Early English Proverbs[96]	14	
Miltons Prosody		8
Wentz Fairies[97]		
Prose Rhythm[98]	8	
The Shirburn Ballads[99]		
Englands Parnassus[100]		29
Coriolanus[101]		37
Raleighs History of World[102]		37
Hakluyts[103]		38
Samson Agonistes[104]		40
Songs of R. Burns[105]		45
Morris Life and Death of Jason[106]		54
Place names		56
Nefrekepta[107]		70

[41r]   Wonder*
Cherry Plum

Negro Folklore Rhymes
    Talley-Macmillan[108]

---

* "Wonder" and "Cherry Plum" written in black ink.

[41v]   √ LLewellyn Jones[109] [?Post]

√ Wm Stanley Braitwaithe[110]
MA DeWolfe Howe[111] 8 Arlington St.
~~Carl Sandburg Chigo News~~[112]
Harriet Monroe[113] 232 E. Erie
j. Clair Minot[114] Herald
~~Edwin~~ F. Edgett
√ Henry C. Canty 20 Vesey

√ {[~~illegible~~]} Van Doren[115]
√ Arthur Pound[116] Herald Ed.
√ Ridgely Torrence New Rep[117]
John Farrar[118]
Bernie Stewart

"I don't see what you have to complain of"

MS. 001170. *Brown soft paper cover notebook with red canvas strip binding, 6¾″ ×*
8⅜″ Stitched pages. Ruled white paper. All entries are in black ink. The first twenty-
six pages are blank, and 27r–30r are torn out of the notebook. "No. 1" written in black
ink on cover.

[27r]   I don't see what you have to complain of you ministers have always had it
pretty much your own way in these country towns. The state is you as you
say.

     Burroughs[1] do you realize that two thirds of the community have always
been against us and only kept ~~under~~ {in subjection} by {sheer} force of ~~righ-~~
~~teousness~~ character. It ~~is~~ {has been a} hard fight for the Levites all down
through history. ~~Those that be for us are more than be against us was not~~
~~written {said} of this more~~ —— And thats why I ask you to take my side
about the ~~books library~~ {circulating} library.

     Why cant we have two circulating libraries one ~~religious and one~~ sacred
for the religious and one profane for the ordinary people.

     Because I don't think it best for the community ~~I have in my keeping~~. I re-
fuse to have ~~it through~~ {my flock}

     ~~Oh come Mr Heald you are beginning to sound too final~~ {flock through
turned out} to indiscriminate worldly reading.

     Oh come Mr. Heald you are beginning to sound [too]{pretty} final in your
tone of voice. Please don't be in a hurry to close ~~the question~~ {in on me}.
Have the library [illegible] {so} it will mean something to me. I don't know

[27v]   The evening will be one of my happy memories. Let the idea stay as much
mine as yours. Don't turn me out

[28r]   who thought of it first you or I. We got it up together—I shall always remember the evening. {Let it be as much mine as yours} ~~Leave me~~ {Don't turn} me
out [of the place] {in the cold} I've simply got to have something to be interested in ~~here~~ {this town} besides the school. {I'm no school teacher really} Its

hard enough for as it is for a person of my freedom to take up with the ~~town~~ village life. Give the mental part a chance. You haven't half considered my list of books. All I ask is that you let in some of them. What possible objection can you have to Rawlinson's History of ~~the World~~ Egypt¹ for instance.

It is atheistical

You say it is that without having read it.

~~If so~~ I venture to say God is not the subject of ~~any chapter~~ {a single page} in it. If he is not the book is godless and godless is atheistical. I say again I refused to have any people corrupted by worldly literature. I will go this far toward compromise however I will make no objection to your bringing the book into town for your own reading. ~~I make a distinction between you I am willing to allow a difference between~~ {That is I'll say nothing about it and you need say nothing ~~about it~~} not the innocence ~~to lose I could wish you had~~ (at stake that most of us have you have}. Books of this kind are one thing for a man of your

[28v]   to be

[29r]   experience ~~wholly~~ {quite} another for simple country people.

But Mr Heald its not my own reading I am concerned about ~~I should take it I was anticipating the pleasure~~ Oh I thought it was. I misunderstood.

What is it then—the reading of your neighbors.

No don't get me wrong on purpose. ~~I was just anticipating the pleasure of work~~ I had set my heart on ~~having something~~ the pleasure of going round to my neighbors on the interesting business. ~~I could how glad they would~~ I'm social. I like ~~people to want to see me coming~~.

You think they'd be be more delighted to see you coming with history and philosophy {under your arm} for a change

They might be Mr. Heald. You give them all the good sermons they need on ~~Sund~~ the Sabbath

Flattery wont help matters.

What do you suppose for the reading of our own statemen at {about} this moment ~~Jef Mr. Jefferson~~ such men as Mr. Jefferson and Mr. Adams.

I can answer for Mr. Jefferson that his reading is probably of the most subversive. He is a godless man. Mr. Adams curiosity may have carried

[30r]   him into ~~strange~~ {dubious} investigations. Allowance must be made for greatness. We must expect to pay the price ~~for~~ our leaders ~~for the extraordinariness~~. They necessarily exceed the bounds of parochial morality.

Will you let me say something?

{Say it} ~~If it is not blasphemous immoral.~~

~~It is that you are immoral.~~

~~Me immoral. Master Burroughs~~

Say it

If I thought there was one morality for the President of the US its and another for the people ~~I should choose for my own observance the morality of the President of the United States~~ I suppose you can guess

[*31r*]   [blank]

[*32r*]   Stephen!—Stephen!—

Yes my dear

Stephen why haven't you come home?

I was ~~just~~ coming home.

The stove's ice cold. ~~What kept you~~ What are you sitting here for in the dark this way. You're not feverish. (She tries his forehead)

No Im as [illegible] cool as the stove. I've been reaching a determination. ~~and I've reached it.~~

Oh Stephen you've given me such a fright. Has something terrible happened to you?

I'm neither killed nor wounded.

Lets go home to the children.

~~I don't know whether I am permitted to go home to the children. I forgot to ask the~~ Sit on my knee—while I tell you something.

~~Stephen~~ Steven you're not right. Get on your feet. ~~Come~~ Oh take me home dear

There must be ~~somewhere~~ some level of society where my traits wouldn't all be ~~faults~~ defects. After all ~~my a thoughts at~~

[*32v*]   is not the result of some momentary injury real or fancied but of a lifelong experience. God knows how I have wanted to prevail with them.

[*33r*]   ~~modesty~~ {modestly now} I can quite hide it from myself that I'm not ~~just a fool~~ altogether a fool and a rascal. I have made my youthful mistakes but my worst mistake has been ~~b~~ abiding too long by the judgement of the simple. Surely it is no discredit to me ~~that I have~~ {to have} stuck to it on principle that they were the best judges were possible judges. But they haven't proved so in my case. It is not too much to say they have failed in my case.

Steven what is it all about? (She ~~kneels at his feet~~ {Lays her head on his knees.}*

Why does it have to be about anything personal and particular?

We weren't going to torture ourselves this way any more. Something has happened to start you off.

You rob me of the beauty of the {my} ~~thought~~ by such small minded assumptions. ~~I talk in general as a~~ Oftener than you would think I speak in general as a philosopher. My grievance against the simple is the result of long experience. {and not of some momentary injury real or fancied.} I wanted to proceed with them. It goes against everything in my nature to give them up. But I have worked it out with myself that it is all over between us. I have given them their chance and

[34ʳ]   That's what you have been about alone here in the cold all evening.

I haven't been alone all the time. The minister has been here some of the time.

Mr. Heald. What Mr. Heald been saying.

~~We~~ He and I have fallen out and he's going to tell on me.

Stephen Ill send for father.

Its too late to do any good. Your father couldn't make the journey from Boston in a week.

Why I thought we were put in Mr Healds care ~~as our~~ {for his} special ~~protector~~ charge protection. How have you lost his friendship.

Do you mean what crime have I committed.

Stephen!

Or what do you mean?

I mean I hate him and I never trusted him Father told him more than he should have. He shouldn't have told him anything.

I ran the risk of being called an imposter if anything came out by accident. You always have to think of that. Your father acted for the best.

Nothing would ever have come out away off

[34ᵛ]   nothing of that in it. Nothing could be more foreign to you. No one would believe it believe him for a minute if he spread that around.

[35ᵛ]   here. We were perfectly — . I wonder how much father did tell him.

---

* Phrase inserted below the line.

Heald called me an imposter today. So I got called one for all our precautions.

How are you an imposter before him?

That goes back to the sermons I preached in Pelham when I wasn't an ordained minister.

Which ~~are~~ is ~~wo~~ the worse imposition {a} good sermon by an unordained minister or bad one by an ordained minister. Yours were good sermons. That goes with the story father must have told. I can hear father ~~in all~~ there.

Heald called me a convict too and a coiner and a seducer.

You were never a seducer. That made out of whole cloth. Father never told him such a thing. That utterly utterly cruel. The story has

I suspect the {dear little} minister has been making some investigations on his own account. You can hear almost anything you want to ~~hear~~ in this world.

Did you tell him he would be betraying confidence if informed on you? Father only let him in as much

[35v]   Maybe ~~sometimes~~ in the morning when I first wake up I am sometimes free

[36r]   as he did so it couldn't be said there was any deception on our part.

He pretends he is only letting the town in so it cant be said there is any deception on his part. He refuses to take the responsibility {a minute longer} of leaving the house unwarned of what it ~~is~~ harboring

Its terrible. I wonder if everybody is {as} afraid of everybody ~~the way~~ {else as} I am. Especially in the dark. ~~Always~~ All my life Im always afraid. Theres something that never lifts. I shouldn't expect to escape it if I were blameless. And I'm always haunted with the sense of blame. Think of the children {right} now waiting for us suffering fear they don't deserve. {That's their start in life and that's [illegible] they will continue} I know you've been crossing. Mr. Heald in something you dear. But it doesn't matter. How could help differing with such a man.

He has been crossing me. He wont let me have my ~~Li~~ Circulating Library.

Why dearest if that's all you asked to sacrifice to keep us together

But it's the principle involved. He's called a lot of good books atheistical just because they aren't bound sermons by Jonathan Edwards[3]

[36v]   Has doing wrong put me in a position where I can't do right
Ethan and Ira Allen
For all I was born into an orthodox minsters family. You weren't lucky you—

Your fathers one of the people that make me think theres another world than the one I'm tormented with and it is not away off somewhere out of reach like ~~heaven or W~~ like the capital of the United States where the President with his cabinet reading anything they please or heaven where God sits talking French revolution. It's right at hand in Boston or New York

[*37r*] and Im going to make him eat his words.

    But if you are not in a position.

    Not in a position to do right?

    You know a person—

    Yes I know I've been to jail. {Say it.} Oh I'm not going to see it through— you needn't hope or fear. I know I haven't the purchase. Im disenfranchised. I'm committed to evil. The world ~~will~~ {wont} let me do wrong but it won't let me do right. ~~But it~~ {Well the world} cant help itself. I'll do which ever I please right or wrong. We'll just see. But I'm not going to fight it out with the minister. I'm going to run away. You are giving home to your father with the children and I am going to fare further in search of a land where my virtues wont be taken as faults. New England isn't everything. The whole world isn't parson ridden. Better priest ridden than parson {Having tried parson ridden a while like my priest} ridden any day. I never was intended for the rigors of orthodoxy. I have to say it for once Im too generous to large for this mean provincialism Im going where religion has some breath of humanity.

    Don't go on so. See here dear

[*37v*] if only we had the chance to get a foothold there!

[*38r*]   I'm only choosing to do what I've got to do so don't {dishearten me} ~~interfere with me~~. If Heald carries out his threat its just a matter of hours when I'll be run out of town with scythes and pitch forks again as I was for preaching good sermons {in Pelham} when I wasn't authorized to preach bad ones.

    Let's go home to the children. You'll be sick from this exposure. Come. – Wont you come. (He gets up stiff and sullen)

    My God Mary Im better than they are instead of worse. ~~That's the startling fact~~. Wouldn't it shock them to hear me say it. That's whats the matter with me: I'm better than they are instead of worse. And its not unbecoming ~~in me~~ for me to claim it because when you stop to consider, it doesn't turn out to be very much to claim. This is just starlight in here. But with no curtain it and so many windows it serves pretty well once your eyes get accustomed to it. When I come out of a trance like that its all I can do to remember what town ~~Im in of all~~ of all our towns I'm living in. This isn't Hanover is it? We've come a long way from there haven't we. Its lucky I've come

[*39r*]   through this afternoon without hurting anybody—isn't it? That isn't the ministers dead body flung over the chair there—is it? No that's my coat which is just what we're looking ~~to go home with~~ for isn't it. Yes lets go home. Im with you. Lets see how old is Willie—five is he? We can settle that later as we go. Do you see my hat. I had it once already to go home. What time do you suppose it is. Take hold of me so you won't fall over anything. Christ I'm ~~gone wi~~ feel gone when the anger goes out of me. I don't think that minister did right

Come on—come on

The curtain goes down as he sits down again

NOTEBOOK 17

"You and I"

MS. 1726. *Soft brown paper covered notebook, 3¼" × 5⅜" with cloth, strip binding on left side. "Handy Notebook" is machine-printed in black letters in the center of the cover surrounded by a black rectangular border. Pages are stitched. Ruled, white paper. Entries in black ink unless otherwise noted.*

[1r–22r]   [A register in Frost's hand of the Amherst class he taught in 1925–26.]

[22v]   You and I.[1]

It seems hardly worth while to differ seriously or violently in principle when our practice is so nearly identical in politics morals and business

[23r]   There came a blight on weeds

Blame. The Bad actor

Just as if it werent as important to me where I staying as it is to them where they're going, the rude honkers

Are some vices worse than others and are the worse ones chosen by society to punish

It aint reasonable it's executive.

The new speaking model that honks words at the man on foot.

[23v]   She didnt know where the feelings were to hurt any more than she knew where they were to touch[2]

1 Make their own trouble without waiting for teachers to make it for them.
2 Turn teacher's claim on them into their claim on the teacher exact reverse of what it has been.
3. Replace examination at set time with self-publication all the time. To publish yourself is to make yourself known and felt (~~with your kind~~.)

4. Lecture on may be a lesson in.

I have wished a bird would go away
And not sing in my yard all day.[3]

[24r]   {That} The Coupler {may have} a free hand I wish
The Intersecting Planes
And just where they intersected I thought was the busiest nosiest place on
earth, it might have been 42nd St and in one plane and I dont just know what
kind of a quiet quiet place but apparently the quietest in all Heaven ~~in the
other plane~~ {on his other plane} a orchard with at most one person and I
couldnot be sure (of him) in it I

Morality is merely organized pity. Pity for bastard embodied in law of inheritance.

The house as a character in a play.   Wild things fear of threshold

[24v]   1 The one who gets slapped by a girl.
2 The one who will encourage others to sin so he can school himself in judging no one.
3 The girl who wants to give all American property to Europeans.
4 The one who wouldnt mind seeing civilization wiped out just to show H.G.
Wells[4] how it would come back inevitably.

Democracy[5] is {only a way of} waiting a long time ~~before~~ open ~~before~~ to details before you close up ~~into meaning~~ light into form idea and conclusion
You and I are the details let in in ~~number~~ larger number than ever in the
worlds history before judgement {was snapped}*

[25r]†   3

One person judges what he has by now much more it is than nothing another
(the self styled idealist) by how much less it is than everything. The real idealist only asks enough for ~~the~~ an idea of the whole. The real idealist is a
synecdochist. One may have the idea of a thing without having all of it.

·   ·   ·

---

* Bracketed portion of phrase continues across the bottom of 25r.
† 25r, 25v and 26r written in pencil.

Your choiceness {exclusiveness} superiority aristocraticalness must be built on a wide basis of democratic inclusiveness and toleration.

Chesterton says papers repeat because no one remembers any more.[6] Papers repeat because no one is sure to have read previous installments.

[25v]   Speaking of contracting enthusiasm from me or any one else see what someone says about Swinburne—Lamb Hugo Baudelaire[7]

1 Homily. Drowning the Woodchuck. After we think we have drowned the boy with literature in class he comes out and goes to some bookstore for a real drink.
2. Cheating. [illegible] In examination question was how many vertebrae in back bone. Boy caught rubbing his own back.
3. Note takers solemnly write down teachers statement and then contrary. Asked if they dont notice discrepancy. Boy says Stop fooling its too near examinations for wasting time.

What is an idealist in tennis, in baseball in law, in government. Is it idealistic to abandon or change form of verse: extend the boundary of beauty: Is anyone occupation any more idealistic than another. Ideal and idea.

[26v]   Was Ibsen in Wild Duck?[8] Emerson? Thoreau. Poe. Is it ideal to be fastidious?

Stop to think that the baby might like to have the distributing of the money when he gets old enough to have Platonic friends.

The whole crowd of you seem to have something to do with producing that baby

If a language really gets you you go over to its nation. Why she despised American scholars: they stay outside of other languages than their own

Puff guns some priest invented in imitation of white mans real guns. See Cook's Voyages.[9]

R. OKeefe & husband—Which had money

·   ·   ·

26v–27r]*   What <u>can</u> you do with a poem besides read it | to yourself or
       to someone else.

Reread it   to yourself and to any new audience that comes along

Copy it   into your commonplace book (so called) if you keep one
      Villon[10] tells of writers in his day who thought they had created a poem
{when they copied it}

Memorize it   Most of our talk is garbled quotation. Make some exact
{Free prayer-prayer book}

Recite it   with the art of the elocutionist or public speaker.

Anthologize it like Untermeyer Monroe Rittenhouse {Strong} and
Palgrave[11]

Plagiarize it[†]   Eddie Guest[12]

Print it   as on a Christmas card with a picture to send to friends

Publish it   like T.B. Mosher[13] and

Sell it   as in the Geoffrey Amherst Bookstore[14]

Emulate it   As the great do emulate great things by doing something as
{great but different}

Imitate it   As Virgil did the Iliad and Odessey {Imitate Christ}[15] Imitate
Hound of Heaven[‡ 16]

Set it to music* *

Grow offshoots on the thought in it.

---

* Entries written across these two pages.

[†] Phrase written in pencil.

[‡] From "Imitate Christ" to "Heaven" written in pencil.

* * Entry written in pencil.

[*27v–28r*]*   Parallel it in part or as a whole

Classify it on some principle Intoning—talking. Elegant - 'homely.'

Rate it comparatively   Best unrhymed poem of fifty lines {between 1915
and 1920} written by a woman under 20

Try it by cannons of art   A poem must be simple sensuous passionate[17]
Brahman writes {Poem must not contain own description.}

Argue about it   At the level of beauty and religion there is at
least less argument than at the parliamentary level.   Dick at <u>Horace
Mann</u>[18]

Say you like or dislike it   like school girls   Pound and the <u>Gardners</u>[19]

Tell why you like or dislike it— but {because it is about your home region
your vocation or} without using those words or their synonyms

Translate it into easier words as you probably did Shakespears and Miltons
{in preparatory school}

Explain what might prove difficulties in it being careful not to underate your
{audience.}

Impart information through it   in geography, history botany etc.

[*28v–29r*]†   Interpret the spirit of it

Tell how the author probably wanted it Taken.   <u>Lindsay's</u>[20] {Preaching
                                                                    Oratory
                                                                    Humor.

•   •   •

---

* Entries written across these two pages.
† Entries written across these two pages.

Get a meaning out of it the author never put into it   Thomas Rhymer
Beauty Truth[21]

Mark Twains Jumping Frog[22]
Captain Price and New Education

Date it   1250 first lyric we have in our language - barnyard[23] {All my war
poems written before the war.}

Relate it to the authors life   Did you once see Shelley plain
Browning[24]

Relate it to the history of his times   Who is the happy warrior {The Isles of
Greece}[25]

Wordsworth[26]

Relate it to philosophy   and science   Tennyson's Locksley Hall[27]

Trace its origins   Robert Bloomfield?[28]   Wordsworth
                       Crabbe[29]   Langland.[30]
                       Virgil Emerson
                       Theocritus Browning.

Make it the basis for philosophic study—as in most graduate schools. Weal
Psychology of Obsolescence.

Correct it {Don't correct it wrong}   Amy Lowells Carpenter on the Roof
The more wrong this
Sugar{ball} is the more effective.   Like a childs wish to be something he
Cant {understand}

29v–30r]*   Scan it {Consider scansion of it}   Show that English meters are chiefly
              iambic {and loose
                  iambic}[31]

Describe the verse forms   First stanza form generally accidental and then
followed

---

* Entries written across these two pages.

with more or less success.   Perfectly repeated in To Daffodils (Herrick)[32]
Describe the sentence forms in the verse forms.   Poem and paragraph a
set of sentences.

Examine language—poetic liturgy vernacular dialect   Idiom

Tell of having done any of the above with it
Tell some adventure with it   }   I call this narative criticism
Tell of associations it has for you

XXX Notes may do all the above.
XXX Ð Star double star triple star the best of them
XXX Do nothing to a poem that it never was written to have done to it

XXX The question is what can you do ~~with~~ {to} anything lovely without offense to anyone in love with it.

How much of anyone of these things or all of them will any one poem
stand up under?

[*30v*]   ~~Sonnet~~

Poem should be a set of sentences. So should a paragraph. How much larger
a form may this be said of. Illustrate by showing variety of structure or tone
~~of~~ in poem and paragraph.[33]

You have to choose whether we are near enough the end of suffering and
strife to give up that which leads to suffering and strife the idea that it is heroic not to mind them.

Obsolescence basis of.

[*31r*]   First Lyric in Oxford Book is barnyard.[34]

Disintegration.

Experience with its repetitions is analytical as well as generalizing or syntheti-
cal. Tasting ingredients

.   .   .

Tiring of a person. &
Tiring of a Good Poem.

Scope

This mans art and that mans scope.[35] Range in the appreciation of beauty.

How to handle a poem without offense to the fresh and sensitive—those in love. What can you do with a poem besides read it without ~~Or Evidence Ruled that.~~ offending against refinement of feeling.

[*31v*]   Birches—Ward[36]
Runaway   Amherst
Witch of Coos   Houdini
Stopping by Woods—New Hampshire.[37] End
Mending Wall   Nationalist*

In the stories it invents or finds to tell you can see the mind heal itself close its gaping differences as where Hueffer[38] makes a regulation person like himself love and yet on with a young rebel like

[*32r*]   Ink.

Fifty lines of verse from Modern American or British Poetry[39], Oxford Book of Verse
Oxford Book of Victorian Verse[40] Palgrave Kipling

~~If~~ {Where} there is thought or emotion pressure the words begin to stretch and change ~~the~~ meaning.

Speaking of Inflaming the {Inflamable} Lynd says Swinburne caught his enthusiasm for the Elizabethan dramatists from Lamb, for Freedom from Hugo for the Devil from Baudelaire.[41]

Poetry as merely the redisposition of a few unchanging elements. Limited vocabulary (countable) countable number of things and words[†]
Lifes a game that one can play

---

* This section, starting with "Birches," written in pencil.
† "words" written up the right side of the page.

With fewer pieces than men say.*

[*32v*]   We have decided to act as if having the home farm was nothing the ~~yo~~ lucky sons were the younger who didn't inherit it. This from [illegible] a de-sire to make it easier for the younger to strike out. ~~It has had the effect on the eldest son of~~ It has made the eldest son feel the worst off and finally follows his younger brothers to the city.

Much character is shown in a person's way of saying excuse me humor-ously carelessly

Pull yourself together and hold on to yourself or the psycho will get you.

[*33r*]† The victim can be forgotten He suffers nothing. It would wrong to make the murderer suffer for one who is out of suffering. It could serve no useful end. So far as victims are concerned there is no reason at all why a murderer should not go on adding to them indefinitely if it were not for what he would do to their friends and relatives. The very basest passions seem to be ~~stirred~~ roused in the nature of friends and relatives. etc.

[*33v*]   Marriage Japanese Dwarf tree

$\left.\begin{array}{l} \text{Pull yourself together} \\ \text{Hold on to yourself} \end{array}\right\}$ before some
psychoanalyst some "specialist" has to do it for you. Before throwing yourself on anyone else make a last draft on your dignity. There is no recovery from spiritual bankruptcy.

Have you a poet who could write another Hound of Heaven.
Francis Thompson couldnt have written another.

The sage say One Que sais je[42]

.   .   .

---

* This entry written at the bottom of 31r, with an arrow from the last entry on 31v point-ing to it. This entry and the two above it written in pencil.
† Page written in pencil.

Better to lose on an uncertainty than to win on certainty. Best of all is to win on an uncertainty Most education of all to lose on a certainty.

[*34r*] Speed—Reach B before you forget A feel the curves of the road and participate in the science of a scientific age. But I say this from far off away up in my superiority to such ~~need~~ property to mark my success. One wants a ~~medal~~ {garter} one wants a star, one wants a PhD and one a Frontier

Temptation to steal came to me in an hour after I had been wronged so that I could not have told whether I stole for a greed or vengeance* against God.

Jack Cade as he fights his way through fights his way up till he is Ramsay MacDonald[43] He wants to be both ends at once but can only be one. When he

[*34v*] rebels against being one he starts on his way to become the other.

Levitt is short for Leviticus

Ulysses was quick witted enough to throw away his stick when the dogs attacked him. The Pole told me to throw mine away.

~~What has~~ No one ever took a wife for wise except by mistake in reading old print Wife Wife

Each takes the view of love will do most honor to his marriage—while that remains happy.

Ma used to be short for Mass when all Mass people were literary or at least literary

[*35r*] ~~Your last teacher~~ A teacher ~~is one~~ may be defined as one who knows how to make trouble for pupils. I only sympathize with pupils in trouble they make for themselves.

Sopsyvine Sops of Wine and Shropshirevine.

•   •   •

---

* Section from "Speed" to "vengeance" written in pencil.

What has become of the name of Aut. I go up and down asking if there is anyone of the name of Barefoot

1 Short stay official wouldnt have thought of never going home. Short history here. 2 No children ended with this stone. 3 All there were cleared out for Canada hating rebels. 4 Maybe here and there a stray out west. But Frosts and Whites and ~~Wa~~ Halls and

[35v]*   Recognition

1st Day All books—all poems
2nd Day Two books—all poems
3rd Day Two books

Most sensible view of Burrough's character.[44] More sinned against than sinning. Conscious or unconscious villain. Child of the times. With or without redeeming traits. Reckless Vicious. Decide beforehand how you'll take him.

Warn you against mistaking m̶ make belief for belief

The house for the deserted for the other they built beside it

[36r]   Cracking metaphors

Every lesson no matter what the subject of it was a lesson in thoroughness. Lessons should be in almost as many qualities as ~~they are in~~ subjects.

He remembered the book too well to be able to read it again and not well enough to make the least use of it

Precious Pair   Jumel   Burroughs

For all your {country} bards
Unprincely accents
He didnt altogether lack sense
You'll own

                    •   •   •

---

* This page, with the exception of the entry that starts "Warn you against . . .", written in pencil.

All he looks for is glinting words.
Swaying whom is nothing.

[*36v*]   to take Gods name off it and put his in its place

One days news in The World.

1st A man offers to give a college forty million ~~to change and take his name in place of~~ to name itself after him alone instead of the three people it has been named after, namely God Jesus and the Holy Ghost. ~~The Opera Club with the President~~ 2nd A German confesses to having bitten 27 people to death and sold their flesh in his butchers shop ~~There~~ 3rd and worst of all the Opera Club of New York with the President of the Colonial Dames ~~speaking~~ at their head begins bringing rag tag and bobtail fired royalty of Europe to America to leven American society.

No one is so agreeable that you couldnt remember enough against him to help you over killing him for his skin if it were worth anything [in the market. (Suggested by killing tame foxes for their skin.*

[*37r*]   12 a day to discuss and mark their Random Remarks on their reading for term

The rich thought of it that the business belonged entirely to them and not at all to the workmen they hired at will. Then the workmen saw it too and said then if it doesnt belong to us we have nothing to lose by wrecking it with revolution. But the wreck of everything and the starting over again taught everybody the business belonged to everybody whether director or working employers or employee, and for awhile they ~~were~~ high and low were brothers till they began to forget again and the whole misunderstanding had to be enacted over again.†

[*37v*]   O Neill's Moon of the Carribees[45]
Austen's Land of Little Rain[46]
Burroughs Memoirs Jan Tuesd[47]
Stevenson's Virginibus
or
Familiar Studies[48]

---

* Bracketed phrase extends onto next page. Entry written in pencil.
† Entry written in blue ink.

Prescott's Conquest of Mexico[49] Tell them Leave out or tell wrong
Dickinson's Poems[50]   They and I read and memorize
Jonson's Silent Woman   Show them reduction
                    or
                    Alchemist[51]
Untermeyer [a] Modern American They & I read ~~they and~~ they memorize
                    and
                    [b] Modern British Poetry
White's Natural History of Selbourne[52] Sir T. Browne[53] *
Conrad's Set of Six[54]
Gilberts Babb Ballads[55]
Russells Where the Pavement Ends[56]
Wells' Thirty Strange Stories[57]
Aucassin & Nicolette[58]
Hakluyt's Voyages[59]
Emerson's Poems[60]
Menken's Trans of Antichrist[61]

[*38r*]   Ballad Book[62]
Columbus Journal of His Voyages.
Oxford Book of Verse.
Importance of Being Ernest[†] [63]
Before you can outlaw war you must first inlaw it.
Can hardly tell whether I act from good taste or cowardice[‡]

[*38v*][§]   Give the name of ~~twenty~~ {fifteen} plays stories or narrative poems
also
   ~~Give~~ the name {also} or in not more than one sentence each the chief
{identifying} characteristic of the hero in ~~as many twenty stories plays and
narrative poems~~. each .

   Name five biographies, five autobiographies
   Give the memorable idea in each of five essays

                    •   •   •

---

* From the beginning of this page to this point is in pencil.
† Entry written in pencil.
‡ This entry and the one above it written in blue ink.
§ This page, except for the last entry, written in pencil.

Give an account of your reading in this course to date. Memorized poetry ~~counts~~ or prose counts (octo)

He made a reed instrument of an empty tomato can by bending it closed.

Repressed force {in one place} need not necessarily break out somewhere else. There is such a thing as stunting artificially dwarfing a tree.*

[*39r*]   Tell   [1]

1 Homer's Long Swim[64]
2 Chaucer's Poisonous Gold/Bocaccio[65]
3 Poe's Masque[66]   Identify 4
4 Hawthorne's Higgenbotham[67]
5 Maupassant's Piece of String[68]
6 Russells Price of a Head[69]

A Lady came into a store and asked for a play (maybe it was a novel) named she was pretty sure the Prisoner of Chillon.[70] She remembered there was a ~~doub~~ duel in it and a case of dual personality if that was what you called it when ~~one~~ {two} people were so exactly alike [~~illegible~~] that they couldnt be told apart.

Still room in the world for the lone wolf who will not run with the pack.

[*39v*]   1 Best idea you have read
            2 Best idea you have heard
            3 Best idea you have had
            4 Best thing you know by heart
            5 ~~What classroom procedure do you~~
            5 Arrange in order of preference the following ways of conducting a class: quizz, lecture debate, conversation
            6 Which of these four does our procedure of this week come nearest?
            7 Take your own way of showing what your books have been to you this year.

                        •   •   •

---
* Bracketed phrase continues onto the next page.

The Presidents Since Washington & My Vote

How much to make sure of A or B. How much to make sure of B or C.

Have modern developements ~~made~~ increased or need of excitement

Speed and Size make new world

[40r]   [note line going down on left side of margin]

Since I saw you last—read Pater's Plato,[71] Caswell's Journal. Vildrac's Love,[72] Plato on imitating the Spartan.[73] Caswell on national prejudice. Vildrac

Connick's[74] Glass Burgers Johnson's Jack Knife

Five invitations to write in 24 hours: Southwestern Review[75] Greenwich Village Theatre.[76]   Eugenics poem[77]   poem on candy Concord Hymn[78]

If you can keep from opening graves long enough it becomes all the more exciting to open them.

Something to announce: that the hope of dynamite goes on the assumption that the other side is up to nothing to offset it.

~~Why~~ What the hurry, modern man? To get to place b before I forget place a ~~so that~~ and make a connection in my mind.

[40v]   A way to find out if you have lost a friend's interest: Watch to see if ~~he~~ when you are interrupted he will remember to ~~g~~ ask you to go on with your stories ~~when~~ afterward.

Striking Women or Two Slaps.

Flawed and irregular glass flaws and irregularities turned to account. Not too realistically.

He's only in his first childhood He says Damn my head. It wont stay up.

This was not driftwood but wood steered

[*41r*]   The new child lay light struck for days staring like china.

Restraint

The strict stem held the force pent all the way up till it burst[79] out at the end as a flower. A little ~~got out as~~ leaked out as leaves on the way [illegible]

Unhappy ourselves all the happiness
We ask is someone to see happy

   Object of schools not so much to fit as to examine for office—examine for what you have learned and for what you are. Hence the constant quizzing. Lecture and quiz. Debate (like politics) and discussion. Best of all converse the communion of minds.

Laboratory Studio Drawing Room

[*41v*]*   Oct.

1 Any idea you have heard or read on election
2 Any {other} idea you have read heard or had
3. Classify in some way The Bottle Imp.[80]

   Book Resort

Not to break it to 'em gently. Break it hard.

You cant be perfectly happy about anything you cant exactly place.

   Was it at once the most cruelly social and cruelly unsocial of our acts—social to its own unsocial to the enemy.

   Deploy and buy what you want to read. End of term write me a good account of yourself in reading

---

* This page, except the phrase "social to its own unsocial to the enemy," is written in pencil. On the last leaf, Frost made three simple sketches in different sizes of the side of a cabin or house.

"Difference between meter and rhythm"

MS. 928940.2. Beige cardboard cover, cloth bound flip pad, 3″ × 5″, stitched pages. Ruled paper. Entries are in back ink unless otherwise noted.

[*1r*]   Difference between meter and rhythm

What do you mean by an appropriate meter.

Come Right Down to It What we really like in poetry.

Analogies again. Bean and Bin.

"Scholars and not voluptuaries"-in dealing with Keats. Oxford

Freeman—freedman

[*2r*]   Analogies for God.

Working hypothesis

Axiom

Spoke once and not since
So did heat once to call the animate out of the manumate—once and never again. In those days there were wonders. From [illegible] wonder we have our breath from the other our faith by a long descent.[1]

Metaphors recently argument formerly poetic. Out of a troubled mind out of a full heart.

If life fundamentally is getting

[*3r*] ~~Nature overtakes and brings down the weakest and slowest. His most danger-~~
~~ous interferences with the course of nature is the way he takes the best from~~
~~his own stock from breeding Natural celibacy of the intellectual The church~~
~~celibacy is merely a {?conflicted} symbol of the natural celibacy of the mind~~
~~and spirit~~

Impregnation theory of the origin of life on earth. By meteor.[2]

[*4r*]   Confidentially
Come Right Down to It
    Let us be merry before we go
    You shine with beauty that is not your own.
    John Gorham.[3]
    The Wood the Wad the Wag[4]
    Song of David[5]
    Runnable Stag
    Ha give me Ale
    Ale does more than Milton[6]
    Piece of Samson Agonistes?[7]
    I know my life
    The Old Cloak
    To me they speak
    Dark Deep and Cold
    The Sleeper. (with Exequy.[8]
    Who hath seen the wind.

[*4v*]   Wolfs Squirrel[9]
In either mood
Uriel[10]
Moses Siege burns
Never Tired Pilgrims

[*8v*]   The Rose Family[11]
Freedom of the Moon
Once by the Pacific
The Soldier
Miracles
Investment

Winter Eden
Times Table
Cocoon
Sand Dunes
Acceptance
Bereft
Cows in the Corn[12]
The Bear
What Fifty Said
Minor Bird
Birth Place
Light of the World
The Same Leaves.

[9r]* The fact sat light ~~behind~~ {inside} a rock
And listened to our foolish talk!

~~Matter~~ {Mind} is matter and matter mind
And God is {the} only one of his kind

[12r] [~~illegible~~]
[illegible] A Stearns

[11v] Ridgley 46 Morton
Louis   Melcher
Holts   62 West 45
Farrar   Alfred Krymborg[13]
Montagu   86 Bank St
MacVeagh
Cross
Mrs Olds   Plaza
Du Chine & Miss Sergeant   3223
Sullivans
Mearns
Chapin   244 W 14   Tel Chelsea 2252
    525 Park Ave   Atwood

---

* Entries on this page are written vertically, against the ruled paper, from top to bottom in
the right hand margin.

Blocks
Mouson
Waldo Frank   Schyler 0193
                     173 Riverside Drive

[*13r*]   Amherst Jan 3—Mar 23
        Wesleyan Nov 29—Dec 11
        Barnard Nov 19 Miss Hubbard
        Parley-Wesleyan Dec 6 Sun afternoon.
        New Jersey College for Women New Brunswick Nov 16

"I learned to laugh when I was young

MS. 928940.1. *Brown soft paper cover flip pad, with canvas strip binding at top, 4⅜"* × 7¼". *Stitched pages. White ruled paper. Entries are in black ink unless otherwise noted.*

[1r]*   I learned to laugh when I was young
          And all my life the habit clung

          People absent turned to devils in his mind.

          Why I don't like "close ups." I never have liked to look too straight in ~~the~~ {a} face ~~when~~ too powerfully moved. It is blinding and averting.

The Report

          But Islands of the Blest! God bless you son
          I couldn't seem to find a blesséd one.[1]

          First you want {wish} to believe it. Then if you can get someone to say it from the outside the trick is turned: you have your religion

          First the rhythm is on the ~~breeching~~ {holdbacks} and then on the tugs. First the donkey pulls the cart then the cart pushes the donkey. [Small stream from the faucet pressed into wrinkles.][†]

          Sold their house in their old age for their board and lodging in it till death

[2r]   Nobody ought to get the Nobel prize I hear whose work hasnt been bullish Hardy[2] has been bearish.

                    •   •   •

---

* Page written in blue ink.
[†] Frost's brackets.

~~Some poetry {critic} tests   How to tell a critic~~
~~Some you have heard of~~

~~Some others~~
  ~~morning cool or midnight febrile~~

How to tell a critic
  Does he simply apply old rules.
  Does he simply ask conservatism or radicalism.

  Can he tell morning cool {*} from midnight febrile
  Can he see the joint the seam the welding.
  Can he see if the original impulse (subconscious intention) has been de-
parted from.
  Does he [illegible] ~~feel~~ know when the rhythm pushes the meter or the
meter pulls the rhythm. Donkey & cart   Sword dance
  Can he put his finger on the place
            Matrix most of poem
  Or if the writer ever wrote exercises (form first
  Can he tell if this idea began before the beginning

[2v] We rightly disparage people who are incapable of being (run away with) (and
swept off their feet.) How much better are those who were never swept off
their feet except by liquor than those who were never swept off their feet at
all? Perhaps a little better Drink is a medicine for the too strict by nature. No
one needs it who has ever lost himself without it.

Rigid people are like poets who tread too strict a measure in the meter. Immoral people are like free versifiers.

Remember the Lake of Nemi[3]

The sentimental gettings together of the cut throat furniture people misunderstood and prosecuted by the government for combination in restraint of
trade. Comedy.

[3r]   A great many deaths went to the making of that squirrel coat.

                    •   •   •

Yes but we dont let ourselves think of that says the furrier.

Just so we dont let ourselves think of the morality that undeniably underlies our decency and saintliness. Come right down to it our actuation is no
doubt necessitous Yes but we don't let ourselves think of that We float living
over we forget what.

Tell me why you are decent.
I refuse to tell you
You dont know yourself
I was ha hardly know and I was happiest when I didnt know at all.—and I
was more decent.

Didnt dialogue long enough to find out if there was anything but his
teachers in the idea that you had to accept as true everything you couldnt re-
fute in public ([?Germans story]) and that the best protective against being
caught with every new / ism is to know all the old isms. He opposed {the}
first to my saying that every one probably had the makings in himself of
some kind {school} of philosophy: it was probably implicit in his deeds and
emergent from his temperament: and it was what he had constantly to come
back to for restarting his study of philosophy

[3v] He opposed the second to my saying the best protective against being too
much invaded was to have started getting up ideas yourself.

Boy
    There are no such things as subject and object: there is to behaviorism[4]
there is only thing; nature. The most fruitful results [illegible] have come
from the assumption that that there are only responses to stimuli.
Man   Responses and stimuli sound strangely like the same old two things.
Boy   Anyway there is no such thing as consciousness.
Man   Wouldnt you be willing to admit consciousness as a response—a de-
ferred response perhaps.
Boy   So that all you think it is
Man   No. I think it is the concomitant of all responses. [It is a generaliza-
tion of the plane of love honor and justice

Wanted a ticket back. All mixed up guess he would go back and to the stations he started from and start all over

[4r]   Crash. There goes another young ideal.

Boy   ~~Whats your~~ You say you hate the word gem.
Man   Not the word at all except as applied figuratively to a poem or pic-
ture.
Boy.   Whats your favorite word?
Man   I have no favorite word
Boy.   My favorite words are silver and twilight. Some people think pave-
ment is the most beautiful word in the language. Pav-e-ment — pav-e-ment.[5]
A boy at the Poetry Society last night had a set of poems all full of the words
silver and twilight and frosted. ~~Thats why~~ I never heard anything I liked
better.
Man.   The first thing frosted taken alone brings into my head is cake
Boy   Dont!
    The question is is it right to educate young people by shock. They are an
undeniable temptation to teachers.

Of two people given their choice of living again ten thousand years hence or
ten thousand years ago: one reasoned that he knew enough already of the
past and so would choose the future the other that he knew just enough of
the past to want to know more and so he would take the past. ~~I~~ The one who

[4v]   chose ten thousand years ago was sacrificed on an altar almost the moment
he was born: the one who ~~was~~ chose ten thousand years hence found himself
the last of the human race and soon perished miserably ~~with nobody~~ of having nobody to talk to (a mental case)

    When I refuse to give you a raise in wages it is from unselfishness for fear
of spoiling you for others. Also: ~~by~~ I am thinking of myself a little. If you go
up ultimately I shall have to go up to pay you. It is easier to fight you down
than to fight my way up: as it is easier to keep than it is to get.

    The Swami. She would marry him in a minute if she were free

    An Undeviating Walker. People of less character make way for him.

[5r]   How shall it be thought of.

    Nothing but a grindstone — puts the universe in its place.[6]

•   •   •

Art is nothing but business. Religion is nothing but business Beautiful good and true. They have to be beautiful in art good in church and truthful in business.

Sitting Out. Trying to live to yourself pastoral in an industrial age.

The river Bath had fleeces.
Salt-suds in the ocean.

The river in spring had a frothy scum
Like wine when it ceases work.
And mixed in the froth were petals of flowers

When we two face the universe confronts itself. We are the two ends of a straight line that in infinity is a circle. We are its extremes meeting.

A drift stick that tried nearing rocks but at last got its exact middle against one so that it kept its balance in the rush of water past its end where the water sank it stayed stranded

[5v] Possibility that one of the lenshaped nebulae seen furthest off is our own universe seen from behind — ourselves seen round a circle.[7]

He takes it like the prow of a ship
That turns dark water white.

Why do we stay with each other in human society — to show self control*

Why do you leave the last part of the {so many} book{s} uncut. — To show my self-control.

Like a person {hard pressed} in an argument we shift the ground to our children and begin the defense of life all over.

Creation is that which parts to meet itself.[8]

•   •   •

---

* "to show self control" written up right side of page, bottom to top.

They say that constriction makes struggle. But constriction is not the re-markable thing in nature. Room is the remarkable thing. There is more space than matter even within the atom.

I will sing of your hero that overcame our hero.

[*6r*]   Mercy and injustice—Jonah's puzzle.[9]
Justice makes men serious. Injustice humorous.
                    Dont have to care.

I seek others—they never seek me. And most of those I seek turn their backs and flee from me. All but the waves. I dont go to the waves. I can stand on the beach and the waves come to me. They never turn their backs on me and run away. They come and come as if they wanted me.

Belief cant be removed by reasons and proof.

More space than matter. Room is the noticeable thing.

What keeps everything moving in place is equality of centripetal and centrif-ugal. What keeps us moving among each other is equality of love and hate

                              Indulgences.

Secret of the entering wedge. Some of the most principled can be told off to be practical and absolved beforehand.

[*6v*]   [blank]

[*7r*]   Pertin.[10]   Just as there are things we dont quite do and things also we can quite bring ourselves to say so beyond that there are even things we cant bear to let ourselves think. And page 1 about close ups.

One nature estimates his gains as it {they} come short of being all it {they} might be. Another as ~~it exceeds anything he had a right to expect~~. {are more than nothing.}*

                      •   •   •

_____
* Inserted below the line.

Remember Sirius and Canopus.[11]

Pardon for sinning against the cause to advance the cause The one chosen for indulgence in as entering wedge.

The find of this anthology is: {for all its straining After youve had Palgrave[12]}
the
Wood the Weed and the Wag[13]
Let us be Merry before we Go[14]
Celia Fell.[15]

The Wedding[16]
Song of David[17]
The Snake {Emily D.}[18]   Tweed to Till.[19]
The Grey Squirrel[20]
In either mood   From harmony[21]

[7v]   Have we got to say whether or no we think machinery destroys art etc.

Im the kind that cant get over things I have to say they have never been. Annul not divorce.   ~~Two~~*

To anniversaries.

All Santayana thinks is that almost all material basis for spirit can be done away with[22]
—not quite all: almost all virtue can be stated in terms of taste[23]—not quite all. The spirit needs not personality nor nationality nor any ~~order~~ place of order at all. But it must have place. Be it no more than chaos. It cannot be thought of in complete detachment. Such being the case I should say the one interesting thing to study is its dependence on matter and it seems to make little difference where you study it in ~~closer~~ more or less close connection.— How few can the spirit make equal to how many in battle Other things how unequal can size lick littleness. —A very useful sin to the church is departing from the principles to deceive

---

* Entry written in pencil.

[*8r*] the enemy. So also is the sin of having children. Both are sure of pardon and absolution. Make it some Klan or Order)

Mingle the hobo tramp {of America} with the holy tramp of Asian type.

Eldorado half way between Incas and Mexicans was the rumor that reached each of the other.

Sitting or standing that what he stands for

Sentenced not to die but to live in prison 480 years.
You mean to say instead of being sentenced to die I am sentenced to live beyond my time—480 years in jail. All right then At least I'll see something of what the world is like then.

Who really did the statue.

"I don't believe in skin."

Dog: Dont ask me to explain. I can't explain. Another dog has adopted ~~this family~~ his: or he's had trouble with his family or he's run himself off his legs

[*8v*] The lonely cow. She was as dissatisfied with America as Sinclair Lewis.[24]
She put her kicking and thrashing on the highest plane.

Our thought masses in space generating heat like little atoms in space. The general shape ~~is~~ {stays} globular. Though for all an outburstof something ocluded here and there bursts the side ~~of the~~ and jets fiercely outward a ~~thousand miles~~ a hundred thousand miles.[25] The furthest ~~it thought~~ is repelled from itself is never far and it is soon reabsorbed into itself as falling dust or rain.

> ~~They are~~ {He is} Nobody's dead
> You can dig up their head
> And nothing said.
> There will be nothing said
> If you dig up his head

The object of life is to feel curves. {You're looking at them all your life.} You'd never feel the {beautiful} curves in the road if didnt ~~get up spee~~ have an automobile to get a speed of more than thirty miles an hour with.

The original wheel ~~to ride on~~ {for traveling}* was a

[9r] hoop to run beside. It took you nowhere and it didnt rob you of your own motion and exercise.

Wife's experiment for her husband to see if his jealous watchfulness of her was all to make sure of the legitimacy of ~~his~~ {the} heirs to his name and property and the purity of his breed.

Mind is matter ~~and~~ matter is mind
And God is the only one of his kind

Theres absolutely not one bit of proof that there is anything wrong with the world. Everything is to be judged by intention.

Edna was there the night the democrat held forth on the final democratic privilege of disinterestedness deference and politeness.[26] She didnt like that. In the country that time she was home she found the only way to feel things over was on errands.

Doctrine of Impurities or of Almost. There is no one quality to which all other qualities may not almost be reduced Any part may almost be taken for the whole.[27]

[9v] Pushing things round—things and people. It may be affectionately or hatefully. It may be affectionately and still roughly. And this more roughly the better. But whether affectionately or hatefully it is always playfully.

A Play no matter how deep has got to be so playful that the audience are left in doubt whether it is deep or shallow.

Poems beginning—
(A Book entitled

---

* Phrase written in blue ink.

Mind is matter and matter is mind
This is the last of my brains
But Islands of the Blest[28]
Etc.

A liberal[29] is one who will allow any {reckless} way of life in others as long as he isnt suspected of that way himself.

[*10r*] Ford's Antique Villages. Edison's High Light.
The ford has taken away and given back Blessed be the name of the ford.[30]

First we learn simple balance as in the balanced sentence. In time we go on to crave the balance of missed and compensated.

Shack near Philadelphia.
English singers versus American compare

We've had the damned language three hundred years which is quite half the length of time they have had it themselves.

Beauty is truth—that sick esthetic monism.[31]

To make a statement and then shore it up with answers to all the questions I imagine it raising in your mind.

To establish by tredle the sense of balance in childhood. And then—live in it if you like your Pope. But if not go on to feel for the balance, missed and compensated; and ultimately to the balance missed almost saved and missed again.

[*1r*]* Dagger aforesaid of the value of 12d certain wooden bucket bound with iron ~~staves of~~ hoops of the value of eight pence

Sameness uniformity monotony of the sky and the sea in comparison with the land. Variety is within us like most things of poetry. Driven inward for variety somewhat[32]

.   .   .

---

* Pages starting here begin at the other side of the notebook and work backward.

Letters Never Sent. Letters Never Written

She Took Her Husband's Side.
    Entertaining the Ladies by getting them some jewelry
    Kings X and Queens X[33]

The bad we scare children with is make believe. The bad we scare grown-
ups with must be real and very bad: It must tempt us to take sides with it to
make their fright serious.

The reference words must chime or there is no style

[2r]   The last time I was Anywhere I heard
                         Blest
But Islands of the Blest, God bless you son
I couldnt seem to find a blesséd one.[34]

Pinney Poppy Show

Suggestion to the Holy Birth Cont Rollers that we all go into that if we can't
be fathers we should all be uncles. Church discovered that long ago

How I worked reason season treason in innocence of the fact that they
were all I had.[35] I should have lost my nerves in that stanza if I had known
that- - - -were all I had. Rhyming dictionary would have disheartened me by
emphasizing my limitation.

Theres is something more grand parental than parental in the fond fuss
they are all making over the most recently generated. You'd think no one had
ever been a grandparent before. But these grand children are not really better
than all previous grandchildren They are merely better than their grandpar-
ents in a great many respects We will all agree that they can beat us in long
distance pissing

[3r]   I have seen them the younger generation in its day piss over the roof of a district schoolhouse. And they can beat us in bathing beauty contests and in pu-
gilism and in eating between meals and in aversion to compromise. Their
weakness is in not thinking of much to do unless we put them up to it.{*}
There lies our safety in the same society with them Suppose they had this ini-

tiative to rise in their relative superiority (they have been chief gainers by the advance of medicine the saving of life has been largely at the baby end) and demand that we meet them on their own ground, say, naked in beauty contests. They'd have us {skun} of course. Lets not be dared out of our clothes by them whatever happens. Lets not throw away the advantage of keeping the comparison in the realm of brains. Lets keep our shirts on. Sans culottes sans chemises[36]

*They lack initiative enterprise adventurousness

*The leaders of the procession {of new youth} I see coming down the street are three or

four greywhiskered old men Shaw[37] Shnitzler[38] etc and one lunatic of the last century

[4r]   1 You come into the knowledge that the good writing comes from the pull of the sentence form you hear in your minds ear on the words that come nearest your meaning.

2 ~~Picking up the idea~~ Beginning the idea at the beginning of yourself i.e. when you are coming out of a sleep or play.

3. Not knowing the limits of rhyme. how many rhyme words Poem a little run of logic (Cuts a figure)[39]

The ~~Freest~~ School Most Free. If they are not asked to do it for marks, shall they be expected to do it for me? I refuse to have their lives turn on my winning ways I aint got none. It is too much to assume the responsibility ~~for their having because~~ {even} the blame with their practical parents for their having become artists thinkers men of taste.

Free man and Freedman   Manumitted.[40]

Aesthetic Conscience

[4v]   Not that meter, though the meter is much and not that tone though the tone is more and not that meter and tone together are enough. There must be cadence cadence cadence

The old metaphors for God and Jesus were really poetic expressions of feeling; the new metaphors are arguments and poetry gone wrong.

·   ·   ·

Our perception of God is that emotion that throws off the metaphors. We know him further from his having disclosed himself when he was on speaking terms with the first men. We have him from them—handed down.

A long distance prediction: just as the {Greeks} slight flicker of electricity has been our whole civilization so our slight intimation of catalysis will be the whole civilization of five thousand years hence. ‖ Sensitivity when understood will be all there is to consider in medicine

The tale of The Fish a Bird.

The fish came to a waterfall
Fool talk is longer than wise talk. There are more things to say of a given subject that aren't true than that are.

[5r] In the Right. Mahetebel Sommes, stay after school. Why what have I done. None of your impertinence miss. Do as you're told. Take your seat. The rest of you ta go. Close the door Sarah, What is it you want. I'll it will do you good to try a little harder to work it out yourself before I help you Take it home with you. You may copy it from the black board. But be quick about it. Dont be all night. I've had all the schooling thats good I need for one day. Thats it off with you. Now Mehe Sommes what have you to say for yourself. She puts her hands in her eyes Boohoo she sobs but turns it into ha ha and uncovers her eyes to look at him boldly {mischievously}*. Arent you ashamed of yourself a big girl like you Come here to me. What is there to be ashamed of. You come here to me. It's the gentlemans place to come to the lady. Well we are getting forward. He walks along the windows to see that no one is lingering about the school house; This room is all windows. So much the better for looking out of So much the better for looking in. too. What would anybody be looking in for. From depraved curiosity to see others suffer punishment. What do you suppose they think I am going to do to you. Make me write

[5v] words {a copy of verses}. Whereas I am going to treat your offense as much an deserving of much more serious penalty. I am going to give you lashes of the whip. Come hold out your hand. You cant make me beg off. Do your worst. There, I should like to be hurt by you. Why dont you strike. Should

---

* Inserted below the line.

you really like to be hurt by me. I shouldn't mind really—as much as you would hurt. Shouldnt you mind my hurting you. Do you mean it. You wouldnt hurt a kitten. He lashes her around the neck gently and leaves the leather in place like a collar. Know your offense. You are too old to be in school and too young for a man to resist. Why do you come disturbing me just when I am all settled down to be quiet and good. Harmless am I. You dont know the kind of fire you are playing with. Its Greek fire that burns under water. What are you keeping me after school for if you are so considerate of my safety. I'm keeping you not because you aren't a good girl I didn't know whether you were a good girl or not but to find out if you were a good girl. Am I a good girl. Im afraid [i̶l̶l̶e̶g̶i̶b̶l̶e̶] you are not Aren't you sorry? Im afraid Mehitable I see someone coming. Its the parson. Hes coming here. You'll have to go. No take your seat and sit c̶o̶n̶t̶r̶i̶t̶e̶l̶y̶ repentant. I'll tell you when

[6r]   you can go. Ill dismiss you after he's been here a minute or two. But first something for you to be repentant for. What do you say. Well. He kisses her – Hurry get your seat ..

Come in. N̶o̶ Nothing important {Mr Searls}. Nothing but this unruly girl. Why Mehelibel S̶o̶m̶m̶e̶s̶ {Wrenn} giving this teacher trouble—a big girl like you. You ought to be ashamed of yourself. What is it We'll spare her the recital I guess. She's been sufficiently punished. You may go Mehitibel. She ducks out at a swift walk almost run. Shes a provoking girl. Yes yes yes. A hard case girl to know what to do with. Its time she was out of school. Her father should be spoken to. T̶h̶e̶y̶ ̶a̶r̶e̶ ̶n̶o̶t̶ ̶t̶h̶e̶ ̶a̶m̶e̶n̶a̶b̶l̶e̶ ̶k̶i̶n̶d̶.̶ Though I am not sure of any good it would do. The family is rather out of jurisdiction. The worser element. There's always a large proportion of the population that refuses to come under the government of the church. And say is what you will outside the church t̶h̶e̶r̶e̶ is n̶o̶ ̶o̶n̶e̶ {outside the} state. T̶h̶e̶ ̶t̶w̶o̶ ̶w̶o̶n̶t̶ s̶e̶p̶a̶r̶a̶t̶e̶.̶ For all our attempts to distinguish them the two remain one and undistinguishable in practice. The godless are the outlawed.

[7r]   He says "Well" and rising slowly leaves the room. He opens the door after closing it. Did you speak. What?
Nothing,
I thought you said something.
What should I say. W̶h̶a̶t̶ ̶d̶i̶d̶ Did you want me to say something.
I honestly dont know.
You wanted me to and I know what it was.

Lets hear it and see if {what} it satisfies ~~anything [illegible] in me.~~

You wanted me to say that nothing we have said or done in the last few months counts .. We are back where we were before all ~~that~~ {the unhappiness}. Isnt that it. You wanted me to do the sweeping of it away

He is silent.

Isnt it.

Im thinking.

Come lets dissipate the illusion. Lets be happy

Its not so easy. No that cant be what I wanted you to say. I doubt if I wanted you to say any thing.

So then.

Don't be angry with me because youve failed to make nothing of it. It cant be made nothing of. Its real

{Nonsense} It isnt. I wont believe it. I wouldnt believe it if anyone else said it I wont believe it

[7v]   even from you.

You wont you think

No.

Do you know I ~~think~~ {believe} I can find a way to make you believe it— give me time.

How.

Some how—give me time.

Ill give you all the rest of my life.

Look it Look it

Aw leave him alone.

[8r]   It is the same kind who always think they have more to contend with in life {and} who think they have a more atrocious enemy to deal with in any war they ~~ha~~ may have.

There ought to be a law made that everybody ~~onl~~ must care. You cant play games with people who would just as lief play as not. To have a good republic you must first of all find some way to drive everybody just crazy to vote.

The {new} mother asked the specialist in child rearing whether the child should ever be whipped. No he answered judicially. I should say not. But on the other hand there is something to be said in favor of whipping him. How much ~~more~~ {less} is there to be said for whipping him on the one hand than on the other? And as a matter of fact I wasn't thinking of whipping him on either hand but somewhere else. I thought it was only teachers never mothers that whipped children on the hands.

[*8v*] At least he ~~was a~~ made a great stir
Oh yes he made a stir all right
You say that as if it were ~~something~~ {nothing}
You say it as if it were something.
I suppose you think it makes all the difference what the stir was about
<u>I</u> do
I <u>dont.</u> Any stir is better than none at all.

Boy ~~that told me~~ frightened into telling me too much about himself. Story of the boy who didnt tell who threw the paper dart.

The prejudice against the wedded wife and in favor of the Anne Rutledge or Jewett[41] is a hang over from the days when people married for position and amused themselves with out-loves, and as a hang over stirs the romantics. Chain armor.

Car stops on the stage. Woman is thrust out and beaten over head with straw hat.

[*9r*] Assignation
Why not take hands and go to the meeting place together

What did he mean by the Cataract of Death.[42] It sounds like something I have been thinking myself.

I'll tell you why all movement is in a circle great or small.[43] It is so every particle ~~can be~~ in it can be looked at directly across by every particle behind it—acted on directly across as well as from behind every particle behind it. The action from across is called environment the action from behind is called inheritance.[44]

The danger of our criticism is judging ~~everything~~ {our literature} from the political level which is necessarily not far below the surface. The political man—we know how he talks in the large for-or-against sloganly, sectional, stentorian. All that distinguishes him from the advertiser is his freedom to attack the other fellow's goods. The political woman will be undistinguishable from the political man. Neither gets down to where their sex differences begin

[9v]   That's where If our criticism succeeded in holding our literature at that exterior superficiality, we'd never have a literature. Personal particularizing, insight scares the politician. It seems morbid—and a waste of time. Talk about us in the altogether, in terms of the two oceans the Mississippi and Rocky Mountains: in terms of wheat corn copper and cotton and you are writing the Great Am Novel or trying to write it, a candidate for the position of G. Am Novelist. What the critics want is Wading in the Missippi

The New Laocoon[45]: the U.S. straining with the Mississippi in his grasp.

Cal controls the Mississippi.

June 4 1928 Do you know the worst thing about a book? It is that it makes such poor fuel. ‖ Do you know the hardest thing in the world {about a person}? It is to know whether a person {he} is sorry enough for his mistakes without your having to rub it in with words.

[10r]   The Baptism of {by} Imersion. Don't touch me.
       You farmer!

Set into the sentence anyway and show your resourcefulness in the way you get out. Just so of the poem. Just as of North Pole

Marriage are made in heaven by for those [illegible] submissive enough to the heavenly influences.

And oh but it was fetching
To see the wretches retching.

Poems Beginning.

·   ·   ·

Llewellan Raney.[46] A Man of Vision and Imagination.

His choking was mental—entirely mental. It might as well have been entirely physical. With most people most things that happen are entirely physical. It is when they are mental on top of physical that poetry arises.

[11r]   Ten Books.

[illegible]
Emerson's Poems   Golden Day.[47]
Panchatantra.[48]   Browns Pseudodoxia.[49]
Pascal's Pensées[50]   Emile.[51]
O Shaugnessey[52] {Bucharest} [Percy's Reliques[53]
Voyage of Beagle[54]   Leviticus
Poe entire.[55]

The physical continuum in love. The broken logic everywhere else. The Lyndes[56]

Many members of society {in spite of their obligation to society to uphold it} shut their eyes and hurry by to avoid being witnesses to a crime and so involved with criminals and the vengeful the rest of their lives. All criminals refuse to see crime enacted in front of them.

I know what I wanted to say to them I know now. That I hate {so sensitively} To be chided rebuked even refused so sensitively that my nature would fain find a principle or principles on which to be beforehand with people, justice or love or honor on which to check myself before another could check me. I would like to deny that I am kept in my place by the conflict

[11v]   of my desire with your desire. Such is my pride. Others can tell me where I must stop: Oh but I don't want to be told. It spoils everything to have to be

Who alone can thank a judge

Your Fist in your hand. A great force strongly held. Poetry is neither the force nor the check. It is the tremor of the deadlock.[57]

•   •   •

There must be something coming from your mind to protect it from infection. A source cant be contaminated.

We are born along submissive to our fate of less and less to do and less and less physical strength till we shall become we know not what

What will you take for it? What will you give*

---

* This entry and the one above it are written in blue ink.

"These are not monologues but my part in a conversation"

MS. 929940.2. Brown stippled leather cover, pocket notebook, 2⅛″ × 3⅞″. "Diary" embossed diagonally in gold on the cover. "Robert Frost/Amherst/Mass/The Webster 45 St." written in Frost's hand in blue ink inside the front cover. Thumb-tabbed calendar for each month of the year, 1929–1930, followed by blank pages. Entries are in black ink, blue ink, or pencil as noted.

[1r]*   [Illegible] These are not monologues but my part in a conversation in which the other part is more or less implied.[1]

[5r]   Unsound financial hobby of my youthful days. Wont say they didnt bother her.

[5v]   Hypocrasy of modesty in woman or man—someone says. We should use all we have of wit beauty or strength. Any lack of assertion is hypocritical. Wow!

    Sick of logic and meaning. Scrape your brain pan for something else. If I say things that wont mean anything to you, they'll have to be things that mean nothing to me.

    A poet had a poetess for child. Percy and Ridgely[2]

[7r]   The moral is
    Don't try to write poetry unless you are pretty sure of success because if you try and fail with your own it spoils you for ever appreciating the poetry of others. You can never be a good critic of poetry. The only critics of poetry are born critics and not made by failure in the attempt to write poetry.

•   •   •

---

* 1r, 5r, 5v, and 7r written in blue ink.

Its the ⌊illegible⌋ middle class English that are so unhappy here. They can stand the upper class over them at home But here they find the middle class over them and they rage*

[7v]† We ask the English what they think about us Someday they may ask us what we are going to do about them.

[8r] No wonder we pleased ourselves to have pulled out such a plum.

She turns her back on the world, he turns his back on heaven. Thence their fond pity for each other

How long would we refrain from seeing if we couldnt win back our position by force—how long would we except the arbitrament of craft‡

[8v] Sin Braggarts   C. Aiken³
Confessing for Everybody

The ~~books~~ {poets} at whose ~~feet~~ metric feet we worshipped and bowed down were Arnold Keats Browning Tennyson Kipling (wooden music xylophone) Emerson Longfellow§

We read their books whole

[9r] Poetry is that in us that will not be terrified by science. Poetry knows best what is best for us—the $9/10$ country.**

"There is a God, but I don't believe in him."

As I go up and down the stairs, I balance myself
But the banisters there to be used at my need
Edna Ogden slide on them

---

* Entry written in pencil.
† Page written in pencil.
‡ Entry written in pencil.
§ Entry written in blue ink.
** Entry written in blue ink, remainder of page written in pencil.

[9v]* Suggestiveness is overflow of meaning. Only preparation for suggestiveness is definite meaning. A curly fume in the sanctum of the heart—that is the love I wish I were sure of.

[10r] Heartiness kept

Story of fraternity marks

Waiting Spirit[4]

Story of Boardman Robinson[5]

How many thing can you do with a poem.

Story of Geo Churchhill's [?Damon][6]

Story of boy who handnt spread

Fire for form.[7]
What can you do with a poem—without outrage to Muse

Find out what it is to have something to say

Meaning beyond [?meaning]

Bearing the weight of Stadium—Sullivan Lewis[8]

[10v] Subjects used in 1906 Eng classes[9]

Something I Used to Think.

Things My Mother Keeps to Remember My Infancy by.

A Person I dont See Any More

My First Book. (Read)

                    •   •   •

---

* 9v and 10r written in blue ink.

Punishments {seen used}* I Have Suffered

Such a thing as being funny about serious things Much modern painting looks like being serious about funny things. Just as we are abstract about the concrete and concrete about the abstract. This is called leaving people behind or carting off followers.

Serious Nonsense. verse

[11r]†   Brainless intellectuals Modish minded Mental fops. Methodologists School of education

A totally absorbed person will deny he ever changed his nature by growth[10] or taking thought. All is a question of absorption. Abstract where concrete is expected and vice versa.

[11v]   [illegible] Nine tenths should be in and individual one tenth out and social

Went to say I was sorry for what I had done. Mustnt speak too at once for fear of seeming too sorry and so magnifying the offence; nor too late for fear of not seeming sorry enough: but just at the right time by the clock to seem sorry enough‡

Spacing the conversation

The Just Moment

[illegible] on word spacing

[12r]   To the High and Mighty Englishman of this time: Come off it!

If Hollywood wanted to do a play of college life it would make the set at Oxford because it looks like a university. Every thing at Hollywood has to look its part. An artist would have to look like an artist.

---

* Inserted from below the line.
† Page written in blue ink.
‡ Entry in pencil, remainder of page written in blue ink.

[12v]*   was the point. It was architectural. It was the steeple I suppose I reminded him of his blocks.

Prescotts[11] laugh ~~when~~ at when the thistle that couldnt get him again.

Form.

Poem to be named Seven Sentences in Three Stanzas.

[drawing]†

Prescotts Laugh said ~~No~~ to the thistle, No you dont not twice. You had one on me Have one on yourself this time.

Aesthetic Beginnings.

[13r]   Details. Ins and Outs of tree trimming.
[drawing]‡
Balance expected missed and compensated for.
Aesthetic Experience
    Child of three passing church stopped on opposite side of the street to laugh at it. What was that laugh? Was he laughing at religion the present state of it in the world? No it was the laugh of one who appreciates sees the point. What

[13v]§   What appreciation is sincerest best most unforced

[14r]**   Not {by} cunning but by belief it is brought to fulfilment.

    Surrender is the one delight Once self should be given in absolute be-fore it learns caution and care. Society should be so formed as to care for us.

•   •   •

---

* Page written in black ink.
† Page written in pencil.
‡ Drawing of three horizontal lines with arrow heads.
§ Drawing of two horizontal lines with circles at the ends of the lines.
** First two entries written in blue ink, last two entries written in black ink.

New art: peculiarity without content.

How does it affect what you do to learn that it wasnt always done and wont always be done?

[14v]*   Saying one in terms of another.

Somebody says glands determine thought. And I say Pretty pretty. Well played. Some one else says thought affects glands—governs determines?

Poetry is that part of everything that you cant mark for?

How Make Poe hard[12]

[15r]†   Another way to deal with it is to treat it as what it is not—language philology What is it. Nice play of enthusiasm that as often takes the form of understatement as overstatement

Imaginative metaphor

Permitted way of saying one thing and [illegible] meaning another

[15v]   Gradients—Christ to Corruption

Ted Lewis[13]—Last Ball Thrown
   Lost in the sun

Eddie Guest's Mirror[14]
C Ruggles[15] Purity

———————————————————————

Good for poetry

Father: God wrote one book

•   •   •

———————————————

* Except the letters "ar" in "mark," which are written in black ink, page written in pencil.
† 15r and 15v written in pencil.

Prof no contemporary

Prof: no American

Dilemma Spoil good poem to teach love of good poetry. Spoil second rate poem in hope of teaching love of first rate.

[*16r*]*   Number Metaphors

$3^2 + 4^2 = 5^2$ Fact

Physics and Chemistry are the metaphor sustained longer than any but religious

Nearer to rate of motion further from place where—this is because of mixed metaphor could tell them it would break down.

Zenos paradox[16] pointed out same thing

Expect it to break down where consciousness begins. Breaks down in world of matter[17]

[*16v*]†   Metaphors:
Machine
Number
Actuarial Statistic
Unknown soldier
Cabbages
Emergent Evol
Evolution[18]
Endemic in broth[19]
Devil can quote
Two in Long Swim
Wounds with Shield

---

* Page written in blue ink.
† Page written in black ink.

[17r]   John Swain—Davidson

Facsimile Text Society
   Columbia University

[17v]*   The one who keeps his heartiness through all the trials of being cultivated

The one who keeps his common sense.

Both speak in vernacular intonations.   Those must have been kept.

Almost by resolution not to be poetical at all that you come to anything newly poetical. Same with philosophical.

Materialist is one lost in his material.[20] Cant get the idea

[18r]†   If she accepted the suicide of the one who couldnt have her, well the one who had had her was not to be out done. But there was a society for scrapping one officer for every ship scrapped

He stood in the box till the last ball batted was returned to him form the fielder who caught it on the fly. He wanted that ball for ~~when~~ the time when you mightnt believe he had been what he had been.‡

[18v]   He ought not to be stopped talking that way The worst he can say will do the world [illegible] less harm than we would do ourselves interfering with him in his freedom.

Final proof of science what synthetic man can do. Poetry only being kept alive in the world now to see if he can write it. Science will arrive when the Robot writes like Shakespeare.

[19r]§   I accuse everybody of being actuated by impurer motives than I am. The Radical. He is a bag of unconnected roots. Bad Talkers and Bad Actors

---

* Page written in black ink.
† Page written in black ink.
‡ "he had been what he had been" written up right side of page, bottom to top.
§ Page written in pencil.

[*19v*]* 1. Zeno & Einstein.[21]

2 Postulate and Axiom

3. Searching subtlety of mathematical science.

4. Pythagoras analogy with numbers[22]

5. Mystic-phallic 10

6 All science domestic science.[23]

7. Except science that trys to equal God in creating life. Just to see what it can do

[*20r*]† No proof life can continue on this continent

Rock Bottome

Any idea you have might be treated as an answer to a question that could be put to a class. W

[*20v*]‡ He said he never lied in his life—except to women. He had never touched a married woman. He had always respected the other man's property rights in a wife. But as to a womans property rights in herself that was another matter. Cheating was permitted there—My

[*21r*] hatred of such a man his fascination for me arises from the unfair advantage his inconsistancy and illogicality give him—I hate him as I hate all unfairness.

Would you let them destroy you just because they are cleverer than you.

[*21v*]§ Right virtue of a president to have been a scholar and have given up scholarship and the company of scholars for the company of trustees ~~and~~ men of the world: his point of view shall be their point of view for rating school maams.

Inexact knowledge versus exact knowledge?

Exact knowledge + some judgement and taste versus exact knowledge

---

* Page written in black ink.

† Page written in pencil.

‡ 20v and 20r written in blue ink.

§ 21v and 22r written in blue ink.

[22r]   How much fire goes to make the form.* [24]

> In religion: conscience
> In art[:]   expression
> In science: curiosity.

*How much spirit goes into matter.[25] How much will goes into reason How the pairs couple.

Inaction. How are they mixed and kept together as a mechanical mixture[26] by the stirring of deeds

[22v]*   In New York I am pressed against it to hard to feel it and know how I felt it with pain or pleasure. This is my right feeling distance. It is also my dealing distance.

The man that made the crash on the Stock Exchange his excuse for being poor.

[23r]   Odrum Rainbow Round[†]

My Shoulder.

Andrew Johnson—Winston[27]

Hemingway Drama of the Forest[‡]

I remember saying once—in
> Chicago
> Terre Haute
> Rourk Bradford[§]

[23v]**   On Pushing things round affectionately or hatefully.

•   •   •

---

* Page written in pencil.
† Entry written in pencil.
‡ "Andrew Johnson . . ." to "Drama of the Forest" written in black ink.
§ "I remember saying" to "Rourk Bradford" written in blue ink.
** 23v and 24r written in black ink.

On mercifully making it as early as possible for your poor friends not to misjudge you.

In justice to these latter years

Policeman and star gazer. Crime and poetry.

Executive in poetry.

They give themselves to [~~illegible~~] build a city. Prophetic

[*24r*]   Be sure it is the right cause or poem and then put everything you have into it. Shall that be your rule? Not in poetry anyway. What you withhold is as effective as what you throw in. You cast a loop a line that goes and returns including much but excluding much like the woods left out of cultivation on a farm. Poetry is measure in two senses. It is a measured tread but it is a also a carefully measured amount of all you have to say. I should have to say only my economies in verse

[*24v*]*   to keep from falsity of thoroughness. Pouring to lees

Huxley Point Counter point[28]
C. E. Montague.[29]
Cunningham-Graham.[30]

    Max Stirner.[31]

The architect and the police man. What are you looking at that bank for at this time of night. None of your business.   But if you want to know it was because I thought it was too ornate. Well it isnt too ornate

[*25r*]   Is it good luck to pray? I never [?liked] say I [?kill] One thing thats bad luck
To laugh. At all- ever? Yes at all ever. I've heard people laughing. I know it
And look at the world.†
I have made a life study of what I can say.

                    •   •   •

---

* Page written in black ink except second entry, which is written in pencil.
† Entry written in pencil, otherwise page is written in black ink.

How would he show his feelings. By saying well I am surprised. Or looking stunned or saying Isn't it stunning?

[25v]*   He had to learn I suppose

Learn what. Didn't he know it ~~anyway~~ {already}

Well he had to learn that he knew it already And maybe that he neednt be so high and mighty about it.

What is his idealism made out of?

Out of ideals possibly

Wrong. Out of ideas. He thinks anything that ranks as an idea is meant to be acted out.

[26r]   [?Donham]

Business Looks at the unforeseen.

Some have to have every thing acted out to think it out.

---

* Written horizontally across the page, from left-hand margin to right-hand margin, in pencil.

"Thick skinned Thick headed"

MS. 001730. *Brown soft paper cover spiral bound flip pad, 4⅛″ × 6″ Ruled pages. "The Spiral no 48" stamped on cover. The first four pages are written vertically from top to bottom of the page, across the ruled lines in black ink, unless otherwise noted. The remaining pages are written in blue ink from left margin to right margin, along the printed lines of the page.*

[1r]*   Thick skinned   Thick headed
               Thick as thieves.   Thicknesses.

Hunters and soldier—can get killed—sporting
Butchers and executioners cant.—unsportsman

Martyrs will die for a cause
Soldiers will too but look out that they don't kill you first

Brittle—literary cant—never used once in mine[†]
Children you are very little
And your bones are very brittle—Stevenson[1] Mistake

Some people think your mistakes and your lies are just your poetry. A young hopeful is one considered imaginative because he cant report the truth.

[2r]   High brow low brow[‡]
         Middle brow and no brow[2]

She had no brow but a mind of her own
She wished the sailors would let her alone
She didnt like sailors she didnt like men

                 •   •   •

---

* Page written in pencil.
† Words "in mine" written in blue ink.
‡ "High brow . . . like men" written in pencil.

All life is cellular in physically and socially[3]

Original sin versus moral sin.
A The first inevitable the second not
    The first is so much darker than the second
    The second doesn't really seem to matter.
    The

[*3r*]   Church religion's greatest cruelty is in sending up to work on steeples where no insurance company will insure their lives for less than their wages. I find it more unbearable to think of them than of men in deep mine galleries or down in [illegible] submarines.*

What angers good teachers is the assumption of the progressives that noone so but progressives ever taught the spirit of the matter. The progressives think they can teach the spirit without the matter.

Know thyself says Socrates Know a woman suggests the Bible.[4]

Liked what I wrote so much I came back to caress it with a touch or two several times later

[*4r*]   The philosopher says dismiss the idea of purpose. And in the same breath he speaks as if the purpose of everything was our purpose to come out on a mountain top level of peace and equality. He thinks we have something in us that wont be got the better of by our needs and greeds. He assumes we have no need of strengthening ourselves in human rivalry to hold our own against nature. {Our dissatisfaction} with we know not what enemy be the evolutionary[5] thing in our bones—a strain—{blind}†

    He who stays out of waste[6] and lives to save
    {His home his money or his very life}
    And {Who} does not join in the unselfish waste
    Of everything who pays not daily tribute
    To the eternal rubbish {refuse}‡ heap of God
    Better beware he will be held a cheat

---

* Entry written in pencil.
† Inserted from below.
‡ Inserted below the line.

[5r]   Things to bear in mind for composure

There is nothing quite so composing as composition.[7] Putting anything in order a house a business a poem gives a sense of sharing the mastery of the
universe.

All life is cellular within the body of a man and outside his world is the
body of society. One chief disposition of life living is cell walls breaking and
cell walls ~~breaking~~ making.[8] Health is a period called peace in the balance of
the two. Sickness a period of war. Health may be too stolid for genius.

There is nothing for it but to learn how to ride phasing along through to
the shape of the whole

[6r]   three score years and ten. Don't let them ~~in~~ supply you with the words to
take tragically the ~~pa~~ phases of love and inspiration for instance. The whole
curve will be from more ethereal than substantial to more substantial than
ethereal. For a poet that would mean he musnt take it hard ~~if the~~ phasing
from lyric to epic in a life time. Lovers may ~~fall out of~~ think they have fallen
out of love when they pass into its next phase. Many a novice gets scared at
getting wiser {wiser}*.

Come to Sunday School with me that you may learn to keep the Sabbath as a
day of waste or sacrifice to God like a libation or burnt offering one seventh
which is even more than a tithe

[7r]   For you learn to be reconciled with ~~the~~ lavish waste of time [illegible] material end yourself and to glory in its generosity. Throw nothing away? You
may have the chance to throw yourself away.[9] [illegible] Who are you that
you should put on airs about purity. Soil your hands. Expect to soil your soul
for good reasons.

There are growths.[10] We know no such thing as growth unlimited. All
growths we know are toward ends—deaths, whether of persons ~~nations~~ trees
or nations. The purpose seems to be rounding off and rounding off and
rounding off. Perpetual rounding suggests a rounding off of the whole of
existance That would be evolution by analogy ~~Th~~ All analogy breaks down[11]

---

* Inserted below the line.

[8r] That means taking too long a view. We cant think of ~~evil~~ good without evil. Neither can come to an end without the other. The rounding off here could only be in the last of both of them.

Expect to keep head above the deluge not by finding a solid peak underfoot by luck but only by treading ~~metaphors~~ the forever failing metaphors

Retreat to Paganism Hold on a minute till I see whether I dont want to retreat further back than to the middle ages further back even than to the beginning of the Christian era.

I am not going to be called

[9r] a Pagan for nothing. I have had to take the nickname over and over again from any easy going Christian that happened along. It never seemed to bother him that he might be too fallible to know what he was talking about. What is it or was it to be a Pagan? If thats what I am lets have a look at me as if I were a Villager of {the} times B.C. just at the point of deciding whether I would step off into the newness of the times AD [illegible] [illegible] {It would be like} making a fresh start of what came [illegible] onto the world out of Judaea by word of Pauls mouth and {Pauls} self importance.

What would I be doing and thinking that I would have ~~to give up~~ either to alter [illegible] or give up entirely to become

[10r] a Christian.

I cannot read it but know what it says 'Daughters of men'[12] it seems there had been men—men always running back {to} time out of mind. Only they had become as is their way once in so often in their history Stale and unsatisfactory to God. So God chose one of them to start all over And inbred Adam [illegible] closely on himself to {make} chosen people of the Jews Conceivably ~~he~~ {God} might have used fresh seed. If he had had ~~on some other star~~ handy on some star not too far off ~~whose~~ [illegible] that sin had not infected.

Questionaire

Do you believe in God
        Yes in some vague way of the Unitarians My confidence to go ahead in life is a faith in life and the future. I believe the

[*11r*]   future in—I believe in God.[13]

—Do you believe in superstition

Yes I sort of believe with the Chinaman who said planting trees made a person live longer.

Do you believe in poetic justice?

Yes it with a much pleasanter smile than I believe in justice. Things do certainly seem to come round on themselves.

Do you believe in justice? I was forgetting to ask you.

Yes not uncontaminated uncorrupted unvitiated by mercy[14]

Do you believe in communication

Do you believe you can be sure you can make a friend understand a word you say.

Well when I met a friend fresh home from his Unitarian Church at about noon on the Sabbath

[*12r*]   I said {spoke} to him as if I was his disciplinary father. Now I said severely do you believe in One God One World One Wife and One Child. He was afraid he wasnt that pure It would be as good a way as any to end the world and have it over with. No violence. No whimper

Just about the time the Western world was setting forth on modern enterprise {at Runnymeade}[15] Marco Polo[16] was in the Eastern world admiring what so many Westerners have admired there but with no disposition to imitate it. Countless Asiatics out of their mortal swarming have escaped to Europe and America for an education in our ways. Now they think they are ready to try our ways against us. We never go to their schools

[*13r*]   to learn their ways with the purpose of using them for their overthrow. Get clean out of there and then see if even with our secrets they can catch up with us and destroy us. Wouldnt it be funny? Just think of this in our arrogance In the Boxer Rebellion[17] the Germans stole out of Germany two astronomical instruments made in the time of Kubla Khan.[18] They were really astrological. But they were something. I understand Germany gave them back.

Speaking of superstition, do you believe anybody can raise anybody from the dead.

Maybe if the corpse hasnt been too long dead.

•   •   •

Can anyone walk on water
Can any one walk much longer.

⌈ 1r ⌉*   We{'d} have the right to know what God's about
Had we the ability for finding out
All we have learned is clouded with a doubt

---

* This page is from the opposite end of the notebook and is written vertically across the ruled page lines.

"True humility is a kind of carelessness"

MS. 001717. *Black buckram loose leaf binder, 6¾″ × 10″, with unruled 6″ × 9½″ three ring loose-leaf pages. Entries are in blue ink unless otherwise noted.*

[1r]*   True humility is a kind of carelessness about the self that stays none to sure the mind is worth educating the soul worth saving any more than the body is worth providing for beyond the next meal[1]

Science pokes into nature as into a dark hole of an unknown wild animal that now and then proves it is there by biting the end of the {its} {his}† poker.[2]

The great rush{ing} of a flow of foliage has in it no to flower a treeful now and then upon its verdant surface. That flood may be on its way to better things. We hardly know. The flowery bursts[3] are no better as they go. A flower is a flower. Athens was one blooming. Rome was one England was one. Byzantium Paris Thebes Memphis. None has been better than Athens.

[2r]‡   Quid-nunc-heads not lunck heads[4]§

Perish the word compromise of me with the rest of things. There is no being or might have been except at the constant confluence of me and the alien.

Shine perishing republic So you sing
My

---

* Entries on this page are written vertically from the bottom to the top of the page, three holes on top.
† Written below the line.
‡ Unless noted, entries on the following pages written horizontally, from top to bottom, three holes to the left.
§ Entry written in black ink.

~~Perish and shine yes shine by perishing~~
Immortal bard and may your will be done
~~May the republic perish like the sun~~
May I both shine and perish like the sun
Perish and shine yes shine by perishing
Perish like you and me and everything[5]

In imitating the Greeks we are not really imitating the Greeks who imitated no one; we are imitating the Greeks' first imitators the Romans.

Two Paranoids Begins with elderly psychiatrist asking his young wife at the breakfast table in the presence of his son by an earlier marriage if she remembered playing the game of {Proteus} What-would-you-do-to-Catch-me. "Yes let's play it now" "Did you call it Proteus?" What does Proteus mean?" A man who can change into anything he pleases to get away as and tease with the shiftiness of his argument. Not a communist but something no

[3r]   The epic could be based on ~~the~~ {our} strange beliefs comparable to the ancient ones Herodotus tells of.[6]

A saint spends his whole effort either (1st) in trying everything short of suicide to ~~keep~~ {get} out of the way and undo the original sin of having been born or (2nd) in allaying the pain and grief men cause each other by the aggression of having been born

School objects: the difficult one of giving pupils ~~the~~ time to mediate. the still more difficult one of making then see what would be a real deed in their subject comparable to winning a game in sports. Object in life is to win-win a game with the play of a poem

~~The one first of honest memory the~~
~~One was of honest memory and one of sainted~~
Chaucer and Langland were contemporary
But one was so intolerant and sainted
~~The other so~~
But Chaucer was too blent of grave and merry
And Langland so intolerably sainted
Small wonder if they never got acquainted.

[4r]*   What's the connection between quality and quantity? There must be one. It is suggested in such a name for a ruler as Artisto-demos. Quality is justice and strength, but quantity can surpass a point where it becomes strength too and justice if it knows what's good for itself ~~had~~ will weaken down to quantity in the same of mercy till some sort of valance is attained between the few and the many.[8] ~~Quality~~ It behooves quality to keep quantity there as reservoir ~~to renew~~ from which to renew itself perpetually.

[5r]   The Dream Killer

1)   His head is on her shoulder. She turns her head away. She says I wouldn't!

2)   He warns her of death in six months. She is silently disapproving of such talk. She is not to be moved.

3)   Crushed to her conformation in all its freshness.

4)   Walking along somewhere. He remembered proof that she must have loved him

[6r]   It had to be accepted that he was worthless and the start made from there.

Undeniably a puzzle for her.

Suggested to her that she better try to love someone more satisfactory. Everyone saw how admirable she was and knew of him as her misfortune.

Scraps of poems. (Voice of long long afterward Dont see how she ever knew with the little there was to go on.

Dark darker darkest.[9]

Pressure on each other. She never ~~put~~ was to put pressure on so hard again. Having pressed him to be sensibly useful and failed to make him change she was ever after on the side of staying useless.

He had told her in a play of fancy once that where lovers paired one turned his back on heaven one turned her back on the world. He was always

---

* Page written in black ink.

to feel that he had turned his on heaven in making her throw away her judgment. He repented a little and thought of heaven sometimes in later life. She
recovered her woman's practical judgement a little toward the end and with
it her power to criticize others at least for not living logically on a sound
financial basis. She refused to be told the governments reckless spending beyond its means was the same as his early indifference in the wherewithal. She
bitterly hated on bitter [?clock] and the sweet president.

[7r]*   Mine enemy has said I have a theory about the sound of sense[9] in poetry. I
have no such thing. {It is his mistake.} There is such a thing as the {a} sound
of sense over and about the sound {of the harmony or inharmony} of the
vowels and consonants {of {the} words, and their harmony and unharmony}
{that make up a sentence.} And there is such a thing as vocal imagination. in
a sentence. The vocal imagination commands it and lives on it. All would
agree no one could be {no} a dramatist who who who had not {could exist
without} the vocal imagination to command it and to involve it {in the context of the} not too ambiguously in the {his} context.[11] I have added nothing
to this except to confess that for me no one can {has} be{en} a poet or even
prose writer who did not command it. In the briefest the slenderest lyric poet
poem even where there is only one character speaking the sentences must
spring away from each other an talk to each other {like repartee} if my interest is to be held. They They must Somewhere in middle life I found on looking back that {I had been rejecting writers}the my rejection had been chiefly
from discouragement with the the literature I had be rejecting had been

[7v]   from discouragement with its a monotony that furnished {provided} me
with nothing to do with my voice but to intone.[12] I speak of my reading
rather than of my writing. I never got far with a poem that offered me no escape my {the} reading voice no escape from the sameness of the meter. I
don't care how much meaning it was loaded with. In fact I sometimes doubt
if I value meaning except as it the sentences act up throws the sentences in to
group relations like the characters in a play and makes them act up with
spirit. More than anything else {That any way is the sup} I have loathed
{loathed in verse free or regular} the rolling sonorousness of straight on sentences about as structural as earth worms [illegible] of earth worms [illegi-
ble] like structure {logey with descriptions} about nature and the weather.

---

* Entries on this page are written vertically from top of the page to bottom, three holes on
top.

They have the structure {and charm} of earthworms placed end for end. {Undeniably} The tone of matter of fact statement is one tone. ~~And it wont bear frequent repetition in the same place~~ {But} A whole composition cannot be made out of it. ~~I should append~~ A poem is not a string but a web: It is like sapling. Set it out-and watch it ramify and proliferate

There anyway meaning attains its height reaches its supreme height*

[*8r*]   It may as well be confessed we democrats[13] ~~have alw~~ secretly or openly have always believed in slavery. And maybe we are right {in this}, and the sentimentalism of the last two hundred years has been wrong in abolishing slavery. Civilization is a partly artificial condition, but it must never become too artificial or it will break down: and it is probable that an entirely slaveless society is too artificial to be healthy {persist}. The present ~~throes~~ social throes {the world over} are no doubt ~~of~~ {toward} a return to ~~nature and~~ the facts of nature in respect to slavery. Some nations unable to ~~take~~ find satisfaction in half measures must needs go back to complete slavery under a despot. They will know their grounds if they have to build allover again from the ground up. They achieve a certain quick clarification we onlooking Americans may well envy. We listen indulgently to their talk of freedom in slavery. There is always freedom in chains where there is consent to chains. The fullness of consent is the measure of freedom. The relief of

[*8v*]   the course they have taken is a great temptation to the spirit.* I am persuaded we will not follow them in it more than part way. But if we think not to follow them at all it will from stubborn unwillingness to face the statistics of the statisticians.[14]

For us these {statistics} are that out of one hundred and ~~thirty~~ {sixty} millions of our people ~~from~~ ten ~~to~~ {or} fifteen millions may hence forth be expected to be entirely taken care of ~~by our government~~ as paupers by our government. The figures are not mine. I take them on faith from the benefi~~cient~~{volent} social branches of the government office. I am enough of a New Englander to be distressed by them but enough of a Democrat {in all my antecedents} to seize on them as new evidence on the side of the proslavery position.

·   ·   ·

---

* Written up left side of page, bottom to top.

Any vigorous society in the freeplay of its energies must apparently have be expected to show a constant elimination in to the poor house not to mention the jail and insane asylum.[15]

[9r]   *Slavery has been kept out of their system too long. They crave too much of it at once. They have been badly off – They are starved for it.

[10r]   The profit motive must be taken out of us-the greed as Pan took drew the pith from the reed to make an artist out of a man.[16]

[10v]   We can only blind ourselves to this to our cost and by {by} put{ting} off the day of reckoning suffer in the end like China for deceiving herself about the facts of force. Ten million at the lowest on our present accumulation of human waste.[17] We have that to go on in our future undertaking. It has come too much to be ignored I agree. The question is what in the large to do about it.

One possibility is to remake our society with the poor in mind so as not to embarrass the {our} poorest {none} {no one}* in possessions position or pride. It has been thought of. All needed is legislation that shall forbid anyone to do the best he can anymore. At the dictates of the heart we can promise not to try too hard. We can try easy. A little control or much control. Teachers have already been forbidden to fail the good for nothing adolescent out into the industries {or army}. Scale standards

[11v]   down to the meanest abilities and virtues. {There shall be no more hindmost and as there long since ceased to be any devil to take the hindmost.}

It sounds humane, but if I know the breed it will refuse arrest at {this or any} any point of its development. It has the ruthlessness for its own salvation. Everywhere in all parties one hears the new brag: Who's afraid to be dangerous? What is dead will be cleanly cut off and the living part will go on with life. Brotherhood where brotherhood becomes us but unsparing rivalry somewhere still as in the whole history of mankind. Our On with this {the} great strife with its chances of loss and total loss lest victory should cease to have a {lose its} meaning. I speak not as of what should be, but will what will be since men are men. They are not going about themselves to the level of

---

* Written below the line.

the pitiable-Either out of weakening {maudlin} ~~sadness~~ or out of resentment toward God for the Lay out or terms of the contract.

You cant tell me the great play isnt going on regardless of some irreparably hurt sensibilities*

[12r]   Those ten million are not going to be allowed to drag down the whole structure with them. They are going to be set apart and handled apart. Protection is their first demand on our sympathy. They shall have ~~that~~ mercy. They shall have the kind of mercy that misusers of words and losers of distinctions nowadays call ~~social~~ justice-social justice.[18] They shall have their protection from want. But no protection without direction. {Big business went to Congress for protection}[†] So much protection must expect a great deal of direction. We will be firm and they must submit to those who know what is good for them. Once wholly protected and directed – that is the definition of a slave. Let us not gag at words. Remember that freedom is not incompatible with slavery. The amount of consent is the measure of freedom in chains.

We have them again self produced with every ~~thing~~

[12v]   sentiment in the world [~~illegible~~] against their ever reappearing. All that remains is to determine how they shall be held en mass by the federal government collectively so to speak like a ~~utility~~ public utility or in severalty by individual owners. I know at least one kind farmer who ~~could~~ would take two and their families. ~~I woul~~ He would have to ask for a good deal of authority over them but I am sure of his essential kindness. I am sure he would treat them better than any ~~govern~~ impersonal government task master. I can imagine his growing very fond of them.*

It should be appended that this slavery will have ~~the~~ in advantage ~~of~~ over the old slavery of the south ~~in that~~ in being white slavery out of which children can always emerge into the master class on proof of character and genius. It will be like the slavery of Greece and Rome. Race prejudice

•   •   •

---

* Written up left side of page, bottom to top.
† Written in left-hand margin.

As foster parents grow fonder of adopted grandchildren than nurses can of orphans in an orphanage.*

[13r]   wont make the insuperable barrier it did between white and black. The mistake of the south was in not enslaving of their own race. But regrets are vain at this distance of time. The south paid for its mistake in blood and is still paying.

The argument is incontrovertible if the statistics it rests on are sound. You are free to hope it is a Must we reorganize then society {then} on an assumption of ten million permanently paupers you are free to hope the number is a goddam exaggeration. We talk of freedom and it is being taken away from us You are still free to hope not too publicly that the number ten million is a

It is interesting to remember that the paupers of a town used to be sold annually to the highest bidder for what {work} could be got out of them above {the cost of} their bed and board.

"Every mans home his own poor house"

[13v]†   A man is better than anything he can name the faults in {he knows whats the matter with}

Isnt there anything you would like to escape yourself. – yes the inessential. – Do you escape it? Not very satisfactorily. – But better than some of the rest of us. Better than some, but worse than some: which pretty well determines my rank and condition in life.

[14r]‡   (Summer) School of the Essay

Not to be a specialist. A little goes a long way

All you remember of some shapely book is some inaccountable detail of physical intensity. Never mind. It is enough for your purpose: all you ask of teacher or book. You will do your own putting of such scraps together.

·   ·   ·

---

* Written in left-hand margin and meant to be inserted after asterisk above.
† Entries are written vertically, top to bottom.
‡ Entries are written horizontally, top to bottom, with three holes on left-hand side of paper.

Symbolic teaching. Express the symbol and leave it. You have to be careful not to perform the same act {of teaching} twice. What did you mean that exercise to teach.

[14v]

earth quake country
unsettled government
<u>all</u> drunk without exception

There Is No Escape

It is desirable that the stage floor should have at least two motions. One bodily up and down, the other see-saw from front to back or from end to end; and that some small pieces of furniture such as smoking stands be left foot loose to tip over ~~as often~~ and roll around as often as stood ~~up~~ on one end.

~~First~~ {T̶h̶e̶ A} Mate Nothing can be ~~determined~~ {decided} till the Captain gets here, but I am very sure he will tell you there is no escape.

The Critic No escape. That's bad news if true. {Listen boys and girls} The comrade here claims to have it from the Captain that there is no such thing as escape.

Mate if you please
~~What's the difference~~
Comrade – mate. What's the difference? Both suggest

[15r]   brotherhood.

But in an entirely different world order. We are now on our tenth {people} revolution {of the masses} if I have kept the count correctly. You must [illegible] ~~keep~~ {bring} your nomenclature up to date.

I simply cant {afford to} have it in my situation that there is no such thing as escape. Come into a ring all you arrested development ~~speak your minds~~ say what you think.

Have it out with the Captain.

.   .   .

You are virtually saying there are no life boats

Thats what it comes to – no life boats that are sea worthy

Why every criticism I ever wrote was based on the idea of escape and here
I am caught where I am told there is no such thing {as escape}. Ill wait and
hear what he Captain has to say.

Here comes the Captain. He enters a small pale frail man

[16r]   and {with a forehead three stories high but} without uniform and without
{or} pretention and takes his seat sideways to the company as if it might embarrass him to be consulted as an authority.

[17r]   I can remember the date almost to a day when I determined to stop reading the {city}* exposure by Lincoln Steffens[19] and his kind. I could see that
since it I was never going to do anything about them it could only go on with
them for the sensational sensation I got out of superiority to politicians big
business men and other voting Americans in general they gave us. I was not
going to have time to be a reformer. It was going to be bad for my will to get
angry fresh every month at conditions on which I never could hope to act.

Crudity[20]

Crudity and why I like it. Man that asked How much a piece do you get for
your books {Mr F}? Why Mr. Poole[21] gets two dollars. Man who said Hell my
wife writes that stuff (And it was true) Telegraph operator who said you
write? "Yes." Poetry? – Your just the person I wanted to find I lost my father
about a year ago and I'd like to get poem written about him. (Taking paper
and pencil) I'll tell you what I want said. Some one out of everything thats
best Harvard, New York, the best {rich} {high} society and literature came
along way to ask me to write something really American to save America. He
was sure I could write something really American if I tried, Crude

Senator and the Dianner on Madison Square Garden[†] [22]

---

* Written in margin.
[†] Entry written in the margin up the left side of the page, top to bottom.

[*17v*]   Long since dealt with.

all of them. But I like crudity. I thank the Lord for crudity which is rawness which is raw material, which is the part of life not yet worked up into form or at least not worked all the way up. We [illegible] meet with another fallacy of the foolish: having had a glimpse of finished art, they forever after pine for a society that shall be nothing but finished art. Why not a world safe for good government and art all things perfectly accomplished. An artist is a~~brute~~ ~~who~~ delights in roughness for what he can do to it. He's the brute who can knock the corners off the marble block. So also is the statesman [illegible] politician, only [illegible] the statesman works in a more protean mass of material that hardly holds any shape long enough for the craftsman to point it out and get credit for it. His material is a rolling mob The poets material is words that for all we say and feel against them, are more manageable than men. You get a few words alone in a room and with plenty of time on your hands you can do almost your will on them.

and drag the imbedded beauty out of bed.*

[*1r*]†   Commencement address [illegible] give to a class that had been educated? on the facts select? of our disappointing civlization. To the hundred in the class the actuarial statistician from Hartford spoke warily on the certainty that twenty five percent of them wold be dead in twenty five years.[23] Countless figures went to prove it. It was a thought for the day. Let them live with it. Cast your accusing eyes one upon another, said the orator, The very one who in assurance of his [illegible] believes himself least likely to be among the fallen ~~is~~ may be the most likely. Memento mori. At the dinner in the evening some irresponsible laugher ventured to show how little such facts signified to any but insurance companies and perhaps governments. Facts of the individual facts of the group. A doctor loses me—not to another doctor. He loses me to death. He comforts himself with remembering that I am but

[*2r*]‡   one of a hundred cases he has treated and he sleeps well on a percentage basis. But what is only a one percent loss to him is a hundred per cent loss to me

---

* Entry written in the margin up the left side of the page, top to bottom.

† This is the first page of material that is still in the ring binder. This page is written in very faded pencil.

‡ Page written in pencil.

– a total loss. And it is not much better if the loss is of the child I love best. I say perhaps the government should see chiefly the facts of death as the doctor and patient see them. What is all to one individual and nothing to another individual must be taken into account in the making of laws.

[*3r–5r*]   [blank]

[*6r*]   The Dictatorship of the Proletariat[24]

It may be this is it. It may well [illegible] be. It would of course come in a new guise in speaking a new language. It wouldnt declare itself openly because it couldnt. It wouldnt recognize itself any more clearly than we recognized it. No one can name [illegible] {in time} a sure sign by which to know it. [illegible] Men will be have suspicions and then will dismiss their suspicions as unworthy of the liberal mind.

Liberalism[25] is virtue at its most charming {amiable} point of relaxation. As it slowly comes round to the point on the dial every thought is taken to hold {pin} it there. Liberty must not become license but what liberal conscience wants the job of censor to keep it from becoming even licentiousness? The liberal feels a sheepishness a squeamishness about imposing discipline and punishment. Leave it to the sheriff and leave the sheriff out of good society. There is no one to check the child or the devil.

It is not written in the stars that

[*7r*]   the forms of government should be made to stand still in their circling any more than the stars themselves. There has been absolute authority easing off into limited authority and from there into the pleasant fancy that there is no discipline but self discipline.

Submissive is too crude a word to be said often said. No If a book seems immoral that is a defect that corre will correct itself. After all what are morals but [illegible] fashion [illegible]. There is no commandment but story upon story has been written to show cases where it has been and should have been violated. Well then!

From the rule of one over all and the principles handed down from God, government has run on the logic [illegible] to where it is asked why should the people if they know what they want not take fresh votes daily to order their affairs. The literature was thought of. Legislation should originate with the people. There should be a referendum before any law goes on the books. Their representatives should be act in office always with a rope around one leg

[8r]   so that they can be yanked from the rostrum. From having been master, the nominal authority has become a slave without authority. His vote is to count as one vote like mine or yours. That is mob rule and the next station on the way we are always traveling.

But happily or unhappily we our journey is circular.[26] We are getting back to things we [illegible] Never mind for the present by what process of reasoning we are getting back to something we have lived before. Chaos the mob itself if you listen to its clamor can be heard calling for order. It wants someone to stay sober or get sober to take care of its drunkenness. Its great heart comes to its rescue with its need for someone to love – a hero. He has got to be godlike. We see him coming. Kind but terrible. Just before {first and then} merciful. The dictator. The absolute authority with no answerability but to God which is another name for the highest in himself. For the next phase consent is at its lowest in government. Having been so much entirely consent that there was nothing to which to consent, it is now practically consentless. Any thing you say O Lord

[9r]   All we ask is bread and circuses.[27] But if he is a great ruler he will cure them of that rotten flesh. They will be whipped into hard words and hard natures once more. If may be after dark ages of slaughter when where only enough people will be left for seed. {with the incentive to sow it.} The worlds great cycle begins anew in simple morals true relationships and the rigorous joys.

The {cool} vision is a very attractive in this hour of hot decadence. The money men the pleasure men the thought men {the work men} have passed beyond liberty and are sick of where they find themselves. In regions w not yet unionized the work men frankly admit they cant be expected to be any good any more till they have union discipline and union bosses over them. Their liberal government and liberal employers are too weak for their to [illegible] com command their respect. They crave stiffening from some where else.* This is the rising note that will save us by bringing us mercifully soon into the despotism that begins it all over again

We are that in nature that catches on anything to resist itself. [28]

---

* Written up left side of page, bottom to top.

[10r]*   Happy drama that has a refuge from science and scholarship in the theater where nobody can approach it except as a play for pleasure. Poetry has the advantage of no such public place. It has the home – is perhaps on better than even terms with drama there. And in America it has a glimmer of new hope in the restoration of the ancient guild of wandering bards. School might be thought of as a resort of the muses, but only by a calamitous mistake. ~~Scho~~ The higher the school the more it is wanted for scholarship. No one ~~wo~~ would dispute the claims of scholarship

As to the way the mistake has {almost insensibly} been made. We go to school to learn to read. (What it is to learn to read will be gone into {in full} else where. Among other things ~~it~~ {and} in passing it is ~~to take our necessary translations with dissatisfaction~~. To be {made} rather miserable over all translations however necessary; and ~~to be~~ suspicious of any ~~report~~ {speech} {anything} oral or written unless sure of ~~the way~~ {how} it is said) We go on to college to be given ~~an~~ a ~~further~~ {another} chance to learn to read in case we havent learned ~~to read~~ in school. But there should be a warning posted. {It has been found} there is an ~~increasing~~ attendant danger increasing every step of advance that we shall learn to study

[11r]   what was only meant to read. And then and there the terrible penalty is we shall never {again as now†} have as raw pleasure again (as Sarah said) in the Ode that Keats wrote to Autumn - or that Shelly wrote to the West Wind. In getting over our ignorance we shall have lost our innocence. So ~~dreadful for us as individuals~~. But dread as {is} the fate [illegible] for the individual it is worse for the nation. From having acquired the habit of ~~re~~studying what was ~~onl~~ written only to read ~~by our next~~ the next we know we shall have to find ourselves writing what was only meant to study. {Must} ~~Literature age[s] a much admired state of needing to be annotated. Is literature to be admired for its need of annotation~~. {the last have to trump may as well blow} ~~Will {Must} we {it} wait for age to give it that charm easily. For us~~ For   It is as if we would try our hand at giving literature the {instant‡} charm of annotation that ~~time {age}~~ {time} alone {was} had ever given it before. Nothing so ~~admired~~ {admirable} as what has aged into [illegible] ~~a line or of text to~~ two lines of blank verse to the rest of the page full of notes.

---

* Entries on this page are written vertically, from top to bottom.
† "again as now" written in black ink.
‡ "instant" written in black ink.

[12r]   He begins anywhere he please and doesnt care where old age may find him.*

           We are on such terms of amiable insult ~~that~~ I hope that you wont mind if I
become your Bently for the

           I dont know how it is overseas where my mother came from, but I am not
of those who like to make an imaginative horror of the abyss that yawns between individuals and ~~peoples~~ {nations}. I like to think that in both good and
bad tendencies ~~we~~ {America and Britain} keep pretty well along side ~~of each
other~~ first one a little ahead and then the other perhaps like [illegible] right
and left foot. {We are on terms of amiable insults I hope} The scholarship I
somewhat grudgingly yield the schools to many ~~have begun with~~ {blame
your} Bentley {for}. I would supposed to ~~know~~ say {Mind you} I admire ~~it~~ [il-
legible]?. Great it is and may inherit it {up all} the earth but the wild hearths
and deserts ~~and~~ {dancing grounds} for [illegible] such dancers as hardly {need
to} touch the earth. The reader (not student) skips lightly from poem to
poem or rather ~~lightly~~ about among the poems. He reads ~~one~~ {Aye} the
better to read Dee (the River) the better to read Aye (eternity) again. Since it
is not a {course or} progress in poetry but a circulation among poems. He
doesn't move through friendships or rise on skipping stones of {his} dead
loves, he lives among friends. He may widen the circle and he may have to
keep moving lazily to hold the circle open.

[13r]   Some of my best friends are pedants. Henry L. Mencken ~~is~~ {'} one of the
best of my best, ~~And he~~ seems of set purpose to want to scare me ~~to~~ in thinking the abyss ~~of~~ has widened ~~on beyond communication~~ out of all communications between the American and English languages.[29] His ~~insight~~ book ~~is to~~
on the subject looks ~~so~~ {as} as mightily {inclusive} ~~I feel sure at times anything I~~ say ~~this must be hell nor am I out of it. I feel as if it feels like~~ {as}
doom. Which this is Hell nor am I out of it.[30] He probably speaks the American language. I have to admit I am perfectly at ease talking with him. {Then}
it must be I speak ~~and write~~ the American language. If I speak it I'm sure I
write it I have ~~never~~ tried to keep my speaking and writing {close} together.
~~The~~ All right then lets abide by the consequences. I am probably so far
gone that I cant understand a word an British book says any more. The
only trouble with that conclusion is I ~~read~~ {mix} all sorts of American and

---

* Written up left side of page, bottom to top.

British books and am perfectly unconscious of any difference in language between in them. A Briticism now and then that I am aware of and an Ameri-
canism

[14r] that I practice myself, but nothing I don't enjoy adjusting to my ingenuity in
adjusting to as in Baris or Burns or Harris.

[15r]   What is it to be a common fellow It is to imagine all sorts of exaggerations
about the manners and customs of the rich aristocratic or merely refined.

Utopia is the mirage arising from all the frustrated farm dreams of city
men Country people are never Utopian. Women are never Utopians.[31] Neither women nor country men waste their time over seed catalogues they
never cant act on.

A west wind made this day
With puffs of white cloud flying
Blanched tree leave turned away
And blackened tree trunks drying

A west wind after rain

[16r]   A Stone a Knife a Hankerchief[32]

There are straight runs like the one that begins in the God Saint and martyrdom, goes on to heroism and success, to power next and the power to do
things worthy of the Gods memory, to be dress beautifully and build beautifully, and so on to modest celebrations and from those to splendid celebrations. But dress processions and architecture and art are wealth which are
no less wealth for having been insensibly arrived at and not thought of as
wealth. {Spiritual} Success and power have found their worldly home in the
treasury. The power to forgive sins against God is a commodity that can be
exchanged for money to maintain God on earth. The end is corruption disso-
lution and the abyss. I dont say religion is on such a run. There might be such
a thing as its being. I am no judge of what is in political situation or human
character. I would not be sure of a crisis if I saw one – nor of a villain. But I
can describe what a villain would be like and I could work one in a story or
not of play

[*17r*]   where I could have my own way with him and hold him to the idea.

    And then there are circular runs like the stone the knife the hankerchief of the Japanese game. The stone is better than the knife because it can dull the knife, the knife is better than {the} handkerchief. The handkerchief ~~because~~ is better than the stone because it can cover the stone. And so on round and round. A College beats B College in football, B College beats C College and then C College beats A College. Nowhere can man seem to check himself in these circulations I am not sure that my first example is not one of circularity too, the God Saint to corruption and the need of another God Saint crying as of old to begin with in the wilderness. No logic runs away into nothingness. The mind of man is an unvicious circle that no desperation can break through. Knowledge is the same.* We get a slight hold on our first poem the better to understand ~~or~~ {our} second, the better still our third and so on till we are back with all our experience of poetry on a day the better to understand our first poem.

The circularity of the mind {the shape of the brain pan} makes the universe look circular a circle that because closed looks finite.*

[*18r*]   Space is said to be circular. I dont know whether it is or not. I suspect the curvature of the mind {which makes us reason always in a circle} would make the universe look curved even in its straightest lines.[33] ~~With~~ Some telescope will be strong enough for us to look at our own back hair.

    A fellow ought to be careful how he uses some of these words and phrases he has just picked up from other people.

    A time for criticizing each others opinions of what money is for.[†]

    ~~Don~~ A fellow ought not to be careless with some of the ideas he picks up now a days. The people that got them up make no claim that they are fool proof.

    Plato and Emersons belief that everything we have is an imperfect copy of

---

* Written up left side of page, bottom to top.
† Two lines in this sentence, downward into one, form an arrow pointing at the last word of the last sentence on this leaf, "money."

a perfect model in heaven. A man womans husband is an imperfect copy of another womans husband[34]

The ever normal granary—one for wheat one for corn etc. One for every thing – money

[19r]   The Man Who Gets Talked About

_____

A rereading confirms me in the belief that the New Testament is the poor man's book and that Christ is the poor mans God[35] and that only as the rich man qualifies when all is said an all the returns are in as a poor thing [illegible] has the book, or the God anything to say to him. The poor the unpretentious the ineffectual and the whipped. We are all but varying degrees of the same poor thing. We are Gods lavish expenditure in a task beyond us an our full understanding and all but beyond him. We have our part in it through him alone.

                          Roughing It[36]

A poem about her father. Tell you what I want said.   Ganesville Tel & Tel

Poem about America Tell you what I want said. Hagedorn[37]

_____

Marceline Cox. Richmond Indiana. She had just had a story "accepted" by the Ladies Home Journal.[38]

[20r]   Liberalism is virtue at its most charming point of relaxation. Virtue spends like another stream. It is going outward into evil*

When electricity from rain water going back to sea takes {extracts} nitrogen and all the rest of our sustenance out of the air we can consider ourselves air plants. Thats where we are going to end up – flying and living on air.

                     •   •   •

_____

* Phrase "into evil" written in pencil.

Whats the constitution between friends the old time Democrat asked. The New Democrat says Whats the Constitution between friends of the poor?[39]

The climax of structural thought and life is nearly reached. One piece more inserted will [illegible] us all together in perfection. You might think so.

Life pretty much always admits of our throwing off minor forms like baskets poems gardens and families. It must be from our success with these we get the illusion that a master politician could make one form of life. A tyrant almost can*

[*21r*]   I'll thank the environment for giving me now and then something I couldnt make up. (invent)

{Dale Carnegie}† How to Make Out Not [illegible] Worry Your Friends[40]

By his trios (sets of three) in talk shall ye know him.[41]

The Thing how as felt {as you feel it} and as you manage to get round it in words spoken or written

See it

Most people cant nail what flits by cant tell how they feel about it and {or} haven't the masterful will to get round it in expression

Think the book—think about the book.

Think the life—think about the life

Equalitarian in feeling most comfortable. And wanting to spend most of my time with people I can treat as equals.[42]

Also by their haste to know whether your remark is meant to be for or against your subject.‡

---

* "A tyrant almost can" written in pencil.
† Written in left-hand margin.
‡ Entry written in black ink.

W Stupidity is shown by most people in their disposition to have it settled at once whether they are better or worse than you are.

Equality is like the meeting of two pin points in mid air.

[*21v*]   It blew three days with a gale from south south east
The gale that ~~blew~~ had blown with rain from the south ~~south~~ {of} east
Was blowing back from the ~~north north west~~ {opposite point} increased
So that we thought this time ~~the woods would~~ it would break the trees
{So that} The clouds ~~replaced were leaving in their wake~~ {dispelled} {that
were driven were leaving in their wake}
T

[*22r*]   12,000000,000
                                                    _____
                                                            290

Theres just going to be one little weak spot where we can break through into the future and one of the surest ways to go about funding it is {to} become an authority on all the solid frame or wall where ~~we havent chance~~ our full strength hasnt a chance of butting through

This is one of the kind of ideas it takes time to get used to My plan would take the shame out of ~~charity~~ {the dole} by forcing everybody rich or poor to accept five {3.} dollars a week out of the national treasury from ~~the~~ his twentieth year till the end of his life. The policy is old that no one shall be impoverished below a certain depth. The administration would be very simple and inexpensive. The outlay rather large—say 12.000 000 000 twelve billion a year. Everybody in the income tax class could be required to give theirs back. [~~illegible~~]

Broke into loud dissatisfaction

You must ~~at~~ love your enemies at home at least better than your enemies abroad or it ends the nation[43]

[*22v*]

Writing must disappear as speech becomes more far reaching. What four thousand years of thinking in printed and written symbols has done to the mind. It has brought out a kind of thinking that can only be deliberate. It has held thought in position to be [illegible] revised and tinkered.

They are sure to go too far with this taking from the rich because it is so pleasant for everybody but the rich—and the rich are in the minority Just what reco is supposed to recommend them: their tenderer hearts toward the poor or their more ingenious minds in word construction.—Both!!

Scotching {to men's} ability may give more pain in the world than starving the poor. It will be hurting the better to relieve the worse. It will be taking the pain from the less feeling part to inflict it on the more feeling part—possibly

I hate the poor dont you? Yes and I hate the rich too. I hate them both the poor as such and hate the rich as such.

[23r]

What song the Siren sang[44]

To all

When you get down to the poverty of a place like China you expect less honesty. The poor Coolie carrying coal in a basket on his back has to submit to having it sprayed with color so he will be found out if he steals so much as a lump of it. The poor are too poor to be good. — And it has been established in our time that the rich are wicked. Nothing is left but the middle to seek virtue in. But the middle are the middle classes {the comfortable and secure} that have been universally damned as the villains of the piece under the name of Burgeoisie. One gives it up in weariness. Saying {they are} all are equally bad is the same as saying they are equally good.[45] We are nowhere after our mental effort.

I have just thought of it afresh (I must have thought of it before) that the poor might bes best be helped if left to themselves to pick up the crumbs of as usual while the enterprising go one with the big adventure of better and better victuals and better and better crumbs.

[24r]

A mistake [illegible] to suppose you can let the mind free all over at once. If you want it to jet you must arrange school so that it will the mind will be actually under pressure except at one or two {chosen} points of release such as in—House or in some writing seminars.

Desiring this mans art and that mans scope[46]
Whitman went in for scope; Poe for art.   Landor[47]

How to take a ~~poet~~ poem

Poe Longfellow Whittier[48] ~~and~~ and Emerson and Sill[49]   How to take a joke. How to take a hint and not to take one when none is intended.[50]

Doctors Directions (mental cases)

Make the patient think he is treating you

Say yes to anything the patient says and then add "not exactly" and finally "not at all."

Family relations teacher gets them ready to find a modus after love is spent. Never occurred to her to prepare them for the sequel phases of love. How to go phasing calmly along to the end. How to go phasing unfrightened through the years of life—and love.

[24v]

The saddest is not to see the poor longing for what they cant have: but to see a poor child happy in the possession of some thing too trifling for any-body else to want. When it is a grown woman it is worse When it is a man it is worst of all. It is a sight to make me willing to bring down the universe in ruins—in carnage.

I hate the poor dont you Yes and I hate the rich. I hate them both as such.

Why do I hate them. Because they bother me so. I have to think of them when there are so many other things I want to think of

The religious fear I have of deadening in anyone what is so soon to die anyway.

[25r]

The Man that Gets Talked About

A grocery store {edge of a small town} just after closing time ten o'clock Saturday night. There is a great pot bellied stove toward the ~~right~~ {left}, a latched and bolted heavy double door with {windows out} with curtains drawn down {over them} at the right, and a long counter and row of shelves with goods across the back. The young grocer is setting things in order for over Sunday His wife is counting money from ~~the~~ a ~~till on~~ cash register on the counter into a bag. A young Doctor in hat and overcoat sits in a comfortable chair ~~facing the~~ {his} face to {the} stove his back to the double door. He picks his chair up without getting out of it and moves back from the heat of the stove. The young grocer comes and sits standing against the front of the counter to talk:

Look Doc I wish I could spring it on you in a sudden flash the way it came over me the other day. First look at the universe.

Big and getting bigger every day as the telescopes get bigger.

And then look at the size of the world in comparison the only ~~spot~~ dot where in astronomy where anything like us

[26r]

has got so much as a toe hold. So far as we know. Can you think of any ~~object~~ {purpose} in the universe more important than to keep the human race going on this planet. ~~We sh~~ It makes all our other interests seem insignificant. {Cant we sink our differences in that} How can we forget it for a moment to quarrel {about trivialities} and run the risk of ~~our own destroying~~ {destroying} not each other but ourselves as a whole race.

I guess we're in easier circumstances than ~~you you imply. You cant worry me into brotherhood work on my imagination to worry me with~~ I d have to see the end of the [illegible] human race more imminent than it is before I'd let myself be worried into brotherhood with three people I ~~know~~ could name. Suppose you have stated the great common cause namely ~~to stay one~~ to maintain the race on earth. Its too easy to worry much about.

Another ~~wa~~ world war like the last one could go a long way toward wiping us out.

Id be willing to bet that after the worst you can imagine, ~~getting swiped by a planets tail~~ a planets tail swiping us, an earth quake that would make

(over

[*26v*]*

land sea and the sea land, another hundred years war,[51] there would still be enough of us in the crevices for seed and enough incentive to sow the seed.

[*27r*]†

Few will dare or deign to dispute that the {prime} object of composing poetry is to ~~make~~ keep any two poems from sounding alike to keep intonations from being worked down into the beauty swill by intoning.

It is neither that rhythm nor that meter, but a {distinct} tune arising from the one being struck sharply across the other. Witness all the poems that ever survived their ~~time~~ age.

[*28v*]

The old Latin Greek philosophy history was really vocational for a large part of the students, those who were to be preachers and teachers.

Latin Poetry

Worldly not scholarly
Number of words left natural in accent
Indifferently Latin of any period. Purity no consideration. (I have just learned (January 31 1950) that the earlier Latin poetry was not quantitative but accentual like ours

~~Inten~~ Concentration on the intention dims and distorts everything not in the center of vision Deliberate distortion is an attempt to treat the not central as central. ~~You~~ {Sight} can only be strictly true to one thing at a time.‡

All art begins at the pleasure end and whatever wisdom it may or may not wind up in.[52] The wisdom may be left to your keepers, your friends, and relatives to provide. You can trust them to keep you from falling off a roof or getting into jail Art is the last of your childhood and may be followed somewhat irresponsibly. An artist will say a lot of wise things anyway without trying to be wise.§

---

* Page written in black ink.
† Page written in black ink.
‡ Entry written in black ink.
§ Entry written in black ink.

[29r]

Much as you love your truth you would deceive him to help him. You would let me go rather than deceive me.

Conscience is a pride of the spirit that is always beforehand with {snub-bers} rebukers and punishers. It is out ahead ~~of~~ as sight is ~~out ahea~~ an extension of touch.[53]

To stay so no [~~illegible~~] {rudeness} no neglect intentional or unintentional can bother you that is to be good natured. To be hurt and offended by every least awkward contact with people in word or deed [~~illegible~~] to be touchy is to be spoiled.*

J C Smith[54] asked me to tell him off hand why at a certain point in Shakespeares Julius Caesar you turn over a leaf and find you are with a new Brutus. I failed him then. Only yesterday it occurred to me when thinking of Dante's lowest Hell. He has Brutus there with Judas.[55] Shakespeare was making a fresh estimate of Brutus from Plutarch but he was partly thinking under the influence of the mediaeval Rome of Dante and the Church.

[30r]†

She
~~She had few words~~‡

A man§ looks at a woman and a woman looks at herself in a mans eyes.

A woman wants a man for her train and a man wants a woman for her tail.

Not for what she is to others in public not for what she is to him <u>alone</u> in private, but for the everlasting contrast between the dignity of her worldly front and her abandon to the pleasures of her—That she [~~illegible~~] who stands so straight should lie so cuddled—so huddled to receive.**

---

* Entry written in black ink.
† Page written in pencil.
‡ Struck through entry written in blue ink.
§ Word written in black ink.
** "so huddled to receive" written in blue ink.

[*30v*]

We are bee like fliers between something that was said to us as we left it[56]
Remember me to —Blank. ~~Remem~~ Everything we leave behind asks us to remember it to something else fruitfully.

[*31r*]

Lessons

The unification of knowledge after you get it If you ~~got~~ {received} it unified
it would only be to break it up before you could use it. Facts come to the
mind as stars come out in the {in the evening} sky, scattered broadcast, thin
at first and then thick enough to suggest constellation. The lines X between
them that bring out the figures are ours, ~~and~~ the final and only conscious part
of our world building. A world you didnt make? Yes you did too. There is
proof that ~~you~~ there were countless offerings to the senses that you kept out
unconsciously. One view of science is that all it does is go back and try to do
more than justice to what in nature we consciously or unconsciously though
we didnt want. (If science isnt that the only possible thing it is is domestic science, bent ~~on~~ more or less {directly} on domesticating the universe.[57] It finds
a gas on the sun that will ultimately be used on earth to bring fresh fruit by
balloon for the kitchen.) In my view of it it is a reconsideration of the thrown
away to see if it wont throw some light on the kept. A going over the refuse
heap

[*32r*]

Look Doc here's a funny word (He brings a box round from a shelf and
sets it {up} on the front of the counter) Tenderized
Yes tenderized prunes. I've noticed it.
Theres {We have} a tenderized ham on the market too. I asked the company salesman what the process was. He didnt know
Probably kicking. {The Hams are} the part of ~~the~~ us ~~anatomy~~ that gets
kicked most.
Its a word for the times. Strange that trade should supply it—yet not so
strange ~~since~~ {when you consider} trade supplies everything. Some of the
best figures come out in advertising and trade names. I call it poetry.
I suppose it is a word for the times. We used to have the holier than thou
to put up with. Now it is the tenderer than thou. Hahn hahn you arent as tender as I am, Jooke

There{'s} ~~are~~ going to be a lot of hard [illegible] hearts {in business} tenderized before this movement is over.

Yes and heads too I dont doubt. Beaten to a pulp. I can ~~tell you~~ tell you what the process is. ~~Bea~~ Breaking down the native fibre. ~~Fibre~~ Fibre used to be a word to live by.

[*32v*]

Must maintain the right to be good for nothing I have had to be good for nothing in the past and I may want to be good for nothing again some time.

I wouldnt dare to do away with poverty ~~for fear~~ considering how much we apparently have owed to it. Theres got to be a less to go from to more. We cant help it some get stuck in the less. Some one has to maintain it like a base in the desert.

Not fool proof—some of this new talk you can pick up.

Perfect world of which this is an imperfect copy[58] ~~The pefection A wifes husband is an imperfect~~ The perfection of which

You've got to fix the blame ~~some where~~ {at some place} to work from.

Jane rings the till and speaks against the profit motive.* When it gets so grocers talk thus {un}grossly. ungrossly

The door to the future may be in getting rid of {the} profit motif There must be some door (The door begins to rattle.) Make a door with your head—butt a breach in the wall

Second person I have seen whose Utopia was the farm he always hoped to buy and retire to. "Its got an orchard." Its an old barn Ive got to close Nothing left but the barn. I lost the house

[*33r*]

Have you got any?

Not much. But that's not the point. Dont make it personal

I was just asking. I havent much myself [illegible]

I can see you dont value it much in a man's composition

~~Tender~~

Being tender ~~is going~~ is a virtue thats going to be more insisted on in the style of the immediate future.

~~How tender do you suppose well have to be.~~ Some standard ~~will have~~ have of tenderness will have to be set up. How tender will we have to be? Legal tender?

---

* Arrow from the word "motive" to the sentence above, "you've got to fix. . . ."

The trouble with you Doc: You're too flippant to be swept off your feet and carried away with anything. Youll never find yourself because you cant lose yourself.

Old sayings are wasted on me

I thought you liked old things, you old conservative

Old things but new sayings. I live by the {my} wits.

What doctor doesn't. ~~Your whole profession is as crooked as the~~ [illegible] {You doctors are as crooked as the lawyers.}

We're not talking about the same thing.

All you accuse me of is being so psychological my patients are deceived into thinking I am [illegible] treating them somatically.

[*33v*]

Must be disinterested enough to take your medicine[59]

Not for their sadness ~~for~~ {over} what they lack but their gladness over the little they possess.

Use the poor but dont use them up leave some of them for other ministering angels.

Turning twenty when you'd rather tell than be told

Giving and Imparting {and Pointing Out}

True equalitarian hates to be thrown too much with those rich or poor who cant treat him as an equal.

Free and equally funny[60]

Right to pride of ancestry.[61]

$\begin{cases} \text{Some teach that which they dont know} \\ \text{Some know that which they cant teach} \end{cases}$

Courses that organize what they don't yet know

Give me a great dump of knowledge

•   •   •

Nothing so composing as composition[62]

Traits all taken away by the government and then restored at the government's direction. Prudence etc.

[*34r*]

√ I am an equalitarian protem. I insist on spending [illegible] {[illegible]} {my}* time {being} mostly with my ~~approximate~~ equals. It gives me an advantage ~~I certa~~ for my part dont enjoy to associate with my inferiors ~~or my superiors.~~ Take someone your size I ~~was exhorted when in my youthful encounters~~ heard the big boy exhorted when he picked on the little boy in the school yard.
I hate the poor yes and I hate the rich. I mean I hate them {both} as such.

√ What you are really up to—as in your dealings with the poor. The fear of being in a position from which to be compassionate

√ One of the quality goes over to those of the quantity.

√ Poor on the brain. Any son of a minister will know where it {virtually} says in the New Testament For Christ's sake forget the poor some of the time.[63] Christ didnt write any Gospel. Maybe he couldnt write. And thats why he made his mark with a cross.[64]

√ Take my word for it Sammy[65] the poor as a lump is bad.

√ Whats the constitution between friends. What the constitution between friends of the poor.

No protection without direction. The rich asked for protection and got it for fifty years but look at what they have brought on themselves Not only direction but humiliating investigation. The poor should take warning and not invite protection. (Thats what they took the census† for—to know what to do to the poor. (David got punished for taking a census.[66]

---

* Inserted below the line.
† Phrase from "(Thats" to "census" written in pencil.

[*35r*]

My reason for holding those ~~views~~ {rule} is not because under them I am surer of success

What we do is lost inside of what is being done with us by God and nature {even with all the carefulness of science}

Cui Lumen Ademptum[67]

Lunkheads and Quidnuncheads[68]

	Pure Science
Spiritual	Spiritual too
	Science[†]

Trueness more important than truth

They Dasent (Venture to Say—Make Bold to Say*

Barnums[69] story of faith with out works The clocks his firm sold the Chinese, the Chinese took the works out of to use the cases for shrines for their Buddas

Don't work, worry, I told a class I left to their own devices for a term. I could say that to the strong and well only.

[*36r*]   To a Governor

If only one could find out the connection between the rich and the poor.

It has been found many times in a small way by marriage. The King {Corphetua} marries the beggar maid ~~Corphetua~~[70]

•   •   •

---

* Entry written in black ink.
† Diagram enclosed in a circle.

It is made over and over again by the rise {from} of boys from poverty to riches in half a life time.

But I mean—Is there no standing connection that can be kept standing.

(A good answer is one that holds long enough for the one who makes it to get away from "buts!)

There is no great {permanent} connection but the greatest and longest lasting is the one one achieved by a demagogue who uses the numerousness of the poor to overthrow the rich and rob them of their riches.
(Taxation.)
The demagogue is usually one of the rich {Cleisthenes, Gracchi, Empedocles Roosevelt.}[71] who from sympathy with the poor goes over to their side.

What does he get out of it for himself? A sense of power. Perhaps a throne. A reign. Empedocles got treated as a god for his pains.
Four elections to the Presidency* [72]
The crown is nearer the poor than to the intervening aristocracy. Extremes meet. Every little while the aristocracy get wiped out.†

_37r–45r_]

[blank]

[_46r_]

The measure of your loyalty is the reluctance you feel to give up an attachment for an attraction.[73]

A poem should{nt}‡ mean it should be[74]
  "   "   "   "   it should be mean.

The nearer a deadline is the less my faculties will concentrate to meet it. The only deadline that doesnt throw me off entirely is the indefinitely far off deadline of my own death.   Does that feel any more definite at 78

---

* This entry and the sentence above it that starts "Empedocles" written in black ink.
† This sentence written in the left-hand margin, from bottom to top of the page.
‡ Inserted below the line.

First comes humanity then your country says D. C. P.[75] (everybody writes in initials now) Yes to that order if you let humanity mean as follows: . . . The word humanity may be used to gather into one all those excessions beyond form, the justice beyond the law, the religiousness beyond the church the love beyond the marriage the poetry beyond the verse, the culture beyond the school the patriotism beyond the nation: which same transcendences are always there smoldering dangerous and ready to break into the revolts rebellions and revolutions toward the renewal of form.

[47r]

Every step is a fall forward off one leg in which you catch yourself with the other. You are more aware of it in running {than in walking}. One of the first signs of age is your ~~having~~ {need} to give up running because you dont always catch yourself {in it} anymore.

That there should be a human race is a burst[76] of force so absolutely different from anything else on earth or in the universe that I am too lost in wonder at it for finding fault with the details or questioning its worth. It may exist for the individuals of it to aim each for himself at getting to heaven. That may be its only purpose. But it would seem strange if the burst itself hadnt a destiny of its own that would become more and more apparent. It would be even sad if it was run for the sole purpose of seeing who could get out of it into a better world. Nonsense. I begin to feel sure sending people to Hell and Heaven is our strongest way of saying how good or bad they are when other words fail. We say Go to Hell to [illegible] our enemies and go to Heaven to our friends.

[48r]*

Close scrutiny {~~scrutin~~} is something in itself
We should be willing to be lost for life in

The primal element, the element
Of elements that seem within our grasp
{Beyond the atom and within the atom}
We virtually have it in our hand
And what is it we have? We have the seed
~~That~~ Of all things that contain them all

●   ●   ●

---

* Page written in black ink.

Only invisably in latency.
It is as if the effort we put forth
~~W~~ Was but to hide from our own eyes
   The multiplicity the seed burst into
   Nothing we live with but was in that seed
   Nothing by time can have been added to it
   And our achievement is attuning to it
   Is to blank out all shapes and colors
   That have emerged ~~into~~ {and manifested from it.}*

[49r]

Joe[77] asked me to name the four greats of the last hundred years. I began
with Darwin[78] and when I hesitated over who came next he helped me out
"Werent the others three Jews." I could do it then: he meant Einstein Freud
and Marx. Leaders are as often as not misleaders. Lets take the four in order
backward. Marx whole mind was in a book called Das Capital[79] the only trouble with which was its ignorance of what capital is namely the dollar ahead
in cash or goods or tools. He is all wrong in his decision as to who should
be the keeper of the dollar ahead. Should rulers be accepted who have taken
to themselves arrogated to themselves the position of keeper [illegible] or
should ~~only~~ those only be accepted who have persuaded us to elect them to
office by campaigning every so often in their own praises. Or mightnt it be
best if they had come up this and that way in the tasks and jobs at hand as by
general consent especially of those first over and around them they have
shown merit? Freud ~~was~~ made to much of sex as the ruling passion. It is
much more likely to be grex[80] or minding each others business. ~~More to me~~
~~than my necessary self~~ Some [illegible] child some cause some art some
friend—something more to me than my necessary self I must have to take
me out of myself and keep my out of myself I must have for strength of
spirit and well being.

[49v]†

Einstein has done nothing but harm with the idea that time is nothing but
a fourth dimension of space and so keeps space from having any fixed points
to work from. Nothing abides long enough to own it or love it. The worst of
it is he sets up to speak with the authority of one too mathematical for us to
try him. He is merely once more speculator in the realm of the metaphyiscal

---

* Written below the line.
† Page written in black ink.

he despises. I am glad to hear from behind the curtain he is not a good math-ematician. As for Darwin look at the harm he had done to the mob by giving them reason to think everything in general and particular [illegible] must be growing infinitely. We know no growth that doesnt round out and come to an end. Everything has counter sides that come up opposed like the sides of a vase to complete a symmetry. All The figure of speech is growth. Darwin ex-tended it by stealth into an eternality that has made fools of many. All four of these people leaders have lead us beyond where their figures of speech break down. Psychoanalysis is based on the sores that need opening up and the cuts that need being kept open with a wick in them for purification. Another fig-ure would be the septic tank that purifies itself by being shut in on its dis-eases.

[50r]

The Woman at the Till

Play opens with Ralph going out of the store angrily.

What's Ralph angry about now.

Was anything said?

Nothing special I guess. He's always angry lately.

I cant and I wont stand it.

What about? Nothing?

No something. I can tell you. Don't you notice how often he says Of course and how angrily he says it. Its about all he says—his total vocabu-lary. He hears every one people gradually talking themselves round into truths he would expect them to have been born knowing—too gradually His nerves can hardly stand the silly approach of their approximation. They are like variables approaching a limit that by their own conditions they cant reach or like the analyzed flight of an arrow getting half way there every half of the time.

Pull the curtain down lock the door. This day is declared done. Lets see how we've come out in the money way. She goes behind the counter to the till.

[51r]

[blank]

.   .   .

[52r]*

Have you thought about rewards a young person recently asked me in a tone as if he feared I hadn't at my age and so didn't perhaps realize that the greatest reward of all was my own self approval. I may rest behind iron bars like John Bunyan[81] under condemnation by all mankind and it is all right if I am sure of my truth and sincerity. The trouble is to be sure. A criminal may have his own self respect as well as a saint ~~may~~ have nobodys ~~good~~ approval but his own. A stuffed shirt is the very opposite: he has given up caring what he thinks of himself and lives entirely on what he can make the world think of him.

No matter how a ~~man~~ {artist} fares he must lean pretty heavily on his own judgement for his rating. For twenty years ~~he is respected by the world, then for twenty years he is praise~~ the world neglects him; then for twenty years receives him ~~The~~ It is for him to decide when the world was right.

We can't help wishing there were {some} third ~~thing~~ test of worth beside that of self and others. We think of God as a possibility, and of Time Oh Time whose verdicts mock our own The only righteous judge art those The scientist seems to have an assurance the artist lacks. He has nature to try himself

[52v]†

by. There was a scene in a revue of fifty years ago ~~in which~~ located Hoosic Tunnel.‡ [82]

[53r]§

And Ripton should like to ask him it isn't true that the world is in parts and the separation of the parts ~~isn't~~ is as important as the connection of the parts.[83] Isnt it true that great demand is for good spacing? But now I do not know the number of his mansion where he lives to write him as much as a letter of inquiry. The mansions so many are probably numberless. Then I must leave it to Jack Harnes in Gloucster

[53v]

[blank]

⋅   ⋅   ⋅

---

* Page written in black ink.
† Page written in black ink.
‡ "Hoosic Tunnel" written in blue ink.
§ 53r–60r written up side of page, bottom to top, three holes on top.

[54ʳ]

Charlie Cole[84] and George Whicher[85] and I just back from having inaugu-
rated the first president of a brand new college at Marlboro Vermont The
College is called Marlboro and the president of it is Walter Hendricks of the
Amherst class of 1917. The excuse ofr found another college where there are
already so many is that this one one is a seedling of Amherst and has much in
its beginning to recall the beginning of Amherst. In the address of the occasion Charles Cole [illegible] drew a ~~beautiful~~ {fine} parallel between the tow
beginnings. I always have an ear cocked for stories of the shoestring start.
That's what I read the obituaries in The Times and the Tribune for when I
read them. I like to think such stories are ~~peculiar to our democracy~~ more
common with us than with other forms of government.

Dorothy Canfield Firsher[86] ~~was there~~ our great lady of Vermont our lady
of the manor was there to praise the new institution as

[54ᵛ]

[blank]

[55ʳ]

obviously partaking in simplicity of the classlessness of Vermont ~~society~~
from the earliest times ~~even~~ down through to the present. No one could tell a
teacher there from a student or either of them from a ~~president or~~ trustee.
The new president confirmed her in this belief. It was as he wanted it to be.

For my part I chose my own private thoughts to look on the new ~~founda-
tion~~ establishment as just one more thing ~~to be loyal to for~~ for people to{ belong to}—more and more people in time with more and deeper and deeper
loyalty in the palin every day sense of the word loyalty. I feel free to make the
most speak of{a} ~~the sentiment on an occasion were we are all gathered like
this~~ we are all here to be bathed in.

But if I am not absolutely sure we are not the only ~~society~~ {country} of
the shoe string start so I am not beyond being shaken in my confidence that
we are a classless society. I was given a scare the recently ~~from~~ a letter asking
me in good faith what ~~considered the prev~~ I could say for the present state of
middle-brow literature. That

[55ᵛ]

~~was are reason~~ Middlebrow! that was a new one to me and I am afraid it was
mean to be for my embarrassment. It was as much as to say ~~invidiously~~ you
old [illegible] what of ~~at~~ the level of intellect so to call it where you at which

you vote and peddle rhyme sheets. It was invidious perhaps. Anyway I was chastened it was all to the good. I was chastened {brought up dull in my slang} and put in my place. But I it was better than good: it furnished me a new refrain for a poem some day.

> High brow
> Low brow
> Middle brow
> And no brow[87]

    With acknowledgments to Polybius and Pound {the poem} it would the story of the girl Hannof the Carlingian captured on the coast of West Africa outside the Gates.[88] It would begin:

> She had no brow but a mind of her own
> She wanted the sailor to let her alone
> She didn't like sailors she didn't like men
> They had to shut her up in a pen.
> She was quite untractable quite contrary [b.i.]

[56r]

[blank]

[56v]

> As the nursery rhyme would say of Mary
> That and the fact of her being so hairy
> Made the Carthginian sailors vote I quote
> To skin the poor girl for {of her}an overcoat

[57r]

[blank]

[57v]*

    It would go on tell how the sailors getting impatiently with her intractabil-ity were permitted to skin her by Hanno to skin her and take her hide home for a trophy of one of the earliest voyages in the Atlantic. They they hung it up in the temple of Ashtaroth as hide [linigue] for harriers. Tunique ought

---

* 57v–60r written in black ink.

to be rhymed somehow with Runic—Runique. It seems as if it could be managed.

Pardon the aside which is not at all aside. The important thing is that in a society which I would fain have classless must now recognized four classes where the last I knew there were only two. {We grow complex as we mature.} You may be curious to determine which the four you belong in. I read of a mother who when asked what service her son had been in during the war proudly answered: The Intelligensia. We musnt let ambition run away with our good sense. We want to be honest with ourselves and take time to consider. We may not want to belong to the highest clan. The word intelligentsia may have unpleasant connotations for us.

Offhand I can think of a {test} couple of tests to settle for us as pretty objectively where on the scale we would place to feel least strained and so most contented and at home.

[58r]

[blank]

[58v]

In looking up potato lately in the Columbia I stumbled on and got hung up on poetry a subject It is subject I never read about before thought I have long been interested in it. I read and was fascinated. Poetry it said (I quote from memory) is largely a matter of rhythm and diction. Meaning is not essential and is often thought to be detrimental. If you laugh enough spontaneously at that you are hopelessly self relegated to out of those lower classes. Don't presume to the style of the more than middle brow at most.

A very prominent article in Harpers Magazine a month or two ago furnished another text to apply . It brings me back to the theme of my address which is loyalty. There loyalty is loftily defined after Josiah Royce and Ralph Emerson (those high binders) as being true to attractions rather than to attachments. Emersons says Verily knows when half gods god the gods arrive.[89] It seems poor spirted to wonder if there aren't sometimes carts ? where quarter gods have arrived. Such thinking would exonerate Benedict Arnold and {Aaron Burr} and I'm told Quisling It certainly helps to their tolerance and understanding. Aaron Burr was a clever man

[59r]

and might well have taken advantage of it his own justification. Shelley might A man should so set his will ruthlessness as to rise on stepping stones of his dead friends to higher things. Always be ready to leave an attachment for an attraction.[90] It runs poor spirited to wonder if sometimes when half gods go if cant quarter godst that arrive and so on down to no gods at all.

~~It is possible for simplicity like mine to fell all mixed up by word play as ingenious play with such ideas as the {admission} attraction and attachment~~ I don't care how far down the brow scale ladder it lands me but

My simplicity {just} naturally resent ~~hates~~ the cleverness ~~ingenuity~~ that would confine me over much a plain matter of fact word as loyalty in its every day use. You and I never thnk of ~~using making it mean~~ meaning {anything by it} a tendency to cling to a present attachment. ~~be it to~~ There is such a thing as having to break with an attachment and go with an attraction. I may be so attracted to Russian that I may want to go there and live for a while I may want to live there for life. I may want to help the Russian [illegible] come here in America even as it is in Russia. But takes a high

This is to denounce the sophistry that would bring it round to the same thing as disloyalty*

[59v]

Platos longing for the utopia of Sparta may have be called idealism but it could be called loyalty to his home town Athens

[60r]

brow sophistication to make that out loyalty.   You and I call it disloyalty. The colonists ~~people~~ who clung to England in 1775 were called Loyalists. We were the disloyalists, ~~and had to accept being put up with the~~ But we faced the fact with reluctance—most of us—nearly all of us but Tom Paine It seemed to cost him no more pain to throw the old over for the entirely new than for Shelley to change girls I don't doubt it cost them something as human not utterly superhuman beings. To that extent they were loyal and to that extent over ~~I have put in verse somewhere~~

The Supreme Court in a lifelong ~~old~~ admiration of mine I should see it denatured or destroy regret to see it denatured {diluted} or destroyed ~~as there is~~ I

---

* This entry written upside down at the bottom of the page along the normal lines of the sheet, in the left margin created by Frost writing vertically across the bottom of the page to the top.

for me there is some thing sacred about regret. I have put it in verse more
than once.

Ah?

[*61r*]

[blank]

[*62r*]*

The History of the United States of American begins has begun with the
sentence: There were two great cities flourishing in the New World and three
great peoples approaching civilization in the New World when Columbus
found it in 1492. The cities would compare in importance with any but even
the best of the line in Europe such as London Paris and Madrid No word of
them came to Columbus—nor word of Columbus to them. They were as
blissfully unconscious of Columbus him as he was unblissfully? unconscious
of them. It would have made all the difference in his career if he had even a
rumor of them and their gold to report to the Queen of Spain who financed
his voyage.

One of the cities had already long been playing with zero in its mathematics.†

[*63r*]‡

You think you ought to be free from all travails outside yourself to think
what you please say what you please and do what you please.

No only to think what I please. I am a freethinker. I believe in change from
day to day.

You mean change from creed to creed from party to party from nation to
nation from love to love. You mean agree with Emerson that any change is
like to be for the better both for you and for the world.[91] You exalt unfaithful-
ness.

We must get on   [forward backward and sideways]§

Yes but don't you think the doctrine dangerous. Shouldn't it be kept from
children till they are of age—and from the merely useful classes. Shouldn't
they be deceived into believing fickleness a sad fault. I remember a story of

---

* Page is written in pencil with noted exceptions.
† Entry written in black ink.
‡ Page written in black ink.
§ Frost's brackets.

mercenaries who surrounded ~~and under fire~~ and given a chance to ~~surrender and take service with the other side~~ change sides refused said it would be ~~bad~~ unprofessional and were slaughtered to a man. Heroic they seemed to me. The poet—says those who change old loves for new pray gods they change for worse. Steadfastness in peace and war has been reckoned a virtue. You

[*64r*]

You think mistakenly.

So has honor

[*65r*]

Thrift: in a writing life of many years I have allowed myself "lovely" twice at mot to my knowledge "beautiful" not once or more than once not a single "indeed"; I have used very few exclamation points, very few O's I have killed all told not a half dozen people.

To the best of my recollection I said at Vassar[92] if there is a thing wrong with the present world and I am far from certain that there is it is our having been led to expect science to deal with more than can be made a science of and worse still science's having been led to expect ~~more than~~ itself to deal with more than can be made a science of. Determine uses? and count them.

To the best of my recollection I once said at Dartmouth if there is a thing wrong with the present world (and I am far from certain there is) it is our un-dereducated ~~confiden~~ overconfidence in the longevity of metaphor.[93]

To the best of my recollection I once said at Chapel Hill if there is a thing wrong with the world and I am far from certain that there is it is progressivism or the neglect of repression to emphasize expression. You must acquire courage to go ahead though in fear you are not quite ready to go ahead. I know someone who has been given money to consider bear one year.[94]

"True humility again lies in suffering"

Boston University, Richards Collection. Black buckram cover with maroon spine and gold lines, maroon triangle corners on right side; 6¾″ × 8¼″. All entries are in blue ink unless otherwise noted. Small leaf pattern cut out of left red cloth on upper left corner. Spine has "RECORD" embossed in gold. Numbers are stamped in boldface onto the right side of the pages. At bottom: 27/R/130./Inside front cover:/American/ "The Line of Quality"/Blank Books/No. 27/Double Entry Ledger/Single Entry Ledger/Journal, 2 Columns/Record, Margin Line/Without Limits/150 and 300 pages [pages torn and cut out].

[1r]   27

True humility is~~~~ again ~~would~~ lies in suffering our self to be admired or not admired by ~~judges~~ the {worlds} imperfect judges—all you have.[1]   This is the deepest humility to submit to ~~the apparently unfair~~ the hasty cruel and unfair judgement of ~~men~~ your fellow men. Who can find out what men want who can find out what God wants. We do the best we can to please God and men and then humbly submit to their [~~illegible~~] awards so incomprehensible rewards of praise or blame. Do we deserve a war, do we deserve the love of a child, do we deserve death [?when] in the middle of good works.

Try to find any place to break the future. The traits are a ring

In the most mutual moment of all ~~neither~~ {no two} can be sure that they [illegible] ha~~s~~ve the same idea of what they are doing. One may think it is fun and the other that it is breeding

[2v]   28

The Christian religion can only succeed in our failure. It is success and the only successful thing yet devised by God or man The only thing that cant fail is our failure.[2]

[*3r*]   29

Like any other great thing   of course*

Poverty has its bad side. Like any other great thing war {too} has its bad side.
Government is concerned with the bad side of poverty to reduce or remove
it.

Dark darker darkest.[3]

"Oh wretched condition of pauverte."[4] That's not in the Bible. ~~Did~~ Wyclife
didnt say it.[5]

Poverty is the inspirer of ambition
Insanity or a touch of it turns ability into genius
Crime keeps ~~up~~ {wars smoldering} in defiance of law {and awe} that bursts
forth[6]
~~Gloriously in revolution~~ enobled into {rebellions} revolutions and war

[*3v*]   30
[blank]

[*4r*]   33

Dark Darker Darkest

Here where we are life wells up as a strong [illegible] spring perpetually
{from} piling water on water ~~in~~ with the dancing high lights {from} upon it.
But it flows away on all sides as into a marsh of it is own making. It flows
away into poverty into insanity into crime. ~~This is a dark truth and it undeniably a~~ dark truth. ~~But dark as it is there is darker still.~~ {Now} like all other
great things poverty has its bad side and so has insanity and so has crime.
The good side must not be ~~overlooked~~ lost sight of. Poverty ~~is the inspiration~~
inspiring ambition. Poverty has done so much good in the world I should be
the last to want to see it abolished {entirely}. Only ~~when~~ brush ~~with~~ {in [a]
touch of} insanity can lift ability {able} ~~gifts~~ ability {~~facilty~~}* into genius.
Crime is that smouldering defiance of law that at times bursts forth enobled

* This word appears to be written below line, though it may be part of the line below it.

into rebellion and revolution. ~~It is the~~ But there is a bad side to all three poverty insanity and crime and this a dark truth and it is undeniably a dark truth.

But dark as it is there is darker still. For ~~wonderful as we all we havent enough~~ to us to govern life and keep it from its worst manifestations. We haven't fingers and toes enough to tend to ~~it in al~~ all the stops. ~~It~~ Life is always breaking at too many points at once Government is concerned to reduce the badness but it must fail to ~~abolish it entirely remove~~ get rid

[4ᵛ]   34
[blank]

[5ʳ]   35
of it. There is a residue of extreme ~~poverty~~ {sorrow} that nothing can be done about and over it poetry lingers to brood ~~if not comfort it~~ {with sympathy}. I have heard poetry charged with having a vested interest in sorrow.

Dark darker darkest.

Dark as it is that there are these sorrows and darker still that we can do so little to get rid of them the darkest is still to come. The darkest is that perhaps we ought not to want to get rid of them. They be the fulfillment of exertion. What life ~~loves~~ craves most is signs of life. A cat can ~~be entertained~~ entertain itself only briefly with a block of wood. ~~A spool is better, A ball is better still.~~ It can deceive itself longer with a spool or a ball. But give it a mouse for [illegible] consummation. Response response The certainty of a source outside of self—original response whether love or hate ~~fear or {ferocity}~~ {fierceness}* or fear.

[5ᵛ]   36
[blank]

[6ʳ]   37
[blank]

[6ᵛ]   38
Why should we be the ones who had to apologize for our existence to the God who imposed it on us.

I'm always being tried for heresy

---

* Written below the line.

[7r] 55

[blank]

[7v] 56

[blank]

[8r] 57

There are any number of impossibilities we dont give a thought to.

The Noblest Temptation. (God the Seducer.)[7]
The only impossibility we cannot resist [illegible] trying
God too is out to win. He has made sure of the defeat of all who cant keep
from reading the Sermon on the Mount.[8]
Many have found it irresistable reading.
Commitment on commitment but none ever deliberate.
Only as we are seduced can we be sure of our sincerity.
Seduced into poetry—into marriage—into war*
Into any form of art or society.
Our fellow climbs to be like God. He give us battle he gives us trial he
worsts us. Then mercy. His final triumph is {in} according mercy. He gives us
libraries, he gives us schools, he gives us hospitals. God breaks us on his Ser-
mon, then gives us Heaven if we own up beaten broken.
*Into looking on the Sermon to be tempted by it to our surrender. The no-
blest the most beautiful temptation
This is where time is requisite—a length of time however short for the trial
to be set, the loss to be conceded, and the mercy to be brought on.
The Doctrine of Excursions.[9] Out from God into a separateness affording
him opposition and so back by defeat forgiveness and mercy into oneness
with him again. The satisfaction must be all His (in one view
The Sermon makes the game like the one at Monte

[8v] 58

[blank]

[9r] 59

Carlo all in favor of the House.

God fixes rigs it in a few loftiest councils so he takes all and then {but} intending always to give us more than our own back. It is like the greatest jest,
but I can find no record or sign of God's having ever laughed anywhere.

Comedy is pagan. The solemn hush of tragedy at the end is the beauty of Christianity.

I think Vespasian died laughing in his "I feel as if I were about to become a God."[10]

The Old Testament knew the Vanity of vanities.[11] A man might be Solomon or Shakespeare but what could it profit him?

God seems first to have become self conscious of {in} his mercy in the book of Jonah.[12]

He thought it all out and exploited it to the full in the New Testament.

Christ sacrificed himself [illegible] rather to show us that we must sacrifice ourselves on the altar of his impossible ideals than to suffer vicariously to save us from [illegible] sacrifice. No atonement quite vicarious.

Justice is a very superficial thin consideration. We strive in the lists, {we are seduced into striving} but the best man often goes down. Job established it that there was no necessary connection between virtue and success or even ability and success.

To the most we can achieve we shall say Vanity of Vanities.[13] How much more is a king than a peasant.

[9v]   60
[blank]

[10r]   61
A pope than a pauper. Before these hard words of the Sermon we are all equally nobodies. The sin of seeking our own advantage that we were seduced into!
That alone is enough to destroy us beyond ordinary forgiveness.

Civilization is a radiance[14]

That Radiance

Civilization has something to do with lights at night
The right to keep late hours (for study or revelry)
The right to hurt yourself with shortened sleep
The right to sit up all night and sleep all day

Avail yourself of lamps to keep late hours
In {cloistered} study or revlery {as} you have the right
Stay waking night an day

For a short life you ~~can~~ {may} increase your powers
By lengthening day at the expense of night

The risk is yours and let it prove in vain
A great state in its greatness can afford
Worse ~~loss~~ {waste}[15] than this

[10v]   62
Few of us but ~~gave up all that to spoil~~
Deliberately ~~left all~~ {consigned} that to spoil
~~We made our choice we left all that to spoil~~
And bringing nothing with us but our fleck
We came away

[r]*   The Minor Bird[16]

I have wished a bird would fly away
And not sing by my house all day.

Have clapped my hands at him from the door
When it seemed as if I could bear no more

The fault may partly have been in me
The bird was not to blame for his key

And of course there must be something wrong
In wanting to silence any song.

[v]   So steep one day ~~was a~~ {made us} heave a load
        As life made ~~a~~ heavy {a} heart
a ~~couple of~~ bags of grain made a heavy load
life made heavy heart

farmer got to saying†

·   ·   ·

---

* The following pages are torn out and inserted into the back of the book.
† This stanza is crossed out with two, sloping vertical lines from left to right.

[illegible] his horse stood still

A sigh for every so many breath

And for every so many sigh a death"[17]

[illegible]ough rolled and stamped in the image*

road that had lost its reason

[illegible] on the mountain with not goal

[illegible] a lilac clump by a cellar hole

that still plows in season

By {the} iron {metal} shoes and tires

The road had lost its reason now

The road had not reason left

[r] 93

Oneanother   I)

[illegible]
One likes to bring up with a sigh
What can't be helped and with a sigh
Dismiss it to the rushing by
As out the window of a car.
His trust is he is not alone
In knowing how with an "Ah well"
To slight the very gates of Hell.
The other echoes it as used
But with the added shade of tone

---

* There is a line drawn in the right hand margin from "image" to the line beginning "By
the metal shoes and tires".

To make the sentiment his own.
And in excelsis there they are.
Both are with fellowship suffused.

And should they ever in despair
~~At being~~ {Imagine they were* being crossed}
From too much going by the book
~~Fear~~ {So} their significance was lost,
The best thing might be to revise
~~From~~ {to} where they started sure and true
In the analogy of eyes
And having reestablished look
Then cautiously come on from there
Into what liberties they dare.

[*v*]   94
So back to where it all began
In infancy as babe to man
When after trying every place
~~One face first found the other face~~
~~And even discriminating features~~
On our analogy as creatures
One face first found the other face

[*r*]   95

2

I mean back where it all began
In infancy as babe to man
When after trying every place
In our analogy as creatures
One face first found the other face;
And even discriminating features
Eyes first found eyes across the gulf
And sent across a signal light
As if to say "yes sight is sight

---

* Beneath this line is an illegible word inserted in the text.

Tis understood. So far so good."
Nor was it far from there to go
In logic to the further trial
Of corresponding in a smile,
As if to say "Yes, yes, we know.
Who said we had to read a book
To find out that we had to look—
Not heliotropic at the sun
But in the universe's middle
Right here where all is said and done?
Let's keep together always so
And not become each other's riddle."
Convergance is the aim ~~you~~ {they} say.
But no tis not what we convey
So much as how we correspond.
We leave the seen and pass beyond

[v]   96
[blank]

[r]   97
To darker parallels within.
One strikes a single note of song
As if to say "Can you do this?"
The other after thinking long
And perhaps asking for it ~~twice~~ (bis)
Arrives at an hypothesis
As to what member of the throat
Deep hidden in the [illegible] {tissue} moved   being
To execute the stricken note,
{Then}* ~~And~~ gets it like a born adept.
~~And~~ Something ~~is~~ {would seem}as good as proved.
{Because of}† ~~The~~ correspondence [illegible] kept.
Wherefrom or self-consciousness of [illegible] ~~God~~?‡
One waves a filament of mind

---

* This word written in margin.
† This phrase written in margin.
‡ This phrase written in left-hand vertically in margin from top to bottom.

And to their fresh success they find
The other can with love unfurl
The self same tendril and with art
Can fling it in the self same curl.
They tremble at how far theyve come
In paralleling part with part
When [illegible] too {from all self consciousness of bent} bent
{They}* [might will have fumbled the intent
And last of all the best and sum
They try the glances of the soul
They give each other glint for glint
Full sure they are each [illegible] {others} kind

And can be trusted grave or droll
To miss no subtlety of hint[18]
But take [illegible] {And take no hint when none designed And yet take none
where}† none's designed‡

[*v*]   98
[blank]

Torn out pages

[*r*]   123

A Cabin in {the} a Clearing[19]
[illegible phrase]
An Eclogue

I don't believe the sleepers in this house
Know where they are.

•   •   •

---

* This word written in margin.
† This phrase written below the line.
‡ These three lines are written up the side of the page in the right margin vertically from top to bottom.

They've been here long enough
To push the woods back from around the house
And part them in the middle with a path,

And still I doubt if they know where they are.
And I begin to fear they never will
All they maintain the pat for in the comfort need
Of visiting {with} the equally bewildered.
Nearer in flight their neighbors are than distance

I am the guardian wraith of starlit smoke
That leans out this and that way from their chimney.
I will not have their happiness despaired of.

No one—not I—would give them up for lost
Simply because they don't know where they are.
I am the damper counterpart of smoke
That gives off from a garden bed at night.
I cotton to their lanscape. Thats who I am.
I am your [illegible] in concern for them.

But lifts no higher than a garden grows*

[v]   124
Let us pretend the dewdrops from the eaves
Are {Is} you and I eaves dropping upon them
And try if we can tell the base from the soprano

[r]   137
If freedom is an object. We show signs
Of a reluctance to break off with Europe
Either from loyalty or homesickness.
See how we take the Indian name for maize
And change it to the English name for wheat.
It seems to do us good to call it corn.
But anyway whatever place it this is,

---

* Line written along the bottom, left-hand side of the page, bottom to top.

Europe or Asia—come to think of it
It can't be Asia—we may dismiss Asia.
Her thrust our way was but a feeble thrust
That yielded to the stronger thrust from Europe.
Any design she ~~may have~~ had in our direction
Waste away among Kanaka islands
Or if it ever reached here spread too thin
A film of Redness over the continent.
~~The wide Pacific was too much for Asia.~~ The wide [?rim] of the Pacific
baffled ~~Asia~~ {Asia}

If the time ever comes when we know <u>who</u>
We are, we shall know better where we are.
But who we are is too much to believe.
~~Is too incredible for us as yet~~ (either for us or for the onlooking world} We
are too sudden to be credible
~~We It is too sudden to be credible~~

Well as I say whatever place this is
We have it and by [illegible] mean to keep it

[r]   139
Why do you swear by Jeptha all the time.

Don't you remember how the [illegible]
Once read our little char to where we are
By quoting ~~something~~ Jeptha ~~said~~ to someone {in [illegible]}
As an enabling text for us stay here.
And not be driven out by comers back
Much less by any {comers} in afresh

Against all comers [?along] here comers back

Against all comers—~~and~~ not {be} driven on
By ~~anyone who thinks he~~ {aboriginal who} wants it back
~~After three hundred years~~
My Muchless

.   .   .

Against all comers
After three hundred years of [illegible phrase]

⌊r⌋*   I

The facing of it should be in
He may be nothing but a curio[20]
But if his instructions were correct
Surely he ought to know enough to know
There could be worse genetics than to claim
He had a mighty monarch for his sire
Nothing less generous or less untrue
Look at him the, What makes his lovely [illegible]
Is loads of mud. For all he is is mud
What of that [illegible phrase]

How otherwise account for the {his} desire
To spend in all direction all at once
The impacted seed that makes his body [illegible]
Look at him listen for the

How otherwise to account for his desire

⌊r⌋†   Who would we say [illegible] it was he parroted
If at this point the [seeming] parrot said
He might be nothing but a curio
Yet he had [illegible] know known {from the first he knew} enough to know
His wing were a [illegible phrase] to fly
Hew would be [illegible] to attempt to the sky
He must not trouble deaf heaven for any answer
Aries Taurus Gemini and Cancer
The lead off cluster of the Zodiac
Only to be snubbed unimportant back.
No his intuitions are correct
His attitude is strangely introspect
It is within himself he would [research]

---

* 6¼″ × 8¹⁄₁₄″ uruled page written in blue ink. This page and the ones following contain
the draft of an unfinished and unpublished poem.
† 5⅞″ × 8″ unruled page written in blue ink.

One could preach worse gestures than to claim
He had a mighty Monarch for his sire
Nothing less generous or less untrue
And that would easily Which easily account for the dense
~~That~~ His parchment body of intensely pith
~~Seemed~~ Apparently was big and bursting wish
To spend in all directions all at once
He feels it mystic in him like a myth.
He was not born so [illegible] food
Has he been kept so vegetable a dunce
As not to know what ailed him was a mood
Of profligate and extravagance
Who would we say he parroted
If at this point the seeming parrot said
His boast was he just had the lack of head
He needed for a prodigal romance

[v]*   Who would we say {it was} he parroted   [illegible]
If it that parrot the ~~[illegible]~~ little parrot said
He might be nothing but a Curio
[~~And yet instinctively~~]
And yet ~~instinctively he seemed to know~~
   from what he knew enough to know
He's ~~pinions were not given~~ {illegible phrase} to fly
He would be foolish to attempt the try
He must not trouble deaf heaven for [~~illegible~~] cries

[r]†   But that his pinions are imaginary
And like a chicken powerless to carry
I wouldnt be [~~put it past~~] {illegible} the Curio
~~To think of canvassing the~~
To canvas ~~the~~ heaven for the answer
Aries Taurus Gemini and Cancer
And so on all around the Zodiac
His down would {only} be to plummet ~~illegible~~ back.
There is no answer any one can know.

---

* 5⅞″ × 8″ unruled page.
† 5⅞″ × 8″ unruled page.

Take what makes his body plump
Is loaded seed for all he is is seed
What more than that is any of us indeed.
And there are there these for nothing but to sow
~~When ripe~~
When Gabriel in the autumn ~~blows~~ sounds his [illegible]
And ripe for sublimation they are freed.
There could be more success than to claim
He had a mighty Monarch for a size
Nothing less generous or less untrue
Why it must account [illegible] for the desire
That his body intensely pith
To spend in all directions and at once
Has he been kept so ~~[illegible]~~ [illegible] a desire
As not to ~~illegible~~ guess what acts [illegible] is a mood
Of profligacy and extravagance
His [illegible] man has just the lack of head.

Apparently is big and brown [illegible]*

[v]†   A fellow needs of a profligate romance
~~Suppose untimely with forced fingers rude~~
So to himself a parrot might have said
So our rebellious might have parroted.
Suppose untimely ~~[illegible]~~ with forced fingers rude[21]
He

[r]‡   Suppose untimely with forced finger rude
He were divested of his outer wrap
In coldness or in the quest of fruit
So far from {being} stripped to flesh and sap
He would be forced to wear an inner suit
Of tiny sequins made to overlap
Like a protective shirt of iron mail.
And these are there for nothing but to sow
And make {it} sure what ever she shall fail

---

* Line is written in the left hand margin from top to bottom and seems directed toward
the line "That his body intensely pith"
† 5⅞" × 8" uruled page.
‡ 5⅞" × 8" unruled.

Pasture and meadow shall not lack for weed
(Speaking of what he knows enough to know)
In quantity they seem to fill a region
Count these if but for the statistics sake
Or let it go at calling them a legion
Yet ~~illegible~~ there are seed and all he is is seed
Is that more than that is any of us in deed

And if his intuitions are correct
His speculation {rumination}* must be introspect

[r]†   Perhaps there wasnt any waste at all
He knew that science [illegible] its universe
A self created self {~~supporting~~} impelled self machine

He knew that some like Lucretius hero[22]
Always in terror lest the next equation
Should land him back in zero equals zero
Set forth from some   rule of thumb

[r]‡   Latest 1

He may be nothing but a Curio
Yet from the first he know enough to know
His wings like barnyard fowls' weren't meant to fly
And there was better reason why
He ~~shouldn't look for reason~~ {would be foolish to attempt} the sky
~~When~~ ~~[earthlings]~~ {mankind} trouble deaf heaven[23] for any answer
The high and mighty of the Zodiac
Aries Taurus Gemini and Cancer
Tis but to get brushed of and plummet back
Not [~~illegible~~] if my intuition ~~is~~ correct
His attitude is [~~rather~~] introspect.
~~[It is inside himself he would inquire]~~ he would turn inward on himself to
search
One could peach loose genetics than to {over} claim

---

* Word written below the line.
† 5⅞″ × 8″ unruled.
‡ 5⅞″ × 8″ unruled.

He had a mighty monarch for his sire
Nothing less generous or less intense
How otherwise account for the desire

[v]   From [illegible]
From many florets one lone carapace
He might feel to responsible are all
Have these on so deciduous a perch
It tends to make one think is such a case
From all the florets lone carapace
[illegible phrase] perch
That he showed some to be the chosen ace
To see that weeds should
From all those florets the lone carapace
Unsafe on too deciduous a carapace
It made him too responsible an ace
Poised there on too deciduous a perch
From all those flowerets the lone carapace
Responsible for

[r]*   Latest 2

His body though of harsh unlikely pith
Nevertheless seems big and bursting with
To spend in all directions all at once.
Has he been kept so vegetable a dunce
As not to guess what ails him in his mood
Of profligacy and extravagance.
Who would the waste be he parroted
If at this point he really spoke and said
My body may have just the lack of head
I needed for a prodigal romancer.
And is {Suppose} untimely with forced fingers rude
He were divested of his outer wrap
In idleness or in the quest of [illegible] fruit
So far from being stripped to [illegible] flesh and sap
He would be found in [still another] {dry under} suit
Of tiny sequins made to over lap

---

* 5⅞″ × 8″ unruled page.

[r]*   Latest 3

    Like a protective shirt of iron mail
    And there are seed for all he is is seed
    What more than that is any of us indeed.
    And ~~there~~ {there} are there for nothing but to sow
    The asking of want he knows enough to know
    When ripe for sublimation they are freed
    So's to make sure whatever else shall field
    Meadows and pasture shall not lack for weed.
    ~~Enough of them they seem to find~~ {They seem in quantity to sow a region}
    Count them if but for the statistics sake
    Or let it go at calling them a legion.
    But ~~let not~~ numbers are {are numbered but } anyone mislead
    From many flowrets one lone carapace

    One thats protective

[r]†   Later

    Into the waste he came of he must go—
    Speaking of what he knows enough to know.
    I {might} doubt there {is} in the
    [illegible line]
    The promise of a single future germ
    And what boots it yet what does it boot
    That paddled along with every seed and flake
    Apparently enough of them to sow a region
    Count them of but for the statistics sake
    Or let it go at calling them a legion
    ~~Is something like a silken parachute~~
    Along with everyone us packed a gift the gift
    Of something like a silken parachute
    With aptitude it seems for sustained lift
    And even something of inspired lift
    To carry away [illegible] a gale
    To carry anew

-----

* 5⅞″ × 8″ unruled page.
† 5⅞″ × 8″ unruled page.

For choice of landing with a chance to root.
The more the tally through the worse the tale
The only way that waste is not to fail
Is when regarded as high sacrifice
For most of these ~~back with the~~ absolute
Of modifying [illegible] {sail and} the sea and air
Into a broth medium ether we can bear
That would be [illegible] race of that [illegible]

[v]   Out of much waste he came and [illegible]

[r]*   2

And these are seed and all there is is seed
(All for that matter is any of us is seed)
Enough apparently to sow the region
And make sure whatever else shall fail
Pasture and meadow shall not lack for weed
Count them if but for the statistics sake
Or let it go {at} an estimated legion.
But let not numbers reawake
In force of numbers to enlarge a race
Where there had been only one of kin
From many flowers but one lone carapace
[Illegible phrase] In an whole ~~dying~~ year one desperate race
[Illegible line]
Now the seeming promise of {a} ~~the~~ life within
[Twelve illegible lines]

[v]   Its destiny was any but a [?lotus]
Or one may go back into the absolute
Or so the dreams
Or so the unrealist would like to dream
              surrealist

[Inside back cover. Stamped in green; "Derry, incorporated/stationers/Boston
and Brookline."]

---

* 5⅞" × 8" unruled page.

"Curiously Enough—as a connection"

MS. 001729. *School theme book, 5¼″ × 7¼″. Front cover missing. Back cover card-board black and white marbled theme book. Stitched pages. Unruled paper. Entries are in black ink except as noted.*

[1r] Curiously Enough—as a connection*

A Bridge over the cows.

Kidney Pond Camp[1]   Greenville
    Roy Bradeen

Northampton
Emmons
Tardiff
    Springfield
Nicholls   Main St.
Italian   970 Main
Kelly   Harrison Ave
Mrs. Beddell 415 Bay
    Greenfield
Parker (Windsor Chair

[1v] A Bad Teacher / An English Teacher

[2r] Not Saying Anything till He Sees[2]

One Art of the Work and Another of Exacting Pay for the Work. Sold for Christmas. He that asking for more hay was like pri self-praise

•   •   •

---

* Entry written in pencil.

One thing you cant make the way you want it—the past to have been other than it was. "I thought that was just what history was for. Each generation re-writes the past to suit itself."

The cross might be taken as the symbol of the way one continuity, the {spiritual} soul, crosses at right angles another continuity, the {physical}* race.

[2v]   The secret hid in the Maya script is that the Maya ~~use~~ knew the bacilli and used them for symbols.[3]

Robbery—no one goes into robbery except for gains. Business likewise—no-body goes into business except for gain. Business and robbery are very much alike. Art is more like more murder in that people may in to ~~both~~ {it} for gain but then {again} may go into ~~both~~ {it} for a variety of other objects—love re-venge, etc.†

How much can you incidentalize or make incidental to the idea—

Discontinuity of material

[3r]   For unaesthetic people they built beautiful houses. At least we seem to think the houses beautiful. We have seen nothing to admire since in our own architecture—Story of the pair from Greenwich Village[4] who rode around with the real estate agent pretending to look for a farm to buy, but in reality looking for fine old New England interior to admire.

For an illiberal people they face the Jewish future of the world with a strange composure.—Story of Mt—'s prophecy from the Bible of how Christ must ultimately come in worldly power to make it right with the Jews for their disappointment.

The young Jews are in a similar revolt from moral and religious strictures with the young Puritans. Their Puritanism is if anything more ~~excessive~~ au-

---

* "Physical" written in blue ink. After the word "race" is a line drawing of a cross, much like a crucifix, tilted toward the right-hand margin.
† Entry, "Robbery . . . etc.," written in blue ink.

thentic. They go to a greater length to revolt. The severity of what they revolt from is

[3v]   I had these higher thoughts long before I had to have them as a refuge in
trouble

An reader
There I have chosen to celebrate
May worship forward the rest can wait

[4r]   partly to blame for this: and their closer relationship with Europe. Their Orientalism has nothing to do with the case. They were the Puritans of the East.
And still Puritans at bottom they are surer than the Yankee to come back to
the home and propriety by middle life or earlier. The Greeks said it was Persian, the Romans said it was Greek, the French said it was Italian The English
say it is French and we say it is English, though sometimes we go back over
the whole series and say it is Oriental.

Outward in space to Beyondness
Backward in time to Beyondness
How much does such Beyondness
Come in ward on us to affect our lives?
The imperceptableness with which
goodness begins in simple poverty
but the better it is and the surer it is[5]

[4v]   [blank]

[5r]   of being thought deserving more of beauty and that lets in art, and the more
beauty the cost and that lets in business and the more cost the more power to
protect it and that lets in politics and the more politics the more practical
morals and that lets in corruption.

The only safety for us Puritans the only place where we can be Puritans
without attracting the attention of the stone throwers is in the bosom of the
Church we came out of in the Reformation. I wonder if we wouldnt have
done better to stay an in and join forces with Loyola.[6]

.   .   .

At a certain point he gave up thinking of politics at all. He had connected political reform with spiritual. But political can only

⌊ 5v ⌋ ⌊blank⌋

[6r] go a little way in bringing up the poor to equal the rich before it comes on the danger of making them richer than the rich.

On what ground do you ask for the release of the political prisoners on the ground that the state has no right to defend itself or on the ground that the state is too big and safe to take any notice of petty plotters against it.

Yes

Let things go to wrack and mine for an idea. Story of the blind old gardener. I guess them—aint a going to bloom. We'd a heard from them ~~fore~~ before this if they was.

Company—the story of the house over back full of wooden dolls.

[6v] [blank]

[7r] Young sure and twenty
Dont cease trying to do
What you dont see why you shouldnt do.
Keep on writing to her after marriage with a view to marrying her later in life when her husband dies.   or fails her.
Every time you have an idea in your work you freshen as a cow does every time she has a calf.
Brad tell that again {like Sidney Cox}[7] for Sibil. Brad's been telling us about the Original Old Nick his first ancestor in this country. Go ahead Brad.
Oh it was nothing. Tell it yourself.
What was it
Why it wasn't anything Sibil to make such a fuss about. I was just saying that according to the best authorities the first two boatloads the Mayflower brought over were all Jews. They were the original Pilgrims. And there ~~were~~ was nothing more original in our annals unless it was the Indian and a certain family of Gilleys Capt. John

[*7v*] [blank]

[*8r*] Smith in coasting along saw dangling their legs and fishing in the waters off the {Isles} {of} Shoals: the Island of Shoals.[8] They were pre-primitive with us. ~~Pirate, or runaway slav slaves servants probably.~~ Exploration is supposed to have come before settlement. But there ~~they were~~ {were} the Gilleys ~~were~~ already settled when exploration came along. {And} I doubt if there being there had anything to do with religion or morals. They were pirates or runaway prisoners probably. The important thing now is that they were getting {and establishing precedence over them}* the start of the Pilgrims and Puritans and establishing precedence over them for their descendants in any [illegible] club of old families that might be formed in Boston forever after.

I know what was the matter with Victorian furniture and decoration: any of us who have any of it are ~~of the the generation just following the~~ children of the newly rich. The newly rich are the only ones who bought

[*8v*] [blank]

[*9r*] much of it and they necessarily bought in bad taste.

The Story Goes—

~~that~~ At one of the State Universities a ~~farmer~~ visiting farmer asked a professor if it was true as reported that (~~such was the present atheism of learning~~) ~~no on~~ the name of God was a forbidden word on the campus. Yes no one was permitted to mention God was the answer but not for the reason ~~that was generally~~ {usually} given. ~~It was found that~~ Swearing was so almost universal that it was thought best to forbid the use of gods name entirely either reverently or irreverently for the time being. It was hard on those who wanted to use it in prayer {or philosophy}[†], but as often happens ~~that~~ for the general good the good had to suffer with the bad.

On Refusing Luck Again: Just because I recognize it as luck that I have ~~th~~ had the chance to be comparatively good, shall I throw away the luck ~~and~~ to put myself on

---

* This bracketed phrase, inserted between lines, appears to be related to the line above it.
† This bracketed phrase written in blue ink.

[9v]   [blank]

[10r]   a level with the unlucky?

The Woodpecker.

The Home-town-hater. (Bickford)[9]

Hypocracy among the Cannibals.

Could the law here be put on the man who had to leave Europe for killing a
man in duel [illegible] and is it (He fired befor the word of command.)

The Slack Farmer.

Wouldnt it be interesting if all the superstitious practices were sprung
from instincts of refinement.

The guide post with the snake

The too rude, rude, polite, and too polite.
The first are {dull} fools, the second [illegible] men
The third are what [illegible] {(and} the nearest right)
The fourth light headed fools—but fools again.

The Barn Doors—A Theatre

[10v]*   A distinguished poetess.

To me who am the author of several rather well known novels of protest. I
may add I am a sensibilist. I make a virtue of suffering from everything that
goes on around me. I hate the whole honking hierarchy tooting hooting boo-
ing barking boosting painting and scraping [illegible] and scraping society
Why this is Hell nor am I out of it, said Dr. Faustus† [10]

.   .   .

---

* Page written in pencil.

† Entry has pencil marks scribbled across it to indicate being crossed out.

Has a larger population of hermits half hermits and [?gnarle] hermits

Van Dore found them not pesants.[11]

I found them not artists and not artisans. I can't bring myself to [illegible] want them all artists with pictures ~~and~~ poems which find a marked for I had rather they
wait—Dr. Faustus, Van Dore

[*11r*]   Nine months of winter—

Postman told me had known a winter when he ~~drove~~ {had driven ~~on runners} to from the seven miles~~ from Franconia to Easton[12] for four unbroken months on runners. I have heard of on {good authority} a temprature in that valley of sixty five degrees below zero ~~but~~ that when I told Mr Stephanson of this record he laughed (he keeps his laugh in working order by reading the Ingoldsby Legends[13] a good deal of the time) and ~~told~~ answered that ordinary thermometers when they drop below a certain point instead of going the rest of the way by degrees just ~~dr~~ fall in a heap.

I suppose its not out of ~~the~~ politeness ~~we alway use with~~ to ladies that we always call what we have with them happiness rather than pleasure.

[*11v*]   My time—I shall. Some midday going out
Along the roads, some ~~midday~~{night} coming home
Along the streets, there will be something said
I cannot laugh at, I shall fail of laughter.
My will shall reach for it in vain and you'll
Have lived to hear me speak without it   Then
Will be your chance to pounce unmerciful
And here I have held you off, young Sure-and-Twenty.

[*12r*]   Young Sure-and-twenty, you must not cease trying
To do the thing that for the life of you
You dont see why you should{nt}* do, For that{s}
~~A way of faith~~ {Is an attack} that something yet may come of.
But now let me explain ~~for~~ {to} you this laughter.

---

* Bracketed letters inserted below the line.

The reason why my laughter is the same
Unvarying in every circumstance
~~Is hidden but~~
And what the {vital} sources of it ~~in me~~ are
I {dont} know ~~not~~ {not} but I grow more certain yearly
It is not inextinguishable in me
As is the laughter of the gods in them.
I am but a poor mortal in my laughter.
And used for everything the way I use it
I shall be lucky if it lasts me out
My time—I shall. Some day there will be something
I cannot laugh at—~~or not~~ {not} {~~my~~ the} ~~heartyly~~ laugh.
Some midday going out along the roads
Some midnight coming home along the streets
And you shall bear it die away forever
My will shall reach for it in vain: and you
Shall hear me left to speak without it. Then
Will be your hour to pounce unmerciful
Where I have held you off. Young sure and twenty

[12v]   [blank]

[13r]   The Real Estate Agent's name was R. Brown. It was a great secret he told me
that the R stood for Rose Ribrea.* She couldn't take his last name: so he took
her first name clasped it between his first and last for a {middle} name

We may all stand criticism of from foreigners when they arent our invad-
ers and masters to act on it. Said the father to his son who had been reading
too much New Rep Freeman.[14]

Science is in penetration and insight.[15] It cant go much of ahead of invention and the uses we put it to.

How from politeness to trees I always ~~made~~ {rounded} a circle to the right
instead of the left when I got lost in the woods.

How Ty Cobb[16] lost the ball in the sun and what came back in place of it.

[13v]   When you dont know wont hurt you
Your ignorance under a fairer name is your innocence. Keep it as long as you
can

---

* "Ribrea" is written in blue ink.

At forty you will know what is the matter with everything anyway and why nothing is worth an effort. All education can do is precocize you bring you to that knowledge at twenty five thus save fifteen years at most of your life.

I educate those who are nothing to me. Those I love I try to console them for not having educated them.

Your novels cant tell them apart as well as you can. Totals are all he knows

[14r]   The Land of the Repentant. Aubrey Beardsley.[17]
     She Spoiled a Good Farmer. Nat
     Girls Will be Choosers.[18] Her College
Boy and Her Home Boy
          A Bad Teacher—of English
     Her Alimony and Her Baby (Adopted.)

What's left of real admirers after you eliminate all those who like you because you are too {un}important to be much helped by their praise; those who like you because they have been told to like you. Those who like you in hope that you will like and help them, those who like you for what you obviously aren't (that is by mistake) those who like you because you are the only writer they have ever met {those who like you because you write about their home town or have named their {your} hero after their family name}*
{Those who like you {so as} to hurt someone else}† Just so what is left of real socialists when {after} you eliminate those who want to attract attention, those who want to "break in," those who want envy the rich, the bad losers the sore heads[19] an the weak and psychopathic. But why go into motives when they are so mixed?

[14v]   Every thing man ever said was All {or that he likened to All} in philosophy is less than All as every comparison or metaphor sometime breaks down.[20] There is nothing the same size as All not even God. Nor is he less than God All on a footing with substance, spirit change idea will force or what you care to name. He is more than All‡

The inhumanity of not letting people understand you and do you justice.

---

* Bracketed phrase written in blue ink and begins in between the lines and extends up the page into the right margin.
† Bracketed phrase written in pencil from bottom to top along the left side of the page.
‡ Entry written in pencil.

[15r] There are some positions things take that they may be trusted to stay it {in} for a while without anybody's holding them.

Her mother died and her father married again. Then she had one parent step parent. [Illegible] Next her father died and her step-mother married again. Then she had two step-parents She committed suicide.

When Bronson brought out the lead horse many ~~children~~ boys came with him riding on the horse ~~shouting and jeering~~ or running behind shouting and jeering.

Nothing is fatal but death. Tattooed Man

Justice is serious and makes those who insist on it serious. Injustice is humorous an makes those that accept it human Tattooed Man

Be Stuck at Nothing.

It might have got him.

Environmental Literature.
Blames the environment for everything. Yet it is well known

[15v] our adaptability will take care of too much or too little warmth or wealth for long stretches of time. Any body but a fool disdains to be changed right off by every change in his circumstances.

Boy ~~wh~~ so happy and American he thought Emily must have meant to be satirical in her The heart asks pleasure first and then excuse from pain etc.[21]

Voice proud Irish would have war.

{Relative} Speech rate ~~differs~~ determines how much talking you will do with a friend

Inelateable

Almost as hard to recover the past as to predict the future.

[16r] What is this that we [?speak and] move to go going through matter?

•   •   •

MLK says nothing persists but all changes.[22] I notice however that he is pleased if his worth to the world persists.

Misgivings of a martyr. Complications unfrocked. How the church is in the world.
Shoot the Police. The girl looking on. (Cabaret party. Go get us some jewelry.

Dry humor is the kind that doesn't seem to appreciate itself {Dry Beauty}.
I wish all literature were as dry in the same sense of the word. Most of it uses the adjectives of self appreciation, that is to say of self description. Use beauty and wonder often enough and your reader will know he is in the presence of poetry. Why not go further and use poetic itself. With poetic [?swollen] eyes she watched the poetic light die in the west.*

[16v]†
An Antique

Just such a
An antique sun power rocker
If a hundred years ago {As the grandma used to know}
{she} You sat in the chair in the sunshine
And it rocked you to and fro
The sunshine made the chair rock
And the rocking made you sew.

But you take a stormy winter
When they didnt get much {hardly saw the} sun
The rocking chair stood by the window
And didn't seem to run
And the Granny said No wonder
They got no sewing done

[17r]
A Dark Winter Year Winter

This is mothers {granny's} sun power rocker
It needs the sun to go.
{Its sunshine makes it go}
mother {Granny} sits in this chair in the sunshine

---

* Entry written in pencil from "that is to say . . ."
† Page written in pencil.

And the s it rocks her to and fro
The sunshine makes the chair rock
And rocking makes mother {her} sew.

{But}* you take a winter {year} {winter} like this one
When we haven't had much sun
The rocking chair stands by the window
And doesnt seem to run
And then you hear {And mother {Granny} says} mother {no} wonder
Why She gets no sewing done

    The {A} sun-power Rocking chair

Oh that's the Paradise in bloom I said
An truly it was not too much to say
Had we but in us to assume in March
Such {The} far advanced luxuriance of May.

[*17v*]   Underfoot.   Pulled rug.

Red ant sandwich

Law for when an ape flies.

Chestnut Blight and White-pine Blister[23]

Cheapen life

What I mean to take with me I will not tell. What boundary line is this the Canadian or heavenly

Standing with me in a rainbow.

1 Parlor magic. A table full of apparatus from the pantry and parlor—alive for my goodness you haven't a besmatterer. Dont know know what it is werent you brought up to call it a besmatterer. Dont you know this thing they scrape the cream off the what you may call it with.

---

* Word written in margin.

2 April first flowers
3 Where to hide something longest.
4 All my flowers in a bouquet.

[18r]   Do something get something done to which to shift your own and other peoples interest to off your self to.

All his ideas the minute they become he has them become opinions.

Not by contradiction. The other fellow has said it; he has the floor: let it stand. ¥ What you might say would sound the opposite if said right then and it may not be the very opposite. It would love nice shading of its difference. You can well afford to keep it even a month till it comes in naturally and
Listen to almost anything like a reporter to tell it again for its character interest. Say to the speaker hold to that belief till I have time to go and tell you.*

[18v]
Stories—the Sabbath-breaker
Flying axehead.²⁴
Not to inquire of the worship of his wife's gods.
A year to till his farm
I have not eaten hero[e]s?
Not to destroy the trees in war:
Tree poisoner. Right to destroy what was her own. This has been thought out too.
Owner of Manna

[19r]
I learned to sleep on my face in

The newsboy in the park at Albany who sold the Boston Herald I gave him and asked for more.

"I hate motives and I hate intelligibility"

•   •   •

---

* This entry written in blue ink.

As through the woods we drove for fifty miles in the dark a man came out of the trees* and stabbed our horse dead—[25]

~~Philosophy is a rounded description of an attitude toward life that roughly implies it~~. I doubt if anybody has philosophized life directly. We simply in philosophy phrase a philosophical attitude toward life that is a part of living.

[19v] The next time I examine a class they will have to ~~ans~~ tell me what I think the world is. The only answer that will be right is Process. — Guess what I think the world is? (Typical question in school.)

[20r] Discipline is a dose of inharmony.

discord[†]

He was no coward. He wasnt afraid to think what must prove his ~~ruin~~ {ruinous}[‡] unhappiness.

Anything you pride yourself in having detected in the book: anything you caught yourself thinking as you read it.

The best you can do is no better than an <u>excerpt</u>[§]

The advances are sudden and swift and somewhat disorderly: such order as they have is a holding over from the {long} intervals ~~of consolation~~ between them of consolidation of gains.[**]

Discipline teaches us how to hold ourselves in a position to give and take Never strike so[††]

[20v] [blank]

---

* This phrase written in blue ink.
† Word written in blue ink.
‡ Word written in blue ink.
§ Entry written in pencil.
** Entry written in pencil.
†† Entry written in pencil.

[*21r*]   hard as to throw yourself entirely off balance and exposed to a fatal counter stroke. Sporting analogy again. But there is an ultimate difference between life and the game.* [~~Illegible~~]

Not to be conceded that the race will never a second time come to such flower.

> Understanding Johnson (the Newbury Col.)[26]
> The Proposed College

The dust lay dead in the dew fall

No city on our skies at night

I like a tree at the window[27]

Psychoanalysis on the assumption that the self deceived need undeceiving

[*21v*]   [blank]

[*22r*]   Shall we tell them all we know even the things we're sorry we know. Yes, for revenge

> So unschooled in the classics that he couldnt tell a Pyrric victory from a
Parthian shot.[28]

> Our combined sheep ranch and bear garden

> Sleep and the Gas-mask.

> ~~The~~ Olds and His Young Red*

> If   Pertinax and Didius Julianus† [29]
>   ⎧ The Detested Puritan
>   ⎨ Who <u>does</u> know what is best for a people
>   ⎩ [illegible] factors – Hostyles

> •   •   •

---

* Entry written in pencil.

† Entry written in blue ink.

Carry the world by storm of belief. Get the belief stated just enough (and not too much) for acting on. A kind of built up narrative answers purpose best. It stays alive longest. It has to be almost blundered into shape out of all sorts of picked up human fragments and mistakes [illegible] observation. Nothing matters if what it figures is right to live by.*

[22v]   [blank]

[23r]†   He could say things on deck to induce St Elmos on the yardarm[30]

The two bumps of ~~idealism~~ {Phrenology} ideality are where the hours almost sprouted in sowing his wild oats.

After babyhood self-improvement becomes a private matter. Physical mental or moral, please attend to it where I cant see you if you care to avoid my disgust. Public primping with a vanity glass is not the worst of it, though bad enough.

The Too Good and the Good Enough. Two Emperors of Rome Pertinax & Diocletian.[31]

Onamatapeia: God said to Adam you wait here till I drive up some of these [illegible] new animals for you to name. So God went over into the woods and pretty soon he came back ~~with a bear~~ driving a bear ahead of him. And he shouted to Adam to have a name ready to ~~illegible~~ {give the bear} as he went by. And Adam made his mind just as blank as he could so that when the bear came into

[23v]   [blank]

[24r]‡   his head there wouldnt be anything else there and he should get a snap result from his first impression. Well the minute he got his full view of him he got it. He made the first sound that came into his mouth, "Bear." "Bear," sai God said," what do you call him that for? "Because it sound the way he looks Dont you think so?" And God said It doesnt yet but probably will when I've heard it

---

* Entry written in blue ink.
† Page written in blue ink.
‡ Page written in blue ink.

in connection with him often enough We'll let it go at that. Men will be children. Stay where you are and I'll drive you up another" Thus was started one of the most dangerous and foolish theories in poetry.

Keats an evolutionist[32] because he tried to write an epic of Jovian hierarchy supplanting the Saturnian?[33] Nonsense. He was thinking only of the final triumph of one infinity over another, definition over indistinctness, the Greek over the Asiatic, form over size.

[*24v*]* This so lovely a thing I know it is
I know it is without your telling me
This is so lovely a thing I promise you
Never to take it from you never never
I know how lovely a think it is to you
More from your motion and the way you speak
Than anything you say though what you say
Is faultless perfect and above the least doubt
If a motive. Oh I know how lovely a thing
It is my beauty and warmth and grace to give you
And I see how you are exalted but I see
How even in exaltation, you are not
(Nay no denial) you are not above[†]
A fear for ~~the~~ {your} security in delight
Fear is not absent from your perfect moment
And I that fear am wrung by to the soul
Love be secure

[*25r*]‡ Some cant help being thrust by the working of our machinery into outer desperation. Most of those so thrust are too blind to know whom to turn on for satisfaction, God, their employers or their own wives and children. They would as soon take it out on a chair they have stumbled over by giving it an extra unreasonable kick as on a throne by revolution. The breeding out of the brain is their curse, and as I say it is a curse that carries with it its own alleviation generally in ~~stupidity~~ stupor. But among those bred ~~to~~ downward in the mind there are always some who throw back and derive from some an-

---

* Page written in pencil.
† The letters "ab" written in blue ink.
‡ Page written in blue ink.

cestor in whom the mind was not recessive. This is the atavism not dangerous to the peace of society. It makes the insubordination of the lowborn who
should have been the highborn. Everything depends on who they make party
with the high born they are most like in nature or the lowborn they resemble
in evolution. In one care they go to [illegible] {serve} the kings in the

[25v]   [blank]

[26r]*   other they rouse the slaves to rebellion. The poor slaves may think by rebelling they are achieving their own freedom equality and supremacy. They are
only making themselves {new} kings out of their own class exalting the low
born high ones.

    These thoughts that I catch glimpses of down underneath my other
thoughts may come to me on the ligaments that connect me with other parts
of my personality in other cities and countries.

    It is not a question of whether you are going to hate or like it like a Puritan
or a Persian. (Persicor odi says the Puritan Horace)[34] but of how you are going to like. Will you like it w like a June bride or like a hospital nurse out of
hours. Where will you have your kick—altogether in the belly. The kick differs according to its connotation for different people.   Along comes a scientist and says the best connotations are biological and

[26v]   Defending God with analogies from science. The fact of your defense is
everything. You fight for what you wont give up.
    You cling to something you{r} {reason} haves never been able to describe.
The best descriptions of it are certain stories that have grown among the
people.

[27r]†   medical. An indiscriminalist says no one {he} has {no} right to choose and no
one has a right to choose for him what his connotations shall be. He must
simply associate with the kick every possible fact he can learn. No choice is
his word. But choice is life—individual and collective. Society is organized to
help you make choices it assumes you will be glad to have help in making.

• • •

---

* Page written in blue ink.
† Page written in dark blue ink.

Believing in God you believe the future in believe it into existence. Belief is the end of the sentence more felt than seen—the end of the paragraph the end of the chapter There is not end so final {no form} so closed that if it hasnt an unclosed place that opens into further form. [?womb]

Just when belated outsiders have it got thoroughly into their heads that as a part of a machine universe they are in danger of having to regard themselves as machines, just when they are on the point of giving up the fight for their souls science calmly announces that the universe itself is not a machine whatever people may

[27v]   ~~Where did we come from~~

As we were driven in flight {by those behind us} so we drive others in front of us and they others in front of them: All is flight from ~~fright~~ and force behind. Progress is escape civilization ~~is~~ sublimation ~~is~~ emerging in terrified flight from someone emerging in terrified flight from someone emerging in terrified flight from God. So we find God again He is the primordial fear that started all this escaping. He started the drive of existence. No one gets anywhere except from the fear of ~~the~~ God.[35]

[28r]   Satirists will tell you that moral virtues are all negative and despicable. Yet who are busier spouting out negatives than satirists. They make their own virtues out of other peoples lacks Escape-talk*

They arent what others are†

It is to them now - - They say not.

Subject people—people thought about but never thinking.‡

About the furthest you can get in disinterestedness is to tell what somebody else thinks as if you enjoyed it for reasons that need not be given.§

---

* "Escape-talk" written in pencil.
† Entry written in pencil.
‡ Entry written in pencil.
§ Entry written in pencil.

The swelling theme—the mighty symbol
Cant tell his symbols from his cymbols*

Look here mister, I'd like to know what you mean by introducing courses in contemporary literature into your curriculum?†

[28v]   The sound is everything. The best means of achieving it are vowels conso-nants met verbal accent meter but the best of all for variety of is meaning.³⁶ Great thoughts are of value as they supply profound tones.

[29r]‡   Story of Dianner and the last fight at Madison Square Garden.³⁷ Some jackass a poet or something. Crowd rearing to go. ~~Who~~ The thing to control you (the mob) would be birth control

> ~~What I've decided not to have shift~~
> ~~The reasons I give shall be fresh every day~~
> In the reasons I give I may change everyday
> Ideas are nothing ~~in which I would rest~~
> I never would choose and idea for rest
> Let my ~~thought~~ choice become a byword and jest

The Ne'er-do-well. / Broken Hill

I have said I would not strive
I will be as good as my word

Another beauty metaphor Time is like a circle is a circle.

We come to loathe the logic of words as it was too exhaustively worked out by [illegible] scholasticism. There is a logic like that in things that when worked out will someday be as profitless and hateful to us.

Which shall we talk about escape and what we can escape from or the in-evitable the inescapable.

·   ·   ·

---

* Entry written in pencil.
† Entry written in blue ink.
‡ Page written in blue ink.

The engineer said it was the easiest thing in the world for one of his profession to see the beauty of a mechanistic theory of the universe. He didn't
need a God to explain things yet when asked he couldn't remember having
seen a machine with no one's hand on the lever of it foot on the pedal. Every
metaphor breaks down.[38]*

[*29v*]   This cult is endemic in brothels. It is the justification of brothels. Once in
so often it gets loose and becomes epidemic in the world. So that even virgins
talk it and more wonderful still wives and mothers.
                [illegible]
He used whores for that part of his nature making a clean breast of it but
for the higher part set up to be unattainable the wife of another man and it
was about her all his poetry was written. The husband might not like to have
his wife so used however unphysically but he was either one of two things (1)
an ordinary fellow who did not count (2) or (2) a brute who deserved his
fate. The wife might not like it but—never mind. The way was to assume she
did.
     The honest man could cross his heart and say he had never touched a
woman who was anyone's else property. He never violated any ones property
rights in a woman unless it was her own property rights in herself.
     Molly Colum[39] men have too meager a sex experience in Am for art. She
may be right. I have been startled to find that it is a conceded fact of history
that there was practically no rape in Shermans devastating raid through
Georgia.[40]

[*30r*]†   Cant you see—cant you see for the life of you see that all they meant was
miracle. They did not know enough to know where exactly it was. If it was
not in turning water into wine {as the story had it} smiting water out of rock
or turning water into wine it was nevertheless somewhere. They knew there
was wonder and mystery. There was mystery no artistry would ever over-
take. They knew mystery was safe. And it still is.

Whats wrong with Genesis is the science in it.
Let science be called on to answer for it not religion.[41] ‡
     We are all ready to give up our white doctors' medicine at the drop of a
hat. For Christian Science for boué[42] for Kikapou[43] Indian Remidies. Ans. Not

---

* Phrase "with no one's hand . . . down" written bottom to top along the left hand side of
the page.
† Page written in blue ink.
‡ Entry written in black ink.

generally till our own white mans medicine has given us up. Our constituted medicine cant blame us if we turn to ~~drugs~~ pills we know not of when abandoned to desperation.

'Thence we sailed on . . . glad to ~~be free~~ {escape} from death but missing our dear companions.

Moral (defined) is to be born into a family—the thinking that comes from being born into a family.

All the state is for is to protect the baby.*

All science is domestic science.† 44

[30v]   This is just a hang over from Puritanism.

What if the only way to describe it was by examples and we had to say we meant such people as Washington Adams Hamilton Bryant Lincoln etc and all our preaching was no more than wishing we could go on having people like those.

Beautiful word pavement or so someone says.45
He stood in rags on the pavement
He didnt know what a shove ment

To get as soon as possible so that at any particular time you don't have to see do or say anything.

[31r]   For the Head   The comb for the non deg man
From the no-deg boy at Bowdoin Commencement46

For God's sake brace up and accept to something you can fool them all yet‡

Lesleys47 thrown room

Cleverness may take away from the charm of goodness: it certainly adds the needed touch of the charm of badness.

Illogic

---

* Entry written in black ink.
† Entry written in black ink.
‡ This entry continues on 34r.

He may be born ~~the~~ without the law and without love, the bastard of a {harlot} ~~prostitute~~, {a child without spiritual ancestors or [illegible]}, representing a break with everything but the material and he need ~~will~~ be no more lacking in sentiment and idea than the most lineally {~~and legiti~~mately} descended from thought from sentiment and idea

It was excusable when the world was new to ~~oppose~~ take sides with form ~~and~~ against matter or with matter against form. Just so suppose it is still excusable in the infancy of experience to take sides with democracy[48] against monarchy. We are about to see that they hold each other up

[*31v*]   [blank]

[*32r*]   by leaning against each other. They offset each other. They depend on each other for opposition like two ~~playing cards~~ {cards} ~~in~~ in building {card} houses. Takes sides with jade against agate

The Ferners are Furiners

Man tells mentality. Mantellity you mean.

My Previous Existences. (Soc. Of Politician A Mill Hand, Etc.

Do you think he won't come home at all if he doesn't get elected?— Someones coming up the steps. Did you lock the front door.

Is that all "the far" you can throw

Jonah's fear that the Lord would weaken and fail him.[49]

Bryans heart[50] was all right in sympathizing with the poor: his brain may have been all right too. It was his finger that was wrong. He was always putting it on the wrong ~~pl~~ thing as to blame for the poverty of the poor.

[*32v*]   Two kinds of pacifists[51] those who ~~think~~ dont want war and those who think you can get along without war. I'm first class

Tecumseh & Ulysses[52] and how were those those for names

•   •   •

These three hundred years of the reformation or protestation will some day be written up in church history as an incident within the church and all souls concerned in it will ~~be forgiven~~ receive absolution from the Pope

Yankee {once used ~~for~~ to mean New Englanders alone} was extended by the war to mean all Americans of the United States. It is but a matter of time when the ~~new~~ name New England will be extended in the same way to cover the whole country. Then because by that time it will be so much oftimes spoken of than ~~Old~~ England it will simply be spoken of as England and England is old England

[*33r*]* My friends are divided into those who try to be good and those who try to be clever and I <u>must</u> say ~~that~~ {it does seem if} on the whole those who try to be good ~~are a good deal more successful~~ {come nearer to being good} than those who try to be clever {come} to being clever.

Isn't that because it is harder to be clever than it is to be good?

That may well be. That well may be

How do people try to be good?

In three ways—by rule from the heart and by rule and from the heart together.

How do people try to be clever

By sharpening their wit on the good.

What is the first prerequisite to that?

Wit.

Isn't it clever to hold the opinion that art is amoral, I mean to hold that ~~and~~ {a work} {or so}[†] may be ~~contrary~~ against morality and yet great art? Isnt it clever {also} to hold that there is such a thing as pure form without content?

No assumption establishes a claim to cleverness. Performance on the assumption is the test—what you are able to do with

[*33v*]   Then we will decide how many Englishmen it will pay us to keep in Old England as an outpost toward Europe. Ten million perhaps for ~~old~~ the sake of the old associations. We English moved in 1620.[53] We havent moved all of our things yet. ~~But~~ By the time I speak of we shall have—all but a few actual parts of the landscape. Those we want to make pilgrimages to clear up to the end and so will want them provided with hotels and keepers. I say this to enrage Canadians rather than Englishmen. ~~If the~~ If the center of empire is going to

---

* Entry written in blue ink.

[†] This entry picks up on an entry begun on 33r.

shift this way they {may} naturally look for it to move to Ottawa rather than to—well Chicago. Well who can you blame them as yet?

[*34r*] the assumption.*

Instance please.

~~You~~ {An} instance you mean of cleverness in making play with either of these assumptions. It was clever ~~for~~ {of} someone to point out that the [illegible] best advocates {in our day} of ~~fo~~ pure form found without content were {not artists but} were the so called Schools of Education wh{ich} spent four years on the forms of teaching with no subject matter {mentioned.}† ~~It was clever for~~ It was clever ~~for~~ {of} me to refuse to {help}‡ save an ~~amoral~~ {immoral} book from ~~the censor~~ being suppressed by the censor. You don't see why. I agreed that it was an immoral thing for the censor to suppress any book or play. But as an ~~imm~~ amoralist I could not concern myself ~~to~~ with his act to ~~oppose it~~ disapprove of it that is any more than I could disapprove of the book. Moral and immoral were one to me form the higher artistic assumption made.

Doesn't know a Pyrric Victory from a Parthian shot crum con from cal cur.§

I know a lady who is suffering from aphasia[54]

[*34v*] You cant ~~say~~ {predict} who in particular will be dead a graduating class ~~in~~ a of one hundred in fifty years but you can say what number more or less exactly for actuarial purposes. Science says ~~it is~~ the same is true of the shooting atom and group atoms.[55] That is there is freedom for the individual and law for the mass. Good metaphor but you make probably as much error in one prediction as in another only it is divided and made to look small compared with the size of the operation

Statically is the way [?I] view the others individually myself and immediates

·   ·   ·

---

* Phrase appears below the line.
† Inserted below line.
‡ Inserted in left-hand margin.
§ See 22r above.

My death to a doctor may mean a one percent loss for the year. For me it means a 100% loss.

[35r] Jealousy is a provision of nature against persons untrustworthiness when it comes to judging himself in his relations with the opposite sex. Louis wife[56] knew long before he did that he was falling in love with his next wife.

The Great Square of Pegasus (the Winged)[57]

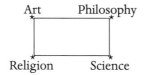

Inability to like the world you've made your bed with is like coldness in married women

Union Station

Play out of How the World Scored Twice off Joan of Arc once ~~enjoying~~ {glutting} its condemnation of her once ~~enjoying~~ {indulging in} magnaminity toward her. Where did she come in.

Medizing Greekes[58]

Over Back[59]

Penny Peep Show (Penny Poppy Show)

Playing Sots. Out fastidiating each other

Putrifactors Hostiles

[35v]
A book should chiefly represent a state the author was in while writing. Half the authors wrote in no particular state at all.

[36r] Someone asks me to get angry and do something about an immoral book's having ~~beingen~~ suppressed by the censor. Surely I am no objector to immo-

rality. Quite right ~~Neither am I~~ to the immorality of books books nor to the immorality ~~in censors who~~ of suppressing them. Both faintly amuse me. On with the arts.

> So now to your life
> Seek your human level

> But Islands of the Blessed God bless you son
> I couldn't seem to find a blessed one[60]

Morality is a few rules to save you from doing what you cant afford to find out about by ~~experience~~ even a single experience—such as killing

A man in Williamstown was loudly lamenting the death of a student worth five million dollars. "Why weep on an uncertainty" I objected. How do we know the boy may not have gone to something better than five million dollars? The answer was He'd be a pretty lucky boy

[*36v*]   O Bertran de Bornagain[61]
Your sword is mightier than your pen

You Can Communicate.

Cheapen Death

Disarming Foreign Jealousy by Self Absuses

Why Lenin Laughed

He was the kind that cant keep from being bad without being good.

[*37r*]   to get two such starts in two lives right off in succession.

The Doctor came with everything to make ~~test complete~~ the examination complete thermometer stethescope and I don't know what all. Ah, so? He said over the prostrate form of the {Miss} poet. "~~Of~~ Such [illegible] being the case I should advise your being loaded on to a special train and sent down to New York at once to see your publisher." It was diagnosis and prescription in one. The poet had not spoken. And when she came to New York and her publishers could be {was} summoned she was still speechless. She seemed at the point of death. She made a motion with her fingers alone to bring him nearer [illegible] {and bend} his head to catch her least sound. IIer [lip] mouth opened sickly wide. Her lips parted further than her teeth like the threat of a wounded tiger. A-ad-*

[37v] Blood is as hard to dam back as water
Just when we think we have it safe {it is impounded safe} in check
It breaks its boundaries {out in} some new-fangled slaughter {new kind of}
{new invented slaughter}⁶² †
It is the force itself

The radio to me
        denied speech at Democratic convention
  Bryan⁶³ on the little portable and aerial ribbon strung to an apple tree
  Earl [?Carrol] of after midnight mocking holiness and purity-and his girls laughing
  Voices toward morning in Missouri singing
  Oh what a morning—When the sun begins to fall.

Mortalities. The toxic man who said you had to fight to live. He would take what he had to. But he the right of way or enough to keep from staring Only he didn't believe in doing it with no gun. The begging little girls Give me a penny {in front of the movies}.
  Give us a penny mister.
  I dont believe a man ought to start giving pennies to little girls on the street. Mammas ought to give little girls their pennies. I wouldnt give you a penny unless I asked your Mamma first. You have a mamma havent you
  First little girl sadly as with fresh loss No sir [illegible] {I have} want them other.
  Second little girl Mar-y!

[38v] Another later.

  I was the calf that now I put into the back of the wagon to take to market.

---

* This entry continues on 38r.
† Line is written in blue ink.

[*38r*]   vertise me she gasped.—Repressed advertising.

Go to Lilley's Proverbs in Euphues[64] for a good start on the way people have taken their metaphors from Quintilian[65] down. Good thesis. As ornament as persuasion as economy. As truth.

Force broken out again in slaughter (cars)   Blood itself

Instead of Rah Rah Rah Radcliffe I cheer "Iambics forever!" Tell the I Amb[66] Jehovah said. Play on prejudices—moral prejudices in subject—iambic prejudices in form. Iambic is etc.

What would I give   You shall not put
For the chance to live   Blue under foot.

The first one I ever made: ~~Every~~ Sentences have a direction of their own back or forth across the penny under the paper. The idea comes out in lines almost at right angles to the lines of the sentences.

Cow lick

One milk maids arm was round the cows foreleg.

A settled time is one in which it is a reproach not to take care of your life ~~and~~ property {and reputation}. A transition time is one in which it is a reproach to take care of any of these.

A lost soul is one lost in the size and complexity of life.[67]

And freedom shall awhile repair*
We were the first that ever burst[68]
I fill this cup to one made up.

The Shadow. A striking unexplained person silent on the stage all through the play

•   •   •

---

* Page written in blue ink.

Everybody is finally going to be privileged to be as gentlemanly to everybody else as gentlemen are to equals.

⌊ *39r* ⌉ We may obscure ourselves in the machinery till we are as hard to find as God is in the universal machine but we will still be there somewhere foot on pedal hand on brake or finger on button. God may show himself then to us as equals in the same situation, expecting us to understand and sympathise.

Life is realizing curves with the body. Deeds are an appreciation of the surfaces gone over. The scythe concaves the hollow

The Entering Wedge and His Indulgence

The prison[illegible] Visitor and the Outbreak (everyone had some little concealed weapon rubbed down from spoon or tool on ~~the~~ his cell walls.) (What did you do that everyone else hasn't done)

The Mummy Warder.

What is the descent into Hades.[69] It is granting the worst. Say your darkest and I'll say it with you.[70] I can go far down before I feel the need to return before I catch any thing to resist the torrent of destruction. For what was I given speed if it was not to run up all streams that spend[71] Nothing can carry me down further than in the luxury of self confidence I choose to let myself be swept away backwards

[*39v*] We {Sloans} tried it in the generation before mine. ~~I don't know that~~ I cant say it failed because it wasnt given a fair chance. There were irrelevant factors that affected the result and kept the experiment from being laboratory clean. The question was was great ability enough itself. The answer seemed to be {in the} negative so far as it went. It went far enough to satisfy us Sloans.

The only ideality is to waste.[72]
Generosity musnt be thrown away or it is not generosity.
The tramp's boy or the lower idealism.

•　　•　　•

Life is that that divides to meet itself as a stranger.[73] The part acts on us from behind in our inheritance and across the curve of the road in our environment[74]

The Tomb Inspector

Attempts to Teach

Thought masses and globulates in space like a {fiery} gass. Its outline is waving and irregular. It ~~shades~~ {thins} into nothingness so imperceptibly etc. It jets violently out from itself in geysers A hundred thousand miles in measure.

[40r] The marvel of it is that it is structural and articulate within itself in layers and wedges the human mind can discriminate.

The Bolsheviki[75] [illegible] give a divorce for conflict of politics or religion. So would I {if at all} All depends on what is thought on what is thought important, unity of body or of mind. Some of the ~~ideas~~ {prejudices} we have ~~of~~ against promiscuity (so as to distinguish between ~~animal~~ {social human} love and ~~human~~ {sex} love) against incest (so as to maintain the distinction between sex love and parental love) against sodomy so to maintain it between ~~sex~~ {animal} love and human love against orientalism so as to maintain it between sex love and divine love.

Topless towers so high[76]—cute on a coin.
It is forbidden you to take away from the beauty and might of Illium.
All right wont diminish Illium for you if you wont America for me.
Are you for or against America. I am too much of it to know the answer.*

Suppose I must be more international or unnational minded than most I have always shrunk so from either bragging of America or finding fault with it: comparing it favorably or unfavorably with other countries. Anymore than I like to compare myself favorably or unfavorably. I like to remove the idea— having from the realm of the ~~adverb~~ [illegible] verb like to the realm of the adverblike

[40v] could

---

* Written below line.

I reel them off with one brain tied behind me.
I wouldnt trust a preacher any further than I could throw a church by the steeple.

A triad: Three [illegible] in killing Three killers: The state the murderer {criminal} the anarchist.

The Two expropriators the state, the criminal but not the anarchist. It is hard to tell the three apart as killers. The anarchist separates himself in theft. I think.

Some think {life is unreasonable and} the little reason in man is broken and defeated by the unreasonableness of life. But no, life is reasonable. It has direction and is bound the way of logic.

[41r]   It has all the errors mistakes you can possibly make listed and numbered in it And every time you obviously avoid making one of them it counts as a figure of speech in your favor.
Every time you avoid making a number {lot} of them {together} it counts as a work of art.

I should think anyone would have to have been brought up on the book to appreciate the such a work of art.
Yes just as on the Greeks Virgil Homer and the Bible to appreciate the literature of the last few hundred years. You have to have some standard of appreciation for any literature.

The Club woman (Her abasement)

How safe! I mean it could be said acceptably in any {modern} company

[41v]   The Mass of Thought. Eclipse

Sex Love and the Other Loves. Philosophy runs things together.

To Say Matter in Terms of Mind[77]

Pursuit of a Pursuit[78]

•   •   •

I blame Philosophy for Running All Together.

The universe a machine without a Pedal.[79]

{Spirit and Matter a Mechanical Mixture[80]
{The Serious Jester
How Are These Two One. Activity.
The Figure Called Synecdoche[81]
The Descent into Hades.[82]
Beauty Not Truth   True Thomas[83]
The Prophet   (It is not enough that I tell you
        what is true now but I must prophesy).
Realism and Rappacinis Daughter[84]
The transitive-intransitive
Dance of Life Believers.[85]
Self shocker and the Boogie Mans Abyss
The Dwarfing by Repression. ~~Not say~~
Not Saying till I See.[86]
The Science is what is defective in the
Old Testament not the religion[87]

[42r] The verb at once transitive and intransitive launches us into the vague vast infinite. For instance, I say How do I know and before anybody can ask What? I continue. I know from certain lives I have seen lived. Infuse an object and take off into my mysticism.

I have heard from the outside

Suppose the last house were the one I saw in Landaff[88] Most of its front was gone facing the north and I could see the furniture in it as in a childs play house. There were children playing around it, all idiot offspring of idiot parents. That would be enough. The only continuity that matters is the continuity of birth. All the other continuities of thought tradition or civilization can be restored at will from that.

I will tell you who my father was   { He kept the boiler
                                        { He was an editor
                                        { He owned mines

                    •   •   •

I am in a Position where I can say almost anything—and mean it.*

I have not wanted to say grief more than archly.

[42v]   When he came to work on the new job he was ignorant: he didn't know what
he neednt do. He had nothing to go by but his own idea of perfection. Experience relieved him. Experience taught him how much short of perfection he
was permitted to come. Science is like that. Science is nothing but practical
experience carried to a greater extent. It ~~lengthens~~ pushes knowledge from
miles to light years. It teaches us on the job what is passable in material
strength {speed} and finish, in the universe what is sufficient to do and think.
It teaches us to forget sentiment not to worry {or be anxious} about sentiment nor ~~and~~ about God who is the King of sentiment. There is a sentiment
of strength in building some builders have had—to last forever. There is a
sentiment people have had in mating to love forever. There is a sentiment
they have had in living—to live forever—as sentiment of immortality. Science
teaches us how much less ~~that~~ than all this it is possible to get along on. If a
man didnt know he might think what perfection was to expect as much jealousy in a wife as he found in himself. Science tells him that the cases are different. His jealous

[43r]   watchfulness is practical it assures him of his blood property in his children. His wifes jealousy—his recognition of that and deference to it is a sentiment.

   [?The] Passions

   Property What I have that you mustnt be jealous {of me} for.
   Because I Fear you. Fear. I have always been afraid

   At the same time I allow jealousy. I want to be guarded and watched [~~illegi-
ble~~] over by the jealousy of a strong nature. Jealousy gives me [illegible]
the sense of being held more than arms around me. I laugh quietly in my
security.

---

* Entry written in blue ink.

Fever Promise

From amphibians or reptiles to mammals was a transition of blood temperature. The coming race will be one that for whom our fever temperature will be normal

Life is that that parts to meet itself with surprise and fright[89]

One who presumes to think for himself is one who is too uneducated to have learned what others have thought for him. So say the professors of the various subjects. All that can be dug out of what we are and where we are has already been dug out. But isnt it a kind of confirmation of the [illegible] truth of thinking of starting fresh and independently that is without too much knowledge of what others have formed we again find the same things true of man God and the universe?

[43v]   This {colonial} thing {the US}
This egg that England has brought into existence her only hope to destroy it is to [illegible] {crush} it [illegible] in her own ~~jaws~~ colonial jaws Canada[90] Australia South Africa and the islands of the sea

Wouldnt we like to know? All we've done the best we could guess. Now tell us. No guess some more. How much more?

Ans. That which parts to meet with surprise and fear*

Mousterian[91] Grief. A ~~race~~ species that sank vitiated and went under. (But worship)

Luxuriation. The mind that loses distinctions our nature makes in practice.

I left myself in England and went back looking for myself.

The patriot: we are going to have culture: but [illegible] whats more we are going to have had all the cultures that any other country ever had Aurignacian[92] [?question]

·   ·   ·

---

* There is a line drawn from the end of this entry outside the right hand margin to the entry beginning "I left myself . . ."

The question is are we {ourselves} eoliths:[93] that is shapes that might have been shaped on each other in the rush of the stream of life or if you prefer by intention for some crude use.

Two that asked in their will to have their bones cleansed petrified and put {side by side} where they wouldn't probably be found for 100 000 years but pretty surely would be then and let it say what it would to the people living then.

[44r]   Not heaped together with animal bones in a river draft

<u>Thee, United   States.</u> Our confidence not that progress will go on because it is progress but because it is a projection of what we can see where we have been and come from.

1. Space is circular? In vain produced all rays return?[94] Time is circular. The furthest from now is on the opposite side of the circle of time to that on which we stand. I believe if space looks circular and time too it is because thought is circular. There is no reasoning so straight that it is not ultimately when followed out a vicious circle. Learning is a vicious circle certainly forever returning on itself. We learn A ~~to lea~~ by which to learn B by which to learn C by which to learn D by which to learn A again and so on round and round.[95]
2. That which parts to meet itself with surprise
3. Alternate legs of the dualism.

Which do you think are more significant Legs or wheels? You mean symbolical?

[44v]   Ministers. If they were what they pretend to be you wouldnt always see them ~~coming~~ in the first ~~class~~ {cabin} pushing for place and provender. Why dont some of them come across with the poor in third class?—If they wanted to be really ~~Christlike~~{ian}* they would walk.
[~~illegible~~]

Travellers

·   ·   ·

---

* Phrase written in blue ink.

Bancroft[96] at Fifty   Cal Boardman
The Work of Art. Tatooing
The Running Gag Man
Mosier.

Let Religion ~~always~~ enter ~~more~~ into combination with the science of the time for it will whether we let it or not. It did anciently with such science as there was in the beginning. It does to day in the mind of the modernist. The science it takes up is always the falsest part of religion however and the part that is most subject to change. The ~~religion~~ science of religion in Genesis seems ridiculous now and the science of religion in early Christian times.[97] The science that religion takes over

[45r]

today ~~will~~ religion will sooner or later drop. The science changes. The religion persists. The religious part of religion has been nearly the same for a ~~thou~~ 5000 years at least.

You can ~~stop~~ hold your breath when you have to get passed a smell of gas or eccersion. But not as long as you can refrain from work or companionship. How long can you refrain form work or human society? It is not known exactly. The camel has a hump to draw on and it may last him through great deserts. (Repressed Jasmine pine.)

Gardiner Jackson[98] says I told him to be a "bum." (There is the first time I ever said or wrote the word. But though I cant have used a word so impossible to my nature I may very well have told him to be something he took as being equivalent to what we meant by "bum." I should think Leonard Cline[99] came nearer the ideal than Gardiner Jackson. The way to be pleasant about it: You're like me—youre a liar. capable of desertion

I trusted myself too much. The boy said
I thought I would live till we married. I didn't ~~think~~ {I didn't think was capable of desertion} And nor you are caught   without a husband. I hope the arrow for my loss will dignify you and make shameless.

[45v]   The play begins with curtain after curtain as if the audience were calling and the actors singly and in groups acknowledging plaudits. It becomes [~~illegible~~] figures in a Curtain call Dance.

A Hitch-Hike Song on a Street Corner at on a stormy night.

A technical philosopher is one who uses an apparatus of words in an attempt to make a science of what is probably only an art. Define your terms! Aristotle begins it.

Two thousand years before there was the right of the Seigneur there was Virgnius and Virginia.[100]

Talk of "service" in our day is just one attempt of the servant to get on top in the transaction.

[46r] For his desire was toward her and his thought
Was toward her with such strength it swept her thought
Back on herself so that she dropt her eyes
Before his eyes and saw but with his eyes
And saw herself {saw} not him at all but saw herself
Mounted upon stone or mountain peak
Beaten upon by light blown round with wind.

A man looks at a woman. Does a woman look at a man? She drops her eyes and in imagination sees herself as he sees her: She is lovely to both of "them." You may read it in poetry by women. Hattie Hatters.

Ends of Debate.

Town planning. He wouldnt let an artist (Lankes)[101] put a large studio window into his garage for fear it would look like a factory. I'll bet he uses the best wild spot in the scenery to [illegible]dump his village rubbish in.

[46v] Please Let Me Flourish[102]

Somewhere on earth where as in heaven
desert doesn't matter.
    The inalienable right to fail.
    To flourish is to play
    Insurance against two things: failure and success,
that is to say, being made a fool of by either or of making too much of either. Philosophy is that insurance. So is an inner circle of friends and lovers. We must have those we can be merely whimsical with, unguarded and undesigning
    When I was young I was afraid of life. I was afraid to touch to disturb to

break and to break silence. Now I am old I am afraid to die. Who are these cheapeners and what are they for. Are they to cheapen life for us by making it less awful And if I could call or let them in on me and credit them could they cheapen death for me and make it less a terror.

The schoolboy's dream. That he had his answer for once to the teacher's brutality.

[47r]   Mr so and so what does Shakespeare mean by that sentence.

The school boy reads it again.

Well what does he mean by it.

Are you expecting me to improve on it in clearness by words of mine. Do you expect me to express it better in unity emphasis coherence clearness force or elegance. Or do you ~~expect~~ want to exalt over me for explaining it worse.

I ask you text for ~~marking~~ rating.

Most of the time I dont want to be rated even in school. I am different from other children in kind. I cant be compared with them in degree.

You refuse to be compared with them in degree.

You ask me to tell you what Shakespeare means. And bid my will avouch it ~~so that~~ in better or worse words of my own so that you can get something on me to measure me by. Wont you reframe you question to say what do you think I think Shakespeare

[47v]   meant.

Well what do you think I think he meant.

That's just it. I cant help wondering as I look at you instead of at the text. You are a great study professor so and so.

Protection. The right ~~to~~ not to stay under people who are too much for you. The right to shirk dealing with them either with ~~yes no~~ ~~or no~~ to their yes or yes to their yes {not to dispute}. So where What springs in you resumes its flow.

As harmless as the shade of trees
Were   of these
If self in me were but at ease.

Much confusion comes from confusing progress with evolution. Progress goes on visably around us mounting from savages to barbarians to civilization to sophistication to decadence and so to destruction. Evolution[103] is a change from form to form invisible imperceptible and only known if at all by inference like the state of a great battle.

[48r]   The wife I tell you of she lived in Lennox
Had taken summer courses in eugenics[104]

                                                    Milieu
                    and if his stuff seemed sillier
He might be at his second juvenilia

The doctor said you want your head trephined?
"I want to let a skylight in my mind."
I got the notion form the ancient Mayas[105]
he didn't understand but answered* Ah yes

Not that man ~~and the~~ is descended from the apes. Nobody now thinks he is. Merely that he is descended from the same ancestor as the apes. That common ancestor though has left no trace. How long ago to look for him. Upwards of 50,000,000. I suppose it will be the same with the horse and the three toed horse there are not in a direct line they have ~~merely~~ merely converge to a common ancestor who vanished and left no trace. Dont all these vanished common ancestors make you suspicious.

[48v]   The new people ~~whom education has taken by surprise~~ who after {the} setting up of high school and college go next {in course} to Europe only to find themselves a laughing stock with class of society over there they are admiting to {by mistake} and then come home to us with the news that it is not enviable in these days to be an American as we were taught in kindergarden but comical as any fool can find out in a summer vacation {in Paris} or {on a} Rhodes scholarship at Oxford. ~~They~~ An access of {self-consciousness} embarrassment might put it into their heads they were speaking for themselves. Education has taken them by surprise and made them ridiculous. The class they are admitted to is too high by half—just half. They are betwixters.
        I'd like to travel the whole country some time staying a week at each lecture place and make a book of Home Travels like Timothy Dwights[106]

                    •   •   •

---
* Inserted below line.

Concerned that the universe started* in several ~~contagion~~ centers of contagion at once broke out in [~~illegible~~] separate places in the sky with [~~illegible~~] mumps measles whooping cough and scarlet fever that spread and interpenetrated to make what we have

[50r]   God owes it to the Jews to keep his promise to have a Messiah who is to come in worldly power so the sermon went But hasnt he come in worldly power.

---

* Phrase written in blue ink.

"America and The Plot"

MS. 001727. *Blue soft paper cover notebook, 6¾″ × 8½″, with canvas strip binding. Pages stitched. Ink varies as noted.*

[*Cover*]   America
              and
          The Plot

              And

          No Way of Knowing
          How Bad the Age

          See Amherst Student[1]

[*Page*]*   The Man in the Tree looked down at me and I looked ~~down~~ up at him. His ~~saw was in his hand and he was sawing off a limb. The tree was apple~~ He had a cross cut in his hand and was sawing off a limb. The tree was was apple leafless now

[*1r*]†   Oh Let Me Flourish[2]

The shadowy first ~~neglect~~ comparative neglect. Denied to books and turned out to play.
    Seek s ~~to~~ occupation where there is no comparision.
    Choice of words choice of anything: No alternatives.
    The unrelinquished worshipper. Only a letter.
    The master who wouldnt say you would do: You neednt go to school anymore.
    Proud but broken ancestry.[3]

                    •   •   •

---

* This page is a torn slip, inside front cover.

† Page written in black ink.

Figure a superiority before you go to sleep instead of praying.

Frightened by the daring of those who ask no friend or home.

All the fears.   Fear of not being found worthy.

[*2r*]* Let me be the one
To do what is done
Let me be the one⁴

Let me tell you the things you want
In the order in which you want them

[Many pages torn out]

[*4r*]† sinners with Hell for a long time after it parted with the mother church. But
~~by that act~~ by the mere act of defying the only church's sentence to Hell it
raised the question whether anyone could send anyone else at all to Hell. The
game was up. The Kingdom of God had come on earth The greatest church
of all was on the way of a billion indifferents whom no priest could scare or
get any hold on.⁵

[*4v*]‡ This is the story of ~~Protestantism~~ {the Protestants}. At first ~~it was~~ {they
were} hardly any less religious than the strictest of the religionists it had broken with. In fact like people ~~now~~ {since} who ~~le~~ {have} neglected the church
they could only excuse themselves {on the ground} that it was because they
were more religious rather than less. But the church saw through them and
saw where the logic of spiritual self reliance however high and devoted
would lead them. It has lead us to where we all are now each a church unto
himself answerable to nobody but himself and his God - ~~a~~ recreant to all
other authority—at home on Sunday in bed in the morning instead of at
Mass. ~~The~~ Freedom or whatever this is ~~The~~ Protestant{ism}§ set out on ~~a~~
{the [~~illegible~~]} the course that has won it for us. ~~Throu~~ From Puritanism to
Unitarianism to Individualism Bless the Protestant or curse him. He has
taken the sting out of what the Church ~~th~~ once thought it could make of

---

* Page written in blue ink
† Page written in blue ink. It is the continuation of the following page.
‡ Page written in blue ink.
§ Inserted below the line.

death if you died without benefit of clergy. ~~The~~ Protestantism still threatened

[5r]*   {We Protes} We Protestants were hardly any less religious than the strictest of [illegible] America.

We moved over in 1630 but we havent brought all our things over yet. We havent finished moving. {A lot of ideas are still ~~to~~ coming to us. ~~Such as that~~} Americans get to meager a sex experience for art. {One idea ~~com~~ yet to come is} (I say it as a foreigner and a lady)—There may be some thing to that. It seems a proven fact that Shermans ~~scourging~~ devastating army of 60 000 ~~moved through~~ went through Georgia and Carolina practically without rape.[6] [Illegible] {Our} men seem not to have heard what's permitted {them} either in war or peace. You are a brave lady here to tell us our lack and perhaps supply our lack.—No I have pointed it out; you must look to your own women to supply it.

Come wouldn't you be Iseult to my Tristram[7]

Which Iseult

The ~~one~~ wife of Mark. Or would that be an Inseult. On the other hand we have an authoress who says ~~sh~~ he cant remember the names of the boys she has slept with (so to speak) because she ~~has~~ slept {so to speak} with so many.

[6r]†   What worries me

She must be suffering from Aphasia to forget {names} like that[8]

Very likely. But nevertheless it says something for the [illegible] liberality of our sex experience {not even to keep an account book}. I suppose you laugh at our quaint provincial attempts to [illegible] be worldly—old worldly

Laugh at you. We 'owl at you.

It is a great shock to some of us to find out that we are laughed at by nations so sure to be right. We graduate from our high schools under the im-

---

* Page written in black ink.
† Page written in black ink.

pression that it is no mean thing to be an American—that it is a proud thing. But that summer we get abroad in a cattle boat {perhaps} and almost the first thing we discover is that in the eyes of Europeans it is a ridiculous thing to be an American. That gives us our first literary impulse which is to go home and tell the folks. {And then again} Those of us who join Europeans in laughing at the rest of us cant be such fools as the rest of us* The ~~only~~ way to disarm ridicule is to ridicule ourselves and before hand with our foreign critics. Arent we comical ~~we~~ the way we suppress obscene books. You English

[7r]† do it more than we {and it seems perfectly all right and dignified}. But when we do it it is really funny. And thats only one of the funny things about us. We are absolutely low comedy. Tell it to the small town and the American Legion. You are too young to remember how the foreign correspondents and all their readers in Europe burst into peals of laughter at the silly battles of our Civil War. We absurd even in our sorrows.

What worries me about your country is that {since your Civil War} it has no compartments to keep ~~all~~ the population or ~~all~~ the business from all rushing to one side ~~of or another~~ of the country when conditions list the least bit and leaving the other side empty. The states are supposed to be such compartments. But the unfortunate outcome of the Civil War virtually did away with the states.

What worries you. ~~What~~ You mean what pleases you. {You've heard that from the States righters.} Don't you distrust your {sanguine} judgement in believing everything we say against ourselves. We join in with you in publishing our faults.

[8r]   Not impressed with our size‡

We say our architecture is made of chewing gum stretched up ward with one pull from the mouth. We ~~say anything~~ recklessly say anything. But mightnt it be to allay the general jealousy we cant help feeling {from around us}. We rather dread the next war till we see more clearly who is going to line up on our side and we are willing to do anything that words can to keep ourselves of contemptible regard. We can afford to talk ourselves down we are so sure

---

* This phrase inserted between lines and written partly up the right side of the page with an arrow pointing to the space under "And then again."
† Page written in black ink.
‡ Phrase written in blue ink.

of ourselves. Thats one thing and another is: {our} self depreciation cant help putting off the evil day when the envy of the world will try to bring us down into the to the classification of the {7} nations in sufferance like Switzerland Belgium and Denmark and Spain.

> You are of a hopeless conceit.
> Did you think you had us grovelling.

[9r]   Dialogue on Humanism

Swain　　A humanist and mollycoddle
Nymph　　A mollycolumnist
Swain: Your are too unrestrained
You {Nymph}: You are too restrained
No Swain: No I am just restrained enough
Nymph I am just unrestrained enough.
Swain: Just restrained enough and just unrestrained enough sounds like meeting in the middle. Lets take hands and dance (They a whirl) a whirl together. (They dance.)
Swain {breathless from dancing.}. But you concede there is such a thing as being too unrestrained?
Nymph Just as you must concede there is such a thing as being too restrained. American men for example lead much too restrained a sex life for the good of American art
Swain You speak as a woman and a foreigner
Nymph　　Exactly

[10r]　Swain. You point out the deficiency. The question is {what} are you prepared to do about it
Nymph. Nothing. I merely point it out and leave it to your own women to do what they please about it.
Swain There may be something to what you say. It seems to be an established historical fact that our most devastating army in the Civil War committed Shermans on its march through Georgia {sacking town and country} committed almost no rape. They plundered without ravishing
Nymph. Your men seem a poor lot. Their idea of a sexual orgy is minding the baby and paying a wifes bills
Swain. They arent romantic are they. Now are romantic arent you?
Nymph. Lets not be persona!

Swain. Wouldnt you if I asked you ~~on~~ on once be my Iseult. I mean the Iseult wife of King Mark. (or would that be an Inseult.

I am 'ere to diagnose your case not to treat it.

Ere says you! 'Ere 'ere. ~~You~~ All the time you were*

[*11r*]   English when I thought you Irish.†

Ungenerous not to leave ~~it some thing to others in keeping you~~ {partly to others}. to keep you from falling off a roof.‡

[*13r*]   We have no way of knowing that this age is one of the worst in the world's history. Arnold claimed that honor for the last age before this. Wordsworth claimed it for the last but one. And so on back through literature. I say they claimed the honor for ~~this~~ their ages. They claimed the honor for themselves rather. It is immodest for a man to think he is ~~up either standing up or~~ going down before the worst forces ever mobilized by God. What it took to stop him is {to be} the measure of his ~~greatness~~ importance on his gravestone.

All ages of the world are bad—a good deal worse anyway than Heaven. They have to befor the world to justify its separate existence form Heaven. If they weren't the world might just as well be Heaven at once and have it over with. One can safely say after from six to thirty thousand years of experience the evident design is

[*14r*]   a situation here in which it will always be {about} equally hard to save ~~your~~ {the} your soul. Whatever progress may be taken to mean it can't ~~be~~ {mean} making the world any easier {a} place {in which} to save ~~your~~ {the} soul or if you dont like ~~your~~ {the} soul mentioned in open meeting, ~~say~~ {you} ~~your~~ {call it} decency, ~~your~~ {~~call it~~ or} integrity.

Ages may vary a little. One may be a little better or worse than another. But it is not possible to get outside of the age you are in to judge it exactly. Indeed it is {as} dangerous to try to get outside of anything as large as an age as it would be to engorge a whole donkey. And the proof is the many who in the attempt have suffered a dilation form which the muscles of the mind have never been able to recover natural shape They cant pick up anything delicate

---

* Entry written in pencil.
† Entry written in pencil.
‡ Entry written in blue ink.

or small any more. They cant use a pen. They have to use a typewriter And they gape in agony. They can write huge gobs of raw sincerity,

[14v]   Any {He} one who has ever tasted {attained to the} {achicved} form to be sure of it is lost to the larger excruciations. I think it must stroke faith in the {right} way it should lie.

Nothing so composing as composition[9]

We dont have to wait till we can get a team together to play them the game before we can play

[15r]   shapeless novels, bellowing with pain, and that's all they can do.

Fortunately we dont need to know how bad the age is. There is something we can always be doing without reference to how good or bad the age is. We can maintain and go on with form {in our modest ways.}. There is at least so much {the} good in the world {that} It permits of form and the making of form. The artist the poet might be expected to be most aware of such re-source {assurance}. But it is really in everybody's sanity to know {feel} and live by it. Fortunately too no forms are more engrossing gratifying comfort-ing and staying than those lesser ones we throw off like vortex rings of smoke, all our own individual enterprise and asking {needing} nobody's co-operation, a basket, a letter, a garden, a room {an idea} a picture a poem. an id The background is hugeness and confusion shading away from where we stand into black chaos and against the

[16r]   background {small} man-made figures of order and uniqueness compact-ness. In us the universe reaches its height of form and through us exceeds it-self.

There are suggestions of form as in rolling clouds realities we excerpt and by a touch at one end or another make less mistakable.

What happiness {pleasanter} than that this simple thing should be so {at all times} {writers we are novelists or economists} If I don't worry about the graded confusion of in its gradations {I cover out upon [illegible] my lec-tures} or tackle it to reduce it It is partly {not just} because I am afraid it would prove too much for me and the democratic-republican socialist-communist or anarchist party but because I like it, I was born used to it, and I have {practical} reasons for wanting it there to play to. To me any little form is velvet is cl. I am content to impose up form nothing {I am lost in} {I assert upon it is velvet} consider how much more it is than nothing. Whereas if I were a {good} Platonist I {suppose} should regret how much less it is than everything.

[17r]   Land has been taken up by trial and error. When the error has been excessive and especially where the government has been a party to the error by advertising {promoting agriculture in} the desert and letting {permitting} the railroads adver promote agriculture in the desert no question but that the government should do something to correct the error. The government is to blame for would have been to praise for having established watches to keep people from going into some land just as it is for having set up light houses to keep people from ships form going ashore. The state is in a position to see more widely than the people can for themselves: and to see further forward. A man should [illegible] take the thought for his children. The state may well take the thought for his grand children's grand children—that is if it expects its flag to wave a thousand years.

It may prove beyond the power of stateliness to make forests grow where there is no {small} water. At least this can restore the buffalo grass to attach the soil in place from wind water.

[18r]   Once there was a d {There once was so refined a child}
So perfectly devoid of greed
His fancy had to be beguiled
If he was to be made to feed.

[19r]   Weather tries the limits of human endurance. We were created between walls of ninety below and one hundred and thirty above and are ever dealt to be held there

---

The leader adds only to the last touch to the harmony of the orchestra, the teacher to that {the discipline} of the class the general to the discipline of the army the President to the order of the United States. If he takes exerts any presiding offices feels called on to exert more than a modicum of influence he will take away rather than add to——

•   •   •

[34v]   The Plot

The farmer who had to have everything right to begin with
The farmer who wanted to industrialize or be industrialized
The farmer whose time was too valuable to walk beside a horse
The farmer who got mad and poured his milk on the ground.
The politician wouldnt tell them what they could do till they saw it for them-
selves.
His don't you see the point speeches. Does it something tell you?

"Since surely good is evil's better half"

MS. 935440. *Cover: Cardboard cover marbled school theme/composition book, 7″ × 8½″; "Amherst upsidedown July 1935 Page 60" written in Frost's hand in the "Name" slot. Ruled pages. Entries are in blue ink unless otherwise noted.*

[1r]* ~~Since~~
  Good is ~~the~~

  Since surely good is evil's better half
  ~~We may as   a merry laugh~~
  It makes you give the world a merry laugh
  ~~Since~~ ~~T~~ that

[1v] All these called revolutions are our having an equalizer once in so often when our relative differences become unbearable to our natures and characters.[1]

[2r] What's all the turn us upside down fuss about Mary How many meetings have you got to address today.
  Ten between now and midnight
  That's too many for a woman with a family. I hope you get beaten at the polls tomorrow.
  Why.
  A dog a woman a wallnut tree
  The more you beat em the better they be.
Beating women ~~at~~ {in the privacy of the} home has gone out for the time being. Their well wishers must be content with wishing them ~~publicly~~ beaten in public beaten at the poles instead of with poles.
  I ought not to let you treat me so flippantly when such momentous things are at stake.

---

* In the upper left-hand corner of the page is a small circle with a cross in the center.

What now, is at stake.

If you don't know

After all my opportunities. I dont want to hear some little insignificant de-tail about this election. Mary I want you to tell me in the large if what you dont think you are bringing to birth as the poem says is a better world

Whose getting pretentious now?

[5r]   Learn the form now and then if you ever have anything to say you will be able to say it well—something to say it in

Same as to learning all past literature before you judge present literature*

No all there is to learning to write and speak is learning how to have something to say

(Making point Making analogy Making phrase Making your weight felt Making observations at nodes and cruxes. Good at premises)

Form without content and form before content are equally hard on us.

I said told a distressed and distressing fo pure formist once that dreamed all one night of trying to pull an empty balloon into shape from the outside.

From what I knew of learning to write I asked Harold Bauer[2] if it wouldnt be possible to learn to play by playing tunes from the beginning without pre-liminary finger exercises. He cheered me [illegible] with the assurance it would. Many second raters present were scandalized. Many Now Children are learning now without finger exercises. Think how much easier their edu-cation is to listen to.

This sounds like the false progressivism in education with all the pain and pains taken out.

[6r][†]   No it means simply that we have found that the satisfaction of meaning can be given children younger than we used to give it them. And of judge-ment

.   .   .

---

* Entry written in black ink. Rest of page written in blue ink.

[†] This page through 9r written in blue ink.

We wouldn't praise a person as much now as once for being willing to work unquestioningly as to ~~wha~~ the purpose of his work. (Story in the readers of the ~~man~~ servant who having moved a stone wall when ordered was then ordered to move it back again and so back and forward till he rebelled and asking a reason was fired.)

Inform is a good word. Let us inform with idea and meaning all we can of work and life. Otherwise those who come under us suffer suspense of nature and character to the detriment {of our young princes. Remember we are not talking of slaves}

But this is not to say spare those that come under us the pains of effort and discipline

They must be [~~illegible~~] {expected to undertake} self discipline.

I heard a false progressive say ~~there was~~ self discipline was the only discipline: and I was tempted to say he who has had only self discipline knows no discipline at all.

We must be taken in hand for our good.

[*6v*]   One of the hardest disciplines is having to learn the meaningless

[*7r*]   And yet a reservation even here. Complete understanding before action we are never going to have. The whole act of life passes but dimly explained. Children must be schooled ~~to free~~ accept their blindness by some daily act of blind obedience. Two reasons might be given for learning a conjugation. First because you can trust your teacher to make it useful that is to say meaningful presently. Second and best because some things we do we are never going to see the good of. We must learn young that it is not all important that we should be given a reason for everything

[*8r*]   For all her {mother} love our mother has to be severe enough with us to prepare us for the ~~slightly~~ somewhat less love and more severity of our teachers.
    The teachers are paid to like what we write better than it deserves. Then come the formidable editors who are paid to like it somewhat less than it deserves.

And so on outward in widening rings till we come to the drill sergeant in war time who only loves a little bit more than the enemy loves us.

The enemy will tell us he comes {("regenerative")} to chasten us with the rigors of conquest for the salvation of our soul, in other words to prepare us for the last judgement. We find it hard to believe the enemy speaking thus concerned for us. We deliberately draw the line at him.

There is nothing for it but to learn to enjoy pains of our own or others imposing.

But as I say life has a right to ask the sustenance of ~~daily~~ some daily meaning—more than we used to think children needed anyway. It is ennobling to be let into the idea—the large plan.

[9r]   Carpe diem[3] they tell us. Only dull clods live in the present They alone have nerves to stand the impact of things ~~to appreciate with appre~~ with appreciation The present is too much for the sensitive who divide to ways to miss and escape it. Once escapes into the future where he can have it {life} as he pleases and with it a superiority to all who cant claim to know what the future is to be. The other never knows what has happened to them till its over and always behind on realization are to be found back there in the past trying to catch up.

[12r]   Wrong Twice

1 He ~~was~~ is for ~~inter~~nationalism who was not long since for internationalism. Wrong twice!

3 He is for the coarsest of content—propaganda-coal in the stocking for Christmas who was not long since for pure form. Wrong twice! {The stocking empty and pulled instead of filled into shape.}*

2 He is for the [illegible] closest sociability like that of a ball of mud worms in a bait can who not long since was heard boasting he was never so social {good for society} as when he was alone. Wrong twice.

Some people have a ~~give~~ {weakness} for cleaving to any extreme just so long as it is an extreme.

·   ·   ·

---

* Written below the line.

For punishment they should be stuck in the golden mean and left there ~~to~~ ~~fancy think themselves Greek~~ in the ward of those whose illusion is that they are Greeks.

They think method is all. The haven't brains enough to equate the power shown {showing} through various methods.*

[*14r*]   A Great Nation in Its Greatness Can Afford Much.[4]

[*15r*]   Federal authority through the Post Office
Now if there was to be a real purge, such as—
I can tell by his looks he doesn't like our uniform.
Can we insist on correct looks?
Yes in an emergency.
Early in the night. Bailys porch[5]
He argues that a great nation in its greatness can afford some slight dissent surely.
    Ball of worms in a bait can
    Most social when he is at work alone[6]
    I know you neighbor Co[illegible] in your disguise
    You wouldnt know what I was talking about if I told you. I wont attempt to tell you.
    Bailys porch later
    Shall I tell you the true reason I wont cooperate to the extent of a sympathetic expression. It would seem to be my

[*16r*]   own sacred affair. It will be thrown away on you.

    You dont believe in the return of the Golden Age.
    That isnt what I was going to say.
    You think it can come back.
    I dont want it back. Who would it be for? For what {remnant} few {in the cold of the sun} would we have all sacrificed ourselves down through the ages?
    Listen to that heresy.
    I think your belief is as ridiculous as any I ever heard in a church.

                    •   •   •

---

* Entry written in blue ink.

The time was ~~fifty~~ {a hundred} centuries after Christ *
The continents were once more getting iced
The staples were getting exorbitantly priced
{So}† he got up ~~the prettiest~~ {a brand new} thing to believe
~~He gave a cunning laugh in his sleeve.~~
And though it was all with no intent to deceive
He gave a cunning laugh in his sleeve

[16v] Sympathy of the middle three fifths must be relied on to save us by its justice
to the lowest fifth and also to the highest fifth.

Then there is the theory that we slowly sink of our own weight till puff a
Christ a Caesar or Cromwell a Mussolini in short a revivalist comes from
somewhere outside to revive us raise us up and make us citizens again (B Ef-
fervescent bubble the speck rides up on‡

[17r] Now you Americans—
Just a minute. May I ask where you come from?-Where you were born?
In Western New York in a small town you never would have heard of sir.
Name it without hedging
Gardenville
One of my best friends lives there—a great American artist. You may
know him. J. J. Lankes.[7]
I have been away at school most of my life
I thought likely. But very scrupulous of you not to try to deceive me as to
your origin.
Scrupulous!
When you might so easily have been tempted to deny the country of your
birth Especially after the beginning you made of thrusting us to arms length
with {your} "You Americans."
Pardon my detachment. I would speak the same way to the British. Surely
you believe in detachment
Not {in} the least. I would attach myself to the anything I touched. I am
worse than a limpet. barnacle

---

* This entry and the lines that follow it on the page written in blue ink.
† This word in left margin.
‡ Phrase starting with parenthesis written in blue ink.

[*18r*]   I am so sorry to hear that of you. What becomes of our boasted internationalism.

Oh you are an internationalist and I take it a Rhodes Scholar with that accent.

I have been told I had an accent, but I have sometimes doubted it myself.

Be reassured. You have one of the richest to my untutored ear. Unmistak-
ably Oxford, but of which particular college I am wouldnt venture to say.
Have you ever been complimented for it at Oxford itself?

Oh more than once and quite good naturedly.

May I ask where you actually live? Do you attempt to live in all countries at
once or in rotation. I mean to be good-natured too. I ask from interest. Dont
be put out with me. If nations are nothing to you how, as I see plainly they
are, how about races? Is there no race to which you incline with imagination
or the rudimentary passions?

The Indian

Specific tribe?

[*18v*]   Everything from Europe has been bad for its kind in America.

[*19r*]   If I had to choose it would be Santo Domingo.

These preferences are beyond reason.

No I have reasons I can give.

Have you Indian blood in your veins?

It is said on good authority that most Americans have: the best thing I
know about them. Mine may possibly have come in through a great great
grandmother who was unfaithful to her respectable husband to the extent of
one wild by blow. There is some such scandal dying away in the family. I must
look into it before it is quite lost. Her weakness for the race would account
for my weakness.

At last I find you. You are an American Indian by election and construction. All you lack is your papers made out and a different accent. I should get
over that Oxford travesty. It distorts your countenance if as if it distressed you
to use it. Its away up in your head, superior to being understood. Come down
to something gutteral. Have you made a start with the Santo Domingan language.

I am told it is very hard to acquire.

[20r]   Not love itself could make Gaelic easy for the Irish patriot. Do you know any Indian poetry?

The poetry is far less important than the wisdom.

The only Indian poem that sticks in my mind is variously translated I use bad shoes, My shoes are worn out My shoes hurt my feet and I swing a wicked shoe (in the shell game). it goes Yaga yaga yaga over and over and over.

It is the wisdom that is the hope of the world.

You think so? You're opening new vistas to for me. Wisdom is better than all.

[21r–25r]   [blank]

[26r]   59

Sauce for the goose is sauce for the gander.

Question of wisom{

Nearer you get to center of culture the more you find him thought of as a poet rather than as a writer.

Kind of person that has things happen to him

Not the way it is used but could be used. Words.

Not fantastic.

Good free-for-all conversation has resemblance to star shower, to everybody's piling hands on hands on someones knee. Roughly a Radial-point.*   Afterwards a radical point for the shower should be calculable on a chart.

[27r]   60

Not Like Other Stories

Brain on the Beach

                        •   •   •

----

* Entry from beginning to this point written in blue ink.

America Hard to See[8]   Plight of Pindar*
                                Green and Marlowe[9]

Relative Importance of Staying and Going

Kingdom Come on Earth.[10] (You've solved it?)

I{n}terpreted into Indian {Divine right and consent
    You can't consent till there is something proposed[†]

Obverse of the Seal of the United States   (I was taken into a high place

old old men[‡]

The Paper ~~Arrow~~ {Dart} in the Ceiling.

The Bottom Drops out of Things at Sixty

The Tattooed Man

The Old Clothes Wearer and the Cars

Her Name between His First and Last. The Clasp
                                        The Locket

The Old age Runaway.

All Men Created Free and Equally Funny[11]
                        Equally entitled to ancestry[12]

Overtures to Micheal Gold   (Lets play we have a terror

                    •   •   •

---

* There is a large arrow-figure bridging the words "Plight" and "of."
† This phrase and "Divine right and consent" written in blue ink.
‡ Phrase written on left side of page above a curved bracket that contains next six entries,
from "The Paper . . ." to the "The Old-Age Runaway."

3

Educ ⎧ Are my eyes green yet?

ational ⎨ Bear horn shapeless and licked into shape

⎩ The Jumping Frog[13]

Over

[*28r*]   61

~~It could yield all to change except except~~

Love your enemies—but love of those at home better than those in other countries.[14]

Make me they liar   Perverted

And Freedom shall awhile repair. }   texts

For Christs sake forget the poor some of the time.[15]

All men created free and equally funny.[16]

All those who change old loves for new   } The problem of leaving an

Pray gods they change for worse   attachment for an attraction[17]

Verily know when half gods go[18]

Art thou poor yet hast thou golden slumbers

Oh sweet content. Dainty sorrow of the rich.[19]

[*29r*]   62

Courses

Patches of History (American)

Applied Romance

[*1r*]   [drawing of an encircled cross]

You can tell how conservative a person is by the length of time it takes him to consent to do what he is going to do at last anyway

I should hate to spend the only life I was going to have in being annoyed with the time I happened to live in.

The great thing about the automobile is that it has made men more individual and more individually skillful and responsible for life than anything in history. Yet we complain of regimentation.

Suffer the athletes' for their prevalence is wh assures that in the physical as in everything else we are better than the savages.

Dont let anyone do you good unless you want them him to or you cant prevent him. Benefaction by force is conquest as by the English in India as by the present government in the United States. Ye proud yeomen stop them.

[*1v*]   The Old Way to be New.[20]

Does Wisdom Signify[21]

Samples of unwisdom Lewis[22]-Yeats-Eliot—Dowson[23] + Moody[24]

Lending ourselves for the duration of the piece.

Where I cant find myself and can. Easier the subversions of Shelley than this seduction.

    Know what I am up to (White mans burden[25]

    Who is putting you up to your propaganda

    Not overinterested in what I didnt get up myself

[*2r*]   The Renewal of Words[26]

The Word-Shift. The displacement

    Not as used but as on second thought one can agree that it could be well used.

Tune (Sound and Soundness. Tone from context. Tune from tone and meter.[27]

Before the Beginning of a Poem[28]

    Land poetry inspired by land sea by sea. Pure poetry

After the End[29] (Trip the body shoot the spirit on

The Lightening Should Fork (Ramify)

    Set of sentences

Parts Not Derivable from Each Other

    Making a system.

Seperateness as Important as Connection.[30]

For a long time a thinker should be content with scattered thoughts. Discontinuity Feat of Words

Poetry as Prowess Performance[31]

Wisdom and Unwisdom (Sinclair Lewis   Dowson

     Does Wisdom Matter. Depths of unwisdom

One Thing in Terms of Another

Fruitless Comparison. (Masculine and Feminine Members)

Imaginative Seizure and Vocal Imagination.[32]

     Where form and content merge.

The Old Way to Be New (Lately dealt with new ways to be new. Emphasis on insanity.

[2v]   Justice has removed the scales from her [illegible] eyes

[3r]   Ode to Bravery

               Ode to Our Length of History

               The Ode to Ancestry

The one great thing to learn is to be brave

     Ode to a Clown

Yes Bravery is all. Yes but How sad to say so.[33]

The important thing about a person is how he has decided to bear his life.*

Cunning to avoid the need of bravery.

     Ode to a Clod.

Seal	The land was ours before we were the lands.[34]
†	The privilege of refraining and diffdeferring
Of U.S.A.	Democracy all to try Of the Crowd but not crowding‡

---

* Entry written in blue ink.

† Between "Seal" and "Of U.S.A." is a simple line drawing of a pyramid.

‡ See 22r below.

Elinor[35] wish that our hope of ~~rel~~ life hereafter depended on something else <u>as well</u> as religion.*

The people I schooled myself as a school teacher ~~were~~ to be tolerant of at whatever cost were the young idealists who thought the world should belong to the laborer who alone made it for his exploiter the capitalist.   It is a hard wrench to turn my tolerance which had become indulgently affectionate to his murderers and executioners though as a matter of fact they are {much} nearer me in practical political philosophy and should be less a strain on my tolerance

[*3v*] ~~I can see looking~~

I can see now how new it must have been

[*4r*] The road was new the mountains new for mountains
People were new in that ~~Sierra~~ {Pacific} country
And for a road the road was new, the mountains
Were new for mountains but the trees for trees
Were old
People were new in the ~~Sierra~~ Pacific country

[*5r*] Our next door neighbors ~~down~~ on the mountain road
Had hollowed out a giant redwood log
And flooded it with icy mountain water
To make their little boys a swimming trough
And any little boys my mother had
~~Must be sent~~ {She must send} down some day to swim with theirs.
She only had one boy I was he)
Well send ~~down his~~ {the one}. So I was fitted out
~~Instructed and~~ {And prayerfully} {One morning and} entrusted to the road.
People were new in that part of the world
~~And for a road the road was new, the mountain~~
~~Were new for mountains~~
So were the mountains new for mountains
~~The redwoods were the only aged thing~~

---

* This entry and the one below it written in blue ink.

[*6r*] Does Wisdom Signify[36]

Not to fear attachment
Not to fear property   Not to stay lost in wonder
Not to fear fear   of {at} what we do not understand
Not to fear {foregone} conclusions
Not to fear principles or generalizations
Maintain action. Matter and spirit are a mechanical mixture is are kept blended only by agitation of a paddle[37]

Partizanship is an honest effort to misunderstand each other as much as possible

Rest in a process

Wisdom of Yeats for instance (that God made the middle class to be preyed on by arrogant kings and arrant beggars.)[38]

[*7r*] Poetry as Performance (Feat of Words)

Is it because I dont value overmuch what happens at college that I dont mind the exaggeration of athletics.

Is it because I like to like the young and I have long since given up trying to like them as ~~intellects~~ {intellectuals} or as any thing but brave and strong and ready

Phasia hyperphasia[39]

[*8r*] The Renewal of Words

~~Like~~ {for a As amazing as} the complaint against the badness of the age ~~for annoyance~~ is the complaint against the oldness of the world and the worness of language.

The world is old {aged} and language worn*

The one-word shift. The ~~whole~~ shift of the whole keyboard. Entirely different set of words apply.

Not ~~the way it is~~ {as} used but as it could be used

•   •   •

Come to think you accept it.

Fetching and Far-fetching.[40]

Displacement by passing through air, water

Norwegian [illegible] spar,[41] mind

[8v]   This had been all the finding to announce
         That once more had the already known been proved
         By psychological experiment
         Once more the already known had been discovered
         By psychological exper[42]

[9r]   There was a vast farm and {a} farm like house
         There was a liveliness few now remember {recall}

[10r] Of all the things that thought upon at night {in bed} {at night}.*
         It does not seem
         It seems as if {as if} I could not rise and do next {by} day
         There
         The one that
         But few

[11r] You wouldn't have thought

         [?Letters]

         I talked with a man in the train
         {One thing}† I wouldnt have thought
         He had something to do with the price of grain
         He had a seat in the stock exchange

[12r]   In the History of Debt

         Mercy is illogical kindness. When Milton said mercy is first he meant in
         the sense of first aid to a race who conceived in sin and from Adams fall

---

* Written below the line.
† Written in left-hand margin.

{down} of no desert.⁴³ In Adams fall We sinned all. He mercly meant that we were so hopelessly bad that there was no use {in our case} in talking of anything but mercy in our case, He wasnt being very exact with the word first. There had first to be sin before there was first aid: Sin failure judgement and condemnation — theres really a whole set up before mercy could be invoked. Nobody could accuse Milton of being a mere New Testament saphead. He faced and liked the harshness of our trial. He was a religious pessamist however and didnt believe there was any such thing as a reward of merit. Not even Cromwells Ironsides were merciful.⁴⁴ We havent had a chance from the day Eve ate that rotten apple. It was probably rotten. Eve wouldnt have known the difference. It was her first apple and look at what city people eat for apples from never having lived in the country and seen apples as they should be

We have to be careful not to run [illegible] {words} all together like the unthinking. Theres {political} cant that

[13r]   makes mercy mean the same thing as social justice "It is only just to be merciful." There is esthetic cant that makes love mean almost anything. It is not what Oscar Wilde thought it was nor what nor Gilbran (Im glad I see less of his art in our houses).⁴⁵ It is not what Marx thought it was. Mercy justice love are three different things or we wouldnt have three such different words for them with three such different histories.⁴⁶

[14r]   School Book

What you are back here for?
                My name's Adult.⁴⁷
I went to school when young with no {out}*⁴⁸ result
And Ive returned to cultivate   a   cult
Take my advice and go and {you'd better} join a cult.
The thing thing for you to do is join a cult

[15r]   Speaking of unspoken words
Words unspoken and repressed
Though at first they hurt the breast

---

* Written below the line.

Need not always hurt the breast
Even as undelivered birds
Native to a ~~shell~~ too thick a shell

But they cannot cut a ring

Though at first they hurt the breast
~~May at least too faint to speak~~
~~Die~~
May at last
Only

[*15v*]   {~~I have staked my claims~~

I have started out my temporary claim
With stars

"The question for the original"

MS. 001896. *Black stippled leather cover three-ring binder, 6″ × 9½″ with loose leaf sheets. Entries are written vertically up the page, bottom to top, and in blue ink unless otherwise noted.*

[1r] The question for the ~~original is whose~~ {an originality}the original is where
Shall [illegible] {he} find refuge from the hasty judges is the impossible
In art or science toward or he knows not what
And does not ~~want~~ {care} to know and much less tell
A sin against the spirit it would be★
To have ~~For him advance~~† {?profane} ~~Himself for any promise~~‡ as promising
As here better ~~hide himself than on~~
                            ~~a disguise~~ hide himself disguise himself
In as a farmer
The question {of the individuality} ~~for the individual~~ is where
Some all he find refuge from the hasty judges
While indulge in suing what will cover
Being what think they have to be.

[2r] ~~He earned a living and a little more and what more he earned~~
~~And what the earning more~~

~~He earned a living and what more he earned~~
~~He spent on~~
~~He earned a living as the saying is~~
~~And~~
The comfort was that he could earn a living
And earn a little better than a living

★ Entries to this point, except "an originality the original is where" and "Shall he find refuge from the hasty judges," written in black ink.
† "For him advance" written in black ink.
‡ "Himself for any promise" written in black ink.

~~If comforted~~

I*

Cant anyone say anything ~~around~~ round here

~~Without its being for more than what he says~~

Without meaning more than what he says?

Not if his if he is a poet   toas

                                        Cant he act

Without his being taken for an actor

[2v]   Thats just your limited idea of poetry

[3r]†   One thing is certain now this it isnt Asia

It came near being but isnt Asia but it isnt

[4r]   His farm was small enough for nothing in it

To get left out of mind. Twas like a house

In being something thoroughness could compass

And he was most like ~~hous~~ a house keeping roman woman

In knowing where ~~the~~ {all things} were in {their} place

And being taken care of ~~in their turn season~~ rotation

He was a little trim man but ~~strong~~ spare

His busy work his knitting as he liked to call it

In his spare time ~~for years was sinking boulders.~~

~~When he had was not to take a gun~~

~~And go out hunting but to take a shovel~~

                              for years was sinking boulders.

~~And~~

He told us that and told me what it was

And afterward they saw him at it.

His ~~coun~~ mountain was so generously strewn

With boulders that to rid the area of them

Would have been {more} like making the world over.

He had never thought of making the world over

[5r]   He told me the extent of his ambition

Had been for the perfecting of a single field

---

* Entries to this point written in black ink.

† Page written horizontally across the page.

~~The idea was perfection but to reach~~
If no more than five a crew.

In a far corner ~~there~~ where will hazel shrub*
~~To give the first stop up~~
~~In flower yellow flower—~~
Takes the first

[6r]   I couldn't ask him I could ask his wife
~~What was the big idea~~
Whats the idea? There is no idea
Its just a notion he has lately had
To have one Perfect Field or almost perfect

[7r]†   ~~Life is a stream that hasn't gone~~
Through may countrys from the start
Before on isles it splits apart
To meet itself down further on[1]
Enough estranged for some surprise
And yet with fascinated eyes
To that see through every disguise.

[8r]   I gave earth an investigating stab
And Nature responded with a savage grab
The Moon begins her [illegible] grind
Looking like a melon rind
Nature
The moon like a melon

[9r]–[16r]   [blank]

[17r]   We did not need a house we had a house
~~But it was almost~~
But we were made almost to wish we hadn't
By this ~~one we that considered from the road~~ {that cried as so to the architect}

---

* These four lines written horizontally across the page.
† Page written in black ink. 7r and 8r written horizontally across the page.

It cried so to the antiquarian
And architect within us for redemption
Touches though simple of the builders art
Declared it had been built for more than use
Pilasters at the corner of the walls
Pilasters ~~beside~~ {by} the door, and ~~glass above~~ and panes of glass
A chimney in the middle of the roof
Proportioned to the block ~~years of~~ {the} house presented.
The ~~glass was broken and the chimney bricks~~ {panes around the door was partly broken}
The ~~were loose brick~~ chimney bricks were loose [?ourselves]
The chimney hadnt lost the house by fire.
Oh irresistible. We let ourselves be drawn

[18r] Which shall I write an epic or a play
~~I'm writing you should be the one to say~~
I'll gladly write you anything you say
To boil the pot and help the Lord persevere
But if I found an epic made me nervous
~~Youd settle with me for a play no doubt~~
~~The question is what will would it be about~~
~~That is if a play it had to be~~
Youd let me off from doing one no doubt*
The question is what it would it be about
I had thought some of taking up Creusa[2]
Whose husband was so careless as to lose her
In the confusion of the move from Troy†
He took along his father and his boy
The boy by hand the old man on his back

She may have perished
in the city's sack‡[3]

[19r] [blank]

---

* This line and the two that follow it written in black ink.
† This line and the two that follow it written in black ink.
‡ These two lines written horizontally and upside-down, in the right margin created by Frost writing vertically up the page.

[*19v*] ~~Then the policeman~~ {And then the daughter}some answered rope
'That he could occupy the only shelf
There was all that left on either slope
So that he couldn't get wedged in himself.

And you do not kill one now and then cumulative

No matter what you do with dust and fume
~~To exterminate~~   To rid the earth of vermin as a breed
There will be more seed left than you assume
And more incentive left to sow the seed.

So spoke the watchman ~~in a tone severe~~ with a wicked sneer
The other answered {feebly} from {fat at} his trap
What have I done that you should be severe
With me for this [?kinman] Mishap

~~You have committed murder~~
You are a murderer and that's the charge

[*20r*]*   fugitives from every verimifuge

~~And far up too fare~~
Too far over him to distinguish features
He saw a {scorched} row of on either idai
Of unusual almost inhuman creatures
Enjoying his discomfort as a wedge

[*20v*]   Moloch[4]

In a deep V shaped crevice of the rocks
Where sides converging had pinched off his shoes
And had {him now} wedged trap tight tightly in his socks
He stood prepared to pay his mortal dues.

He had not stepped a step ~~for many hours a day~~ {sunny yesterday}
~~To think that there was no one left out~~

---

* Page written vertically down the page, top to bottom.

He neednt have mourned that in the last of him
The human race was being swept away
The last survivor of the [?Arakius][5]

But looking once from habit up above
He saw something dangling in the light
~~And~~ And heard a {sudden} ~~loud voice~~ cry. As god is love
   Boys sure he is even got him dead to right.
   And dangling like a spider near his head
   He asked ~~him if he hand one expressed~~ {about the poet that expressed}
   A wish the whole damn human race was dead
   You may consider yourself under arrest.

     I wished it religiously
   It is what Punch Moloch
     Would demand
  You did not understand
       hate
   exterminate

     murder thought
   I didn't mean a thing

We have to do some*
   sacrificing right along

Just as we wave to do some dancing
   To keep from the one or granted dance[†]

[*21r*]   Moloch

The religious need for human sacrifice

A certain man was heard to overhead to say

       •   •   •

---

* This line and the three that follow it written in black ink.
† Entries from "I wished it religiously" to here written in the right margin Frost creates by writing vertically up the page.

In a deep V shaped crevice of the rocks
Whose sides converging had pinched off his shoes
So that And And now had wedged him tightly in his socks

He stood prepared to pay his mortal dues.
He stood arrested tightly in
He stood with feet wedged in his socks
With no thought but to pay his moral dues.

[22r]   Let me not be prophetic but I fear
(There's something tells me we are dealing here
With who those {men} it will not be enough to bet
Your {The bottom} dollar with {of} your capital

[23r]   As if in answer. It was Preston Hall Prisby
The doctor a few still had is the belief
That when he was himself and {when he} wasn't drugged not overcome with drugs
He was a genius. There were Stories had got round
About the practice He was the more a genius for sins their habit
There was no genius like him anywhere in the country
The story was his practice had once had been he once had had a practice
Among the rich and great and San Francisco
Or some said Washington and anyway
He never failed to come when he was able
And then Moreover Beside that   was not expensive for the poor and not wasn't
And whats more never charged the poor too much and
What was more   Wasn't particular about collecting bills
He had his drug kit, with him with him He stood waiting for them
With one foot on the doorstep of his car.
And with a smile of greeting not annexed of kindly mockery {not unkindly amusement}
With irony at what he took to be
A situation
At what he took to be a situation
No children of her own from restlessness

[24r]   A double row of houses all alike
Such as child might draw as a beginner

Stared at each other with unlidded eyes
Across the cinders in a treeless street.
Clinkers and cinders ~~in a midday sun that the midday sun~~ {the noon sun had fired}
~~As hot as Heated about as hot as from the~~
~~Had fired~~ almost us hot again as from the furnace.
The question was which house should be the one
~~In all that wealth of sameness to select from.~~
With all the wealth of dreariness to chose from
The seventh on the right had some one said?
There was the doctor coming out of one
As if in answer. I was ~~doctor Wade Woodbury~~ Preston Hall
He had his ~~tool~~ {drug} kit. He ~~waited for them~~ stood waiting for them
With one foot on the door of his car
~~To see if they were after what he guessed~~
~~He smile was kindly~~
~~His smile greeting seemed not unamused~~
~~At what he took to be a situation.~~

~~The doctor some still had for all the talk gossip~~*
~~About~~
The doctor once a few still had in the belief
Then when he was himself and wasn't drugged
There was no genius like him in the ~~state~~ country
There were authentic offices of the practice

[25r]   The doctor coming out ~~was~~ (to call him doctor—
~~Was~~
What there was left of ~~one~~ him—the story was
He had once had a practice in ~~Chicago~~ Amsterdam†
Or ~~some said, in New York~~ {Montreal some said} among the rich
~~And a few had Some people~~ him still in the belief
That when he was himself not under drugs
He was the more a glue for his frailty
And anyway he came when he was able
~~Was easy on the poor and was it~~ <u>too</u>

---

* These six lines written horizontally upside-down, in the right margin created by Frost writing vertically up the page.
† "Amsterdam" written in pencil.

~~Particular about collecting bills.~~
Never charged poor folks much and wasn't too
Particular about collecting debts.
Suppose we don't say who he was by name
Bid leave it that all made excuses for him

[26r]   He was the victim of experiments
He had made on himself in the pursuit
Of science.

[27r]   The epitome savannah of wild grass
Was is no more threatened danger by invading trees
Than were a valley of volcanic glass
Or the ~~stark black salt~~ water of ~~the middle~~ {Atlantic} seas. Mid brine of the
Atlantic seas*
~~And~~
Its venture ~~has been to react~~ is with spears to be a legion
~~All And be responsible to overwhelm~~
~~So that~~
 Impossible for woods to overwhelm
 And ~~be~~ {make} not a locality or region
 But constitute a spiritual realm.

 Upon its holies I have no design
 [illegible] it be to take you to its middle most
 And

[28r]   Which would you rather come ~~yourself~~ {yourself} and see
If such a place as I describe can be
Or take my word for it

The only reason why the [~~illegible~~] grass
Can keep the better of trees

So close we mow the grass

    • • •

---

* "Mid brine of the Atlantic seas" written in pencil.

In all our histry ~~man~~ {we} has never ceast
~~We wont someone to worship~~ {To look for someone as the} as anointed
The Kind as statesman as warrior or the King as priest
We have tried ~~often~~ {both these} and been disappointed
We might do worse as worshippers and clients
To by give ourselves a King as man of science
The scientists ~~agree~~ {cry yes} with one with one accord
Why not then say leave everything to them

~~The don't know all~~
~~They~~ But waiving all that talk about the Lord*
    And any mention of a diadem
    ~~They will say~~ {The justice to themselves} for themselves they ought to
mention
    They know a lot about the Fourth to mention

[*29r*]†   Well here you I ve brought you to this door
His front door ~~so to speak~~
        ~~And~~ That there No admittance Sign
~~Is his law shingle with his name~~ on it
~~You can read what it says. Not its~~ for you
~~To~~
His front door so's to speak as I agreed
~~That~~ you're a good guide / / you can't say I winked?
I never could have found the way myself
~~Its changed so since~~
Through all this wasted wilderness[6]
~~It changed so since I was a {little} girl~~

That ~~the~~ No Admittance sign there on the tree
So his law shingle with his name on it
~~I've done my finding. Here's where I~~
~~Here~~
It

[*30r*]   As everybody should know how to cook

          •   •   •

---

* These five lines written horizontally upside-down, in the right margin Frost creates by
writing vertically up the page.

† 29r–39r written horizontally across the page.

Last say before the logic closes in
On the star point from which

Again from which I spread

As everybody should know how to cook
So everybody should know how to use asked
be forced to learn
Science enough to take part in his time

[31r]*   Someone put on the market a device
I took t
That I took to and shape my habits to
But it was taken to by no one else
Or so it seems for when I wore mine out
Or wore the blade {part} out in that was vital
And tried to find another in the store
There was [illegible] to be had
I tried to tell the dealer what it looked like
And what it did. It had the Roman name
In some town in New York State
Of some small western village in New York State
I said must have seen the village from the train
So had the dealer he had been there too
Few but
Not many but get everywhere {I said} today
What
And he agreed and added Not many now adays.
What with almost as many
What with
I said I couldn't do without the tool.
But then they couldn't make it just for use
Nor for its own sake like a work of art
It had to sell and if it didn't sell—
But all the same the it had undoubted {a kind of [illegible]}
It wasn't plastic
It wasn't plastic the idea of which

_____

* 31r–32r written in black ink.

~~I understood do~~
Came from the burnt food stuck to the kettle bottom
~~I was It was good honest wood and metal~~
~~It was too bad~~
I [?clasted] had come
It meant some hope and enterprise
That put in capital ~~out in~~ and built up
A small story

[32r]*   ~~So scraped together~~
That put as scraped together capital
And built up a little factory
To give employment to the out of work
~~But now it is shut up~~
And made the village almost businesslike
But now the factory is shut up and empty
~~I know just how it looks~~
~~I may be~~ and seek Ive {seen the very one} or it by just one like it
We have one here down by the railroad track
With its windows all knockin by stoning boys
All that keeps ~~glass in windows~~ {windows in a home}†
Is people in the home looking out the windows and he agreed
Too bad a thing like that cant last I said
And he agreed ~~not a feel but didn't feel as sorry but we but with~~ less grief
than I felt
One good thing was we didn't blame the intered?

[33r]‡   Someone put on the mark of a device

Above you close peak
That star rise going on
Is of a height too weak
To constitute a dawn.

                    •   •   •

---

* Page written in black ink.
† Page, except "Someone put on the mark of a device" and "With sacrificial feasts," written in black ink.
‡ Phrase written below the line.

~~And yet with bloody feasts~~
~~And~~
Yet it has had its priests
And has been ushered in
With sacrificial feasts

We can do nothing to the stars
That is to say as yet
And design we have on Mars
Is but an idle threat

[34r]   Tendencies Cancel[7]

If ever tendential force
Ran out of its logical course
The alarmist might be scared
But tendencies seem to be paired
And there seems to be a provision
The pairs shall end in collision
The many collisions enlace
And entangle and mean in space
And that's what makes the sun
~~And it is then~~ {To give an idea of one} comes ~~in the One~~
That where the One comes in
It has let the action begin
And let a lot get done
And been at no least expense
~~Not~~ getting the least intense

[35r]   The time of year might have been any time
But winter

For all there was to tell the dawn by
T
The door the doctor with his bag came out of
Was too close to the street; the the street ~~was of~~ {was} cinders
(That part of town served was all bound out to cinders)
~~There was no leaf of tree nor spear~~
~~There was no spear of grass or leaf of shrub~~

~~To tell~~
For all that ~~leaf tree or grass~~ said to the contrary
The time of year might have been any time
All that was sure was that it wasn't snowing

For all that leaf of tree or spear of grass
Said to the contrary like time of tear
Might have been

[*36r*]   The Let-up

coming to the bat*

~~Flecked~~

~~The barn ball batter at the plate~~
~~Wild~~
~~Does better~~
Finds he does better to have been welding

The greater weight
Of two bats on the sidelines

So manage always to have just been doing
Some thing much harder ~~than the thing in hand~~

~~The easing off will give a case?~~
                          than you're doing now

The starrise going on
Above the mountain peak
As if a light too weak
To constitute a dawn
Or so you would suppose

Avent? Wind after rain
Tha

_____
* "bat" written in black ink.

With ~~haycocke flat as cake~~
~~And ?~~
That filled the land with lakes
And wet the haycocks ~~down~~
As flat as fallen cakes

And yet I here have been left*
Its unpretentious pay
For.
Yet there [illegible] a cent left

[37r]   A young Jew swore to me ~~he had this~~ {that in a} dream
~~And I believed it knowingly where he got it.~~
He was cupbearer to the Persian King[8]
~~I Babalon and in the banquet hall~~
~~The~~ throwing   ~~that one~~ night
Who in the banquet hall ~~in Babalon~~
Took notices of him for his sober cooks.
~~And all~~
And a hush fell on everyone to listen
To the rebuke that singled out ~~the~~ {a} slave.

[38r]   Bancroft in the Pullman   Horace Fletcher[9]
Tatooman Noting fatal   Marceline Cox[10]
                but death
          Restaurant
Hiring a Teacher   Perpetual Motion. Doctor
The Press in the Gore   Level of Franklin Edison
Brought to be Exibited   Carl Burell[11]
                    related by marriage to Amy

His wife from Northernmost Newfoundland.

~~Pair as in~~
~~In Pairs like Plutarch[12] only here in instead~~
Of Greek with and Roman ~~I've have take Urbane Rustic and Urbane~~

---

* These four lines written in the right margin to the right of "The starrise going on."

I want belongings but I want to be a belonging*
Paired as in Plutarch only here instead
Of Greek with Roman it is Rustic with Urbane
No one has found the thing to say about success.
No inspirational but fortificational
All is a matter of belongings and belongings.

Story of the Gaget Gimlet† no Longer Manufactured.
    "   " Hiring the One-armed Teacher
    "   " The Woodpecker's Daughter.
   Nothing Fatal but Death Stigma
Of an [?Albenes] Tatoo
Brat buster
Do you read [?Serviss]

Psuedo science more than as much of you wet at a time as bad as more than
so much of your skin burned.

[39r]   Lost: out beyond the borders of the world
A Border Collie answering to the name
Of Gillie—answering ~~to the name of~~ Gillio[13]
~~Or the least word~~   with an a
Of Gillie—answering with an anxious
~~He wont like   to find out in life~~
~~What is expected of him~~
      And with anxiety
~~To figure out what is expected of him~~
Not to miss any thing expected of him
~~Almost too touching for a man to bear~~
Almost as touching as a human being.
He has a listening vocabulary
Of many common words for anyone
~~Coming this way whose hold?~~
To try him with who may encounter him
~~He loves our speech and has a liking~~
~~Vocabulary of~~

---

* This line and the one below it written in black ink.
† From "Gimlet" to "Tatoo" written in black ink.

~~He loves words~~

~~He goes by signs and words. He loves our words our speech~~

~~And has a listening vocabulary~~

~~Of many words for~~

He loves our language ~~has a listening~~ has a very large

Vocabulary of our common words

For anyone to try him with

[39v]   Lost out beyond the border of the world*

A border Collie with the heavy coat of black

~~But white socks white shirt~~

Lost out beyond the border of the world

A border collie answering to the name

Of Gillie ~~has the right with anxiety both ours~~ annoyance to please

~~Not to miss~~

~~To~~

With

He has the {two} colors called for in the breed

Blanche and white free from brown. ~~His heavy coat coal black~~ {coat black as coal}

~~Coat black his shirt and~~

~~His socks shirt and socks and tail tip~~

~~His shirt front socks and tail tip white as snow~~

His shirt bosom ~~socks~~ and tail tip white as snow

~~His tail tip with a tail light in the dark~~

~~His tail tip like a tail light in the dark~~

~~A head~~

~~His~~ his tail tip in the dark almost at night

Shows like a tail light

Loves our language

Understands more words than he speaks but shakes

A word or two particulary out

With Distinct and with varying distinctness

---

* These three lines written horizontally; remainder of page written vertically down the page, top to bottom.

[40r]*   I heard at one time there that you had died
      And then I heard you hadn't
                            Which was true?
      Its me all right and yet I really died
      My death was by ~~known~~ {the} doctors certified
      Now don't be tiresome. Tell me something new.
      That's an old story—risen from the dead
      Like Lazarus.[14]
              That wasn't what I said
      I simply say I died yet this is me.

      Pinch you and I will find you ~~to be~~ {solid} flesh
      Or is it spirit you pretend to be
      A ghost perhaps or transmigrating soul

[41r]†   On your way ~~to perform~~ in

[42r]   If free from this in that then go

43r – 44r]   [blank]

[45r]   N

      What was this bitterness of mine about
      ~~That after all the justifying creed~~
      ~~Tall? Leaves~~   ~~of a doubt~~
      ~~It was no deeper than a jealous jealous haste~~
      ~~If life is nothing but the will to work a wish of seed~~
      Was it about the general wash of seed
      That after all the justifying creed
      Still leaves the haunting flavor of a doubt
      ~~It went no deeper in the bitter.~~
      ~~Those I future was still a bitter in his milk~~
      ~~It was age.~~
      The bitter went no deeper in his milk
      Than jealousy of ~~other~~ waste[15] that others made

---

* 40r–46r written vertically up the page, bottom to top.
† 41r and 42r written in black ink.

[46ʳ]   That first to put you off in your research investigation {to baffle you in your
request}
But lift a few of them with careful
That first to baffle you in your inquest.
But left a few of them with careful read
And you will the secret of the weed
And what this bitterness is all about
(The bitterness detected in the milk) We have detected in the flow of milk
It is if waste is for the supreme decreed
Which may stay in doubt which may no longer now remain [illegible]
And yearning is but toward the waste of seed
And only incidentally
And yearning is but

NOTEBOOK 28

"Having Learned to Read"

MS. 936940.2. *Marbled cardboard school theme notebook, 6¾″ × 8¼″. White label in center of cardboard cover stamped "National." White ruled pages. Entries are in blue ink unless otherwise noted.*

[*cover*]   Having Learned to Read

    1 A Further Range[1]
    2The Year Two Thousand[2]
    3Preface to S.C. Book[3]
    4 [illegible]

[*6v*]   Harsh divorce between

Ideal—sensible

He cant have you to idealize while I have you to practice on.

The woman gets the worst of it (Erskin[4]

Kindness and severity.

Crudity[5] and disorder are my meat and opportunity. Toward refinement and system is my course.

Piecework almost automatic rating—but not quite. One wants more stock and turns out a poorer product though he works faster. A penny earned is better than a penny saved.[6]

Better to give birth than to save from death.

[*7r*]

The Year Two Thousand

Now for the Millenium

Is there progress by the final test?
Will the world ever be an easier place to save your soul in?[7] Save your decency in
Never while it is the world.

New sources of increased unrest that is no doubt prophetic of the crisis of the sounded second thousand Some of the signs.

Take an equalizer—(that is a revolution) for {the health} of the body politics[8]

[*8r*]   # The Trajectory

There is an individual physical progress or life trajectory from less to more.[9]

And over and about it there is the spiritual problem of saving your soul by not being made a fool of by less nor made a fool of by more nor made a fool of by failure to achieve more.

(From little or no family to more family

"	"	" "	money	"	"	money
"	"	" "	fame	"	"	fame
"	"	" "	understanding	" "		understanding
"	"	" "	assurance	"	"	assurance
"	"	" "	personality	"	"	personality
"	"	" "	physique	"	"	physique

Then there is the slow decline and dissipation of all these at different rates till they are all gone. It seems to have been the same for nations and for individuals Yet we long to assume that it may be different for the human race as a whole.

[*9r*]   Race Spiritual

The progress of the race is likewise from less to more

And over and above it there is a spiritual problem to solve of equal retroactive nobility for all concerned from least poor slave [illegible] of a slave under the lash of the pyramids to the richest man that ever failed to get through the eye of a needle.[10] (He founded the Western gate in his son Segub.)[11]

[*10r*]   The Trajectory Not from
Cut throat Survivalism to Pater Mater Fraterism.[12] Evolutionism[13] to Marxism
Neither get N Nor from individualism to socialism

From absolute monarchy to limited to democracy[14] to socialism is not a progress but part of a circle or round for the next step is mob rule which is no rule and only saves itself by dictatorship that is once again absolute monarchy.

The race trajectory is simply from less to more. Less to more people. Less to more comfort. Less to more apparatus—Then again form more to less.

[*11r*]   Neither or Both.

Meditation as dwelling on the truth

As getting up something to say or do.

The separateness of parts is as
Important as their connection.[15]

Walking or something as automatic a walking (hoeing for instance or knitting or lieing awake peacefully in bed at night) may be the secret of meditation.

To be judged for whether an original intention has been strongly spent or weakly lost. Strongly spent is as good as kept.[16]

A little weeding where ever I find myself in the garden or woods. Advance tree flowers and hills and put down baffling weeds as M Arnold would say.[17]

[12r]   The Kingdom Come on Earth[18]

As it is in

[13r]   It is not our vices alone that stand in the way of utopia it is even more our virtues. If it were vices we yielded to we could be called defeatists.

Take severity. The small severity of our mother is to prepare us for the greater severity of our teacher the teacher for the greater still of the world at large theworlds for the greater still of the drill seargant the drill seargant's of the almost intolerably severe discipline of the enemy.

[14r]   No sin but against the state. No more possible to sin against yourself

[15r]   Dark Darker Darkest[19]

[16r]   Exploitation Reported in the Dept. of Kazan
A Play Someone has hired a man. They both confess. Yes Sar/Sah Commisar Gold for Christman—the very poor*

[16v]   Question Can ~~God~~ the Devil make his followers happy
            Can the Devil make Gods Followers unhappy
            Does each work to make the other followers unhappy.
            Is that why practically everybody is unhappy
            Does success or failure mean anything in Gods view
            Isn't the aim so set in the sermon on the mount as to insure our failing into the arms of Jesus.†

[17r]

The custom {once} was ~~in the days before progressivism~~ for us to be asked every evening at supper table Well what did you learn today? Education has progressed to a point where it is not now ~~permissible~~ {good form} for me to ask you what you have learned in the last four years at Burr and Burton Seminary.[20] You many know but might not be able to tell in a word or a sentence.

Many wise people don't know what you may be supposed to have learned.

---

* Entry from "Someone" to "very poor" written in black ink.
† Page torn out after 16v.

And as they are all at sea about what you may have learned so they are all the more at sea about what other children like you should be expected to learn in school after the war.

To save embarrassment all round instead of asking {you}. ~~Why don't~~ I {will} hereby undertake telling you what you have learned—in these last four years in these last twelve if you like.

You have learned to read.

I mean in school.

You have learned to read letters and numbers.

The greatest thing of all is of course to get the hang of life. (The figure is no doubt from our experience with tools and implements such as

[18r]   the hammer the scythe the brush the bat the needle the knife but I can think o f no figure of more universal application)

School is but a part of this—I don't say how large a part. Apprenticeship perhaps a larger part—{and} one ~~that is~~ {on the way} in danger of {being} missed by a generation forbidden to work by law to work for hire till they are twenty one.

We have to bear in mind that school never would have needed to exist but the for the invention of letters and numbers. Over ~~its~~ {every school} entrance I would have carved the rhyme of dedication:

$$A \quad B \quad C$$
$$\&$$
$$1 \quad 2 \quad 3^{21}$$

Other things for other places, but these two primarily for school. I

When I say you have learned to read ~~my conviction is~~ {assume} that by the end of high school you have ~~reached a place~~ {got} where you can be trusted to read on alone. You can be left to see to it that everything you do has a proper admixture of reading Letters and numbers have been bestowed on you to go with

And if not—if you haven't taken these means to hear the chances are {this will happen:} you will be back at school {again} in your forties or fifties for some adult education.

[19r]   ~~And when asked~~
~~What are you back here for?~~

~~You will answer say~~ ~~My names Adult~~[22]
~~I went to school when young without result~~

I can just hear the colloquy that would ensue.
"What are you back here for?" "My name's Adult
I went to school when young without result."

"You don't want culture what you need's a cult."

And very close to the mark in my opinion. Books failed with you. Either they never touched you at all or they made a book fool out of you. You didn't learn to read and you are back to another try at it.

Teachers have had more directly to do with you than they will ever have again even if you go to college. ~~In colleges you would be thrown with them~~ In college you would be thrown with them but less as your instructors and disciplinarians than as your examples {to emulate} ~~in performance~~ in thought and expression. There will be only two kind of you ~~from~~ from now on, the self made in college and the self made out of college.

A final word about what it is ~~to have learned~~ {have it put into your head} to read.

First it is to have put into your head that there

[*19v*] But first ~~let me explain~~ what it is not. It is not have come into a system of rules by which to judge the wisdom of everything in or out of books

[*20r*] is a book side to everything farming [~~illegible phrase~~] carpentry war fishing politics thinking science and domestic science[23] ({but} all science is domestic science in ~~a~~ {the} sense that it is only world-keeping as ~~only an enlargement of~~ domestic science is house keeping.) housekeeping

{You have got so} you will never be at a loss about what to read next, saying what <u>is</u> there to read. You will know ~~one book can~~ you can trust one book to lead to another by bridges of reference. There will always be the comfort of a cloud of books ahead ~~you mean to read~~ you can ~~choose~~ take from at your need

[*21v*] But first let me explain what it is not. It is not having come into a system of rules by which to judge the wisdom of everything in or out of books

[*21r*]   You have learned to read. Perhaps it would be more impressive on your memory to leave it at that statement or leave it you and your ~~ability to read~~ reading to find out what that statement implies.

[*21v*]   be it in art politics school church business friendship love or marriage—in a piece of work or in a career

[*1r*]*   [lined theme book]

How to take a soldier Those who went don't like to think you could know without suffering what they suffered. Of course not –won't do. No† It wasn't God they found on the battle field. It wasn't man. Nor peace Nor disillusion. Nor was it just nothing. Don to guess. What would be the use of their hav [illegible] gone if you could understand it without [illegible] gone. They didn't go to report it to pe[illegible] who didn't know it already. They tell it to each other slowly between pipe puffs at their secret meetings.

When losers come around us in the dark
To lose us to ourselves in peace and war
By morning bounds and rubbing out a mark
Our name has helped us cling to what we are‡

V

I asked the fate of man anxiously
If the new way to farm might be to ask
Lest science ~~for~~ of poor ~~farmer~~ country me
   I mean mightily my the task
   And leave me easy in my [?talk]
   ~~fate man only answered No~~
   ~~Move if I would stay alive~~
   I said The strain the strain already I said too great the strain
   If there are more things I must know is more I have to know

---

* Loose ruled page torn from another notebook and inserted here.
† "No" written in black ink.
‡ Page from "They tell it to each other" to the end written in black ink.

Im going somewhere to [?complain]
Im going to find somewhere to go
I thought the country city was designed
For people crafty in a craft
The country should not call for mind
I do not want to use my mind shouldn't have to use my mind
He smote me on the back and laughed

"Democracy"

MS. 001720. *Soft light-brown paper-covered school notebook, 6⅜″ × 8″ unruled pages. Black cloth-strip spine. All entries are in blue ink unless otherwise noted.*

[*Cover*] Democracy[1]

See Amherst Page 60

Disappointed in the Ocean[2] ⋆

[Hand Sketch of Four Mountain Peaks]

[*1r*]   If things get too bad here I shall know where to go. It wont be to New Zealand Australia or the Scandanavian countries. Those are bad already but may have to get a good deal worse before they get better. I shall go to Russia where they have had it and got over it or practically over it. –What an inexpensive experiment theirs has been for us. I mean inexpensive for us.

We have to have little victories to give us confidence ~~They~~ {and} strengthen ~~us perceptibly.~~ Instead of being weakened by disease it seems to me I am stronger after every big sickness I overcome.

Is nature for us or against us? It must be more for us than against us or we shouldn't have kept the thread of our existence unbroken all down through the thousand of years. Mightnt that merely prove we were better than nature? If we are too much for nature then nature is good for us. Incontrovertable. It may be as much as ever that we have prevailed.[3]

[*2r*]   The one hatched needs a solution of broken codfish eggs[4] to grow up in.

•　　•　　•

⋆ Underneath the phrase "Disappointed in the Ocean" Frost sketched four mountain peaks.

It has destroyed faith to consider how many eggs a codfish lays to one it hatches. But think of all the eggs a hen lays to one she hatches.[5] Our beings overlap How many grains Ceres grows.

Come see   kill a vase

Make them good and break them [illegible] bad.

Proposal to vacate five states.

Russia Germany was defeated and Russia was defeated. Italy was all but defeated. France is all too sensible of her obligation to England and the United States for her continuance as a nation. {She feels compromised.} England and the United States were alone victorious. {For Russia Italy Germany and France} Not for us all then these shifts of the unfortunate for the restoration of their self respect. We are free-[illegible]spirited people strong in the faith that much will good will happen of itself unforced. We are not ready to be taken in hand for stricter governing. Government of course. We have been years reaching

[2v]   a balance to our liking between government and freedom. Why should we try to act as if we weren't reasonably satisfied as far as we have got with our developement? Possibly for the appearance of modesty and to save the less favored from embarrassment and envy. Very great nonsense.

Consummate {blight}.

But oh for all the oceans being free vast[6]
Its separation of us from the Old
That should have made our New World new and gold
Its barrier had given way at last

I counted on the oceans being vast

We have been disappointed in our gold
And I in ocean that could be so vast

[3r]   I chose my own shell from the dryer sand

.   .   .

The ocean had been spoken to before
But if it had no thought of giving heed
To words of mine   I had a place to go
Where I need ~~give~~ listen to its ~~beat~~ {note} no more
Nor taste its salt nor smell its fish and weed
Nor be reminded of ~~it~~ {them} in a blow

So far inland the very name of ocean
~~Is never heard~~ {Goes mentionless} excepting ~~perhaps in school~~ {when with a class}
The teachers own experiences fail her
And she can only give the ~~young~~ {class} child a notion
By {of what it is} pointing ~~to the~~ {[illegible]} ~~apples~~ {water} on a ~~pool~~ glass
And ~~saying~~ telling them her cousin was a sailor
                                    that Sinbad was {~~Columbus was~~}

We were deceived in thinking it so great
Its separation of us from the Old
Had made our New World ~~for a while~~ {seem} new
But no for all its being vast
~~It hadn't~~ The separation hadn't seemed to hold
Or ~~made~~ {make} us different ~~by~~ in a single trait

[4*r*] Where is the place of the place of the ideal and
Who is {its} custodian ~~of the ideal?~~

The poet. He may be the most abhorrent little workman.

The feminine more than the masculine?

Is it some one who has been given ~~a view~~ into heaven opened a view of the perfect chair table and bed so that he is forever dissatisfied with the furniture on earth: and credited by his fellows with divine unrest?

~~It is~~ I should like to think it was the skilled artizan who came to his work by apprenticeship.

But it is any one who insists on form in a given material.

•   •   •

No one will find any calling ideal who hasn't strength {or patience} to put his own ideals into it. That is why the casual laborer is always struck with the unideality of all the jobs he tries. He is too noble for ambition and lack of ambition is lack of mastery.

Commitment not by deliberate by by being seduced. Then the charm of the way the adjustments ({major} compromises) are taken or made

[5r]   The Retentive

Enough has been said of the damage to {the} initiative
  "   "   "   "   a   "   "   {the} competitive
What of the retentive in man's nature?
Clay is more retentive than sand and would make a better reservoir.
    Shall our retentives be chosen by vote or shall they be brought out in the exigencies of business.
    Shall formal vote assign every body to his place?

                    More than Enough

    Security lies her in more than enough. Too much What may have proved too much more than enough has gone to character and gifts and endow-ments at the discretion of the sucessful. There is an end of all that in the will of the unsucessful to seize {the superfluity} rather than to be beholden for gifts. to want for them to be bestowed.

[6r]   Historical Sense Forward[7]

    Now about our historical sense. It shows backward in our genealogical pride—pride of race and pride of family[8] and pride of nation. It shows itself in forward in desire of fame and a monument but as such much as anywhere in the need to endow heirs and descendants. Shall it be denied the individual

    While it is yet ours to give
    Let us well satisfy the need to give.
    Suffer the ephemeral man to stretch his days.

[7r]   Protection and Direction
    Those that live by passion and those that are last prepared to be reason-able. Passion for one love. Passion for the poor and suffering.

[*8r*]   The Unification of Knowledge
                                              or
                          A School of <u>One</u> Subject.

ɪ   President of a College (Hears it may come to that)
2   Teacher of Writing (An Essayist himself)
3   Teacher of Unsystematic Philosophy (An Essayist himself)
5   Alumnus in Business (Remembers all his teachers
                                      (as essayists on occasion.
4   Student of Politics

[*8v*]   As {M̶ Alice Meynell}[9] the Catholic to Christ, so I say to Democracy
Thou art the Way. Hadst thou been nothing but the goal I cannot say if thou
hadst ever met my soul.

Free and equally funny.[10]

Upstart nation of individual upstarts and shoestring starters

Right to ancestry[11]

Dainty sorrows.[12] Daintiest of the dainty to sit back and say Vanity of
vanities.[13]

Trusted in locomotive engineers

If [illegible] not better m̶e̶n̶ {and soldiers} from democracy then it should
perish from the earth t̶i̶l̶l̶ and wait to come back when the fight is heard no
more.

All the best people went to Canada[14] or so we hear it proved. Accept the
premise. But nothing has happened in Canada since they went. Ergo nothing
good ever comes of the best people. Another possibility Nothing like Emerson Thoreau Whitman Longfellow Dickinson Howells etc ever happens in a
colonial state.

"Whats the constitution between friends" of the poor[15]

*But if child rearing is the figure. Mercy comes first in a mother to prepare
the way for our facing the rigors of justice.[16]

[9r]   History of the United States

The Land was ours before we were the land's.[17]

The right to ancestry. (Captain of the ship to Glasgow[18]

He who makes the law is above the law. King in monarchy
                                        Mob in democracy.

Whose tongue it was and is.

When we moved we didnt move all our things.

Accorded rights, but also privileges as of not crowding, {though we belong to
the crowd.}

America is a hard country to see.[19] (Second coming of Columbus. He could
see right through America to Asia but he couldn't sail through. Lock him
through to get rid of him.)

[Of the crowd but not crowding. Giving more than is asked. Refraining.
Seeking not his advantage beyond a self-set limit.

Justice! and the next word you think of is mercy What holds those two together what holds any pair? Action. Life is a mechanical mixture[20] in which
matter and spirit are made one by the paddle of action. Mercy alone is the socialists state. But mercy is a ~~byproduct~~ {opposite} of justice. On the battle
field of life justice comes first; mercy moves on like the ambulance*

[10r]   Jefferson and the others ~~sat for~~ painted the Constitution. Washington sat
for it.[21]

But you have a great general of your own to praise. You praise ours too
much. So ~~with~~ from gentlemen we would deprecate our victory. No refinement nor sensitiveness of a superior class could out do these feelings of
the common man abut his own success.

                              •   •   •

---

* This discussion continues at the asterisk in 8v.

Natural for the defeated to wish us ill of our victory. Ill they argue it has brought us to ill They are willing to share in the ill for the sake of having it on us.

Willing to have us all lose our State rights since they lost theirs

When they say we have no faith—this is a lull between faiths—we are on the verge of a faith to come and until it comes there can be no art: there is an answer. We are at ease in the assurance that much good can be trusted to come of itself unforced. We have faith in the refusal of power. Our first rulers refused more than so much

[10v] for themselves. No one wants all he wants of anything. The constitution is a memorandum.

reputation.* [illegible] If I had a choice of two personalities to call mine I should take the better one. Motives deeds. Nobody knows his motives. Ask others what they remember you to have said and done. Thats the objective and only you. Have the good sense the kindness of heart and the harmoniousness to come to bed with me.

[11r] To take an extreme position for the fun of battle

Politics is an honest effort to misunderstand one another.

If there is a big design beyond us it is made out of the little designs within our powers, not out of the general confusion. The big aim is made out of our small aims in {of} our concentrated moments.

The Self-torturer.

Play. Subject offered by husband for life tragedy We have a reputation for good sense for kindness of heart and for having lived together in harmony. Our good sense has been a gift for making phrase and epigram proverb (we have never known what we were doing.) Our kindness of heart has been only dramatic and in general (Our follies have entailed great suffering) Our har-

---

* This entry is a continuation of a passage that begins on 11r.

mony has been superficial. She says: You are trying to make a contribution to the mask theory of life. I'm going to accept my[*]

[11v]   in the intimacies of individuality[†]

[12r]   No rivers to the sea[22]   Slogan

        Bug confusion[23]

        Rebel poetry its form and content. (A newspaper world in a tone of hatefulness)

        First yourself (No) then your own then your neighbor, then your state then your nation then, you might argue, your humanity. (This is not any order of merit.) You of course realize you must first be personal before you are interpersonal.[24] There must be points established before there can be lines of interaction. You must be national in order that there may be international relations. And there is an illusion about internationalism that arises from extremes meeting. When you get out there far as you have gone from home you still find personal friends and fraternizing between the armies. The realities of family and state and nation are surprised and swept away you are back

[12v]   Brave yourself more to change

        ~~But stay~~

        Stay as you are and be our stay[25]

        Ð To the Rest of the Country (not to be afraid of New England and fear keep talking against it.)—Harvard

        No rivers to the sea!![26]

        A law forbidding a man to sacrifice anybody but himself to in starting an enterprise of any kind. He may go short of clothes and food but he may not ask his employees or even his wife and children to take less than {a} standard

---

[*] There is an arrow indicating this passage continues on 10v.
[†] This entry completes one begun on 12r.

livelihood. No more starting on a shoe string like Robert Bruce—or on {one thread of} a spider web[27]

[13r]   Keeper[28] of School   Teacher and how much more

Keeper of the stars that fall to us

Keepcr of the text.—to the least jot and tittle.[29]

Keeper of the past-Priest of the sense of history

Keeper of the relics

Keeper keeper!

So on to keep what has been kept.—300 years

But is the ~~sense historical~~ {sense of history} one wholly backward[30]

Trees planted money willed foundations laid are from a forward sense of history It may be shorter ~~dimmer~~ {weaker} than the backward {~~sense~~} {reach} The longing for extension in both ways

~~Let no state take from us~~

Let no state think to take away from us the the investing planting and endowing ~~or~~ and assume to do it for us.

This is a sense that must be gratified in each {at least} as much as in the mass.

[13v]   [~~illegible~~] I have a key to put away where I can find it. {a year from now.} ~~But if I put it away unthinkingly with no sense of the danger of forgetting~~ But if I trust the act itself ~~to store my memory to make to~~ be memorable. ~~But it is not enough I must pause to make it memorable. I must make the act an event. I must press it into my mind with all my weight. I must rouse myself to the danger of forgetting.~~ He I learned this at school and it was all I learned This is school—strengthening memory with fear.*

·   ·   ·

---

* Part of this passage is cancelled with four vertical lines.

The weight of the event itself isnt enough to make It memorable you I have to add my own weight to it to make the impression deep{er } enough {I have to put my mind on it deliberately heavy} Perhaps I have to scare myself a little with the danger of forgetting That is school and all there is to school. I learned so much there and it was all I learned or needed to learn.

[14r]   Are you confused? (Parlor game for the psychoanalytical.)

When you are told we can have no litera art now because we have no faith we are in a lull between two faiths. Have you nothing to say for your democracy? Namely the faith that most if not quite all goodness can come unforced. Namely that power can have learned from experience to refrain from its own logical complete fulfillment.

When you are told of the superman [illegible] either developed from us or sprung at a lea an evolutionary[31] leap of excess energy from our ribs rather than our loins. Are you worried to decide how that should affect our conduct. Should it at all?

When you are told by Wells[32] of the improvement of the environment. Will the world become an easier and easier place to save your soul in till finally you are born saved. That

[15r]   is the only effort {worth considering}.[33] There is the effort for comfort, the effort for peace. The only thing that matters is the soul's adjustment to comfort or discomfort peace or strife, rivalry or concert. (Even in a relay race where four are banded together for one {four hundred-yard} victory, there is rivalry and often bad feeling about who does his part {own hundred yards} best.

About behaviorism.[34] Is there nothing but use? Or is motivation single. Have you no sure sense of {the} how soon you may trade on a friendship.

About your being lost in a statistical statement of men. To the doctor your death is a very few percent for you the year fewer in a lifetime of practice. It is a hundred percent for you. For the lawyer who loses your defence in a trial for murder in the first degree. Statistics are our way of looking at everybody but ourselves[35]

It is immodest to say in an age like this that you are not confused.

[15v]   said No matter if her vote was offset. She only voted to assert herself—not to win elections.

Let alone I might arrive sooner or later at the same ~~conclusions~~ convictions as they. They are quicker joiners than I that's all. They don't have to think their way through. They can take it in a step.

Should have taken white slaves. Then there wouldn't have been the problem of absorbing them after emancipation. We were too sentimental to hold white slaves any more.

I have too much on one quotation from Moses in First Deuteronomy.[36] Dictator.

~~The young~~ {We} are original in poetry when young or we never are. In mathematics too and in science and even in philosophy. Maybe in politics, but you wouldn't know it from any thing the young are moving to do nowadays.

[16r]   Abelard and William[37] of never settled it about the one and the many. ~~How can~~

Are you confused about your sex as some are. I leave you to some Freud. The libidinists

The greatest freedom is to be able to talk and think free from the fear of being {regarded as} either ~~for~~ pessimistic or optimistic for or against creation ~~or~~ the age ~~or~~ the program or creation.

Fascist and communist are not opposites but both are opposite to democracy. We are in a day of new vigorous dynasties rising.

With his rank on his sleeve and his time on his wrist

All men were created free and equally funny.[38] The gentleman was henceforth to be no less funny in literature than the yokel.
equally entitled to ancestors.

Town-apiece Club.

Cancellation Club. A mens club for rendering womens vote ineffective by voting the other way. One woman*

---

* Entry continues with the last entry on 15v.

[16v]   No more talk of having to be so hard on the wicked as to hang them for robbery

No more talk of being so hard on the worthless as to starve them to death. [illegible]

We are going to express charity in the very form of government.

School education is an approach to the life of our time and country through letters and numbers. ABC & 1–2–3[39]

One thing I am sure of after reading Ecclesiastes there is nothing so valuable that anyone should want to have more of it than another. money wisdom slaves public works, men singers and women singers

Remember all is gone out of those old books for which you hang on the lips of your living friends and loves. It may be a good exercise for you to supply it from your imagination*

[17r]   Our Darkest Concern.[40]

Marking for Taste and Judgement

What has Democracy Still to Show.

No more generalities such as that the truth shall make you free. Our freedom is half a dozen hard won specific items right to trial by jury, habeas corpus, free speech and conscience. Shall we by all this fuss and fury add one more item to the list What will it be? Suggestion: a law that though a man may sacrifice himself for obscure beginnings he may not take advantage of the needy to sacrifice them.

imagination. But the effort is not one you can expect yourself to sustain always

---

* Last word of entry is written half on this page and half on the next. This entry continues in the last entry of 17r.

[*17v*]   What Became of New England[41]

She was nearer having drawn off and nearer having been cast off from the mother country into a nationhood of her own than any other of the colonies. She had not much more but a little more than Virginia to give up in ~~merging with~~ losing herself in the federation. Once she thought of the loss she accepted it and never looked back—or hardly ever.

It takes more country to make a unit in the West than in New England (that's all.)
Another cruelty is not to let ~~yourself~~ {the world} understand you.

So love your loves that you can never be disillusioned about them. The worst cruelty is to be disillusioned about a person or country. It is [~~illegible~~] cruel to yourself (and you will probably think of no one else) but it is cruel to both and crueler to the person and the country

[*18r*]   There are fallen stars in Aggasiz[42]

[three musical notes]

<u>What <u>Has</u> <u>Become</u> of <u>New England</u>?</u>

Ford Maddox[43] said the Catholic peasantry of Europe renews itself: the Protestant peasantry of America has run out and disappeared in six or seven generations.

A Mexican Interlude[44] says the Puritan stock has run out and been displaced by a new stock too smart for the old.

Brooks virtualy does the Spengler[45] in treating New England as an example of nations that flower and fade.

Santayana has done the Last Puritan.[46]

·   ·   ·

It was by way of becoming a little nation of great religious political and race homogeneity up to the point of declaring its independence. It broke in the war of 76 with the provinciality that had kept it from having arts of its own.

But as it happened it wasn't able to make that break unaided. It had no recourse but to make common cause with Virginia

[18v]   and Pennsylvania and New York. It would have been interesting if she could have got out of it alone. But England would not have tolerated an independence so small.

She took the decision more or less unconsciously to merge with the greater nation that was to be. All she was gradually was disolved into the larger nation. Not so soon that she didn't come into some of the rewards ~~she~~ of initiative she was trembling on the verge of. The first authors of her victory were strictly her own. But only her first. Any that came after must necessarily be American authors rather than New Englands. She pooled everything in good faith. She sacrificed her identity [~~illegible~~] to contribute her blood traits and family names to the United States. She even spread out into the whole land with all there was of her. She left New England pretty thinly populated and in many parts empty. She was not disposessed in any sense of the word. [arrow]

[19r]   A ~~village~~ {town} with six street lights and few [illegible]{houses}
Than I could count

Two thousand miles southwest in the empty plain.
A town of six street lights flashed past my window
Its ~~few mean~~ houses black with after midnight sleep.

Who shall deny the village could have had them

The new races that came in came in to her leavings. She had gone in two directions. She had gone abroad to the nation and she had gone up into the seats of government and business. Her family names will be found in both places. There is no run out stock left on her soil. Most of her families are simply gone. Any that remain still have their importance.

It is not a case for Spengler[47]—not a case. OVER*

[*19v*]   {To try for is not to pretend to lofty things like disinterestedness[48]
             {To try for truth without illusion.

Sin against ones self versus treason or sin against the state.

Fear of not being found worthy.

Breadth of base is surely one factor in height.   But it must be mounted from or it nothing but baseness.

New England schooling: designed to establish two habits, taking thought to add your own weight to deepen the impression anything gives you, and taking another look to see if you first look was right. ~~Fear~~ Cultivates the fear of forgetting and the fear of mistake—To exhaust in a moments survey the possibilities of mistake.—all the places you could go wrong

[*20r*]   The thirties seemed strange numbers to write in {a} dates

_____

_____

_____

Good delusion! Once you recognize the delusion it ceases to be good.

As a {the best} man is always just one jump ahead of his own insincerity. So are we as a race always just one jump ahead of our falsity. It is only the tired who give in to the pursuer with an After all, all is false. Let deceit have me so long as it is a good deceit. Let me find a gentlemanly Horatian way to accept miracles Superstition keeps a man from bleakness. With such doctrine Spain went out into nothingness. Santayana was the Spaniard with us. The War of 1898[49] unmasked him. His philosophy is nothing but a complicated defense of the Spanish attitude toward life.

•   •   •

_____

* "OVER" written vertically up the right margin.

The last Puritan would be the final man to spare himself no disillusionment in his quest

[21r]   of the sense of truth. Perhaps that is like coldness on the nose a fish [illegible] holds the stream that is passing away.[50] Everything aside in all directions. There is truth to feel somewhere. He will hug no delusion however comforting. There will the harsh Protestant as long as their is the easy Catholic. There are plenty of good Cat Puritans in the Catholic Church—more there than anywhere else—so many that I don't know how to judge the Catholic Church.

Santayana was caught in the wrong place by the War of 1898. He took it out on us (his fault. He shouldnt have been where he was) by attacking us philosophically so as to seem as disinterested* as possible. James common sense trial and error in the highest is most us.[51]

The only part of logic you have to be good in is premises.

The Freudians should not object to the alternative name of Libidinists.

*We know we must seem disinterested. We {can} seek to be or we {can} pretend to be.

[22r]   All this idealism in Roosevelts speeches sounds so good as to be goody goody. It would be a relief to see where the bad came in. So I said till it dawned on me from a rising note I hear in them of late. The bad is toward {the} foreign nation. What he asks for is a mighty nation to weild threateningly against the world. He will pay any price to have it well tempered and wieldy. His present policy is the tempering of the people. [illegible] {He will bribe them if he must, but he will have them love not just the Democratic party but their country. He will have them patriotic.}[52]   I will keep trying to understand him on the assumption that he cannot intend foolishness. No doubt he craves power inordinately. But he will have more power than he could have any other way more power than most powerful men in history if he is President of the most formidable people power in the modern world {times}—if he makes it {and passes it along to his successor} more harmonious therefore more formidable than he found it. and if

Answer over

[*23r*]   But he will defeat his own aim if he makes his people too harmonious. A nation is not meant to be as harmonious as a family It is one step further toward the severe in the gradations of discipline. Perhaps two steps. ~~I have told~~ Here lies the noble seeming fallacy of the socialists. ~~From~~ {By} the Jew Marx they have been brought back to God the father from having worshipped with Darwin[53] in the temple I was going to say but no in the [illegible] {gymnasium} of God the fight-promotor. A nation should be just as full of conflict as it can contain, physically mentally, financially. [Paragraph sign] But of course it must contain. The strain must be short of the bursting point—just short.[34] The citizen must love his enemy within [illegible] more than he loves his enemy without.[54] Otherwise the boundaries will go down the song of the International will be heard [illegible] and [illegible phrase] chaos [illegible] come back. Classes have cast★

[*23v*]   proletarian† and aristocrat alike.

[*24r*]   questioning looks outside the country in doubt whether they have not more ~~with their own class~~ in common with the same classes there than with the different classes at home. This is the peril of the moment. The individuality of the person may have to be sacrificed a little to the separateness of the nation. There must be some merging of men to save us from too much merging of nations.

   Have I told you about the gradations of discipline.

   You told me once about the gradations of decay—from Christ to moral corruption. Your defect is that you end in distinguishing between opposite principles: where as existance for all of us is a varying blend of those opposites. You will find that you will always be out in not being able to accept the particular blend of the party of the majority. We have thought of all you mention and from where you leave off we go on to our collectivism.

[*24v*]   Aleviate for our comfort

[illegible] Russia is moving faster toward the right than we are to the left. I hope she will get to democracy[55] in time to save our tottering reason. Noble document that latest Russian Constitution.[35] Provides for the thing that from the outside we were most worried about namely[56] personal greed and acquis-

---

★ This entry continues on 24r.

† This passage is a continuation of an entry begun on 24r.

itiveness.[57] The individual can own something more of it than his neighbor if he has it in him to a sense of thrift to satisfy.[58] I am much relieved to find I wasn't wrong about the good of that trait. But a limit is set to growth. No one shall have farm enough or household enough to hire to use a hired man or a hired girl. No one shall rise to be a little leader and no one shall sink to be a little follower. There shall be no leaders but big leaders and they shall be voted into their positions in the bureau. There shall be no mounting except by election*

[25r] Any way our disagreement comes to no more than a quantative one. We both see that God is a double God. He is the God kindness fostering kindness and of [illegible phrase] {disciplinary cruelty}. If we can unite him he the God of

You think we cant afford to have any less for our good of the cruelty of competition.

Perhaps the government must take everything over before it hands it back into severalty so as to make us all realize whose we are and through whom we have anything we can call our own.

———————————————————————

———————————————————————

There is something in human nature[†] they havent got to yet. I shall be waiting for them to see it afraid all the time that I may be wrong about it and it may not be there to see. If they wont be impatient with me why I wont be impatient with them. I cant help thinking young people may well start as servants and some of them stay servants all their lives. It is good for them and developing for those over {them}

[26r] WBY says {there are} the artist has a choice of some seven poses.[59] One of them he must assume. Don't believe it children. There is such a thing as sincerity. It is hard to define but is probably nothing but your highest liveliness escaping from a succession of dead selves. Miraculously. It is the same with illusions. Any belief you sink into when you should be leaving it behind is an il-

---

* This entry continues on 25r, below the two lines.
† This passage is a continuation of an entry begun on 24v.

lusion. Reality is the cold feeling on the end of the trouts nose from the stream that runs away.[60] Ɏ W.B.Y. and G. S.anta.[61] are two false souls.

[26v] Mr Dee Tractor persists through the administrations

A lot (33) of their men they most approved of have apparently come to disapprove of their form of communism. It ought to make us reconsider ~~their~~ the Russian experiment. These men are accused of wanting to go back to capitalism for entirely selfish reasons. I should have suspected Trotsky of having stayed too idealistic for the people who have the responsibility of practical government. The Russian government has come right faster than the American government has been going left. What is it to be a counter-revolutionary anyway. I have been called one I am told. Is it because I am suspected of believing that to allow farmers to hold property in severalty is to ~~surrender~~ abdicate our original position of no greed and no jealousy and no possessiveness. Or is it because I believe that if you can let a man have a farm you*

[27r] You'd expect if† you expected good to come up ~~unimposed~~ from anywhere—you'd expect good to children to come up naturally out of mothers.

But apparently they have let their children work before eighteen all these years. No we can't trust any good to come out of anyone except by law imposed from without.

But but! I am troubled to know where the good in that law originates. It must originate in [illegible] human beings don't you assume? It must be in some very good man or men. Some ~~no~~ kingly noble man, or I was going to say congress. Have you ever seen or met congress. They are all right, but first rough and ready Democrats brought up to do what they have to for victory. Tenderness would be the last thing I should look for in So and So for instance. I should far rather look for it in mothers. I cant get over it that

[27v] can let him exploit‡ one little hired man. I'd only go ~~on~~ that much further than the present Russian Constitution. I think some people are meant to be hired men. They mortgage themselves out of ownership into dependence

---

* This entry continues on 27v.

† This passage continues an entry that begins on 28r.

‡ This passage continues an entry that begins on 26v.

and the dependence might as well be on a neighbor as on a central government. I can see that once yo started on this road it is hard to know where to stop. But I know, I wouldnt have the precious fruits of the revolution lost.

[28r] the quality of mercy* had to wait to make its appearance in such {so} unpromising a quarter.

It just shows you that as no one sees himself as others see him, that is that a man sees another better than himself, so the only way the world advances is by minding each one's minding everybodys business but his own. The obsolete gospel was look out for No 1. The new gospel we give unto you as a surprise this last election is look out for No 2
Am I fool enough to think that story of the fight for the poor for a larger share has come to an end?
The King the crown the throne finds always some one new to exploit to keep itself the top power. It wasnt at the money man the usurer the middleman the bourgeoisie that overthrew the lord of the feudal system. It was the King using the money man the capitalist The King has reeled and his throne tottered before the might of the capatalist he conjured up.

[28v] Again he seems about to save himself from his creature with the help of his next creature the proletariat.[62] Power is invincible and must prevail if only by playing its own against its own. The new class it brings to bear may expect to come in for great favors privileges. Money will not be as important as it was has been since Henry VII.[63] It may have about the influence it had in feudality. The usurers will survive but will go in fear.

Then what. Can we see far enough into the future to make out what estate the King will invoke to save himself predominant over the proletariat. "No I think the proletariat exhaust the possibilities. Then comes the end of the world." I hope so for the mind's sake. Further thinking seems intolerable." It is not required of us. The human race has arrived where it can afford to take a long long rest from speculation about the future. Probabably it means the end of the world. That would seem to be the only logical conclusion.

Authority never forgets the crown.†

---

* This passage finishes an entry that began on 27r.
† This phrase written vertically up left margin.

[*29r*]   There should be nothing more appealing to the mother instinct than a
puny little squalling minority.

What no underdog at all?

All plunging headlong to look out for Number 2. The question is who will
be the heap big Looker-Out-For No 2. He will be heap big Number One!

One reason for doing good to the poor is that they are too weak to resist
you—poor things Let them alone. Take somebody of your own strength or
position in society to impose on. Christ had his run-in with the great ones of
the earth.

Instead of a barn raising a spire raising.*
*The broader the base the higher the point.

[*29v*]   And kept a million days of school

300
2̲0̲0̲
60,000

~~And keep~~ through revolutions scaith
And

~~The~~ Engraven on thy ports the faith
~~Of~~ In ABC and Θ 123[64]

dedicate
[~~illegible~~] above thy gate.

[*30r*]   The street was dirty and mean
The house was shabby and small
But out of the house a voice

The mother had sent a son

---

* After this phrase Frost drew a spire depicted as a cone with three intersecting lines facing
the right margin.

[*30v*]   His reasons sordid
              Are not recorded
              Details are lacking
              But he ~~started~~ {took to} packing
              The Holy of holies
              With Tugwells and Moleys[65]
              And anybody
              However shoddy

              And it didnt go over
              At all with Jehovah
              You couldnt water
              His priestly order
              Not if he knew it
              You couldnt do it

[*31r*]   In the old reliable
              [~~illegible~~] King Jameses Bible
              (~~ask~~{Now} Simon-Shuster's[66]
              The Bible-boosters)
              There's Jeroboam
              Deserves a poem
              ~~By some~~ {In his} New Deal[67] he
              He Promoted freely
              Everybody
              However shoddy
              ~~However~~ {The very} lowly
              (~~Like~~ {The} Tugwell ~~and~~ {the} Moley)

              By some New Deal he
              ~~Took~~ {He raised} {Advanced} too freely
              To ~~raising the lowly~~
              {The} Tugwell{s} and Moleys
              To the Holy of Holies

[*32r*]   Form is only the last refinement of subject matter[68]

                         •   •   •

In theory all property belongs to the King who speaks as We. That is to say it belongs to all of us in common first. Then it is allotted to us individually ~~as a loan~~ in parcels as loans.

I had always thought it belonged to us individually first and was pooled theoretically to make safer our possessions.

It was never either way in practice. The most primative practice contained both elements.

Nothing but injustice. Shall we take it with humor or tragedy?*

Enough of these freely had and freely scattered and a figure begins to come out like a constellation in the sky.

We are told to love our enemies But we should be sure to love our enemies in the home country more than those in the other countries

Historical sense backward always?[69] How about it forward and for the individual.[70] How long a foresight shall be encouraged—or permitted

[*33r*]   All depends on what you take off from, negatively as from a father a town a class of society you hate or positively from discoveries you like.

What would be a sample ideal.

[*34r*]   I{d} ~~should~~ go to him and {say} Ah Great Duress
You could take all. But take a little less
Forego a little that you may have won
And And {~~That~~ ~~You shall be extolled~~} {You shall be praised aloft} with Washington
And Till all you ~~our~~ history is said an done
~~Halting the just short of~~ {And breaking with the} logic [~~illegible~~] {of} suc[c]ess

~~For~~

.   .   .

---

* "dual" precedes this line on blank left-hand page.

Not too much order

A little chaos in our composition[71]

[35r] So suddenly that flower had come
Some sort of cypripedium[72]
And bloomed there without root or stem
And been served by its Seraphim
Being found as if by miracle

[36r] I{'ve} have seen [illegible] {it} all not reasoned out but acted out. I{'ve} have seen case put in pawns disposed upon the checkered board of life. And then was no denying everything {all} we have and are and think {and are} we have it all from [illegible] you, the King, who speak for all of us as We. You gave it and can take it back. We had forgotten how it stood with Property. You let us have it, you reminded us, {granted us the loan of it} to play to work to strive with. But it multiplied and varigated and became so strange past all recognition{zing} what it was and whose it was. We stand reminded. It is yours who speak for all of us as We. And it was weapons tools utensils homes land. Yes it was waterfalls and lightening in a wire. And it was servants and {slaves} each other. It was children. It was books, opinions. It was everything in trust great trust and ever growing greater; till the management at times seemed too much for our strength At times we wielded

[37r] it; at times we failed. And then we cringed from our temerity. The sensitive cried out to you the King to take away the properties. We hurt each other with them [illegible phrase] {We had lost}* the hang of what we had elaborated in our overconfidence. And this though we were brothers in intent. Take back the waterfall Take back the child. Take back the land who long long since took back the sword Take all in one sweep. Take the responsibility and let us sleep.

I saw it all {thus} not reasoned out but acted out. The King who speaks for all of us as We, took all. He took the waterfall. He took the tree. He took the railroad as he had the road. He took the cloth so that for not one moment of the day did we could we forget the clothes we wore were regimentals of a

---

* Written under the line.

king {in state} and both of them confest ~~Though they used the euphemism~~
quibble ridiculed plead   working guest.

For bringing sin against oneself again into the world

Yates is a kite with a one Pound tail

Strike a mournful note over what you will.

They are not afraid to be dangerous

A conservative is one who approves of all previous reforms but none of the
latest proposed.

The world is old the race weary and our words worn out. So where is the
hope of literature or of anything else for that matter Is it an excuse for themselves or a spiteful way involving others in ~~their own defeat~~ {their own fail-
ure}, or ~~a way of making~~ {of getting an effect of tragic} sadness ~~and tragedy~~
~~for literature~~ {in it}. The ~~disco~~ delight of the discouraged must be in discouraging. ~~In speaking for themselves~~ They are willing to despair for themselves
if at the same time they may despair ~~for the lively~~ {for us all}. Just as the comrades are willing to submit to the harshest discipline and completest loss of
freedom for themselves if they can have the satisfaction of forcing others to
submit too.

   As to the worlds being old no one knows how old it is comparatively. It
may be young comparatively. Some of the race is no doubt weary, {and} was
in fact borne tired. And if words as we find them seem worn {out} with daily
use it is for poetry to renew them. Poetry if it ~~is~~ {has been} nothing more has
always been ~~in and ou~~ both in and out of verse primarily the renewal of
words.[75]

How words are renewed the shift the displacement
                    in the refraction of light

   The only words not immediately susceptible of renewal are those in everybodys poems.

·   ·   ·

soldier in the ranks. He made it sweeping and of right Acknowledg
universal—total

I saw it thus not reasoned but acted out as in no other age of h
King's

[*37v*]   No child could sin against himself. This was the nadir of the
drama

[*38r*]   predicament was ~~like~~ Moses {like} whose cares became so many
delegation.[73] There were committees ~~things~~ cares that called for (
fices that called for countless officers to fill them And the Kingc
coming an Officialdom.[74] There was no sin except against the st
could sin [ex] against himself. ~~Offence was capital~~

The King said nothing but decided to relieve himself of som
fore it bore him down. And first he gave the subject back the
against himself. He gave him back a sheep a cow a horse a hen,
let me hear from these again. Theyre yours to keep or lose bi
them friend, you get no more from me so theres an end. I c
you're going to hurt your neighbor with such innocence as she
do {dont} come to me about it: you and he can weep.

So many things had happened {and} so hard to understand
political economy that ~~there wasnt~~ {it was as if} in the land ha

[*39r*]   sent to college or at least to boarding school The land could
solitary fool. ~~The~~ He ate the only sheep he had before the cre
{And} Thus having sinned against himself to that extent wi
made a porridge of the grain he should have kept for seed ar
{He couldnt seem}* to tell the time to take his cow to bree
was in middle life as good as dispossest   He went to live w
a sort of working guest. But gossip soon got started {up} ti
got excited Though but a solitary case a man had ~~been~~ {got}
he and his employer were brought ~~beneath~~ {in dire} arrest I

---

* Written under the line.

But in saying poetry is the renewal of words is no more than using the part for the whole although perhaps the chief part. I might rest the case entirely on words. Words are enough.

But poetry is also the renewal of principles

Principles have got to be lost in order to be found.

Wisdom as thinking is better than wisdom as learning. Pity some would say to think a thing out only to find that Plato or St. Thomas had thought it out before. Scorn of

The classicists so contemptuous of the romantics but so romantic about None so romantic as the classicists about their classics and their classicism.

[41r]   The best thing to be said of the classics is that they have been good enough to survive. But they are prunes not plums. They are not fresh fruit. A classic has to be translated into fresh slang for every generation. Much depends on the translator. The housewife puts the prunes to soak. But water soaked is not infused with juice.

Other things being equal (mind you) a book of your own day and people is has the advantage of the classic. One reason is that it asks for judgement as no

Trust ourselves to come out somewhere near the old ones but not so near {as to} we have had our labor for our pains. The slight difference is everything It is the cambium

We cant miss coming out in the principles more or less. Natzi Fachist would put the law on us to make sure. They are of little faith—excusably after the overthrow of their so state and society. They begin timidly with brute force in handling delicate things

[41v]   Again and again we scrap all for a fair restart to see where we will come out and if any other world is possible

.   .   .

I am one of the kind of radicals who would be willing to destroy Jerusalem for the fun of seeing it crystal comeback in shooting crystal after crystal. I should like to stand on the edge with some of the heterohopeful and see one character of after another show itself. Look there's a priest, look a wife, look a policeman, a judge a secretary of Labor. Nothing more different than a little refreshed.

It is for the renewal of principles that we never tire of hearing and seeing case put in pawns disposed in plays and novels. We get the same answer only different.

Aristotle says we go to the play for purging Drama is drastic. That is one of the great {psychological} figures.

[42r] Not nearly so good is D H Lawrence;[76] we go to see for the superiority we feel over the poor put upon wretches on the stage.

We really [illegible] go to hear the question restated—to get a fresh glint of reality off the old question.

Spes alit agricolam: Miles et in mensa pingere castra mero:[77] the same yesterday as today. My classical teachers would not let me think believe there was anything to say that the Greeks had not said before me. Einstein says the more exactly we know how fast a body (Gin a body meet a body coming though the rye) is travelling the less exactly we know where it is and the more exactly we know where it is the less exactly we know how fast it is travelling.[78] But Zeno[79] the disciple of Parmenides the disciple of Anaxagorus[80] demonstrated in Elea more more than two thousand years since the impossibility of stating motion in terms of both time and space at once.[81] Again my audience of the classical department {of Mass} refuses to let me have it that Plato has not quite covered all the ways of knowledge when he says in Ion that they are two the specialists and the

[42v] He's like peroxide more or less
He makes corruption effervesce
And bubble into nothingness
Youll {know} what this implies I guess
If ever you had wounds to dress

. . .

poets (inspired by Appolo.), one by experience and the other by frenzy:[82] and refuses to let me have it that Aristotle said all in describing tragedy as kathartic.[83] I felt as if I was back in school again with the system on top of me and not under me.   And yet I [illegible] {was} willing to exibit {expose} myself as one doubting if his what he had found out about art by trial and error was quite covered by the great Athenian. Perhaps Ion should have shown Socrates that the poets knowledge comes largely from our all being specialists in human intercourse. (The psychologist has set up to be the real specialist there in modern times) But Ion would have done better*

[43r]   Just as Lord Hid in Aberam killed
Bid the {Laid the} foundation lay {stones} of Jerico[84]
(And Joshuas prediction was fulfilled)
We
So we did plant our trees or nearly so
    or very nearly so
Some ourselves some fifteen years ago
    not half
In our Ambassador to Modern Greece
So we our Apple trees of Mac Intosh
Did plant in the Ambassador to Greece
Did plant our Northern Spy and Mac Intosh
As there in the {our} Ambassador to Greece
Lately come home from having followed {fought with} Foch
We armed him with the implements of peace
    implemented him for deeds
We we first put the shovel in his hand
And taught him digging who has since progressed
To dig in a much more important land
Than any in our unhisto
    our despised and unhistoric West.

[43v]   if he had merely pointed out† that with people of imagination and insight (artists) a {very} little goes a long long way. Exhaustive knowledge may not help to meaning it may prevent meaning. The generalizations of philosophy are not derived from complete knowledge. There is no such thing as complete enough knowledge for perfectly safe action on the part of the king. A

---

* This entry continues on 43v.
† This passage finishes an entry begun on 42v.

king [illegible] see to {must} act on generalization less grounded than a philosopher would conclude on. A word to the wise—one word. One fact to the
wise. Facts may get so thick that nobody is extricator {enough} to break free
of them to with their idea. No artist can afford to be a specialist Special
knowledge is his ruin.

[44ʳ]   A Benefit Performance

                   Scene 1 Off stage—wings to right

                                    .

The   is being interviewed in his shirt sleeves
by the   of the Daily Questionaire . . .

    You want it understood then that it is a benefit performance. For the bene-
fit of whom? The actors. The Johnstown flood sufferers.[85]
    No but {for} the sufferers from inability to think things out. Most people
cant think things out they have to see them {things} acted out.
    You mean on the stage

                   Another Play Within This Play

You cant tell a criminal from an idealist

    The artists that wouldnt educate his children

    The moving French Canadian

Who cant? The truant officer the policeman and the righteous. Capture of a
tramp.

As a matter of fact arent isnt the idealist a criminal and dont the two extremes literally meet? Say the hard heads and the humanists.

    Shelley doesnt know what he's up to Making thy lyre[86]

    God the Seducer may not see his results.[87] Springs another love season on
the year

[45r]   What do you think of our Tuneses Walter Duranty[88]
I really dont know how to answer you Anty
He can ~~generate all sorts of argument~~ {[illegible] rattle it off with assurance}
can't he
The offhand way in a ~~recent~~ {Sunday} Times I got
He tells of Stalin's ~~having~~ {taking} the Lukewarm <u>Trotski</u>[89] ~~people of~~
Gen[. . . .]
The off

[46r]   A Voice said youve ~~have~~{got} some thing there
That might make all the difference in your fate

[47v]   Make the stuffed shirt sit up and face the court.
He cant ~~you[r]~~ Exelency. He's overdone. He's been through too much.
Question him and I will take his whispers. I'll act as loudspeaker for him.

[48r]   You say you're a Collectivist {~~Luke~~}. Justify. Tell us what you mean by a
Collectivist.
A collectivist is one who collects postage stamps.
No that is a collector But
You keep out of this Luke till it comes your turn.
Well a Collectivist is one who believes in encouraging others to collect
stamps.
Meaning whom invidiously
Do I have to say?
Luke Luke. I'm afraid you will end in being made an example of for Luke-
warmness.
That's as much warmth as I'm capable of I can't help my name can I?
We should all give up our Christian names since we have all ceased to be
Christians. Havent you heard what they are doing to people in batches out on
the Colorado for Lukewarmness
Why not lukewarmth. It's a sounder word? Which Colorado. Have you
ever stopped to

[48v]   Tonight each member is expected to make good his membership and de-
clare his character that in future meetings he will sustain.
An absolutely continent continent.
Nothing escapes us.

[49r]   consider what the Colorado means. Colorado! Naturally! Colorado I should say so.

Luke you're irrepressible.

Speaker comes forward to edge of the stage and speaks toward audience: For the benefit of those who have come in late I should explain that this is the first meeting of the Variety Club successor to the old Rotary Club of the Capitalist system now gone with the Feudal

[50r]   In {the} an anteroom of {Judge [-]} of the Court before the morning session three ladies are being presented to the famous Judge Romboyd.

Mary Isnt it fun to be merciless. Are we going to have a very merciless morning of this morning Judge Romboyd
Two Why Mary.
Mary I mean isn't it good to find it necessary to be merciless. I mean in a way. I mean for a while. Dont misunderstand me Judge Romboyd
Three. Mary means for an idea.
Mary] yes of course for an idea. It brings back something into the world that has been sadly lacking I should say for the last three hundred years.
Two Especially if the idea isn't your own and you never had an idea in your life.
Mary. Don't be sarcastic and unsimple any more under the new dispensation. Yes especially if the idea isnt your own. Because there is nothing like the rigors of submission for the good of the south.
Two)   I could submit for the pleasure of getting onto the posse to make others submit.
Mary For mercy sake judge Romboyd why don't

[51r]   you say something to settle this.
Two) Because as judge he can do nothing for mercy's sake.
Clerk (pale young with too high forehead) Who has been waiting to speak to the judge on business) I will say this for the young people of my generation, they dare to be dangerous.
Mary Yes for an idea
Two) Though they never had an idea
Clerk. Are you reflecting on the young people of my generation? Do you dislike the young?
Two {Some people} I know some who hate the old

Clerk Age I do abhor thee. Shakespeare himself said.[90]

Mary It seems to me that cant be quite right. We must all be old sometime

Two. Not nearly as many of us as must be young

Mary. But thank God none of us is very old not even the venerable Judge

{At this point}Here the Judge having found {the} a little of this enough bows {with} from a thick middle and backs off cautiously to avoid stepping on anyone (Romboid head romboid trunk. Legs far apart at top and bottom)

[*52r*] The clerk lingers a moment more from sensitiviness than good manners–

Mary. Our prattle is nothing to the judge; {and that} which is as it should be.

Clerk. I shouldnt say that. The judge was deeply moved {by your waiting on him} by the attention of {such} girls from such families as yours have been. He is very awkward except in court. And he carries a heavy burden of responsibility. (The Clerk is about to follow the Judge but the girls detain him)

Mary. Have you some interesting cases on the docket today. Arent you the Professor Sibley who taught social science at Greenmawr before the Fourth

Two) Mary means the Fourth Revolution not the Fourth of July.

Mary Well Im Mary—My sister was in your confessions class and some of the things she confessed to were my sins. She didnt do them at all. I did them. So theres another confession.

Clerk All that seems far away now in this new world.

Mary Yes doesn't it? These are my friends —— ——

[*53r*] But about the {budget} docket

Well theres the ordinary run of cases. Two or three to be dealt with for lukewarmness.

That calls for severity according to my Walter Duranty[91] I swear by my Walter Duranty and always keep it by me.

And theres a Sloganite to be tried.

A Sloganite.

Yes a person who gets up a Slogan

More than one Slogan

Probably not more than one. A Sloganites mind dies after one slogan like an animal that dies after once breeding.

Cant you tell me what his slogan is.

Better stay and hear it.

Please Mr. Sibley tell us now. There arent any seats left out there. Isnt it fascinating Babara Barbara is as barbarous as I am. She believes in cruelty if its for an idea. My brother has a wonderful short argument in favor of it. I wish I could remember it for you.

What

[53v] We've had a lot of trouble with him. We've nicknamed him Surge. Because he can't get it through his head that we have done all the surging forward we are going to do. Its no joke for him though. Its become a life and death matter.

[54r] else. Have you any third degree cases.

One a very strange one {a} very momentous one Everything else is trivial by comparison.

That will call for some severity I guess

It has called and will call for more. It may prove beyond the competence of this court. It is very puzzling in its ramifications.

Oh dear oh dear How too bad.

Mary means too bad it should be puzzling. Now she finds something to be feminine about. We girls cant be expected to be hard hearted all the time. The strain of these days almost makes me hysterical.

What else

Theres a prophet—a fellow talking about a hundred or two years ahead of his time. He

Awful.

{That's} Surging forward has got to be stopped now. If I had time I could tell you why. The ruler uses the capitalist to destroy the landlord (under Henry VII)[92] then the ruler uses the proletariat[93] to destroy the capitalist Thats the way the ruler keeps on top himself. But after he gives power to the proletariat what

[55r] has he left to reduce them with. Unless he goes back and uses some of the old ones the feudal landlords or the capitalist usurers over again. Best not think that way. We've got to stop somewhere and it may as well be now. I hope the {world}play world ends exactly when the curtain goes down.

Oh Mr Sibley

And theres a whole roundup of flippant fellows who have been running a secret society in mockery of the old Rotary clubs.

No harm in that surely.

But they've been making fun of collectivists

How in the world. Whats funny about a collectivist.

It has gone around town that they define a collectivist not as one who collects postage stamps but as one who encourages others to collect postage
stamps.

The rapscallions. Mr Sibley just one more {word} question before you go.
Do you think foreign nations will ever understand our American

[*55v*]   A case of exploitation down in Goff county

[*56r*]   way of administering justice. Our humor is to[o] hard for them dont you
think. No two nations can ever agree on what is funny.

A buzzer goes off and the Dist Att. (not Clerk) excuses himself. Nine oclock.
To work to work.

Barbara. Did you ever hear the story of how Romboyd bit the cow   well
In his farm hand days a cow kicked the milk pail out from between his knees
when he {was} milking: which I'm told is the worst offense you can commit
on a farm. First Romboid threw his stool at ~~the~~ her then {looked for a pitch-
fork and finding none} leaping on her and seizing her [illegible] {back} in
both hands fastened his little teeth in her backbone. It brought a bellow out
of her. Well ~~he answered~~ was his response who began it darn ye. There spoke
the future justice. But from the story you ~~get not only~~ derive not only a sense
of the judges herculean strength ~~to~~ [illegible]{double teeth all round} that
could penetrate the sensibilities of a cow: you get also an equalitarianism that
scorns to hold itself above you and talks with a beast.

[*60r*]   O

Oh where oh where is the underdog gone
Oh where oh where can he be
That I always lavished my sympathies on

I don't want to hear you put your lyric gift to such base and ironical uses.
Haven't I had provocation.
What has anybody been saying to you.
Anybody has been saying ~~Where is~~ What has become of the sympathy I
used to have for the poor. I used to ~~write~~ show it in my ~~writing~~ songs And
now when [illegible] the chance offers I simply refuse to make the ~~world~~
{state} over for them.

You claim the right to change your mind and ~~to~~ even to be inconsistent.
Neither I never change my mind and Im {nor am I} ever inconsistent.
Yet you used to sing the sorrows of the poor and now refuse to vote for
them.

I told—I never would have sung their sorrows if I had thought for a moment anything was

[61r] going to be done about it. I didnt mean to help bring {on} any revolution. Is
this a world of dogs revolving so fast that my mind can't keep up with them. I
want my underdog to stay under long enough for me to get attached to him

As long as some dog is undesirable I dont see what you have to complain
of.

A complete revolution would be all the way round to where we started
from. Only a half revolution would put the bottom on top.

[62r]   Disinterestedness versus Humaneness

Poetry ~~for fame and money~~ Can the love of it be separated from love of fame
{and} money?

Principle   Can the love of it be isolated?

Drink   Can the passion for it be found almost pure. Or is it always too
much adultered with sociability—or unhappiness

There are fabulae meant to show ~~that~~ love of principle almost pure

To be sure no man can think entirely from one such document as the constitution. Extraneous considerations must enter into the base of his premises.
Those are things that change from generation to generation.

Whats the constitution between friends?
Whats the constitution among friends of the poor?

Should think the word appeasers would stick in the throats of the party
whose boast is that they have prevented the war of the classes by appeasing
the proletariat[94]

[63r]   Boast of their early disadvantages when they come out on top. Boast of
their advantages when young on the unlikelyhood that they will ever amount
to much.

•   •   •

The Drafted. That is what all are in peace and war who didnt get up the idea—all who work for Ford—all who fight for [illegible] Gen. Eisenhower. They are dragged in and dragged along. I never understood before their sadness and my sympathy with them. For them the Bible is right in calling work a curse.[95] ~~It is never a curse~~ Their object is to get as much of a living as possible for as short hours as possible. For their leaders who sustain the idea (and got it up) the Bible is wrong. They feel like volunteers. [illegible] They are the princes who spare no time nor effort. Leading or misleading they get all the fun The ~~enemy's~~ leaders {of both parties} think if only ~~their~~ the the followers of the other {party} could be made to see they would change leaders. The Russians think ~~the illegible~~ our proletariat would join their proletariat if they weren't kept under.

[63v]   Kipling was sure the Boers wouldnt for a moment have fought England if they had half a chance to see what it was all about "They were lead by evil counsellors the Lord shall deal with them.[96]

~~They~~ We turn from counting forward from the start to estimating backward from the end

Santanas idea that we must know everything said before we start to speak ourselves: that is if we want to avoid repetition[97]

[68v]   When footsteps interrupted

[69r]   <u>Epaminondas</u>[98] came home {from} cleaning up
~~He came home~~ {One morning} furious at having found
A pair of wretched legs in pant and boot
Stuck out of {a} tipped over garbage can
Like somebody's whose murder wasn't wort
Reporting. But the {wretched} legs weret dead [illegible]
~~They~~ Or not so dead they didn't come to life
{When interrupted on approach of steps}
They stirred and drew back from the garbage can
　　　　~~As man drew from it bearded to the eyes and the beard~~
　　　　~~Was foul with feeding and the eyes were guilty.~~
As ~~and~~ A whole man drew back from the garbage can
Full bearded and {his} beard was foul with feeding

His eyes were guilty as if caught in something.
He stayed on hands ~~until the interruption~~ {and [illegible]}
    And knees ~~and waited out~~
                though waiting out
                [illegible]
The interruption

Epaminondas ~~was cursed? the poor.~~
        cursed ~~until his~~ [illegible]
My dear my dear we mustnt hate the poor

[69v] You tell my dog that Im the boss
~~You mean of you as well as him~~
Go find the Boss you always say

[70v] me and so on Till the bourgoise papers begin to notice it. Just make believe
of course. What can you do in such a cheerful country but behave like cheerful idiots.

[71v] I am told you have been calling me a counter revolutionary. Well I am going to call you a bargain counter revolutionary You don't mind! ~~I only mean
cheap.~~ It is all in good fun to stretch our vocabularies ~~I don't mean I mean
cheap. Not too cheap~~ But read on and get my qualifiers When I say cheap I
don't mean too cheap. You do the best you probably can in a country where
~~you cant~~ {the law forbids your} actually inciting to open violence. We have a
shackled press. Things may ease up later. Meanwhile I have a proposal to
make ~~It will kill Time~~ It will help us kill Time since there is nobody else we
can kill. Lets you and I play we [illegible] have a Terror in this country. And
lets take turns shooting each other against the wall. First you shoot me
against the wall. Ill let you have the first turn. Then Ill shoot you and then
you shoot me

[72r] Star of stars—pride of Holywood.[98]

My sister
I know all about your sister. I didnt expect to find you here. (She unobtru-
sively brings out a small note book.) Tell me
Im under contract not to give interviews to anybody except from certain
papers.

But tell me It wont hurt for you to give ~~first part~~ a poor little home town reporter just one weeny answer to a question.

All right, one

Two

Two then

Lets see what they will be. I must make them crucial. Well here's the first one. Do you think this is a revolution.

> Revolution?   Half a revolution is better than a
>   A whole one because a whole one would
>   be right back.
>
> Yes revolution You know. (She makes her hand go round and round.
>   Monkeying with calendar

[73r]   It showed them up all right Full of incest and hypocracy and selling slaves to the nobility of South Carolina. Witch burning too.

Ive heard about it. I wonder why they were called Puritans? Because their motives were pure?

Did nt they land some where?

It was the Pilgrims that did the landing.

Maybe it was the Pilgrims I meant. There was one character named ~~Pilgrim in reverse~~ Mr. Grim Pill which I suppose was just Pilgrim in reverse. I had the leading part. I suffered in silence [illegible] from an unnatural relationship with someone very religious.

Oh my goodness (standing up with {sudden} respect) you arent—

No Im not my sister if that's what you were going to say. My sister isnt expected till tomorrow. Im plain [illegible] Amory Reeches

[74r]   You mean as in so many thousan revolutions a minute.

Never mind that question. Heres a better one You are of one of the oldest families in Baltimore arent you?

Yes my sister and I both are. The Reeches pronounced Riches. Its a sure sign of a very old word where you get double ee pronounced i as in creek seek em and breeches. ~~You~~ {Im told} Mrs. K's claim to connection with us is an odd one. My sister is her daughter in law by ~~a former~~ {one of her earlier} marriages She chooses to keep up the connection on ~~account of~~ account of genealogy. Mrs. K {entering} Disgusting. Animals I call them. No checks. Anything that is physically possible between them is wholly possible. You dont know what I'm talking on about. Ive just had an engagement announced to me in the

[75ʳ]   kitchen—between my former maid and present gardener. There's a news item for you ~~Miss~~ little Miss Scavenger. (She glances at a card she has been holding in her hand pushing it away from her and feeling for her pince nez.) Why Sibyl Simpson. Why didnt you speak up for yourself. I didnt recognize you in the office of a reporter. So youre a reporter now She looks at the card. For {The} Intelligencer that my {own} grandfather founded. And you thought you might pick up something about the splendid people that are coming to my party to meet Mrs Sobier. {You belong to the best yourself} You have a right to ~~as the equal of anybody of any of them~~. {anything you want to know} Its wise policy for The Intelligencer to send out into society the equals of any of us. Adele this is Sybil Simpson—Bragg on her mothers side The Simpsons could always do anything

"Alcie That Socratic boy"

MS. 001672. *Brown paper cover spiral notebook, 5½" × 8½". Image, possibly of a fruit or melon, drawn on the center of the cover. "Ask for No. 855C Another MAPLE LEAF product" is stamped on the bottom center of the cover and a maple leaf is printed on the top left corner of the cover. White ruled pages. All entries are in blue ink.*

[*1r*] Alcie That Socractic boy[1]
Left the ship at Thursoi   Left the Syracusian fleet
~~That was when he got descreet~~
That was where he ~~jumped the fleet~~

Knowing what was good for him
~~Luckily hw learned how to swing.~~
Luckily he learned to swing
While he got sophisticated.

[*2r*] It seems the honking horns of theater cars
That in homes going got their bumpers tangled
And the shouts of their owners with cigars
That got down in the dirty street and wrangled
Were the first sounds of men to reach the stars
That the sky over New York City spangled
It seems it didn't seem to bother Mars
That we the people had small love [illegible]
And that hope of war need never wither
But Venus poor dear sympathetic Venus
~~But Venus~~
The star of Love was thrown out a delta.
~~And it was Venus sent the saucer hither~~
And (at the expense no doubt of some – Marcians)
Twas venus sent the flying saucer hither.

[3r] ~~That by my publisher ha~~
That by my publisher was just reported
As having landed out near Hollywood
And though by lack of English somewhat thwarted
Got satisfied she had misunderstood
~~The state of love~~
The love she was afraid no longer sported
She founded California good.
Was flourishing out ~~out there and it was good~~ and she pronounced it good
The saucer had rays round like a Saturn
But twas from Venus Hollywood attracted
It pilot ~~girl~~ was a girl a lovely slatter
Dishevilled as if recently contacted
She know what love was knew by matter
No matter what was said. Twas [illegible] acted

She knew what love was by its tactile pattern
Not Not by its language but by how it acted.*

[4r] The first time any of the surrounding stars
Ever took notice of our [?going things] here
Was the night of the last jam of cars
          In Broadway

The first time the surrounding skies
Took notice of us and struck out their eyes
At people here was
At us was af
Of people here was after theater

[5r] The first time ever the surrounding skies
Took notice of us and stuck out their eyes
That happened to be Juppiter and mars
Was the night the final jam of cars
In Broadway ~~after~~ after theater too late
The impatient cars began to honk with hate
Policeman had come in vain to bid them hush

---

* These two lines written up left side of page, bottom to top.

The cars head on would lock together and push
Until they stood each other up on their hind wheels
More like ferocities than automobiles.
~~Then they began to~~
The crumpled up into a pyramid
And in the name of the suburban Id
~~And a man with the~~
And with the authority of the great I am
Pronounced to have the general Traffic –
The end of Every thing is End for end.

[5*v*]   No [illegible] heavens very eyeballs bulged
At the earth extent that was then divulged
Earth was a morgue of chances and spare parts
~~Looking~~   men had lost their hearts
A morgue of
Where seldom came back for spare parts
Where seldom men came looking for their hearts

[6*r*]   Some of the poem is merely headway in getting on in hopes of a lucky incident now and then and a lucky end.[2]

Tempter of Love as at Corinth and Alexandria
Tempter of Chance as at Las Vegas
More true Love more true chance outside the [illegible]

Our democracy most like the traditional bill of fare
Russian democracy more like

Clutching at words like feeling for chords on the lute strings of the heart that
do it to you.

How to keep [illegible] the child like country

"Three of those evils parsed in half an hour"

MS. 001275. *Off-white canvas cover bound diary-notebook, 7¼″ × 10¼″. Unruled white paper. The letters "rf" embossed in black on the spine and on the front cover. Entries are in blue ink unless otherwise noted. Numerals in Frost's hand are written in throughout the notebooks.*

[1r]   [blank]

[2r]   Three of those evils parsed in half an hour

      [illegible] [illegible]

[3r]   2

Mustnt forget   Poet in Residence[1]

                                         Poet in resistance

Slow readers found to have been slowed up by the habit formed in reading poetry which can be read no faster than it is read aloud or ~~in~~ silently in the minds ear

    Slow readers found to have been slowed up by maturity. To think the book is of course faster [that] {than}* to think the book and ~~to think~~ at the same time think about the book For the originating reader there is besides the induced current of the text itself the super induced current of things occurring to him that he values most. (All this came up {in my head} when Brown the state superintendant of New Hampshire (successor to Henry Morrison) made some experiments in rapidity of reading in the New Hampshire schools in 1915 or 14[2]

                   •   •   •

---

* Inserted below the line.

Have someone say he hoped people who had gone to heaven didnt know any more about what we were doing here than ~~the~~ we know about what they are doing there.

Have someone else say he had begun to notice he had been doing better in this world as the [number] of his friends were and by death [illegible] what he might call his party in the other world.

The particularity of Dante on the subject of Hell is only figurative and poetic (the inspiration of it ~~so sustained~~ could only have been sustained by hate in a disagreeable nature The particularity of Swedenborg is a literal report. He said millions were happy in Hell.[3] I have forgotten but didnt he say they couldnt stand Heaven when they tried it.
There had been cases.

[3v]   Kenny's[4] rebuking me for joshing a convert as if he were as shabby as a turn-coat.

Kierkegaard gets a whole new theology out of Abrahams near sacrifice of Isaac[5] as I got one out of the idea of our ~~having~~ lacking the support of even the slightest recollection that we chose ourselves beforehand with open eyes before we were born.[6] Abraham is assumed not to have blamed God for what he was going to do to Isaac—I mean in his talk to Isaac—as he led him to the altar. He was a nobler murderer for not excusing himself and being willing to pass for wicked. Fun playing with tales from the Bible. Inexhaustible book. Only danger is if people arent brought up on it a poet cant track on it.

189 Voyage to New York (by the Fall River Lines
    Carrie Nation[7] on board. First encounter with
    Murder in a N.Y. dining place

Later 1954 Taxi man who carried my bag clear into the elevator at Holts.[8] He had told me all ~~about~~ what life meant to him. Drunks he said often over-tipped you and often didnt even pay you. He said he had shown his disregard for either tips or pay by turning a man abruptly out of his cab because he blasphemed three times. He wouldnt tell me ~~wh~~ what his curse words were. They were too bad. I remarked there was such a society in his church as the

Holy Name society.[9] He said yes there was. He didnt say he did or didnt belong to it. He didnt deny the church was his.

[4r] 3

~~Our part is the bees our part is a go between~~
Remember me to—

The bees are go between's and so are we. Anything we leave and say goodbye to says {back} to us. Remember me to any <u>whose</u> any pollen will take effect.[10] ~~Every~~ Our part in remembering one thing to another*

We can do absolutely nothing about our own evolution[11] into anything else better or worse. We havent the least idea ~~about~~ where to go about it at what trait to break forward or out. But maybe this inexplicable dissatisfaction we talk about so much is the obscure [?force] of [illegible] Oh what is being done with us we ask in patience.

Enthusiasm may be eloquent

Even close in in

But rapture is a still small silent thing

From Artistotles regard for deduction came {the} natural ~~piety of~~ or nature piety of the nature poets and the pursuit of science. Wordsworth's "natural piety."[12]

[4v–5v] [blank]

[6r] 5

You snap the grip and Pegasus prances

[6v]   Us Us and the Russ[13]

A run of luck to a completion[14]

                    •   •   •

_____

* Entry written in black ink.

I dont believe no line can be straight
I dont believe space is round or anything but flat Euclidian
I dont believe time is a dimension of space
I dont believe the speed of light is an absolute.[15]

Light turning red with distance is light dissipating as all waves dissipate and as this particular universe is dissipating.[16]

Handicapping needed if the human race is to be a race of* justice and mercy. Mercy to the weak is handicapping the strong

People who have a conscientious concern for poetry and ~~art~~ {painting} and music toward their own improvement—as distinguished from people who have a weakness for the arts so that they cant let them alone.[†]

The Hoped She Would Get Over It. So they sent her to college: they sent her travelling. They gave her all sorts of people to meet.

Peach orchard with [illegible] petal carpet

Horse sense. Horses have no special sense more than a cow or chicken. Horse sense means the sense a man has in trading and handling horses

Our kind of government is purposely left ramshackle. ~~It rains and~~ The parts of ram crack almost apart but stay shackled together Like an old time freight train. Penny saved is [?mean] penny ~~saved~~ is {earned is generous} Liberty and equality—justice and mercy[17]

[*7r*][‡]   6
Three Obituaries in Today's Paper

Old Thayer ~~born~~ sixty nine. His own grave and stone Paquin the demented He didnt fool me. {Gold for Christmas}[§]
Will Morell the cowman

•   •   •

---

* Section starting with "A run of luck" to here written in black ink.
[†] Entry written in black ink except where noted.
[‡] Page written in black ink.
[§] Inserted partially in the margin and written in blue ink.

The early Christians knew their difference with the state was over the altar of Victory in the Senate

Pertinax the Puritan the Praetorians loathed.[18]

Waste[19]   Penny saved = penny earned?*[20]
Getting drunk is the glorification of waste—pouring libation {to the God of Waste} not onto the ground not onto the fire but into yourself.[21] It is squandering with complete submissiveness to the nature of things your time your wealth your faculties. An altar found in the jungle had a single {short} word on it that has been translated to mean night soil. The medium in which alone life can flourish is perished matter.[22] The little that lives organized lives in a bath of broken down organisms—disorganisms.†

Enough for the symbol—enough for us to get the idea. The savage doesn't make himself see with less than the slaughter of less than hundreds of cattle and even men. But it is the same God of Waste we waste pour [illegible] the wine to.

Epimmonadas[23] conducts the rites in Thebes in his working clothes as city scavenger—garbage man‡

The tree stands growing in its own waste—the bark it sheds the branches and the bark it sheds

There is no evolution[24] there is only growth of something in its own waste. The figure for the whole is a tree—Igdrasil.[25] The longest life is the great

[7ν]   growth that comprises the many growths. The It is only a growth though and must have its time limit. So far as we can see its material goes round and round except for a central pinnacle that seems to thrust [illegible] toward something outside the circulation Our grief our pain are our feeling of being cast off from and this thrust and seemingly wasted so to speak

The danger in the word evolution as used is that stealthily introduces the idea of eternality into the idea of growth. Growths is a better idea than growth§ (sing.)

•   •   •

---

* Phrase written in blue ink.
† Word written in blue ink.
‡ "garbage man" written in blue ink.
§ Page to this point written in black ink.

It is anticipating old age to get enticed of the delights

It is anticipating old age to get enticed of the delights

Nolo Contendere
$\left\{\begin{array}{l}\text{For small favors} \\ \text{For a place on foot in the road} \\ \text{For a place for poetry.}\end{array}\right.$
"I wont play"

"I cant and wont"—most desperate mood of all.
But answer to a question is How can you ask it

      This May Be it The Waste of Seats in cars
A thousand cars with all seats in them empty
Except the drivers: Havent the carless a right to the empty seats.

    The universe would turn out to be circular because all reasoning is in a cir-
cle (however wide for receptiveness) and all reassuring is in a circle because
the head—round-the brain pan[26]
    But if space is curved no bodies in it can be straight away from my explo-
sion to expand the universe The redness of the more distant suns must be
from the deterioration of light far spent not from our own receeding sources

[*8r*]*   7

Did Shelley[27] know what he was up to? I hate to think I cant count on people
to know when I am being figurative and when I am not being—when I am
hinting and when I am not hinting.† [28]

      Waste[29]

I was in a trance with poetry that made it as distasteful to listen to the
Kitridges[30] talk about poetry as it would have been to read Freud or Havelock
Ellis[31] or Kraft Ebbing[32] when I was in love. That really was why I [illegible]
out of college. I was willing to be a sacrifice to [?certacy]. I wasnt afraid to be
wasted to the maenads.

              •   •   •

---

* Page written in black ink.
† Entry written up side of page, bottom to top.

All is expense. All is waste that is not expense to a purpose—namely US.

Waste disturbed the boys*
Pertinax talked to the ~~bro~~ boys (not brothers Romulus and Remus[33] about 1
How you find yourself in convictions. 2 The notion you value most what has
cost you the most pains. 3 Gentrification of waste—pouring a libation into
yourself. *4 The courage to go ahead on insufficient knowledge 5 When you
leave an attachment for an attraction.[34] 6 You many yourself know what you
mean but do you know what you are up to? Make-Make Wasnt it different
~~once~~ {[then]} {once} from what it is? Once loyalty was that ~~with~~ with which
we stayed
~~With what were no longer held by love~~
Where love no longer could [~~illegible~~] {pretend} to hold us.

Stayed with a meaning that had lost its meaning
Stayed with a lover for what once he meant.

I do not like the way you shift your eyes
When you say things like that of late Vizier[35]
You waver in the breast. You shake the throne
With a distrust ~~of intellectuality~~ {I am ashamed to own}
Stand up and to {make} our fellow banqueters revellers
Share in our ~~intellectuality~~ [?laugh]
~~I want the queen to hear this~~ [~~illegible~~]
We ~~cannot~~ must not always laugh our lives away
I want the Queen to hear this. [illegible] Listen
Mordecai[36] has a novel definition

[8v]   Affability was the same five thousand years ago as now science hasn't
changed it

Aquinas takes a Greek {Aristotle} to rationalize the New Testament.[37]
Spinoza takes the Greeks to rationalize the Old Testament.[38] Einstein picks
up some Spinoza to sanctify his science.[39]

~~The~~ The great characteristic of all four of the beliefs I have enumerated[40]
(and several more I could have brought in) is their strength to go forward in

---

* This line and the one above it written in blue ink.

spite of in the truth of any facts that may be brought against them. Scepticism (facts) may baffle them to death in the end—and it may not.

One thing can be said that though reason wont undertake to rationalized the beliefs it cant help respecting them. It may never know what to make of them it may not need to. Let it stand there in awe of them.

Humility.![41] The successful can afford to be humble who have now nothing more to press on for.

[9r]   Loyalty is the trouble and their order of importance. When to leave one for another. When to forsake an attachment for an attraction.[42] When to take a chance on new gods. When it gather in the people to a head in one man for taking this chance.

The brute ugliness of driving unaimed by history and its rationalities. You might think history as a closed form like the human body but it is open at the muzzle for newness as the body is open for newness at the crotch.

The trouble with the Supreme court and the Oliver Wendell Holmeses[43] is that they want to keep changing things so fast as to rob the radicals of the fun of rebelling against the conservatives. Their laws go through the state too loosely to nourish its weight and strength.*

Life is always one third shorter than
[Illegible]
you are accustomed to think because you forget
[illegible]
about sleep.

Hunter — butcher
Soldier   executioner.

Is there excuse for some falseness of propaganda that How insincerely] shall work to put the soldiers dander up in fight (and so make his hardship more bearable)

You could stay getting knowledge in school all your life without losing your innocence.

The opposite of the thing is irreducible [illegible] {minimum} that wont be brought in to the generalization you are making.

---

* Page to this point written in black ink.

[9v]   The reason the universe turns out to be round: I wouldnt trust any concate-
nations of syllogisms or equations to be carried out any distance without returning on themselves to where they started from and thats because the
brain pan is more or less circular. We can't help reasoning in a circle some
peoples circles are wider than some other peoples.[44]

Someone once asked if Dead Souls[45] was a great book
Someone else answered All books are great.
Someone then asked was Dead Souls worth reading
No book is worth reading
                    died down passion
Shame is merely lack of passion
                    ashes

I dont change my watch every time I see a clock it differs from

We know now pretty well that sin is what the Pope doesnt do what priests
dont do what Mary didnt do. But sin is only wicked when not confined to
The wedding ceremony, marriage is a sweeping of confession that takes care
of in advance of all the sins of a lifetime.

How much has American prosperity to do with American happiness that
wants to make other nations prosperous and happy. I assume our interfering
ways derive from a Christian wish to make the whole world happy. Maybe a
mistaken idea of Christianity which may have no purpose other than to save
us {in our unhappiness.}*

[10r]   9
Alone in front of the empty shack
I looked far after those gone away
I had no language for calling back†
There are thing I live amid
Of which I'd rather be rid

{Some}‡ I [illegible] change [they] watch everytime {whenever they} I come
On another timepiece it differs from.

---

* Written vertically up the right-hand margin.
† First three lines written in black ink.
‡ Inserted in left-hand margin.

Some
I change my {[illegible]} {the [illegible] scared members of each other}
watch whenever {illegible} revue
On another timepiece it differs from-

The meaning is not that God rested from labor on the seventh day but ~~that he~~
simply that he rested his case. The last thing he did was to put in a good word
for it and pronounce it all right He summed up for the defense The seventh
day the Jews set aside of to do seventh of their time to this God who loves
sacrifice{ial} waste — pure sacrifice.   Heave offerings, and wave offerings
are not true offerings[46]

~~Landlord or tenant choose which one to be~~ {one part to plan} you will
Where and with whom I found myself by accident
I always found most apt to make me think and dream

Tentatives vs tenets
Griefs vs grievances[47]
Lunkheads and Qudidnunc heads[48] ([?Sehin] heads)
Civilization and Utopia
Liberty and Equality (Justice and Mercy)[49]
Penny saved<penny earned

[10v]   ~~We~~ Our schools are free. We are free to go to them. We are free not to go to
them. And there our freedom ends. We are not free to go to no school at all.
~~But in~~ That should be all there is to say except that really a considerable number manage to get by without an
education.
     One God One World One Woman and One Child
Make that your creed
That I believe would be the best way out

     Titles
~~And That Was That~~
Take it from me   Sez you
Talk Talk
A Straight Crookednes (in a cane)[50]
I make bold to say

The Right to Know—anything you are smart enough to find out—anything you are deep enough to understand. ~~Is it a right~~ There is the Right to Tell for our consideration. The things we are in honor bound not to tell in many places we can **perhaps tell** in poetry and drama. We have a right to tell anything we know how when and where to tell.

A wit is never a bore   ~~a wit is a right~~
As long as he's witty   [~~illegible~~]
       Youre all right if your witty
       You musnt be a witty
       Your all right if you are a sit
       You mustnt be a witty
    The article a [illegible] It

[*11r*]   11

A Murmur of Inner Voices

Abigail says John ~~told~~ {tells} her this ~~was~~ {is} Europe
And always will be.*[51]

Latest: Sabbath keeping is not for rest but for sacrifice of seventh part of a lifetime. It is sacrificial and not recreational. Thats why Neamiah[52] was so high minded in his insistance on the observance of Sunday.

So I didnt rest from labor. He rested his case and prejudiced it as much as possible to our judgement by declaring it good.

But he had to try three times before he got the people he wanted. Adam was his first fresh start after something went wrong with the aboriginals. Noah was the second when things went bad again. Christ was the third— God in person himself. It remains to be seen if he may not have to come back for a second time in person. {It is} So prophesied.

To be above the us of our feet is one of our chief ambitions. The earliest Bible reference is to a [~~illegible~~] {woman} so refined that she has never set her feet on the ground[53] (curse in Leviticus[54]) Chinese women aimed at the atrophy of feet.[55] Cowboys disdain to walk the shortest distance even. I saw half a

---

* Page to this point written in black ink.

dozen ~~girls~~ college girls waiting for any car that would pick them up for a lift. A car stopped for them and took them all in. I ~~watched to~~ followed to see how far their need was. They rode one block and all got out for a class apparently. To be sure it was uphill somewhat. Everybod stands thumbing for a ride longer than it would take to reach [illegible] a destination.

Kinsey[56] says young couples do it three and one half times a year. One suspects the first sign there of the [frigidity] of woman. [Illegible] She may very well be the one that fails once out of four tries.

School where choice has to be made between being landlord or tennant.

Every barn should have hanged like a millstone round [?the] neck the ownership of twenty acres of land

[*11v*] Ever since I began to see the relation of Aristotle to Plato[57] I have had a growing suspicion that it is even worse than Aristotle ~~said~~ when he ~~said~~ we must reject not only the a priori but equally the a posteriori: what comes up is as important as what comes down. Plato would have it that nothing down here below but is an imperfect copy of the ideal idea above.[58] Aristotle broke that when he turned to study nature with the same respect reverence piety that he used in thinking the thoughts Plato believed nature derived from. One day in my reading it was revealed to me that what Wordsworth meant by "days bound each to each by natural piety was"[59] by nature piety. In a loose way he had been take{n}* (by me perhaps by nobody else) as ~~a~~ meaning a religious piety that was natural for all of us to feel. He was talking an Aristotelian philosophy contrary to the Platonic. Maybe Rousseau[60] set him in the right way. But Aristotle should have ~~set~~ set us all long ago. I have a growing suspicion that might line me up in disloyalty to the humanists that nothing comes down from above but what has ~~com~~ so long since come up from below that we have forgotten its origin. All is observation of nature (human nature included) consciously or unconsciously made by our eyes and minds developed from the ground up. We notice traits of nature—thats all we do. The so called nature poet so tiresome

---

* Inserted below the line.

[*12r*]*   12

A Murmur of Inner Voices

Abigail says John tells her this is Europe.
~~That's all it is and all it needs to~~ be.
And that is all it is ~~in his opinion~~ or ever will be
John is a seaboard sentimentalist.
For him revolt rebellion revolution
Meant no break with the old worlds complications
{Im sure He Would give anything to know I think}
~~If he had any way offending out~~
How ~~bad~~ {wet} an weather was today in ~~Bost~~ London
So he could dress accordingly in Boston.
He
~~I [illegible] He He wants us in our roominess~~
~~He didnt see wh~~   contention
He doesnt see why all our roominess
Might not except in which it [lacked]
Before the bottle gurgled
From suffering the pained economy {bill}
Of ~~their~~ {the} constriction of a tiny island.

---

to some toils not neither does he spin[61] like a natural scientist but it is to the natural scientist he is nearest of kin in his fresh noticing of the details[62] that prove he has "been there" as the expression is (low down). Little to choose he finds [illegible] background nature (rocks and trees [illegible] and wild animals) and foreground nature the portrait of a man neither laughing nor weeping but with features qualified by having laughed and wept: The proud humanists [illegible] would be right if they said they held themselves above the part of nature not yet human. Or nearer rights when they put on airs of disdain for the praise of out doors that without exclamation of wonderful and beautiful pays tribute by reporting details not previously mentioned

[*12v*]   Thats nature poetry and nature science. You have to be careful with the word natural—with all words in fact. You have to play the words close to the reali-

---

* Line drawn [or ink spill] across this page, diagonally, from right to left. Entry up to line/ ink spill written in black ink.

ties. And the realities are from below upward and from outside inward. There is such a resevoir such a stock pile accumulated above to do our thinking from that it gives the illusion of always having been up there of itself absolutely. My growing suspicion is that practically all is from down up and from out in. The great difference to discriminate between is the old and seasoned harvest or vintage and the new harvest or vintage and the new harvest green from the garden before it has time to wilt spoil and ferment into inspiration that has no flavor of its derivation

¶ True many {if not all} of our words show traces of a metaphorical origin. But in daily use they have become obsolete. Like lead at the dead end of things once radioactive. What a comfort to think of what has come to final rest be it word or substance.

[13r]   13
          [blank]

[13v]   [blank]

[14r]   15
          Who Ruled
From Garfield to Truman[63]*

Several ladies have come out with it in polite conversation that [illegible] lately that they were going through the change of life. They often [spoke] out about their bitches being in heat. Next I know they will be telling me frankly they are in heat themselves. I must be ready for it. I mean so I wont seem shocked. I have always managed so far not to seem shocked.

Go phasing along with self submission. These things said in parable so the wrong people wont understand them and get saved[64] — {maker poetry and religion} — sound aristocratic and esoteric—until I take time to arrive at the recollection that all the misinterpretations of my poetry have been at the worst when done by the educated and the bible says elsewhere "except ye become as little children[65] and neither toil a you the meanings nor spin them out of shape[66] you are the wrong people We dont want to see saved

                    •   •   •

_____
* Entry written in black ink.

||

She could have told you what he wouldnt tell you
But for the she for the same reason wouldn't either.
They both looked on you with dark disfavor
For [running] to assume you could be saved
The need of having to live through it all
By any story anyone could tell you.

[14v]   Education Seventy Years Afterward.

Couldnt it be that besides being all that you and I want it to be and have given lives toward making it be there are still left several old fashioned things it would be too bad to have seen left behind. Such as

The formation {of} the habit of looking at least once back at what's said and done to catch yourself in any mistake in it to correct before anyone else hurts your self respect or pride by correcting it for you.

The formulation of the habit of adding the weight of your will by getting on top of any impression with determination to make it press press it down and in and deepen it partly for the sake of depth and partly to make it more lasting and memorable. As when you take an order of goods to bring with you from the store. You even get mnemonic devices with ingenious humor.

Getting it in readiness like a fire engine house for any emergency. So that when spoken to unsympathetically attack ally as by a hostile lawyers in a law court your thoughts don't scatter. Your training has just put you into a more or les perpetual state of readiness to answer up. You have regretted your failure to think of the right thing to say on the spur of the moment and the harsh attack that you have got more present minded and greatly improve in repartee.

Thus there is another rule of life I never {always think of when} I see a player serving two or three bats once before he goes to the plate to fan pitcher with one bat. Always try to

[15r]*   have arranged that you were doing something harder and more disciplinary [illegible] than what you the picktie exhibition you have before you are about to make of yourself.

                    •   •   •

---

* Page torn at the top.

Lastly [~~illegible~~] (for the time being anyway) I can conceive of a person going further from having been squeezed almost too tight in school just as a pip
might shoot the father in to the world the tighter it has been pinched between the fingers

I have always quoted someone who said in [illegible] Those who will may
and those who wont must self discipline Sure for in choice spirits is enough

(next page

[*15v*]   But he has never taken discipline at all I was almost saying who has never un-
dergone discipline of the parent the teacher the policeman and the drill
seargant. But society will take care of that. I have trusted the ideal to venture
pretty far with a sort of flower pot [~~illegible~~] policy with the young [~~illegible~~]
plant: open unlimited at the top but at the bottom closed and shut in tight except for perhaps one small hole for drainage that you may make the most of
for a symbol

[*16r*]*   Old Gold for Christmas[67]

"You stand and let me lean on you a minute
Till I can think. Don't ask me who I am.
I'm all mixed up from having been retired."
He rued a bloody knuckle in the street light
As a girl gloats on her engagement ring.
I helped him shoulder one of his suspenders.
I've been down on ~~in the dirt~~ {some ice} and lost my coat.
The empty trolleys buses at this time of night
Are so insane to get home to their car barns
They'd as soon knock you down as pick you up.
I must have thrown my coat away at one.
The place I want to get to is a farm
And nothing but a farm will satisfy me†
Thats out here on a side road with two rows
Of sugar maples leading up to it—
The airs lit up with seven burning maples‡
In case you had a mind to take me there,

---

* Page written in black ink except where noted.
† Line written in blue ink.
‡ Line written in blue ink.

Or ~~root~~ out someone else to do it for you:
You're on foot walking so you can't yourself.
It's where I live and claim my residence
To vote at ~~though Im no great of a voter,~~ {when there's anything to vote}
{when I see the need of voting*}
The house is not much, but the barn is standing.
There! Midnight, I suppose, or one o'clock.
~~When the lights all go down~~ and out on one breath
The really should be careful what it does to people
~~Like candles on a birthday cake my brains lurch,~~
They shouldnt be so sudden with their lights
Blowing them all out on one breath {like can}
~~I loose my consciousness, it seems as if~~
They ~~say~~ {tell me}† its due to hardening of the heart.
The thing for us is to stay propped together
Till I can think—till both of us can think.
{you angry you have to think what you will of with me}
~~It cant hurt either of us to stop and think~~
I've got to think what I will till my daughter
I have to think what I will till my daughter
Who {she} will be worried waiting up to see
If I have thrown away my coat again.
She's not my daughter, but my daughter-in-law:

They shouldn't be so sudden with their lights
Blowing them out on one breath‡

[16v]   Since it had seemed to do his grievance good
To stand there holding forth and holding on
I hadnt forced him to let go of me.

Your silence means you don't believe my story
Or else your {[[illegible]]} ~~meditating where to [illegible]~~ {thinking where to
go with me.§}

---

* Phrase written below the line.
† Phrase written in blue ink.
‡ Lines written up right side of page.
§ Phrase written below the line.

But whats the matter with our staying here
You dont seem to appreciate at your age
~~Feeling~~ {Stomping} your feet on ground too frozen hard
~~For you~~ For them to dig your grave in if you died
It might help if I told you who it was
You'd captured or been captivated by
I have been called the Gold for Christmas Man
I used to get my pay in gold for Christmas
As a reward for having served the shop
Longer than anybody but the owners

You know what I think. Think your daughter there
Waiting up for you {~~sitting up waiting for you [illegible]~~} live That old house
you live in
And not one way off somewhere in the cold
Not one away off somewhere in the cold
Who ~~else.~~

[*17r*]*   Which explains why ~~she's been so strict with me~~ {she has to be so strict}†
~~About seed catalogues, though as for that~~
My wife was not much easier I guess.
You can't blame ~~wives~~ {women} for being on their guard
Against ~~the tendency men always~~ have {the tendency ~~to farm~~ men have to
farm}
~~To give up everthing that's comfortable~~
~~And get back back down to earth like on a farm~~
The tendency ~~some have~~ to fish and hunt ~~is different~~
~~Is not so dangerous to peace of mind~~
Because, though taking men away from home,
It doesn't drag home with them back to nature.‡
~~Women do right to stick to city life.~~
~~You take it where the pump is in the yard—~~
~~But why get conscientious about what~~
~~I havent even done but only thought~~
~~Of doing to the women in my day~~

---

* Page written in black ink except where noted.
† Phrase written in blue ink.
‡ There is an arrow after this line pointing to the first entry on 16v.

With the excuse of what I had to do
To earn their living and respect myself."

"Oh, isn't it about my turn to talk!
You have to think what you will tell your daughter:
I have to think what I will do with you.
I saw but one light in the neighborhood
And that had gone upstairs almost to bed.*
But its been putting notions in my head.
Who would it be awake up there so late?"

"No one I'd care to introduce you to.
He's a church preacher and a baseball pitcher—
Combined. He pitches for us Saturdays
And preaches to us on Sundays. He can pitch.
Only they claim he's too wild for his strength.
Catchers cant hold him, or he'd make the league.

[17v]†   I saw but one light in the neighborhood
And that had gone upstairs almost to bed

[18r]‡   He's not our kind. He don't believe in farming.
He thinks the future of the world's in mills.
You stir him up and all you'll get is talk—
You'll see—about dependence on the weather
Being the reason there's no hope in farming.
My daughter turns him onto me sometimes."

"Do you know I'm beginning to suspect
That light's your daughter waiting up for you.
I'll bet That {very} house right there is where you live,
And not away off somewhere in the country cold
Where have my faculties been all this time?"

"Its no such thing. I made the first down payment,
Yes and have receipt for it here in my pocket,
Or would have if I hadn't lost my coat.

---

* There is an arrow in the left-hand margin pointing to the last entry on 16v.
† Page in black ink.
‡ 18r-21r written in black ink except where noted.

But whats the matter with our staying here?
You don't seem to appreciate at your age
~~Feeling~~ your feet on ground too frozen hard
For them to dig your grave in if you died."

~~Since I could see this plainly wasn't drink,~~
~~But the and last end and the best of may come to,~~
~~And since~~ it seemed to do his {grievance} ~~trouble~~ good
To stand there holding on and holding forth
I hadn't forced him to let go of me.
~~But now when I had let myself be leaned on~~
~~Enough for one night's charity I said:~~
~~"Tell me the rest of it indoors you'll have to.~~
~~I'm frozen Let's {go over and [illegible phrase}}"~~
~~He let himself be dragged since it was gently.~~

~~My door knock frightened me with its results.~~

[*18v*]   I'm glad he wanted to come here. We're friends.
{and to pitch}
I pitch I may {and} say. He was once {my} catcher
In the bare handed days before the mitt
Look at his knuckles will you! He and I
Speak the same language, don't we Grandsir?
That's why he ~~comes~~ {came} to my church when he ~~comes~~ {came}

[*19r*]   The householder proved too big for his house.
Bringing him downstairs almost brought the house down
The windows rattled and the dishes must have.
He turned the porch light one us like a spot light
Before he unlocked and flung wide the door.

"See what you've captured—Gransir Rice again!
He runs away from second childishness."

"I didn't capture him; ~~he captured me~~ {he rose up}
He rose up* from the ditch and captured me."

•   •   •

---
* Phrase written in blue ink.

"What did he, make a flying tackle on you?
He's torn the very patches off his knees.
He runs away from old man's craziness.
Cant you tell by the slyness of his look
He knows he's done {in the} wrong? But he isn't bad, though
Just naughty like a child you hate to punish.
That's my wife telephoning for his son.
To come and get him as {is} [illegible] customary
You didn't get much out of him I guess."

"Oh,* the contrary I got words and words"
"About that non-existant farm of his?"

"I wasn't fooled. I knew it was the dream farm
We all indulge in all our city lives.
"We'll hurt his feelings if we talk like this won't we?
Our talk like this will hurt her feelings won't it?†
He's taking it all in—stunned as he looks.) dull
He told me if we found we were mistaken
And wanted to undo what we had done,
The first stage backward would be back to farming
The next to hunting and the last to fishing."
"Did he say things like that?"
                    "Well something like that

[19v]   [blank]

[20r]   ("He knows hes being talked about all right.)
He opened up with you. At home he's sullen.
Because we don't keep bringing up his past.
No one would guess to see him bowed down there
He once was someone."
                    "Someone of importance?"

"Yes let me tell you who it is you've taken.
He didn't tell you?"

---

* Word written in blue ink.
† Entry written up left side of page, bottom to top.

"No he didn't brag."
"That was the trait that gave him his importance
He never would declare how good he was.
Shall we wait for his son and let him tell you
A story he has I wouldn't want to spoil
Called Gold for Christmas? It's a story about
What a great man this is now gone to nothing."

"You'll tell it now."
                    "Well good Samaritan
You have been gentle with one worthy of it.
His son will be found gentle with him too
And that because unlike most of the family
He has been patient with his stubborn father"

"About the farm?"

                    "No this was something else.
He thought if he was worthy of more hire
It was for ~~someone~~ {others} not {for} him to say so.
I can ~~say what~~ {speak as} his son can hardly speak.
His wife and children were forever at him
To get ~~a~~ {his} pay raised on a family duty.*
Their learning only mad him lower his head
With obstinacy as its lowered now
We shouldn't talk so in his hearing should we?
The children were brought up to the idea
They had been robbed of what he handn't earned.
They thought too meanly of him, I'm afraid—
Considered him poor spirited. But that was
Just what he wasn't. He was proud enough.

[*20v*]   [blank]

[*21r*]   Pride was his sin if any, but it was
             The modest pride or pride of modesty

---

* "There is an arrow in the right-hand margin indicating insertion of the next three lines,
which are written in the up the right-hand side of the page, bottom to top.

That many talk without understanding.
He would not have objected to the praise
~~That took the form of a flattering pay raise~~
Or flattery in the form of better pay*
To ask for it would be as bad as boasting.
To fail of it was failure to be sure,
But failure kin of any decent kindness
Would not have brought out into open meeting,
There's one art of the work, they made him argue,
Another art of getting paid for it, And how he hated to be driven to argue
One was enough for ~~him to establish~~ {one man ~~to display~~}
I've ~~talked with~~ {[illegible]} him about it. Candidates
For office may legitimately spend
One year in four in talking up themselves.
But for a sober worksman at his trade
Self praise was a ~~sick~~ {poor} substitute for praise.
He was an old-fashioned laborer—that's all."

"The kind employees took advantage of
Until advantage must be taken of them."
"Ever since my forerunner named John Ball
They ve had their chance to be magnanimous
And be beforehand with the demands.
They missed it and their hats should be blown off
~~To say the least.~~"
                        "They'd be a moral lesson
Chasing their blown off Derbies in the traffic.
What was his work? How much did he get?

He fired the furnace at the factory,
He blew the whistle morning noon and night
For forty years, and all he got a week
Was twenty dollars to support a family
He was a {village} name with us faithfulness."   Village

"His bosses must have thought he was a god-send"

[21v]*   I wasn't fooled as someone else was fooled
            No so long afterward by all this talk
            About his farm of refuge.

            His son was a policeman

            He'll run off once too often

            His son arrived. He was a policeman

            Don't be too hard on the old man. As I said

            But someday he will run off once too often.

            Don't you lay hands on me you   brute

            All he gave me to go on

            He got away this time for good and all

[22r]*   "O yes, they liked him, everybody liked him.
            His bosses even showed signs they admired him.
            I'll tell you what they did: they gave him gold.
            A double eagle twenty gold for Christmas"

            "Extra you ought to mean, but don't, I guess."

            "A double eagle, no not double pay.
            The same pay but in gold the week of Christmas"

            "They must have felt the deepest satisfaction.
            Was there a presentation ceremony?"

            His son had come in and stood listening
            With nods in confirmation of the story.
            He caught the old man's eye and with a smile
            And a crooking finger beckoned him away.

                                    •   •   •

_____
* Page written in black ink except where noted.

I wasn't fooled by his farm refuge talk
As someone else was evidently fooled
Not so long afterward. ~~In the newspaper~~ {I heard about it}*
~~This afternoon his story was completed~~ {concluded}.
The someone ~~must have given him a lift~~
~~Or so he~~ had come forward and admitted
He'd given the old runaway a lift
And on his one too plausible ~~petition~~ request
Set him down at the bottom of the side road
That led to where he said he lived. He'd be
All right from there on. I could just imagine
How he had got his way with crazy cunning.
He didn't want it seen there was no house.
The house not much? There was no house at all.
Only a cellar hole. There <u>was</u> a barn.
And there they found him fast asleep for good
In ~~not~~ {hardly}* enough waste hay to cover him.
The {early}* snow helped out that sifted through the cracks.
~~Eaked out~~ The winter had been ~~softening~~ {mellowing} with snow
In storm on storm the ground it first had hardened

[22v]   [Blank]

[23r]   Of loyalty it may be ~~said~~ {aptly}* said
Tis something for the lack or loss of which
Your gang will kill you if they catch you at it
Your gang will be the judges out of court
Alone too concerned [~~illegible~~] {about} the evidence
And if you doubt it you don't know your gang.

For gang read king the prince of wales suggested

I like gang better said the queen his mother freely
executively ~~as an executor~~

All down the {banquet}* table there was silence
As of rebelliousness about to break

                    •   •   •

_____
·* Phrase written in blue ink.

Stand up don't sit*

In lines like this the Enthusiast was saying
Everyone should should stand ready
                              With his mind [illegible]
To set off ~~at~~ {headlong} {heavenward} at moments notice
Fr
Loyalty is a somewhat different thing
Word has come

[24r]   Gold for Christmas

"You stand and let me lean on you a minute
Till I can think. Don't ask me who I am."
I'm all mixed up from having retired."
He rued a bloody knuckle in the street light
As a girl gloats on her engagement ring.
I helped him shoulder one of his suspenders
I've been down on some ice and lost my coat.
The empty ~~trolleys~~ busses at this time of night
Are so insane to get home to their car barns
They'd as soon knock you down as pick you up.
I must have thrown my coat away at one.
The place I've got to get to is a farm
That's out here on a side road with two rows
Of sugar maples leading up to it—
The air, lit up by seven golden burning maples.
In case you had a mind to take me there
Or rout out someone else to do it for you.
You're on foot walking so you can't yourself.
It's where I live and claim my residence
To vote at when there's any need to vote.
~~There midnight~~ The house is not much but the barn is standing
There! Midnight I suppose or one o'clock!
~~When all the lights go out at once like that—~~
~~Like candles on a birthday cake on one breath~~
My brains lurch sort of {and} lose consciousness
They ~~say its~~ {tell me} due to hardening of the heart.

––––––––––
* Page to this point written in black ink.

The thing for us to stay propped together
Till I can think—till both of us can think
It cant hurt any of us to stop and think.
Or for that matter to stand propped together.

That light the air like seven golden candles*

[24v]   The ~~city~~ {village} should take care and not blow out
All Its street ~~lights suddenly in on~~ breath once so suddenly
~~Light~~ the ~~lights~~ candles on a birthday cake

The city ~~should be careful how it~~ blows
Its street lights ~~out~~ all out on one sudden breath
Like candles on a birthday cake (like that)
~~It makes my brains lurch and lose consciousness~~
~~They say its due to hardening of the heart~~
~~The thing for us~~

[25r]†   ~~I wasn't fooled the least by all that talk~~
~~About a farm I knew if for the place~~
All wives must be afraid
You've got to think what you will do with me
I've got to think what I will tell my daughter.
She will be worried waiting ~~up for me~~ to see
If I have thrown away my coat again.
She's not my daughter but my daughter in law
Which explains why she has to be so strict.
My wife was not much ~~easier~~ {less so I guess} ~~guess~~ I suppose
And you cant blame ~~the wives~~ {the women} ~~for~~ being on their guard
~~Against the tendency men seem to sho~~
Against the [illegible] {our mens} tendency to want to farm.
Our ~~the~~ tendency to fish and hunt is different
Because though ~~taking them~~ {drawing us} away from home.
It doesn't drag home with ~~them~~ {us} back to nature.
You take it where the pump is in the yard—"
And the water needs to be ~~brought~~ {lugged} in ~~in pack~~
~~Since I could plainly see this wasn't drink~~

---

* Entry written up the right side of the page, bottom to top.
† Page written in blue ink.

~~And~~ since it ~~seemed~~ {appeared} to do his grievance good
To stand there holding on and holding forth
I hadn't forced him to let go of me.
But {I had} ~~been thinking about him~~ {been considering all the time}
~~There I saw~~ but one light in the neighborhood
And {I saw} that had gone upstairs almost to bed.
Might it not be his daughter waiting for him
Might not the house be where he really lived
And not away off somewhere in the ~~country~~ {cold}?

~~I can tell guess from the way you don't reply~~
~~You don't know whether~~
~~You don't believe doubt my word. I'll~~ {Lets} tell you who I am

[24v]   But I'd been taking thought about his future

[25r–25v]   [blank]

[26r]   ~~I guess your silence~~ {your silence either} means you doubt my word
Or else you're planning what to do with me
It might help if I told you who it was
You'd captured or been captivated by
~~Im well~~ {am} known as the Gold for Christmas man
Because I used to get my pay in gold
The week of Christmas, twenty dollars ~~gold~~
~~Just the~~ {Not extra the same} twenty I always got
(And brought up half the number of children on)
Only in gold for Christmas to reward me
For faithful service to the company
~~I fired~~ {?primed} the furnace ~~got up~~ for them forty years—
Blowing the whistle morning noon and night
And My wife was at me almost all the time
To stand up for my self and strike for more
To strike for more. You know how women are.
She brought the children up to the ~~ide~~ idea
They had been robbed of what I didn't earn
Theyd didn't think much of me Im afraid
If you had time I tell you my idea
Of what ~~I was back then~~ {felt it used to be}. It isn't now.
I've changed, and yet I haven't very much.

There's one art of the work I used to argue
Another of getting paid for it.
You ~~seldom find a man who has them both.~~
~~If~~ you had time I'd tell you which I have
~~A I need to tell you which I'd rather~~ have
Or anyway I had
I used to think Id rather have the first
But now I ~~wish~~ guess I wish I had them both.
You seldom find a man who has them both.

[26v]* I woke some people in the nearest house
And showed him to them in the light they lit.
Why Gransir

~~The workmans art I venturd to suppose~~
~~Was learning how much less he has to do~~
~~Than he might fear would be expected of him.~~
~~That is called getting settled down I guess~~

~~The workmans art I ventured to suppose~~
~~Was learning how much less he has to~~
~~Than he had been afraid he had to do {feared would to be expected of him}~~
~~That I supposed was getting settled down~~

~~He heard me. I attracted his attention.~~
~~He looked at me with~~
~~If you had time he said I'll show you how why~~
~~That doctrine though its deep is not is a bad [illegible]~~
~~But you seem restless~~

[27r] Since it appeared to do is grievance good
To stand there holding on and holding forth
I hadn't forced him to let go of me.
But what to do with him was now the question
Never mind what I did expect to say
I found him so he wasn't further lost.
~~All that proved true about the~~ Gold for Christmas

•   •   •

_____

* First three lines in black ink.

Never mind what I did with him that might
I took care of him and found out who he was
Found him that is to say when he was lost.
~~He was just that I found him so to speak.~~
All that ~~was~~ {proved} true about the Gold for Christmas
~~His people said~~
His I had it from his people from a son
Who came to fetch him when I telephoned.

~~From a house I had gently dragged him to.~~
He runs away from second childishness
~~The son explained~~

He talked to you
                You should have heard him talk

He doesn't talk about home. He's ~~thinks he's not~~ {cross with us}
Appreciated, but he is. We all
Remember what he did to bring us up
Yes that's all true about the Gold for Christmas

[27v]   [blank]

[28r]   Dear Mr. [?Levine][68]

    You are too busy milling around down there in New York and the turn over is great on your staff what with marriages and ambitions for you to know much of the time who is responsible for what. But let me tell you one or more of your girls and boys (I am credibly informed by one of them that they dictate {their so called} in chores) got me glaringly wrong in your department of mostly Hollywood [?sexpletives] the other week. And would it be too much of a departure from any policy you may have adopted lately to be faintly disagreeable wherever possible for you to admit for the benefit of my public which may be part of yours that on second reading you can't find a I have ever {single word} {or easy description of} in praise of hard work—The Ax Helve[69] ~~they~~ you mentioned is about not in praise of education with a big E a la Hutchins.[70] As for the other waywardness of your article I can only calculate you got them from quoting me ~~in far California~~ my talk in far Clifornia far out of context. What I said was that poetry is no industry and I had never been industrious in it. Hard work had been my lifelong vacation from it.[71] This is more of a rebuke than a correction and in fairness my friend as I had been led to suppose you were I think you may well decide to print it in the department where ~~the offense was given~~ that was done

[28v]   That not say a no joke should be explained A joke has now and then to be explained as a form of punishment as much to say don't let {ever} us catch you being so stupid again.

[29r]   To have so lived that when your [?success] come from the statue of Liberty to the figurines of Tenagra[72]

The way to a poem is through as many as possible of all other poems that were ever written.*

The Prerequisites[73]

~~A peface to a poem is too late to be of any help so is a footnote while is going on. The read reader is robbed if he has~~ The heart sinks when it is robbed of the chance to see for itself what the poem is all about. Just as it does when it has to have the joke It ~~comes~~ [illegible] upon the court of poetry in a state of poetry prepared in and out of books for the utmost of poetry ~~which is the figure and the figureine all the way from the figure to the figurine~~ [illegible] is all figurativeness from the statue

Any preface to a poem would be like cramming for an examination. It would be too late. So would any foot note which the poem was while the poem was going on. Too late too late ~~and dismal~~ And dismal for the spirit for the spirit to mention.

~~The preparation for a poem~~

There is the poem before you. Your preparation for it must have converged on it ~~from far away and from~~ many {sides} directions. You had to begin somewhere. You read A the better to read B the better to read C the better to read D the better to read A. {again}. So the approach was only fitfully a progression. It was more like a circulation. The instinct was to get among the poems and works of art in general. ~~No poem is~~ A poem is best read in the light

---

* Entry written in black ink.

of all the other poems that were ever written. So without had we most be getting about them.

That's not to say no ~~poem~~ joke or poem should not be explained. One reason for this being explained is as a reprimand of stupidity as much as to say. This is it this time but don't let me ever catch you being as stupid again. [illegible] had to be told*

[*29v*] You come to the play from a long experience of the make and like of metaphors not only in books but all the talks with ~~figures~~ {in figures} which we keep on top of [illegible] You are good taking figures. You get them with agility. You can make them too when you have to

And except in school you can afford to dismiss a poem that you are not up to. You can have it like some day you may happen upon it again better prepared.

{A young reader I remember}

Sixty years ago {for example} for example encountered Emerson's Brahma saying

> They reckon ill who leave me out
> When me they fly I am the wings
> I am the doubter and the doubt
> And I the hymn the Brahmin sings.[74]

I felt myself quite equal to that stanza end liked the idea that my God included the doubt as well as the faith But the next stanza there's one off [illegible] for the being out of the poem where [illegible] where I remained busy with other interests til last year.   I saw I was wrong about the other stanza

even

> The strong gods pine for my abode
> And pine in vain the sacred seven
> But thou meek lover of the good
> Find me and turn thy back on heaven

That was so much too much for me that I refused to be bothered ~~with it~~ {further}. I should have gone to college about it or to India. I don't know why I gave up so easily unless it was in confidence that

---

* Written along the left side of the page, bottom to top.

[30r]   if I didn't go to college and India, college and India would sooner or later come to me maybe in time before I got around to read Emersons in to read the poem again. And they did. By accident [illegible] an [inclusion] that made the poem mine. Meek lover of the good. I know that there his rather too darkly occluded the whole doctrine of detachment from lust and ambition. Turn thy back on heaven. Something better than heaven. Nirvana of course. The only nothing that is something I feel better but not quite satisfied that Emerson was giving us a fair chance to show what our aptitude at poetry. I can do that now. But there are cult symbols I cant do and don't care if I dont

In one of the following poems I speak of the language of ants. Formic. The acid language of satire {of criticism} Did you get it without my help. I fail if you didn't.—whoever you are as Whitman would say.

[30v]   [blank]

[31r]   All a poem asks is that it shall be read in the light of all other poems ever written.[75] A beginning has to be made somewhere. The first poem has to be read more or less as a sacrifice. But let it wait patiently to see how it can be taken care of. The first is read the We read the first the better to read the second, the second the better to read the third the third the better to read the fourth the fourth the better to read the first again if it so happens.

[31v]   Natural Piety

The only praise of nature (praise be to nature) is fresh observation of its traits and particulars, remarking on what is remarkable in experience.[76] Aristotle set us acting in that direction. Plato was nothing but a priori—from above downward. There is nothing up there but a reservoir or stockpile of observations collected and generalized from below so long ago we have forgotten where they came from, ie from below.[77] All is inductive—deductive means well seasoned inductive. Aristotle authorized both science and what is called nature poetry in one stroke. What then is the difference between science and poetry? It should be charm. That one is more charming than the other. But that wont do. Maybe one is lovely and the other facinating. Maybe the difference is depth. One knows better than to go any deeper than we live. Neither will that do. We We Theres nothing deeper than the atom and this as an age living with the atom.[78] I wont quite venture to say dos agreeably

[32r]   We all know each other so well we

                            •   •   •

Whether you will value yourself as one of the majority or as one of the minority. Thomas and John[79]

Victory for the weak side

Do you like to feel overwhelmingly right

Does
                    [geometric figures]*   oblong as long as
                                                          you please.

Some {more} absolutes: wholes of ascending magnitude
Particles even of force

Up and down are relative but out and in are absolutes. Both {extremes} look
infinite unless they curve and meet

All life is cellular — cells cells cells — walls making and breaking inside of us
and outside of us.[80] Another absolute is expense.   Extent

Kings are so far outside of us they have to rule us by statistics—and so we
have to take ourselves partly by statistics—but only in part, not chiefly. We
treat others more than ourselves by {statistics and} averages.[81] But the nearer
we come to our loves and hates the more we are thrown on the same judgements we use on ourselves. Are they true in their approval of us. {Are they
really on our scale—good form.} Thats for us to say with temerity. Are we
true to God. That is to say is our sacrifice of body and soul in war and art acceptable in his sight. {Thats for God to say.} The ache of doubt that is always
there. We give ourselves up as creatures of mixed motives probed too deep
for certainties Meredith[82] One of the doubts forever is whether we could
know more if we were given more time. It rather looks as if the opposites
run up in balanced lines of beauty from the base of the vase to one extreme
difference only to those in for symmetry in approximately seventy years
whether we [illegible]

[32v]   our last chance is to do something pretty to the lip of the crater [illegible]
vase or what you call it

---

* Frost sketches a triangle, a pentagon, a square, and two rectangles.

The extent of your moment.
The natural bounds of science.

The story of my not getting Irwin Edmunds joke[83]— good fences make good burglars[84]
The story of the man who didnt get till years afterward what the girl meant when she said she would do anything in the world for him.
A joke is something created so you will kick yourself for failing to get it without help pronto So is a figure of speech. And if so isnt it is a dreary retrospect to look back over all the hours of being told in school [illegible] {what} the poems meant. If you were being reproached taunted and insulted into seeing for yourself all right. ~~you~~ That was one more joke you failed to get at the time unprompted. There are two kinds of republicans in a party divided against itself as everybody know is this year of 1954.[85] The difference that tells them a part is nicely shown by an experiment I tried on them with the joke going round about egg heads.[86] We already have Workers of the world unite you have nothing to lose but your chains, and the ~~play on~~ further play on ~~that~~ workers of the world unite you have nothing to lose but your brains. Now comes Stevenson with

[33r]   a better one Egg heads of the world unite you have nothing to lose but your yokes. The lively left (Rep) wingers (strange that the left wing should be livelier that the right wing when it is usually the right wing that is livelier that the left) the left wings [illegible] got the idea instantly with a laugh [illegible] of scorn for anyone who thought to make political capital out of talking as if we {wild Americans} were all yoked cattle, but the old guard right wings after a {deep} moment ~~of deep~~ remarked vacuously Why I thought the yolk was the best part of the egg.

They Also Serve Who Only Service Cars[87]

The old question came up at Brandeis[88] whether poets or their patrons rank higher in the sight of God. Story of the magnate who felt as if the bottom dropped out of everything for almost everybody at the age of fifty. Story of the man in Borrow[89] who thought right up to the end that his business of dogfighting and bearbaiting was of undisillusionable interest to everybody— even clergymen of the church of England—and the Pope of Rome.
{Story of the Sickenic and the Zipper Man}
The Puritans came out outright with no pretense of apostolic justification.

The extreme of the Puritans were the Independents who thought everything they pleased individually and even when together they sang each his own separate song in hubbub. The Congregationalists are the Independents descendants. The Episcopalians

Cromwell[90] *

[*33v*] hired a Philadelphia lawyer the original Philadelphia lawyer whose direct heirs settled along the Main line, to construe ~~them~~ {Henry VIII} apostolic succession to look almost as good as that of Rome.

Premedical pre preaching preteaching ~~pre~~ presearching. You have to admit literature is not taught as much now as prescholarship The new is introduced as it should be and as much of the old should be to try ourself on.

A poem is a ~~series~~ {chain} of lucky ~~thoughts~~ {words} that could be called a run of luck.[91]

The Fear not and Be not afraid complex of our last three rulers.[92]

What begins more ethereal than substantial in the lyric[†] ends up more substantial than ethereal in the epic (or novel). The stars deepen from white to red with age.[‡] [93]

[*34r*] Since it appeared to do his grievance good
To stand there holding on and holding forth
I hadn't forced him to let go of me.
But what to do with him was not {became} now the question.
Never mind what I did to except to say
I found him so he was no ~~further~~ longer lost.
All that proved true about the Gold for Christmas
~~His~~ The son confirmed it who came after him.
He runs away from second childishness
~~The son explained~~ {Wise the sons words.} It seems he talked to you
He didn't talk at home. He thinks hes not

---

* Written horizontally and upward, in the left-hand margin of the above paragraph.
† Phrase written in black ink.
‡ Entry written in black ink.

Appreciated. Well he is. We all
Remember ~~all our~~ bringing up he gave us.
He's torn the very patches off his knees
You could tell by the slyness of his looks
He knows his hes being talked about all right.
Yes that's all true about the Gold for Christmas
To show the appreciation of ~~the~~ his bosses.

Extra you ought to mean but don't I guess

A double eagle—no not double pay
The same pay but in gold the work of Christmas

There must have been a presentation ceremony

~~He didn't fool me with his talk~~
I wasn't fooled by all that talk of his
About the farm. I recognized the dream farm dream
~~We indulge thought of all~~
Men will ~~People~~ will indulge in all their tales
Im glad you captured him. He captured me
He rose up from the ditch and capture me

[34ᵛ]   I wasn't fooled as someone else was fooled
A few weeks later after snow set in
Some more gullibly humane than I
Who gave the poor old ~~child~~ the humane the satisfaction
Of ~~seeing~~ having his future story ~~finally~~ {at last} believed in
         heard
~~I read about it and inquired about it~~
~~Which was a great thing~~
~~The happiest thing that ever happened to him~~
~~Who knows perhaps the~~
~~The happiest thing on earth perhaps~~

[35ʳ]   He's stronger minded than he ever was.
You can tell by the shyness of his looks
He knows hes being talked about all right

Stranger ways we have of going off the scene
                              Getting out of here

~~I wasn't fooled as someone else was fooled~~
~~As someone else was fooled soon afterward~~
I wasn't foold by his farm refuge talk
As someone else was fooled soon afterward
~~The someone had come forward and~~ {confessed} ~~admitted~~
According to the story in the paper,
Someone more kindly gullible it seemed
Had given the old runaway a lift
(Not that same {hard} night of bare ground on more [illegible])
A few quick [illegible] aged snow set in
And on his none too pleasureable appeal
Set him down at the bottom of the ~~side road~~ lane
That lead to where he said he lived. He'd be
All right from there ~~on~~ no need of coming with him.

[35v]   The place I'm trying to get to all my life
          Is a farm out here on a side road somewhere
          ~~With two rows of rock samples leading to it~~
          ~~With sugar maples leading up to it—~~
          In case you had a mind to take neither

[36r]   "You stand and let me lean on you a moment
          Till I can think. Don't ask me who I am.
          Im all mixed up form having been retired."

          He rued a bloody knuckle I the street light
          As a girl gloats on her engagement ring.
          I helped him shoulder one of his suspenders.

          I've been down on some ice and lost my coat.
          The empty ~~busses~~ trolleys at this time of night
          Are so insane to get home to their car-barns
          They'd as soon knock you down as pick you up.
          I must have thrown my coat away at one.

The ~~place I've got to get to is my farm~~ farm in life like to get away to
And nothing but a farm will satisfy me.
In case you had the mind to take me there
On ~~sout out someone~~ else to do it for you
You're one fool walking so you can't yourself
~~It's where I wanted~~ {I want to claim} claim my residence.
[illegible phrase]
The house is not much but the barn is standing.
There! Midnight I suppose or one o clock.
The city should be careful it does
Blowing its lights out all at once ~~so suddenly~~ on {on people}
Like eighty candles on a birthday cake.
It makes my brains lurch and lose {my} consciousness.
~~They say~~ This is my due to hardening of the heart ~~they tell me~~
The thing for us is to stay propped together
Till we can think—till both of {us} can think.
~~You what your going~~
You've got to think what you will do with me
Ive got to think what I will tell my daughter
Who will be worried waiting up ~~for me~~ to see
~~To see~~ I have thrown away my coat again.
She's not my daughter but my daughter in law
Which explains why she has to be so strict

[36v]   He doesn't mind my staying home from church
Or so he ~~claims~~ as a Christian has to claim.
But we are not the friends we used to be
He claims so but you know how {illegible} Christian
~~Not~~ [illegible] as about as ~~Christian~~ {natural} as the rest of us.
I used to catch him when he was a pitcher
Hes better in the box than in pulpit
Except that hes too wild for his strength
Or hed have made the majors we always said

[37r]   ~~I'll~~ bet you ~~to avoid an argument~~ [illegible phrase] an argument That lights
your daughter waiting up for you And that is your house and that is where
your house Not some way off some where in the ~~cold~~ dark and cold. It would
be a mistake of both our likes if the idea was the get rid of me [illegible

phrase] ~~That's where the preacher lives~~. He might cannot go. ~~He's an exhorter~~ That's where the preacher lives. He might convert you.

On the door step, of that [illegible] that's where the preacher lives. He might exhort*

[37v]   ~~I charmed~~

Im charmed with your wife Job, God said.
Yes I could see you were
You once were charmed with Joseph's wife
See what it did to her

[Illegible] What was the greatest
of all who done it stories
the immaculate conception

[38r]   [blank]

[39r]   The driver of hard bargains who is he
But the shrewd judge as quick to see
As take advantage of with out contrition
The weakness of the other mans position.
The almost perfect field (of Old Thayer Belt)
Water gushed up so flushly from the ground
That water piled on water in a mound

One of the first provisions of a progressive school is that in it academic questions should be barred.[94] An [illegible] {academic} question is one that the asker of already knows the answer. The best student shouldnt hesitate to rebuke it by saying ask me something you dont know. The second provision is the teacher should only tell the students what ~~he~~ they haven't heard before. The only way of making sure they havent heard it before is to make sure he himself hasn't thought of it before.

·   ·   ·

---

* Written along the left side of the page bottom to top.

Emerson is right about consistency.[95] Dont hope to say or do anything {with which} you will never say or do anything else inconsistent. Thats the simple reason pacifists[96] who turn the other cheek to be smitten on can talk in the same book about coming to bring out peace with a sword.

The charitable assumption is that our schools assume the [illegible] by learning thoughts will learn to think.

Learning thoughts is not quite the same as learning to think. Thoughts are only or chiefly worth learning as examples of or models for our emulation.

[39v]   [blank]

[40r]*   Thoughts on Having Held Your Own[†]1)

When the fact of Evolution[97] came up to shake the church's certainties about the creation and the date of it 4004 BC.[98] I bade myself be not discouraged. The old idea we were asked to give up was that God made man out of mud at one stroke I saw that the new idea would have to be that God made man out of prepared mud[99] that he had taken his time about working up gradation. I was not much put off out or off my own thinking. There was as much of a God in it as ever.
    When the waste of codfish eggs[100] to produce one codfish not to seem too disillusioning for young Bostonians to bear and stay even Unitarian I would have come to their rescue if they would have listened to me with the suggestion that the death of all those eggs was necessary to make the ocean a froth for fit for the one codfish to live in. But I would go further to day in standing my ground. There is no waste and all that looks[101]

[40v]‡   3)
to accept our position; but I see no way out of it. There is apparently not a soul but us alive in the whole business of rolling balls and eddying fires, and long distance rays of light. It makes any coziness in our houses here all the

---

* Page written in black ink.
† Entry written in black ink.
‡ Page written in black ink.

more heart warming. Some are not like me in this respect. While I hug myself in a corner they are out rolling up their sleeves in readiness to see if we cant do something about occupying a star or two besides this one.

So I have found that for my own survival I had to have phrases of salvation if I was to keep anything worth keeping

Truth what is truth? said Pilate and we know not and ~~no~~ no search can make us know, said someone else[102] But I said can't we know? We can know well enough to go on with being tried every day ~~we~~ in our courage to tell it. What is truth? Truth is that that takes fresh courage to tell it. It takes all our best skill too.

[41r] Before we leave this place for places*
Let us be [sure] we have exhausted this
How do we know we have expressed the juice
To the last drop

We thought [?must] [illegible] we were extract
[~~illegible~~]
Rays of our own we did not know we shed

— |2

---

like waste is some form of sacrifice like tithes to the Lord, absolute Sabbath. Keeping (throwing the day away entirely) and flowing out {a} libation on the ground or fire. It is once wasted on the ground It is twice wasted ~~poured~~ down the gullet of the worshipper. Then it not only washes the liquor but it also wastes the man

Was I thrown off myself when I had to change from the Ptolomaic geocentric ~~unive~~ to the Copernican no centric universe.[103] It seemed to me a not very different universe I felt just as much at home in only if possible a much more magnificent great space for us to be the only living thing in I felt our importance almost exaggerated It has taken me some years of my life†

---

* Poem written in black ink.
† This entry, from "like waste" on, written in black ink.

[41v]*   4)

You {I} begin with your {my} native preference saying I may not know [illegi-ble] what [illeglble] is supposed to be or what a really educated person ought to believe, but I know what I like and I mean to stick to it or at least not give up more than a part of it and that {or any part of it} without a struggle I come throu expect to come through not unaffected by influences and attacks {friends and enemies} but I trust not altered beyond recognition I hope to keep my basic features of eyes nose and ears.

I have had to tell myself what at bottom I mean by loyalty in a time like this. No different than {from what} I would mean at any time. It means changing, adherence leaving with regret. "As if regret were in it and were sa-cred."104 The different problem of getting from an attachment to an attrac-tion. The possibility that when half gods go not whole gods but quarter gods arrive.105 All those who change old loves for new Pray gods they change for worse. The realest statement of loyalty is: that for the lack of which your gang will slay you if they catch you in it. And without trial by jury.106

[42r]†   To the Freudians I say, not sex but grex is the ruling interest in passionate man. Grex is minding each others businesss so that we have to fend each other off with the expression Mind your own business once in so often.107 I decided one might when confronted with an inquisition that I didnt have to be [illegible] of the alternatives offered me extrovert or introvert "swan or just plain" vert from Vermont.

You have to have speak up for yourself if you are going to [illegible] hold your own—

Hold your own I mean rather with than against your playmates.

[42v]   [blank]

[43r]‡   All our all nature does is to keep throwing out hints for us to take in science or art. Nothing in science or art counts unless [illegible] as the result of hint taken.108 No matter how slow we are to get it through our heads what is be-ing suggested, time seems endless for us and natures patience too. Think how

---

* Page written in black ink. 41v–43v written in black ink.
† Page written in black ink.
‡ Page written in black ink.

en tirelessly the thunder kept roaring and the lightning fiercely flashing before Ben Franklin[109] took the hint that there was something there for [~~illegi-
ble~~] {our} consideration And think how many apples must have fallen to the
ground before Newton took the hint to any purpose. They say one had to fall
right on his head before it occurred to him that apples would fall to be rejected as mere wind falls (though hot a breeze was blowing) unless they were
picked first and lifted down. Think of all the boys who have found and {per-
haps} earned their way through {scientific courses in} college by lifting them
down into boxes and baskets for the market.

The unpardonable sin for the reader of nature and particularly of poetry
is to take a hint where none is intended. It is almost as venal for the poet
never at all to hint more than he says in verse. The game between him and
[~~illegible~~] the reader is no more than that to see if he can catch the reader out
missing

[*43v*][†]   "[illegible] [?hope] from India*
there are and taking hints there arent. I say in ~~good nature~~ charming good nature {like the [illegible]} and not the least grim like the school room. No one
is being improved ~~We are merely hav~~ The sprite is merely testing our intelligence and trying us for our life. The sprite peeps like lightning flashes
through the clouds or through the meshes.
There is a humor involved too hard for mere jokers of jokes.

Take me for example how much alcohol ~~have I seen drunk~~ did I have to see
drunk to get ~~it suggested to~~ get a suggestion that might help my enemies or
doubters with an idea about me that I had never had before and they would
probably never {have} had in their condition of daily cocktails if they had
waited till there were nothing left in politics but conventional radicals. Let me
help them to it. It is theirs to my question which cant be too many years off.
(I am well past their age) If my ~~innards~~ {stomach} hated wine and liquor as
much as my [?mouth] ~~it would be too~~ [illegible] I would risk drinking in polite society I am {more} fastidious than I ought to be about physical function.
Some dont mind doing anything in public that they [illegible] as in private
privacy or [?privity] and their ultimate [illegible]. But I did happen to confess
the other day to a not inordinate pleasure

---

* Entry written up left side of page, top to bottom.
† Page written in black ink.

[44r]*	in the draft of heavy port I was lapping in steadily in my hand to be sociabil-
ity [illegible] ~~I gave my reason, which was my mistake~~	And for socia-
bility that is merely for something to say I gave my reasons {And gave myself
away} Moral, means purely—more pure And a good Roman thought ~~nothi~~
of nothing as pure but pure evil. {~~When he said pure~~ [illegible] He only
needed to say pure to be understood by} The poet says the soldier home
form the front dips his fingers in the "pure" and draws a picture ~~with it w~~ of
the camp with it on the table[110] You would resent my Latin for it but it exists.

Then I went on inculpate myself by admitting I wanted no drink so pure I
couldn't taste in it what it was made from ~~corn rye potatoes~~ What was rejecting {all} but ~~grapes~~ wine of grapes. [Illegible] These whiskies ~~an~~ {an} rums
~~from~~ that [illegible] {kept} no reminiscence of their original corn rye or bar-
ley were to abstract form Sorvas the rum I wouldnt know came from sugar. I
could endure the port because it tasted of grapes.

The rout of Comus[111] were all over me at once It was as in a dream and
may have been a dream. One of them was a lady whom the others playfully
called [illegible] brogans because ~~because~~ her shoes were so dainty {they
were} almost no shoes at all the very opposite of brogans. She didnt trample
with them she cut. {The sharp stilletoes} ~~She~~ bled my ~~face~~ old scarred face.
She wasnt the only one. {Another} ~~One~~ of the party was [illegible] an old
tried friend whose faithfulness to me had been ~~too~~ so greatly in contrast with
his faithfulness to women.

[44v]†	I wont say drink wasnt a help with it. But thought riotous it was hardly orgi-
astic and among acquaintances and competitors all in good wholesome fun.
Their triumph was natural. I had given myself away. But by this time some of
them must know how I am. ~~My~~ {From} genial contempt for their wit ~~has
never~~ I have often laughed with them at my own expense. Do I suppose they
would have thought of it if I hadnt underlined the symbolism of my liking
port because it was so strong of grapes. They <u>were</u> all were as symbolical as
they could be ~~and as abstract~~ they were specially good at giving or taking
hints but as professed symbolists they did the best they could. And most of
them were abstractionists. They might have been ashamed to take it from
me, but they forgot themselves in the clarification I furnished them with. So I

---

* Page written in black ink.
† Page written in black ink.

virtually told them not to say. "He might as well drink Welchs grape juice. [Il-
legible] They clamored it. They had been so long without an idea they [illegi-
ble] didnt know ~~they~~ this wasnt theirs but mine They were all Freudians. I
wondered if what they would make of all this as a dream I like dreams dont
you. When they say a girls a dream it should and no doubt does put ideas ~~of~~
~~he~~ into her head of running for Miss Universe. A kind of {tasteful} men will
measure her for her hips bust [illegible]

[45r]   A Mild Surmise

The {particular} terror or event that put the idea into your head may not
have been a case of the idea (you were wrong there—you missed your quest
but there was such a thing in general.

[45v]   [blank]

[46r]   What thoughts have you what stories have you that dont come under the
critics favorite heads of frustration escape or complex. I should think that was
the question.

[46v]   I knew a child that had to have a leash
~~Just like a dog. The leach ran on a Th~~
The leash was on a trolley over head
He was so unafraid of ~~getting lost~~

He was so unafraid of leaving the house
And getting lost in the whole universe
It may as well have been to him at his age
The leas ran on a trolley overhead
To give his nature a better play
Around the yard. It wasn't good for him
It was a bad thing for him.

To check his fearlessness of leaving home
For the wide world some nearer may go
Some and amid leaving for the universe
Some in the baby cradle of the ages
Start reaching for the moon with hands and feet

And thcy shall have moon for what its worth
And

[4ﾉ1]   Gold for Christmas 3

Didn't I tell you it would be like this?

She's calling up your son to take you home

I'll bet she is. She knows whats good for you

And everybody else.

                    <u>Shes</u> a good woman.

Anyway here she comes I say no more
Take care of yourself. I'll take care of mine
Don't let her draw you out or obligate you
The door popped open ~~like~~ {as on} a cucoo clock
For her to say take in [?make] coffee for him
He runs from second childishness
Then shut again as on a cucoo clock
The the door shut as on a cucoo clock.
[illegible] I'm [~~illegible~~] {always} better after {I've} had my spell
   But mums my word. Didn't you let I'm better
   I'd ahave come out all re[illegible]
   She [illegible] social workers working me
   I'm just a social case to he
   She's got to let her have her satisfaction

[47v]   If we dispute each other hard and long enough it might this [~~illegible~~] good
might come of it that we might get some least idea how our positions were
arrived at. We might.

[48r]   The commonest fault to find with education in this country is ~~that its~~ that
it is slower than in the old ~~world~~ {countries}. ~~Never~~ France England and Germany for instance. Never quarrel with the premises. Contradiction is too
much like a head on collision for polite society. Let who will go to Europe "to

get rich quick." But let those ~~dont~~ {who [illegible] averse to} travel console
themselves with the possibility that there is ~~enough to be said for not being in
hurry~~ no {great} object in being in a hurry. ~~about anything unless it be to
keep up with some procession.~~* For if there is a time for everything and
plenty of the years between our ~~twelfth~~ {tenth} (say) and our twentieth are
appointed for our hanging around till we catch on. We may read or right or
talk to look as if we were busy but the main thing is that we be with the right
people who have already themselves caught on. It is a slow process—very
slow toward a state that will be cheap and shoddy if hurried into. It is more
like ripening to the flower than anything else, whether on the tree or picked
hard and stored away to become perfect. There is no harm in learning some
what from books in those years but care taken that it should seem carelessly
worn. I have seen something of the harsh product of the French driving discipline It is [illegible] idea of a bourgeois slave than efficiency.†

[48v]   The genius of the region is not grass
But trees of all kind irrepressible
The grass is but a holding company
To save the soil from being washed away
~~While trees~~ While we put trees to use for fire and
Grass the channel ~~it will~~ all be wood again
You mean no pluralism can end us
If that is all. I can go with you there.
I mean that's one anxiety the less
For writers will tell us in magazines

Sick is the way of all anxieties
You can dismiss them one by one like that
Till there is none [illegible] by the anxiety
Not to tell this. That what I'm coming to
The lie of lies is saying you believe
More than in church or out of
Is that the hardest way to hold the truth

---

* Entry to this point written in black ink.
† Sentence inserted in left hand margin, written vertically from top to bottom.

⌊ 49r ⌋*   The Club House

~~Our grief these in~~ {meek}† happened to us
~~The grief we feel of failure to attain~~‡ {but more occurs} to us.

Your asked to make a motion of the mind
That possibly you never made before
It will delight us both if you can make it
We will be friends away not in advance
~~Of the crowding~~
Of the confusion due to being crowded.
~~Of an~~ the trial of a motion
Trial on you by me on you by you
We've kept together found each other hand
For reassurance in the dark around us
Communication is not it but correspondence
It is as if I asked you Are you there
I have not lost you have I on the path.
The answer is I get it. I am with you
Yes I can see now that is as much as {that} might be.
Looking afar off into nonthingness.
How I enjoy your look of easy effort
As you perform on the [illegible] far
Between the finite and the infinite.
More than mean we can't down man bar
But often were surprised with what we can
And that's what it is we are to one another
Communications not [illegible] correspondence
You thin I must be putting of a mass
With all this hesitating with misgiving
We never [illegible] all this to do before
Looking back I can see ~~nothing~~ no awkwardness
In the approach to novelty before
If this something hard it most be false
Not a fair list for either one of us.

---

* Entries from 49r to the end of the notebook written in black ink unless otherwise noted.
† Entry to this point written in black ink.
‡ Entry to this point written in black ink.

[49v]*   I believe I believe you
        Every word you say
        This world solidity I heard
        Is particles on particles on their way

        Or if not particles themselves
        Their residue
        Some scurf or other waste they shed
        That's dying if not dead
        How true how true

        You've come to know
        The welling flood
        That's going on this flow
        That passing through
        Includes my flesh and blood
        Well be it so

        As sure as I am I
        I've long been on the verge
        Of thinking ~~some such thing there is~~ {some such thing beside me†}
        Something I cant deny
        Is ~~going on~~ on the verge
        Or going by
        ~~Outside me~~ I can't deny
        Some demiurge some [~~illegible~~] {source} king
        Is blowing ring on ring
        Of cosmic smoke that only incidentally
        [~~illegible line~~]
        Results [illegible] in folk.

[50r]   ~~This one‡~~
                      ✓   ✓   ✓
        ~~This~~ This man or mill hand in a country town
        And his ideal ~~creas~~ {based} on the idea
        That there is one art of the work itself

---

* 49v and 50r written in black ink except where noted.
† Phrase written below the line.
‡ There are three large check marks made to the right of this entry.

Another art of getting paid for it.
~~He would have soon~~
He didn't have—reasoned to have the second.
~~He would as soon have asked a raise in pay~~
~~To~~ Ask ~~in~~ {in a} for record of pay was as bad as boasting
He would as soon have asked or struck for [illegible]
As asked for praise. I had heard all about him.
He served the company for forty years
Before it was remarked that twenty ~~dollars~~ {a week}*
Was all he had to raise a family on
His work had been to fire the [illegible] {factory†} furnace
Where hats were manufactured for the head
Threre were two colleges [illegible] in the town besides
Where ~~something also——doing~~ {brains were manufactured}‡ for the head
For all of <u>him</u> they might have been in Heaven
I met him in the middle of my life§

[*50v*]   [blank]
[*51r*]

I like to get so [illegible] {slept out} tired of sleep
[illegible line]
As restless almost over me so wild
~~Everything for a change~~
I have to get up something for a change.
What do you mean by something for a change?
Something to change the structure of the world?
Some way of putting something to myself
Or someone else like being back at ~~growth~~ work
~~Like spring—spring after winter~~
Or rather {back} at growth again like spring
Spring after winter—after being dormant
I like to come unblinded suddenly
On what have been blind to all the years
And don't for myself so ~~that the~~ I wonder
It took me all this time to notice things what

---

* Phrase written in blue ink.
† Word written below the line.
‡ Phrase written in blue ink.
§ Line written in blue ink.

I had been ~~seeing~~ looking at from childhood.
It is without regret without complaint
It shouldn't have been sooner. I might rejoice
It had been kept from me. Since kept from me
Me was kept from me to dawn on me in the dawn

Sounds revolutionary or original.

Not even ~~original or~~ very original I guess
No better than making a remark that tells
Its all I hang around for all I hope for
For it to happen again. It has to happen
Since it has happened to you nothing else
Much matters while you wait for its return
Arnold tells how the school boy left Oxford
And forsook scholarship and learning thought

[51v]   To go in quest of having thoughts.[112] Heavensent
He calls them. There's no mystery about them
They're ~~simply~~ the relief from having overslept
The From being almost tired to death with rest once
The great relief from rest is that once it is tasted
There ~~are~~ {is} that other mind that others find.
In drudgery ~~as dangerous in their way~~ {almost as dangerous}
Though they {it may} seem less dangerous to friends
~~Who are less anxious for you when you drudge~~
Or parents relatives who feel less ~~anxiety~~ {anxious} for you
~~Where you are safely~~
Whey you are safe where they can see you drudging

It sounds like being struck with an idea
Have you been struck with any lately.

~~One was that driving in~~
Flat driving in the middle of the road
Would be a straddle of {the white line there} ~~the middle white~~
The figure works out this way if you drive
~~And~~ {As} of the class that drives your safety lies
Whether you drive a bad class or Ford

In keeping to the right and aristocratic
But if you walk and live pedestrian
You naturally for safety keep the left
And Belong that to to the left that in politics.
Doesn't that seem to settle something
And I would claim it feels settling

[52r]   It please me to have a chance to call
Under the pillared firmament of science rotten
Is rottenness
Makes the scientists produce particles
They only know by name as yet Neutrino.
I quote the scientists. I like to catch them
Talking about an absolute like us
The speed of light for instance (which is doubtful
But this one far more absolutely sure

[52v]   There were two brothers come home from their trial
They took off their coats with a terrible smile
And one of them calmly said to the other
The court says we didn't kill father and mother

The court's word in such things is final for men
Our neighbor can never accuse us again
The works then they can say to us under the laws
Is someone was guilty: if we weren't who was?

With the judgement of God we may still have to cope
But not for a good many years let us hope

[53r]   Power comes to us we know not what to make of
Let alone use. What power it is we wonder question
That nations come to us about their wars
To make their quarrels ours, and in their ordeal
Save men to be our fellows in [illegible] the danger
Sometimes we [illegible] {are sure} we know know not who we are—
Well not to define. Because the mystery
Of whence we came has yet to be resolved
Out of the very earth we treat per perhaps

The fairest bolt of map has rolled to east and cut
Between the earth's two oceans in a ~~zone~~ belt
~~So perfect~~ almost too perfect to have been our choice.
We ~~will~~ {dare} not presume to ask ~~from~~ {to} shall traits in ourselves
Of mingled race or pure we owe ~~our~~ {the} strength*
~~Of unpremeditated~~
Of our position unpremeditated
Even by the most forseeing of us all
(I mean besides the natural resources.}
Darkening ~~a~~ than our fathers felt into the future

[53v]   [blank]

[54r]   Believe me as your anthropologist
~~You Truth~~ is you haven't any sire
~~And that is why long to be a frog~~
~~And as an amateur ventriloquist~~
~~Believe me as~~ {Take it from me} your anthropologist
Your trouble is as an anthropoloywog
~~Is that~~ you ~~wish long to be a native frog~~
Is that you really want to be a frog
And as an amateur ~~ventriloquist~~ ventriloquist
Set solitary in the {[illegible]} animal mist
~~And from~~ {Upon} a slowly sinking log
Proclaiming love to the [illegible] {[illegible]} bog
D
The trouble with you is a lack of sex

[54v]   I'll be your anthropologist
You be my anthropolywog
~~I want to study~~
I've study why {so} ~~should~~ insist
In being nothing but a frog

It must be to attain a sex
To set there on a waterlog

_____
* There is an arrow drawn from this entry to the end of the entry in parentheses four lines later.

And with you Breck a Reokcoex
Ventriloquize the tranquil bog

[illegible]
Believe me as an anthropolog
Your trouble as an anthropolywog
Is that really want to be a frog
An as an [illegible] ventriloquist
And bet all night [illegible] {long} in a [illegible]

[55r] One of Nature's lessons
Is that Nature [illegible] Lessons   Is She always lessens
It is of the essence
Nature that her face powers {she shall diminish} diminish
Toward some conclusion {final} finish
Likely Certain to [illegible] astound
Any one around
Hit by a comet
Or a man made bombette

[55v] [blank]

[56r] When the French King requested me of late
To a recommend a suitable court fool
It took me some to collect my wits
And recollect France hadn't any King
And somebody was talking on my ship
Or I was preternaturally [?awoke]
And this was many hundred years ago
And asking out of sheer considerateness
Was gently hinting I propose myself how about myself
And fools being made official fool
I had been saying many foolish things
And doing many [illegible phrase]
From willingness to [illegible] be laughed at when [?incorrect]
Had I been doing anything so very funny
Comedy isnt often [illegible]
I had been talking standing on my head

[56v]   It must be a great comfort when youre liked
           To tell yourself and neighbors you were tricked

[57r]   Two fellows in unselfishness competed
           One of them said hed rather be the cheated
           In trade or argument than be the cheater
                    Philosophy or rhyme and [mutter]
           When all is said and done there be the cheater
           The other replied in rhyme and meter
           Youd rather be the beaten than the beater
           Don't get me wrong for I believe in wrong
           By letting your opponent do the sinning

           It seems there was a hero in our time
           Who was convicted of a heinous crime
           He did to save his girl from doing wrong

[57v]   [blank]

[58r]   Take Alcie that sophisticated boy[113]
           Who had to jump the ship at Thasir
           Because the house police were after him
           The story doesn't say he had to swim
           It only says he safely got away
           To

[58v]   We saw leaves go to glory[114]
           Then almost migratory
           So half way down the lane
           And then to end the story
           Get beaten down and pasted
           In one wild day of rain
           We heard Tis Over! roaring
           A year of leaves was wasted
           Oh we make a point of storing
           Of saving and of keeping
           But only by ignoring
           The was of nations daylight sleeping
           The waste

[59r] Since it appeared to do his grievance good
To stand there holding on and holding forth
I hadn't forced him to let go of me.

[59v] And all the water has to be lugged in—
You're watching something. You're not listening.
If you let go of me Ill run off further
I see but one light in the neighborhood
And that has gone upstairs almost to bed
You want to be know what I begin to think
[illegible line]
That lights your daughter waiting up for you
[illegible phrase]
That is your home and the right there where you live
Not way off somewhere in the dark and cold

Since it seemed to his presence
To stand there holding on and holding forth
I hadn't forced him to let you [?pace]
But there are limits limits to my [illegible] spirit {social sense}
I've got to help you find out where you are

I know who you are from off somewhere
Youre in the printing business in the city
I've heard how much you get for book expense
I want to [illegible] {make} a statement you can use
I'm not a fugitive from any sin
Except for
Except for a stale old family joke
Of books called the Gold for Christmas man
I always hate to hear a joke explained
You want to hear me yodel who I am

Don't yodel youre not crazy.

Your not either
I know what ails you've feet got cold feet
[illegible] Of course you don't appreciate your age
Stomping on ground like this frozen hard

For them to dig your grave as if your dead
Say I may have to yodel for relief

[60r]   And all the water has to be lugged in—
Your watching something. Youre not listening.
I ~~saw~~ see but one light in the neighborhood
And that had gone upstairs almost to bed
Since it had seemed to do her grievance good
To stand there holding on and holding forth
I hadn't forced him to let go of me
~~But I'd been then busy. To you~~
~~That But~~ the light put a notion in my head
You want to know what I begin to think
That is your daughter waking up for you
That is your home and right there's where you live
Not way off somewhere in the dark and cold

If in your hurry to get rid of me
You left me on the doorstep of that house
It might be the mistake of both our lives
{That's where} ~~We don't know who what he might be getting in for~~
Im not familiar with this side of town
[~~Three illegible lines~~]
Because he wouldn't want his friends to think
That his response was just [illegible] to his sermon
[~~illegible line~~]
He's better in the pulpit than the box
But every [illegible] [illegible] for his strength
Or hed have made the league. He's giant size

[60v]   You'll wake the dead up in the graveyard
The dead.
He's better in the box than in the pulpit.
But even there he's too wild for his strength

If in your hurry to get rid of me
You left me on the doorsteps of that house
It might be the mistake of both our lives
That's where the parson lives or used to live

Im not familiar with that part of town
He's better in the box than in the pulpit
But {[illegible]} [illegible] he's still too wild for his strength
He Or he'd have made the league. He's giant size
He should have been a giant with the Giants
They say he had a try out with the Giants
He has a hand as big as Honus Wagner[115]
Too many {batters} got their bases on balls
Or got know down and carried off the field
He has a [illegible] {fist} for force and mouth for fraud
Something between a soldier and a lawyer
Or else between the army and the ~~legislative~~ senate
    Say I may have to yodel for relief

You cast me off and [illegible]

[illegible]*

[61r]   He should have been a giant on the Giants
They say he had a tryout on the Giants
He's got an arm for force and mouth ~~for~~ fraud
You cant tell when he's liable to convert yours

Still it appeared to do his greatness good
To stand there holding on and holding forth
I hadn't for [illegible] to let got of me
But there were limits to my public spirit
~~I've got to find and for who you are~~
If you let got of me Ill run off further
~~I said we can stand talking here all night~~
I've got to find out for you who you are
If you desert me I'll run off further.
I now what ails you You have got cold feet
~~You don't seem to~~ {It seems you don't} appreciate your age
Stomping ~~your feet~~ {like this} on ground frozen hard
For them to dig your rave in if your dead.

---

* Written up left side of page, bottom to top.

I know who you are. Your from off somewhere
You want to have me yodel who I am.
I want to make a statement. Im not balmy
~~Im not a fugitive from anything~~
~~Except a worn out fraternity joke about me~~

You'll wake the dead I that little graveyard

The dead in that there graveyard's doubly dead
No ones been buried there since Moses was
By Neber mountain in the land of Moses.

Whats going on here
                    Nothings going on hrere
Didn't It tell you I would be here this
We're under arrest to all intents. [illegible] For loitering
There in that blaze of their piazza light
His wife and conscience.

We're under arrest for all intents for loitering*
That [illegible] large as {life} That she has
There in the blaze of light the piazza
His conscience and the conscience of
Into his hand we may [illegible]
We're caught as [illegible] picture

[61v]   [blank]

[62r]   I want to make a statement I'm not balmy
          There needs to be a song that went like this
          When I was young I never joined the army
          But there are times I only wished I had
          For then the stuff that makes them feel as balmy
          Is not the [illegible] of [illegible]
          I'm not a fugitive form anything

---

* This line and the five that follow it written diagonally in the bottom right corner of the
page.

Except a stale old family joke
[illegible] {Of calling me} the Gold for Christmas Man
You want to be [illegible] who I am?

Don't yodel. Your not craz

Youre not craz either
Your just weary
You are just sick and tired of doing good

I like to listen to the way you like {your} running on.

That's nothing. I am an [illegible] that's all
I always have to hear a joke explained.

The [illegible] light had been put out, the stars
Had been put out by empty cloud
[illegible] Out of the darkness doubledyed a voice spoke

I may have learned that in the British army
Or maybe I was in the Foreign legion
My fathers are from the Orkneys the Norwegian

[62v]   He rose up from the ditch beside the road
And made a sort of flying leap on me
I see you know him so

We know when you are if you don't know us
You're in the printing business in the city
As I heard someone say in his Post office
He said how much you got for both apiece
And if we don't take care you'll
[Two illegible lines]
I'm with you

You've had a great successive success
Commiserating the depravity of life
In villages like ours. I'm wholly with you
In run out villages like our own

Im with you. Im a sociologist
[illegible line]
From [illegible phrase]
You [illegible phrase]
Enochs[116] named for the Governor of Maine
Lincoln [illegible phrase]
Lincoln capital of Nebraska
The governor was
Lincoln Nebraska capital was named for

There isn't much escape distract
[illegible line]

[63r]   Leah

Well Enoch Lincoln here we are again
See who you've captivated with your kindness mercy
He runs away from second childishness
He ought to have a harness round the waist.

Didn't I tell you it would be like this?

He captured me I didn't capture him.
He {it} didn't fool me with his farm or refuge talk.

As he fooled someone else {just} the other day
And got himself dropped out there in a snowstorm—
The [illegible] place
The Brewster place: He's got it on the brain.
A posse of us [illegible] {had} to bring him back
But we knew just where to find him.

                    He told me
The house was not much but the barn was standing

The barn is standing but there is no house
We all say Issac Brewster burned it down
To make her husband build another better
But he refused He moved across the road

Set up house [illegible phrase] stables the harness
[illegible line]
Or sale of farmers [illegible phrase] I the barn
[Two illegible lines]
And passed her off on down road to live herself
   In the old district school house [illegible] loved
   She didn't stand it, She lit out for somewhere

But he refused. He moved across the road
And {with} the things left over from the farm
Set up housekeeping in the harness room
[illegible line]
He passed her off down road to live herself
In the old district school house we abandoned
Shed didn't stay long. She lit out for somewhere

[63v]   Old Brewster died. His stuff was sold at auction
But there were things that weren't accounted for
Keepsakes of hers he got way from her
It was supposed and he'd been in the barn
That was the gossip. Just this kind of [illegible] story
[illegible line]
Enoch might very well be one of those.
I wouldn't put it past him. Anyway
Jane Brewster was his sweetheart long ago
It may have been some [?talisman] between
That spoiled her marriage with another
Alma how you run on. You've absolutely
Nothing [illegible]. He ins't like that.
What is he like. Since you [illegible] {claim} to know him.
I only offered this suggestion
To the reporter that his some [illegible]
We know who you are if you don't know
And had a lot of help to get acquainted
Your in the printing business in the city
As I heard someone say in the post office
He much for books apiece
And if we don't take care you'll write us up
With And if what I supply you with [illegible]

It will be [illegible] when you're through with
You've had a great success of successes
Commentating the depravity of life
I run our little onestreet village
I'm with you in your overdogs
There isn't much escapes a district [illegible
[Three illegible lines]
Lets have it for our purposes Enoch Lincoln

[64r]   Not who he is but who he thinks he is.
Sometimes he seems to think he is Enoch Lincoln
He talks that way the early governor
Who fought a boundary battle with the English
A figure of the first heroic age
The poet of a [illegible] book the Village
I should be able to lay hands on for you
I had two copies of it. Here it is.
A copy of it used to be on exhibition
When I was out there in Nebraska
Lincoln the capital named for him
That our history you never heard
The

[64v]   If such an understanding they arrived
The could discuss such words as {being} [illegible]
In etimology and in the throng
How vivid they still seemd and show
[illegible line]
Shed didn't likely later it was son wrong
Why any likely men that came along
She did [illegible phrase]
[illegible phrase]*

[illegible line]
All is {was} still courting for {her} girls for the consent
She only really give him where she went

---

* Preceding on the page written in black ink, following in pencil.

[65–73]   [blank]

[74v]*   Didn't I tell you it would be like this.
You want to learn.
It wouldn't be polite
We are connected. But I told you so
In her hand do [?reign] my future

[2r]†   Leila

Faustine

[3r]   Two girls one light and one dark prepare to sell at a small table in the lobby
of the lecture hall in the [illegible] {Gilley} Settlement House.

Leila (the dark one) you havent enough money there to make change on the
first ten dollar bill.
Steen (the light one) With luck I have. Depends on how many tickets the ten
15 {its} for. – But you dont like the hobo, do you? Do you like him?
Leila I'd marry him in minute if I were free.
Steen Arent you free?
Leila Well he isnt.
Steen Oh its got as far as his telling you that has it? We all know the meaning
of that kind of prospect. My dear my notion would be you are in serious danger and your best bet would be to run for it. The place for you till this blows
over is back home in the parsonage with your father and mother. I only tell
you since you ask me.

[4r]   Leila. You know he's not a hobo Steen. He's a genius. He can do anything
with those big hands. Watch him work the modeling-clay in the work room.
Steen. But he's done time.
Leila Not long
Steen Time is time. Leila I wouldnt dare to stay round here another minute
in the state youre in {[illegible]}. I wouldnt trust myself. (She is interrupted
to sell a few tickets.) Speaking of those big hands of his they me the shivers.
Is he in the work room tonight?

---

* Page written in black ink.

† Pages starting here begin at the other side of the notebook and work backward. Entries
written vertically across the page, bottom to top.

Leila. I dont know. (She is interrupted by more sales). ~~Lei~~ Steen please don't scoff if I tell you I have figured him out as a philosophical anarchist—like To-lstoy.

Steen. Hoh! he's been reading Tolstoy has he? Or Carl Marx?

Leila You know he doesnt read. He hasnt the literary languages educated lingo go to say it with but he hates society and he hates all the condensation of the upper class to the lower that this [illegible] settlement represents. And so do I.

[5r] Steen. What do you and he propose to do about it?

Leila I'm going to initiate him into my cell of the party, thats what Im going to do tomorrow night. Ive got him all explained out to himself. You may laugh. His resentment can be channeled to great purposes I'm sure.

Steen. I must have a ~~real~~ {better} look at him. Next time youre in the post of-fice you take a real look at the rogues pictures there as wanted by the police and see if you dont find him among them. I had a notion I did. I think hes some fugitive from justice who may be hiding ~~with us behind our [illegible]~~ {I bet hes one of the wanted}

Gault. (among a group waiting for tickets) Wanted did I hear someone say? Who's wanted? Leila you're wanted. I want you. Come

Leila Im selling tickets.

Gault (He gathers both her wrists into one hand with his other hand reaches for the tickets.) No youre not. Im giving them anway. Whats on tonight. A lecture on <u>what</u>? The Poverty Vow. Whats that.Here have these free all you poor people. Every mans house his own poorhouse. Thats my motto. Its the [illegible] motto of the President of the United States.

[6r] I heard him say it to Tobius Teamsters. Have one – have one.

Leila Let go of me – you! You hurt. Don't treat me like this before people. (She breaks free for a moment)

Gault. Dont be so ~~glum~~ sulky. (He recaptures one of her wrists. She slaps his face.)

Leila. I hate you.

Gault. I'll give you something to hate me for. (He rumples her hair clear over her eyes)

Steen Call Dr. Butter someone? This is a scene

Leila What'll you give me you big brute.

Gault It's a four letter word.

Leila Say it so people can see what you are

Gault L-O-V-E. Are you coming along peacetully or must I drag you by the hair of the head (He muses her hair again)

Dr Butter Whats all this? What are you doing to Miss Lamprey.

Gault. Shes my wife I mean shes my sister Ive got one wife already and I want her to come home to her my children but she wont. You better not interfere between us. She pledged and unarmed   you

[7r] I warn you

Dr Butter Call the police

Leila   Dont   No   Dont   Kills von Kiells*

Steen   Yes—the police

Gault. Blondie behave. If you're her friend your mine. You come on with us {[illegible]}if you're worried. I got a table reserved at Klills This is a serious business. that calls for a chaperone.

Steen. Im selling tickets.

Gault. No you arent No one is. They're free tonight for our celebration Im giving them away. Here every body. Disperse to your seats in the hall {what there of you.} Come on ladies. Tumble out of here. (He runs them out roughly) The police arrive as the curtain goes down and the lecturer comes in from the hall

A police man with a big long billy brings guides the introducers of the lecturer through the {small} crowd.

[8r]   A darkish room a killes von kulls. The three have hardly got seated at a small table when the lecturer {introducer}on the Poverty Vow and the big policeman comes quietly in.

Lecturer Catherwood I was sure everything was all right. But I just came along with this officer to be sure there was no bloodshed. They werent quite satisfied this wasnt a case of disturbing the peace. I excused myself from the audience in an emergency. There werent many of them.†

Steen. Everything all OK officer. Let me assure you we are just two humane college girls seeing life. This giant is a discovery of ours. A study you might say. I majored in psychological relations (The police withdraw

Catherwood: you see how it is captain, (hes no captain). Isnt it all right on duty for a warming up at the bar. On me! (He goes to the bar door with the

---

* Phrase justified to right margin.

† These last two sentences appear to be added in between the preceding and the following sentences.

policeman but returns while the party at the table is getting ~~settle~~ interested in their menus. ~~and~~

Gault (rising to him.) Professor! Youre a feller. But I ought to say this is ~~going to~~ planned to be a very unusual sort of party indeed ~~that~~ it might bother your principles to sit in on. I wouldnt want you to be any the worse for what you have tried to do for us. That you for quieting the cop. ~~But~~ No knowing how much you may have helped. You have done enough. You

[9r] probably feel more at home from now on somewhere else. We wish you the friendliest good [illegible] {bye}. And ~~let me remember~~ if you are ever in trouble in the streets of this wicked city at night remember the mere mention of my name at the top of your voice may be enough to save your life. And for the love of dope what became of your audience you were introducing the lecturer to.

Catherwood: Which means that I must leave your to your fate ladies.

Steen Whatever it is. Im curious.

Catherwood (dubiously) Good ~~night by idea~~ ([illegible])

Gault Till we meet again. At the grave or beyond it

Steen Dont you know who that is ~~you~~ – you ignoramus

Leila I know I was on the posters—Old Catherwood who hates society as much as we.

Steen But with more humor that keeps him ~~from~~ out of jail. He says more things {in a day} he ought to be shot for than you and I together Leila learned in four years of sociology in College. I dont know how he gets by. He's a dear. I know Gault would like his ~~lectures~~ ideas

Leila No he wouldnt.

Steen. Why not?

[10r] Gault: While you ~~ladies~~ girls are settling me and getting the foot order I a'm going to ask to be excused ~~while~~ {to} wash my hands I may be gone awhile longer than you have patience for. Dont spare me. Say anything you please ~~about me~~ behind my back. Quite the contrary. I shall return to find the touch on this occasion that will make it as memorable as a wedding.

Leila Are you going after a priest?

Steen Or more policeman.

Gault Now you're talking.

Leila No priests Gault. No mocking like that. I was brought up in a parsonage—remember.

Gault Dont be sullen. Dont pout.

Leila Well. I am a serious rebel. And I think at bottom you are. Steen may not be. She is teacher-taught. Easy come easy go. Shell be raising children in a progressive school when you and I will be facing our last jury for the fourth offence. Then perhaps the world will get the big idea.

Steen. Let's pause at this point for indentification of the big idea

Gault That's the talk. You girls can talk while I act on the assumption.

(He leaves)

[11r]   Steen. Listen to that, act on the assumption! ~~No words you say~~ And you say he haven't the words to fulfill himself. Act on the assumption. When did he make that up. I like it's what shall I say? What's he after?

Leila. Wait and see.

Steen Do you know?

All I know is he said he would to any any length to ~~express~~ {show} his respect for me.

How do you mean respect

He said he had half a mind to open a jewelry store for me.

You mean go into the jewelry business

In a manner of speaking yes. As a matter of fact Steen I have reason to think he has gone off after a ring for me.

A marriage ring! Leila!

No just an engagement ring as yet.

But theres no jewelry store open at this time of night.

I told you he intended to open one. He wanted to make the occasion dangerous.

Those police may be back.—Isnt it funny about property. Society is an agreement to let money accumulate in the hands of a few till the rest of us cant stand it a minute longer and have to take it away from them ~~Ive arrived at that~~ conculsion arrived at signed and sealed.

The rest of us can even things up any time it occurs to us to start a revolution because the rest of us are the vast majority have the weight of numbers on our side. It seldom occurs to us in our own cogitations. We have to want to have it pointed out by a leader of from the other class*

[12r]   Leila. You've ~~done~~ pretty well for a school girl.

Steen School girl yourself. What are you but a school girl? I may have to show you by deeds. I'm past all definition. Aslong at its a case of breaking and entering I hope the [illegible] brings off some small keepsake for me to

---

* Entry written upside-down horizontally across the page, right to left, in the left margin created by Frost writing vertically up the page.

show ~~for the risk~~. my grandchildren for the risk were taking. How much'll you bet those police wont be back here tonight?

Leila Gault has his heart set on putting ~~a ring~~ the costliest ring on me he can find—the costlier the better. He said he wouldn't care if cost him his life. Someday he's going to have to shoot it out with society. It might as well be now as anytime. Though he hates to die young ~~and leave me when he has me~~ on me.

Steen Why Leila I hope you know what youre doing. I dont know what Im doing. You better step off home while you can. Before you get incriminated I believe I will. No. I want to see what happens. Where are you going?

Theres a big old deserted mansion with groun [illegible] river. Its called the Cuyler place. Its boarded up but Gault ~~says~~ has been

[13r] in and out of it.

Steen Here he is. No. (Come one comes toward them, but veers off)

Leila He says theres antique furniture in one or two rooms. Its quite liveable. He's got the water on. We could use candles. He says its a fortification.

Steen What's the big idea

Leila May be with Thoreau's home at Walden Pond.

Steen. Isnt this suspense awful. Let's drink. Waiter! (They give their order) You know who I think that was coming in,. Your professor Catherwood wasnt it. I saw it was someone you recognized. Who are those he's with.

Leila Yes. He signaled. I ought not to tell you but he belongs to the party I see him at the meetings. He's all right. One of the intelligent I wish Gault could see something of him. He's in a position to do a lot of good.*

Steen. Heres where we part company my dear. Its getting so you can scare me. I can keep up ~~with you~~. As I understand it you're making the Cuyler Mansion your home.

Leila Not forever. Just long enough for the idea. The same as Thoreau. To show our contempt for the gaudy set up. Life can be as inexpensive as you care to make it. Who ~~cares~~ asks for a given freedom. [~~illegible~~]

[14r] The liberties we take ~~that~~ are all that count.

Steen Heres where we part company. This exceeds the educational {the experimental} process.

Leila You must come and see us. You will need Gaults guidance in We will probably give a house warming party.

---

* Arrow drawn from beginning of this last sentence to space in between ". . . intelligent" and "I wish" . . .

Steen You deceitful friend. You have this whole thing planned and didn't let on. Are you intend to winter there? How will you manage the house warming?

Leila. Theres a big fireplace in our intended living room. We can burn some of the furniture and the banisters and the panelling if worse comes to worst. We can burn the house's insides out.

How about the smoke

At night it wont show much. – though it is a risk. Let the neighbors get used to it.*

I smell disaster. Your professor has a protective eye on us. Why dont you call him over. (She does)

Catherwood Where's your young man gone ~~ladies~~ girls?

Steen On some errand of benefaction Leila claims.

Cat Has it occurred to you he may not be able to come back.

[15r] Leila. What do you know? Anything?

Coling Nothing special. Only I think those policemen are staying with him. I didn't like the way they went ~~and~~ off. They me all right very pointedly. Where do you think the boy is?

Steen You didnt go back to your lecture. You suspect something.

Leila If I thought –

Steen Somethings gone wrong I know.

Col I dont want to stampede you girls, but if I were you I'd get up and go quietly one at a time ~~and go~~ {one at at time and} somewhere else. Theres a man over there in the corner I dont like the looks of.

Steen Come home with me Leila out all this sinisterity

Leila Don't you see I can't. You go. Mr Collingwood will stay with me.

Steen Well {as} I'm no good to anyone ~~I suppose~~ and maybe worse than no good I suppose I may as well – here he is, out of the kitchen in some waiter's blacktie. Oh my god! Look at him there with a [illegible]{menu}† and a napkin. He's going to take our orders. Dont laugh

Leila Who're but you?—Gault!

Gault. (Handing each a ~~bill of fare~~ {wine list} and ~~showing a~~ at the same time showing to all a saphire ring on the first joint of his little finger.) As good as

---

* Phrase written in blue ink.
† Word written in blue ink.

our word Leila. But no ceremony here tonight. They're on my trail too close
A ring for me braclets for me maybe costly ring [illegible]

[16r]   But its not for this job something else theyve got a [?guarantee] or think they
have. Weve got em all stirred up. Theres a congress of them outside in the
outer room. Better disperse. Everybody for himself. They know I shoot for
[?practice]
Catherwood.   ~~Here~~ Take my order then. I'll order for everybody. My address is 333 East 23rd Street appartment 28. You wrote it down the The rest
can memorize it. Do you get it – 333 East 23. Ahh 32. You're all invited right
off tonight. I have a word to say to you children. We can have any ceremony
[~~illegible~~] {needed} there. OK?
Steen. We girls can take off together.
Cath. I'll put you in a taxi: Cocktails first though. Get us past anything (~~while~~
Gault ~~fails to~~ goes and fails to reappear. They call another waiter) I wonder if
it isnt another case of being crosses in love of country You dont think so
Leila. What is it then? Disappointed in patriotism is what many of his generation are in our judgement.
Leila Gault must know what patriotism. He dont know what a country is. All
that highfalutinism.
Cath He was led to expect something that couldnt be. ~~I'll be~~ I find it a relief
to his kind if they are helped to take it out on the people that mislead them
[illegible] given a chance to talk their resentment off intelligently.
Leila. Im like that. You might do something for me. Then again you might
not. My minds made up and so is yours

[17r]   yours [~~illegible~~] JimCatherwood. It goes down deeper than something personal Mob revenge is the only prescription, you know it. Ive heard you say so
in class [illegible]. The magnates had their chance and ruined it .. ~~They deserve to have~~ {I want to see} their hats blown off.
Cath. All right lets go to ground. The boy is not coming back. Give you an
hour or to to reassemble. Take your time. You start along. I'll take care of the
bill. You'll come wont you.
Steen. I may not. Ill see. Ive got house work to do.
Bath So have I—papers to mark
Leila youre way off in your theory about us, professor. I have one open [illeg-
ible]. Ive already explained him to himself beyond anything you are likely
to say.

Cath Ill have another ready when you get there. And there's the ceremony.
Leila We'll come [illegible] I feel awfully observed. But here gocs. Bye He'll
know where we've gone. It all over here. We re too obvious. We here gues.
Dye.*
Catherwood. Your turn to bail out next. Font fail us. Just my sort of situation
[illegible] to deal with. Do you more good than a classroom lecture.
Faustine goes out and two men come and sit at the table with Batherwood.
They are not officers apparently: they are in plain clothes. But on of them
with an air of finality. Well!

Curtain.

---

* Word written in blue ink.

"Leila. What have you brought him into the house for?"

MS. 001731. *Brown paper cover spiral notebook, 5½" × 8½" ruled pages. All entries are in blue ink. "Ask for No. 855C/Another MAPLE SAE Product" stamped on the cover. "Prefaces etc." written in what appears to be Frost's hand on the cover, below a maple leaf machine stamped on the cover..*

[1r]   Leila. What have you brought him into the house for? I suppose because you've got next to no one else to love.

Mother. He's a good boy. You used to like him yourself. Your father and I went to look him up in his trouble. We thought we might use him as a leader up here teachers don't like to come {are so hard to bring}. He'll have to learn to write all over with his left hand. It was his right he lost in the saw mill.

Leila. As To my recollection he never good wright with his right. He wasn't much in school.

M. No but we thought he might be made to do.

Leila Who is there for him to teach.

M. Not many but theres the Tiochbusy family coming up and one or two other scattering

Leila I hear he died from the infection.

Mother. He he

~~M. I don't want to see him But don't treat him inhospitably on my account. I'm transient.~~

Mother. He came near it for the flies on his open wound. You should have seeen the quarters we received from in Millville.

[2r]   Liela I don't want to meet him. But don't treat him inhospitably on my account I'm transient. This is no home of mine—never was. I fled ~~him~~ back in ~~an~~ {my} extremity. Edna and Fred Blethin are coming to get me.

Mother Is that the Fred Blethin ~~we used~~ we used to know summers in Montclair. Bradford? Whats he doing now.

Leila. Hes busy with the courts taking the Fifth Amendment to keep his job as a professor of sociology at Brooklyn University. Any objection?

M. None the least for my part. ~~Your father~~ Kind of a communist ~~I suppose~~
{wasn't he?}

L. Marxist

M. You are too.

L No Im an anarchist like Emma Goldman[1] if you get me. He looks toward
Moscow when he {kneels to pray}. I look toward Barcelona. Any objection?

M. ~~I do if~~ Your father might mind. I don't pretend to know the difference. Is
Edna one?

Leila. Yes shes one or both. She's confused. She's as bad as you {are}. She
doesn't discriminate {between the} in rebellions. She just rebels the way you
do at heart come right down to it. I got it from you. I'll bet your in love with

[3r]   this poor one armed lumberjack you old Latharioress

M. don't call your mother unintelligible names.

Leila. But aren't you?

M. Arent I what you silly. But there all sorts of love. He's the kind of man I'd
marry in a minute if I were free—and he'd see me at my age. {As it is} I have
place for him just as for a son.

Leila. We might as well cry as laugh about things I say. Do the places for him
include you.

Mother. Do you know I think women have lost in coming from behind out
into the open of politics and affairs. Their undisclosed influence was what
counted. Let me tell you something. This township has sent anyone to the
{mother} legislature for some time. We has a right once. I could have gone. I
got him elected to go six votes to none the same as in in Russia. So its as a
Representative you meet him,

L. did he make a name for himself

M. It was only his first session. But he did a nice thing that got talked about.
He got the portrait of that early Gov—

[4r]   brought out from behind an open door that that covered and hung in a decent place in the State House.

Leila That's him in the kitchen. Probably thinks Im ashamed to meet him.

M. Too unthinking he is to think of such things.

Leila. Two such things. You know things I suspect. We have yet to say them
to each other. One is that I am going to have a child and the other is that its
father is in the death cell at Sing Sing. Want to see the ring he gave his life to
get me. (She take it draws it out of her breast on its string about her neck) It

is too grand to wear. Im no homing dove. I fled to you. I escaped from and es-
capade.

Mother. It was in the papers, some of it.

Leila does your pretty boy know that my pretty boy must die. I hear a car
coming up the mountain. Must be Fred and Edna. Bring on your paramour. I
want a glimpse of im for old times sake before I go. He wrote me love letters
when we were thirteen fourteen. I don't know what I am in for. I may have to
{go} beg the body. Fred will have found out.

[4*v*]   Copy

    The reason of my perfect ease[2]
    In the society of trees
    Is that their competing struggles pass
    So far below my social class
    For me to share them or be made
    For any thing I hold afraid

[5*r*]   {They say} Some Boston boys when they were faced
    By science with the awful fact of waste[3]
    That from a million codfish eggs one ~~egg~~ cod
    Is all we ever get, went back on God
    And suicided with a lightening rod

    Nothing ever so sincere
    ~~That if it went out of sheer~~
    That unless its out of sheer
    Mischief and a little queer
    It wont prove a bore to hear

    Peace give us peace though great I Am
    Let us lie down together
    You be the lion we'll be the lamb
    You cant mistake us for a ram
    We look more like a [illegible] [?wolves]

[6*r*]   We are not talking about the small fry intelligentsia who are thrown into consternation and confusion by an avalanche of new dictum appearing. Some-

thing has to be done to for them to be. The King has his editorial writers and article writers to sooth them down

[7r]⁴ Another thing that comes up for consideration is the question of the Superman. He is a leftover from the great period of Evolution.⁵ By estimating the distance the animals [illegible phrase] how far it is to what comes next after the monkeys to us any school ought be [illegible].

[8r] Another thing that comes up for the kings

[9r] The challenge of the sciences to government takes the form of asking what will you do with the [illegible] latest? Will you use it as weapon or a tool or both. If you ignore it we small try on your {some} rival government If you try to suppress it we will do the same.

The challenge of science to the small fry intelligentsia takes the form of asking what are you going to say to our latest? How are you going to take our having hit the moon for the Russia? With chagrin rightly. You should hate not to win. It must be Nothing can be done with people who don't mind losing. You are not that bad. If the best we been harder {more powerful} for you to {be beaten in} the race for the moon than the races at Melbourne. You [illegible] thrown in consternation and confusion by the new words fuel by the truck load of new words for fuel we have forced rattling down the chute into the your old coal bin in the cellar. Find something to say to [illegible] our posess you must learn to sass the Sphinx. It seems a shame to once on you will our {new} novel when you are hardly up around after what Darwin Spencer and Huxley⁶ did to {you} last century. But you will be taken sure of this time as you were the last time by our editorial writers and column writers and our commentators.

[10r] The next thing we are confronted with is the question of the Superman who is to succeed us.   He He ought to be no further beyond us than we are beyond the monkey. Every school boy brought up on anthropology and the comic strips {can tell you} knows how amusing short a distance that is. Shall we {We can}liken it to what the mystic Carl Marx likes to call historical necessity to the distance or stake {we can} we take with our further evolution into our own hands and make what we please of ourselves our labor Will the laboratariians messing around rays or genes for mutation sperm and ovules for eugenics⁷ (Galton's word not mine)⁸ But Im As far as I can see men with my eyes shut men will be acting {[illegible]} as of that thought they [il-

legible] were giving [illegible] its best chance by pairing for love and money like Europa and Danaa. [illegible] I forsee no society where artificial insemination will [illegible] in good taste.

All this talk as science were way things but its not as if I know its not. It is mans greatest enterprise. It is his venture into nature. It is his own substantiation. Bu it does not belown to itself. It is a part There never was a scientist King any more than there will be a philosopher king. The only poet King was Henry VIII who took poetry

"Prophetic"

MS. 001721. *Brown soft paper cover notebook with black canvas-strip binding, 6¾″ ×
8⅜″. Pages stitched. White ruled paper. Entries are in blue ink unless otherwise
noted.*

[*Cover*]   D*
Prophetic†

Thy Kingdom Come¹
The Hicksites² Daughter.

[*1r*]‡   Deeds as prophecy   And now thy matchless deed's achieved
                                   Determined dared and done³

Deeds as judgement   Mercy and injustice—Jonahs puzzle.⁴

1   Great Snake (Vedder)⁵ glides off—Arizona

On the contrary I think the very highest of prophecy:

Gambling is the abuse of prophecy.

Kings are more prophetic than philosophers and even poets and that is
why those are wrong who would set philosophers or poets over states as rulers. Every deed [illegible] {arises from} prediction of what can be done and is
a proof of that prediction.

Put up or shut up.

•   •   •

---

* Written in Frost's hand.
† Written at a slight upward angle.
‡ Page written in black ink.

Nothing more salutary for the prophet than to have his prophecies prove false. Humiliation of

The ways of knowing
Nature an infinite paraqueet.[6] One scent to hyson & to wall flower

Got to be killed back to the ground almost and come up from the roots again.

[1v]*   If there were any justice I might go ahead.
I think you want me to go ahead just to satisfy your curiosity.
Well Im not going to prophesy—thats all. Let somebody else do it. He is alone—talking to unheard voice
I believe in that voice But I dont trust it
Do you think its a liar
No I think it means what it says when it says it but it wont have the firmness to carry out its promise.
You think pretty poorly of him.
Youd think so wouldnt you. The very opposite is the fact Its all because I think the

{Running away from what
{Something you know not of   Station platform
{None of our business hey. He admits hes a fugitive from {Justice}

Yes I dont believe in justice
your back
Yes Im back
How far did you get. You look as if you had a been {in a railroad wreck}
{I've been in worse I've been} As far as getting a rope round my neck
You a rope round your neck. For what in the world
Nothing
You havent had time to do anything. What were you accused of doing.
I was misjudged—mistaken for someone else who had
‖ Serves you right for running away from me

[13 pages torn out]

_____
* Page written in black ink.

[2r]*   that it isnt partly mental just as theres none so mental that it isnt partly physical. {And no it doesnt much matter it which} end you start the treatment the
mental {or the physical}†,

Dr. Truell has thought of pretty much everything hasn't he

Pretty much.

I ask for sympathy and this is what I get. You take his side g against me.

My dear boy I should think we could both concede this system that
much—his system say—not mine

What, that we're all mental cases more or less

When we're cases of any kind. Some of us arent cases at all. You're not a
case. You have no business in here

[2v]   Especially where there are too many syllogisms to hold in the mind at
once.

Give give but see to it that in giving you do not take away more than you
give.

And remember the best gift you can give may be discipline by contest.
(Discipline by contest being happier and healthier than discipline by prohibition

[3r]   ~~The Very Focal Point~~
                      The Other Thing
                            or
                    Thy Kingdom Come[7]

Some people cant think a proof ~~or disproof~~ out. They have to act it out.

Take a simple statement like Carl Marx' that is only an extension of our
Quaker pacifism:[8] We dont need to hurt each other with war; neither to do
we need to hurt each other with trade. The only way to find out if we neednt
is to try it out. I am prepared to go to any length in ~~soe~~ the social experiment.
For what do we pray saying Thy Kingdom come on earth if it isnt some such
brotherhood and equality as the communists ~~advocate~~ {promise}. Either stop
praying for it or join in to help bring it now. Ours is the responsibility on this
globe as we are the best people on this globe [illegible] Any ~~Utopia we~~ heaven
on earth will be of our achievement. How do we know we are better than
Africans

---

* Page written in black ink.
† Written beneath line.

[*3v*]   Captive minds. Anyone may be considered a captive to any contract or [il-legible] promise made when conditions were more favorable.

Utopia is the opposite of Civilization.⁹

[*4r*]   and {even} Asians. Because we dominate them. Christendom has {had} all the say for a thousand years and is today wholly dominant. We can beat Buddism Confuciansim Shintoism Mohammedism any time in fight and what with [illegible] {plenty of} energy to spare {left over} to fight each other within Christendom when we are not fighting them without. You'd think we had proved ourselves sufficiently in force to lay force aside {if we pleased.} Anyway as we decide the it the world will have to be. So plan well nobly ide-ally. It must have been a bad church and clergy in Russia that kept the Bolsheviks from realizing their unanimity with Christianity. Perhaps events will bring them to their senses and they will yet take up the cross and the leadership of Christianity. It is a hope. The democracies {We} seem about prepared to go with them to the

[*5r*]   logical conclusion of our democracy.¹⁰

Resentia the ministers bad wayward girl.

[*6r–8r*]   [blank]

[*9r*]¹¹   There was never naught   weighty thought
There was always thought
But when noticed first¹²
It was fairly burst¹³
Into having weight
It was in a state
of atomic one   of atomic One
Matter was begun –
Was in fact complete
One and yet discrete
[Illegible]

[*8v–24r*]   [blank]

"What is your attitude toward our having robbed
the Indians of the American Continent?"

MS. 001893. *Blue paper cover, 6¼" × 9¼", binding torn off, some stitching still intact. White unruled pages. All entries are in blue ink.*

[*1r*]*   What is your attitude toward our having robbed the Indians of the American Continent?

Why do you ask?

Because I am gathering statistics on the subject for a Doctorate in the graduate school of the University of Chicago.

Do I have to answer your question.

Dont you dare to answer it?

Cant you think of any better reason for my not answering it

You may have answered it already and are too proud to repeat yourself

Yes several times over in my published books. The first poem I ever wrote, La Noche Triste[1] still extant ~~deals~~ {would} ~~shows~~ {where} my sympathies lie and so ~~so~~ also would several later. But as I can't expect you to have read me I must ~~find~~ {give} a better reason still for finding your question merely academic, namely Darwin.[2]

You mean Darwin made one lump sum of our ruthlessness in the struggle for prevailing.

Darwin unified all that just as Freud tried to unify the details of personal conduct, Einstein the details of force and matter and Marx

[*2r*]   the conflicts of society so that we wont have to hurt each other even in peace any more.

You bring Darwin and Marx into seeming contradiction by mentioning them so close together.

Yes Darwin held something loves being done with as by natural selection

---

* Entries on this page and 2r are written vertically down the page, top to bottom.

that could have little to do with directing or keeping from hurting us where it had to toward its unforeseeable end. Our blind rivalries were our chief guide. Marx thought our rivalries could be ameliorated or done away with.

Cant they be

No.

Just no!

Our rivalry with the Indians race with race is over ~~to~~ however and not worth our lingering regret. If we have absorbed ~~any of~~ them there is seemingly nothing to show for it beyond a few words and place names. I have a sentiment for those.

Would we have been degraded by their absorption?

I like to think not. They had much of the first virtue of a <u>virtutis</u> bravery

[*2v*] They gave us many noblemen to remember and more than one high culture all their own.

You ~~are~~ {have to be secretly} sorry for their fate ~~secret~~ because you are a good Darwinian. To the victor belongs the responsibility for the future. But may well prove a sighing matter. Is that it. May I quote you so. And one thing more while I am about it. Can there be any such show down between us and the Negro as there was between us and the Indian.

Our struggle to hold the Negro off is about over. He is not going to overwhelm us with either his superiority or inferiority. From his history in Africa we might be justified in the fear ~~he's~~ his being drawn into our blood would be damaging. But I am going to say his traits ~~mi~~ absorbed might do us good by letting us down or relaxing us just enough in our over strained civilization like the new happiness pills. Tinting toward them might restore the physical where it was getting lost in the intellectual. The happiness pills are a new resource for the same purpose. But we have always had drink to rescue the emotional and [?generative] imaginative from the rational.

[*3r–4v*] [blank]

[*5r*] That o is or finished C
And are unfinished o
In all I needed to know

~~His~~

~~Whose lightness as~~

He has tightness wad of thrift
Is a resolve to the world his gift
Shall be of the least possible avail

His lightness that suggests a wad of thrift
Is but a [illegible] resolves his passive gift
Shall be of the least possible avail.

[5v]³   Out of sheer nervousness the jester spoke
Is loyalty not something we invoke
To break it gently to a lady friend
When we feel passion dying to an end?

"After the lady in the case has cried
She can be counted on our pride
To be the hesitater go along
And not be so afraid of doing wrong."

The King consults the timepiece on his wrist
We've heard the amateur psychologist
Nor the professorial idealist
Will give the verities a needed twist.

"In times like this; the unhappy statesman faltered
The value as we say are getting altered
In a great hope that never may {any} scare
Need mankind do each other harm in war.

And Marx had found a way form him to learn
From doing one another harm in peace.
And that to some might seem an end in view
Worth leaving parents wife and country too

From too much flag the spiritual shall go
We weary of our nationalistic brags
And it is {Malthus} figured nations need not crowd
If all his children were're allowed.
The [illegible] I look at Absalom your son
Rebellion with a boy may be for fun

But all the same ~~he can but feel the~~ {we're in a kind of} glory
Oh taking to the mountains in out-lawry
That a king should flourish in outlawry

[6r] He had to save his head to save his face

He had to lose his head to save his face
These were not times for talking [?commonplace]

What ever they were like—what ~~were~~ they like?
He wished he knew the poker note to stick
-He knew he was handing in his resignation
-He knew he was with a sublime sensation
~~He knew it didn't matter what he said~~
~~In many like thoughts~~
~~He was as good as speaking from the dead~~
~~His account changed from cynical to hard~~
His face was all that [?withered] now to save
He was as sad as speaking from the grave
All that remained
~~All that remained~~ now {was} for
To say ~~was~~ hard a death it was to be
Some forms of death
The king himself thinks some forms of death too good for ~~some~~

[6v] The king—he formed the subject no less grim
For being house personal to him.
So many [illegible] held their breath.
The wall became {was like} a vacuum of death.
So many
And when he spoke the verdict of the king
~~was that~~ Left loyalty about that same old thing
In times like these ~~the same~~ {in fact} in any time
Disloyalty in Blackstone is a crime
Against the throne for which you cant expect

Treason he said according to Blackstone
[~~Is an suspect~~] {[illegible]} crime against the throne
Disloyalty is that for which your gang[4]

Without trial shoot you with a bang
Will end you with a whimper and a bang[5]

They need not take you to the chopping block
But some might whey our fumbling at the lock
Of your front door to ~~your~~ {to meet} loyal wife to meet
Battery of.

[7r]   [blank]

[7v]   A dog is loyal to his source of grub
One kind of man is loyal to his club

"Pertinax"

MS. 951490. *Brown soft paper cover notebook with canvas strip binding, 8⁵⁄₁₆″ × 6⅝″.*
Pages stitched. Ruled paper. All entries in blue ink unless otherwise noted.

[*Cover*]*   No 1   Pertinax¹
                         Pertinax in Name

              Pertinax
              August 1951
              <u>Cocktail Bar in 45th St</u>
              July 52

[*1v*]   Do you believe in signs.
              The only signs I believe in are the first steps taken in carrying out an idea.

[*2r*]   Diddius (Julianus) says to someone How should you like to be Caesar for
              a day?
              Better than for a half a day or no day at all.
              Why do you ask? What would it indicate if I said I should?
              ~~Wh~~ How much would you give?
              All you have and then as much again
              Because the first thing you could do in power would be to recover it in taxes.
              Is there any wish you had rather wish if you could have your wish.
              I should have to think. But shouldn't I be wasting my time.
              How better could you waste it than in a dream that might come true.
              What chance is there? You mean there is a chance for someone.
              To me it has been offered—if I will be at Caesars portico tomorrow at an
              hour—to bid the Empire on at auction with impunity.

---

* Page written in black ink.

[*3r*]   The Practorians will sell it to whosowill presume.[2]

You lie to please me

Word has been ~~pr~~ passed me secretly about who has the means and courage the ambition.

The bidding will be [illegible] open?

Yes and no. ~~But who would dare to bid under encouraged? They fear to~~
~~hold the auction~~

But fewwould dare to bid—

perhaps none unless encouraged—given assurance the sale was in good faith.

For ~~jus~~ just a day.

A day a year It could not in the nature of the case be long

A day would not suffice to taste full savor of the palace let alone the city let
alone the Empire.

The hope could be for longer than a day.

And then comes death

We do not have to say the word

But do we think the Empire should be bought

[*4r*]   or sold at auction.

We do not know. What physically may be theres nothing to prevent.

The Caesar in the Palace now—What will [illegible] become of him

We do not know—we do not ask to know

Didius I do not believe the Empire will be sold at auction to the highest to
the only bidder. What is the price suggested.

All that I have

It is a trick to take your all and give you nothing.

Im not prepared to think Rome come to this.*

Do you believe in signs.

Then are there signs.

The {only} signs that I believe in are the first steps taken to carry out a new
idea. A new Rome dawns. Rome has been what it has been. Rome hence forth
shall be wealth realized wealth enjoyed—Wealth to the wealthy—pleasure

[*5r*]   unrefined. {The ascent is} From discipline[†] to power to ~~we~~ riches that can
command both power and discipline. Money can hire the discipline of troops
the power of brawn the power of brain—retainers counsellors entertainers.
Tis in the air. Why be blinded to it.

---

* There is a line from the beginning of this phrase that connects it to the phrase above it.
† There is a caret between "discipline" and "to", but appears to be no corresponding word
or phrase to insert.

There are not signs in heaven.

No in politics.

I shall have to think.

For me as friend

Who was your father Diddius

A slave

From what land

Asia Minor

It is like Rome for opportunity. No one so humble but he may be bearer if he deserves Hail then.

Tis nothing yet. Come to see the sale tomorrow and stand by me—if it be not too dangerous.

What shall I be in the new government.

[6r]   a new portfolio

The one to prompt me in my pleasures.

Dip where you will

To reconcile these when the conflict. To see that the greater arent lost sight of in the lesser. Some order {even in orgy} must be ~~observed even in~~ {kept} orgy. Some measure of one {delight} is justice to another.

~~Shall~~ Must I devise a system.

But not obtrude it in ~~our~~ {my} thoughts. ~~Yo~~ It must be kept from me. Thats what the orderly are for so that the free may be more free. {They must be dependened on to keep the drunk from falling off the roof. sober enough}

We talk as if it had come true.

~~All is~~ {More is} arranged than I have said.

I do not believe {Rome} will be sold at auction.

The hour—even now—Rome ~~is without a ruler~~ may be rulerless

You know? You are in the plot

I know enough. Go home. But ~~stay wait~~ {stay} my friend.

[6v]   He gets much for a little.

But he gets death with it.

[7r]*   Divine right   This palace is not occupied

Fear of delight   —not used

·   ·   ·

---

* Followed by notes.

Conscience but an extension of the fear of punish[e]ment or rebuke (which is punishment enough for the proud) as sight is an extension of the sense of touch.[3] It is a pride away-way out {to be} beforehand even with the least thought of reproach from others. It is one of the last refinements and most exquisite of luxuries the cultivated can [illegible] attain to.

Philosopher king. We prophesy most in action in a deed. We prophesy in {a} deeds as we can {at all} in {a} word.

King {and a} sliding scale of democracy[4] to

Caesar Kaiser
Emperor
Imperator
General as dictator
Indefinitely continuum
in office

Art forever puts case.

Refusing power   Ventures to say*
Refraining in power

Idea of it makes the practical ugly
Soul of it makes the flesh ugly.

Bring more people	People grew far away from
Within the circle where	the ruler in his palace, till his
the trial of character goes on.	palace guards were his only con-
stituency	
Dormancy of generations not very evil.	with the power of election and
recall	

[7v]   [illegible] {love} I hear of thing done sweepingly
        Sweeping is what small natures fear to be

[8r]   One story I would never tire of telling
        As long as I found anyone to listen

---

* Phrase written in black ink.

Concerns a boy a cup bearer at court
~~Whose look of sorrow made the king rebuke him~~
Who ~~looked~~ {wore} so sad ~~it~~ {a look} ~~made~~ the king rebuked him
~~Listen it cheers you to be cheering one~~
~~Far better were you serving in the kitchen~~
~~You far better serving in the kitchen~~
The task of charming me should make you cheer up
A ~~glum~~ {sad} cup bearer would be summoner
What ails you boy? The cupbearer made answer
You would be sad if your home lay ruined

Tell me about it. you man name the town.
What would you do about it boy?
                                        Restore it.

Nothing was said about who laid the town {defenses}
Nothing was said about the power required
To wall it in ~~against~~ again against all comers
Whether the king himself or merely neighbors

[9r]   How much time would you have to be away.

~~The story goes he named a time~~
The young man name a time. The chances are
Much shorter than it looks. He took twelve years.
~~The King sat waiting for him all that time~~
He couldnt have come back the same cupbearer
As he had been. They made him something else
Perhaps a governor. He had the traits.
The king sat waiting for him all the time.

How was it. Tell me how the story ended?

I managed it by gates. I got subscribers
I got one ~~family pledged to build the~~ wall {pledged to build a [illegible] of wall}
~~From one gate to the next~~
To the next gate when ~~they~~ {he} redeemed the pledges
(I wager it had to be there was no money)

I named the gate for him and in his honor
The difficulty was with the neighbor races

[9¹¹] Good natured affability in kings
Was the same thing three thousand years ago
As now. There is no [illegible] of such things

[10v] ~~The~~ Whose land was given us ~~we could~~ take it from them
{It had been given us to take the land from}
Yet we had never wholly ~~eliminated~~ [illegible] gyped them out of it}
~~It was~~ {T is} ~~to defend the place from them and from you~~
~~Oh king I wanted to restore the wall~~

~~Who cares whom you built the wall against~~
It was against those neighbors and not you*
Oh king I wanted to restore the walls.

I do{nt}† care whom it was against. Go on.
Did they stand by and let you build in peace

We did it armed, ~~a sword in one hand~~ {a trowel in one hand}
A sword in one. They scoffed at us. I kept
The name of one Sanballat it was the worst.
He threatened me with you. But I repent
It was against ~~them~~ {him} and not you I built.

Sanballat has no ~~preference~~ {influence} with me.
How many people made a city for you?

[11r] Pure, forty thousand

Were they truly grateful

They wept in unison the forty thousand
When told the restoration ~~for them~~ {of the wall}

---

* There is a line from the beginning of this line to the end of the line, "Yet we had never
[~~illegible~~] {[~~illegible~~] gyped them out of it}"
† Written beneath the line.

Would mean restoration of the law.
Was the law cruel. Were you too severe.
I only said they must live moral lives.
Whom was much hurt by that?
                          You should have heard them
I had to threaten them with you and God.
I don't see how you differed from Sanballat.
Let me explain our faith.
                          No dont explain.

[11v]   Girls can be beautiful in many styles
          [illegible]

[12r]   Religion ~~shouldnt bother a cupbearer~~
          The names of honor on the city gates
          ~~That was a good idea~~
          Was an idea I give you credit for
          Were they wise laws they said they had to keep?

          ~~They had to be~~.
          Simple they had to be. I said but two.
          The first was they mustnt marry out
          The second that they mustnt break the Sabbath

          Almost too simple   Insignificant
          Why all the waiting

                          There were loves involved

          Oh oh and love is terrible with some
          But why is it so wrong to marry out
          Girls can be beautiful in many styles*
          All races do don't they from love
                          ~~Their~~ {Ours} is the worlds
          First trial of exclusively human breeding
          The same with the animals and plants

          ---
          * This entry is from 11v (plus there is an additional, illegible word). Its inclusion is indi-
          cated by an arrow to the left margin of the page.

[13r]   Live breeding called to the see what comes of it

It shouldnt matter on so small a scale.
Not to disturb an empire I should say.

Thats as it seems to you. And Sabbath keeping
That is a symbol of our waste[5] to God
Things on the alter like a ~~lamb~~ votive lamb.
So we ~~wi~~'ll regard the awareness of waste.

It shouldnt matter on so small a scale
Poor forty thousand I can hear them wait.

[14r]   Of tales retellable ~~one I like~~ best is {the} one {one of the best}
~~concerns~~ {about} a boy a cupbearer at court
The King No one needs have been frightened at the scene*

Of tales retellable (one of the best)
Concerns a boy a cupbearer at court
Who bore himself seriously it seemed
To please ~~the~~ {a} king. The King stopped everything
To ~~ask him if he didnt know his~~ remind that as cupbearer his} task
Was to look happy making others happy.
The ~~banquet hall~~ {court need not have} trembled [illegible] ~~boy~~ {at the scene}
The King was only being affable
And affability was the same thing then
~~In great one over kings to~~
In the high might as it is today
~~All of the science makes~~ {have made us} ~~no difference in it.~~
~~All science has not changed it in the least~~
All science has not made it any different
In its design to bring the lowly out.

[15r]   One of the best of tales retellable
When out of reach of books rereadable

---

* This phrase written vertically in the left-hand margin and connected by an arrow by the
preceding word "King,"

And after poems memorized give out
By firelight {somewhere} in the wilderness ~~some~~ {at} ~~night~~
Concerns aboy cupbearer to the King
Who gave the {king} offense by looking moody
The king stopped everything to ask the boy
Didnt he know a good part of his task
Was to look cheerful making others cheerful.
~~There need not have been~~
The court need not have {~~been frightened~~} {trembled} at the scene
The king was only being affable[~~illegible~~]
And affability was the same thing
~~Back~~ then as {it is} today ~~after all these years~~
Science has made no difference in ~~the trait~~
All the King wanted was divertisement
At any ones expense he happened on.
Tell us ~~about your~~ {what you are sad about} he urged
~~He may have liked to [illegible] a [illegible] of shadow~~
He may have craved some shadows for relief
From all endless revelry at court.

[*15v*]   About this marrying out you object to
Tell me the story if it is a story.

It goes back to the arbitrary act
Where God in disappointment with mankind
Chose one man ~~out to start a chosen race~~ {from the such to start all over}*
~~And cast him in a concentration camp~~[6]
And to concentrate on him and his future
He cast him in a concentration camp

[*16r*]   You would be sad the cupbearer replied
If your home town had been laid waste in war.

Your town has been laid waste? Who laid it waste?[7]
~~He no doubt liked to feel to hear it was his work.~~
~~He liked to think of rules he had wrought~~ {of pride he had brought low.
He no doubt hope to hear it was himself.

---

* Written beneath the line.

{He could afford to be good natural}
Both sides can be good natured about war
After it has receded far enough {in the past.}

Jerusalem the boy said. There was silence
The King remembered having laid it waste
Or having it laid. He forgot the reason.
What would you do about it boy

                              Restore it.

Your restore it with your own hands

[17r]   My English Witch
             In the name of the Demons

         Hasin odat
             Aeleus   Megalistus Ornereus
             Lick [illegible] Nicon Moscromas and Zeper

[18r]   It goes back to an arbitrary act
          When God in disappointment with the people
          He had [?invested] The prime prehistoric nature with
          Decided to take one out of the ruck
          And put him in a concentration camp
          {Where}* To {he could} concentrate on his development {[?him] alone}
          To the exclusion of everybodys else {and oblservation}
          Of everybody else and start all over.
          God didnt mind acknowledging [?recklessness]
          He gave the dung hill
          Thus early in time where no one critical
          Was round to [illegible] of {smile at} the acknowledgement
          He cheerfully threw years of work away
          Seeing it wasnt good and with a will
          (Which was {the} trait that most distinguished him
          Projected a brand new experiment in {breeding}
          [Illegible] {A species} from his failure with genes.

---

* Written in left-hand margin.

He found an Adam that he thought would do
But couldnt find a woman ~~that~~ worthy of [illegible]
So like the gardener he was he sprung a{n}* ~~woman~~ {Eve}
By budding as it were from Adams side.
Purity was his watchword from the first
And has been ever since in everything
~~Scien~~ Religion Science Art and Government .

[19r]   Inbreeding closer never has been tried.
All well ~~from~~ and good clear for a beginning.
The first thing that went wrong ~~he~~ {God} lost his patience
~~With them he loved because They broke some rule~~
[Illegible] Because his favorite broke some garden rule
And [?punished] them by punishing himself
~~He turned them out of the one place~~ {where he needed them}
He turned them out of the one place on earth
Where for his plans he needed them to be.
[Illegible] So that they never again got back to it.
      Or {ever} could find out where it had been
      Somewhere between the Tigres and the Euprhates
      They looked and many after them have looked
~~The next thing that went wrong with this~~.
The next thing that went maddeningly wrong
With this experiment in high eugenics[8]
~~God didnt prosper them~~
God didnt have much luck in Adams children
Both of them boys: one of them killed the other.
There were no girls perhaps for fear of incest
Yet that seems inconsistent with the promise

[19v]   Editors note three thousand years thereafter

[20r]   ~~Th~~ ~~Tha~~† That all the hope we have is in inbreeding
Well since they had no suitors they could marry
They had no choice: they had to marry out
~~So from the first~~

---

* Written beneath the line.
† Written in left-hand margin.

So the experiment was vitiated
Daughters of men they had to take for wives.
So that the doctrine not to marry out
Now has become
I know one of those counsels of perfection
We observe by being sorry not to keep.
{Those are what sinners speak of as ideals}
Wait till you see the faith called Christian
That I predict will terminate the world.
{By selling the least poor soul on the impossible.}
By setting souls to [illegible] of the

[21r–27r]   [blank]

[27v]*   Another question is are they aware of me†
Off on a corner
Down from the country in there by myself‡
In the dark background with my ginger ale

[28r]§   Theres {An all} pervading unreality

In

You I can be wrong

They To hear their talking {babble} at the cocktail bar
They sounded as if they had the authority
To send send me {me} down to hell for being wrong.
One question is have they an authority
They or their ups in orthodoxy
Another question would be am I wrong
And how important is it if I am
Im glad that [illegible] I may be wrong in many ways
And yet not sent to jail

---

* This is the beginning of "The Cocktail Bar in 45th Street"
† These lines are in blue ink.
‡ There are a series of arrows in blue ink pointing to this line from the line on the next page, 28r, "Another question would be am I wrong".
§ Page is in black in ink except where noted.

And merely sent to Hell not sent to jail.

There are a lot of things I can be sent to jail for.

It's something that I can't be sent to jail.

For thinking falsely or believing falsely

For swearing falsely is another thing

[*29r*]*   The would be perjury and criminal

Suppose I was prepared to take my battle

With Epicurus[9] that there was no God

When it is common knowledge and belief

There is one maybe even more than one

Would that be punishable perjury?

I can rest reassured but I tell them

They'd better burn me for my heresies

Here where they have me in the flesh to burn

And {And} Not put off the burning till the next world {in Hell}

I've a soul and may like Helium

Prove The solar gas prove incombustible.

How do these after theater knowitalls[†]

Half lying face around on the cocktail bar

Their pretty bottoms

Their [illegible] pretty tails in bottoms overflowing

In abundance the high stools they sit in on.

Their bare arms

Bare arms flung forward frowardly [illegible]

And they have matches for their cigarettes

To set my clothes on fire if they want to[‡]

[*30r*][§]   To the Bartenders Joe {not Jove} for his opinion

As between old friends and coreligionists

Joe had by rote the a lot of rules to go by—

How did these {sinners} know if I was wrong

How could I tell myself? I wished I could.

They knew because they had just been to a play*

---

* Page is in black ink except where noted.

† This word is in blue ink.

‡ These two lines are written in blue ink in the left margin of the page, bottom to top.

§ Page is in black ink except where noted.

About it all the play it sin of or seemed to say

About it all, the formula of which

Was that to save your soul you had to sin

More deeply the more greatly to repent.

Sin fast one said and get it over with

So you wont get run over unrepentant.

{Must have been a Marxist}*

With any luck you could allow yourself

Till say for sin—with any luck.

There it was the same gamble here as at the races.

You had to take your chances in there to start

You had to chance it when to start repenting.

One said he knew someone who knew the author

I wasnt of the festive company

*They brought in Dante they had been to college
   Has even been to Europe most some of them†

[30v]   There was

An air of unreality pervaded all

[31r]   But [and] set off in a corner with a glass of ginger ale‡

In a dark corner thinking by myself

They wre not being personal condemnation

I might have been sorry if

Should I by speaking up attract attention§

Could she rent to hers by talk of theirs.

What did they know about Pelagius[10]

What did they know beyond the latest news

From theater land or motion picture land

If women gave us pleasure it was sure

But when they gave us happiness it wasnt

---

* This line is written in the left margin just beside the lines "Sin fast one said and get it over with / So you won't get run over unrepentant." It is blue ink, written bottom to top.

† Frost's note is in pencil, written in the top, right hand margin of the page and circled.

‡ The first four lines of this page are in black ink.

§ Line is in blue ink.

[*32r*] Original sin ~~was it they were on~~ {and the mystery of it}
Seemed to delight their minds with superstition {superstitiousness}
I wanted to say if I knew a sin
Original enough to get reported
In the ~~great~~ {big} papers I would go and do it
And still sat there ~~in~~ [illegible] deep in my dark corner
~~And~~ dared ~~not~~ With ~~my~~ perhaps my third glass {of ginger ale}*
Getting my courag[e] up with ginger ale
To trick into their [illegible] {fashionable} attention.
Suppose I spoke and they all looked at me
They would at once see I was from the country
~~And would be~~ shocked at my
And [he] shouted at me for an original
Might laugh and say Another country heard from.
I was not equal to it. ~~I was~~ shy with a crowd
But now came closing time or time perhaps
For some of them to catch the last train home
To Somerville [?servicedale] before the revolution
No not the last that night the last forever
    Latest but the very last

[*33r*] they straggled ~~forth~~ {out} into the dying traffic
{Talking of rotten but whatever it was}
The door revolving gulped them [they] were gone
And I would speak I had to speak to someone
~~And the barkeeper he~~
~~The barkeep~~ The
I took the barkeep you say confidences
~~[illegible] and [illegible] my chair back~~
~~I snapped my chair back~~
Since I began on him and scraped my chair back
It is not any thing ~~we so or do~~ a ~~person does~~ {a man commits}
~~Like giving birth to~~
~~Lik~~ Like fathering a child
    Legitimate or illegitimate
Tis not in giving birth but being born
It has in the first out cry for the alteration

---
* Written beneath the line.

That some one else might have and better have
It is our doom {in life} but to know now
To keep There is no way out for us to be selfish
That From that hour forth The Barkeep {said I guess}^
    If a mans sense talk the thought arises from

[34r]†   What has some one else is kept from having
        Think of the people who are kept from drink
        The ginger ale Ive had from you tonight.
        That is what is my [illegible] the Barkeep said I guess

[35r–37r]   [blank]

[37v]‡   Like the bald tops of [illegible] {the tops of priestly} heads of priests
        Who had been buried standing in their graves
        A fringe {of grass} around them like at tonsure
        Many a one had gone down at his hands
        And left no trace in a surveyors {his surveyors} sight.
        If you asked him in the larger view {through what he was doing}
        Or thought he was {in} putting stones underground
        When he himself would scarce be underground
        Before his field would all go back to woods.
        The genius of this region wasnt grass
        But trees and trees would soon with groping roots
        Getting the feel
        But trees and {trees} trees and no one else but trees
        Would Would be aware of what he'd put away
        Trees by their Trees {only} by roots feeling in the dark
        Would be aware of what he'd put away
        To her discredit for the waste of time.
        That would be some advantage

[38r]   [blank]

[38v]¹¹   So near it as to call but a touch
        (A crow bar touch perhaps) to tip it in.

---

* Written beneath the line.
† Page torn out.
‡ 37v, 38v, and 39v written in black ink.

There upon satisfaction in the homing thud
Of such a solid tons weight in conclusion
{And there should be to read or write about it}
But Thayer didn't want [illegible] aid ~~about it~~ out loud
Fanciful ~~small~~ {farm} talk made him but a fool
~~His notion was~~
~~A fairer {smoother} field was all {what} he had in mind.~~
~~If that were fanciful~~
~~If it was fanciful to have in mind~~
~~A {perfect} fairer field for [illegible] mowing than was needed~~
~~The he less said so~~
A perfect field as worth a mans ambition
The less ~~emotion~~ {exhaustion} over it the better
He was wearing ideals on his sleeve.
As far as he would go {to the sentiment} ~~was to concede~~
~~In the five acres~~
~~[Illegible] in the~~
~~[Ther] she was to concede in the five acre piece~~
There had been twenty boulders to the acre

[39r]   The old tried way our fathers liked to use
With boulders to sink them in their place
In situ as the educated say
~~Old Thayer was~~
Now if a city lawyer has a farm
He wants to make a show of he ~~calls in~~ invokes
~~Road machinery [illegible]~~
~~The road~~
Great megatherium like road machines
To push ~~their~~ {his} boulders off to one side down
The mountain out of sight among the bushes.
The glazier ~~was~~ strewed [illegible] {stone} eggs too lavishly
(~~It has been thought~~ by critics of creation)
Foundering they were but token eggs
Non meant to hatch, ~~any that hatched were~~ {their hatching ~~was~~ unheard of}
Old Thayer was the last to deal with them
In the old way of sinking them by hand.
The process was to dig a hole beside one
So deep as to be sure of burying it
~~Two feet~~ {A foot} below the ~~surface~~ furrow of the plow

"And it would satisfy something in him"

MS. 001673. *Brown paper cover spiral bound notebook, 5″ × 8″. "Coiled-bound/Note-book/No. C-190" stamped on cover. White ruled pages. All entries are written verti-cally across the lines of the page, bottom to top, in blue ink.*

[*cover*]   Pursuit of a Pursuit[1]

[*1r*]   ~~He~~ And it would satisfy a something in him
          Or so he thinks (a penny for his thoughts)
          If he could make a sunrise in the west
          As Scott got laughed at once making one.
          He would stand ready by his phaeton

[*2r*]   [blank]

[*3r*]   He stands by his peregrine machine
          And about wingless bird stripped to a bullet
          That no one knows but he what he can ask of

          T
          It was not the moon he wanted all the time
          The moon was far this side of what he wanted

          ~~We kno~~
          But The one thing sure we know he isn't
          He is no fugitive

          How has he qualified ~~himself to think~~ particular thought
          ~~In what school in what~~ in what school in

[*4v*]   The being in the Races' baby crib
          His uniform a diaper and bib
          With nothing on but dia

[5r]   [blank]

[5v]   The Being on the ram's baby cradle
         Wherever that was by whatever river   kicking and reaching
         Cried for the moon and got himself long laughed at.
         But he shall have the moon for what its worth.
         No hurry. He has all the time there is
         He likes to tell the friends impatient for him.
         He can afford to have been ~~laughed at~~ among the laughed at.
         ~~To reaching with on his back for hand are feet~~
         For what he cant have and besides not knowing {For with knowing what he
         couldn't have}
             Or would do with if he attained.
         ~~What to do with it if he ever attained got it.~~
         The moon is far this side of ~~it either design he craves~~ [illegible]
         So is the sun. They both are but his baubles
         Tonight he mounts his peregrine machine
         Beside his chosen Princess of adventure
         To show [illegible] how ~~to trifle with the sun~~. What he could do with the sun

"If his own intuitions were correct"

MS. 001674. *Brown paper cover spiral flip pad, 8½″ × 4¾″. "The Spiral No. 580-CD" is stamped on the cover in block letters. White ruled pages. All entries are written vertically across the ruled lines of the page, top to bottom, in blue ink unless otherwise noted.*

[1r] If his own intuitions were correct
~~He'd~~ His ~~quest of knowledge~~ way to face it would be introspect
He might be nothing but a curio[1]
~~Of~~ A curiosity but even so
He shouldn't be too upside down to know
~~Into the waste he came of he must go~~*
Who would it be but us he parroted
If in dry bitterness he spoke and said
Into the waste[2] I came I must go   It seemed to need
~~My~~ His body ~~may~~ must have just the lack of head
It ~~needed~~ ought to have for a prodigal romance   was Resqusite
~~For profligacy and extravagance~~
There could be worse genetics than to claim
He had a mighty Monarch for his sire
Nothing less generous or more untame
How otherwise account for desire

[1v] And so it must be ~~rusty~~ honest pachyderm
If I may like ~~him~~ you with another term
If we look outward into the universe
There we see nothing but ~~expense~~ expense
~~That was a~~
He

---

* Arrow to line "Into the waste . . ." below.

[2r] His ~~body though of~~ harsh unlikely pith
        Nevertheless seems big and bursting with[3]
        To spend in all directions all at once
        He ~~had been~~ kept must have kept to vegetate a dunce   slayed
        Not to have guessed what ailed him was a mood
        Of profligacy of extravagance
        Suppose untimely with forced fingers rude[4]
        He were divested of his outer wrap
        In idleness or in the quest or in the quest of fruit
        So far from being stripped to flesh and sap
        It would be found in still another suit
        Of tiny sequins set to over lap
        As tight yet supple as a coat of mail.
        But there are seed and all he is is seed
        (What for that matter we are indeed)
        And seed—enough ~~of seed~~ to sow a given region Sufficient seed

[3r] And make sure whatever else should fail
        Meadow and pasture should not lack for weed.
        Count them if but for the statistics sake
        Or let it go at calling them a legion.
        The more the rally thing the worm the tale
        Alas what boots it though what does it boot
        That every seedy sequin scale or flake   It makes ~~the further~~ it all the
        more   more
        Has packed with it a silken parachute   beyond dispute
        With a capacity ~~of~~ for sustained drift
        And even at hints of inspired lift
        To carry it off on light and airy sail
        ~~And~~ On not ~~a~~ too strong and hurry up a gail
        For choice of landing with a chance to root.
        In vain in vein ~~No Tall~~ it will be a lucky germ
        Of all embodied in ~~anothe little~~ our pachyderm
        (To like him with another honest term)

[4r] More than gets back into the absolute.
        Lucky to get back there beyond dispute
        ~~Where~~ The Bramin tell us

[4v]   And so it must be honest pachyderm
If I may like you with another term
You're not so upside down you need be told
Not.

[5r]   He may be nothing but a curio
Of curiosity ~~but even so~~ this pachyderm
If I may like him with an honest term
But if his intuitions are correct
He's not so upside down ~~as not to know~~ upon his perch ~~His perch~~

[5v]   If any great reality of hold
Can be I on so deciduous a perch
He surely has no need of being told—and if his intuitions are correct
It has been settled for him from of old
The great inquiry must be introspect.
He has but to turn inward his research
Instead of outward into the universe
To find ~~out~~ theres nothing but expense—expense
Who would it be but us he parroted
If not unquizzically he spoke and said
This body of his has just the lack of head
That it needed for a prodigal romance.
But ~~If His it intuitions are wont be correct~~ He may be nothing but a curio
Of curiosity but even so
The chances are he knows enough to know
In the waste he came of he must go

[6r]   He may be nothing but a curio
Of curiosity poor pachyderm
(If he'll accept anothers I may praise him with the honest term
But I ~~suspect~~ we'll he knows enough to know
If his own intuitions are correct
And ~~if~~ theres ~~is~~ reality in the that hold
So upside down he has upon his perch:
Into the waste he came of he must go
Not off into the infinite universe
Must he pursue his optical research
~~Not off in~~ To find out there is nothing but expense
It has been settled for him from of old

The great inquiry should be introspect.
Who would it be but us he parroted
~~If he looked in~~ If not unquizically he he spoke and said
~~If with self If out of self~~

[6v]   ~~There could be worse genetics than to claim~~
There could be worse genetics than to claim
He had a mighty Monarch for his sire
Nothing less generous or less untame
How otherwise account for the desire
~~That~~ His stolid body of unlikely pith
Apparently is big and bursting with
To waste in all directions all at once
He feels it singing in him like a quire
~~H [illegible]~~

[7r]   His body ~~had must~~ may have just the lack of head
It needed for a prodigall romance
~~His genius~~ All he embodied was extravagance
Suppose
Hasn't ~~his~~ my body just the lack of head
It needed for a prodigal romance

[8r]   No wit so poor as not to
No one so poor in with as mot to jest
No so witless in his great chagrin
~~At having~~
Over the lunar round we didn't win
As not
No one so
As in the lunar ~~round~~ race we didn't win
We cant be blamed for any joke or quip
We find to cover our profound chagrin
In being worsted ~~in the~~ for ~~a~~ one comicstrip.

[9r]*   The only real freedom is in departure[5]—before the crowd can catch up with
you with the new ruler

•   •   •

---

* Entries from 9r to the end of the notebook written horizontally along the ruled lines of
the pages.

Where poetry is posted—on the brink of spiritual disaster[6]

Warp warp

No matter how straight forth ~~you think to go~~ may have gone
The reasoning is in a circle man[7]
And that's because the minds a cyclotron
And ~~the~~ brain ~~as is~~ goes [illegible] circling the brain pan
Because of the round shape of the brain pan
Your brain pans round like Pans own

You reason always in a circle [?reason]
Your mind moves always like a cyclotron
Because of the round shape of the brain pan

The circle of the idea or the ideal is a true
Circle and has only one center: Good
The circle of a ~~body~~ moving body in practice
is an oval[6] and has two centers Good and Evil
The Sun is where good is. The 2nd one
we never see. Sinister took word for it

[10r]   No matter how straight forth you think you've gone
You've always thought as in a cyclotron
You ~~'ve always~~ reasoned in a circle man
Because of the round shape of the brain pan

The straight lines [illegible] around has always
So that we end by saying space is curved
And every little while we get profound
~~And say the universe~~
And the universe is round

It may be one lobe of the brain is stronger
~~And just exactly~~
~~And just as~~ I often think when on leg is often longer
The {length of [illegible] the work is}
The c   imagine
Has a
The ~~tendency~~ pull of the [illegible] way the

Tends ~~to~~ to pull them around with us
[illegible] ~~Pull~~ To.
So that the way the unmatched couple [illegible]
Tend to insure their money in a circle

[*11r*] ~~We~~ employ soldiers to obtain in peace
And then to keep it we employ police
Soldiers in war time try to get us peace
In peace time we depend on the police
Soldiers dont care what time ~~they had to~~ of day they fight
Policemen are most active in the night

If you dont ~~the~~ form the habit of making point and phrase in talk and prose as you live and write ~~to~~ (letters for instance how can you expect them to oc-cur to you in the emergency of ~~your~~ poems. They should become any mod-est pride you have in your mind. They ~~must~~ are the ~~the~~ high water marks on your wall of memory you have a right to preserve.

  Regret is the most ~~when~~ important when it is that you werent ready enough with your answer in a situation. It {Regret}Regrets deep enough and hard enough ~~that~~ will ~~improve your~~ quicken your wit. Whatever else regrets may do for you.

[*12r*] Aries Taurus
Gemini Cancer
Arise in chorus
Whats the answer

Tell oh tell us
If it be a
Blend of Hellas
And Judea

Who and what'll
Solve the poser
Aristotle
Or Spinoza

[*13r–17r*] [blank]

"There is a shadow always on success"

MS. 001728. *Brown paper cover spiral flip pad, 4⅞″ × 7⅞″. White ruled pages. "The Spiral No. 580-CE" is stamped on the cover in black letters. All entries are in blue ink.*

[1r]* There is a ~~sense~~ shadow {always} on success
Often mistaken for a sense of sin.
Left to ~~themselves~~ {himself} for any length of time
The best ~~of us~~ {man} will become aware of it.
~~And~~ Not just old age at the [illegible] effort end
In being laughed at for ~~knowing~~ having known
What use to make of ~~wealth or fame when won.~~
                              Money when achieved
Money or fame ~~whe~~ or any such reward

[2r] The many things the Bible doesn't mean
Are often plainer than the few it does.
For instance when it calls him man the first
It doesn't mean he was the first and only.
Others are spoken of

[3r] The many things the Bible doesn't mean
Are often plainer than the few it does.
In setting Adam up as Man the First
It doesn't mean he was the first and only
Others are spoken of as having daughters
His sons could nearly.[1] All he represents
Is a fresh start God had to start with someone.
~~God was a great starter~~ one of his {Gods} three ~~great~~ fresh stars
~~We have recorded.~~
The very Bible is a record of.

---

* 1r–4r written vertically up the page, bottom to top.

Adam comes first. His human predecessors
Must have been formed unsatisfactory
Must have some wrong in some respect not given.
At any rate here we have God apparently
Entering on his first experiment
~~On this earth in eugenics~~
~~In Eugenics In the eugenic or race purity~~

[*4r*]   To make the experiment a clean one
He took precautions to create the kind
Of man he wanted and then breed him from himself
~~His wife~~ The man and wife were literally one flesh
Not merely figuratively as became the history
Perhaps that was the blunder anyway
Something went wrong again

[*5r*]   Poetry

Poetry is prowess[2]
Poetry is the renewal of words[3]
Poetry is the dawning of an idea
Poetry is that which tends to evaporate from both prose and verse when
translated.
Poetry is the Liberal Arts. The Liberal Arts are Poetry.   A poem is a mo-
mentary stay against confusion[4]
Rhymes and meter are an excess ~~of needing~~ [illegible phrase]
Words and syntax interpose resistance enough you would think. Rhyme and
meter are taken on extra to show—
Rhymes are less limited than is apparent. They are merely the last syllable on
the various phrases just as ly and ation are on the ends of many words. Many
more phrases than you would think have any off hand chosen word for an
ending.
    Difference between smoke and smoke rings.
Pure poetry pure science pure valor are for glory rather than use. Use is incidental. Pure eagerness pure love for their own sake

    They none of know and but you. You swell up and call them all books. Till
on a day

[5v]   It amuses you that you should have been so sure they weren't thinking of you as a book. You mature to humor in philosophy. Jokers don't understand humor.

[6r]   Here and there in the gone backward side of town where it basks on the railroad there still stand among new make shift storage sheds and small businesses houses {dwelling} of some pretense in their day brick with stone lintels and corniers. They are still dwelt in dingily People go home to them and light lights in them and keep them burning away into the night where the rest of the shabby neighborhood is deserted and dark except for the small street lights far apart. I know someone who lives in one of them. And he has his reasons quaint and original, that save him from having to be quaint and original or careful of anything else in any other way. And he hath neither child nor wife. I go there to set up with him till daylight doth appear. He is particularly romantic or philosophical about a long abandoned nearly ruined factory with all its window broken by delinquent boys but still with

[6v]   name on it of the small business it was once in. The immanent manifest Nature of a tool I have looked for in vain recently in hardware stores—a gimlet. (as in gimlet eyes. The store keeper laughed at it as a literary word) My friend says resignedly to the ways of the world. Nothing keeps a window pane from being stared out but a living face behind it. He says he likes to show his face behind when his when the gangs come raiding by. The big trains freight and passenger ~~go roaring past~~ shake the well built house as they go roaring past behind us. They shake our argument and beliefs to. We cant ignore them and the question of where they think it worth going to; Detroit; Chicago San Francisco Los Angeles, St. Louis or merely New York or Washington. He likes the darn things as a symbol of transition. But they come as much as they go I protest. But the people in them must go more come less

[7r]   than they go or Florida and California those two extremities wouldn't be growing faster than any sate in the union. We are turning our backs on Europe he likes to claim. Struck is his social and economic fancy. But one fancy in those realms is as pretty as another. He quoted me a poem of his own once that I remember part of

Europe might sink and the wave of its sinking sweep
And spend itself on our shores and we would not weep
Our cities could not even turn in their sleep

·   ·   ·

Our faces are not that way or should not be
Our future is another west on the other sea

No need of going into that too far. He gets up a [illegible] to take care of a whole set of problems he gets up as to our intercourse with the borders on the Pacific in a pacific world, us and Canada and Mexico and Chili and Peru and New Zealand

[7v] And Australia and the Phillipines and yes and some Asia. He stops where he gets into trouble then or I stop him and say good night. I don't meet a soul as I take my way. A train passes raising a cloud of dust and cinders that reach me but only as a token.

[8r] His poems don't sit very well
If I may be permitted the structure
And he looked like a cherub from Hell
If I'm any judge of a picture

[9r] Poet is a master of sentiment

Introduction: How would it be to put it this way? Then a poem Then a significant silence as much to say do you get it?

Grace without works. Justification without sanctification. Sidney had the saint quest. Could you be so sure of anybody's grace, could you be sure of your own. The church has ventured to canonize those it was sure had grace. Self search apt to go crazy. There is absolutely no outward sign. I ask you have you grace. You may answer Yes or no and I neednt believe you in either case. Maybe a power to perform miracles proves something. Lets be sensible like Episcopal conclusion is and not canonize any one. I think I can now and then catch something in a word that could only be from the soul of grace in religion or poetry

[18v] To the traveler going sidereal
One danger they say is bacterial
I don't know the pattern
On Mars or on Saturn
But on Venus must be venereal

• • •

A Poem about the Lemming

And so without hawing or hemming
This poem's concerning the lemming
It is not much to quote
But its something I wrote
To say what I owe Mr. Fleming

At least it's a sort of feeler
To find how he feels as a dealer
About not paying debts
I got into hi bets
I hope he don't think I'm a squealer

"If we are too much given to reflect"

MS. 001894. *Brown paper cover spiral bound flip pad, 7¾″ × 5″. "The Spiral No. 580-CD" is stamped on the cover in black letters. White ruled pages. All entries are in blue ink. First two pages are torn out and inserted into the front of the book.*

torn page,   If we are too much given to reflect
recto]   Or doubt best excess for the defect
           Is that our world has not light of its own
           And shines but by reflected light alone

           He wore out the virtue of coffee
           He wore out the virtue of tea
           He wore out the virtue of whiskey
           He wore out the virtue of me

           When nothing was left to {excite} ~~inspire~~ him

           ~~The latest news is that~~
           ~~Why speak like that it simply isn't true~~
           ~~To say the earth's ray of radiance is through~~

           That's libelous it simply isn't true
           To say earths day of radiance through[1]
           It gives off

torn page,   It is right in there
recto][2]   Betwixt and between
           The orchard bare
           And the orchard green

                 •   •   •

That we fear the worst
When

And that may be a [illegible] proven
So no one came out of here [illegible]
So one will attempt by a decision
So that no right creeping to derision
Will hope to will say [illegible] to yet his outer space
Further than back into his starting place

No matter how straight forth you think you have come
You reasoned in a circle as a man[3]
You always land back where you started from
Because the round shape of your brain pan

The reason why think your getting on
Is that your circling a makes a circling span
The brain pan {still} is the the same old cyclotron
Your brain pan still the same old pan of Pan

[1r–2r]   [blank]

[2v]   God long worked up prepared mud
Into
God took his time to work up the mud
Through ages of animal flesh and blood

Before he
God we the dust to [illegible] mud
Then worked that up into flesh and blood

We weren't made directly out of mud
But out of animal flesh and blood

A mud prepared for

We weren't made directly out of mud
It was But mud {first} prepared as flesh and blood[4]

·   ·   ·

Through years of animal life on earth
Reforc—were given trial birth

To see if we couldn't reciprocate

[*3r*]⁵   When the significance is lost
From ~~symbols getting double~~ crossed
From dictionaries getting crossed

The best thing may be to return
~~To where we started and try~~
To the analogy of eyes.
I mean back where it all began
In infancy as back to man
When after trying every place
In our ~~comparison of~~ {ideal of} creation
One face first found the other face
And even discriminating features
Eyes first found eyes across the abyss
And ~~lashing~~ [illegible] {gave a look of} signal light
As [illegible] {good as} say sight in sigh
Tis understood so far so good"
~~We wondered at~~
I t was far thrown from home to go
In peals of lightening like them
[illegible line]
As if to say help we know
We didn't have to learn to read
To find out that our taking heed

[*3v*]   We didn't have to learn to read
To find out that our paying heed
No heliotropic toward the sun
But toward the universal middle
Right ~~where everything is done~~
Right where all is said and done

[*4r*]   Not heliotropic to the sun
Was {toward} the universal middle
Right where ~~everything~~ {all is said} and done

Lets keep together somehow
And not become each others riddle
Communication some would say
But no tis not what we convey

[5r] When all significance gets crossed
From language getting double crossed
~~When our vocabularies get crossed~~
~~So all signs forever lost~~
The best way might be to revise
To the analogy of eyes
I mean back where it all began
In infancy babe to man
When after trying every place
One face first faced another face
And gave a look of signal light
As if to say yes sight is sight
Tis understood so far so good.

[6r] When axes lost their heads
By flying off their helves[6]
And killing [illegible phrase]
They ran and hid themselves

When axes lost their heads
By flying off their helves
And killing people dead
We went and hid ourselves

[7r] ~~That by the milk herd~~
~~That was our foster nurse~~
And by the milk herd
That was our foster nurse

[8r]   The Couplet

The bees [~~illegible~~] {are only} gobetweens
And as from flower to flower ~~we~~ {they} go

Remember me to so and so
With pollen dust the ~~flowers~~ means.[7]

My rhyme is but the figure of
The far with and near the old and new
By saying "May be likened to"
My couplet couples as in love

[9r]   The bees are only go betweens
And as from flower to flower they go
Remember me to sound so
(With pollen dust) the flower means

"I wont be talked to by a woman, tell her"

MS. 001880. *Black and gray cardboard bound notebook, 6⅜″ × 9⅜″. Unruled white paper. "Robert Frost" stamped in red letters on the bottom half of the cover. Entries are in blue ink unless otherwise noted.*

[1r]   [blank]

[2r]   I wont be talked to by a woman, tell her[1]

Oh yes you will. You will let me deal with him
You go and get him something in the [illegible]
I know the case. I know where he belongs
Where he can be protected from himself
He runs away from second childishness
You're {Enoch} [illegible] Hill the Gold for Christmas man
And {you and I are fated} [illegible] ~~going~~ to be friends

Who said we were

[3r–6r]   [blank]

[7r]   I asked him
More to embarrass him than anything
Because there was a lady ~~with me~~ in the car
~~I asked him who tipped better men or women.~~
I asked the taxi driver who tipped better
Women or men. ~~How~~ He answered ~~boldly~~ Men {of course}
And you see why. Men are the source o fmoney,
Money belongs to men to make and spend
The more the men they are ~~It's in their nature~~
    ~~They need to show~~

•   •   •

~~They need~~
~~To show~~
~~The making means more than the spending it~~
They chiefly value ~~the more their glory~~
~~In making it~~
Once more they proved themselves in making money
~~They don't care what~~
Theres nothing like more than spending it
On those they ~~may~~ have outdone in making it.
They don't care where it goes to charity
~~Or education~~
Or tax use, to schools or hospitals.
They ~~cash in their~~ greatness either way.
    get their greatness out either way
Thus spake the taxi driver of Manhattan.
~~And so in my pursuit lifelong~~
~~And so in my pursuit lifelong pursuit~~
~~And so in my pursuit of the statistics~~
And so in my pursuit of the statistics
Of lifelong ~~for~~ like a income tax collector
I asked him which tipped better drunk or sober
Sometimes a drunk will give you all he has

[8r]   Sometimes a drunk has nothing ~~left to~~ give.
But you and I are {really} ~~wholly~~ {always*} money minded
~~The very day I asked I turned a man out of this car~~
This very day I turned a ~~man~~ passenger
Out of this car for his profanity.
~~I heard him take the name of God in vain~~
~~Three times behind and three times~~
He took the name of God in vain three times
~~Out of this car without his fare~~
~~This very day I threw away a fare~~
~~Not to~~
I threw away a tip and even fare
~~This very morning~~
~~When I got out~~

———————————
* Word written below the line.

[9r]   More to embarrass him than anything
Because there was a lady in the car
I asked the taxi driver of Manhattan
Which of us tip the better men or women
The Men {do} of course. They are the source of money
Money belongs to men. ~~The more the men they are~~
                To spend on women
You don't find women spending it on men.
You'll say for me the more the men they are
The more their interest is in making money
Once made they don't care what they do with it
~~Give it back to~~
Lavish it or squander it ~~on hospitals luxury~~
~~Or colleges or women as I say~~
~~Or charity or schools and hospitals~~
Maybe the {their} height ~~of their satisfaction is~~
To give it back to those they've made it out
In colleges museums hospitals
But some get greatness ~~out of secret~~ {private} gifts
They get no credit for to tramps and beggars
~~And~~
Or to the next grade higher in the scale
The tipable
But some {feel} get all the greatness they require
In private gifts they get no credit for
To tramps and beggars ~~in the~~ out [illegible]
Or to the next grade higher in the scale
The tippable like all the taxi drivers
The porters waiters.   chamber maids

[10r]   ~~The important thing do not~~ to know how much
~~To let to~~
~~The important thing~~
~~One thing to know how much to tip~~
Its something to know who you can or cant tip.
They say you cant tip no one in the country.
Thus spake the Taxi driver of Manhattan
And so to keep from getting out of depth
~~In social question~~

                   •   •   •

I asked him who tips better drunk or sober

Sometimes the drunks will give all they have
Sometimes they haven't anything ~~they have~~ {to give}
Once after having had his ride confess
He hadn't even a cent to pay his fare
You would have liked the

[11r] ~~Because I hoped I would embarrass him~~
To
Hoping the question
Because we had a lady in the car
To make the question an embarassment
I asked the Taxi Driver ~~of Manhattan~~ which ~~of Manhattan~~ tip better
Which of us tipped the better men or women
He said ~~the~~ men. Men are the source of money
~~Money belongs to men~~
~~They look on it as made for them to make~~

I asked the Taxi Driver which the better
Women or men. ~~He~~ You men of course he said

~~Men are the source of money. It makes~~
Men are not interested in keeping money
It ministers to the creative in them
~~Once they have made it they don't care how much~~
~~To be the makers of it~~
~~To feel that the everything~~
~~To feel that~~
To have the feeling ~~they make everything~~ {all the made their}
~~Without them nothing; made what in you get the point~~
Nothing that's made is made except by them
~~Once~~
~~Money~~

[12r] Because we had a lady in the car
To make the question an embarrassment
I asked the Taxi Driver which tipped better
Women or men. He answered men of course

[13r]²

The Birches 1	~~Birches~~
The Hill Wife 2	
" Bon Fire 3	Old Man Winter
	~~The Bonfire~~
Out Out 1	
New Hampshire 14	~~In the Homo Stretch~~
" The Census Taker 2	
" Star Splitter 2	~~Maple~~
Maple 4	Fountain a Bottle 6
" Ax helve 4	
Paul's Wife 4	~~The Census Taker~~
Wild Grapes 4	
" Witch of Coos 7	
" Pauper Witch of Grafton 2	~~The Roadside Stand~~
Two Look at Two 2	
" Lovely Shall Be Choosers 2	~~A Blue Ribbon 3~~
West Running Brook 3	
Two Tramps in Mud Time 3	
" White Tailed Hornet 3	
" Gold Hesperidee	
" Roadside Stand 2	
Build Soil 10	
" Literate Farmer	
Directive 2	
From Plane to Plane 4	
Old Man Winters Night 1	
In the Home Stretch	
Snow 15	

[14r]   A thousand years ago in Rome
And I was in a catacomb
~~Upon a rosmary shelf~~
Stretched out upon a strong shelf
I had entirely to myself
I lay apparently becalmed
From having died and been embalmed
With toes upturned arms composed
And you would never have supposed

What I lay there a thinking of
Of many things but mostly love
Venus with who wrote Anchises lay
So far from having had her day
Her reigning was just begun
She was is the one and only one
The element of elements
That all the universe creates
That when the elements were brutes
Was observing was
From having been so obvious
The atoms are a hundred plus
She no [illegible]
Of needing less or more of them
She is the came the
She is a [illegible] so refined
That gives what little extra weight
That [illegible]
To
You must lose you
Loves the cause not the effect

[15r]

Birches 2	The Star Splitter
~~From Plane to Plane~~	
Two Look at Two	A Fountain a Bottle
West Running Brook 3	The Literate Farmer
Paul's Wife 5	The Ax Helve
Witch of Coos 7	
Pauper Witch of	An Old Man 1
Grafton 7	
Wild Grapes 4	~~Two Tramps in Mud~~
Maple 4	The Star Splitter 3
Lovely Shall Be	The Ax Helve 4
Choosers 2	
Two Tramps 3	Blue Ribbon 3
Snow 15	Out Out 1
Masque of Reason 20	From Plane to Plane 4
70 50	Build Soil 10

Directive
The Census Taker
The Bonfire 3
Gold Hesperidee 2

New Hampshire 14
Brown's Descent 2
Directive 2
Vanishing Red 2
70
20

[16r]

Into My Own
My November Guest
Mowing
Tuft of Flowers
October
Reluctance

Mending Wall

The Death of the Hired
Man
Home Burial
After Apple Picking

The Wood Pile
F

The Road Not Taken
An Old Man's Winters
Night
Hyla Brook
Bond and Free

Spring Pools
Peck of Gold
Once by the Pacific
Bereft
Tree at My Window
A Winter Eden
The Flood
Acquainted with the
Night
The Lovely Shall Be
Choosers
West Running Brook

Sand Dunes
A Soldier
The Investment
The Birthplace
Sitting By a Bush in
Broad
On Looking by Chance

The Lone Striker

Two Tramps
The White Tailed
Hornet

Birches
Two Witches
I Will Sing You One O
Fire and Ice
In a Disused Graveyard
Dust of Snow
~~To~~ The Runaway
Stopping by Woods
The Onset
To Earthward
Looking for a Sunset
Bird
Misgiving
On a Tree Fallen By the
Road
The Need of Being
Versed
~~Spring Pools~~

Drumlin Woodchuck
In Time of Cloudburst
Departmental

Lost in Heaven
Desert Places
A Leaf Treader
Neither Out Far
Design
Not Quite Social

[16v]

The Silken Tent
All Revelation

Come In
I Could Give All to Time

Carpe Diem
The Most of It
Never Again Would Birds
Song
The Subverted Flower
The Gift Outright
Triple Bronze
A Considerable Speck
The Lost Follower
November

November

A Pod of the Milkweed
Away
A Cabin in the Clearing
A One More Brevity
Escapist—Never
The Gift Outright

Accidentally on Purpose
Accidentally on Purpose
Forgive O Lord
Parts of Kitty Hawk
Auspex
The Draft Horse
Ends
Peril of Hope
Questioning Faces

A Young Birch   Lines Written in Dejection
Something for Hope   In Winter in the Woods
~~November~~
One Step Backward
November
To an Ancient
The Night Light
Bravado
On Making Certain
The Courage to Be New
Iota Subscript
The Middleness of the
Road
Take Something Like a
Star
Closed for Good

[17r]   East and West and North South and North
         We unite to praise the Fourth
         And the greatest of the great
         Whose decision fixed the date
         First of all comes Washington to is
         Who when all is said and done
         Well might be the only one

[18r]   [An address not in Frost's hand]

[19r]–[23r]   [blank]

[23v]*   Something there is that doesn't love a wall
         Something there is that does and after all
         Oh guileless children house and pastures
         [illegible] Cant you bet taught [illegible phrase] {that since the world began}
         All life upon it has been [illegible] celular³
         [illegible]
         [illegible]
         Inside and outside cells are are all we are

---

* 23v–39v written upside-down horizontally across the page, right to left.

[24v]   Oh California my native state
          I never have esteemed you less than great
          But is your certain greatness so immense
          That any pleasantry at your expense
          Is treated as a capital offense
          You must forgive me
          In venting with the monarchs of late
          To show them I had heard of them before
          [illegible] them as bit of childhood lore
          They still were [illegible] as

[25v]   There {is} no question you will rule the elm
          You will restore the orchard save the elm
          You'll poison every bug you ought to poison
          And get control of agriculture's foison
          That has been giving us the great alarm

[26v]* Whether [illegible] to see a scientific sky[4]
          Or wait and got to Heaven when they die
          In other words to wager their reliance
          On {plain} religion or religious science

          They hope to crash the puzzle of their God
          As Alexander crashed the Gordian knot
          [~~illegible phrase~~]
          Or as we crashed the barrier of sound
          To best the very world's speed going round

          Yet what charming earnest world it is
          So modest we can hardly hear it whiz
          Spinning as well as running on course
          It seems to bad to steer it of by force

[27v]   With what unbroken spirit naïve Science
          Keeps hurling our Promethean defiance
          From our atomic ball of rotting rock
          At the divine Safe's combination lock

                •   •   •

---

* 26v–48r written in blue ink.

In our defiance we are still defied
But have not I as prophet prophesied
That {sick} of circling round and round the sun
We will resolve that some shall be done

Now that we've found the secret out of weight
So we cancel it it however great
And what await lofty engineers
~~And~~ If we cant take the planet by the ears

Or by the poles or simply by the scruff
And saying simply we have had enough
Of numbers and monotony on earth
Where nothing's going but death and birth

And mans of such limited longevity
And our in the confidence of new found levity
(Our gravity has been our major curse
We'll cast off hawser for the universe

Taking along the whole race for a ride
Have not I prophesied and prophesied
All voting viva voce where to go
The noisier because they hardly know

[28v]   [blank]

[29v]   Whether to seek a scientific sky
Or seek to go heaven when they die
[~~illegible line~~]
And crack the puzzle of our human lot
As Alexander did the Gordian Knot
[illegible line]
Or as we crashed the barrier of sound[5]

They hope

[30v]   Why wait to go to heaven when we die
When we can have seen lie sky
The moon and Mars in fact the heavens

Now that we have found the secret out of weight
So we can cancel it however great

[31v]   ~~To g~~

And head this old thing staying {space ward} far and wide
Take the race with for a ride
Forgetful the of the limited longevity
~~But glorying in their new~~
But filled with glory in their new found levity
All viva voce voting to go
~~The choice is all Lets go~~

Whether to go to Heaven when we die
To stay alive and and have the sky
Or wait and go to heaven when they die

All
All voting viva voce where to go
The noisier because they do not know
Whether to seek the scientific sky
Or wait and go to heaven when they

A [illegible phrase] ~~mean to solve the lock~~

But they say

Whether to seek along the present sky
Or wait and go to heaven when they die
~~They~~ The combination puzzle of then
    They mean to en crash it with a Gordian
    Or as they crash the barrier of sound
    To [illegible] than the world [illegible] round

[32r]   [four illegible lines]

[32v]   With which unbroken spirit modern science
      Keep hurling our Promethean defiance

From this atomic ball of rotting rock
At the Divine Safe's combination lock

In our defiance {we are still} [illegible] defiant
But have not I as prophet prophesied
That ~~now~~ that we have found the cause of weight
So we can cancel it however great

~~We will cast off our hawser to the sun~~
Something
It will not be something we will be done
~~We cast off ou~~
We will cast off our hawser to the sun
Ah what avail our countless engineers
If we ever our planet by the ears

All that is altered something [illegible]
Tired of forever circling round the sun
~~And having resolved are~~
Having {solved} resolved the mystery of weight
So we can cancel it however great
A what avail our wonderful engineers
If we cant take their planet by the ears
Or by the poles or simply by the scruff
And saying firmly we've had enough

Cast off our hawser boldly to the past
[illegible] Or any prejudice we have to cast
And set forth

[33v]   With one unbroken spirit modern science
Keeps pushing our Promethean defiance
From this atomic ball of rotting rock
At the divine Safe's combination lock.

Why want to go to Heaven when we die
When we can stay alive and have the sky
By grace of having found the cause of weight

So we {can} cancel it [illegible] however great

The fate of
[illegible phrase]
Thus far has our defiance been defied
But have I not as prophet prophecied
Now that we've almost found the cause of weight
So we can cancel it however great

The everything is to {levitate} [illegible] the earth
Where nothing goes on but death and birth
And [illegible] [illegible] about longevity
Let take advantage of our stolen levity
And
The [illegible] thing we will [illegible] steer the earth
with nothing going on but death and birth
[illegible line]

[34r]   In our defense we are still defied
But have not I as prophet prophesied
Even of forever circling round the sun
We will rise or that something shall be done

Now that we have found the secret out of weight
So we can cancel it however great
Ah what avail our {mighty} [illegible] engineers
If we cant take this planet by the ears

Or by the poles or simply by the scruff
And impatient of this
And

[34v]   Why wait to got to heaven when we die
When we can stay alive and have the sky
And get away from this eternal row
And have all this
[illegible line]
[illegible line]

[35v]   With what unbroken spirit modern Science
          Keeps hurling our Promethean defiance
          From out atomic ball of rotting rock
          At the divine Safe's combination lock.

          How long has our defiance been defied.
          But as I prophet I have {have not I as prophet} prophesied
          That when we've severed the force that causes weight
          And can never again, however great
          [illegible]
          [illegible]
          We'll seize by poles as by the ears
          By grace of [illegible]
          And steer the [illegible]
          With its whole [illegible] of many colored ray
          All viva voce voting where to go
          Which will depend what they want to know
          [illegible]
          Whether to stay and reach the sky
          Is the same thing as heaven when they die
          Whether to stay alive and have the sky
          Or wait and go to heaven when they di

[36v]   There was
          Once a great queen refused to be amused
          But Juppiter is verily enthused
          To take this [illegible]
          As in his worship [illegible] has [?regulats]
          To send the vultures to attack the mortals
          [illegible phrase] by all the strain of [illegible]
          To watch the children at their [?scene]
          Even to the utmost point of good defiance
          He takes it as praise {of him} [illegible] his [?regulats]
          To send the vultures to attack their vitals
          And if it were the
          And if the vitals weren't the [illegible phrase]
          The [illegible] might make for modern art

[37v]   What has mans mastery of of his teachers tool
        What it has done for him is still a mystery
        And what it may do more is even moreso
        ~~He problem's still [?out] be a fool~~
        He is the same Old figure [?hunched] torso
        He finds it still as hard to live by to live by rules

[38v]   I had been taught to call a spade a spade
        But ~~recently~~ {lately} I began to be afraid
        In my upbringing I had been betrayed
        At home have learned to call a spade a heart
        ~~[illegible line]~~
        ~~[illegible]~~
        ~~[illegible]~~
        Not just because its now considered smart
        To call ~~thing~~ {words} what they weren't in modern art
        But bitterness and agony apart
        Because of what they both were symbols of
        No more on earth than on the moon above
        When Noahs rocket {that} released a door
        The heart depends on love but when the love
        Is too heart sick for medicine to save
        The shovels always there to dig the grave
        You bet [illegible phrase]

[39v]   Whatever else we have to say of Science
        It is a [illegible] Promethean defiance
        If any Unknown God to stay unknown
        Unknowable on her Olympic thrown
        Man's Agnostic [illegible phrase]
        To [~~illegible~~] find out of from want of room men suffer
        Their premium may very

        What ever else we have to say of science
        [illegible] Has Prometheus [~~illegible~~] a defiance
        From this little ball of rotting rock
        Life's safe with a secret lock
        At the whole universe's secret lock
        I wonder if

Prometheus called down lighting from the skies
To set the waves on fire when they were dry
The Universe called down [illegible]
We [illegible] know by whose
If anyone in the firmament

[40r]   Birches 2
From Plane to Plane 4
And Old Man's Winter Night 1
The Bonfire 4
The Star Splitter 4
Two Witches 8
Pauls Wife {5} Two Look at Two 2
New Hampshire 10
Blue Ribbon at Amesbury 2
The Literate Farmer 4
                    -Brown's Descent 3
Wild Grapes 4
Maple 4
The Hill Wife 3
Snow 8
Build Soil 10

[41v]*   He asked what she was thinking of
She should answered simply love
But said the self [illegible] as you
[illegible line]

[42v]   He didnt have to pop the question
Or have to make the least suggestion
Believing nothing then had been said
But here they were undressed in bed
Intent on mutual distraction
They needed no set [more] introduction
Than this
Except his strangeness into [? her]

                    •   •   •

_____
* 41v–45r written vertically up the page, bottom to top.

One a physical suggestion
There's been nothing done or said

He asks what she was thinking of
She didnt answer simply Love
But [illegible] by the same thing as you
He said you simply by [illegible]
But simply the same thing as you
But may be the same thing as you

[43v]   He turned the letter over in his hand
And got all out of he could unopened
The way some do even when its theirs to open
(It wasn't his to open it was hers
And then instead of placing it for her
And then instead of pulling it for her
At her place at the table he stood with it
Waiting to give it to her when she came.

[44v]   i

He stood there watching with it in his hand
To give her when she entered. Yes she said
And put in by as if it didn't matter
Then they sat down

               Then put it by in some fold of her dress
               As if it didn't matter at all to her
               Or much to her
Then both of them sat down opposed for breakfast
In a long tacit give and take of thought

He read the letter all from the outside
And then instead of [illegible] it for her
He stood there [illegible] with it in his hand
To [illegible] her when she entered yes she said.
And put in y in some fold of her dress
As if didn't matter much to her
Or matter at all to him. And {let it} [illegible] wait.
And then they their seats apposed for breakfast.

[45r]   Whats mine is yours but whats yours is not mine

But what if I don't want him in my life

He read the letter all over from [illegible]

[46r]   But there it is miraculous to tell
It is a sort of fiendish Land of Nod
~~When not from water on the brain or~~ weight
~~But from~~
Where from the sin of intellectuallity
Not water on the brain or over weight
Really as appropriate reward
For all the people they to sleep have poured
The inmates unable to hold up the heads
And yet [illegible] {kept} polite to go to bed
It is the Devils latest principality
The address of the ~~that~~ elected there to dwell
(The first they know their heads begin to swell
A look at ~~was called~~ {seemed} the business of ideality
~~And~~ But are imparted horn that didn't sprout
If the photographas of [?Israel])
The address ~~then is somewhat~~ {post office is aware} still in doubt
But someone further {down} circle [illegible]
And ~~not~~ yet not down as deep as circle six or eight
That is seven down between the graveyard sod
Or from the landing of the River Stix
Which would be more ~~than forty~~ {than six*} down from Heavn
The circle was an after thought of God
That had to be squeezed into the need
~~But~~ {And} the Post office ~~has~~ recently appeared
[Three illegible lines]

Nothing in any circle can exceed
The mining of them that nod and not
Till they are bored {down} coppling on {all fours} ~~on the floor~~
Too heavy with great thought if not with brains

---

* Words written below the line.

In one stage mainly on all fours
And standing [illegible] on the head
Kicking high legs [illegible] cake bread

Trying to bring their poor feet down in vain*

[47r]† Well down along the circles of sad hell
~~There have been recently set up by God they tell of~~
~~There has been one set up by God of late~~
~~That Dante in the wisdom of hiate~~
That in the usurpation of his hate
Dante provided for us all so well
Is one he didn't bother to create
~~Or didn't think it worth his while to tell~~
~~Maybe he left~~
~~May he left to be done by God~~
Or left it {to have it done} [illegible] by God
~~But then it is miraculous to tell~~

[48r] Apparently was big and bursting with
To spend in all directions all at once.
He felt it ongoing in him like a choice
Had he been kept so vegetable a dunce
As not to guess what ailed him was a mood
Of profligacy and extravagance?
A propiting toward old prodigal romance
Or so he might have asked since parrots spoke
Suppose untimely with forced fingers rude
He was divested of his outer cloak
In colleness or in the quest of fruit.
Hew would go far from stripped entirely nude,
Be poured to wear another inner suit
Of overlapping sequins scale on scale
[illegible] {As crafty} as a shirt of iron mail.
And there are seed and all he is is seed.
(What more than that is any of us indeed?

---

* Entry written vertically up the left side of the page, bottom to top.
† Page written vertically down the page, top to bottom.

He might {have} arrested the thinking folk.)
And then there are seed enough to sow a region
So's to make sure whatever else shall fail
Pasture and garden shall not lack for weed.
Grant them if but for the statistics sake
Or let the go at an estimated legion
He may have other plans for them than sowing

"Dedication of The Gift Outright"

MS. 1881. *Light brown cardboard cover spiral notebook, 5″ × 7⅜″. "National" stamped on bottom left-hand corner of the cover. White ruled paper. All entries are in blue ink.*

[1r]

Dedication
of
The Gift Outright
on
His Inauguration as President[1]

[2r]   [blank]

[3r]   [blank]

[4r]   Before the headsman takes you by the zone
Milord I want a word with you alone
I want to help you with the word you want
The trouble with you is you're too avant

~~Tis your misfortune your before~~
Your bad luck is your lame before your laws
That may not be as terrible a cause
On any books as treason is or theft
But it is just a little too far left

In politics you have to use your head
Or you you will get beheaded good and dead
I fear you've got beyond my jurisdiction
And you will have to disappear in a flash

•   •   •

But just some history before you go
And just a bit of prophecy as so
When people were already round the pace
~~God spotted took one fellow~~ A
   the chose one fellow of the human

And stated an expense

[5r]   The still depended on the human Jew
A Justis of the chosen people thus
And had a son [?before] in her virginity
For both of them to stone in his diadem

This time God undoubtedly had in mind
To make a chosen race of all mankind[2]
The rigor of the natural was unfrozen
And all the human race became the chosen

Chosen to be the children of his Son
Who was to have no children. He was done
With his experiment in human breeding
Trying so many years and succeeding

The trouble was the boys would marry out
That's what the people's rage was all about
Warned them don't by more than just talk
To pretty daughter of the Canaanite

They warned them such experiment would fail
If they would [?traffic] with the girls of Baal
And God would punish them by [?turning] in
The see like ~~farces of the~~ the King of Babylon

[6r]   He was resolved to bear sure as sass
His great experiment with man will pass

Respect the variant nature soil
Though with the future always
~~This look-on~~

~~This wasn't to have been the way~~
This seems to me to be the way it all was planned
And I must say
And if it was I [?now] beautiful and grand
This was the ~~vision~~ {dream} ~~that Jehovah~~
                    {God may have} dreamed
The object of his attempt
And no so missed as removed cut as will
And in our that in our time take to
                    see fulfilled

The [serialist] in all his arrogance
May be the point of the variance
The [?outcome]   the successful shirk
Of [illegible] at this Bible eases the case of work

[6v]   We wait for girls when they are really girly
Their charm is to breathe late then early
At rendezvous in the [art] of early mating
No gentleman ~~must needs~~ {will} keep a lady waiting

Girls keep us waiting when they are really girly
Their charm into be rather late than early
~~At~~ At rendezvous

A girl may keep one waiting. To be girly
Her charm is to be rather late than early
But in the rendezvous—or art of mating
One must not keep a lady waiting

A girl keeps you waiting. If she's girlie
Her charm to be rather late than early
~~At the street corner or in the act~~
~~At the rendezvous or in the~~

[7r]   To start them in up the evolution ramp[3]
He put them in a concentration camp

                    •   •   •

He split a man in two to start the fun
~~And But [illegible]~~ {Tell them} act as instincts as one

But god was reckoning without the snake
Which some account [illegible] obvious mistake
~~But God was reckoning without the snake~~
[illegible line]
That education [illegible] would come along
And mix us up about with right and wrong

They were just the first in being best
And ~~for~~ beautify they
All could the pleasure
And they were surely something

[8r]   And
       But
       From the very first to some extent
       ~~They~~ God vitiated {his} experiment
       By blessing [illegible] people he chose
       Who loved so well I say [illegible] their
       [illegible line]
       By blessing their [illegible] joys
       With nothing but a pair of [illegible]
                              [?boys]

"One Favored Acorn"

MS. 02348. *Blue hardcover buckram notebook, 6″ × 9¼″. Unruled white paper. Entries are in blue ink unless otherwise noted. This notebook contains drafts of several published poems, including "The Bad Island" and "The Draft Horse," which according to Frost, was written as early as 1920. It also contains drafts of several poems that Frost did not publish, one or two of which may be extremely early.*

[*recto*]*   [~~illegible~~]   One Favored Acorn¹

~~More than a million~~ {A million acorn}seed
1   Most of which must fail
    And go for squirrel feed.

    Some had got for themselves hurled
. 2   In the equinoxal gale
    Far out into the world

    Some when the wind was still
3   Had fallen plummet direct
    (But may have ~~rolled~~ {bounced} down hill)

    In a hollow ~~some~~ {there} lay in a heap
4   Not knowing what to expect
    Tow or three acorns deep.

    Already at one extreme
5   ~~Some~~ By autumn dampness' aid
    Some were showing a toothwise gleam

                    •   •   •

---

* This page, written in blue ink, is from a sheet of 7¼″ × 10³⁄₁₆″ unruled white paper inserted into the notebook. "Hotel Roosevelt New York A Hilton Hotel" is embossed on its verso side.

Or what might have been a fuse
6   To some small devil grenade
Fat loaded ready to use.

But practically {To think} all that must perish
7   Unless I should intervene
And pick up one to cherish

I might plant one in a yard
8   To alter a village scene
And of long regard.

But whether with blindfold shut
9   Or frankly open eyes
I hoped it would I could hit on a nut

That would be most appreciative
10   And feel the most surprise
At being allowed to live.*

R.F.

[1r]   Kays² after she gets through copying

R.F.

[1v]   [Blank except for a small drawn figure which appear to be a crown on top of a head in the bottom right hand portion of the page]

[2r]   [blank]

[2v]   [blank]

---

* The last stanza is written vertically on the bottom, right hand side of the page, bottom to top.

[3r]   Traces*

These words have been loved in and wept in
It is [?can't] {not supposed}† to be his own
That of two that came loving together
But one came weeping alone.

Yet the conifers sight to the warblers
That lisp in their lofty tops.
And their bark sheds tears everlasting
Of silvery rosin drops.

                          My First Rejection³

Once in a Californian Sierra
I was swooped down upon when I was small
And measured but not taken after all
By a great eagle bird in all his terror

Such auspices are very hard to read
My parents when I ran to them averred
I'd been rejected by Joves royal bird
As one who would not make a Ganemede

Not find a bartender to Jove in me?
I have resented {it} ever since that day
When any but myself presumed to say
That there was anything I couldnt be.

[4r]   The Bad Island—{called}‡ Easter Because It Hasn't Risen Again⁴

         On a Head from Easter Island in the
         Portico of the British Museum (I think)§

---

* Poem written in black ink.
† "not supposed" written in blue ink.
‡ "called" written in blue ink.
§ "I think" written in blue ink.

That primitive head *
So ambitiously vast,
Yet so rude in its art,
Is as easily read
For the woes of the past
As a clinical art.

For one thing above,
The success of the lip
So scornfully curled,
Has that tongue of stone
Been brought in a ship
Halfway around the world

They were days on that stone.
They gave it the wedge
Till it flaked from the ledge.
They gave it a face.
The with tackle unknown
They stood in place
On a cliff for a throne
They gave it a face
Of _what_ was it?—Scorn
Of themselves as race
For having been born
And then having first
Been cajoled, then coerced
Into being beruled?
By what strangers
Was their cynical throng
So cozened and fooled
And jollied along?

[5r]   Were they told they were free
And persuaded to see
Something in it for them?

---

* There is a rounded bracket written in blue ink around the right hand margin of this stanza with a line drawn into the left hand side of the page.

Well, they flourished and waxed
By executive guile
By fraud and by force,
Or so for a while;
Until over axed
In never and resource
They started to wane
They emptied the isle
Except for a few
That can be but described
As a vile residue—
And a garrulous too.
They were punished and bribed ..
All was in vain.
Nothing would do.
Some mistake had been made
No book can explain,
Some change in the law
~~Except as a~~ That nobody saw
Except as a gain.
But one thing is sure
Whatever kultur
They were made to parade,
Whatever altrur-
ian thought to attain,
Not a trace of it's left
But the gospel of sharing
And that has decayed
Into a belief
In being a thief
And perishing in theft
With cynical daring

[6r]*   Rather Pointed⁵

With a lantern that wouldnt burn
In too frail a buggy we drove

---

* Two pages are torn out prior to this page.

Behind a great Percheron horse
Through a pitch dark limitless grove

And a man came of the trees
And took our horse by the head
And reach back to her ribs
Deliberately stabbed her dead.

The cumbersome beast went down
With the crack of a broken shaft.
The night sighed {through} the ~~world~~ grove
In ~~in a row it is ended~~ {one long terminal}* draft

The most unquestioning pair
That every accepted fate.
And the ~~least~~ {most} disposed to ascribe
~~Any~~ No more than we had to to fate,

We assumed the man himself
Or someone he had to obey
Want us to get down
And walk the rest of the way.

[7r]   One Favored Acorn[6]

More than a million seed
Most of which must fail
And go for squirrel feed.

Some had got for themselves hurled
In the equinoxal gale
Far out into the world

Some when the wind was still
Had fallen plummet direct
(But may have bounced down hill)

_____
* The phrase is written beneath the line.

In a hollow some lay in a heap
Not knowing what to expect
Tow or three acorns deep.

Already at one extreme
By autumn dampness' aid
Some were showing a toothwise gleam

What might have been a fuse
To some small devil grenade
Fat loaded ready to use.

All that must perish
Unless I should intervene
And pick up one to cherish

I might plant one in a yard
To alter a village scene
And of long regard.

But whether with faithfully shut
Or intelligently open eyes
I wished I could choose a nut

That would be most appreciative
And feel the most surprise
At being allowed to live.*

[8r–13r]   [blank]

---

* The last stanza is written vertically, on the bottom right hand side of the page, bottom to top.

"First Answerability Divine Right"

MS. 1694A. 5″ × 8″ *white ruled pages torn from a spiral flip pad. All entries are in blue ink.*

[1r]   First Answerability Divine Right

Separateness of the Parts[1] All life is cellular[2]

For story and for Use

Individuality of Nations of People within Nations[3]

Religion Science and Gossip

Philosophy nothing but theology or an attempt to rationalize religion The God question. Religion is superstition or it is nothing. It is still there after philosophy has done its best. Very feminine what with Eve and Mary not to mention the other Marys

[2r]   Philosophy strangely lacking in the feminine. No woman in all the worlds history has ever made a name for herself in philosophy. Women have perhaps felt the unconscious antagonism of <u>Xantippe</u>[4] toward it as the enemy of unreason and sheer belief. As to the second of the three parts of life namely science; all science is domestic science[5] our domestication on and our hold on the planet[6] just one jump ahead of the exhaustion of resources. Another feminine thing about it is that its laboratory is but a glorified kitchen, which is peculiarly the womans room in the fathers house of many mansions. Here I am as if taking the womans side in argument

[3r]   when all I set out to do was indicate a difference between philosophy and wisdom when I got round to it From the innateness of the word philosophy it should seem to be the same thing as wisdom. But all it is is a tradition of hard

working system builders from Thales[7] on doubtfully down till it tapers off in a tail end of doubting the word terms it has to doubt with. Or else it gives up and manfully throws itself existentially in with the last of my trio, gossip or th endless record of what goes or what we think goes on. A definitive definition of gossip is our guessing at each other. It is the luxuriant garden of wisdom-unwisdom. We would be prigs and prudes not

[4r]   to enjoy ourselves in it. Wisdom-unwisdom mind you. It has hardly ever in beds of any one kind. A flower here and or flower there quite contrary like the Mary that had the garden in the nursery rhyme. I often revert to the nursery rhymes for wisdom. Athens was the head quarters of philosophy but Sparta wisdom. Plato is my authority.[8] He says the Spartans had the wisdom and when they {he} felt it coming over them to talk wisdom he ordered all strangers out of town so they couldn't profit by it. How like Marks saying Christians in their exclusiveness must talk in parable so the wrong people wont understand them and so get saved.[9] Many people consider Plato infallible. Sometime

[5r]   I mean to round up a lot of wise saying such as I suspect we have from the Spartans such as Good fences make good neighbors.[10] My guess would be we owe most of them to the wise woman of the tribe or family. They are the thoughts of our guesswork as it amounts to journalism to cronicle to history to literature in novel drama and poetry. We disport ourselves in venturing making bold to say. But do our utmost as in a careful court of law, we are all being tried, the lawyers the judge and the jury as well as the defendant. Times verdicts are supposed to mock our own. "Speak after sentence? Yea until the end of time."[11] The lives of great men have to be rewritten {for} almost every generation I suppose so

[6r]   The End of Colonialism means the multiplication of nations.

Separateness of the parts is as important as the connection of the parts.[12] As Pax Britannica[13] fails and the British Empire breaks up the emphasis in the big world shifts to the separateness . The colonies draw off into nations on their own. The individuality of units becomes the ideal. Strange that this should be so when within the nations the tendency is toward the loss of individuality in socialism. The citizens are grouping up while the countries are ungrouping. Still every individuals first answerability is to himself. His immediate second to his fellows

[7r]   First the highest is himself The King's divine right like the Presidents (for ~~Glory and For Use~~)is to act on the two responsibilities in that order.

All life is cellular No living particle of matter however small has yet been found without a skin—without a wall.[14]

"Last Refinement of Subject Matter"

MS. 1694B. 5³⁄₁₆″ × 6¹⁄₁₆″ *white cream paper. Entries are in black ink unless otherwise noted.*

[1r]   Last Refinement of Subject Matter[1] Vocal Imagination[2] Voice as Subject Matter★ [3]

The Sound of Sense†[4]—The Sound of Poetry A Content of Sound‡

If you were to Ask {me} if I make the sound of poetry a matter of vowel and consonant sounds, a matter of alliteration and assonation, {and} my answer would have to be "No", but it might be any one of a great many kinds of "No" all spelled exactly alike with the same vowel and consonant yet all quite distinct. I might say that poetry was a matter of vowel and consonant sounds; or No, I tell you No! Lets hear no more of that or Oh, no, you don't understand; or No, I can't hear to it, no; or No you wait a moment and I'll tell you. These nos noes are not merely negative In addition to being negative the first is lenient, the second is al but angry, the third is contemptuous, the fourth is short and final, the fifth merely by the way and preliminary to the

[1v]§   The Sentences must spring from each other and talk to each other even when there is only one character speaking.[5]

You mean to say he wants two hundred dollars for that old warhorse?

[2r]   2

explanation I am about to give.

★ Written vertically on the left side of the page from bottom to top in blue ink.
† Phrase written in blue ink.
‡ "A Content of Sound" written in blue ink.
§ Page written in blue ink.

But don't think that because these Nnoes are given as examples that they are not to be taken seriously. I mean every one of them at once. You are to dismiss the idea that the sound of the letters in the word "no" or in {any} other word is the real stuff of poetry.

Still the point is not so much as it is that neither is the simple negative sound of the "No" the stuff of poetry. That would be too characteristic, too unimaginative. It is the extra sound the "No" gets when in addition to being negative it becomes lenient angry contemptuous, {or} short and final ~~what you please~~

Shall I go on? Or have I said enough?* [6]

The thing to notice {is} that orally in each case the "No" stands safely on its own legs alone. It can be made to convey its extra meaning without the help of any context. But in writing it is otherwise: in writing it begins to need the help of a setting

[3r]   3

of other words to determine its character. It has to take its place in a sentence, the other words of which shall act as a sort of notation to indicate what particular "No" it is, the lenient, the angry, the scornful, the short and final ~~or what you please~~

There are many yes tones as no tones on our lips, I suppose, and probably more oh tones than either. In speaking I can make the bare "Oh" express many things. In writing I have no way of making it express anything beyond exclamation except as it stands in a sentence.

Here we come one of the principle use of the sentence.

~~Poetry~~-Poets have lamented the lack in poetry of any such notation as music has for suggesting sound. But it is there and has always been there. The sentence is the notation. The sentence is before all else just that: a notation for suggesting significant tones of voice. With the sentence that doesn't suggest significant

[4r]   4

tones of voice, poetry has no concern whatever.

---

* "Line is written vertically on the left-hand side of the page, from bottom to top, in blue ink."

There is place in the world to be sure for a kind of sentence like a mathematical formula that is content to convey no more meaning than belongs to a [i̶l̶l̶e̶g̶i̶b̶l̶e̶] grammatical set of words. Such a sentence serves for much necessary workaday writing and also for certain over intellectual writing that most of us find dull—for two extremes hasty journalism and heavy philosophy. It goes toneless or in the lifeless tone of matter-of-fact statement. It has no part in poetry. No mechanical attempts to vary it by structural device can save it to poetry.

Once and for all the sentence that takes rank as poetry must do double duty. It will not neglect the meaning it can convey in words; but it will succeed chiefly by some meaning it conveys by tone of voice.

You hear the tone of lofty scorn in the first line of Yates's Rose of the World "Who dreamed that beauty passes like a dream."[7]

[5r] 5

tennis with the net down[8] – tug and [?breeching] – scotch sword dancer

the weariness of it all in the first lines of <u>Tennyson's Ulysses:</u>

It little profits that an idle King
By this still health, among the barren crags,
Matched with an aged wife I unite and dole
Unequal laws unto a savage race:[9]

   The hate in Brownings <u>In a Cloister</u>[10]
Grr! There go my heart's abhorrence,
Water your damned flower pots, do!

   The delight in Brownings

The fancy I had today![11]

   The man's longing <u>in Kiplings</u>

      •   •   •

Put me down somewhere east of Suez where
    The best is like the worst.[12]

Under everything in all these lines you have the metrical beat of the verse. I take that more or less as a matter of course although some of my friends don't nowadays. The writers of free verse dispense with it altogether. I'm not sure that it isn't horrible to do without it. As it happens I don't do without it myself. I seem rather to want it where it is as something to for the rhythm

[6r]   6

of the vocal tones to play across, to make a figure in, to posture in—say it as you like. It has its purpose.

But at the same time it is to be regarded as a danger. There is always the certainty that the voice will fall prey to it if there is nothing worthier to engage the attention. The only refuge from the deadly singsong of the verse provided by real poetry is the tones of meaning clearly and sharply imagined and set down in black and white for the recognition of the reader. The sentence must never leave the reader in doubt for a moment as to how the voice is to be placed in it. So only will it save {us} from death by jingle.

I speak of imagination as having some part in the sound of poetry. It is everything in the sound of poetry; but not as invention nor creation—simply as a summoner. Make no mistake about the tones of speech I mean. They are the same yesterday, today, and forever. The were before words were—if anything was before anything else. They have merely entrenched themselves in words. No one

recognition and Lowes* [13]

[7r]   7

invents new tones of voice. So many and no more belong to the human throat, just as so many runs and quavers belong to the throat of the cat-bird, so many to the chicadee.[14] The imagination is no more than their summoner—the imagination of the ear.

It is the imagination of the eye we think oftenest of in connection with poetry. We remember the poet's injunction to poets to write with the eye on the object.[15] We value poetry too much as it makes pictures. The imagination of the ear is more peculiarly poetical than the imaginative eye, since it deals

---

* Written vertically along the left-hand side of the page, bottom to top.

with sound which is what poetry is before it is sight. Write with the ear to the speaking voice. Seek first in poetry concrete images of sound—concrete tone images. Poetry is a dwelling on the fact, a gloating over the fact, a luxuriating in the fact. It's first pleasure is in the facts of the voice.

So much for what the sounds of poetry are, where they come from and at what summons (the summons of the imaginative ear. It remains to show

[8r]   8

Bother {is} the only emotion not poetical★

That ~~there is~~ not all tones {of voice} have the same poetical value. I am not so much afraid of vulgar tones or what might be dismissed off hand as vulgar. You never know what is vulgar till you try to see ~~how~~ what you can carry off with thinking no evil. A scolding tone would seem to be hopeless for poetry. And yet—you never can tell. Bookish tones are surely to be avoided, such as belong to the balanced sentence, for example, and all {tones} that depend altogether on conjunctions and conjunctives. There are the tones of grandeur of sweetness of invocation that poetry has had rather too much of. It could well get along with less for a while. There are dull tones of plain statement which are almost no tones at all. They require no imagination in the summoning. Anybody can get them down on the page. And about half the poets are getting them down on the page by the bookfull.

What attests the imagination of the poet are significant tones of voice we all know and easily recognize, but can't say we have grown familiar with

[9r]   9

from having met {with} them in books.

I have gone to poets of the past for such examples of poetry as I have used {for} ~~to support~~ my theme. But there {are} poets of the present as we have all been made very much aware of late. I have decided to leave you these as material to try by my principles or try my principles by. You know their names. Which of them have no tones but those of plain statement? Which haven't tones enough for a refuge from the jingle of their verse? Which have none but the old familiar bookish tones? Which have none but the tones long established in poetry? And have nothing to show that they have observing ears.

★ Written vertically on the left-hand side of the page, top to bottom in blue ink.

"Sentences may have the greatest monotony to the eye"

MS. 1694C. *Two 6½″ × 6⁷⁄₁₆″ thick white sheets of paper folded into halves. Entries are in blue ink.*

[1r]   Sentences may have the greatest monotony to the eye in length and structure and yet the greatest variety to the ear in the tones of voice they convey.[1] As in Emerson's prose—and verse too.

Sentences must talk to each other.

The imagination of the ear flags first as the spirit dies down in writing. It is the part of the expression {ceases to be spirited} nearest to the spirit. The imagination of the eye can be or ~~less feigned or kept up~~ {stretched} in appearance by effort.

Even in lyric the great thing is that every sentence should come from a different dramatic slant. The separateness of the parts as important as their connection.[2]

Fool psychologists more systematic than observing have dealt impartially with the five sense elements in poetry. But they are not all equally important and there are more than five of them. The

2

[1v]   tone of voice element might be regarded as almost the whole thing. It is the continuous flow on which the other are carried along like sticks and leaves and flowers.

Some of the high spots, the most vivid imaginative passages in poetry, are of the eye but more perhaps are of the ear.

All poetry does is try to catch you off your guard with reminders of old sights and sounds.

The vocabulary may be what it will, though I prefer it not too literary; but the tones of voice must be caught always fresh and fresh from life.

Poetry is a fresh look and a fresh listen.

·   ·   ·

I remember trying to show some children in those days exactly what I meant. I told them a "Primer" story in three sentences about a cat.

The cat is in the room.

I will put the cat out

The cat will come back

All in the tone of statement. Let's see what can be done with them just mechanically to bring them to life and put tones of extra meaning into them. (Extra)

There's that cat got in.

Get out you cat!

No use—she'll be right back.

I once went round talking of Vocal Realism and Observations of the Voice, Where Form and Substance Merge[3]

[2r]   3

It is one thing to hear the tones in the minds ear. Another to give them accurately at the mouth. Still another to implicate them in sentences and fasten them printed to the page. The second is the actors gift. The third is the writers.

I need no machine to tell me how long this syllable or that is. The length of syllables for practical purposes is entirely expressional, that is, dependent entirely on the tone of voice of the sentence they occur in. "Oh" may be as long as prolonged agony or short as slight surprise.[4]

We are not considering the sound of vowels and consonants but the sound of sense, tones with a meaning

Some have proposed inventing a notation to make sure the tones intended

Some have tried to help themselves with

[2v]   adjectives in the margin. But the sentences themselves, whatever else they are, are a {context} notation for initiating tones of voice. In fact a good sentence does double duty: it conveys one meaning with words and syntax another by the tone of voice it indicates. In irony the words may say one thing, the tone of voice the opposite.

Take six interjected Ohs and write them in a column. The all look alike but I want them said all said differently. My best way my only way to get them said differently is to write them as of [if] sentences. (In speaking I can get along very well with the Oh's alone)

Oh I see now what you mean

Oh isn't he lovely
Oh you sad fool why would you?
Oh I slipped. Let me try again.
Oh murder   help   murder!
Oh King live forever This is commenest in poetry—too common

The brute noises of our human throat that were all our meaning before words stole {in}. I suppose there is one for every shade of feeling we will ever feel, yes and for every thought we will every think. Such is the limitation of our thought.

The tones dealt in may be the broadest or again they may be the most delicate. I must have cited The Garden[5] and Magna Est Veritas[6] for contrast to show what different levels the theory held good, one almost colloquial, the other in the grand manner.

One might make a distinction between intoned poetry and intonational poetry. The two interpenetrate.

And so on ad lib. I have only said this way and that over what Jack[7] says in his paper. It comes to little more.

NOTEBOOK 46

"Many speak as if it was a reproach to the Puritans"

MS. 1694D. 6³⁄₁₆″ × 7³⁄₁₆″ Heavy-woven beige paper. Entries are in black ink unless otherwise noted.

[1r]   I

   Many speak as if was a reproach to the Puritans that the freedom they initiated was not for everybody for all time. They never can have imagined it was for anybody but themselves for the time being. ~~Just so~~ They were not going to have it spoiled right off by any Ann Hutchinson's or Roger Williams's or ~~before it was all begun.~~ {Mortons of Merrymount}[1] Just so with the heroes of the American Revolution the freedom they set up was a particular freedom for their own care and comfort for the time being—for say a thousand years more or less. A thousand years all the song asks.[2] [paragraph sign] Any freedom set up is as precarious ~~enough and will bear~~ as an organic compound and with all the conditioning care in the world cant be expected to stay stable forever. No one can hope we have

[1v]   Every revolution has its heroes whose names become household words and are best involved to describe it. ~~Washington~~ When losers come around us in the dark to lose us to ourselves in peace and war there are always Washington Adams Jefferson Hamilton Madison and Marshall[3]

[2r]   II   2

seen the last revolution. ~~Perhaps~~ More than half the great names of history have been heroes of change. They appeal to more in us than merely our imagination. There will certainly arrive new heroes to make fresh adjustments of the law to the restless spirit of enterprise. There will be new people to whom they will be heroes. ~~No one can hope other wise~~ {hope otherwise} To ~~doubt~~ it would be to count on some such catastrophy as the earth's exploding in its asteroids.

                              •   •   •

Nothing can prevent it but the earth's exploding into asteroids.*

Heroes The heroes of

When losers come around us in the dark to lose us to ourselves in peace
and war. our best A surer stay against confusion than the Constitution itself
might {well} be the roster of the heroes who gave us the Constitution—men
like Washington Adams Jefferson Hamilton and Madison. Their lives {was
maybe} maybe are the best definition of what we are. Abstractions are a dry
substitute for the story.

[3r]   III

Even now the next revolution may be stealing upon us {by way of} in the
monstrous {shape of} industry we have conj out of the machine or by way
{in the person meek per} meek religion. It will have its new heroes to establish its new freedom Both the fre new freedom heroes and the new freedom
may be in sight. I may be looking right at them and not see them. For I still
have the old heroes and the old freedom at heart and am ready to take action
offense at the first signs of their betrayal. Heroes must have people to be
heroes to. {Martin} Luther and {John} Milton and the Duke of Marlborough⁴
have me to be heroes to for long time I am far from getting all having got all
there was to get out of either the Protestant Revolution or the American Revolution. The freedom they charted still does me very well.

[4r]   IV

I hear good Britishers say their freedom feels freer to them than our freedom.
To them I should expect it of course {To them of course. Be it granted.}
They are naïve only when they expect their freedom to will feel freer to us. It
may to a certain kind of American that neednt be considered too leniently
here. I am willing to believe a great number of Russians find they move
round get all the freedom of spirit mind and body they need out of their institutions. I trust it is no treason {on} to my part to hope so. Treason either to
them or to us.

In a country like this of ours and in the eyes of our admirers there has
never been one like it never been another quite like it. The great national ob-

---

* Written vertically along the left-hand side of the page, bottom to top.

ligation {of course} is to encourage the liveliness of life, ~~To be sure~~ Limits must be ~~set to be~~ assumed to exist. But how are ~~must not~~ we be too certain sure where the bounds ~~the lines~~ are unless we make bold to try them.

We don't like to deaden by repression what's soon to die⋆

[5r]   V

And this hold in art religion {business} and politics in our day, though less liberally in {the} business and politics. ~~Anybody~~ Heresy and modernism flourish⁵ unchecked {by anything but satire}. We are reluctant to deaden at all what is soon soon to die. Nothing but what I might surface with I venture to say or I make bold to say is worth saying I am honestly far less interested than I may seem from all this talk in ~~liberty~~ {our} Freedom ~~with a big~~ {given me by law}. I value myself on the liberties I take. What keeps the balloon expanded is ~~everybodys~~ a million {imprisoned} little heads bumping against it from within.

Some plainly ask for the freedom to be disloyal ~~now and then~~ {more or less} at their own discretion. Well {in a country like this} you ~~can~~ will at worst get called names for changing your party ~~(mugwump)~~ mugwump⁶ between elections, ~~for getting converted to a new religion for foreskaing old friends giving~~ mugwump ~~or~~ or giving up your religion (apostate) or forsaking one love for another (jilt) or for

for giving up your country (expatriate)†

[5v]   putting your friends behind you underfoot like stepping stones to rise to higher things (climber)

⋆ Written vertically along the left-hand side of the page, bottom to top.
† Written vertically along the left hand side of the page, bottom to top.

"All thoughts all passions all delights"

MS. 910940.2. *Loose pages of various sizes and undated except where noted. Some are from notebooks but not matching the other intact volumes. Entries are written in blue ink unless otherwise noted.*

[*recto*]*   All thoughts all passions all delights

Separateness of the masses as important as their connection.[1]

Making a set   Making a costume out of all things in this garret.

†(Despair of finding five strings separate enough (underived from each other) for a play.

Before the beginning is the dictionary {of words} and the dictionary of rhymes—neither of which can be wielded

No alphabetical listing of tones of voice[2] though it is evident only a limited number belong to our throats.[3]

Nor of ideas.

Several I strewed ahead like the boulders in my Franconia pasture.[4]

Positions taken.

Recklessness of life in family whose modesty forbids it to believe it could produce a poet.

---

* 6″ × 8″ white sheet.

† There is a line drawn from this open parenthesis to the sentence ending with the word "connection" above.

[1r]*   The cruelest thing ~~in the world is to think~~ you can do to others is not to let them understand you {at all.}† {It is a species of sadism.}   You may well make it hard for them to understand you. For the most tonic thing you can do to others is to {make} let them discover for {themselves} why kindness is your severity.

From every fraction of disjected truth ~~th~~ a school of art may be expected to spring up. Take the delight of being wronged by the stupid. You can indulge it {yourself} to feel there by the simple formula of putting your [illegible] ~~idea~~ {wisdom} so far ~~out of~~ {to} reach that as many as you like will seem as stupid as you like. ~~You Someone has thought of that ahead of you and you can act on it.~~ You may thus increase the canaille under your feet to the number of the whole human race minus one. {This has already been} Strange one had thought of ~~this ahead of you and~~ acted ~~on it~~ {upon}. ~~So~~ No originality {credit for} ~~his not~~ originality is left ~~in~~ get at of the idea

[1v]   Much of ~~the~~ {our} {recent} literature {prose and verse} has no intrinsic pleasure for anyone. It is only to be enjoyed ~~by those in~~ {by those in on} [for]? the theory on which it is {written}‡ ~~written~~ {and} ~~subjective in on that that theory~~. The pleasure is all outside of it like that of the [illegible] which you cant taste but ~~you~~ {nevertheless} relish on the strength of the articles about them {it} in the Sunday papers.

You are supposed to have a good time being baffled by one kind of poetry. All right ~~you~~ you obediently have a good time. You have been taught better than to look for epithet phrase epigram or point.[5]

[recto]§   Against our opposites. Over against the desire in us to save from war disease death madness is set is our lifes most sacred love

~~Life lo~~

What life loves is signs of life. Response Something to which to respond Cat and block spool mouse and another cat.

Life is ~~that which divides~~ roun[d] is a stream that divides round islands great and small to meet itself further on again with recognition but surprise.[6] As many have been deceived by the [illegible] [illegible] of the stream as by [illegible] parelling the stream

---

* 6″ × 8″ white sheet.
† Inserted below the line.
‡ Inserted in right-hand margin.
§ 6″ × 8″ white sheet.

Life breaking unexpected into the utmost manifestations.

We would not do anything to deaden what is soon to die. To have it various from [illegible] formidable down to appealing

The next time I go to a hotel

Im tired of a lot of things the treasured cant of radicals no less that of conservatives

Not stuck in the golden mean but sweeping wide as [?matter] head is advanced and now the feet.*

[1r]†   But the whole is too much for us. {At some point} we desist ~~in sorrow but with regret at some point~~. And This our darkest concern that we must give in and let {be} what ought not to be.[7] But darker still is a suspicion that perhaps we ought to let {be} what ought not to be—that we ought to condone suffering. It comes over us from an opposite extreme of our nature to the ~~one~~ saving one that would save life save souls save money. Utopia has dogged our steps in some guise or other ~~and sooner~~ from Plato to Carl Marx and ~~even~~ {down to} Edward Bellamy of Chicopee.[8] Man. And it may get us before all is said. Right now the fight is on to see if it will get possession of our colleges. Its champions claim that academic freedom {invade the colleges} to try to talk them away from the state as it is and deliver them over to the state that is ~~to be~~ possibly be. The presidents of the colleges are ~~supposed~~ expected to look over impartially and not take sides in the contest. We have them

over

[1v]   intimidated‡

[recto]§   One of my {still} unchastened crudities is[9]

Curiosity as to what you are reading in the train on the boat even in the house at homes. I am more eager to know than I ought to be.

You are a special person if you leave a book in your hand. I am tempted to seek your acquaintance presuming not on a weakness in you but {on} a freemasonry of letters between you and I

---

* Written in the upper left hand margin, vertically, from bottom to top.
† 6″ × 8″ white paper written in black ink.
‡ Word written in black ink.
§ 6″ × 9½″ lined 3-hole ring binder paper. Entry written the length of the page from top to bottom in black ink.

I am not unproud of my skill in leading up to the object of my curiosity without offense.

In the case to be observed between readers it could be really no great offense if I went over to a stranger and took his book form him with a penny for whats going on in your mind here. Sympathy would be my excuse.

What more do you want? You have come right up to the hive of the alternatives and made your choice between them pair by pair in such number as you needed to to get a life out of. Or in practice you find yourself taking them blended

It took ~~our~~ hands free   packs on our backs*

[*recto*]†   Your vote is asked for as a symbol of acquiescence in the ~~state~~ government you maintain an live under.   ~~We have you~~ The world has you by your weight and can insist ~~on~~ not only on your doing but on your being what it prescribes.

By my insight and and ~~my aversion to suicide~~ {my love of life}.

Don't be frightened We have instruments of precision with which we can safely torture you within an inch of your life and {even} within a fraction of an inch.

[*recto*]‡   Soul and body are a mechanical mixture[10] that is only kept together ~~by~~ and the body kept from settling to the bottom of the by the paddle of action.

One of the most obnoxious violations of taste is in carrying the analogy between numbers and things beyond the point of breaking down. The attempt to determine units of feeling as such as heartbeats or respirations and then count them for a meaning is one of the most obnoxious violations of the taste acquired ~~in~~ {by} poetry. The ~~analogy vast~~ {vastly discussed} analogy between numbers and things must like any other be taught its limits. So far shall it go and no further. The exquisite sense of how far any figure may be carried is nowhere cultivated as well as in poetry.

•   •   •

---

* These two phrases written in left-hand margin, vertically, from top to bottom.
† 6″ × 8″ white paper.
‡ 6″ × 8″ white paper.

One of the most vastly successful figures of thought is the comparison of numbers with things. Relying on it science has penetrated far into matter. ~~It is~~ {When} poetry [illegible] warns us that there must be a point ~~beyond which it cannot at which it must break down~~ like any other {pretty} figure however unpretentious[11] ~~There~~

[recto]*   Poetical license is a redundancy. Poetry is license

Off hand poetry might be called licence to be wrong, wild ~~and~~ foolish, {sickly impossible and dangerous}. It is supposed to have won to freedom from all restraints but those of rhyme and metre and from even those ~~of~~ lately. ~~A popular excuse for inexactness is that it is poetry. to shrug and say "poetry" the word poetry. Any inexactness is popularly expressed as poetry. Error cant err.~~ The name of poetry covers and excuses any inexactness. Oh poetry you know. Poetry belongs to the part of human nature that defies organization.

[recto]†   The real freedom is in departure[12]—before the word can catch up with you with a new rule

The Book of Worthies[13] — Old Testament

   Hard Head

Phsychology + Sociology   New Testament

   Combined Sorehead and saphead

Where Poetry is Poised—on the brink of spiritual disaster.‡ [14]

The Adventure into Materiality   God Substantiated[15]

In Praise of Lord Clive and the East India Company[16]

Insubordination.

[~~Illegible~~] Poetry is the only way to tell yourself or confess yourself with good taste.

•   •   •

---

* 6″ × 8″ white paper.

† Torn out from a spiral notebook, with spiral along the spine, 5½″ × 8½2″ white ruled paper.

‡ There is a line drawn from the beginning of this sentence to the sentence below, "Poetry is the . . . with good taste."

1 Sore heads—hungry radicals

2 Sap heads—the well to do who cant help helping the sore heads

3 [?Hard] Hard heads—who can manage to bear it that there must be good and bad

    losers.[17]

The first two merge to make a democratic party in a democracy.[18]

The [illegible] third should make a republican party in a republic.

The first two might welcome monarchy to save democracy back to save democracy

    from the oligarchy the republic tends toward.

[*recto*]*   distressful question is always what is a big enough way. We have to be sure our civil disobedience our rebellion isnt on trivial or rediculous grounds. If we werent too sure of our grounds we might end up too soon by letting someone else pay our taxes for us and get out of jail the worse only for anti-climax. My guess would be our best emulation of such great writers would be in great writing. By all means by every possible means lets have more it before the written word is given up for features on screen and television. I sigh with the luxury of passages in Walden[19]

[*recto*]†   Plato assumed there were tw but two ways of knowledge, the specialists and the geniuses {[illegible]}. He asks how a poet could know how to drive a chariot in a race? And concludes only by inspiration from Apollo.—the truth is the specialist is never quite satisfied with the poet's deer invasion of his specialty. The poet knows as the common observer knows. He has the better of the specialist and the common observer in his ability to hit off characteristics. Plato never had heard of the common the knowledge we speak of in law.[20]

    The ancient philosophers and the modern poets draw together in their use of metaphor. Ancient poets believed metaphor merely ornamental and of the surface.

[*1r*]‡   The war or something has roused the nearly all the college presidents I have encountered lately to take thought about the [illegible] {dry} bones of

---

* 10″ × 6″ torn ruled three-ring binder page, entry written lengthwise across lines, from bottom to top.

† 8¼″ × 6¼″ torn three-ring binder page, entry lengthwise bottom to top.

‡ 9¹⁄₁₂″ × 6″ white paper. A group of three separate sheets.

education. We owe much to war, particularly in science, though war like everything else of course has its bad side

Then {First} Brown he read a paper and he
  reconstructed there
From those same bones an animal that
  Was extremely rare.
But Jones he asked the chair for a
  suspension of the rules
Till he could prove that those same bones
  were one of his lost mules.

I have been to some trouble to find out what threatening or promising in pedagogy. The question is to have our rulers ~~anything~~ in mind to propose anything entirely new ~~in~~ or are they going to be satisfied with a change of emphasis by playing up one subject and playing down another. One President tell me it is impossible to mark (~~school slang can~~ as the school cant ~~word~~ is) it is impossible to mark for library writing.

[*2r*] have been particularly hard to estimate the worth of public men. ~~To Brutus it must have~~ Brutus must have seen Caesar like in the Garden giving the state "a shog maist ruined a'." [Illegible] We can say at this distance Brutus was probably wrong.[21]

Cant we be sure he was?

Sure but {not} absolutely sure.

I trust I have a proper sense of my own unsureness. Sureness and security, there it confronts us again the same idea in a different word.

You and I dont think {the} talk about social security goes deep enough. Do we know ~~any one who doesn't suffer from~~ one in a position ~~he is~~ of wealth or honor he is sure of holding? If he gets ~~to~~ [illegible] to worrying about it openly he is on the way to the doctor's office. The most that is permitted {his} manliness is a gleam of malice now and then toward his ~~threatening~~ rivals. ~~Wherever we~~ [illegible] Society reminds me of so many sleepless beetles ~~in a~~ climbing over each other in a bottle. The one question is who better or worse than ~~you~~ {whom}. A {full} professor {with permanent tenure} even in the sheltered life of {an} endowed institution ~~is flatte~~ needs the {self}* flattery of thinking he is better than anything he ~~knows the~~ he can find ~~the~~ fault with. He has to guard against the [?wrankles] of higher criticism. The

---

* Inserted in left-hand margin.

absolutely [~~illegible~~] permanent civil servant has to have ~~to have the better of~~
[~~illegible~~] {to have ~~some~~ ~~[illegible]~~}*

[*3r*]   Its a noble story of two souls with but the single thought of abolishing
poverty.

And yet you dont give in to it.

I can lead myself to it for the duration of the piece. It doesnt antagonize
me and never did. I feel as if it was a dream I was giving to remember to tell
next day. But living by daylight dissipates it into thin {the} air.

You know how I feel about poverty. So much good has come of it that I
shouldnt dare to abolish it.

Yes yes ~~but its a noble story~~ and everything {poverty and} even war has its
bad side. {They have to have} Allowances ~~must be~~ made {for them}. But the
dream of security for every one is a noble one. Every one so secure the only
gambling will be gambling pure.

I dont know about subscribing to that {sentiment} if it makes reality seem
base by contrast. ~~Some people use the soul to make the body look unseemly.~~
~~The unseemliness~~ It seems to me the unseemliness is all the souls when [~~il-~~
~~legible~~] the soul is used to make the body look unseemly.

But I stick to it that the story is a noble one sincerely ~~spread out~~ and humbly spread out for judgement.

You sound like Anthony on the subject of Brutus at Caesars funeral.[22]

There was an age for you when it must

[*recto*][†]   Alert to push the minute the word relaxes.

Not how it is used but it must be granted it could be used.

[*recto*][‡]   Of those who distrust the mental part of poetry and would either give it a
{silly} mind or no mind a[t] all let us deal with the ones

Let us ~~divide~~ [~~illegible~~] cut in two horizontals the throng who would either
~~give~~ {grant} the poetry a silly wind or deny it any mind at all and deal {first}
with the half nearer [~~illegible~~] {[~~illegible~~]} and less tormenting ~~first~~. With
them poetry and license are the same thing. Poetic license is a pleonasm.

---

* Inserted below the line.
† 7¼″ × 10½″ white sheet.
‡ 8″ × 6″ white sheet.

⌊*recto*⌋*   Marathon[23] clung to for the comparisons.

As much as can be [?wrong]

Think scornful of barriers (Mulvaney[24]

Great thoughts grave thoughts

Incidentality of ⎧ Old rivals in sagging leather
⎩ Our selfless forager[25]

My defect in neatness ⎧ Martyr
⎨ Soldier
⎩ Executioner.

Skill when in danger.

Emotion harnessed to the wit mill

[?moves] the words.   {Not as they are
                                  As they could be} dis
                                                        place
                                                        ment
Aventure   Get in and get out   Displacement of whole vocabulary

Self surprise

You dont want to understand whats happening to you. You have only to comfort yourself in it and through it.

Performance in poetry and in life is recognition and admission of the fact that
things are not to be too well understood

Sentencing from all directions.

Sets and systems

---

* 7½″ × 11″ white sheet written in black ink.

[1*r*]* Scotts poem called the Outlaw²⁶ ~~as well~~ [illegible] which were as well called Romance and Reality sounds like ~~an~~ a duet in an opera between a maiden (soprano) on a castle wall who voices romance and an outlaw (baritone) on the forest edge without the wall who voices reality, grim reality.

    Going to school is a game like running the gauntlet in which the object is to see ~~who~~ if you [illegible] can get through without being hurt too much by the books in the hands of the teachers.

A [illegible] self-experimenter ate several pounds of salt and could not find that it made his blood {appreciably} more saline ~~by one percent~~ A hundred textbooks {~~appreciably~~} studied do not make the average pupil one per cent more intelligent.

    Follow truth if it takes you to Hell—
(but it won't take you.)

[2*r*]   Pointing with the head in the direction of your thought indicates

Wheel derived from Huile† ²⁷

Man begins where summer leaves off.

It is business opportunity {for women} that has take marriage out of business

Poetry is that good in human nature which can never become habit.

A fool is one who says what other know as well but will not say is one who never knows what is happening until it is all over it is one

Not a question so much What is it about as
What is it?

Poetry is synecdoche: the part for the whole‡ ²⁸

        •   •   •

---

* First of two 5″ × 9″ white sheets.

† From the end of this sentence to the top of the page written in pencil. Rest of page written in black ink unless otherwise stated.

‡ The beginning of this sentence to the bottom of the page is written in red ink.

Must contain the general in the particular

Sub
The Striped Road.

Sub
The Right Love of Autumn.

Sub
When Drudgery Touched Me Not. Mill Town

[1r]*   When Adam delved and Eve span {spun}   And yet it is.
        Who was then the gentleman
        Adam, Eve; and gentlemen have been the effeminate ever since.
        Evidences of progress   Levellers²⁹
                                        Gracci³⁰
                                        Albigenses³¹
                                        Gower† ³²
                                        John Bull³³
                                        Milton was one‡
                                        Abolitionists

        Debtors progress.   All men born equally funny.³⁴
        Right to ancestry.³⁵

        We take an equalizer for our health.³⁶

        Dainty sorrows for all. Dainty sorrows of the rich.³⁷

        {Diffusion of responsibility for life and death}
        Every man a licensed locomotive engineer with a [illegible] ton of [illegible]
        armor and the power of life and death regardless of class. Diffusion is the
        word for it all. Diffusion of providence (providing for ones our future—the
        historical sense forward.³⁸

                              •   •   •

---

* First of two 8¼" × 7" ruled school theme book pages.
† This entry is to the left of the column, and inserted via an arrow.
‡ A line with an arrow from the end of this phrase to the word "Levellers," above.

Daintiest of all sorrows to put your feet on the mantelpiece like {the Preacher} Solomon and sigh Vanity of vanities.[39] {American authors} deprecation of last 40 years.

Ultimate privilege {of the crowd} not to crowd. Not to go till stopped others. To stop yourself before you are bumped—before you are spoken to—before you are looked at severely as daggers. The conscience is simply an extension of [illegible] {fear of punishment} sensitiveness as sight is an extension of touch.[40] It hates the slightest punishment and manages to be a long way beforehand with it. The pyramid on the Seal refuses to come to a point.[41] {Men will learn at last to refuse their ultimate fulfillments. We have Democracy when rulers refuse full rule.} These are the very grandest things to keep me form believing in progress. But if there cant be progress a priori I refuse to accept it a posteriori.[42]

[1v]   Accorded regrets but also privileges
         Privilege of not crowding

Explaining our lawlessness. The king is always above the law and so scarcely bound by it. The common man is now king. To be a Yankee in these days is greater than to be a King.
    Often wonder if democracy may not be weakening of the forces so that nobody shall come out on top. But no it is a refraining.
    Whats the constitution between friends of the Poor[43]
Leave him his historical sense forward as well as backward.[44] Leave him prudence. Shall there be nobody prudent but the State. Or does insurance mean we cant average wrong or a loss
    As the Catholic to Christ so I say to Democracy Thou art the Way. Hadst thou been nothing but the Good. I cannot say. If thou hadst ever met my soul

Isnt God to great a simplification? Yes hence all these Saints [illegible] {he has [illegible]}

[recto]*

Whatever else you come to know you'll never know that any better than you knew it at sight. You come to wonder at the strength with which you knew it in comparison with all your more studied knowledges.

          •   •   •

---

* 7¼″ × 10¹/₁₂″ white sheet.

All reasoning is a circle I say. At any rate all learning is in a circle. We learn A the better to learn B the better to learn C the better to learn D the better to learn A. All we get of A is enough to start us on the way to take it up later again.⁴⁵ We should circulate among the facts not progress through them leaving some forever behind.

Every sentence has got to have a way with it.

~~Leave progress to take care of itself.~~

The object of it all is to get among the poems where they throw light on each other.—to get among the ideas too

[*recto*]* By hypothesis the world is always going to be a hard place to save your soul in.⁴⁶ Such being the case we may as well settle down to a basis of suffering mixed with pleasure and see what we can make of it.

The lines turn Italic.

By coming at it again and again and ramming in fresh wads till it is overstuffed.

The logic must be flowed not pieced out.

Think a poem out or feel it out.

Some very great explorers have sent out parties ahead of them to plant bases all but to the pole. They were pioneers only in the last brief dash [~~illegible~~] from the last base.

[*recto*]† The greater affirmations that seem to show as thoughts are [~~illegible~~] really sentiments. A feat of words a feat of wit a feat of sentiment.

[?Pease] won't climb dry brush.

---

* 7¼″ × 10½″ white sheet.
† 7¼″ × 10½″ white sheet.

[*recto*]*   Nothing that ever came over me[†]

How far can we carry the ideal of human responsibility befor{e}[‡] the strain becomes too much and we break down from civilization and have to start over with talismans and luck and faith

All that clings [~~illegible~~] to me[§]

No rules can be made so fool proof that a bad poem cant be written under them.

[*recto*]**   Poetry need not be afraid of being regarded as knowledge if it is Knowledge come by in the right way.

[*1r*][††]   The only idealisms I have had to give up Several visions and the conviction that virtue was one.[‡‡]

I have envied the four moon planet.

Life is a ~~taking~~ punishment. All we can contribute to it is gracefulness in taking the punishment.

I had rather be wise than artistic.

We shall never understand   We shall never be shaken off this world. Our understanding is inferior to our resourcefulness.

Modesty keeps our best from insisting on what they have more than knowledge[§§]

---

* 7½" × 9" white sheet.

[†] Entry written in pencil.

[‡] Inserted below the line.

[§] Entry written in pencil.

** 8½" × 7½" white sheet written in pencil.

[††] 7" × 10" white sheets written in black ink unless noted.

[‡‡] Entry from "The only idealisms . . . virtue was one" written in pencil.

[§§] Entry written in pencil.

Happiness makes up in height for what it lacks in length.[47]

Radicalism is young ~~foolish~~ folly:
Conservatism is old stupidity.[40]

What is deep? And instant tells of colliding tendencies*
                                        Will talk give out?
You'll have plenty to do just keeping honest—that is to say reporting ~~on~~
your ~~yourself truthfully~~ {position}. ~~Your state of mind~~ truthfully from phase
to phase.

[1v]   Checked
                                                                        by
                                                                   B.L. Young

                                                                   What is
                                                                    deep

                                                                   Never
                                                                   Under
                                                                    stand
                                                                 happiness
                                                                   height

                                                                 Radicalism
                                                                   Young
                                                                    Folly

                                                                 Power to
                                                                   Hurt

[verso]†   {teacher   It cannot be
      [~~Illegible~~]
          No progress in any real sense seems possible

                              •   •   •

---

* "And instant . . . tendencies" written in pencil.

† 8″ × 7″ ruled theme book page.

Prospect of any denouement to history I bad for two three reasons

1.) Our virtues prevent a Utopian* outcome   {Originality} courage of originality
2.) The layout on earth is a place where a man may try himself and probably find out ~~what he's~~ [illegible] if he's any good
3.) Time limitation that may lie in the {possible} violence and abruptness of {the} sidereal situation of the world. Comet's tail

   The opposite of civilization is what? Eutopia[49]

A Dark darker darkest[50]

B Not to be made a fool of by either success or failure

C By theorem a hard place to save your soul. When all souls are saved that are going to be saved, then the kingdom of heaven will come earth.[51]

*From martyrdom to soldiership to martyr dom again

   The difference between a liberal and a practical politician is that the liberal feels sorrier than the practical man about [illegible] doing wrong[52]

It was exciting while it lasted.—Yes it was exciting enough-

You say that as if was unimportant.—You say it as if it [illegible] was {[illegible]}

The return to slavery in the circling years
   No protection without direction.

[*recto*]*   We find ourselves I the middle of our times that is if we are middle aged: and I see nothing for it but talk from them.

What goes on in one art goes on in another. What goes on in all the arts goes on in politics science and religion. In politics ambition {insatiable} in science

---

* 7½″ × 11″ white sheet written in black ink.

curiosity {insatiable} in religion belief {insatiable} {[illegible]}* in the arts de-sire ~~desire~~ love {(and hate} insatiable

Whose [illegible]

[illegible]

Your way and you will have it.

Many many stars and one desire (whose worth's unknown although its height be taken.[53]

[illegible]

We can understand art no better than in terms of two {human traits} ~~op~~ that have come up in ~~our~~ modern ~~minds~~ {consideration} as essential to be got rid of before we can have the perfect state

[recto]†   Outer form, inner form

Great scholar is one who has kept his heartiness through the discipline and la-bor of learning. Whose modesty forbids him to insist on what he has more than learning.

Logic of the emotion is what the eye of the poet picks up ahead.

No one can imagine a planned poem.

Have I an idea for April 19   August 17

When is an idea.

[1r]‡   Before the beginning of a poem are all the words in the dictionary and all the rhymes in the rhyming dictionary.[54]

•   •   •

---

* Written below the line.
† 7½″ × 11″ white page written in black ink.
‡ The first of a set of five 8″ × 6″ sheets of white paper.

Separateness important as connection

How many years of thinking must have gone to ~~the emo~~ make the lightness of the line

Here without regret one sees!   Who has given

me to this sweet

Ranks conditions and degrees

~~The poet had been through all the phases~~

It sounds as if the poet had been through all the phases of social thought only to find himself where he was in the beginning. The last ~~two~~ {three} ideas [illegible] catch myself having concern the name of Shirley's poem Death the Leveller[55] and the possibility of filling the world with any one thing rabbits or security [illegible] we ~~else~~ attended to it and nothing all of us, and how society would look if it were the same at both ends: it be the only living thing without [illegible] head {and} tail. The questions [illegible] are such thoughts evaded. No because you never know when years of them will flower in one good line or couplet.

The [illegible] has been to distrust the mental part of painting, poetry and music. The poetry

[1v]   purists as I like to call them from {the title} [?Brements] book, have been misunderstood I think in their position about subject matter and thought. Should a poem be on a subject. No but it should be a process of discovering a subject and not only to the reader but to the writer.

(Life is ~~stream that~~ river that divides That goes apart round islands great and small[56]

[2r]   By wrong, I mean inexact, careless [illegible] {with} facts: {as in} having the sun rise in the West, hav{ing}* Cortez discover the Pacific[57] have{ing}† a carpenter shingle the roof from the ridgepole downward: ~~being~~ Whatever poetry loves it seems not in love literal truth. It is vulgarly a synonym for ~~untruth~~ harmless untruth.

By wild I mean ~~outside the fences~~[58] {outside} ~~scornful~~ offences civil and

---

* Written beneath the line.

† Written beneath the line.

domestic. {Poetry} It is the real{m}* where all of man not brought in and broken still runs [illegible] impulsive. ~~It incurs debt lightly.~~ It reaches {the} highest of generosity {in giving away} with what doesnt belong to it. Gener-ous again it loaves [illegible] to friends to keep it from falling [drunken] off the roof ~~when drunk.~~ {But}† Altruistic it thinks only of some other mans wife {By inadvertence it may have a wife of its own}.

It is Shelleys Episychideon[59]

It is Vachel Lindsays Pony[60] that wouldnt be broken of dancing.

By foolish I mean silly about beauty and its {own} sensitiveness to beauty. There is always about as much beauty as it can stand. One more touch and it will cry or die or fly Any thought [illegible] to make plain men ashamed

[2v]   is peculiarly poetic.

[3r]‡   If {we} ~~count all the kinds of success in the world~~ {big and little} ~~there is re-ally a great deal of success. More than most think.~~ Success is the experience of completing consummating and rounding out any form of whatever size. If we count all the sizes of success ~~there a there are really more~~ [illegible] there may [illegible] {easily} be more success in the world than failure [illegi-ble] at least there may be enough to give the elusion ~~of~~ in retrospect of hav-ing been more. That is to say {total} success may be higher than {ideal} fail-ure is long.

The maladjusted and the frustrated ~~are~~ are {often} simply those who can-not ~~in their natures~~ {or will not} ~~have the size~~ and just their ambitions to the size of ~~achievement~~ {[illegible]} ~~it is~~ {it is} within their natures, ~~and ambition~~ to achieve. They even make a merit of having failed of what was too much for them. They boast of a divine [?dissatisfaction]. They expect to be at once admired and and pitied for their plight. They would rather have failed to be Shakespeare than {have} succeeded in being Longfellow. Their misfortune may have been the accidental choice of a moment when it was still open to them either to laugh off their misplaced of ambition or

[3v]   to perish braving it out: ~~Once they become public cases they are of~~ {to make light of it or make} heavy. Once they become public cases to [illegible] They are [illegible] when they become public cases of braving it out: ~~They are~~ like

---

* Written beneath the line.

† Inserted in left-hand margin.

‡ Page written in black ink.

the first offender who if young enough may be permitted by ~~society~~ {circumstance} to regard his fault rather ~~as a crime~~ prank on society than as a crime against society.

[4r]*   I have word

_____

It does seem as if viewed ~~from~~ as widely as [illegible] we now see ~~that~~ good had been [illegible] and ~~we are~~ the world was better than it used to be

Havent you heard of the new belief I am come into the world to teach. The last teacher. No more will be needed

"Oh I see"—and after looking long—"I see."[61]

The most terrible of all is the countless lives that have gone out in ~~darkness a~~ {blind} sacrifice to us and our happiness here at the end of time in the cold of the sun. I dont [want]? their sacrifice. Going back to the wretchedest nameless slave who died under the lash building the ~~pyramids~~ first ~~pry~~ pyramid
    Shall we bring in the She Serub to cleanse him of this pessimism. He'll take the permission out of [illegible] (You ought to see the Glee [illegible]

[4v]   Vote or war may change the frame. Our life stories will shape much the same. We lose our loves

~~Do~~ {Are} reforms then nothing to us at the [-] {people's} level? We join in the shouting in the street. When we go home we are let down from our excitement. What is for us is love and what follows [illegible]. The scarcely touches us

Is no state better for us than another. Was feudalism as good as what we call capitalism. Was the eleventh century no worse than now.

Suppose there is Progress. {Which} Which I halt stupidly asking moves imperceptibly but moves to heaven.
We are taught to pray saying Thy Kingdom come on earth

_____

* Page written in black ink.

I have taught otherwise. I have defined the world I should scorn to profit
by the sacrifice of all who have perished miserably

*But even if I am wrong and heaven is to come in the cold of the sun
There is still the objections of to a final civilisation based on all the slave ages
of the buried past.

over

[5v]   I have a word that may alter your position.

No one has ever gone to heaven. All there will ever be there are angels than
which we are always to be a little lower.

His kingdom is to come on earth.

When here at last bring it it will be for all the dead arising to come into. [Il-
legible]. They are waiting they are pressing for a conclusion. The lurking are
places are full their latent potential.

Individual goodness is the ground grip the purchase on which the larger race
goodness can rely to swing its self forward.

I want you to stop doubting to give up obstructing with your doubts. The
kingdom is to come and for all who ever contributed the least of lives toward
it. None shall be left out.

Vote or war may change the frame
Life stories shape about the same
You take my doctor's middle name†

[1r]‡   To begin with I assume that you are a radical?

From the fact that twenty young {one} and twenty?

I make haste to say that I know as well as you that the dividing line between
radical and conservative cuts across the line between youth and age at right
angles and almost exactly at the middle.⁶² and in the same way across the line
between the sexes and the line between the ric poor and {the} rich. Some of
the {The} extremist radicals {may} have a private yachts and as many [illegi-
ble] as a rascal has aliases. One of the poorest and lowest jokes [illegible]

---

* There is an arrow with line from "But" to the beginning of the sentence, "I should scorn
profit . . ." above.

† These three lines written upside-down.

‡ 6¾″ × 9¾″ white paper.

{and} latest jokes on our human{ity}* [illegible] ~~will have it~~ {is} that a conservative is one who has something to conserve.† I refuse to have it that young foolishness makes a radical old ~~conservatism~~ stupidity a conservative. Radicalism and conservatism {go deeper ~~than that~~ deeper down} are greater than that. [Illegible] {The poem says} We are born to one [illegible] or the ~~other the poet says~~. other as the poem says} ~~They~~ {the [?two]} create [illegible] [illegible] {by interaction} other and each gets its share of the best brains {and natures} in the choosing up of sides. I will listen to now low reflections neither.

But after all who knows what a radical is any more.

Dont ~~yo~~ use that [?smoke] {[?cover]} on me I have [illegible] heard it too often from Maine to Georgia

[2r]   ~~The only one I admire~~ I give all my admiration to the one who used it first. I wouldnt keep a parrot.

~~I dont ask for your~~

Nobody asked for your admiration. ~~We~~ Im not {conceited} going to refuse wisdom merely because I didn't get it up myself. ~~I'm not so egotistical.~~

You should {be} if it is merely contemporary wisdom. Permit nobody alive to impose ideas on you. You will have little enough room left for your own thinking {to move [illegible] round in} after you have filled your mind with the {proven} wisdom of the ancients. Mental activity {the [illegible]} is the greatest thing [illegible] {of all}. The product must be put up with. It will gradually [illegible] close in on you ~~and~~ press on your arms at your side and bring you to a stop. But see that it is your own product that takes up the [?last/least] last of your {precious} open space. But you were young to tell me you were a communist or at least a socialist.

How do you know

By a certain resentful [?wretching/twitching] of your cheeks. You neednt be afraid to confess. I am no informer. I know ~~who~~ {a}man who writes for a most radical magazine under one name and for a conservative magazine under another name. ~~In fact I know two men~~ In fact I know two of this kind. The radical paper is in the [illegible]?. I dont tell on them I respect their position. They [illegible] on themselves as on a [illegible]. [Illegible] [And] ~~deception~~ The are under no obligations   [illegible] with an

---

* Written below the line.

† There is a line drawn from the end of this sentence to the start of the sentence above, beginning "Some of the {The} extremist radicals . . ."

[1r]* "Great men talk about ideas: mediocre men about events: low minds about people"[63]

[Illegible]   Add: Dramatists about all three.

                            What this man is in a word*
            I   3   2
Grex Sex Rex and the greatest of these is grex.[64]

To do unto others. To teach them. To preach to them. To convert them. To doctor them. To psychoanalyze them. Interference is the strongest trait in human nature. We stick into each other in all directions. We are inextricably one. We are a grex. {[illegible] Co ex co ex co ex. The grex in me.} We flourish only by minding each others business. And [illegible] doing each others business.[65] It's a sad fool that obeys the injunction [?{Mesa}] Mind your own business. He shall perish of his obedience as [illegible] it were {of} a disease. The disease will be called offishness (as opposed to offishness.) The Herd Made One. {Significant that we spend so much time keeping each other at even a reasonable distance by endlessly repeated Mind your etc.} But still it must be remembered The separate ness of the parts is quite as important as the connections of the parts.[66] And this is so of the parts of the society and equally so of the of the smalles parts of the smallest poems. The effect is better if the parts are not derivable from any one part. Members of one another.

integrated into.

*Always a muddle head present to exclaim: To great a simplification. Things arent
not so simple as that. When you try for any oneness.

[1v]   Democracy is   and maintaining   the best soldiers from privates
                                                          {[illegible}]}
The best way to find the best people, the best generals the best statesmen the best thinkers the best artists, the best soldiers the best common people. If not it will perish in favor of the older ways of feuding and maintaining the best people the aristocracy. If not the best soldiers from democracy then it should

---

* 8″ × 7″ ruled school notebook page.

perish form the earth and wan ton abeyance to come back when the fiery fight is heard no more.

Jefferson Franklin Adams and others collaborated to paint the Constitution. Washington sat for it[67]

[1r]*   Melancholy of having touched form and seen the form [illegible] of life by comparison. (Some find form in their own works of art and are at rest)

Melancholy of having got the idea of what was beginning to be or happen— having got the whole idea and so see in the young institution as it will be when completed in its old age

Melancholy of finding your mistakes in thinking that ~~what~~ {salvation} can had by the individual is within the reach of the race

Artist of very high degree. He is neither moral religious nor patriotic

Some thing to study ~~and relate~~ [historicaly] ~~and phil~~ {in its historical} and philosophical relations.

Positive thrust of personality and belief

Many words many ideas.

You have to feel queer to queer the words

Displacement refraction [?If so]

[1v]   I note something ~~in~~ o to prove it

You may not have noticed but Im talking in metre. and poetry is the least given to question, of all literature.

Lowes says[68]
On the contrary it quotes entirely

Elevated— {already} in the work—queer

•   •   •

---

* 8″ × 6″ white page.

⌈doodlings in ink⌉

Some people find trouble

Distinction

[1r]*

Sad –sad irony

[From] {[illegible] His art} what how far

Emotion   From what how far

Recognition

Quoting   yes quoting ~~from the~~ dictionary words

the

Fragmentary is {the} impression on the mind

~~The a~~ aristocracy

The aristocrat is one who finds himself
Worthy on grounds of loftiness too low

How shall sincerity perform cut capers
[~~Illegible~~] {Teacher} I come to school {again} to you to ask you
What else is everything in [~~illegible~~] poetry

What did I tell you yesterday ~~was~~ it was
So and so says no similes are needed
You mustnt quote one teacher to another

{And}† How {in} poetry ~~shall be~~ made pure

Bards of passion and of mirth

[1v]   The psychology of [~~illegible~~] poetry is the same as that of desire—which is
blind
All this talk of poetry without thought—pure poetry

The strength of a man is in the extremity of the opposites he can hold together by [?main] force   Law-rebellion-Will-reason

---

* 8″ × 6″ white page.
† Inserted in left-hand margin.

Form—content   Poor weak partisans
of either one alone
          I thought you said

Grazing—refracting

Politics will bring the Golden Age for all

Poetry is the Golden Age for whosoever will
                              [So also can the farm or]*

The president ~~the wife~~ {the policeman} the bishop the wife

Ideal in love is a triangle.

Want you to write them as an aphrodisiac on? the apothecary.

          Recognition J.L. Lowes   You have to see what a phrase is form to see
how far the poet has fetched it. Fetching and farfetching.[69] over

[1r][†]   Lack of faith keeps its pressure to much on the steering wheel.

You can feel a moment of shifts working as just after you have dialed a telephone before the bell starts at the other end.

A poem can afford to be misunderstood somewhat if it is going to be a long
time here.

Poor ye (save always } No economics
                              for him
Render unto Caesar[70]

Old Testament wrong in science only.[71]

[2r]   It is going to be {poured} run ~~no~~ and flowed not pieced together—returned
to and renamed with words of beauty till it is {an article} overstuffed furniture.

---

* A line is drawn from sentence immediately above to middle of this bracketed phrase.
† First of six sheets of 8½″ × 5½″ white paper written in black ink.

It slides on its own emotion as a snail on its own flow of silver.

Paved the future with things that have happened to me and things that equally of their own motion have occurred to me

They're like stones God has scattered over my pasture and no one has picked off

They lie so undisturbed they grow in size

The separateness is important as the connection.[72] ~~There~~ Three lumps

[3r]   Beginning Im not an idealist. Nothing God does can disappoint me.

The only things I ever wished were different were the moon and goodness I have wished not that the moon were green cheese or that it were within our reach or that it were inhabited. I have wished that it were not single.

God can trust me not to be captious. So can my friends. I am never heard suffering from their failure in my eyes. I have nothing to judge things by except the way I find them except by themselves.

And yet I can lend myself to the extravagances of idealism upon action as in a Shelley or a Lenin.

~~Propaganda~~ {Political belief} only good as it comes in through what you are.

Seeking political belief for material as silly as seeking experience for material {for material.}*

You neednt worry you'll have both and both will show {[~~illegible~~]} {[~~illegible~~]} {through you.}[†]

[4r]   Happiest thing is to ~~have someone~~ [?wanted]

The fear of loving the suffrage the [?convert]

The fear of not being kept up with. He can do little

False pride in being unintelligible Sadism.

Always a figure of ~~of~~ manhood to be realized in politics a statesman in religion a saint

in business a magnate

---

* This phrase written below the previous two words.

[†] There is a line drawn from the word "show" to these three phrases, which are written above the previous sentence.

in poetry a lover. [Illegible] I omit kings. There was [illegible] when the king combined in his office all

Happy is the

We have had too much of escape as an explanation the idea that we have come to who arrived where we are by flight.

Changing the rules

How much in the books—thus far.

The perfection of happiness is to be wanted as much as you want. [Illegible] to have to have someone [illegible] want understand you as much as you want to be understood.

Value themselves on having got up something to {lover}* expect that can never be. I have never wished [illegible] asked for the moon. Just to know how it feels to be an idealist I have let my permitted myself a wish that the earth might have been blessed with more than one moon

[5r]   four or five deploying and [illegible]

[6r]   On being carried away with the eagle and being carried away by the eagle. Imaginative [?anyone] Rush of being is becoming. Becoming is a rush of being to the {heart and} mind. Fresh access of the old first longing.

Every poem is

	Fear of not being different
Sight and insight	Fear of superficiality.
	Fear of habit seeing
	Fear of not being wanted

Fear of un genuineness. Things that happen to you and things that just as much of their own emotion occur to you.

Guide right   Guide left

•   •   •

---

* This word written in right-hand margin.

The snail has two feelers {out ahead}. We have two eyes {further out} — and two of whatever more it is that is aware of dangers to avoid without really having {to have} them in mind.

Fears give us most to talk about
A subject like economics is concerned with nothing out fears to right and left of our pursuit. There is not such thing in the department of knowledge of ~~unity~~ reconciliation of left and right transcendence of party.

[1r]* but a {with} ~~stranger~~ a stranger's surprise.[73] So it melts in the encounter of a beast and its prey of lover and lover a man and a monkey. The least possible case of it is seeing your own face in the water or a looking glass. The fascination of literature is analogous. It gives you your traits back in the characters of the books.
      Are these facts material.
      No they are merely thrown in for your improvement by the way.
      Is improvement [?worth] which in the eleventh hour.
      People have taken college degrees at the age of seventy.
      It is indecent. No one ought to be caught improving himself {or being improved} after school age. Grooming and primping are private matters. The use of lipstitch and howdy ~~should be forb~~ in public should be forbidden by law. But after all it is not

[2r] a question of my age. I am still young. [Illegible] what interest have I in education [?when/whom] you are about to be made short work of
      Yes if you will not vote
      I am obdurate.
      We first try persuasion before resort to coercion.
      Neither persuasion nor coercion can ~~touch~~ {corrupt} the sources of the will. You cant poison a living spring.
      The kings mercy lies in ~~not~~ punishing {not} for contumacy but for error only. It remains to measure the extent of your error. The case is one presumably of conscientious objection to participates{ating} in what you consider a hollow mockery You say you do not believe in sex. What are some of the other things you [?doubt] believe in—if you are really with them on your tongues end?
      Voting war relativity rabies ~~and~~ sleep evolution[74] Freud and Marx

---

* First of four 8″ × 6″ white sheets written in black ink.

[3r]   As I say they havent got through with me yet. The propose to show me.
How? In this room? Why does it have to be in this chamber of horror?
It is a good ~~room~~ {place}. Any given time in the world is just such another
to a person living in it—a confusion of dangers like a crossing of three or
more streets in a metropolis at midday. It ~~is~~ seems hardly to make sense.
But haven't you given in?
Only the first point at issue—progress. I have granted that there is prog-
ress. And there is. I see it now

[4r]   So you have elected to be judged by a jury of men rather than women.
The better to be understood.
Because men are more understanding
Of women as women are of men.
Is it true that you were taken in the act of refusing to vote.
I confess it to save you the trouble of adducing proof.
Refusing to vote after all the fuss that has been made for a hundred years
to get you the vote.
I didnt make it.
But your sex did.
I don't believe in sex
Then you dont understand life
Not entirely. Are you prepared to define it.
Lif[e] is that which parts ~~round~~ like a river round islands great or small to
meet itself further on with recognition

[recto]*   Once atom molecule

A poem may turn out to be propaganda
 "   "   "   "   "   " an exercise.

Poems are made out of trust in what will be
Propaganda as we [~~illegible~~] know it in general is made out of fear of what
may not be

To be an actor with no [illegible] muscles but ~~the~~ of the mouth and throat.

·   ·   ·

---

* 6¾" × 9¾" white sheet.

Take you by both hands and pull you over the last line in to more than you cared to say.

What sounds last the longest

[illegible]. Diagnosis.

1st Word Shame   {speech   bring yourself to say
                      writing
2   Theme shame {What you can talk about varies
                      With your different ages
    sentiment false*
3   Wealth shame   Sense of too much.   Strange reflex not tested
                                                 Image not tested.
4   ~~Cheating for what you like.~~
5 Metaphor a fanciful marriage
6 Sense of stops.   Too susceptible to mere words. Stump and skunk.
7 {What}† Goes to the spot—Italic)
8 Measure of a mathematician
         Burns so in the stomach it seems it must be doing good.
9 Mischievousness to scare people about this poisonous

[*recto*]‡   up from where we are

    That is the thought that in

It goes against us not put our arms around to retain

We know things we could do

But taken together they are too much for us

That is our darkest concern. That is my theme.

Dark it is that there is this waste.[75] ~~Darker~~

                •   •   •

---

* There is a line drawn from this phrase to the word "Strange" on the line below.
† Word inserted below the line.
‡ 8″ × 6″ white sheet.

Darker still that it is beyond us to check it

Society as it has grown up is some check upon it.

Reform would have it that a society could be declared ~~of~~ out of whole cloth
to check it entirely.

Utopia has dogged our steps.

It will get us.

I name our dark concern and our darker. There is still our darkest that perhaps we ought not to want to end want that we should condone sorrow.
~~That is the thought that in the hour of~~ [?revelry] ~~comes between us and~~

[1r]* If ~~it~~ {farming} gets to be too much of a {scientific} thing to learn. If ordinary
wits and character wont do for it. Why some of us have go to perish. Do you
mean to say that if I want to sink to the primitive level.
     On his [illegible] ugliness with which he ~~hates~~ finds so much to hate.
     Do you mean to say that if the new farming proves to be too much of a
scientific thing for me to learn, that that ends it: there is going to be no life for
me to live? I shant be permitted to be slow ~~an~~ stupid and clod like at the task
of breaking clods. There will be left me on old farming for a refuge. Some
times I am frightened for my faculties. I am sure I am inadequate I am not
chemist economist financier {banker} enough to be one of the chosen few
holding up the agricultural end of our system. For God sake let me not rot
my days out in the old peasant fashion on some neglected bit of land ~~left~~ left
out of account. I could be crossed off and my offspring could creep back into
the social scheme as servants as common soldiers if any such be still called
for in the day of efficiency.

[1v] I will not try to say

I will not try to make you see
How deeply in a wood beside a tree

[1r]†   I demand to speak with God

•   •   •

_____
* 10″ × 6¾″ white sheet.
† 6¾″ × 8¼″ white sheet.

What is your business with God

I couldn't explain that to anybody but God

There is not God

So much the better perhaps. Because that rules out half my business. If there is no God there can be no future life. The present life is all I should have to worry about.

There is no future life. Are you worried about the present life.

Even more so because there is no future life to defer to. I see all salvation limited to here and now. Happiness cannot be put off. I must ask to see the highest authority at once.

You aren't mocking the saints are you?

<u>Saints</u> No! those bare-faced church introductions. Who introduced them to the church? Nobody but themselves. Let me see the highest authority there is on

[1v]* The blaze is within you The combustibles touched off are piled up every-thing of your first fifteen years of life. The light you see is the fires reflection on the walls of the night on the walls of the universe. What lures you is the walls to go through. There is a not well defined or sure of a gate there or it is of a man or of a poem or a painting. The Look in your eyes and lips is greed for that goal—hunger and thirst for it.

Set men free for their daintier troubles. {Despairs,} sorrow of love ambition and sincerity and adjustment.

I'm a plain man I'd rather be worried about a living than any lazy mans fantasticality

•   •   •

---

* Page written in black ink.

The style controllers wife says there is no need of any change of style in [illegible] womens clothes: so there will be none. Change always threatening

Thought come out as unviolently as when a fog burns off

[recto]*   Last expression of what you bear
for belief

It is the chastisement that none but
the most distant can give you

Near is dear. There must be some
one far enough away to chastise
you more than the near and dear
can be expected to.

[verso]   A Business Letter

The Waiting Spirit[76]

~~The~~ A Moment When You See One
Composing in Things

Skin I suspect is partly from flesh and partly from skin. Just so words
are partly from things and partly from other words. R.F 1935
These old scraps may amuse you.

[recto]†   On what similarity have the following groups been made?

1.   [illegible]

Masefield's Sea Fever[77] Stevenson's Romance[78]
Caremen's Joy's of the Road,[79] Kipling's L'Envoi[80]

---

* The remaining pages are from the Barrett Collection of the University of Virginia library
(6261-bb and 6261-y). This is the first of two sheets on a 5″ × 6″ unruled cream-colored
page written in black ink and dated 1935.
† 4⅞″ × 6″ unruled cream-colored page. The remaining pages are written in blue ink.

2. [illegible]

Johnson's Statue of King Charles[81]
Bottomleys to Iron Founders.[82]

3

OShuahgnessy's Fountain of Tears[83]
Margaret Woods' the Mariners, Blunt's[84]
    Deviate City,[85] Swinburne's Hesperia[86]
Dobell's Return,[87] Davidson's Runnable Stag[88]
    [?Dometh's] Christmas

4

Rosetti's Blessed Domozel[89]
Morris' [?Sailing] of the Sword[90]
Tennyson's Lady of Shalott[91]

5

Ingelows High Tide[92] Stevenson
Christmas at Sea[93] Davidsons Runnable Stag, Gibsons Fannan Isle.[94]

6

Patmores Magna est Veritas[95]

[verso]   Locky Lampson's At Her Window,[96]
Christina Rosetti, Italia,[97] Francis
Thompson's Daisy[98] Synge's A Question[99]
Flecker's Rionperoux[100] Davies Liesure[101]
Henleys England my England[102]

    I.   Ans. Wanderlust*
    2.   Ans. Spirit of reaction
        [illegible phrase]

---

* The remaining entries on this page are written upside-down.

3.   Ans. Sonorousness

4.   Ans. Pre-Raphaelite picture-writing

6: Narrative

6 Nothing at all. Just a jumble

[recto]*   Capital in parenthesis

took up an interest

machinery—worm at its core

to rather relish

birds of a feather—work in same channels

Time is one of those things you save have

To cruelly pay

mutual agreement 112

Alright Chap 7

147 there was little sign of struggle in parenthesis

118 waste of motives   bull by horns not sure

122 shudders body—shudders <u>at</u> rain

123 Son on   go on

    132   Who had killed whom

              Who had chased whom

    133   the <u>events</u> had <u>synchronized</u> or the times had coincided.

[verso]   135 (she had fallen into a restless sleep) [illegible]

    138   religious instead of Catholic or else call it strange instead of pre-
posterous.

            emerged <u>in</u> a new world

147 <u>sinfully</u> cruel.† I'm surprised shes etc

---

* 5″ × 6½″ unruled cream-colored page.

† The period after "cruel" is circled.

148 I wondered when?
152 flare in this business?
171 Doubt if I'd mention that horrid
    Strange Death of Pres Harding
174 follow her lead? not leader
175 [illegible] It would have taken a dozen murders to shake
18 rather to balance
210 recourse

Such grand writing is [?in] the three or four kinds needed to build a novel
Intensities of imagined scene (you grew up on this) Intensities of imagined
dialogue intensities of insight into character and situation. Too good to be a
disaster story.

[r]*   This patched up God
       What God is this with whom we are consoled
       Unless
       This God that put together from all the scrapps
       And leavings in the science laboratory
       The shreds and patches of the last perhaps
       Lip service still accords him all the {power} and glory
       But only
       But all he sums and personifies
       Is what as yet our science cant comprise

       His doom it is to shrink as science grows
       As {man} we reduce {diminish} {reduces} what to thought is waste
       God shrinks as man inexorably knows
       And follows on to know impatient haste

---

* White unruled sheet, 6⅛″ × 8″.

"Nothing more composing than composition"

MS. 002336. *Black buckram notebook with red and gold bands at the top and bottom.* 10½" × 8¼". *"Record 278 B-R" stamped on the cover and "National: Green-white Hammermill paper" stamped on the inside front cover. White ruled pages with numbers printed in the upper right hand corner. All entries are in black ink.*

[1r] Nothing more composing than composition[1]
The holiness of wholeness though it be no larger than of a basket a horse-shoe a nail or an apple. I asked a teacher if he had ever had a whole experi-ence ~~with~~ of a pupil—so that it made a story. Tell it. Would he have recog-nized himself in your narrative? Yes I ~~told~~ gave one the idea once for a novel. And first he went and lived the idea and he wrote the novel. The idea was that the sin is love—original sin—according not only the priests of our reli-gion but the pagan (see Atlis) and the least sever punishment for it the mild-est of all is marriage.
      The boy and girl who in elopement

[2r–79r] [blank]

[80r] And in the end

[81r] As the slave owns the owner of the slave
The people always ruled in being ruled
Not so they may have noticed it at first
Appearances were that they feared the King
More than the king feaed them in end Accad.
~~The truth was that it was from fear of them~~
~~And feasting with them~~
It was from fear of them and ~~of~~ and feasting with them
{He} But it was only {out of} in the fear of them
      And fear of fasting with them {he recognized} he was king.
      {With Tyrannically. And he always failed}

{Time after time he had his hold on them}
{He was afraid they weren't enough afraid
{And in the His fee}
He was afraid (the people) (his subjects) weren't afraid
And in the end they weren't. He always failed.
And there was no more kingdom in the desert.
Someone else tried one with them {elsewhere} somewhere else
On a new principle {of better men} of balanced fear
Being less terrible with laws himself
{Having} And having them less terrible insecurate?
{Now they were satisfied} To any punishment he neednt inflict.
{He raised them to appreciate up to an appreciation}
Now were they satisfied? They never were.

Notes

Acknowledgments

Index

Notes

1. Frost here may be referring to James Arthur Hunter (1824–1889), an Australian writer and pastoralist.

2. This is a draft of one of Frost's earliest poems from his Lawrence years:

> The reason of my perfect ease
> In the society of trees
> Is that their cruel struggles pass
> Too far below my social class
> For me to share them or be made
> For what I am and love afraid.

Frost's comment in the upper-right corner of the page, "Old old nineties," was probably written decades later, when he came back to the notebook. Frost wrote a copy of the draft and marked it as such in Notebook 32, 4v.

3. References to "Waste" continue throughout this notebook. See also 4.13r; 31.7r, 8r, 10r, 40r, 40v; 32; 37.1r, 5v, 6v; 22.10v; 13.8r; 12.7v; 9.10r; 24.39v; 21.4r, 7r; 27.29r, 45r, 46r; 5; 47; 23.10r; 35.13r, 16r.

4. See 22.1r, 47r; 12.10r; 37.2r; 7.3r, 4r; 33.9r; 8.58r, 58v; 17.41r; 19.8v; 24.38v; 29.23r.

5. This line recurs throughout this notebook. See also 37 and 47.

6. The poem in draft here is an early version of "Pod of the Milkweed," which Frost published as a Christmas poem in 1954. It also has phrases in verse of what appeared as his talk entitled "The Future of Man" on the occasion of the centennial of the publication of Darwin's *On the Origin of Species* in 1959 in New York.

7. See Frost's "Pod of The Milkweed" (1954): "But waste was of the essence of the scheme. / And all the good they did for man or god / To all those flowers they passionately trod / Was leave as their posterity one pod / With an inheritance of restless dream." And from "The Future of Man" (1959). "He's a god of waste, magnificent waste is another name for generosity of not always being intent on our own advantage, nor too importunate even for a better world. We pour out a libation to him as a symbol of the waste we share in—participate in. Pour it on the ground and you've wasted it; pour it into yourself and you've doubly wasted it. But all in the cause of generosity and relaxation of self interest."

8. Enoch Lincoln (1788–1829), a Congressman for Massachusetts and Maine when the two states were one. When Maine was made separate, he represented that state from 1921 to 1926. He was elected governor of Maine in 1827 and served until his death. See 31.72v.

9. This page is an early draft of what became "A Concept Self-Conceived" (1963). One large "X" is drawn over the first two stanzas, and another is drawn over the third stanza.

10. See 24.14r; 47.

11. See 4r; 4.1r, 12r; 12.5r; 24.32v; 33.3r.

12. See Matthew Arnold (1822–1888), "A Progress" (1852): "The Master stood upon the mount, and taught. / He saw a fire in his disciples' eyes; / 'The old law,' they cried, 'is wholly come to nought, / Behold the new world rise!' / 'Was it,' the Lord then said, 'with scorn ye saw / The old law observed by Scribes and Pharisees? / I say unto you, see *ye* keep the law / More faithfully than these!'" (ll.1–8).

13. See 4.1r; 29.38r; 33.cover, 3r; 25.41r; 26.27r; 28.12r; 47. See also Frost's poem "The Lesson for Today" from *A Witness Tree* (1942), ll. 98–103: "Earth's a hard place in which to save the soul, / And could it be brought under state control, / So automatically we all were saved, / Its separateness from Heaven could be waived; / It might as well at once be kingdom-come. / (Perhaps it will be next millennium.)"

14. See 1r; 4.1r; 12r; 12.5r; 24.32v; 33.3r.

15. In 1872 William Prescott Frost, Jr., Frost's father, graduated from Harvard College and became principal at Lewistown Academy in Pennsylvania.

16. These are significant dates in the biography of Frost's family. Frost's parents were married in March 1873; 1874 is the year RF was born; 1875 is perhaps the year that RF recalls for the birth date of his sister, Jeanie Florence Frost, though it was actually 1876. 1885 is the year that RF's father, William Prescott Frost, Jr., died.

NOTEBOOK 2

1. See 28.6v; 31.7r.

2. Frost took up poultry farming in 1899, renting a house and barn in Methuen, Massachusetts, with financial help from his grandfather. In 1900 he moved to a 30-acre farm in Derry, New Hampshire, where he continued poultry farming for the next decade. From 1903 to 1905 Frost published a number of stories and articles in several poultry magazines, including *The Eastern Poultryman* and *Farm-Poultry* (see later in this notebook).

3. Cecil John Rhodes (1853–1902). British Imperialist, mining magnate, and later philanthropist.

4. Dante, *Paradiso*, XVI, 121 (Caponsacco).

5. See 24.46v; 31.7r; 14.4v; 47; 25.1r; 46.5r; 12.10r.

6. See 10.2r.

7. William Shakespeare, *Richard III*, Act I, Scene I.

8. The Roycroft was a reformist community of workers and artists which formed part of the arts and crafts movement founded by Elbert Hubbard in 1895 in East Aurora, New York, near Buffalo. The name derives from the 17th-century printers Samuel and Thomas Roycroft, and the group took as its "creed" a quotation from Ruskin: "A belief in working with the head, hands, and heart, and mixing enough play with work that every task is pleasurable and makes for health and happiness."

9. A possible reference to Kimball Flaccus (1911–1972). Frost had a copy of *The White Stranger: Poems* (1940) inscribed "To Robert Frost with deep respect from Kimball Flaccus. New York City, Jan. 26, 1940."

10. German psychologist Jacques Loeb (1859–1924).

11. Slumming parties in the late 19th century were groups that visited slums for philanthropic reasons.

12. William Jennings Bryan (1860–1925), Congressman who was defeated by Republicans in the 1900 presidential election after running on an anti-imperialism, pro-silver plat-

form. By "symposium" Frost may be referring to the Chautauqua, a movement in the late 19th and early 20th centuries that held assemblies across the United States after starting as a summer educational group on Lake Chautauqua in upstate New York. Bryan's lectures on temperance and other issues made him one of the most popular speakers at the assemblies.

13. "Trap Nests," a story Frost wrote for *The Eastern Poultryman,* February 1903, p. 71.

14. "Old Welch Goes to the Show," a story Frost wrote for *Farm-Poultry,* August 15, 1903, pp. 334–335.

15. Theodore Roosevelt (1868–1919) was vice-president under President William McKinley (1843–1901). McKinley was assassinated early in his second term, and Roosevelt assumed the presidency. Roosevelt was president from 1901 through 1909. "Rough Riders" was the nickname of the First U.S. Volunteer Cavalry Regiment, which Roosevelt organized and helped command during the Spanish-American War.

16. Mentioned in Frost's poultry stories. Dr. Charlemagne C. Bricault.

17. An axolotl is an aquatic salamander native to central Mexico that never matures past its gilled stage, thus providing a real-life representation of the imagined water babies in Rev. Charles Kingsley's children's novel *The Water-Babies, A Fairy Tale for a Land Baby* (1863).

18. See also 4; 6.22r; 8.56r; 14.17r; 15.33v; 20.11r, 16v; 21.4r, 7r; 22.49r; 24.24r, 47v; 28.10r; 29.14r, 23r; 31.4r, 7r, 7v, 40r; 32.7r, 10r; 34.1r, 2r, 2v; 41.7r; 47.

19. *Times Saturday Review,* founded in 1858, began as a review in opposition to *The Times* of London. Toward the end of the nineteenth century, it had a reputation for stylistic and scholarly standards. *McClure's Magazine* (1893–1929) was a popular monthly published and edited by Samuel Sidney McClure (1857–1949), an Irish-born publisher who in 1884 established the first newspaper syndicated in the U.S. and went on to found the magazine that bore his name. It was intended to present at a small price the work of the most famous contemporary English and American authors, as well as to report current scientific knowledge and world affairs. It became a leading vehicle for the muckrakers, producing lively articles on complex subjects, and was a spearhead of the reform movement, investigating every aspect of American life. Its contributors included O. Henry, F. P. Dunne, Jack London, and W. A. White, and among the leading articles were "The History of the Standard Oil Company," by Ida Tarbell; "The Shame of Minneapolis," by Lincoln Steffens; and "The Right to Work," by R. S. Baker. Its period of significance passed with the waning of public enthusiasm for reform, and McClure's own success diminished. The work he called *My Autobiography* (1914) was written by Willa Cather.

NOTEBOOK 3

1. See the conclusion to Frost's "Education by Poetry: A Meditative Monologue" (1930): "There are four beliefs that I know more about from having lived with poetry . . . And then finally the relationship we enter into with God to believe the future in—to believe the hereafter in."

2. See Frost's preface to *Collected Poems, 1939,* "The Figure a Poem Makes": "No tears in the writer, no tears in the reader. No surprise for the writer, no surprise for the reader."

3. See 24.30r; 28.20r; 20.19v; 43.2r; 22.31r.

4. In his pamphlet against the Church Prelates *The Reason of Church Government* (1642), John Milton prefaces the second book of his argument with an elaborate discussion of the

cultural and historical studies at his father's estate, Horton, from 1632 to 1638. He justifies his vocation of poetry and asserts that political prose is something he does only "with the left hand." He concludes by stating his reluctance to interrupt the very studies that might make one worthy to speak of the gospels, in stark contrast, he believes, to the vapid rhetoric of current Prelates: " . . . Neither do I think it shame to covenant with any knowing reader, that for some few years yet I may go on trust with him toward the payment of what I am now indebted, as being a work not to be raised from the heat of youth, or the vapors of wine, like that which flows at waste from the pen of some vulgar amorist, or the trencher fury of a riming parasite, nor to be obtained by the invocation of Dame Memory and her Siren daughters, but by devout prayer to that eternal Spirit who can enrich with all utterance and knowledge, and sends out his seraphim with the hallowed fire of his altar, to touch and purify the lips of whom he pleases. To this must be added industrious and select reading, steady observation, insight into all seemly and generous arts and affairs, till which in some measure be compassed, at mine own peril and cost I refuse not to sustain this expectation from as many as are not loth to hazard so much credulity upon the best pledges I can give them. Although it nothing content me beforehand, but that I trust hereby to make it manifest with what small willingness I endure to interrupt the pursuit of no less hopes than these, and leave a calm and pleasing solitariness, fed with cheerful and confident thoughts, to embark in a troubled sea of noises and horse disputes, put from beholding the bright countenance of truth in the quiet and still air of delightful studies to come into the dim reflection of hollow antiquities sold by the seeming bulk, and there be fain to club quotations with men whose learning and belief lies in marginal stuffings, who, when they have like good sumpters, laid ye down their horseload of citations and fathers at your door, with a rhapsody of who and who were bishops here or there, ye may take off their packsaddles, their day's work is done, and episcopacy, as they think, stoutly think, vindicated."

5. See the concluding lines of Milton's *Comus: A Masque* (1634), spoken by the Spirit: "Mortals that would follow me, / Love Virtue, she alone is free, / She can teach ye how to climb / Higher than the sphery chime; / Or if Virtue feeble were, / Heaven itself would stoop to her" (ll. 1018–1023).

6. Frost is referring to an article by William Johnson, "How Air Travel Began," *The Outlook*, June 25, 1910, pp. 375–380. Curtis is Glenn Hammond Curtiss who flew from Albany to New York on "a half-tone of machinery, guided by a daring aviator, rose by its own power high in air at Albany, and, in far less time than the fastest train could make it, descended safely in the metropolis one hundred and fifty miles away" (375). Curtiss "not only broke all records for fast flying, he not only made the longest flight but one [Paulhan's London-to-Manchester flight a few days before] anywhere in the world, but he demonstrated successfully for the first time the possibility of aeroplanes being used in travel between cities."

7. Robert Fulton (1765–1815) engineered the first steamboat and piloted it up the Hudson from New York to Albany on August 14, 1807.

8. Maurice Francis Egan, the American minister to Denmark. Egan was marginally associated with the Cook scandal when he received Cook in Copenhagen in September of 1909. Before Cook's claim that he had reached the North Pole was found fraudulent, Egan escorted him to the University of Copenhagen where he received an honorary doctorate and the silver medal of the Royal Geographic Society. Shortly thereafter, Peary reached

the North Pole. See "Dr. Cook in Copenhagen," *Century,* September 1910, pp. 759–763. The editors, however, have been unable to find any direct comparison made by Egan in print between Peary and Columbus.

9. Walter Wellman led a failed attempt to cross the Atlantic in a dirigible balloon on October 15, 1910. The journey, which started in Atlantic City and got as far as halfway between Nova Scotia and Nantucket Island, ended three days later four hundred miles off the coast of Cape Hatteras when the crew was rescued from dangerous winds.

10. See "Kitty Hawk" (1956).

NOTEBOOK 4

1. Matthew 6:10 : "Thy kingdom come. Thy will be done on earth, as it is in heaven."

2. See 29.38r; 33.cover, 3r; 25.4r; 1.1r; 26.27r; 28.12r. See also Frost's poem "The Lesson for Today," Notebook 1, note 10.

3. See 12r; 1.1r, 4r; 12.5r; 24.32v; 31.39r; 33.3r.

4. See 21r, 24r; 29.8v; 47; 26.28r.

5. See 28.8r, 9r.

6. See "The Constant Symbol" (1946): "We may speak after sentence, resenting judgment. How can the world know anything so intimate as what we were intending to do? The answer is the world presumes to know. The ruling passion in man is not as Viennese as is claimed. It is rather a gregarious instinct to keep together by minding each other's business." See also 31.42r; 22.49r; 47.

7. Joseph Albany (born Albani) (1924–1988), jazz pianist.

8. Frost bought a farm, known as the "Stone Cottage," in South Shaftesbury, Vermont, in 1920. (He had previously lived in Franconia, New Hampshire, from 1915 to 1920.) He gave the farm as a wedding present to his son Carol and daughter-in-law Lillian LaBatt in 1923.

9. Ganymede, the handsome son of Tros, was carried off by an eagle to be Jove's (Zeus's) cupbearer. See *The Homeric Hymn to Aphrodite* (5. 202–217).

10. Discussion of Darwin and evolution continues throughout this notebook. See also 2.16r; 6.22r; 8.56r; 14.17r; 15.33v; 20.11r, 16v; 21.4r, 7r; 22.49r; 24.24r, 47v; 28.10r; 29.14r, 23r; 31.4r, 7r, 7v, 40r; 32.7r, 10r; 34.1r, 2r, 2v; 41.7r; 47.

11. The Cod is the state symbol of Massachusetts. See Notebook 25 in which Frost presents the cod as a symbol of nature's waste.

12. See 28.10r.

13. The tiny (64-square-mile) volcanic island in the South Pacific is one of the most isolated inhabited places on earth. It has suffered ecological disasters and severe fluctuations in its population that some believe have led to cannibalism. See "The Bad Island—Easter" in *In the Clearing* (1962).

14. Glastonbury, Connecticut, was founded in 1693.

15. Tristan da Cunha (also Tristan d'Achuna) is a remote island in the South Atlantic Ocean discovered and named by the navigator Tristao d'Achuna in 1506.

16. Tiberius Sempronius Gracchus (d. 133 B.C.) and Caius Sempronius Gracchus (d. 122 B.C.), brothers, Roman statesmen, and social reformers who championed the redistribution of wealth and land. See also 22.36r and 47.

17. John Bull, the English equivalent of Uncle Sam, first appeared as a character in John

Arbuthnot's *The History of John Bull* (1712). He is usually depicted in cartoons as an honest, farmer figure. See also Notebook 47.

18. The Albigenses were a neo-Manichean religious sect that flourished in southern France during the 12th century. They opposed the authority of the Catholic Church and held to the heresy that there were two mutually opposed principles of good and evil. See also Notebook 47.

19. The Levellers were English political reformers active 1645–1649 whose ideas influenced the English Bill of Rights (1689) and the United States Constitution. See also Notebook 47.

20. See lines 5–9 of Frost's "Our Doom to Bloom," first published as Frost's Christmas poem of 1950 and later in *In The Clearing* (1962): "The Sibyl said, 'Go back to Rome / And tell your clientele at home / that if it's not a mere illusion / All there is to it is diffusion— / Of coats, oats, votes, to all mankind.'"

21. George Meredith (1828–1909), from *Modern Love,* sonnet LVI.

22. See Frost's *A Masque of Reason* (1945), 354–355 [God speaks]:

"Disinterestedness never did exist,
And if it did, it wouldn't be a virtue."

See also 15.19v; 19.9r; 22.33v; 24.28r; 29.

23. Frost's comment is a reference to what Jesus said in John 12:8: "For the poor you always have with you but me you have not always." See also 23r; 22.19r, 34r; 26.28r.

24. "What Became of New England" was the title of a commencement address Frost gave at Oberlin College, June 8, 1937.

25. Here Frost may be referring to some of the repartee that took place when he met with Wallace Stevens in Key West, first in 1935, then later in February 1940. Of this second meeting Lawrance Thompson writes: "Frost and Stevens traded literary gossip before resuming the playful teasing of each they had started in 1935.

'The trouble with you, Robert, is that you're too academic,' said Stevens.

'The trouble with you, Wallace, is that you're too executive,' retorted Frost.

'The trouble with you, Robert, is that you write about—subjects.'

'The trouble with you, Wallace, is that you write about—bric-a-brac.'"

From *Robert Frost: The Later Years,* p. 61.

26. See 47v; 29.12r.

27. A possible reference to Sara Teasdale's (1884–1933) book of poems *Rivers to the Sea* (1915). Cf. Frost's letter to Louis Untermeyer of August 7, 1936: "To hell with these baubles gewgaws kickshaws. I'll write 'em a poem the last night before I face the mike. I will and be damned to all the uncontrolled rivers in the country. (I've got a new slogan in for one party or the other. I hadn't broken it to you, had I?) It is the name and the theme of an eclogue I have written. This is it. No Rivers to the Sea! No water shall go back. Meanwhile, I am mowing some, chopping some, and digging a little. How could man die better?" The eclogue Frost mentions may be "Too Anxious for Rivers" (1947). Frost owned a copy of the 1915 edition inscribed to him by Teasdale as well as a copy of the 1927 edition. See also 47v; 29.12r, 12v.

28. Louis Brandeis (1856–1941), Justice of the United States Supreme Court, was a vehement opponent of large corporations and trusts. He became known as "the people's attorney" because of his devotion to public causes and his emphasis on the importance of

civic responsibility. In a speech delivered at Brighton, Massachusetts, December 2, 1904, Brandeis praised politicians for their commitment to public life: "It is customary for people to berate politicians. But after all, the politicians, even if their motives are not of the purest, come much nearer performing their duties than the so-called 'good' citizens who stay at home."

29. Brandeis was the first to cite "Privacy" as a right. Brandeis along with Samuel Warren wrote the paper on Privacy for the *Harvard Law Review,* Vol. IV, No. 5.

30. See 15r; 23.10r; 39.

31. See 5.19v; 26.14r.

32. See 42r; 33.3v; 47; 31.10r; 22.15r.

33. Pericles (470–399 B.C.E.), Athenian statesman and soldier.

34. Alcibiades (450–404), Athenian general and statesman, student of Socrates, known for his beauty.

35. Critias (460–403), Athenian philosopher, rhetorician, and poet.

36. Native people of Arctic coastal regions of North America.

37. The Navajo are the largest tribe of native North Americans and live primarily in the southwest United States.

38. See 22.17r.

39. Cf. Frost's "A Masque of Mercy" (1947): "*Jonah:* My name's not Joe. I don't like what she says./It's Greenwich Village cocktail party talk—/ Big-city talk. I'm getting out of here. / I'm—bound—away. (He quotes it to the tune.)" See also 13.12r; 24.3r; 11.29v.

40. Frost may be referring to "The Goose Girl" (1819), one of Grimms' Fairy Tales, though in that tale the girl does not lose a goose from her flock.

41. See 1r; 1.1r, 4r; 12.5r; 24.32v; 31.39r; 33.3r.

42. See 29.44r; 23.8r.

43. See 31.7r, 8r, 10r, 40r, 40v; 32; 37.1r, 5v, 6v; 22.10v; 13.8r; 12.7v; 9.10r; 24.39v; 21.4r, 7r; 27.29r, 45r, 46r; 1; 5; 47; 23.10r; 35.13r, 16r.

44. See 8v; 23.10r; 39.

45. Arthur Schopenhauer, *The World as Will and Representation* (1818). Frost also said in talks and interviews that he was most influenced by a book he had never read but had thought hard about the title, *The Vision Concerning Piers Plowman.* See Lawrance Thompson, *Robert Frost: The Years of Triumph* (1970), p. 700.

46. Cf. Frost's "New Hampshire" (1923), ll. 353–354, "On coming nearer: 'Wasn't she an i-deal / Son-of-a-bitch? You bet she was an i-deal.'" And "Build Soil" from *A Further Range* (1936). See also 22r; 29.31r.

47. Eleanor Roosevelt (1884–1962).

48. Ralph Waldo Emerson. In 1939, Frost was named the Ralph Waldo Emerson Fellow in Poetry at Harvard University and held the position for two years.

49. Robert Browning's "Waring": "What's become of Waring / Since he gave us all the slip, / Chase land-travel or seafaring / Boots and chest or or stuff and snapp, / Rather than pace up and down, / Any larger London town."

50. Award given annually since 1919 by Yale University for a book of poems by an author under 40. Archibald Macleish and W. H. Auden both served as judges.

51. Frost's "Introduction to Edwin Arlington Robinson's '*King Jasper*'" was published in 1936. In it Frost wrote, "Grievances are a form of impatience. Griefs are a form of patience."

52. Frost delivered "Education by Poetry: A Meditative Monologue" to the Amherst Alumni Council in November 1936.

53. See 29.32r; 44.1

54. "The Figure a Poem Makes" was the title Frost gave to his preface of his *Collected Poems* (1939).

55. Frost gave a talk to Amherst seniors on May 28, 1935, called "Our Darkest Concern" about the dangers of the extreme political left and right. See also "On Emerson": "I don't like obscurity and obfuscation, but I do like dark sayings I must leave the clearing of to time. And I don't want to be robbed of the pleasure of fathoming depths for myself." See also 32v; 47; 23.3r, 4r, 5r; 28.15r; 22.6r; 29.17r; 24.39r.

56. See Frost's "An Equalizer" from *A Witness Tree* (1942). See also 26.1r; 28.7r; 47.

57. John Webster, *The Duchess of Malfi* (1623), IV.ii.56–57.

58. William Allingham (1824–1829), "The Fairies."

59. *Acquitted: A Play in Three Acts*, by Charles Elton Openshaw (1900–1985), no publication date on play. Imprint: London: Steele's Play Bureau. See also 10.iv.

60. Region (and city) in southwestern Mexico.

61. Matthew 5:44: "But I say unto you, Love your enemies, bless them that curse you, do good to them that hate you, and pray for them which despitefully use you, and persecute you."

62. See 22.22r; 26.28r.

63. Cf. *A Masque of Reason* (1947), 105–106: "Jesse Bel. Your courage failed. The saddest thing in life / Is that the best thing in it should be courage." See also 52r; 26.3r.

64. See lines 41–42 of "The Tuft of Flowers" (1906) from *A Boy's Will*, "'Men work together,' I told him from the heart, / 'Whether they work together or apart.'"

65. See "West-Running Brook" (1928), ll. 56–60: "The Universal cataract of death / That spends to nothingness—and unresisted, / Save by some strange resistance in itself, / Not just a swerving but a throwing back, / As if regret were in it and were sacred."

66. Charles A. Lindbergh (1902–1974), American aviator and first to cross the Atlantic. Frost may be referring to a Lindbergh's controversial stances in favor of American isolationism before World War II.

67. Sports and entertainment arena in New York City. Frost probably refers to its third location on 8th Avenue (1925–1968). See 24.29r; 11.1r; 22.17r.

68. See 22.33v; 29.8v, 16r; 26.27r, 28r; 47.

69. See "The Generations of Men" from *North of Boston* (1914), ll. 82–83, "What will we come to / With all this pride of ancestry, we Yankees?"; 29.6r, 8v; 22.33v; 25.1r; 47; 26.27r.

70. See 1r, 24r; 29.8v; 47; 26.28r.

71. See 23.9r; 29.8v; 47.

72. Christina Giorgina Rossetti (1830–1894), Pre-Raphaelite poet.

73. See 12.4r, 12r; 22.6r; 29.28v, 54r, 62r.

74. Sinclair Lewis (1885–1951), novelist and author of *Babbitt* (1922). Theodore Dreiser (1871–1951), novelist and author of *Sister Carrie* (1900).

75. Cf. "America Is Hard to See," *In the Clearing* (1962) (first as "And All We Call American" in the *Atlantic Monthly*, June 1951). "But all he did was spread the room / Of our enacting out the doom / Of being in each other's way, / And so put off the weary day / When we would have to put our mind / On how to crowd but still be kind." See also 12.22r; 29.9r; 26.27r; 5.5r.

76. See 8.37r; 17.25r; 22.8r, 8v; 24.31r; 28.10r; 29; 33.5r; 35.7r; 47.

77. See 47.

78. See 15r; 29.31r.

79. II Samuel 18:1. "And David numbered the people that were with him, and set captains of thousands and captains of hundreds over them." See also 8.42v; 12.22r; 22.34r.

80. Cf. Genesis 12: 10–20. When Abram entered Egypt, he disguised his wife Sarah as his sister, fearing that they would kill him.

81. The book of Job has forty-two chapters. Frost concluded his *A Masque of Reason* (1945) with "(Here endeth Chapter Forty-three of Job)."

82. See 6r; 22.19r, 34r; 26.28r.

83. Invasion of Britain by Duke William of Normandy, 1066.

84. The last major battle of the American Revolution was fought October 6–9, 1781.

85. See 1r, 21r; 29.8v; 47; 26.28r.

86. See 4.24r; 24.43v; 29.8v.

87. See 27r; 48.1r; 21.5r; 29.34r; 25.14v; 22.33v.

88. See "Our Hold on the Planet."

89. See 22.34r.

90. See 22.23r.

91. See 25r; 48.1r; 21.5r; 29.34r; 25.14v; 22.33v.

92. See 22.8v; 29.15r; 31.32r.

93. Cf. Milton's "On Time" (1633), l. 4.

94. Cf. "The Figure a Poem Makes" (1939): "It begins in delight, it inclines to the impulse, it assumes direction with the first line laid down, it runs a course of lucky events, and ends in a clarification of life—not necessarily a great clarification, such as sects and cults are founded on, but in a momentary stay against confusion." See also 30.6r; 31.33v.

95. Lucretius (98–85), Roman poet and author of *De Rerum Natura,* a didactic poem based on the thought of Greek philosopher Epicurus (341–271 B.C.E.). Cf. Frost's "Too Anxious for Rivers" (1947).

96. *Anthony and Cleopatra,* III.xiii 195–197 [Enobarbus]: "Now he'll outstare the lightning; to be furious / Is to be frightened out of fear, and in that mood / The dove will peck the estridge; . . .'"

97. Stephen Crane (1871–1900), American novelist and poet, author of *The Red Badge of Courage* (1895).

98. See John Keats, *Endymion* (1818), I.1–5: "A thing of beauty is a joy forever: / Its loveliness increases; it will never / Pass into nothingness, but still will keep / A bower quiet for us, and a sleep / Full of dreams, and health and quiet breathing."

99. See Emerson's "Give All to Love" (1846), ll. 43–49: "Though thou loved her as thyself, / As a self of purer clay, / Though her parting dims the day, / Stealing grace from all alive; / Heartily know, / When half-gods go, / The gods arrive." See also 26.28r; 31.41v; 22.58v.

100. Aldous Huxley, "The Importance of Being Foreign," *Vanity Fair,* November 1928; reprinted in Aldous Huxley, *Complete Essays,* Vol. II, *1926–29,* edited by Robert S. Baker and James Sexton (Chicago: Ivan R. Dee, 2000), pp. 126–127: "Now, with the exception of two or three perfect and unalterable pieces, the poems of Edgar Allan Poe are tinged with a subtle vulgarity—a vulgarity that is not in the subject matter (for Poe was a great spiritual aristocrat), nor in the broad lines of the composition (for Poe had many qualities of a

great poet), but in the verbal texture of his poems, in the rhythms and harmonies of his verse."

101. Cf. Thomas Gray's (1716–1771) "On the Death of a Favourite Cat, Drowned in a Tub of Gold Fishes," ll. 37–42:

> From hence, ye beauties undeceived,
> Know, one false step is ne'er retrieved,
> And be with caution bold.
> Not all that tempts your wand'ring eyes
> And heedless hearts is lawful prize;
> Nor all that glisters, gold.

See also 44r.

102. See also Frost's "A Masque of Mercy" (1948); 35r; 22.4r, 12r; 31.6v, 10r; 29.9r; 33.1r, 1v; 24.32r; 21.11r; 26.12r, 13r; 19.6r; 23.8r, 9r.

103. See 4.32r; 14.15r; 24.39v, 43v, 44r; 19.5v; 27.7r; 47.

104. See 20.10r; 8.37r; 13.6r; 14.12r.

105. Frost gave a talk to Amherst seniors on May 28, 1935, called "Our Darkest Concern" about the dangers of the extreme political left and right. See also "On Emerson": "I don't like obscurity and obfuscation, but I do like dark sayings I must leave the clearing of to time. And I don't want to be robbed of the pleasure of fathoming depths for myself." See also 17r; 47; 22.6r; 23.3r, 4r, 5r; 28.15r; 29.17r; 24.39r.

106. Cf. Frost's *A Masque of Reason* (1945), ll. 201–204:

> Job's Wife. God, who invented earth?
> Job. What, still awake?
> God. Any originality it showed
> Was of the Devil . . .

107. John Milton, "Lycidas," l. 71.

108. Shakespeare, *Henry VIII*, III.ii 441–2.

109. Rudyard Kipling's poem "The White Man's Burden," published in *McClure's Magazine* in 1899, exhorted imperialism and touched off a feverish reaction in the American press for nearly two years.

110. See "Frost on Emerson" (1959): "Emerson supplies the emancipating formula for giving an attachment up for an attraction, one nationality for another nationality, one love for another love. If you must break free, 'Heartily know, / when half gods go / the gods arrive.'" See also 46r, 47v; 22.46r, 59r; 26.28r; 31.8r, 9r.

111. Cf. "The Lesson for Today" (1942). A variant phrase also appears on Frost's gravestone: "I had a lover's quarrel with the world."

112. See 36r; 15.28v; 43.1r, 6r; 45.1r; 47; 28.11r; 22.53r; 26.2r, 47.

113. See also Frost's "A Masque of Mercy" (1948); 32r; 22.4r, 12r; 31.6v, 10r; 29.9r; 33.1r, 1v; 24.32r; 21.11r; 26.12r, 13r; 19.6r; 23.8r, 9r.

114. Matthew 5:30, "And if they right hand offend thee, cut it off, and cast it from thee: for it is profitable for thee that one of thy members should perish, and not that thy whole body should be cast into hell."

115. J. B. Bury (1861–1927), *History of Greece* (Macmillan, 1913).

116. The Greeks, led by Themistocles, defeated the Persians at Salamis in 480 B.C.E.

117. The Sicilian Greeks defeated the Phoenicians at Carthage in 480 B.C.E.

118. See 34r; 15.28v; 43.1r, 6r; 45.1r; 47; 28.11r; 22.53r.

119. A possible reference to Hervey Allen (1889–1949), poet and friend of Frost's.

120. Thomas Campbell (1777–1844),"Ye Mariners of England": "Ye Mariners of England/That braved our native seas; / Whose Flag has braved, a thousand years, / The battle and the breeze . . ."

121. Cf. Frost's "Letter to The Amherst Student" (1935): "Whatever progress may be taken to mean, it can't mean making the world any easier a place in which to save your soul." See also 28.7r; 29.17r, 15r; 47.

122. Thomas Bulfinch (1796–1867), *The Age of Fable: Stories of Gods and Heroes* (1855).

123. See 29.16v, 29v; 15.22r; 28.18r; 9.19r. See also Frost's "Kitty Hawk."

124. Edgar A. Bancroft (1857–1925), *The Chicago Strike of 1894* (1895); Horace Fletcher (1849–1919), self-taught nutritionist popular in the first part of the twentieth century and nicknamed "The Great Masticator" because of his doctrine of "Fletcherism," which advocated chewing all food until it turned to liquid before swallowing. See also 28.38r.

125. John Keats (1795–1821). In addition, of course, to his "Ode on a Grecian Urn," Frost would likely have had in mind Keats's letters, especially the one to Benjamin Bailey of November 22, 1817—"What the imagination seizes as Beauty must be truth"—and the letter to George and Tom Keats of December 21, 1817, in which he discusses "negative capability." Frost would quote the phrase "beauty is truth" from Keats's "Ode on a Grecian Urn." See 19.10r and his letter to Sidney Cox of December 14, 1914: "You are not influenced by that Beauty is Truth claptrap."

126. See John Keats's sonnet, "When I have Fears that I may Cease to Be": "When I behold, upon the night's starr'd face, / Huge cloudy symbols of a high romance, / And feel that I may never live to trace / Their shadows with the magic hand of chance."

127. Francis Turner Palgrave, editor of the *The Golden Treasury* (Macmillan, 1861).

128. Cf. Emily Dickinson's "The heart asks pleasure first":

The Heart asks Pleasure – first –
And then – Excuse from Pain –
And then – those little Anodynes
That deaden suffering –

And then – to go to sleep –
And then – if it should be
The will of its Inquisitor
The privilege to die –

129. Colley Cibber (1671–1757), actor and dramatist, satirized by Alexander Pope in *The Dunciad, in Four Books* (1742).

130. Arthur Quiller-Couch (1863–1944), editor of the *Oxford Book of English Verse* (1900); Louis Untermeyer (1885–1977), editor of *Modern American Poetry* (Harcourt, Brace and How, 1919). Untermeyer's volume was one of the first anthologies to champion Frost.

131. Thomas Carlyle (1795–1881), *On Heroes, Hero Worship, and the Heroic in History* (1841). Carlyle held against prevailing scientific and materialist views (or historical material determinism), and asserted that the great man of genius was the most important creative force in history.

132. See 9r, 10v; 33 3v; 47; 31 10r; 22 15r.

133. G. W. F. Hegel (1770–1831). Hegel's doctrine of opposites, called by him *dialectic,* is a triadic formulation serving to ascertain truth. Commonly conceived in shorthand as: thesis + antithesis = synthesis, Hegel's formulation presupposes that any predicate (i.e. thesis) is inherently self-contradictory and requires its opposite (antithesis) for resolution. But even the resolution (i.e. synthesis) is inadequate, and so the process begins anew.

134. This formulation does not appear in Frost's essay, "The Constant Symbol" (1946).

135. See 15.24v; 19.9v; 22.6r; 47.

136. Catherine Drinker Bowen (1897–1973), biographer of Oliver Wendell Holmes, Sir Edward Coke, and John Adams. She was a speaker at Breadloaf in the summer of 1944 and a faculty member in 1945.

137. The 19th-century English Christmas carol attributed to A. H. Bullen begins "God rest ye merry gentlemen, let nothing you dismay, / Remember Christ our Savior was born on Christmas day; / To save us all from Satan's power when we were gone astray."

138. After the repeal of prohibition, Eleanor Roosevelt argued that liquor in itself was not an evil and that responsibility for its use rested with individuals:

> During the last few days I have been bombarded by a series of postcards from Chicago which seem to be inspired. The writers insist that every evil in the country is due to the manufacture and consumption of liquor. They all seem to forget that once we tried the experiment of legislating virtue through prohibition with very little success, and that we have now gone back to the longer, but perhaps more successful, effort of trying to make our homes and our schools and perhaps our communities produce young people with character enough to control themselves and live with moderation.
>
> A very beautiful woman who came to see me yesterday afternoon announced that she was 85 years old and that she laid her looks and her ability to keep active to her moderation in living. (From Roosevelt's syndicated column, "My Day," of December 5, 1945.)

139. Cf. Frost's "A Masque of Mercy" (1947), lines 700–704:

Keeper   But not the fear of punishment for sin
(I have to sin to prove it isn't that).
I'm no more governed by the fear of Hell
Than by the fear of the asylum, jail, or poorhouse,
The basic three the state is founded on.

See also 22.8v; 11.53r.

140. See 31r, note 97.

141. See 33v, 47v; 22.46r, 59r; 26.28r; 31.8r, 9r.

142. Cf. Frost's "On Emerson": "Loyalty is that for the lack of which your gang will shoot you without the benefit of trial by jury. And serves you right. Be as treacherous as you must be for your ideals, but don't expect to be kissed good-bye by the idol you go back on. We don't want to look foolish, do we?" See also 31.41v; 34.6v.

143. See 35.15v.

144. Frost here refers to the opening sentences of the Preamble of the Declaration of Independence: "We hold these Truths to be self-evident, that all Men are created equal,

that they are endowed, by their Creator, with certain unalienable Rights, that among these are Life, Liberty, and the Pursuit of Happiness."

145. The phrase has been associated with the legend of the Pied Piper of Hamelin since the 16th century.

146. Dwight Morrow (1873–1931) was a lawyer, U.S. Senator from New Jersey, and Ambassador to Mexico. He was also the father of Anne Morrow Lindbergh, the wife of Charles Lindbergh.

147. Along with the Armours, two prominent Illinois families who made great fortunes, from the mid-nineteenth century onward, in the meat-packing business.

148. Although there are several antecedent plays concerning "bloodthirsty" moneylenders, see in particular the character of Shylock and the "pound of flesh" in Shakespeare's *Merchant of Venice* (c. 1596 or 1597), Act I, Sc. III, Act III, Sc. III, and Act IV, Sc. I.

149. The first point of Woodrow Wilson's "Fourteen Points" speech before Congress of January 8, 1918, was "Open covenants of peace, openly arrived at, after which there shall be no private international understanding of any kind but diplomacy shall proceed always and frankly and in the public view." Wilson was demanding that all of the belligerents in World War I make clear their aims and that morality and ethics become the basis for the development of a foreign policy.

150. Donald Culross Peattie (1898–1964), naturalist and author acclaimed for his lyrical prose. His works include *Green Laurels: The Lives and Achievements of the Great Naturalists* and *Forward the Nation* (1942). Frost's library includes a copy of *American Hardwood* (1949), inscribed to him by Peattie. During the Second World War, Peattie's writings included polemical moments against American nationalism. See, for example, this selection from the essay "Flag of Stars," included in Peattie's *Journey into America* (Boston: Houghton Mifflin, 1943):

> But in America's house are many mansions . . . Their names make a poem, however you say them. Names of queer states, Maryland, Virginia, Carolina, names like flowers carried between smiling lips, Florida, California . . . And then the one name, that Tom Paine found—the United States of America.
>
> So no part is greater than the whole. To believe that it can be is the essential fallacy. No state on earth can be so sovereign that it stands above consideration of the interests of others. This planet is the mansion of the human race. To set that house in order must be what we are fighting for; doubt that it can be done breaks faith with all our past which has flowered in so nearly a perfect union. Among the nations we are Fortune's heir, and with great fortune comes responsibility. To accept it is to kneel for the crown of true sovereignty. (Peattie, p. 273.)

See also 22.46r.

151. See 33v, 46r; 22.46r, 59r; 26.28r; 31.8r, 9r.

152. See 7r; 29.12r, 12v.

153. See 7r; 29.12r.

154. Jean-Baptiste Lamarck (1744–1829), French biologist who proposed a theory of biological change by inheritance of acquired traits. Charles Darwin's theory of speciation by natural selection superseded Lamarck's but biologists continued to argue over the role of will in evolutionary change. Darwin himself praised Lamarck's emphasis on the impor-

tance of environment and adaptation in biological change even though he disagreed with the theory of the mechanism.

155. See 7.4r; 37.9r; 31.7v, 9v; 14.1r, 2r, 11r; 22.8r, 12r, 17r, 18r; 24.44r; 15.3v; 39; 47; 19.5r, 5v, 9r.

156. All radioactive elements. Uranium was discovered as an element in 1789 and in 1896 found to be radioactive. Radium was discovered in 1898 and metallic radium was isolated by electrolysis in 1910 by Marie Curie and André Debierne. Plutonium was discovered by Glenn Seaborg, Arthur Wahl and Joseph Kennedy in 1940 in Berkeley, California.

157. Thucydides, *The History of the Peloponnesian War,* Book II, LXXIV: "Upon these points he tried to reassure them by saying: 'You have only to deliver over the city and houses to us Lacedaemonians, to point out the boundaries of your land, the number of your fruit-trees, and whatever else can be numerically stated, and yourselves to withdraw wherever you like as long the war shall last," translated by Richard Crawley (Random House, 1910). Frost owned a copy of this edition.

158. "A Reflex" (1962): "Here my rigmarole. / Science stuck a pole / Down a likely Hole / And he got it bit. / Science gave a stab / And he got a grab. / That was what he got. / 'Ah,' he said, 'Qui vive, / Who goes there, and what / ARE we to believe?' / That there is an It?'" See also 22.1r.

159. See 22.1r; 23.1r; 31.8v, 5.1r.

160. From 1893 to the end of World War I, Mr. Dooley was one of the most recognizable figures in American popular culture, a character created by newspaper columnist Peter Finley Dunne (1867–1936). In weekly columns, Mr. Dooley, a Chicago saloon keeper, held forth on all aspects of urban life and became particularly noteworthy for his witty repartee and characterizations that transcended stereotypes of Irish immigrants.

161. The Brookings Institution, located in Washington, D.C., was founded in 1916 for independent policy research.

162. See Frost's "How Hard It Is to Keep from Being King When It's in You and in the Situation," first published in *Proceedings of the American Academy of Arts and Letters and the National Institute of Arts and Letters,* Second Series, Number One (1951) and later in *In the Clearing* (1962).

163. Frost's satiric name for T. S. Eliot's play *The Cocktail Party* (1950).

164. From Catullus (84–54 B.C.), 65, l. 4. Frost quotes the phrase in "Kitty Hawk," l. 390 and discussed it in a talk he gave at Kenyon College in 1950: "mens—mind, and animus— the spirit, see . . . And I suppose that's what we've been talking about today. The order— mens, the order of my wildness . . . see that's the way I translate the enterprise of the spirit . . . that's the animus, that's the enterprise, that's the spirit that breaks the form." In a talk at Oxford University in 1957, Frost said: "Poetry is the thoughts of the heart. I'm sure that's what Catullus meant by *mens animi.* Poetry is hyphenated like so many British names. It's a thought-felt thing. Poetry is the thing that laughs and cries about everything as it's going on—and makes you take it. A momentary stay against confusion."

165. Thales of Miletus (62?–546 B.C.), Greek natural philosopher and astronomer and important source for Aristotle's theories of matter.

166. See 45.1r; 17.30v; 24.28v; 19.1r.

167. Cf. *A Masque of Reason* (1947), 105–106: "Jesse Bel. Your courage failed. The saddest thing in life / Is that the best thing in it should be courage." See also 19r; 26.3r.

168. In 1909, the Frost family took its first botany excursion to Lake Willoughby, Vermont.

NOTEBOOK 5

1. See 4.49r; 22.11r; 22.2r; 31.8v.

2. References to "waste" continue throughout this notebook. See also 4.13r; 31.7r, 8r, 10r, 40r, 40v; 32; 37.1r, 5v, 6v; 22.10v; 13.8r; 12.7v; 9.10r; 24.39v; 21.4r, 7r; 27.29r, 45r, 46r; 1; 47; 23.10r; 35.13r, 16r.

3. See 27.8r.

4. Title of Frost poem, "America Is Hard to See." First published as that title in *In the Clearing* (1962). Previously published with the variant title, "And All We Call American" (1951). See also 12.22r; 26.27r; 29.9r; 4.21r.

5. See 28.19r; 26.14r.

6. See 17.40r; 24.48r; 32.10r; 35.19r; 41.7r.

7. See 24.48r.

8. Shinto is a form of religious belief native to Japan that began to borrow elements of Buddhism and Confucianism during the fifth century when Chinese writing was adapted to the Japanese language. Traditionally, the Emperor has been the highest religious figure of the faith. During the Meiji period, many of the old ways of Shinto were reinstituted. After the Second World War, connections between Shinto and the State were disestablished.

9. Perhaps Troy, New York. Claims for itself "birthplace" of the idea of the name of "Uncle Sam." Frost was in Troy, New York in 1921.

10. See Frost's "Provide, Provide" (1934).

11. This is an early draft of "A Bed in the Barn," which appeared in an early manuscript of *Steeple Bush*, but was not included in the final published collection.

12. See 4.9r; 26.14r.

13. See 31.32v; 43.5r; 47.

14. See 12.22v, 23v; 22.30v; 31.4r; 39.8r.

15. According to archeological records, Moab was located near the upper eastern region of the Dead Sea beginning in the thirteenth century B.C., in what is now Jordan. The Moabites claimed kinship to the Hebrews.

NOTEBOOK 6

1. Cf. Frost's English curriculum for the Pinkerton Academy in 1910: "The general aim of the course in English is twofold: to bring our students under the *influence* of the great books, and to teach the *satisfaction* of superior speech."

2. Robert Newdick was Frost's first biographer. The book was barely begun when he died in 1939. It was later published as *Season of Frost: An Interrupted Biography of Robert Frost,* ed. William A. Sutton (Albany: State University of New York Press, 1976).

3. Frost continues this discussion on 37v. "The Waiting Spirit: How Long Will It Wait" was a lecture Frost gave at the Pinkerton Normal School in 1916.

4. See 4.48r; 37.9r; 31.7v, 9v; 14.1r, 2r, 11r; 22.8r, 12r, 17r, 18r; 24.44r; 15.3v; 39; 47; 19.5r, 5v, 9r.

5. Mark Twain (1835–1910). Twain's first short story was entitled "The Celebrated Jumping Frog of Calaveras County" (1865). See also 12.1r; 15.19v; 17.28v–29r; 26.27r.

NOTEBOOK 7

1. In 1911, Frost taught psychology and education at the New Hampshire State Normal School in Plymouth. In the courses he assigned Williams James's *Psychology: The Briefer Course as well as writings by Rousseau, Pestalozzi, Spencer, and others.*

2. Francis Gotch (1853–1913), British physiologist. In 1899, Gotch discovered the separation of nervous impulses by a "refractory phase."

3. See also 2.16r; 4; 8.56r; 14.17r; 15.33v; 20.11r, 16v; 21.4r, 7r; 22.49r; 24.24r, 47v; 28.10r; 29.14r, 23r; 31.4r, 7r, 7v, 40r; 32.7r, 10r; 34.1r, 2r, 2v; 41.7r; 47.

4. Plato (c. 429–347 B.C.), *The Republic.*

5. Michel de Montaigne, "Of the Education of Children" (c. 1580). See also 8.3r; 17.33v.

6. Johann Heinrich Pestalozzi (1746–1827), "Leonard and Gertrude" (1781), a portrait of Swiss peasant life. Frost used these works including Pestalozzi's *How Gertrude Teaches Her Children,* instead of the traditional textbook to teach girls at the Plymouth Normal School.

7. Louis Agassiz (1807–1873) was a professor of natural history at Harvard, 1848–1873. Nathaniel Southgate Shaler (1841–1906), a professor of paleontology and geology at Harvard from 1869 to 1906, described in his autobiography (1909) an experience he had as one of Agassiz's students:

> When I sat down before my tin pan, Agassiz brought me a small fish, placing it before me with the rather stern requirement that I should study it, but should on no account talk to anyone concerning it, nor read anything relating to fishes, until I had permission to do so. To my inquiry "What shall I do?" he said in effect: "Find out what you can without damaging the specimen; when I think that you have done the work I will question you."
>
> In the course of an hour I thought I had compassed that fish; it was a rather unsavory object, giving forth the stench of old alcohol, then loathsome to me, though in time I came to like it. Many of the scales were loosened so that they fell off it. It appeared to me to be a case for a summary report, which I was anxious to make and get on to the next stage of the business. But Agassiz, though always within call, concerned himself no further with me that day, nor the next, nor for the week.
>
> At first, this neglect was distressing; but . . . I set my wits to work upon the thing, and in the course of a hundred hours or so thought I had done much—a hundred times as much as seemed possible at the start. I got interested in finding out how the scales went in series, their shape, the form and placement of teeth, etc. Finally, I felt full of the subject and probably expressed it in my bearing; as for the words about it then, there were none from my master except his cheery "Good morning."
>
> At length on the seventh day, came the question "Well?" and my disgorge of learning to him as he sat on the edge of my table puffing his cigar. At the end of the hour's telling, he swung off and away, saying, "That is not right." I went at the task anew, discarded my first notes, and in another week of ten hours a day labor I had results which astonished myself and satisfied him." (*The Autobiogra-*

phy of Nathaniel Southgate Shaler [Boston and New York: Houghton Mifflin Co., 1909], pp. 98–99.)

As a student at Harvard in 1898 and 1899, Frost took courses in evolutionary geology with Shaler.

It is also interesting to note that Ezra Pound recounted a version of the story to open his *ABC of Reading* (1934).

8. Friedrich Wilhelm August Froebel (1782–1852), German educational theorist who founded the kindergarten system.

9. Herbert Spencer (1820–1903), English philosopher and sociologist and leading advocate of social Darwinism who coined the term "survival of the fittest." Against the idea of public education and the traditional curriculum of history, literature and languages, he advocated an elite system of private schools where science and the more mundane skills necessary to survive were to be the central components in the curriculum.

10. See G.K. Chesterton's "On Mr. Rudyard Kipling and Making the World Small": "The real poetry, the 'true romance' which Mr. Kipling has taught, is the romance of the division of labor and the discipline of all trades. He sings the arts of peace much more accurately than the arts of war . . . Everything is military in the sense that everything depends upon obedience . . . We may jump upon a child's rockinghorse for a joke. But we are glad that the carpenter did not leave the legs of it unglued for a joke. So far from having merely preached that a soldier cleaning his side-arm is to be adored because he is military, Kipling at his best and clearest has preached that the baker baking loaves and the tailor cutting coats is as military as anybody. Being devoted to this multitudinous vision of duty, Mr. Kipling is naturally a cosmopolitan." Following Chesterton's sense, Wordsworth would express this sense of duty not only in "Ode to Duty" but also in the character of the leech gatherer in "Resolution and Independence." See also 8.5r; 17.25r.

11. See 24.34r; 25.6r; 11.51v; 26.7r.

12. Henri Bergson, *Creative Evolution* (Henry Holt, 1911), tr. Arthur Mitchell, p. 11: "There is no reason, therefore, why a duration, and so a form of existence like our own, should not be attributed to the systems that science isolates, provided such systems are reintegrated into the Whole. But they must be so reintegrated. The same is even more obviously true of the objects cut out by our perception. The distinct outlines which we see in an object, and which give it its individuality, are only the design of a certain *influence* that we might exert on a certain point of space; it is the plan of our eventual actions that is sent back to our eyes, as though by a mirror, when we see the surfaces and edges of things. Suppress this action, and with it consequently those main directions which by perception are traced out for it in the entanglement of the real, and the individuality of the body is re-absorbed in the universal interaction which, without doubt, is the reality itself." See also 9.4r.

13. See 43.1r, 7r; 31.32r; 21.2r, 5r; 40.23v.

14. Robert Louis Stevenson's (1850–1898) novel *St. Ives: Being the Adventures of a French Prisoner in England* was completed posthumously in 1898 by novelist, poet, and critic Arthur Quiller-Couch (1863–1944).

15. *Marius the Epicurean,* novel written by Walter Pater (1839–1894) in 1885.

16. Peter Mark Roget (1779–1869), English physician and lexicographer. Published his *Thesaurus of English Words and Phrases* in 1852.

NOTEBOOK 8

1. O. Raymond Drey (1885–1976) was a literary critic and essayist who wrote for *Tyro,* a journal edited by Wyndham Lewis. Drey was married to the American painter Anne Estelle Rice.

2. Cf. Frost's "A Hundred Collars" (1913).

3. A variation on a couplet from "A Shropshire Lad" (1896) by A. E. Housman (1859–1936): "And malt does more than Milton can/ To justify God's ways to man." See also 18.4r.

4. See W. B. Yeats' *Folk Irish Peasantry* (1888): "Through this door of white stone, and the other doors of that land where geabheadh tu an sonas aer pighin ('you can buy joy for a penny'), have gone kings, queens, and princes, but so greatly has the power of Faery dwindled, that there are none but peasants in these sad chronicles of mine."

5. Charles Mudie (1818–1890), an English publisher, established Mudie's Select Library, a highly successful and influential lending library in London. In the interest of his library, Mudie often purchased entire first printings of both nonfiction prose and then-popular fiction and also encouraged publishers to publish fiction in three-volume editions.

6. William Shakespeare, *Venus and Adonis* (1593).

7. Que sais-je? Fr. What do I know? The theme of Montaigne's essay project, his skeptical approach to knowledge, and especially self-knowledge. This phrase was carved on the wall of his octagonal study. See also 6.22r; 17.33v.

8. Sir Edward Levy-Lawson (1833–1916), Lord Burnham, established the *London Daily Telegraph* and lived near Beaconsfield, where Frost resided for more than a year during his stay in England. In a letter of 7 January 1913, Frost wrote: "Beaconsfield is a fairish-sized town fifteen miles form the largest city in the world. It has no library for child or man. So much the more need for a working library in the school. What I was shown interested me. I heard its history. Lord Burnham, the school patron, keeps it up by occasional gifts of books that come to his newspaper office for review. It is what Lord Burnham didn't want and what not one of his office assistants wanted—leavings."

9. See Frost's "A Hundred Collars" (1913).

10. G. K. Chesterton, *Orthodoxy* (1908), ch. 1, "In Defence of Everything Else": "For if this book is a joke it is a joke against me. I am the man who with the utmost daring discovered what had been discovered before. If there is an element of farce in what follows, the farce is at my own expense; for this book explains how I fancied I was the first to set foot in Brighton and then found I was the last . . . I freely confess all the idiotic ambitions of the end of the nineteenth century. I did, like all other solemn little boys, try to be in advance of the age. Like them I tried to be some ten minutes in advance of the truth. And I found that I was eighteen hundred years behind it. I did strain my voice with a painfully juvenile exaggeration in uttering my truths. And I was punished in the fittest and funniest way, for I have kept my truths: but I have discovered, not that they were not truths, but simply that they were not mine. When I fancied that I stood alone I was really in the ridiculous position of being backed up by all Christendom. It may be, Heaven forgive me, that I did try to be original; but I only succeeded in inventing for myself an inferior copy of the existing traditions of civilized religion . . . I tried to found a heresy of my own; and when I had put the last touches to it, I discovered that it was orthodoxy." See also 8.5r; 17.25r; 6.25r.

11. The process of reproduction without fertilization in invertebrates and lower plant species.

12. "Life can only be understood backwards; but it must be lived forwards." Soren Kierkegaard (1813–1855), *Works of Love* (1847).

13. C.f. Frost's "The Wood-Pile," ll. 10–16.

A small bird flew before me. He was careful
To put a tree between us when he was lighted,
And say no word to tell me who he was
Who was so foolish as to think what *he* thought.
He thought that I was after him for a feather—
The white one in his tail; like one who takes
Everything said as personal to himself.

14. Possibly John D. Rockefeller (1837–1937).

15. The planchette typewriter was invented in 1853 by a French spiritist. It is an offspring of the tipping table: a triangular polished board on rollers, resting on a pencil in the socket at the apex. The medium places his hand on the board. If it moves the front leg, the pencil leaves markings on the paper placed beneath. These markings may assume the form of letters and spell out connected messages.

16. The river Leadon, in Donnington, Herefordshire.

17. See 32r; 22.8r; 26.2r; 44; 45; 13.9v; 12; 15.13r; 47.

18. Cf. Frost's lecture at the Browne and Nichols School, "The Unmade Word, or Fetching and Far-Fetching" (1918). See also 26.8r; 47.

19. See 9.15r; 12.15v; 45.2r; 47.

20. See 56r; 24.41v; 9.8r; 47; 19.9r.

21. King Alfred the Great (ruled 871–899?).

22. See 15r; 22.8r; 26.2r; 44; 45; 13.9v; 12; 15.13r; 47.

23. Joseph Conrad (1857–1924), *Mirror of the Sea: Memories and Impressions, with a Personal Record* (1902).

24. John Galsworthy (1867–1933), English novelist and dramatist, author of *The Inn of Tranquillity: Studies and Essays* (1912).

25. Cf. Edmund Gosse's (1849–1928) *Father and Son* (1907), an autobiography in which the author describes the conflict with his father, Philip Gosse, a Christian fundamentalist and naturalist who resisted Darwin's theory of natural selection.

26. George Bernard Shaw (1856–1950).

27. George Moore (1852–1933), Irish writer, author of *Hail and Farewell: Ave, Salve, Vale,* a memoir. Frost had three of his books in his library: *Fragments from Heloise & Abelard, Heloise and Abelard,* and *The Making of an Immortal.*

28. Mrs. Rosamund Marriott Watson (1863–1911) (*The Poems of Rosamund Marriott Watson* [London and New York: John Lane Co., 1912]). Frost owned a copy of her *Tares.*

29. Gerard Manley Hopkins (1844–1889), English poet.

30. Cf. G.K. Chesterton's *St. Thomas Aquinas* (1933), chapter III: "Most of the Schoolmen, if informed by the only informants they had that a unicorn has one horn or a salamander lives in the fire, still used it more as an illustration of logic than an incident of life. What they really said was, 'If a Unicorn has one horn, two unicorns have as many horns as one cow.' And that has not one inch the less a fact because the unicorn is a fable."

31. Maurice Hewlett (1861–1923), English poet and novelist. W. Y. Evans-Wentz (1878–1965), British anthropologist and author of *The Fairy-Faith in Celtic Countries* (Oxford, 1911), which was dedicated to W. B. Yeats.

32. The "Olympian pair" is a reference to Ares and Aphrodite, who were caught in the act of adultery by Hephaestus, husband of Aphrodite. In *The Odyssey*, Book 8, Homer has the pair laughed at by an audience of the gods. This phrase is also found in RF's January 21, 1913, letter to the English poet F. S. Flint.

33. Katherine Mansfield (pen-name of Kathleen Mansfield Beauchamp) (1888–1923), New Zealand short story writer.

34. The reference to "beer" is probably an allusion to lines from the last stanza of Chesterton's poem "The Secret People" (1900):

> We hear men speaking for us of new laws strong and sweet,
> Yet is there no man speaketh as we speak in the street.
> It may be we shall rise the last as Frenchmen rose the first,
> Our wrath come after Russia's wrath and our wrath be the worst.
> It may be we are meant to mark with our riot and our rest
> God's scorn for all men governing. It may be beer is best.
> But we are the people of England; and we have not spoken yet.
> Smile at us, pay us, pass us. But do not quite forget.

Frost also refers to Chesterton's essay "Charles II" from *Twelve Types* (London, 1910), 97: "It is a commonplace that the Restoration movement can only be understood when considered as a reaction against Puritanism. But it is insufficiently realized that the tyranny which half frustrated all the good work of Puritanism was of a very peculiar kind. It was not the fire of Puritanism, the exultation in sobriety, the frenzy of restraint, which passed away; that still burns in the heart of England, only to be quenched by the final overwhelming sea."

Chesterton's view of history is given succinctly in "The Fear of the Past" from *What's Wrong with the World* (New York, 1910), p. 34: "Now in history there is no Revolution that is not a Restoration. Among the many things that leave me doubtful about the modern habit of fixing eyes on the future, none is stronger than this: that all the men in history who have really done anything with the future have had their eyes fixed upon the past."

35. See lines 99–103 of Frost's "Black Cottage" from *North of Boston* (1914): "Only—there was the bonnet in the pew. / Such a phrase couldn't have meant much to her. / But suppose she had missed it from the Creed / As a child misses the unsaid Good-night, / and falls asleep with heartache—how should *I* feel?"

36. Texas A&M University.

37. See 4.32r; 20.10r; 13.6r; 14.12r.

38. See 4.22r; 17.25r; 22.8r, 8v; 24.31r; 28.10r; 29; 33.5r; 35.7r; 47.

39. Marcus Aurelius Antoninus (A.D. 121–180), Stoic philosopher and Roman Emperor.

40. Marcus Aurelius Commodus Antoninus (A.D. 180–192), Aurelius's son and successor who lost the lands that the previous emperor had gained.

41. In "Economy," the first chapter of *Walden* (1854), Thoreau wrote: "Yet they honestly think there is no choice left. But alert and healthy natures remember that the sun rose clear. It is never too late to give up our prejudices. No way of thinking or doing, however ancient, can be trusted without proof. What everybody echoes or in silence passes by as true today may turn out to be falsehood tomorrow, mere smoke of opinion, which some had trusted for a cloud that would sprinkle fertilizing rain on their fields. What old people

say you cannot do, you try and find that you can. Old deeds for old people, and new deeds for new."

42. On June 22, 1906, Congress passed a joint resolution stating that "the people of the United States are horrified by reports of the massacre of the Hebrews in Russia, on account of their race and religion. Congress also expresses sympathy with the sufferers."

43. Thomas Hardy (1840–1928).

44. The Franco-Prussian War (1870–71) led to the rise of Germanic Imperialism and the founding of the Third Republic in France, as well as a loss of independence for the Papal States, which were subsumed into Italy. Because of unresolved matters on both sides of conflict, this war is said to have contributed to the outbreak of the Great War (1914–1918).

45. See 4.23r; 12.22r; 22.34r.

46. Much of William Butler Yeats' edition of *Fairy and Folk Tales of the Irish Peasantry* (1888) is concerned with fairies.

47. Robert Grant (1852–1940), novelist, poet, essayist, journalist. Along with the "adoptive American O'Reilly" he wrote *The King's Men: A Tale of Tomorrow* (1884); *The Opinions of a Philosopher* (1894); *The High Priestess* (1915); *Their Spirit: Some Impressions on the English and the French during the Summer of 1916* (1916); *The Married Man: The Reflections of a Married Man* (1925).

48. See 22.7r; 44.3v.

49. Frost's library held Robert Reynolds' *In Praise of Gratitude* (1961).

50. In an August 20, 1932, campaign speech in Columbus, Ohio, Roosevelt invoked Lewis Carroll's *Alice in Wonderland* while addressing the climate of 1928 and those responsible for the stock-market crash of 1929. The relevant text follows:

> It has been suggested that the American public was apparently elected to the role of our old friend, Alice in Wonderland. I agree that Alice was peering into a wonderful looking-glass of the wonderful economics. White Knights had great schemes of unlimited sales in foreign markets and discounted the future ten years ahead.
>
> The poorhouse was to vanish like the Cheshire cat. A mad hatter invited everyone to "have some more profits." There were no profits, except on paper. A cynical Father William in the lower district of Manhattan balanced the sinuous evil of a pool-ridden stock market on the end of his nose. A puzzled, somewhat skeptical Alice asked the Republican leadership some simple questions:
>
> "Will not the printing and selling of more stocks and bonds, the building of new plants and the increase of efficiency produce more goods than we can buy?"
>
> "No," shouted Humpty Dumpty. "The more we produce the more we can buy."
>
> "What if we produce a surplus?"
>
> "Oh, we can sell it to foreign consumers."
>
> "How can the foreigners pay for it?"
>
> "Why, we will lend them the money."
>
> "I see," said little Alice, "they will buy our surplus with our money. Of course, these foreigners will pay us back by selling us their goods?"
>
> "Oh, not at all," said Humpty Dumpty. "We set up a high wall called the tariff."

"And," said Alice at last, "how will the foreigners pay off these loans?"

"That is easy," said Humpty Dumpty, "did you ever hear of a moratorium?"

And so, at last, my friends, we have reached the heart of the magic formula of 1928. Strange as it may seem, the road to abolition of poverty was a constantly increasing maze of machine production. The absorption of the surplus was to be through what I quoted before, the "development of backward and crippled countries by means of loans."

51. William Ashley Sunday (1862–1935). Early in his life he was a player for the Chicago White Stockings. Later in his life, when he had found God, he traveled the country giving countless sermons to an estimated total of 100 million people.

52. See 18v; 24.41v; 9.8r; 19.9r; 47.

53. Cf. Frost's letter to Louis Untermeyer dated January 1, 1917: "What I like about Bergson and Fabre is that they have bothered our evolutionism so much with the cases of instinct they have brought up. You get more credit for thinking if you restate formulae or cite cases that fall in easily under formulae, but all the fun is outside saying things that suggest formulae that won't formulate—that almost but don't quite formulate." See also 2.16r; 4; 6.22r; 14.17r; 15.33v; 20.11r, 16v; 21.4r, 7r; 22.49r; 24.24r, 47v; 28.10r; 29.14r, 23r; 31.4r, 7r, 7v, 40r; 32.7r, 10r; 34.1r, 2r, 2v; 41.7r; 47.

54. John Eliot (1604–1690), American colonial clergyman. He was born in Hertfordshire, England, and emigrated to America in 1631. He became a minister in Roxbury, Massachusetts, in 1631 and began preaching to the Indians in their own tongue in Newton in October 1646. He translated the Bible into Algonquin in 1663.

55. Cf. Frost's "Education by Poetry": "Greatest of all attempts to say one thing in terms of another is the philosophical attempt to say matter in terms of spirit, or spirit in terms of matter, to make the final unity. That is the greatest attempt that has ever failed. We stop just short there. But it is the height of poetry, the height of all poetic thinking, that attempt to say matter in terms of spirit and spirit in terms of matter." See also 15.10r.

56. See 58v; 22.11r, 47r; 12.10r; 37.2r; 7.3r, 4r; 33.9r; 1.34v; 17.41r; 19.8v; 24.38v; 29.23r.

NOTEBOOK 9

1. George Bernard Shaw (1856–1950).

2. From an old folk song: "You can buy joy for a penny, through the door." In Gaelic: Geabheadhtuan sonas air pighin (W. B. Yeats, *Celtic Twlight*, Kidnappers, 1902).

3. In a letter of 7 January 1913, Frost wrote: "Beaconsfield is a fairish-sized town fifteen miles from the largest city in the world. It has no library for child or man. So much the more need for a working library in the school. What I was shown interested me. I heard its history. Lord Burnham, the school patron, keeps it up by occasional gifts of books that come to his newspaper office for review. It is what Lord Burnham didn't want and what not one of his office assistants wanted—leavings."

4. Lesley Frost (1899–1983), Frost's eldest daughter.

5. Maria de Montessori (1870–1952), Italian educator and physician. Beginning by addressing the educational needs of retarded children, she applied these principles to normal preschool-aged children. At the beginning of the 20th century, she and her followers be-

gan to export these methods abroad. The Montessori Method is predicated on the idea that children will learn if their environment is suitably enriched with the materials they need to learn. The method attempts to promote self-education by allowing the child to exploit on his own the resources found in the classroom. These resources include games, toys, domestic items, and so forth. See Frost's letter of January 7, 1913, in which he describes the principal of the Beaconsfield boy's school: "He is a gentle body, well read in a different way from most of our men. He knows the literary names better than the educational—He had not heard of Montessori. Neither for that matter had the teacher of the kindergarten."

6. The "he" in the above quotation refers to Mr. Baker, the Superintendent of Schools of New Hampshire. Earlier in the letter he refers to George Bernard (GB) Shaw, and, given Mr. Baker's interest in the common man, the SK may refer to Søren Kierkegaard.

7. Katharine Tynan Hinkson (1861–1931), English poet, anthologized by Arthur Quiller-Couch in the 1919 edition of *Oxford Book of English Verse*.

8. Melanism refers to darkness of color resulting from an abnormal (but not morbid) development of black pigment in the epidermis or other external appendages (hair, feathers, etc.) of animals, as opposed to albinism. In a letter dated November 19, 1912, to the publisher Thomas B. Mosher, Frost said he had planned to entitle one of his verse collections "Melanism."

9. Henri Bergson (1859–1941), French philosopher and author of *Creative Evolution* (1907; English translation, 1911). Frost owned and annotated a copy of *Creative Evolution,* which he read in late 1911 and which is now in the Fales Collection at New York University. See also 8.28v.

10. Harriet Monroe (1860–1936). Cf. "Rhythms of English Verse, I," *Poetry,* Vol. 3, November 1913, pp. 61–68; and "Rhythms of English Verse, II," *Poetry,* Vol. 3, December 1913, p. 100.

11. Andrew Carnegie (1835–1919), Scottish-born American industrialist and philanthropist; Kaiser Wilhelm II (1859–1941). Carnegie Steel was subsumed into United States Steel in 1901. At that time, US steel made sixty-seven percent of the country's product. Under Wilhelm's reign, Krupp Steel became a large steel producer, filling the need for German armaments and the requirements of the Kaiser's navy. Its output was significantly reduced after the Treaty of Versailles (1919), which marked the end of the First World War.

12. Cf. Frost's letter to Sydney Cox of December 1914 (from Dymock, Gloucestershire): "Just so many sentence sounds belong to man as just so many vocal runs belong to one kind of bird."

13. Ulysses S. Grant (1822–1885).

14. Robert Southey (1774–1843), "The Battle of Blenheim" (1798): "'It was the English,' Kaspar cried, / 'Who put the French to rout; / But what they fought each other for, / I could not well make out; / But everybody said,' quoth he, 'That 'twas a famous victory'" (ll. 31–36).

15. The Battle of Chevy Chase was fought in 1388.

16. The International Sunshine Society was incorporated in 1900 by Cynthia Westover Alden. Inspired by the ideals espoused in Alden's "Sunshine Column" of *Ladies' Home Journal,* in particular that of "passing a kindness on," chapters of the organization across the United States perform a variety of charitable acts in members' local communities.

17. Possibly Mary Lynch, wife of John Lynch, an Irish-born farmer of Bethlehem, New Hampshire, with whom the Frosts stayed several times in the early part of the twentieth century.

18. See 8.18v; 12.15v; 45.2r; 47.

19. Robert Louis Stevenson's "Christmas Prayer": "Oh, God . . . / help us rightly to remember / the birth of Jesus, that / we may share in the songs / of the angels, the gladness / of the shepherds, and the / worship of the wise men. / [stanza break] / May the Christmas morning / make us happy / to be your children."

20. Cf. Emerson's "Uriel" (1846), ll. 21–24: "'Line in nature is not found; / Unit and universe are round; / In vain produce, all rays return; / Evil will bless, and ice will burn.'"

21. See Ezekiel 38.1. It is the description of a foe that comes from the north to destroy the promised land.

22. Esther 6 and Ezra 4.

23. In the Upper Valley region near Dartmouth College, Hanover, New Hampshire.

24. See 29.16v, 29v; 15.22r; 28.18r; 4.38r.

25. See 7.3v; 20.10r; 47.

26. Stephen Crane (1871–1900), novelist, short-story writer, poet. He is best known for his war poems and *The Red Badge of Courage* (1895).

27. William Sharp (1855–1905), Scottish poet and critic who wrote under pseudonym Fiona Macleod.

28. Possibly William Cullen Bryant (1794–1878), poet, editor, lawyer, who wrote two of his best poems "To a Waterfowl" (1815) and *Thanatopsis* (1817) at an early age.

29. Frost wrote to Louis Untermeyer in an unpublished letter of 1915: "If I must be classified a poet, I might be called a Synechdochist, for I prefer the synechdoche in poetry— that figure of speech in which we use a part for the whole." See also 19.9r; 24.41v; 47; 8.36, 105.

30. Cf. Frost's "New Hampshire" (1922), ll. 188–192: ". . . Still Corners (so called not because / The place is silent all day long, nor yet / Because it boasts a whisky still—because / It set out once to be a city and still / Is only corners, crossroads in a wood)." See also 10.1v.

31. *In The Voyage of the Beagle,* one of Frost's favorite books, Darwin discusses the conditions of those living in South America (near the Strait of Magellan) for the breeding and multiplication of horses: "They are well stocked with horses, each man having, according to Mr. Low, six or seven, and all the women, and even children, their own horse. In the time of Sarmiento (1580), these Indians had bows and arrows, now long since disused; they then also possessed some horses. This is a very curious fact, the extraordinarily rapid multiplication of horses in South America. The horse was first landed in at Buenos Ayres in 1537, and the colony being then for a time deserted, the horse ran wild; in 1580, only forty-three years afterwards, we hear of them at the Strait of Magellan! Mr. Low informs me, that a neighboring tribe of foot-Indians is now changing into horse-Indians: the tribe at Gregory Bay giving them their worn-out horses, and sending in winter a few of their best skilled men to hunt for them." (*The Voyage of the Beagle* [New York: Natural History Library, 1860, 1962], pp. 234–235).

32. See 4.13r; 31.7r, 8r, 10r, 40r, 40v; 32; 37.1r, 5v, 6v; 22.10v; 13.8r; 12.7v; 24.39v; 21.4r, 7r; 27.29r, 45r, 46r; 1; 5; 47; 23.10r; 35.13r, 16r.

NOTEBOOK 10

1. Cf. Frost's "New Hampshire" (1922), ll. 188–192: " . . . Still Corners (so called not because. / The place is silent all day long, nor yet / Because it boasts a whisky still—because / It set out once to be a city and still / Is only corners, crossroads in the woods)." See also 9.9r.

2. See 4.18r.

3. Cf. Frost's poem "The Witch of Coös" (1922).

4. See 47; 24.11r.

5. Bungay, which is also known as Bungee or Bungey (see earlier on this page), is a lost town in Coos County, New Hampshire, near Franconia, with a great deal of local folklore attached to it. One example of this is the "Bungay Jar." A "jar" is an old logging term for a "strong wind." In the early spring there is a wind unique to the geography of the valley where Bungay allegedly once existed. The wind blows in a strong, almost hurricane force, in pulsing pattern from south of the valley. The wind forms and comes down from Moosilauki Mountain and Kinsman Notch in the Landaff area. The wind became known as the "Bungay Jar" because of the alleged village, known as either Bungay Corners or Bungay Valley, located at the south end of the valley.

Folkore concerning the origins of Bungay Corners varies, but it is rumored that in the late 1700's a group of religious zealots from the United Kingdom settled in the area and built a temporary living community. The legend is that this group believed in the apocalypse, and their consequent salvation at the final judgment day, taking place at a specific date and time. When the date came and went without the arrival of the final judgment, the entire community left the area in the middle of the night. In the local dialect of the region the term "bungay" has been used as a verb, meaning to leave quickly. See also 13.11r and Frost's "New Hampshire" (1922), ll. 201–209:

New York (five million) laughs at Manchester,
Manchester (sixty or seventy thousand), laughs
At Littleton (four thousand), Littleton
Laughs at Franconia (seven hundred), and
Franconia laughs, I fear,—did laugh that night—
At Easton. What has Easton left to laugh at,
And like the actress exclaim, 'Oh, my God' at?
There's Bungey; and for Bungey there are towns,
Whole townships named but without population.

6. Probably John T. Bartlett, a favorite student of Frost's at Pinkerton Academy in Derry, where Frost taught from 1906 to 1911.

7. See 22.54r, note 86.

8. Frost is likely referring to Hannah Anthony Mosher, sister of Susan B. Anthony, one of twelve women who registered to vote in Rochester, New York in 1871.

9. Saint John Fisher (c. 1469–1535), English prelate, cardinal, bishop of Rochester (1503–1534). Known for his scholarship at Cambridge, he was chosen confessor to Margaret Beaufort, mother of Henry VII. As vice chancellor of the university (1501–1504) and chancellor thereafter, he helped carry out her plans for establishing St. John's College and Christ's

College. As bishop he was firm in his denunciation of abuses by the clergy; however, he resisted reforms, like those of Martin Luther, that affected the doctrines of the church. Giving his support to the new learning, he brought Erasmus to lecture at the university. Fisher, who was confessor to Katharine of Aragón, was the only English bishop to oppose the invalidation of the marriage of Henry VIII and Katharine. He refused to acknowledge the king as supreme head of the church and to accede to the Act of Succession, which declared Katharine's child (Mary I) illegitimate. In 1534 he was imprisoned in the Tower and deprived of his bishopric. Pope Paul III, to show his support, created Fisher a cardinal in May 1535. Henry, infuriated, pushed the trial forward. A fortnight before Sir Thomas More was executed, Fisher was beheaded on Tower Hill. He was canonized as a martyr in 1935. Most of the Latin writings that he left were published in 1597. Some of his English works still remain in manuscript. Feast: July 9.

10. Cf. Dante's *Inferno*, Canto V, ll. 82–142. A pair of lovers condemned to the second circle of hell for an adulterous love affair that they began after reading the story of Lancelot and Guinevere.

11. See 2.5r.

12. Cf. a variation of these lines in Frost's "Immigrants," from *West-Running Brook* (1928): "No ship of all that under sail or steam / Have gathered people to use more and more / But Pilgrim-manned the *Mayflower* in a dream / Has been her anxious convoy to shore."

NOTEBOOK 11

1. Bertran de Born (1140–1214) was a troubadour known for his belligerent politics and condemned in Dante's *Inferno*. Biographer Lawrance Thompson recorded in the notes of *Conversations with Robert Frost* that on March 1, 1940, during a conversation in Miami, Frost told him that while in England he had addressed Ezra Pound as Bertran de Born Again. See also 51v; 24.36v.

2. Lascelles Abercrombie (1872–1956), English poet with whom Frost associated when he lived in England during the early part of the twentieth century before *A Boy's Will* (1913) was published. In 1914, after Abercrombie claimed that poets should return to Wordsworth as a source for inspiration, Pound sent him a note which read: "Dear Mr. Abercrombie: stupidity carried beyond a certain point becomes a public menace. I hereby challenge you to a duel, to be fought at the earliest moment that is suited to your convenience. My seconds will wait upon you in due course. Yours sincerely, Ezra Pound." Frost paraphrases this note later in this notebook on 31v.

3. See 4.20v; 24.29r; 22.17r. "Dianner" is probably Frost's play on the pronunciation of "Diana" by a person with a New England accent. See also 24.29r.

4. Cf. Frost's "A Masque of Mercy" (1947): "*Jonah:* My name's not Joe. I don't like what she says. / It's Greenwich Village cocktail party talk— / Big-city talk. I'm getting out of here. I'm—bound—away. (He quotes it to the tune)." See also 4.12r; 13.12r; 24.3r.

5. Arnold Bennett (1867–1931), English novelist. Bennett was a regular contributor to the *Yellow Book*, a miscellany of short stories, articles, poetry, and drawings. It was able to draw material from writers with wide differences of style and viewpoint, but its emphasis was on the bizarre, the "modern," and the aesthetic. Among its other contributors were Oscar Wilde, Max Beerbohm, John Davidson, Richard Le Gallienne, William Butler Yeats, Ernest Dowson.

6. Rabindranath Tagore (1861–1941), Indian philosopher, sociopolitical activist, and author of poems and novels in English. He was awarded the Nobel Prize in Literature in 1913.

7. Max Beerbohm (1872–1956), English essayist, caricaturist, and parodist. He contributed to the famous *Yellow Book* while still an undergraduate at Oxford. In 1898 he succeeded G. B. Shaw as drama critic for the *Saturday Review.* A charming, witty, and elegant man often called "the incomparable Max," Beerbohm was a brilliant parodist and the master of a polished prose style. His works include *A Christmas Garland* (1912), a collection of parodies on such authors as Joseph Conrad and Thomas Hardy; *Zuleika Dobson* (1911), an amusing satire on Oxford; *Seven Men* (1919), stories; and *And Even Now* (1920) and *Mainly on the Air* (1947), essays.

8. See 1r; 24.36v.

9. Aspasia (ca. 469 BC-?), writer, rhetorician, and philosopher who came to Athens from Miletus and exerted much influence on 5th-century Athenian intellectual and political culture, particularly on Socrates and Pericles. She was known to have been Pericles' consort.

10. See 24.34r; 25.6r; 11.51v; 6.27v; 26.7r.

11. Cf. Frost's "A Masque of Mercy," ll. 700–704:

Keeper   But not the fear of punishment for sin
(I have to sin to prove it isn't that).
I'm no more governed by the fear of Hell
Than by the fear of the asylum, jail, or poorhouse,
The basic three the state is founded on.

See also 22.8v; 4.44r.

12. Robert Burns (1759–1796), Scottish poet who produced works both in English and various Scots dialects and collected folk songs from across Scotland that he later adapted. Burns is widely regarded as the national poet of Scotland, and has since become a cultural icon for many people of Scottish descent.

NOTEBOOK 12

1. Discussion of voice, its tones, and its realism in poetry continue throughout this notebook. See also 22.8v; 26.2r; 44; 45; 13.9v; 15.13r; 47; 8.15r, 32r.

2. Frost may be referring to Wilson's initial isolationism and pacifism that he expressed to a group of recently naturalized citizens in Philadelphia on May 10, 1915: " . . . A nation that is not constantly renewed out of new sources is apt to have the narrowness and prejudice of a family. Whereas, America must have this consciousness, that on all sides it touches elbows and touches hearts with all the nations of mankind. The example of America must be a special example . . . There is such a thing as being too proud to fight. There is such a thing as a nation being so right that it does not need to convince others by force that it is right." Frost may be referring to Wilson's ambivalence toward recently naturalized Americans, an ambivalence that would eventually grow into fear. In the same speech to recently naturalized Americans he warned: "You cannot dedicate yourselves to America unless you become in every respect and with every purpose of your will thorough Americans. You cannot become thorough Americans if you think of yourselves in groups. America does not consist in groups. A man who thinks of himself as belonging to a particular national group in America, has not yet become an American, and the man

who goes among you to trade upon your nationality is no worthy son to live under the Stars and Stripes."

3. See 12r; 4.21r; 22.6r; 29.28v, 54r, 62r.

4. Cf. Frost's early cellar poems, especially "Ghost House" (1906), "The Generations of Men" (1913) and "An Old Man's Winter's Night" (1908).

5. See 1.1r, 4r; 4.1r, 12r; 24.32v; 31.39r; 33.3r.

6. Shakespeare's Sonnet XCIV, l: "They that have the power to hurt and will do none."

7. See Emerson's "Uriel" (1846), ll. 34–41:

A sad self-knowledge withering fell
On the beauty of Uriel;
In heaven once eminent, the god
Withdrew that hour into his cloud;
Whether doom'd to long gyration
In the sea of generation,
Or by knowledge grown too bright
To hit the nerve of feebler sight.

8. G. B. Shaw (1856–1950). Frost may have in mind, among other things, Shaw's pacifism and utopianism, as in *Back to Methuselah* (1921), as well as his pessimistic view of the bourgeoisie, as portrayed in *Heartbreak House* (1919). Shaw's disparaging comments about family structure and relations as the basis for social tyranny can be found in his *Treatise on Parents and Children*.

9. Frost may be referring to Wilson's support of the Clayton Anti-Trust Act of 1914 that excluded both labor and farmers from antitrust prosecution as well the Federal Farm Loan Act of 1916 that made farm loans more available to small farmers but also evened out the income that could be made from farming.

10. See 4.13r; 31.7r, 8r, 10r, 40r, 40v; 32; 37.1r, 5v, 6v; 22.10v; 13.8r; 9.10r; 24.39v; 21.4r, 7r; 27.29r, 45r, 46r; 1; 5; 47; 23.10r; 35.13r, 16r.

11. Max Eastman (1883–1969), critic and poet. Taught at Columbia, edited Marx, and was an editor of two socialist-oriented journals, *The Masses* (1911) and *The Liberator* (1917). During the twenties, became disenchanted with Lenin and Stalin, though he still followed Trotsky. By the Second World War, he became a reporter for *Reader's Digest*. By then, he had broken with his previous beliefs and wrote many pieces critical of Communism. Frost characterized Eastman as one of Louis Untermeyer's "Red friends."

12. Emerson wrote two essays called "Nature." The first was collected in *Essays: Second Series* (1844) and the second, longer essay was published in *Nature: Addresses and Lectures* (1849). See also 13.8r; 22.18r, 32v; 31.11v, 31v.

13. John Boyle O'Reilly (1844–1890), Irish-American journalist, novelist, and poet. Born in Ireland, naturalized in America. He was a "Fenian" and agitated for Catholic equality in Protestant Boston. His collections of poems are *Songs from the Southern Seas, and Other Poems* (1873) and *Songs, Legends, and Ballads* (1878). He was also anthologized by Yeats and Quiller-Couch. Frost had read him since high school.

14. Ernest Mach (1838–1916), Austrian physicist and philosopher.

15. See 24.46v; 31.7r; 14.4v; 47; 25.1r; 2.4v; 46.5r.

16. Wilson cabled his May 20, 1919, message for the opening of a new session of Congress from the Paris Peace Conference. It was published the following day, on May 21st.

His views on international tariffs, to which Frost refers, suggest contradictory attitudes toward foreign nations, including defeated Germany:

> There is fortunately, no occasion for undertaking in the immediate future any general revision of our system of import duties. No serious danger of foreign competition now threatens American industries. Our country has emerged from the war less disturbed and less weakened than any of the European countries which are our competitors in manufacture . . .
>
> Nevertheless there are parts of our tariff system which need prompt attention. The experiences of the war have made it plain that in some cases our great reliance on foreign supply is dangerous, and that in determining certain parts of our tariff policy domestic considerations must be borne in mind which are political as well as economic. Among the industries to which special consideration should be given is that of the manufacture of dyestuffs and related chemicals. Our complete dependence upon German supplies before the war made the interruption of trade a cause of exceptional economic disturbance . . . Although the United States will gladly and unhesitatingly join in the program of international disarmament it will, nevertheless, be a policy of obvious prudence to make certain of the successful maintenance of many strong and well-equipped chemical plants. The German chemical industry, with which we will be brought into competition, was and may well be again a thoroughly knit monopoly, capable of exercising a competition of peculiarly insidious and dangerous kind.

17. A New Hampshire town about 15 miles west of Concord.

18. See 8.18v; 9.15r; 45.2r; 47.

19. See 31.12r.

20. Perhaps a play off of Frost's poem "The Witch of Coös" in *Two Witches* from *New Hampshire* (1923) and Henry Holt, Frost's publisher.

21. Possibly Rex Beach's (1877–1949) *The Spoilers* (1905), a western adventure story about Alaska, or Jean Henri-Fabre's (1823–1915) *The Spoilers* (1915).

22. Cf. *The Egyptian Book of the Dead: The Papyrus by Ani,* trans. E. A. Wallis Budge (1895).

23. Cf. Frost's *A Masque of Reason* (1945): "Job: I am a name for being put upon. / But, yes, I'm fine, except for now and then / A reminiscent twinge of rheumatism. / The letup's heavenly."

24. Amenhotep IV also known as Akhenaton was the enigmatic Pharoah of Egypt who reigned from 1350 to 1334 BC and became known for moving the capital of the kingdom, reducing the powers of the priesthood, and replacing the old theriomorphic gods with the Aten or sun-disk. Interest among archaeologists and Egyptologists in Akhenaton and his kingdom in Amarna grew in the early 20th century. See, in particular, Arthur Weigall's *Akhnaton, Pharaoh of Egypt* (1907; republished in 1910) and his *The Life and Times of Akhnaton, Pharaoh of Egypt* (1911; reprinted in 1922, 1923, 1933, and 1934).

25. William Dean Howells had praised Frost in *Harper's* magazine (September 1915). Frost later acknowledged his "great debt to Howells." See Edward Martins, "W. D. Howells," *Harper's Monthly Magazine,* July 1920, and Booth Tarkington, "Mr. Howells," *Harper's Monthly Magazine,* August 1920.

26. Friedrich Wilhelm Heinrich Alexander von Humboldt (1769–1859), German naturalist and explorer.

27. Henry Adams (1838–1918), American historian and biographer. His best-known work is *The Education of Henry Adams* (1906, 1918).

28. From Geoffrey Chaucer's *Canterbury Tales.*

29. Probably the "Nun Priest's Tale," from the *Canterbury Tales.*

30. Giovanni Boccaccio (1313?–1375). A tale from the *Decameron* (composed 1349–1351). John Dryden later adapted the work as his "Theodore and Honoria, from Boccace; in heroic verse," *Fables, ancient and modern* (1700).

31. See 19.11v.

32. Cf. the title of the Frost poem, "The Census-Taker" (1921). See also 4.23r; 8.42v; 22.34r.

33. Cf "America Is Hard to See," first titled "And All We Call American" (1951). See also 29.9r; 26.27r; 5.5r; 4.21r.

34. Cf. Frost's "West-Running Brook" (1926) and "The Master-Speed" (1936).

35. See 5.26r; 22.30v; 31.4r; 39.8r.

36. Named for its alleged resemblance to the dolphin, the annual *Delphinium,* or Larkspur, has lacy foliage and a tapering bloom that ranges in color from white to carmine, light pink, scarlet, light blue, and dark purple.

37. Cf. Frost's "The Strong are Saying Nothing Until They See" (1936).

38. Lesley Frost (1899–1993), the poet's eldest daughter.

39. See 25r below; 21.2r; 22.55v.

40. John Milton's *Comus: A Masque presented at Lundlow Castle* (1634).

41. The titles of short stories and tales by Robert Louis Stevenson (1850–94), "The Bottle Imp" (1891), "The Isle of Voices" (1893); Nathaniel Hawthorne (1804–64), "Mr. Higgenbotham's Catastrophe"; Mark Twain (1835–1910), "The Celebrated Jumping Frog of Calaveras County" (1865). For more references to Twain's story see 7.38r; 15.19v; 17.28v–29r; 26.27r.

42. Possibly Emily Gradidge, *Nell, the Clown's Wife: or, How the Poor Help Each Other* (London: Charles H. Kelly, 1892).

43. Cf. Matthew Arnold's (1822–1888) *Culture and Anarchy: An Essay in Political and Social Criticism* (1869), chapter V. In it he outlines the "Hebraic" and "Hellenic" "sides of humanity," characterizing the former as "strict consciousness" and the latter as "loose consciousness," and discusses how they work in opposition to each other.

44. These are allusions to Matthew Arnold's poems "Sohrab and Rustum" and "The Scholar Gypsy." Frost echoes them again in his poem "New Hampshire," ll. 383–385. From "The Scholar Gypsy," l. 184: "His seat upon the intellectual throne." From "Sohrub and Rustum": "And stood erect trembling with rage" and "was choked with rage; at last these words broke away" (ll. 449, 456). And from the same: "A foil'd circuitous wanderer—till at last / The longed-for dash of waves is heard" (ll. 888–889).

45. Cf. Frost's "New Hampshire" (1923), ll. 232–33, "I'm what is called a sensibilist, / Or otherwise an environmentalist," and ll. 343–44, "The more the sensibilist I am / The more I seem to want my mountains wild."

46. The Frosts first met Fobes and his wife, Edith Hazard Fobes, in June 1915 when they bought a farm in Franconia, New Hampshire. The Fobeses' estate, used by them as a summer residence, lay adjacent to the Frosts' new farm. In later years the Frosts often re-

treated to Mrs. Fobes's guest-cottage to escape the worst hay-fever weeks in lower New England.

47. Cf. Frost's "The Star-Splitter" (1923).

48. See 22.1r, 47r; 37.2r; 7.3r, 4r; 33.9r; 8.58r, 58v; 1.34v; 17.41r; 19.8v; 24.38v; 29.23r.

49. See 4r; 4.21r; 22.6r; 29.28v, 54r, 62r.

50. Probably Sarah N. Cleghorn (1840–1959), a socialist-reformer and poet. Frost wrote a preface to her *Threescore: The Autobiography of Sarah N. Cleghorn* (1936).

51. Madison C. Bates was president of the Poetry Society of Southern Vermont and headmaster of Burr and Burton Seminary in Manchester, Vermont. Frost visited his home in the early 1920s. See also 28.17r.

52. Tinmouth Pond is located near the town of Tinmouth, in southwestern Vermont.

53. See 24r; 21.2r; 22.55v.

NOTEBOOK 13

1. Northern Democrats who opposed Union aggression, favoring instead a negotiated peace with the South. Frost's father was allegedly a Copperhead.

2. Wool was cleaned and dyed before being sent to the carding room where carding machines typical of pioneer mills prepared the fibers for spinning. Large revolving cylinders shaped the wool into a flat web of brushed fleece similar to cotton batting. Rollers then divided it into yarnlike ropes, which were wound onto large spools. The spools were mounted on machines that extended and twisted the ropes into finished yarn. Yarns were then arranged on a reel and rewound onto loom beams. After weaving, the cloth was treated in a fulling mill. Dry cloth from the fulling mill was napped, sheared, or pressed, often by machine.

3. Bungay, which is also known as Bungee or Bungey, is a lost town in Coos County, New Hampshire, near Franconia. See also 10.1v and Frost's "New Hampshire" (1922), ll. 208–209: "There's Bungey; and for Bungey there are towns, / Whole townships named but without population."

4. Frost's father was of English stock and his mother of Scottish stock. See Frost's Preface to "This Is My Best" (1942): "My first two books were published in England by the Scotch and English, to whom I am under obligations for life and my start in life."

5. See the conclusion of Frost's "The White-Tailed Hornet" (1936):

Won't this whole instinct matter bear revision?
Won't almost any theory bear revision?
To err is human, not to, animal.
Or so we pay the compliment to instinct,
Only too liberal of our compliment
That really takes away instead of gives.
Our worship, humor, conscientiousness
Went long since to the dogs under the table.
And served us right for having instituted
Downward comparisons. As long on earth
As our comparisons were stoutly upward
With gods and angels, we were men at least,

But little lower than the gods and angels.
But once comparisons were yielded downward,
Once we began to see our images
Reflected in the mud and even dust
'Twas disillusion upon disillusion.
We were lost piecemeal to the animals,
Like people thrown out to delay the wolves.
Nothing but fallibility was left us,
And this day's work made even that seem doubtful.

6. Cf. Frost's lecture at the Browne and Nichols School, "The Unmade Word, or Fetching and Far-Fetching." See also 8.15r; 26.28r; 47.

7. Rheims is a small city in northwestern France. The Rheims Cathedral built in the 13th or 14th century and noted for its great stained glass windows was virtually destroyed during World War I and rebuilt and restored by 1938 with funds from the Rockefeller Foundation. Cf. Frost's letter to Louis Untermeyer of May 24, 1916, concerning teaching and lecturing at Amherst College, among other things: "Dear Old Louis: Seriously I am fooling. And so are you with your crocodile you'llyou'llations. Come off. I thought you and we was going to be rebels together. And being rebels doesn't mean being radical. . . . It means busting something just when everybody begins to think its so sacred it's safe. (See Rheims Cathedral—next time you're in France.)"

8. See Frost's "The Gift Outright."

9. See 4.32r; 20.10r; 8.37r; 14.12r.

10. Probably Nancy Hanks Lincoln (1784–1818), Abraham Lincoln's mother.

11. Percy Bridgeman (1882–1961), Harvard researcher who won a Nobel Prize in Physics (1946) "for the invention of an apparatus to produce extremely high pressures, and for the discoveries he made therewith in the field of high pressure physics."

12. See 4.13r; 31.7r, 8r, 10r, 40r, 40v; 32; 37.1r, 5v, 6v; 22.10v; 12.7v; 9.10r; 24.39v; 21.4r, 7r; 27.29r, 45r, 46r; 1; 5; 47; 23.10r; 35.13r, 16r.

13. Cf. Plato's allegory of the cave in *The Republic*, book 7. See also 12.9v; 22.18r, 32v; 31.11v, 31v.

14. Similar to "rock, paper, scissors," "stone, knife, handkerchief" is a Japanese game also known as *janken*. See 22.16v, 17r; 15.3v.

15. See 22.8r; 26.2r; 44; 45; 12; 15.13r; 47; 8.15r, 32r.

16. Sir Roger Casement (1864–1916), poet and Irish Nationalist. Serving as a British diplomat for the Colonial Service from 1892 to 1912, he revealed atrocities in the Belgian Congo and in Peru. Resigning his post in 1912, he joined the Irish Nationalist movement. He attempted to work from Germany against England and for Ireland's independence. After having been brought to the Irish coast by a German U-boat, he was arrested, brought to London, and hanged for treason, sabotage and espionage. His was the subject of celebratory verse by Padraic Colum among others.

17. Bryn Athyn, a city in the state of Pennsylvania, is also the name of the College based upon the teachings of Swedenborg. Frost may be referring to the metal door(s) on the Bryn Athyn Cathedral. The Cathedral has several metal doors, both exterior and interior. The west door is of monel metal and glass, the south door and the door to the Mi-

chael tower are of solid metal, a combination of copper, silver and monel. Work on the cathedral began in 1913 and it was dedicated Oct. 5, 1919. However, the Council Hall and Choir Hall were not completed until 1926 and 1929 respectively. Frost may have been referring to the metal door of the Michael tower, completed around the time of the choir hall and connected to it. The monel and glass west door is the most striking of the doors on the cathedral, but it wasn't finally installed until the seventies, an oak door having been temporarily installed in 1919.

18. Agnes Gillet Boalt Crain taught architecture at the University of Cincinnati.

19. At the end of a collection of manuscripts Burns made for his friend Captain Robert Riddell, he wrote, "Let these be regarded as the genuine sentiments of a man who seldom flattered any, and never those he loved."

20. Cf. Frost's "A Masque of Mercy" (1947): "*Jonah* My name's not Joe. I don't like what she says./It's Greenwich Village cocktail party talk—/ Big-city talk. I'm getting out of here. I'm—bound—away. (He quotes it to the tune)." See also 4.12r; 24.3r; 11.29v.

21. Persepolis was a city of ancient Persia, the ceremonial seat of the Achaemenid empire of Darius I and his successors. Sitting on the Tigris river, Nineveh was the capital city of the Assyrian Empire in what is now Iraq. The palace of Sennacherib (cf. Byron's poem) was located here. A ruined city 20 miles southeast of Baghdad, Ctesiphon is the former capital of ancient Parthia and later of the Sassanid empire. It is famous for a huge vaulted hall, the remains of a palace known as the Taq-e Kosra (Throne of Khosru I). It is mentioned in "The Ingenuities of Debt," *Steeple Bush* (1947).

22. See Frost's "Education by Poetry": "Another metaphor that has interested us in our time and has done all our thinking for us is the metaphor of evolution . . . It is a very brilliant metaphor, I acknowledge, though I myself get too tired of the kind of essay that talks about the evolution of candy, we will say, or the evolution of elevators—the evolution of this, that, and the other. Everything is evolution. I emancipate myself by simply saying that I didn't get up the metaphor and so am not much interested in it." See also 21.6r; 4; 6.22r; 8.56r; 14.7r; 15.33v; 20.11r, 16v; 21.4r, 7r; 22.49r; 24.24r, 47r; 28.10r; 29.14r, 23r; 31.4r, 7r, 7v, 40r; 32.7r, 10r; 34. 1r, 2r, 2v; 47.

23. See 4.22r; 8.37r; 17.25r; 22.8r, 8v; 28. 10r; 29; 33.5r; 35.7r; 47.

24. Publius Helvius Pertinax (126–193 AD), Roman emperor who ruled for 87 days in 193 AD. "Sale of an Empire" may refer to the Praetorian camp that became the site of an auction for the throne of emperor in the wake of Pertinax's death as Flavius Sulpicianus, Pertinax's father-in-law, and Didius Julianus attempted to outbid each other in the size of their donatives to the troops. When Didius Julianus won the throne with a bid of 5,000 sesterces, he was allowed into the camp and proclaimed emperor. How Didius Julianus seized the throne, through the "Auction of the Empire," proved to be the most memorable event in his two-month reign. See also 31.7r; 24.22r; 35.

NOTEBOOK 14

1. See 11r; 7.4r; 37.9r; 4.48r; 31.7v, 9v; 22.8r, 12r, 17r, 18r; 24.44r; 15.3v; 39; 47; 19.5r, 5v, 9r; 23.4r.

2. Ben Hecht (1893–1964), novelist, journalist, dramatist. He edited the *Literary Times* and wrote plays and films including Alfred Hitchcock's *Notorious* (1946). Michael Arlen

(1895 1956) was born in Bulgaria and naturalized in Britain; author of racy novels, he later wrote screenplays in Hollywood, one of which, *A Woman of Affairs,* starred Greta Garbo. Arlen tried to hide his Armenian background while living in England while Hecht was an open advocate of Jewish causes in the Chicago press.

3. See 24.46v; 31.7r; 47; 25.1r; 2.4v; 46.5r; 12.10r.

4. The Rosenwassers were a Jewish family from Europe, residing in Cleveland, and comprised of several generations of doctors. Marcus Rosenwasser's (1846–1910) diaries and papers are archived.

5. See 31.10v; 15.9v.

6. Leo Frobenius (1873–1938), German archeologist and anthropologist.

7. Sir Thomas Malory (d. 1471), *Le Morte D'Arthur* (writ. 1469–1470, pub. 1485), Book IV, chapter 16, "How the Damoysel of the Lake saved kynge Arthur from a mantel which shold have brente hym." "And than was sir Gawayne ware how there hynge a whyght shelde on that tre, and ever as the damsels com by hit they spette upon hit and som threwe myre upon the shelde. Than sir Gawayne and sir Uwayne wente and salewed them, and asked why they dud that dispyte to the shelde." This [particular part? of the] story is retold in Mark Twain's *A Connecticut Yankee in King Arthur's Court* (1889).

8. Named after Andrew Volstead, Republican congressman from Minnesota, the act enforced the Eighteenth Amendment, which prohibited the manufacture, sale, and transportation of intoxicating liquors within the United States. The amendment was in effect from 1920 until its repeal in 1933. Cf. Frost's mention of the act in "New Hampshire" (1923): "I met a poet from another state, / A zealot full of fluid inspiration, / Who in the name of fluid inspiration, / But in the best style of bad salesmanship, / Angrily tried to make me write a protest / (In verse I think) against the Volstead Act. / He didn't offer me a drink / Until I asked for one to steady *him.* / This is called having an idea to sell."

9. J. M. Barrie (1860–1937), journalist, novelist and playwright who developed the character of Peter Pan, who first appeared in the novel *The Little White Bird* (1902) and subsequently in his play, *Peter Pan* (1904). In his library RF had: *Dear Brutus, Half Hours, A Kiss for Cinderella, Representative Plays, Sentimental Tommy.*

10. This line appears twice in Frost's poetry. Once in "Away"(1958): "Unless I'm wrong / I but obey / The urge of a song: / I'm—bound—away!" and next in *Masque of Mercy* (1947) as "My name's not Joe. I don't like what she says. / It's Greenwich Village cocktail party talk— / Big-city talk. I'm getting out of here. / I'm—bound—away. (He quotes it to the tune)." Frost was probably echoing the words "I'm—bound—away" from the well-known folk song "Shenandoah," one of the several songs he was fond of singing aloud. The pertinent refrain in this song is "Bound away, I'm bound away, 'cross the wide Missouri."

11. See Frost's "Etherealizing" (1947): "Then when the arms and legs have atrophied, / And brain is all that's left of mortal stuff, / We can lie on the beach with the seaweed / And take our daily tide baths smooth and rough. / There once we lay as blobs of jellyfish / At evolution's opposite extreme. / But now as blobs of brain we'll lie and dream, / With only one vestigial creature wish: / Oh, may the tide be soon enough at high / To keep our abstract verse from being dry."

12. See 1r, 2r; 7.4r; 37.9r; 4.48r; 31.7v, 9v; 22.8r, 12r, 17r, 18r; 24.44r; 15.3v; 39; 47; 19.5r, 5v, 9r.

13. William Ellery Leonard (1876–1944), American poet and professor of English at University of Wisconsin. Of his numerous volumes of poetry the most famous is *Two Lives*

(1922), a sonnet sequence relating the tragic story of his first marriage, which ended in his young wife's suicide.

14. See 4.32r; 20.10r; 8.37r; 13.6r.

15. See 4.32r; 24.39v, 43v, 44r; 19.5v; 27.7r; 47.

16. See Frost's "The Literate Farmer and the Planet Venus" (1941): "We need the interruption of the night / To ease attention off when overtight, / To break our logic in too long a flight, / And ask us if our premises are right."

17. See Shakespeare's Sonnet no. 116: "If this be error and upon me proved, / I never writ, nor no man ever loved." It also appears in variation in Fulke Greville's (1554–1628) *Caelica:* "I say, if this false be proved, Let me not love, or not be loved."(1633). See also *Macbeth* V.v.22: "And all our yesterdays have lighted fools / the way to dusty death," and Milton's "Comus," ll. 611–613, "If this fail, / The pillared firmament is rottenness, / And earth's base built on stubble."

18. Carter Goodrich (1897–1971), a 1917 graduate of Amherst, was originally a literature major who studied with Frost and worked with him on the *The Amherst Monthly* and then switched to an economics major. Frost liked Goodrich's poetry and mentioned him favorably in a letter to Lesley Frost. Goodrich went on to become a notable population and labor economist.

19. Gorham B. Munson (1896–1969), American literary and social critic and author of *The Dilemma of the Liberated* (1929) and *Aladdin's Lamp: The Wealth of the American People* (1945). He was an early exponent of creative writing programs and a regular faculty member at Bread Loaf. Munson also wrote *Robert Frost: A Study in Sensibility and Good Sense* (1927), though Frost remarked on its "nonsense about my noble ancestry."

20. See also 2.16r; 4; 6.22r; 8.56r; 15.33v; 20.11r, 16v; 21.4r, 7r; 22.49r; 24.24r, 47r; 28.10r; 29.14r, 23r; 31.4r, 7r, 7v, 40r; 32.7r, 10r; 34.1r, 2r, 2v; 41.7r; 47.

21. At the time of his death, Frost had in his library Walter Murdoch and Alan Mulgan, eds, *A Book of Australian and New Zealand Verse.*

22. Marcus Clark (1846–1881), journalist and novelist who was born in London and emigrated to Australia in 1863.

23. Adam Lindsay Gordan (1833–1870), sometimes credited as founder of the "Bush Ballad." Lawson and Paterson (see notes 17 and 21) followed him in this tradition.

24. Rolf Boldrewood (1826–1913), pseudonym of novelist Thomas Alexander Browne, who was born in London and emigrated to Australia in 1830.

25. Henry Lawson (1867–1922), short-story writer and writer of ballads that revealed a sympathy for democracy and the working man.

26. Jeannie Gunn (1870–1961), b. Jeannie Taylor. Australian writer of fiction.

27. Henry Kendall (1839–1882). At the time of his death, probably the most highly reputed poet of Australia's colonial period.

28. Possibly Henry Lawson (1867–1922), Australian poet and bush-ballader.

29. Andrew Barton Patterson (1864–1941), author of "Waltzing Matilda." Along with the poet Lawson he participated in the "bush-ballad revival."

30. Roy Bridges (1885–1952). Journalist and novelist.

31. Clarence Michael James Dennis (1876–1938).

32. Ethel Turner (1870–1958).

33. Bernard O'Dowd (1866–1953), Irish-born Australian poet.

34. Tom Collins (pseud. of Joseph Furphy, 1843–1912), early Australian novelist. His diaries were published as *Such Is Life: Being Certain Extracts from the Diary of Tom Collins* (1903).

35. Marcus Clark, *For the Term of His Natural Life* (1892).

36. Rolf Boldrewood (pseud. of Thomas Alexander Browne), *Robbery Under Arms*, an account of swashbuckling through the Australian bush. First serialized in the *Sydney Mail* in 1882.

37. Henry Kingsley (1830–1876), English journalist and novelist who left Oxford before taking a degree and for a time lived in Australia. Kingsley wrote *The Recollections of Geoffrey Hamlyn* (London, 1876).

38. Henry Lawson, *While the Billy Boils* (1896).

39. Jeannie Gunn, *We of the Never-Never* (1908), is an extended anecdote on the vicissitudes of life in the Territory and has given Australian literature several memorable characters.

40. Bernard O'Dowd, *The Bush* (1912), a Nationalist Australian poem.

41. John Holmes (1904–1962), Professor at Tufts University. His *Address to the Living* (1937) was the only publication for which Frost ever wrote a blurb.

NOTEBOOK 15

1. Frost accepted an appointment at Amherst in 1923 after President Meiklejohn was dismissed by the trustees. He taught one course in philosophical judgments and one course on literature, and this notebook contains notes for classes Frost taught between the fall of 1923 and the fall of 1924. The first two pages of this notebook list names of Amherst students from the class of 1924, as well as unrelated random addresses. One student listed, Eugene R. Whittemore, appears again on 12r.

2. See 7.4r; 37.9r; 4.48r; 31.7v, 9v; 14.1r, 2r, 11r; 22.8r, 12r, 17r, 18r; 24.44r; 39; 47; 19.5r, 5v, 9r.

3. Similar to "rock, paper, scissors," "stone, knife, handkerchief" is a Japanese game also known as *janken*. See 22.16v, 17r; 23.9v.

4. Benedetto Croce (1866–1952), *History: Its Theory and Practice* (New York: Harcourt, Brace and Co., 1923).

5. James Anthony Froude (1818–1894), English historian. Froude himself was a devotee of Carlyle and Froude championed the study of history as an academic discipline.

6. Cf. Emerson's poem "Uriel."

7. Lev Nikolayevich Tolstoy (1828–1910), *The Death of Ivan Ilych* (1884–6).

8. "Polikúshka" (1863), short story by Tolstoy.

9. Julia Pastrana (1834–1860), Mexican-Indian woman born with congenital hypertrichosis, a condition that caused her small body to grow copious amounts of hair and an ape-like protruding mouth. Billed as the "baboon lady," she spent much of her life—and afterlife as an embalmed corpse—being exhibited around America and Europe to shock and titillate curious circus-goers and scientists.

10. Svyato-Danilov Monastery or Holy Danilov Monastery is a male monastery on the right bank of the Moskva River in Moscow founded in the late 13th century by Alexander Nevsky's son Danilov. Since 1983, it has functioned as the headquarters of the Russian Orthodox church.

11. Valdai is a city located almost exactly halfway between Moscow and St. Petersburg that became an important staging post after Catherine the Great decided to build a "road palace" there in 1770. Craftsmen in the area fashioned bells that adorned the troikas, or

stagecoaches, that would warn fellow travelers of an oncoming troika on the road between Moscow and St. Petersburg.

12. Nickname for the Boston American League Ball Club, or the Boston Red Sox.

13. A variation of a line from "Escapist—Never" (1962): "A crooked straightness yet no less a straightness." Also, from "The Constant Symbol" (1946), "The mind is a baby giant who, more provident in the cradle than he knows, has hurdled his paths in life all round ahead of him like playthings given—data so called. They are vocabulary, grammar, prosody, and diary, and it will be too bad if he can't find stepping stones of them for his feet wherever he wants to go. The way will be zigzag, but it will be a straight crookedness like the walking stick he cuts himself in the bushes for an emblem." See also 31.10v; 14.5r.

14. See "Education by Poetry": "Greatest of all attempts to say one thing in terms of another is the philosophical attempt to say matter in terms of spirit, or spirit in terms of matter, to make the final unity. That is the greatest attempt that has ever failed. We stop just short there. But it is the height of poetry, the height of all poetic thinking, that attempt to say matter in terms of spirit and spirit in terms of matter." See also 8.58r.

15. See 4.16r; 47.

16. Ernest Christopher Dowson (1867–1900), English poet whose most famous poem is "Non Sum Qualis Eram Bonae sub Regno Cynarae," in *Cynara: A Little Book of Verse* (Portland, Maine: T. B. Mosher, 1907).

17. John Davidson (1857–1909), "A Ballad of Hell" (1895).

18. Frost entered Dartmouth College in the fall of 1892 and dropped out in December. In 1893, he went to work in the Arlington Woolen Mill in his hometown of Lawrence, Massachusetts, quitting in February 1894.

19. See 22.8r; 26.2r; 44; 45; 13.9v; 12; 47; 8.15r, 32r.

20. George Borrow (1803–1881), British novelist who traveled widely as an agent for the Bible Society. During his travels he spent a lot of time in the company of the Romany, who almost adopted him. *Lavengro* (1851) was the title of one of his semi-autobiographical novels.

21. Shakespeare, *Coriolanus* (ca. 1607–1608).

22. Aldous Huxley (1894–1963).

23. Sherwood Anderson (1876–1941).

24. See 29.42r; 20.19v.

25. Cf. Frost's "The Figure a Poem Makes" (1939).

26. See 4.6r; 19.9r; 22.33v; 24.28r; 29.

27. Mark Twain (1835–1910). See also 7.38r; 12.1r; 17.28v–29r; 26.27r.

28. *Dr. Johnson's Table Talk, or Conversations of the late Samuel Johnson, LL.D., on a Variety of Useful and Entertaining Subjects* (London: G. G. J. and J. Robinson, 1785), or possibly John Selden's *Table-Talk*, which Frost received as a prize *pro insigni in studiis diligentia* while an undergraduate at Harvard.

29. Herman Melville, *Typee: A Peep at Polynesian Life* (1846).

30. Cf. Frost's "The Figure a Poem Makes" (1939): "Scholars and artists thrown together are often annoyed at the puzzle of where they differ. Both work from knowledge; but I suspect that they differ most importantly in the way their knowledge is come by. Scholars get theirs with conscientious thoroughness along projected lines of logic; poets theirs cavalierly and as it happens in and out of books. They stick to nothing deliberately, but let what will stick to them like burrs where they walk in the fields." See also 25r.

31. Christopher Marlowe's *The Tragical History of Doctor Faustus* (1604).

32. See 29.16v, 29v; 4.38r; 28.18r; 9.19r. See also Frost's "Kitty Hawk."

33. Cf. Walden, Chapter 1, "Economy": "And when the farmer has got his house, he may not be the richer but the poorer for it, and it be the house that has got him. As I understand it, that was a valid objection urged by Momus against the house which Minerva made, that she 'had not made it movable, by which means a bad neighborhood might be avoided'; and it may still be urged, for our houses are such unwieldy property that we are often imprisoned rather than housed in them; and the bad neighborhood to be avoided is our own scurvy selves. I know one or two families, at least, in this town, who, for nearly a generation, have been wishing to sell their houses in the outskirts and move into the village, but have not been able to accomplish it, and only death will set them free."

34. See 19.3v; 29.15r.

35. See 4.42r; 19.9v; 22.6r; 47.

36. Cf. Frost's "The Figure a Poem Makes" (1939). See also 20v.

37. Willa Cather (1873–1947) short story entitled "Paul's Case" (1905).

38. Guy de Maupassant (1850–1893), "The Diamond Necklace" (1885).

39. Cf. "The Ax-Helve" (1917): "Mrs. Baptiste came in and rocked a chair / That had as many motions as the world: / One back and forward, in and out of shadow, / That got her nowhere; . . ."

40. Cf. Frost's letter to Louis Untermeyer of March 10, 1924: "I owe any form of humor shows fear and inferiority. Irony is simply a kind of guardedness. So is a twinkle. It keeps the reader from criticism . . . Belief is better than anything else, and it is best when rapt, above paying respects to anybody's doubt whatsoever. At bottom the world isn't a joke. We only joke about it to avoid an issue with someone to let someone know that we know he's there with his questions: to disarm him by seeming to have heard and done justice to his side of the standing argument. Humor is the most engaging cowardice. With it myself I have been able to hold some of my enemy in play far out of gunshot."

41. See 43.1r, 6r; 45.1r; 47; 28.11r; 4.34r, 36r; 22.53r; 26.2r; 47.

42. Emily Dickinson (1830–1886). "T. Hardy" is Thomas Hardy (1840–1928).

43. This could be either Frost's assessment of an aspect of Santayana's thought or an assertion of Frost's own. Santayana never wrote that "behavior is a belief" but parts of *Scepticism and Animal Faith* (1923) may be considered in those terms. In the chapter "The Implied Being of Truth," Santayana wrote " . . . In general I think that the impulse of action is translated into a belief in changed things long before it reproaches itself without having made any error about them. The recognition of a truth to be discerned may thus be avoided; because although a belief in things must actually be either true or false, it is directed upon the present existence and character of these things, not upon its own truth. The active object posited alone interests the man of action; if he were interested in the rightness of the action, he would not be a man of action but a philosopher." (264). Frost's own use of the phrase "believe in" in *Education by Poetry* (1930) suggests action in relationship to belief: "There are four beliefs that I know more about from having lived with poetry . . . the literary one in every work of art, not of cunning and craft, mind you, but of real art; that believing the thing into existence, saying as you go more than you ever hoped you were ever going to be able to say, and coming with surprise to an end that you foreknew only with some sort of emotion. And then finally the relationship we enter into God to believe the future in—to believe the hereafter in." See also 19.7v.

44. Babylonian monarch who reigned BC 562–559.

45. In the United States, the funds needed to wage war had required the federal government to institute death or inheritance taxes (e.g. during the Civil and Spanish-American Wars). In 1916, the federal government began to institute a progressive inheritance tax. About the same time in England, death duties were imposed. This tax and the Great War were frequently credited in England as contributing factors to the reorganization of and loss of power to the older social orders.

46. See also 2.16r; 4; 6.22r; 8.56r; 14.17r; 20.11r, 16v; 21.4r, 7r; 22.49r; 24.24r, 47r; 28.10r; 29.14r, 23r; 31.4r, 7r, 7v, 40r; 32.7r, 10r; 34.11r, 2r, 2v; 41.7r; 47.

47. (Joan) Rosita Torr Forbes (1893–1967), British author who wrote a book on an early-20th-century Berber chieftain, *El Raisuni: The Sultan of the Mountain* (London, 1924).

48. Chase Salmon Osborn (1860–1949), literary critic and author of *Madagascar, Land of the Man-eating Tree* (New York, 1924). A copy of Osborn's *Iron Hunter* was in Frost's library at the time of his death.

49. Christopher Columbus (1451–1506), *Journal of First Voyage to America* (1493).

50. Warner may be a mistake for William Morton Wheeler (1865–1937), author of *Social Life among Insects: Being a Series of Lectures Delivered at the Lowell Institute in Boston in March 1922* (New York, 1923).

51. Charles Howard McIlwain (1871–1968), *The American Revolution: A Constitutional Interpretation* (1923).

52. A. L. Kroeber (1876–1960), American anthropologist who published prolifically. He specialized in North American Indian language and culture and the natives of Peru. Frost is probably referring to Kroeber's *Anthropology* (1923, rev. 1948).

53. Pierre Loti (1850–1923), *A Tale of Brittany (mon frere Yves)* (1900, 1930).

54. Gilbert Seldes (1893–1970), who was widely credited as America's first systematic student of the "Popular Arts." See his *The Seven Lively Arts* (New York, 1924).

55. Frank Hurley (1885–1962), *Pearls and Savages: Adventures in the Air, on Land and Sea— in New Guinea* (New York: G. P. Putnam's Sons, 1924).

56. "Greenland" and "Rasmussen" are in black ink.

57. Knud Rasmussen (1879–1933), Danish explorer and the author of *Greenland by the Polar Sea: The Story of the Thule Expedition from Melville Bay to Cape Morris Jesup* (1921).

58. Edward Gibbon (1737–1794). Commonly known as his *Autobiography,* more properly as *Memoirs of His Life and Writings* (1796).

59. Jean-Jacques Rousseau (1712–1778), *Emile* (1762).

60. William Hickling Prescott (1796–1859), author of *History of the Conquest of Mexico* (1843) and *History of the Conquest of Peru* (1847).

61. John Dryden (1631–1700), *All for Love* (1677).

62. Ralph Waldo Emerson (1803–1882) *Representative Men* (1850). Composed of essays on Plato, Swedenborg, Montaigne, Napoleon, and Goethe.

63. Henry David Thoreau (1817–1862), *Walden* (1854). See also Notebook 47.

64. Francis Brette Harte (1836–1902), also known as "Bret Harte," American short-story writer and poet. "The Luck of Roaring Camp," *Overland Monthly,* Vol. 1, No. 2 (August 1868) was a picturesque account of life in the west.

65. George Herbert Palmer (1842–1933), Frost's teacher at Harvard and translator of *The Odyssey of Homer* (1884).

66. Henry Houghton initiated the Riverside Press in 1852. In 1880 he began a partner-

ship with George Mifflin. Shortly thereafter, the Riverside Literature Series was born. The series printed well-bound and well-edited editions for the educational market and the discerning general reader.

67. Jacobus de Voragine (1230–1298), *The Golden Legend,* or *Legenda Aurea* (though originally titled *Legenda Sanctorum*), is a thirteenth-century collection of stories and tales designed to inspire devotional living.

68. Kostes Palamas (1859–1943), Greek poet. *Immovable Life* is probably *Life Unshakable,* a collection of verse (1904, partial tr., 1919, 1921).

69. Ernst Boerschmann (1873–1949), *Picturesque China: Architecture and Landscape; a Journey through Twelve Provinces* (1923).

70. Brentano's was a prominent New York bookselling and publishing company, the first to publish G. B. Shaw in the United States and controversial books by Margaret Sanger on birth control. The Brentano's New York bookstore, managed by Arthur Brentano, was a social landmark from the late nineteenth through the first decades of the twentieth century.

71. Founded in 1846, Charles Scribner's Sons, a New York publishing house, released titles by many of the great authors of the early to mid-twentieth century including F. Scott Fitzgerald, Ernest Hemingway, Thomas Wolfe, et al.

72. Percy Bysshe Shelley (1792–1822), *A Philosophical View of Reform,* ed. T. W. Rolleston (1920).

73. Alexis de Tocqueville (1805–1859), French critic, best known for his observations in *Democracy in America* (vol. I, 1835; vol. II, 1840).

74. R. B. Haldane (1856–1928), *The Doctrine of Degrees in Knowledge, Truth and Reality* (1919).

75. T. J. Haarhoff (1892–1971) *Schools of Gaul: A Study of Pagan and Christian Education in the Last Century of the Western Empire* (1920).

76. Mrs. Sinclair Stevenson (1875–1957), *The Rites of the Twice-Born* (1920).

77. Arthur Berriedale Keith (1879–1944), *The Samkhya System: A History of the Samkhya Philosophy* (1918).

78. Vincent Taylor (1887–1968), *Historical Evidence for the Virgin Birth* (1920).

79. Arthur George Heath (1887–1915), *The Moral and Social Significance of the Conception of Personality* (1921).

80. William Matthews Flinders Petrie (1853–1942), *Eygptian Stories.*

81. C. W. King, *Antique Gems: Their Origin, Uses, and Value as Interpreters of Ancient History* (1860).

82. William Collins (1721–59), English poet.

83. John Clare (1793–1864), English poet.

84. Edward John Trelawny (1792–1881), *Recollections of the Last Days of Shelley and Byron* (1858).

85. Mary Wollstonescraft Godwin (1759–97) or perhaps her daughter and the poet Shelley's wife Mary Wollstonecraft Shelley (1797–1851).

86. Diary of Japanese poet Ki Tsurayuki (ca. 870–946), containing his poetic theories. Published in English as W. G. Aston (1841–1911), trans., *An Ancient Japanese Classic (The "Tosa Nikki" or Tosa Diary)* (Yokahama, 1884), and William Ninnis Porter (d. 1929), trans., *The Tosa Diary* (London, 1912). Tsurayuki was apparently a Japanese poet of some talent. He compiled anthologies, held government posts, and discoursed on love.

87. A fictional account (mystery and detective fiction) set in India. Meadows Taylor (1808–1876), *Confessions of a Thug*, 3 vols. (London, 1839).

88. Lucretius (ca. 95–55 B.C.), Roman poet whose *De Rerum Natura* ("On the Nature of Things") was based on the the Epicurean philosophy. Cf. Frost's "Lucretius versus the Lake Poets."

89. A whaling chronicle set in New Zealand. George Hempleman (1799–1880), *The Piraki Log ("E Pirangi ahau koe"): or, Diary of Captain Hempleman*, trans. F. A. Anson (1910).

90. *The Trial between Lieut. Trelawney, Plaintiff and Capt. Coleman, Defendant, for Criminal Conversation with the Plaintiff's Wife, including the Amorous Love Letters, &c.* (1817).

91. Edmund Horace Fellowes (1870–1950), *The English Madrigal* (1925).

92. John Donne (1572–1631), *Donne's Sermons*, ed. Logan Pearsall Smith (Oxford, 1920).

93. John Aubrey (1626–1697). His posthumously published (from manuscript, 1898) *Brief Lives* were biographical sketches of poets, philosophers, etc.

94. H. J. C. Grierson, *Metaphysical Lyrics & Poems of the Seventeenth Century: Donne to Butler* (Oxford, 1921), or *The Poems of John Donne*, ed. H. J. C. Grierson (Oxford, 1912).

95. Edmund Spenser (1552?–1599), *The Poetical Works of Edmund Spenser*, ed. J. C. Smith and E. De Sélincourt (London: Oxford Univ. Press, 1912).

96. Walter W. Skeat (1835–1912), *Early English Proverbs, Chiefly of the Thirteenth and Fourteenth Centuries* (1910).

97. W. Y. Evans-Wentz (1878–1965), *The Fairy-Faith in Celtic Countries* (1911).

98. Albert Curtis Clark (1859–1937), *Prose Rhythm in English* (1913).

99. *The Shirburn Ballads, 1585–1616*, ed. from the ms. by Andrew Clark (Oxford, 1907).

100. One of three English poetic miscellanies published in 1600. The others were *England's Helicon* and *Belvedere, or the Garden of the Muses*.

101. William Shakespeare, *Coriolanus* (1607–1608).

102. Sir Walter Raleigh (ca. 1552–1618). See also 19.7r; 18.4r.

103. Richard Hakluyt (1533–1616), *Divers Voyages Touching the Discovery of America* (1582) and his magnum opus: *The Principal Navigations, Voyages, Traffics, and Discoveries of the English Nation, Made by Sea or Overland to the Remote and Farthest Distant Quarters of the Earth at Any Time within the Compass of These 1600 Years*, 3 vols. (1589).

104. John Milton (1608–1674), *Samson Agonistes* (1671). See also 18.4r.

105. Robert Burns (1759–96), Scottish poet who collected folk songs across Scotland and adapted them into lyric poems. The most prominent examples of these are "Auld Lang Syne" and "Scots Wha Hae."

106. William Morris (1834–1896), *The Life and Death of Jason: A Poem* (1867).

107. Possibly Gilbert Murray (1866–1957), *The Story of Nefrekepta from a Demotic Papyrus, Put into Verse* (Oxford, 1911).

108. Thomas W. Talley (1870–1952), *Negro Folk Rhymes, Wise and Unwise, with a Study* (New York: Macmillan, 1922). Talley was a black chemistry professor from Tennessee.

109. Llewellyn Jones (1884–1961), *First Impressions: Essays on Poetry, Criticism, and Prosody* (New York: Alfred A. Knopf, 1925). The first and second essays are on E. A. Robinson and Robert Frost, respectively.

110. William Stanley Braithwaite (1878–1962), American editor, literary critic, and poet.

111. M. A. De Wolfe Howe (1864–1960), critic and editor of American letters.

112. Carl Sandburg (1878–1967) wrote for the *Chicago Daily News*.

113. Harriet Monroe (1860–1936), critic, poet, and founding editor of *Poetry: A Magazine of Verse* in 1912.

114. John Clair Minot (b. 1872).

115. Edwin F. Gay (1867–1946), American writer, editor, and journalist.

116. Arthur Pound (1884–1966), newspaperman (1913–40), professor at the University of Pittsburgh (1935–36), and a state historian of New York (1940–44).

117. Ridgley Torrence (1875–1950) was an American poet, dramatist, journalist, and editor; the poems in *Hesperides* (1925) express his transcendental faith. Frost dedicated the poem "A Passing Glimpse" in *West-Running Brook* (1928) to Torrence.

118. John Farrar (1896–1974), head of the Breadloaf Writer's Conference prior to Frost. The two met at Yale in 1917 and Farrar reviewed with praise Frost's *New Hampshire* in 1923.

NOTEBOOK 16

1. Stephen Burroughs (1765–1840) served in the army, which he deserted, and attended Dartmouth College, which he left without a diploma; he became "notorious" for impersonating an ordained minister with plagiarized sermons and for counterfeiting. Burroughs later went to Canada, converted to Roman Catholicism, and became a respected tutor of the sons of wealthy Catholics. Cf. Frost's "Preface" to *Memoirs of the Notorious Stephen Burroughs* (1924). Here Frost seems to be in imaginary dialogue with Burroughs.

2. George Rawlinson (1812–1902), professor of ancient history at Oxford University and author of *History of Ancient Egypt* (1881).

3. Jonathan Edwards (1703–1758), American Congregational preacher and theologian who defended Calvinist theology and Puritanical doctrines. He is best known for his sermon, "Sinners in the Hands of an Angry God."

NOTEBOOK 17

The first twenty-one pages of this notebook contain a grading ledger for a literature course Frost taught at Amherst, between 1923 and 1925. Frost taught a full-year elective course for juniors at Amherst in 1923–24, described as "a course of extensive reading in poetry, drama, essays, and short stories." He taught two elective courses in 1924–25, one for juniors and one for seniors. The course for seniors is described in the college catalogue simply as "Advanced writing."

1. A possible reference to Harriet Monroe's (1860–1936) *You and I* (1914).

2. See Frost's "A Servant to Servants" (1914), ll. 7–9: "I can't express my feelings any more / Than I can raise my voice or want to lift / My hand (oh, I can lift it when I have to)."

3. A variation of the first two lines from a "A Minor Bird," *West-Running Brook* (1928): "I have wished a bird would fly away, / And not sing by my house all day." First published as "The Minor Bird" (1926).

4. Herbert George Wells (1866–1946), English novelist and political reformer. Besides those works for which he is well-known (e.g. *The Time Machine* [1895] and *The Invisible Man* [1897]), see *The Outline of History* (1919; 1930), *The Science of Life* (1929), *The Work, Wealth and Happiness of Mankind* (1932), and *The Fate of Homo Sapiens* (1939). See 29.14r.

5. See 4.22r; 8.37r; 22.8r, 8v; 24.31r; 28.10r; 29; 33.5r; 35.7r; 47.

6. See 8.5r; 6.25r.

7. See note 42 below.

8. Henrik Ibsen (1828–1906), Norwegian playwright and poet. One of Ibsen's plays is entitled *The Wild Duck* (Norwegian, *Vildanden*, 1884).

9. Captain James Cook (1728–1779), *A Journal of a voyage round the world in His Majesty's Ship Endeavour, in the years 1768, 1769, 1770, and 1771; undertaken in pursuit of natural knowledge, at the desire of the Royal Society* (London, 1771).

10. François Villon (1431–1474), French poet.

11. Louis Untermeyer (1885–1977), *Modern American and British Poetry* (New York: Harcourt, Brace, 1928); Harriet Monroe (1860–1936) and Alice Corbin Henderson (1881–1949), *The New Poetry: An Anthology* (New York: The Macmillan Company, 1920); Jessie B. Rittenhouse (1869–1948), *The Little Book of Modern Verse: A Selection from the Work of Contemporaneous American Poets* (Boston: Houghton Mifflin Company, 1913); C. Day Lewis (1904–1972) and L. A. G. Strong (1896–1958), *A New Anthology of Modern Verse, 1920–1940* (1941); Francis T. Palgrave (1824–1897), *Golden Treasury of English Songs and Lyrics* (London: Macmillan & Co., 1861). On anthologies, Frost had several memorable things to say: In a dialogue that occurs in "Poverty and Poetry," his address to Haverford College, October 25, 1937, Frost remarks: "Poor thing. If anthologies are bad, so is all criticism, for anthologies are just a form of criticism. There's no better way for you to approach Shakespeare's sonnets than through reading the selections Palgrave made of them and the selections Quiller-Couch made of them. It's the example without too many words. Maybe the anthologies are bad; on the other hand, they are good, too. Maybe the poor are unfortunate, but on the other hand, they may be fortunate." Frost would also lecture on the topic, "The anthology as the Highest Form of Criticism; survival and revival tell the story."

12. Edgar A. Guest (1881–1959), poet.

13. Thomas B. Mosher (1852–1923), a publisher who reprinted English works for American audiences. He championed a very simple, plain look for bindings, dust-wrappers, and text.

14. Jeffrey Amherst Bookshop in Amherst, Massachusetts, since 1943.

15. "De Imitatione Christi" *The Imitation of Christ* (ca. 1425 or 1427), traditionally ascribed to Thomas à Kempis (1379/80–1471). A very popular devotional work on the withdrawal from worldly care and the retreat into the contemplative Christian life.

16. Francis Thompson (1859–1907), English Roman Catholic critic and poet. "The Hound of Heaven," one of his best-known poems, was published in *Poems* (1893).

17. Milton's description of poetry, one of the organic arts, made in his tract "Of Education" (1644) in relation to rhetoric and logic: "To which poetry would be made subsequent, or indeed, rather precedent, as being less suttle and fine but more simple, sensuous, and passionate."

18. Horace Mann is a preparatory school in the Bronx, New York.

19. Isabella Stewart Gardner (1840–1924), art collector and literary socialite. With her husband, Jack, the founder of the Isabella Stewart Gardner Museum in Boston.

20. Vachel Lindsay (1879–1931), American poet, known for dramatic performances of his work.

21. An English ballad called "Thomas the Rhymer" by Thomas the Rhymer a.k.a.

Thomas of Erceldoune (1220?–1297?), a Scottish poet reputed to have prophetic gifts. Frost commented on the poem in "Remarks on the Occasion of the Tagore Centenary." John Frederick Nims transcribed Frost's remarks from the tape and published them in *Poetry 99* (November 1961): 106–19: "Some people think that beauty is truth. They aren't ineffable enough to know that that isn't so. Keats didn't pretend to be ineffable when he said that: 'Beauty is truth, truth beauty . . . ' No. One of the poets a long time ago wrote like this: he got up a story about a fellow called True Thomas; it's in an old ballad: 'True Thomas lay on Huntley Bank, / And a wonder came riding by,' something supernatural came riding by,' a beautiful lady. And he rose up from where he was, and 'louted low down,' it says, 'to his knee.' And she says: 'Rise up, Thomas! Who do you think I am?' He says: 'You're so beautiful, you must be the Queen of Heaven!' And she says: 'Oh, you couldn't make a greater mistake! I'm only the Queen of Fairyland!' You see, she was the Queen of Beauty, but not of Truth." See also 24.41v; 19.10r.

22. Short story by Mark Twain (1835–1910), "The Celebrated Jumping Frog of Calaveras County" (1865). See also 7.38r; 12.1r; 15.19v; 26.27r.

23. The first poem in the *Oxford Book of English Verse, 1250–1918* (ed. Arthur Quiller-Couch) is the anonymous "Cuckoo Song" dated ca. 1250.

24. Cf. The first line of Robert Browning's (1812–1889) poem "Memorabilia": "Ah, did you once see Shelley plain, / And did he stop and speak to you? / And did you speak to him again? / How strange it seems, and new!"

25. George Gordon, Lord Byron (1788–1824), "The Isles of Greece," from *Don Juan*, Canto the Third, LXXXVI (1821).

26. Cf. the first lines of William Wordsworth's (1770–1850) poem "The Character of the Happy Warrior": "Who is the happy Warrior? Who is he / That every man in arms should wish to be?"

27. Tennyson, "Locksley Hall" (1842).

28. Robert Bloomfield (1766–1823), English pastoral poet. *A Selection from the Poems of Robert Bloomfield*, preface by Edmund Blunden, ed. J. L. Carr (Kettering, Northants: Campaigner, 1966).

29. George Crabbe (1754–1832), English poet.

30. Langland or "William Langley" (ca. 1331–1399?), English poet, author of *Piers Plowman* (ca. 1362).

31. Cf. Frost's "The Figure a Poem Makes" (1939): "All that can be done with words is soon told. So also with meter—particularly with our language where there are virtually but two, strict iambic and loose iambic."

32. Robert Herrick (1591–1674), "To Daffadills" (1648). Frost discusses this poem's form in *A Constant Symbol* (1946).

33. See 4.51r; 45.1r; 24.28v; 19.1r.

34. See note 23 above.

35. Cf. Shakespeare's Sonnet XXIX.

36. The poem "Wild Grapes" (1920) was written at the request of Susan Hayes Ward (1838–1924), editor of *The Independent*, who published Frost's first poem "My Butterfly" (18). She asked Frost to write a poem that would do for girls what "Birches" (1915) had done for boys.

37. "Stopping by Woods on a Snowy Evening" is included in *New Hampshire* (1923).

38. Ford Madox Ford (1873–1939) (b. Ford Hermann Hueffer).

39. Untermeyer's anthologies—which were combined into one.

40. Arthur Quiller-Couch, *The Oxford Book of English Verse* and *The Oxford Book of Victorian Verse*. These anthologies went through several editions.

41. Robert Lynd (1879–1949), Irish Protestant, prolific essayist, critic, and writer with sympathies towards Irish nationalism. Cf. Lynd's "A Note on Elizabethan Plays": "One day, when Swinburne was looking over Mr. Gosse's books, he took down Lamb's Specimens of the English Dramatic Poets, and, turning to Mr. Gosse, said, 'That book taught me more than any other book in the world—that and the Bible.' Swinburne was a notorious borrower of other men's enthusiams. He borrowed republicanism from Landor and Mazzini, the Devil from Baudelaire, and the Elizabethans from Lamb. He has not, as Lamb had, Elizabethan blood in his veins. Lamb had the Elizabethan love of phrases that have cost a voyage of fancies discovered in a cave. Swinburne had none of this rich taste in speech. He used words riotously, but he did not use great words riotously. He was excitedly extravagant where Lamb was carefully extravagant. He often seemed to be bent chiefly making a beautiful noise" (*The Art of Letters* [New York: Charles Scribner's Sons, 1921], p. 83). In another essay entitled "Jean Valjean" (1932) in *Books and Writers* (London: Dent, 1952), on Hugo: "There is probably no critic writing to-day who would say of him, as Swinburne once did, that he was 'the greatest writer born in the nineteenth century.' His rhetoric faded with time, his propaganda of a past age; his characters belong to melodrama rather than to the fiction of human nature; and his sentimentality is as unpalatable to many modern readers as that of a tract" (p. 156). In another essay, entitled "Swinburne" (a two-part essay collected in *Old and New Masters* [Charles Scribner's Sons, n.d.]), Lynd writes: "He had little of his own to express, but he discovered the heretic's gospel in Gautier and Baudelaire and set it forth in English music that he might have learned form the Sirens who sang to Ulysses. He reveled in blasphemous and licentious fancies that would have made Byron's hair stand on end" (pp. 189–90). And: "Still, even to-day, once cannot but enjoy the gusto with which he praised Trelawney—Shelley's and Byron's Trelawney—"the most splendid old man I have seen since Landor and my own grandfather" (p. 190). And: "Swinburne, it seems, was easily pleased. One of his proudest boasts was that he and Victor Hugo bore a close resemblance to each other in one respect: both of them were almost dead when they were born, 'certainly not expected to live an hour.' There was also one great difference between them. Swinburne never grew up" (p. 191).

42. Que sais-je? Fr. What do I know? The theme of Montaigne's essay project, his skeptical approach to knowledge, and especially self-knowledge. This phrase was carved on the wall of his octagonal study. See also 8.3r; 6.22r.

43. Jack Cade (d. 1450), an English political rebel and organizer of popular rebellion, possibly of Irish birth. James Ramsey MacDonald (1866–1937), a Scotsman, was British Prime Minister during 1924, and from 1929 to 1935.

44. Stephen Burroughs (1765–1840) served in the army, which he deserted, and attended Dartmouth College, which he left without a diploma; he became "notorious" for impersonating an ordained minister with plagiarized sermons and for counterfeiting. Burroughs later went to Canada, converted to Roman Catholicism, and became a respected tutor

of the sons of wealthy Catholics. Cf. Frost's *Preface* to *Memoirs of the Notorious Stephen Burroughs* (1924).

45. Eugene O'Neill (1888–1953), American playwright. *The Moon of the Caribbes* (1919) is a one-act drama.

46. Mary Austin (1868–1934), American author interested in North American Indian and native life. Her *The Land of Little Rain* (1903) describes life in the deserts of the western United States.

47. Stephen Burroughs (1765–1840), *Memoirs of the Notorious Stephen Burroughs of New Hampshire, with a Preface by Robert Frost* (New York: Dial Press, 1924).

48. Robert Louis Stevenson (1850–1894), *Virginibus Puerisque* (1881) and *Familiar Studies of Men and Books* (1892).

49. William H. Prescott (1796–1859), *History of the Conquest of Mexico* (1843). See also 15.38r.

50. Emily Dickinson's poems, only a few of which were published during her lifetime. Most were published at the end of the nineteenth century.

51. Ben Jonson (1572–1637), English poet and playwright, author of *Epicœne, or the Silent Woman* (1609) and *The Alchemist* (1610).

52. Gilbert White (1720–1793), *Natural History of Selbourne* (1788).

53. Sir Thomas Browne (1605–1682), English prose writer and Christian thinker. Best known for *Religio Medici* (1643) and *Pseudodoxia Epidemica* (1646). From the beginning of this page to this point the writing is in pencil.

54. Joseph Conrad (1857–1924), *Set of Six* (1915).

55. W. S. Gilbert (1836–1911), *The Bab Ballads, with Which Are Included Songs of a Savoyard* (1924).

56. John Russell (1885–1956). *Where the Pavement Ends* (1919) is the title of a collection of short stories.

57. H. G. Wells (1866–1946), *Thirty Strange Stories* (1897).

58. Aucassin and Nicolette, a 13th-century legend of Provence, which has been translated or adapted by F. W. Bourdillon, Swinburne, Andrew Lang, and Eugene Mason. With "Amis and Amile" (see Amis and Amiloun) it forms the subject of one of Pater's "Studies in the History of the Renaissance." The original is in prose interspersed with songs. Aucassin, son of Count Garins of Beaucaire, loves Nicolette, a beautiful Saracen captive. The father forbids their marriage and immures Nicolette in a tower, and subsequently, after further dissension with his son, imprisons Aucassin himself. The damsel escapes and is followed by Aucassin, and the story is concerned with their simple adventures and faithful love, which is finally rewarded.

59. Richard Hakluyt (1533–1616), *Divers Voyages Touching the Discovery of America* (1582) and his magnum opus: *The Principal Navigations, Voyages, Traffics, and Discoveries of the English Nation, Made by Sea or Overland to the Remote and Farthest Distant Quarters of the Earth at Any Time within the Compass of These 1600 Years*, 3 vols. (1589). Cf. Frost's "The Discovery of the Madeiras: A Rhyme of Hackluyt" (1942).

60. Ralph Waldo Emerson (1803–1882), *Poems* (1847), *May-Day and Other Pieces* (1867), and *Selected Poems* (1876), among other uncollected pieces.

61. H. L. Mencken (1880–1956). Mencken translated Friedrich Nietzsche's *The Anti-Christ* in 1920.

62. Possibly William Allingham, *Ballad Book: A Selection of the Choicest British Ballads* (Cambridge, 1865). Frost had a copy of Allingham's *Ballad Book,* which he received from his mother, in his library.

63. Oscar Wilde's (1854–1900) play *The Importance of Being Earnest* (1895).

64. In Book V of *The Odyssey* Odysseus swims to the Island of the Phaeacians after a storm raised by Poseidon destroys his raft.

65. Geoffrey Chaucer's "The Canon's Yeoman's Tale," whose protagonist eventually repudiates alchemy.

66. Edgar Allan Poe (1809–1849), "The Masque of the Red Death" (1842).

67. Nathaniel Hawthorne (1804–1864) "Mr. Higginbotham's Catastrophe" (1834).

68. Guy de Maupassant's (1850–1893) short story "The Piece of String" (1884).

69. John Russell (1885–1956), "The Price of the Head," in *The Red Mark and Other Stories* (1919).

70. Byron, *The Prisoner of Chillon* (1816).

71. Walter Pater, *Plato and Platonism* (London, 1893).

72. Charles Vildrac (1882–1971) *Livre d'amour* (1910), translated into English as *A Book of Love* (New York, 1923).

73. See Notebook 43, note 6.

74. May refer to Charles J. Connick (1875–1945), the great 19th-century American stained-glass maker.

75. Possibly *Southwest Review,* beginning with Vol. 10 in Oct. 1924; previously *Texas Review* (1915–1924).

76. Greenwich Village Theatre in lower part of Manhattan Island in New York, New York, was a forum for one-act plays, including those by Eugene O'Neill, Sherwood Anderson, and e.e. cummings, among others.

77. See 5.8r; 24.48r; 32.10r; 35.19r.

78. Ralph Waldo Emerson (1803–1882), the "Concord Hymn" or "Hymn: Sung at the Completion of the Concord Monument, April 19, 1836" is collected in *Poems* (1847): "By the rude bridge that arched the flood, / Their flag to April's breeze unfurled, / Here once the embattled farmers stood, / And fired the shot heard round the world."

79. See 22.11r, 47r; 12.10r; 37.2r; 7.3r, 4r; 33.9r; 8.58r, 58v; 1.34v; 19.8v; 24.38v; 29.23r.

80. Robert Louis Stevenson (1850–94), "The Bottle Imp" (1891). See also 12.1r.

NOTEBOOK 18

1. Cf. Frost's "Sitting by a Bush in Broad Sunlight," from *West-Running Brook* (1928).

2. Frost may be referring to the theory of panspermia—literally, "seeds everywhere"— which argues that life could come from space. In 1871, with the support of British physicist Lord Kelvin and Swedish chemist and Nobel laureate Svante Arrhenius, German physicist Hermann von Helmholtz wrote: "who could say whether the comets and meteors which swarm everywhere through space, may not scatter germs wherever a new world has reached the stage in which it is a suitable place for organic beings" (*Selected Writings of Hermann von Helmholtz* [Wesleyan Univ. Press, 1974], p. 284). In the first decade of the 1900s, Arrhenius theorized that bacterial spores propelled through space by light pressure were the seeds of life on Earth. In 1911 the American geologist T. C. Chamberlin argued

against the idea that spores driven by light pressure could travel across the universe, transporting life from planet to planet. In a paper he coauthored with his son in 1908 called "Early terrestrial conditions that may have favored organic synthesis," he suggested that "planetesimals," the small bodies from which planets were formed, may have been a source of organic compounds for the primitive Earth. Based on findings of organic matter in meteorites, he wrote: "the planetesimals are assumed to have contained carbon, sulphur, phosphorus and all other elements found in organic matter, and as they impinged more or less violently upon the surface formed of previous accessions of similar matter, there should have been generated various compounds," among them "hydrocarbons, ammonia, hydrogen phosphide, and hydrogen sulphide gases," which could be "mingled with the ordinary gases carried by the planetesimal furnishing rather remarkable conditions for interactions and combinations, among which unusual synthesis would not be improbable" (*Science* 28 [1908]: 897–910). See also Frost's "A Star in a Stoneboat" (1921).

3. Poem by E. A. Robinson (1869–1935).

4. Sir Walter Raleigh (1552–1618). From "To His Son": "Three things there be that prosper all apace, / And flourish whilst they are asunder far; / But on a day, they meet all in one place, / And when they meet, they one another mar. / And they be these: the Wood, the Weed, the Wag: / The Wood is that that makes the gallows tree; / The Weed is that that strings the hangman's bag; / The Wag, my pretty knave, betokens thee. / Mark well, dear boy, whilst these assemble not, / Green springs the tree, hemp grows, the wag is wild; / But when they meet, it makes the timber rot, / It frets the halter, and it chokes the child. / Then bless thee, and beware, and let us pray. / We part not with thee at this meeting day." See also 15.40v; 19.7r.

5. Christopher Smart (1722–1770), *A Song to David* (1763). See also 19.7r.

6. A variation on a couplet from "A Shropshire Lad" (1896) by A. E. Housman (1859–1936): "And malt does more than Milton can / to justify God's ways to man." See also 8.2v.

7. John Milton (1608–1674), *Samson Agonistes* (1671). See also 15.40v.

8. Cf. Edgar Allen Poe's "The Sleeper" (1831). See also Frost's letter to Bernard DeVoto of 12 April 1938: " . . . [Poe] used a cadence from the exequy to make the whole of his poem The Sleeper."

9. Humbert Wolfe's (1886–1940) "The Grey Squirrel." See also 19.7v.

10. Poem by Ralph Waldo Emerson. Job paraphrases a line from the poem in Frost's "A Masque of Reason" and refers to it as "the greatest Western poem yet."

11. Some of the following entries on this page are titles of Frost poems: "The Rose Family" (1927); "The Freedom of the Moon" (1930); "Once by the Pacific" (1926); "A Soldier" (1927); "The Investment" (1930); "A Winter Eden" (1927); "The Times Table" (1927); "The Cocoon" (1927); "Sand Dunes" (1926); "Acceptance" (1930); "Bereft" (1927); "The Bear" (1928); "What Fifty Said" (1930); "A Minor Bird" (1926; as "The Minor Bird," 1930); "The Birthplace" (1923).

12. A very short one-act play Frost wrote sometime between 1918 and 1927.

13. Alfred Kreymborg (1883–1966), American poet, novelist, playwright, and editor.

NOTEBOOK 19

1. Cf. "An Answer" (1946): "But Islands of the Blessèd, bless you, son, / I never came upon a blessèd one." See also 9v, 2r; 24.36r.

2. Thomas Hardy (1840–1928), English poet and novelist.

3. Cf. the opening lines of Sir James George Frazier's (1854–1941) *The Golden Bough* (1922), ch. 1, "§I. *Diana and Virbius.*—Who does not know Turner's picture of the Golden Bough? The scene, suffused with the golden glow of imagination in which the divine mind of Turner steeped and transfigured even the fairest natural landscape, is a dream-like vision of the little woodland lake of Nemi—'Diana's Mirror,' as it was called by the ancients."

4. See 15.23r; 29.15r.

5. Cf. Chapter 6 of Arnold Bennett's *Literary Taste: How to Form It* (1909), titled "The Question of Style": "When you read a book there are only three things of which you may be conscious: (1) The significance of the words, which is inseparably bound up with the thought. (2) The look of the printed words on the page—I do not suppose that anybody reads any author for the visual beauty of the words on the page. (3) The sound of the words, either actually uttered or imagined by the brain to be uttered. Now it is indubitable that words differ in beauty and sound. To my mind one of the most beautiful words in the English language is 'pavement.'" See also 24.30v.

6. Cf. Frost's "The Grindstone," *New Hampshire* (1923).

7. See 9r; 7.4r; 37.9r; 4.48r; 31.7v, 9v; 14.1r, 2r, 11r; 22.8r, 12r, 17r, 18r; 24.44r; 15.3v; 39; 47; 23.4r.

8. See 4.32r; 24.39v, 43v, 44r; 14.15r; 47; 27.7r.

9. See Frost's "A Masque of Mercy" (1948); 31.6v, 10r; 4.32r, 35r; 22.4r, 12r; 29.9r; 33.1r, 1v; 24.32r; 21.11r; 26.12r, 13r; 23.8r, 9r.

10. See 31.7r; 13.16r; 24.22r; 35.

11. The two brightest starts in the constellation *Canis Major.* There are several myths of Indo-Greek and Egyptian origin.

12. One of Frost's favorite books, Francis T. Palgrave, *Golden Treasury of English Songs and Lyrics* (1861). Palgrave followed this work with other anthologies, the *Treasury of Sacred Song* (1889) and the *Golden Treasury* (1897).

13. Sir Walter Raleigh (ca. 1552–1618). From "To His Son": "Three things there be that prosper all apace, / And flourish whilst they are asunder far; / But on a day, they meet all in one place, / And when they meet, they one another mar. / And they be these: the Wood, the Weed, the Wag: / The Wood is that that makes the gallows tree; / The Weed is that that strings the hangman's bag; / The Wag, my pretty knave, betokens thee. / Mark well, dear boy, whilst these assemble not, / Green springs the tree, hemp grows, the wag is wild; / But when they meet, it makes the timber rot, / It frets the halter, and it chokes the child. / Then bless thee, and beware, and let us pray. / We part not with thee at this meeting day." See also 15.40v; 18.4r.

14. John Philpot Curran (1750–1817). Title of poem included by Padraic Colum (1881–1972) in *Anthology of Irish Verse* (1922).

15. An early American song, "Poor Celia Fell Sick" (ca. 1776).

16. Anton Chekhov's (1860–1904) play "The Wedding" (1889).

17. Christopher Smart (1722–1770), *A Song to David* (1763). See 18.4r.

18. Emily Dickinson (1830–1886). There are three Dickinson poems with a snake in them: "A narrow fellow in the grass / Occasionally rides"; "Sweet is the swamp with its secrets, / Until we meet a snake"; "It came his turn to beg – / The begging for the life."

19. See the short lyric entitled "Two Rivers": "Says Tweed to Till – / 'What gars ye rin

sae still?' / Says Till to Tweed— / 'Though ye rin with speed / And I rin slaw, / For ae man that ye droon / I droon twa.'" Anonymous, 17th cent., in Arthur Quiller-Couch, *The Oxford Book of English Verse* (1919).

20. Poem by Humbert Wolfe (1886–1940), English poet, critic, and civil servant. He wrote a popular and memorable lyric:

Like a small grey
coffee-pot,
sits the squirrel.
He is not

all he should be,
kills by dozens
trees, and eats
his red-brown cousins.

The keeper on the
other hand,
who shot him, is
a Christian, and

loves his enemies,
which shows
the squirrel was not
one of those.

21. First few lines from John Dryden's (1631–1700) "A Song for St. Cecilia's Day" (1687): "From harmony, from universal harmony / This universal frame began."

22. While a student at Harvard, Frost may have heard Santayana discuss the relation of spirit and matter. The view that Frost here attributes to Santayana can be found in a variety of his writings but especially in *Scepticism and Animal Faith* (1923). In the chapter entitled "Discernment of Spirit," Santayana argues for the independence of his concept of spirit from dependence on matter: " . . . The investigation of substance and the law of events is the province of physics, and I call everything that science may discover in that direction physical and not spiritual. Even if the substance of things should be sentiency, or a bevy of souls, or a single intense Absolute, it would be nothing but matter to what I call spirit. It would exercise only material functions in kindling the flame of actual intuition, and bearing my light thoughts like bubbles upon its infinite flood. I do not know what matter is in itself; but what metaphysical idealists call spirit, if it is to be understood to be responsible for what goes on in the world and in myself, and to be the 'reality' of these appearances is, in respect to my spiritual existence, precisely what I call matter; and I find the description of this matter which the natural sciences supply more interesting than that given by the idealists, much more beautiful, and much more likely to be true. That there is no spirit in the interstices of matter, where the magicians look for it, nor at the heart of the matter, where many metaphysicians would place it, needs no proof to one who understands what spirit is; because spirit is in another realm of being altogether, and needs the

being and movement of matter, by its large and sweeping harmonies, to generate it, and give it wings" (*Scepticism and Animal Faith,* pp. 287–88). See also 15.32r.

23. Santayana discusses the relationship of taste and morals, aesthetics and ethics, in a variety of works. The opening of his 1896 Harvard lectures, collected and published as *The Sense of Beauty* (1896), strikes a dominant chord in his thought when he argues that the sense of beauty and aesthetic preference is primary in all realms of judgment: "The philosophy of beauty is a theory of values. It would be easy to find a definition of beauty that should give in a few words a telling paraphrase of the word. We know on excellent authority that beauty is truth, that it is the expression of the ideal, the symbol of divine perfection, and the sensible manifestation of the good. A litany of these titles of honour might be compiled, and repeated in praise of our divinity." Later in *The Life of Reason* (1933), in the chapter on "The Criterion of Taste," Santayana will argue that the preference for one beauty over another is fundamental for judgment: "The very instinct that is satisfied by beauty prefers one beauty to another; and we have only to question and purge our aesthetic feelings in order to obtain our criterion of taste. This criterion will be natural, personal, autonomous; a circumstance that will give it authority over our judgment—which is all moral science is concerned about—and will extend its authority over other minds also, in so far as their constitution is similar to ours" (*The Life of Reason,* p. 368). See also 15.32r.

24. (Harry) Sinclair Lewis (1885–1951), American novelist and first American to be awarded the Nobel prize (1930). Best known for *Main Street* (1920) and *Babbitt* (1922).

25. See 22.11r, 47r; 12.10r; 37.2r; 7.3r, 4r; 33.9r; 8.58r, 58v; 1.34v; 17.41r; 24.38v; 29.23r.

26. See 4.6r; 15.19v; 22.33v; 24.28r; 29.

27. See also 24.41v; 47; 8.18v, 105; 9.8r.

28. Cf. "An Answer" (1946): "But Islands of the Blessèd, bless you, son, / I never came upon a blessèd one." See also 1r above and 2r below; 24.36r.

29. See 4.42r; 15.24v; 22.6r; 47.

30. In 1912, Henry Ford began, in Dearborn, Michigan, what would be the re-creation of an "authentic" American past that celebrated the quotidian elements of American rural life. He constructed a village and museum dedicated to preserving this early American culture. Ford would send people out around the country to find exemplary pieces of American architecture and, taking them apart, reconstruct them back in Dearborn. In 1929, Ford dedicated the museum to Edison, calling it the Edison Institute Museum & Greenfield Village. Upon the death of Ford in 1953, the museum was renamed the Henry Ford Museum.

31. See also 24.41v; 17.28v–29r.

32. See 4.51r; 45.11r; 17.30v; 24.28v.

33. Cf. Frost's poem "U.S. 1946 King's X" (1946).

34. Cf. "An Answer" (1946): "But Islands of the Blessèd, bless you, son, / I never came upon a blessèd one." See also 1r and 9v above; 24.36r.

35. Cf. Frost's poem "Reluctance" (1912), particularly, "Ah, when to the heart of man / Was it ever less than a treason / To go with the drift of things, / To yield with a grace to reason, / And bow and accept the end / Of a love or a season?"

36. Fr. "Without breeches, without shirts." A play on an old American phrase "keep your shirt on" and the name of a French revolutionary group.

37. George Bernard Shaw (1856–1950), Irish-born playwright and critic.

38. Arthur Schnitzler (1862–1931), Viennese dramatist and novelist. He was also a practicing doctor influenced by libidinal theories of Sigmund Freud.

39. Cf. Frost's "The Figure a Poem Makes": "I tell how there may be a better wildness of logic than of inconsequence."

40. Cf. Frost's poem "The Literate Farmer and the Planet Venus" (1941) ll. 371–2: "'The slave will never thank his manumitter; / Which often makes the manumitter bitter.'"

41. Anne Rutledge (1803–1835) was an alleged mistress of Abraham Lincoln. Edgar Lee Masters (1888–1950) wrote a poem about her using her name for a title in his *Spoon River Anthology* (1915). Sarah Orne Jewett (1849–1909) was an American novelist and short-story writer. See esp. *A Country Doctor* (1884).

42. Cf. "West-Running Brook" (1928): "The universal cataract of death / That spends to nothingness—and unresisted, / Save by some strange resistance in itself, / Not just swerving, but a throwing back, / As if regret were in it and sacred." Also a line from Henry Wadsworth Longfellow (1807–1882): "Though, half-way up the hill, I see Past/ Lying beneath me with its sounds and sights,— / A city in the twilight dim and vast, / With smoking roofs, soft bells, and gleaming lights,— / And hear above me on the autumnal blast / The cataract of Death far thundering from the heights." *Mezzo Cammin* (1842).

43. See 5r, 5v; 7.4r; 37.9r; 4.48r; 31.7v, 9v; 14.1r, 2r, 11r; 22.8r, 12r, 17r, 18r; 24.44r; 15.3v; 39; 47.

44. See 24.39v.

45. In Greek mythology, the priest of Apollo who warned the Trojans not to touch the wooden horse made by the Greeks during the Trojan War. While he and his two sons were sacrificing to Poseidon at the seashore, two serpents came from the water and destroyed them. The Trojans interpreted this event as a sign of the gods' disapproval of Laocoon's prophecy, and they brought the wooden horse into the city. A Greek statue by Agesander, Athenodorus, and Polydorus, unearthed in Rome in 1508 and now in the Vatican, shows Laocoon and his sons in their death struggle.

46. Llewellan [sic] Raney is M. Llewellyn Raney (1877–1964), librarian at the University of Chicago and chairman of the American Library Association's Committee on Photographic Reproduction of Library Materials. He was an early advocate of photographic reproduction, archival and portable storage systems. Also wrote on Abraham Lincoln with Carl Sandburg in 1935, which is probably after this notebook.

47. William Dumas (b. 1858), *The Golden Day and Miscellaneous Poems* (1893).

48. A collection of animal fables written in Sanskrit and compiled ca. 500 AD for the instruction of young princes.

49. Sir Thomas Browne (1605–1682), *Pseudodoxia Epidemica* (1646), otherwise known as *Vulgar Errors,* is concerned with the suppositions and hypotheses of scientific thought.

50. Blaise Pascal (1623–1662), *Pensées* (1657–58).

51. Jean-Jacques Rousseau (1712–1778). A work concerned with a child's growth, *Emile* (1762) is an important book in the development of educational thought.

52. Possibly Arthur William Edgar O'Shaughnessy (1844–81), English poet. Loosely affiliated with Rossetti and the Pre-Raphaelites.

53. Thomas Percy (1729–1811), *Reliques of Ancient English Poetry* (1759).

54. Charles Darwin (1809–1882), *Journal of Researches into the Geology and Natural History of the Various Countries Visited by H.M.S. Beagle* (1839).

55. Edgar Allen Poe (1809–1849).

56. Robert S. Lynd (1892–1949) and Helen M. Lynd (1896–1982), teachers, sociologists. Born in Indiana and Illinois respectively. Their reputation was established with the classic studies on an American small town, *Middletown* (1929) and *Middletown Revisited* (1937). Robert Lynd became Professor of Sociology at Columbia in 1931, and his wife was Professor of Social Philosophy at Sarah Lawrence College. Her two major works are on England in the 1880s: *Toward a Social Basis for Freedom* (1945).

57. See 12.22r.

NOTEBOOK 20

1. See 44.1v.

2. A possible reference to Percy MacKaye (1875–1956) and Ridgely Torrence (1875–1950), both of whom were poets.

3. Conrad Aiken (1889–1973), American poet and critic. Edited several anthologies in which Frost's work appeared. Aiken held the post of Consultant in Poetry to the Library of Congress from 1950 until Randall Jarrell was awarded the position in 1956 and held it through 1958. Frost held the position from 1958 to 1959.

4. See 7.3v; 9.20r; 47.

5. Boardman Robinson (1876–1952), American painter and cartoonist born in Somerset, Novia Scotia. He contributed to the *New York Times,* the *New York Tribune, The Suffragists,* and *The Masses,* a radical journal that published a cartoon of Robinson's that was charged by the U.S. government to be in violation of the Espionage Act.

6. George Bosworth Churchill (1866–1925) was an Amherst college professor and United States congressman from Massachusetts. Frost was offered a teaching position at Amherst College in 1917 when Churchill resigned to assume his congressional post.

7. See note 25 below as well as 4.32r; 8.37r; 13.6r; 14.12r.

8. A possible reference to Louis Henry (Henri) Sullivan (1856–1924), American architect and mentor to Frank Lloyd Wright. Sullivan, however, did not design stadiums.

9. In 1906, Frost was teaching English part-time at the Pinkerton Academy in Derry, New Hampshire.

10. See also 16v; 2.16r; 4; 6.22r; 8.56r; 14.17r; 15.33v; 21.4r, 7r; 22.49r; 24.24r, 47r; 28.10r; 29.14r, 23r; 31.4r, 7r, 7v, 40r; 32.7r, 10r; 34.1r, 2r, 2v; 41.7r; 47.

11. William Prescott Frost (b. 1924), the poet's grandson and son of Carol Frost.

12. Edgar Allan Poe (1809–1849).

13. Ted Lewis (1872–1936), pitcher for the Major League baseball team the Boston Beaneaters, 1896–1901, who threw a shutout in his last game in 1901. Later Lewis became the president of the University of New Hampshire and a friend of Frost's.

14. Edgar A. Guest (1881–1959), prolific American poet (b. England) syndicated in newspapers.

15. Carl Ruggles (1876–1971), American composer. His major compositions include *Men and Angels* (1925) and *Men and Mountains* (1951).

16. See 29.42r; 15.18v.

17. See Frost's "Education by Poetry" (1935): "What I am pointing out is that unless you are at home in the metaphor, unless you have had your proper poetical education in the

metaphor, you are not safe anywhere. Because you are not at ease with figurative values: you don't know the metaphor in its strength and its weakness. You don't know how far you may expect to ride it and when it may break down with you. All metaphor breaks down somewhere. That is the beauty of it." See also Notebooks 24.29r; 21.7r; 47.

18. See also 11r; 2.16r; 4; 6.22r; 8.56r; 14.17r; 15.33v; 21.4r, 7r; 22.49r; 24.24r; 47r; 28.10r; 29.14r, 23r; 31.4r, 7r, 7v, 40r; 32.7r, 10r; 34.1r, 2r, 2v; 41.7r; 47

19. See "Education by Poetry": "Take the way we have been led into our present position morally, the world over. It is by a sort of metaphorical gradient. There is a kind of thinking—to speak metaphorically—there is a kind of thinking you might say was endemic in the brothel."

20. See "Education by Poetry": "Materialism is not the attempt to say all in terms of matter. The only materialist—be he poet, teacher, scientist, politician, or statesman—is the man who gets lost in his material without a gathering metaphor to throw it into shape and order. He is the lost soul." See also "On Emerson": ". . . All you have to do is to amount to something anyway. The only reprehensible materiality is the materialism of getting lost in your material so you can't find out yourself what it is all about." See also 24.3v.

21. See 15.18v.; 29.42r.

22. See "Education by Poetry": "Once on a time all the Greeks were busy telling each other what the All was—or was like unto. All was three elements, air, earth, and water (we once thought it was ninety elements: now we think it is only one). All was substance, said another. All was change, said a third. But best and most fruitful was Pythagoras' comparison of the universe with number. Number of what? Number of feet, pounds, and seconds was the answer, and we had science and all that has followed in science. The metaphor has held and held, breaking down only when it came to the spiritual and psychological or the out of the way places of the physical."

23. See 24.30r; 4.1r; 28.20r; 43.2r; 22.31r. The phrase "domestic science" also appears in *The Future of Man* (unpublished version, 1959).

24. See "What Fifty Said" (1930): "When I was young my teachers were the old. / I gave up fire for form till I was cold. / I suffered like a metal being cast. / I went to school to age to learn the past."

25. See "The Trial by Existence" (1906): "And God has taken a flower of gold / And broken it, and used therefrom / The mystic link to bind and hold / Spirit to matter till death come."

26. "The Mixture Mechanic" is the title to part four of the poem "Kitty Hawk" from *In the Clearing* (1962). See also 9r; 26.6r; 47; 24.41v.

27. *Andrew Johnson: Plebeian and Patriot* by Robert W. Winston (1928).

28. Aldous Huxley (1894–1963), *Point Counter Point* (1928).

29. Charles Edward Montague (1867–1928). Born in London of an Irish family. Novelist and journalist at the *Manchester Guardian* for thirty-five years.

30. Robert Bontine Cunningham-Graham (1852–1936), Scottish author.

31. Max Stirner (1806–1856), Prussian philosopher. Translated Adam Smith's *Wealth of Nations* into German (1847) and best known for his treatise *The Ego and His Own: The Case of the Individual against Authority* (1845, trans. 1907).

NOTEBOOK 21

1. Robert Louis Stevenson (1850–1894). Cf. the opening lines of "Good and Bad Children" from *A Child's Garden of Verses* (1885):

Children, you are very little,
And your bones are very brittle;
If you would grow great and stately,
You must learn to walk sedately.

2. See "Speaking of Loyalty," an address at the Amherst College Alumni Luncheon, June 19, 1948: "I had a questionnaire the other day from an editor. He asked, 'What in your opinion is the present state of middle-brow literature in America?' That was new slang to me. I'd got behind a little bit, being off in the country. I hadn't heard of 'middle-brow' before. What he meant to say was, 'You old skeezix, what's the present state of your own middle-brow stuff?' There was something invidious, I am sure, in that. But right away I thought of a way to use it, not here but in verse, in writing. You make it like this: '/ High-brow, low brow, / Middle-brow, and now brow.' There is a refrain for the next poem. 'High-brow, low brow, / Middle-brow, and no brow.'" See also 12.24r, 25r; 22.55v.

3. See 5r; 43.1r, 7r; 31.32r; 6.29v; 40.23v.

4. "Know thyself" is the *sententia* of the Oracle at Delphi. The greek is *"gnothi seauton."* In the Bible, when Adam *knew* Eve, it was carnal knowledge.

5. See also 7r; 2.16r; 4; 6.22r; 8.56r; 14.17r; 15.33v; 20.11r, 16v; 22.49r; 24.24r, 47r; 28.10r; 29.14r, 23r; 31.4r, 7r, 7v, 40r; 32.7r, 10r; 34.1r, 2r, 2v; 41.7r; 47.

6. See 7r; 4.13r; 31.7r, 8r, 10r, 40r, 40v; 32; 37.1r, 5v, 6v; 22.10v; 13.8r; 12.7v; 9.10r; 24.39v; 27.29r, 45r, 44r; 1; 5; 47; 23.10r; 35.13r, 16r. See also Frost's letter to Louis Untermeyer of July 9, 1931: "We were brought up on principles of saving everything, ourselves included. The war taught us a new gospel. My next book is to be called The Right to Waste. The Right? The Right? The duty, the obligation, to waste everything, time, material, <u>and</u> the man."

7. See 29.34r; 48.1r; 4.25r, 27r; 25.14v; 22.33v.

8. See 2r; 43.1r, 7r; 31.32r; 6.29v; 40.23v.

9. See 4r; 4.13r; 31.7r, 8r, 10r, 40r, 40v; 37.1r, 5v, 6v; 32; 22.10v; 13.8r; 12.7v; 9.10r; 24.39v; 27.29r, 45r, 46r; 1; 5; 47; 23.10r; 35.13r, 16r.

10. See also 4r; 2.16r; 4; 6.22r; 8.56r; 14.17r; 15.33v; 20.11r, 16v; 22.49r; 24.24r, 47r; 28.10r; 29.14r, 23r; 31.4r, 7r, 7v, 40r; 32.7r, 10r; 34.1r, 2r, 2v; 41.7r; 47.

11. See Frost's "Education by Poetry" (1935): "What I am pointing out is that unless you are at home in the metaphor, unless you have had your proper poetical education in the metaphor, you are not safe anywhere. Because you are not at ease with figurative values: you don't know the metaphor in its strength and its weakness. You don't know how far you may expect to ride it and when it may break down with you . . . All metaphor breaks down somewhere. That is the beauty of it." See also 24.29r; 47; 20.16r.

12. Genesis 6: 1–2. "And it came to pass, when men began to multiply on the face of the earth, and daughters were born unto them, that the sons of God saw the daughters of men that were fair; and they took them wives of all which they chose."

13. Cf. the conclusion to "Education by Poetry" (1930): "Now I think—I happen to think

that those three beliefs that I speak of, the self-belief, the love-belief, and the art-belief, are all closely rooted to the God-belief, that the belief in God is a relationship you enter into with Him to bring about the future."

14. See Frost's "A Masque of Mercy" (1948); 31.6v, 10r; 4.32r, 35r; 22.4r, 12r; 29.9r; 33.1r, 1v; 24.32r, 20.12r, 13r, 19.01r, 29.01r, 9r.

15. King John granted *Magna Carta* at Runnymeade in 1215.

16. Marco Polo (1254–1324) traveled in China from 1275 to 1292.

17. Uprising in 1900 by a Chinese secret society opposed to foreign influence.

18. Emperor of China (Mongolia), 1215–1294.

NOTEBOOK 22

1. See 4.49r; 23.1r; 31.8v, 5.1r.

2. Cf. Frost's "A Reflex" (1962): "Hear my rigmarole. / Science stuck a pole / Down a likely hole / And he got it bit. / Science gave a stab / And he got a grab. / That was what he got. / 'Ah,' he said, 'Qui vive, / Who goes there, and what / ARE we to believe? / That there is an It?'" See also 4.48v.

3. See 47r; 12.10r; 37.2r; 7.3r, 4r; 33.9r; 8.58r, 58v; 1.34v; 17.41r; 19.8v; 24.38v; 29.23r.

4. The Latin "qiud-nunc" means "what now?" and indicates a gossip. Cf. Frost's "The Milky Way Is a Cowpath," ll. 1–12:

On wings too stiff to flap
We started to exult
In having left the map
On journey the penult.

But since we got nowhere,
Like small boys we got mad
And let go at the air
With everything we had.

Incorrigible Quid-nuncs,
We *would* see what could come
Of pelting heaven with chunks
Of crude uranium.

See also 35r; 31.10r.

5. Frost made the title of Robinson Jeffers's 1923 poem "Shine, Perishing Republic" the epigraph for his 1962 poem "Our Doom to Bloom."

6. In *The History*, Herodotus begins his discussion of the beliefs of the ancient Egyptians with pragmatic acceptance: "As for the stories told by the Egyptians, let whoever finds them credible use them. Throughout the entire history it is my underlying principle that it is what people severally have said to me, and what I have heard, that I must write down" (*The History*, 2.123, tr. David Greene). David Greene noted that Herodotus's *History* "is as much about what people believe and think as it is about events that happen—and less about whether events *did* happen than that people thought they did. Because history for him, is the total fabric of a moment and an era and a nation or civilization, where

thought is as important as acts or events" (Herodotus, *The History*, translated by David Greene [Chicago, 1987], p. 185).

7. William Langland (ca. 1332–ca. 1400), putative author of the dream-vision *Piers Plowman* and contemporary of Geoffrey Chaucer.

8. See also Frost's "A Masque of Mercy" (1948); 12r; 31.6v, 10r; 4.32r, 35r; 29.9r; 33.1r, IV; 24.32r; 21.11r; 26.12r, 13r; 19.6r; 23.8r, 9r.

9. Frost gave a talk to Amherst seniors on May 28, 1935, called "Our Darkest Concern" about the dangers of the extreme political left and right. See also "On Emerson": "I don't like obscurity and obfuscation, but I do like dark sayings I must leave the clearing of to time. And I don't want to be robbed of the pleasure of fathoming depths for myself." See also 4.17r, 32v; 47; 23.3r, 4r, 5r; 28.15r; 29.17r; 24.39r.

10. See 8.49v; 44.3v.

11. See 26.2r; 44.1r; 24.31r.

12. See 44; 45; 13.9v; 12; 15.13r; 47; 26.2r; 8.15r, 32r.

13. See 8v; 4.22r; 8.37r; 17.25r; 24.31r; 28.10r; 29; 33.5r; 35.7r; 47.

14. See 4.27r; 29.15r; 31.32r.

15. Cf. Frost's "A Masque of Mercy" (1947), ll. 700–704:

Keeper   But not the fear of punishment for sin
   (I have to sin to prove it isn't that).
   I'm no more governed by the fear of Hell
   Than by the fear of the asylum, jail, or poorhouse,
   The basic three the state is founded on.

   See also 4.44r; 11.53r.

16. See Elizabeth Barrett Browning, "A Musical Instrument" (1862): "He tore out a reed, the great god Pan, / From the deep cool bed of the river; / The limpid water turbidly ran, / And the broken lilies a-dying lay, / And the dragon-fly had fled away, / Ere he brought it out of the river" (2nd stanza); "He cut it short, did the great god Pan / (How tall it stood in the river!), / Then drew the pith, like the heart of a man, / Steadily from the outside ring, / And notch'd the poor dry empty thing / In holes, as he sat by the river" (4th stanza); "Yet half a beast is the great god Pan, / to laugh as he sits by the river, / Making a poet out of a man: / The true gods sigh for / As a reed with the reeds of the river" (7th and final stanza).

17. See 4.13r; 31.7r, 8r, 10r, 40r, 40v; 32; 37.1r, 5v, 6v; 13.8r; 12.7v; 9.10r; 24.39v; 21.4r, 7r; 27.29r, 45r, 46r; 1; 5; 47; 23.10r; 35.13r; 16r.

18. See also Frost's "A Masque of Mercy" (1948); 4r; 31.6v, 10r; 4.32r, 35r; 29.9r; 33.1r, IV; 24.32r; 21.11r; 26.12r, 13r; 19.6r; 23.8r, 9r.

19. Lincoln Steffens (1866–1936), one of the great American "muckraker" journalists and editor at *McClures'*, among others. He was the author of *The Shame of Cities* (1904) and *The Struggle for Self-Government* (1906).

20. See 4.11r; 28.6v; 47.

21. Perhaps Ernest Poole (1880–1950), Chicago-born New York novelist and social reformer.

22. See 4.20v; 24.29r; 11.1r.

23. At this time many of America's insurance companies were located in Hartford, Connecticut.

24. See 4.21r; 12.41r, 12r; 29.28v, 54r, 62r.

25. See 4.42r; 15.24v; 19.9v; 47.

26. See 12r; 18r; 7.4r; 37.9r; 4.48r; 31.7v, 9v; 14.1r, 2r, 11r; 24.44r; 15.3v; 39; 47; 19.5r, 5v, 9r.

27. "Bread and circuses" is a derogatory phrase which can describe either government policies to pacify the citizenry, or the shallow, decadent desires of that same citizenry. In both cases, it refers to low-cost, low-quality, high-availability food and entertainment, and to the exclusion of things which the speaker considers more important, such as art, public works projects, democracy, or human rights.

28. Cf. Frost's "West Running Brook" (1928).

29. Henry L. Mencken (1880–1956), fierce journalist and political pundit, was editor of the *Smart Set* and author of the The *American Language: An Inquiry into the Development of English in the United States* (1919, 4th ed. 1939; supplements, 1946, 1948). Cf. Frost's reference to Mencken in "A Romantic Chasm," written as the introduction to the British edition of *A Masque of Reason* (London, 1948): "It took an American, a friend, Henry L. Mencken, to rouse me to a sense of national differences. My pedantry would be poor and my desert small with the educated if I could pretend to look unscared into the gulf his great book had made to yawn between the American and English languages."

30. See 24.10v. Christopher Marlowe (1564–93), *Doctor Faustus*, I.iii: "Faustus: How comes it then that thou are out of Hell? / Mephistopheles: Why this is Hell, nor am I out of it" (74–75). See also Frost's poem "New Hampshire" from *New Hampshire* (1923), ll. 242–243: "Kit Marlowe taught me how to say my prayers: / 'Why, this is Hell, nor am I out of it.'"

31. See 4.9r, 10v, 42r; 31.10r; 33.3v; 47.

32. Similar to "rock, paper, scissors," "stone, knife, handkerchief" is a Japanese game also known as *janken*. See 17r; 13.9v; 15.3v. See also Frost's "The Doctrine of Excursions" (1939): "Bread Loaf is to be regarded then as a place in Vermont where a writer can try his effect on readers. There as out in the world he must brave the rigors of specific criticism. He will get enough and perhaps more than enough of good set praise and blame. He will help wear out the words 'like' and 'dislike.' He will hear too many things compared to the disadvantage of all of them. A handkerchief is worse than a knife because it can be cut by a knife; a knife is worse than a stone because it can be blunted by a stone; a stone is worse than a handkerchief because it can be covered by a handkerchief; and we have been round the silly circle. All this is as it has to be where the end is a referee's decision. There is nothing so satisfactory in literature as the knock-out in prize-fighting."

33. See 8r, 12r; 7.4r; 37.9r; 4.48r; 31.7v, 9v; 14.1r, 2r, 11r; 24.44r; 15.3v; 39; 47; 19.5r, 5v, 9r.

34. Cf. Frost's letter to the poet R. P. T. Coffin dated February 1938: " . . . I am not the Platonist Robinson was. By Platonist I mean one who believes what we have here is an imperfect copy of what is in heaven. The woman you have is an imperfect copy of the some woman in heaven or in someone else's bed. Many of the of the world's greatest—maybe all of them—have been ranged on that romantic side. I am philosophically opposed to having one Iseult for my vocation and another for my avocation; as you may have inferred from a poem called Two Tramps in Mud Time." See also 32v; 12.9v; 13.8r; 31.11v, 31v.

35. See also 34r; 4.6r, 23r; 26.28r.

36. *Roughing It* (1891), Mark Twain's narrative tale of his travels in the west.

37. Herman Hagedorn (1882–1964), poet, playwright, and biographer of Theodore Roosevelt, Edwin Arlington Robinson, and Albert Schweitzer.

38. Marcelene Cox (1900–1998), columnist for *Ladies' Home Journal* and contributor to *Reader's Digest* and *Good Housekeeping,* among other publications. See also 27.38r.

39. See 29.8v; 47.

40. Dale Carnegie (1888–1955) was a salesman who became a successful author of books about public speaking and personality development. His *How to Win Friends and Influence People* (1936) sold more than 10,000,000 copies.

41. Cf. Matthew 7: 15–16: "Beware of false prophets, which come to you in sheep's clothing, but inwardly they are ravening wolves. / Ye shall know them by their fruits. Do men gather grapes of thorns, or figs of thistles?"

42. Cf. Frost's comments on his friendship with Sidney Cox in the preface to Cox's *A Swinger of Birches* (1957): "We differed more in taste perhaps than in thinking. But we stood up to each other to support each other as two playing cards may be made to in building. I am a great equalitarian: I try to spend most of my time with my equals."

43. See 4.19r; 26.28r; 29.23r.

44. Cf. Sir Thomas Browne (1605–1682), *Urne-Burial* (1658), chapter V: "What songs the Syrens sang, or what name Achilles assumed when he hid himself among women, though Questions are not beyond conjecture."

45. See 4.27r

46. Cf. Shakespeare's Sonnet XXIX.

47. Walter Savage Landor (1775–1864), English Romantic poet and brilliant prose stylist.

48. John Greenleaf Whittier (1807–1892), American poet.

49. Edward Rowland Sill (1841–1887), American poet and educator.

50. See 23; 31.8r, 43r–44v.

51. The Hundred Years' War (1337–1453) was a war between England and France over, among other things, England's right to disputed territory in France.

52. Cf. Frost's "The Figure a Poem Makes" (1939): "The figure a poem makes. It begins in delight and ends in wisdom."

53. See 29.13r, 32r; 35.7r; 47.

54. John Cruickshanks Smith (1867–1946), Oxford literary historian and author, along with H. J. C. Grierson, of a *A Critical History of English Poetry* (1944).

55. Cf. Dante's *Inferno*, Canto XXXIV, ll. 61–67, which describes Judas Iscariot, Brutus, and Cassius each being eternally eaten by Lucifer's three mouths.

56. See 5.26r; 12.23v; 31.4r; 39.8r.

57. See 24.30r; 28.20r; 3.1r; 20.19v; 43.2r.

58. See also 18r; 12.9v; 13.8r; 31.11v, 31v.

59. See 4.6r; 15.19v; 19.9r; 24.28r; 29.

60. See 29.8v, 16r; 4.21r; 47; 26.27r, 28r.

61. See "The Generations of Men" from *North of Boston* (1914), ll. 82–83, "What will we come to / With all this pride of ancestry, we Yankees?"; See also 29.6r, 8v; 4.21r; 25.1r; 47; 26.27r.

62. See 29.34r; 48.1r; 21.5r; 4.25r, 27r; 25.14v.

63. Cf. Frost's "Poverty and Poetry," Haverford College Address (1937). See also 19r; 4.6r, 23r; 26.28r.

64. Frost probably refers to the Gospel of John 8.8. After Jesus admonishes those who would condemn the adulterous woman, "he stooped down, and with his finger wrote on the ground." It has never been determined what Jesus wrote.

65. See 4.26v,

66. See II Samuel 24: "And again the anger of the Lord was kindled against Israel, and he moved David against them to say, Go number Israel and Judah." Later, David believes that in taking the census he has sinned: "And David's heart smote him after that he had numbered the people. And David said unto the Lord, I have sinned greatly in that I have done: and now, I beseech thee, O Lord, take away the iniquity of thy servant; for I have done very foolishly." See also 4.23r; 8.42v; 12.22r.

67. Virgil, *Aeneid* 3, 658: "Monstrum horrendum, informe, ingens, cui lumen ademptum" or "and seeking the well-known shore—a monster awful, shapeless, huge, bereft of light."

68. See 2r; 31.10r.

69. Phineas Taylor Barnum (1810–1891). The story refers to the Jerome Clock Company, in which Barnum invested $110,000 and in the same year (1855) lost it. From *Struggles and Triumphs*: "The Jerome clocks were for sale all over the world, even in China, where the Celestials were said to take out the 'movements,' and use the cases for little temples for their idols, thus proving that faith was possible without 'works'" (392).

70. Cophetua was a legendary king of great wealth who fell in love with a beggar maid. See also Tennyson's "The Beggar Maid": "Her arms across her breast she laid; / She was more fair than words can say; / Barefooted came the beggar maid / Before the king Cophetua . . ."

71. Cleisthenes (ca. 570–508 BC), considered the founder of Athenian democracy. The Gracchi were brothers who invented the idea of senatorial representation for plebeians. For the Gracchi see 47 and 4.3r.

72. This statement refers to Franklin Delano Roosevelt's unprecedented four-term election to the presidency of the United States from 1933 to 1945.

73. See 59r; 4.33v, 46r, 47v; 26.28r; 31.8r, 9r.

74. Cf. Archibald MacLeish (1892–1982), "Ars Poetica," ll. 23–24: "A poem should not mean / But be."

75. Donald Culross Peattie (1898–1964), American naturalist and author of several works on trees, flora, and fauna. See also 4.47r.

76. See 1r; 12.10r; 37.2r; 7.3r, 4r; 33.9r; 8.58r, 58v; 1.34v; 17.41r; 19.8v; 24.38v; 29.23r.

77. Joseph W. Ballantine (1888–1973), American diplomat and educator. He and Frost's daughter Lesley were married in 1952.

78. See also 2.16r; 4; 6.22r; 8.56r; 14.17r; 15.33v; 20.11r, 16v; 21.4r, 7r; 24.24r, 47r; 28.10r; 29.14r, 23r; 31.4r, 7r, 7v, 40r; 32.7r, 10r; 34.1r, 2r, 2v; 41.7r; 47.

79. Karl Marx, *Das Kapital* (1867; first English ed., 1887).

80. *Grex* in Latin means "herd" or "flock" and provides the root for English words such as "gregarious," "aggregate," "segregate" and "egregious," etc. See "A Constant Symbol" (1946): "The ruling passion in man is not as Viennese as is claimed. It is rather a gregarious instinct to keep together by minding each other's business. Grex rather than sex. We *must* be preserved from becoming egregious. The beauty of socialism is that it will end the individuality that is always crying out mind your own business. Terence's answer would be all human business is my business. No more invisible means of support, no more invisible motives, no more invisible anything. The ultimate commitment is giving in to it that an outsider may see what we were up to sooner and better than we ourselves." See also 4.1r; 31.42r; 47.

81. John Bunyan (1628–1688), English preacher and author of *Pilgrim's Progress*.

82. Frost probably refers to the Hoosac Tunnel in northwestern Massachusetts which runs 4.82 miles under the Berkshire Mountains. It took 22 years to complete (1851–1873), and was considered a major 19th-century engineering feat.

83. See 15.28v; 43.1r, 6r; 45.1r; 47; 28.11r; 4.34r, 36r; 26.2r; 47.

84. This is a draft of Frost's address "Speaking of Loyalty," delivered to an Amherst Alumni luncheon on June 19, 1948. There are significant differences between the versions; in particular, the draft is far more risqué in what in what Frost says about Hanno. Frost also says more in the draft version about social hierarchy and democracy and about tests of loyalty.

85. George Whicher (1889–1954), Professor of English at Amherst College; Charles W. Cole, President of Amherst from 1946 to 1960. Whicher originally submitted a transcript of the "Speaking of Loyalty" address to Frost for revision and eventual publication.

86. Dorothy Canfield Fisher (1879–1958), American educational reformer, social activist, and author. Fisher brought the Montessori Method of child-rearing to the United States, presided over the country's first adult education program, and served as a member of the Book-of-the-Month Club selection committee from 1926 to 1951. Under the names Dorothy Canfield and Dorothy Canfield Fisher, she wrote 22 works of fiction and 18 of nonfiction. Among these are *Fellow Captains* (1916) and *Nothing Ever Happens and How* (1940), both with Frost's long-time friend Sarah Cleghorn, who is mentioned elsewhere in the notebooks.

87. See 12.24r, 25r; 21.2r.

88. In the first published appearance of "Speaking of Loyalty" in the *Amherst Graduates' Quarterly*, Whicher supplied the following note: "The episode as recorded by the Carthaginian navigator who first came in contact with pygmies (not anthropoid apes) on the coast of Sierra Leone runs as follows in *The Periplus* of Hanno, translated from the Greek by Wilfred H. Schoff (Philadelphia, 1912), p. 5: 'In the recess of this bay there was an island, like the former one, having a lake, in which there was another island full of savage men. There were women, too, in even greater number. They had hairy bodies, and the interpreters called them Gorrilae. When we pursued them we were unable to take any of the men; for they all escaped, by climbing the steep places, and defending themselves with stones; but we took three of the women, who bit and scratched their leaders, and would not follow us. So we killed them and flayed them, and brought their skins to Carthage. For we did not voyage further, provisions failing us.'"

89. See Emerson's "Give All to Love" (1846), ll. 43–49: "Though thou loved her as thyself, As a self of purer clay,/ Though her parting dims the day,/ Stealing grace from all alive;/ Heartily know,/ When half-gods go,/ The gods arrive." See also 26.28r; 4.31r; 22.58v; 31.41v.

90. See 46r; 4.33v, 46r, 47v; 26.28r; 31.8r, 9r.

91. Although the idea of change is everywhere in Emerson, see especially his *Nature* (1836).

92. Talk at Vassar, Dec. 9, 1959, for which there is no transcript.

93. In 1948 Frost gave the "Great Issues" series lecture entitled "Some Obstinacy" to graduating seniors at Dartmouth College.

94. In June 1953, Frost received the twenty-fifth honorary doctorate of his career, from University of North Carolina, Chapel Hill.

NOTEBOOK 23

1. See 4.49r; 22.11r; 31.8v, 5.1r.

2. See 26.16v

3. Frost gave a talk to Amherst seniors on May 28, 1935, called "Our Darkest Concern" about the dangers of the extreme political left and right. See also "On Emerson": "I don't like obscurity and obfuscation, but I do like dark sayings I must leave the clearing of to time. And I don't want to be robbed of the pleasure of fathoming depths for myself." See also 4r, 5r; 4.17r, 32v; 47; 28.15r; 22.6r; 29.17r; 24.39r. In a letter to Louis Untermeyer of June 24, 1935, Frost wrote, "I'm in favor of more discrimination and then some more. Here without regret one sees rank consideration and degrees. Go to your more discriminating anthology—so long as in discriminating against others you discriminate in favor of me. It was designed to be a sad world, how sad we won't keep telling each other over and over, as we would have to if our heads weren't thick. You should have heard me holding forth to the boys at commencement on Our Darkest Concern. I darkened the sunny day fine day for them inexorably."

4. See the opening of Chaucer's "The Prologe of the Mannes Tale of Lawe": "O hateful harm, condicion of poverte." The phrase seems to have been in general currency in the Middle Ages. Also note, there is line drawn from the beginning of this phrase to the words "of course" at the top right of this leaf.

5. John Wycliffe (1320?–1384), religious reformer, theologian, and translator of the Bible into English. His disciples were called "Poor Preachers."

6. See 4r; 22.11r; 12.10r; 37.2r; 33.9r; 8.58r, 58v; 1.34v; 17.41r; 19.8v; 24.38v; 29.23r.

7. See 4.13r; 29.44r.

8. See Matthew 5–7.

9. Also the title of Frost's preface to *Bread Loaf Anthology*, ed. W. S. Lee (Middlebury, Vt.: Middlebury College Press, 1939).

10. Vespasian (9–79), Roman emperor whose legend is recounted in Suetonius's *The Twelve Caesars* and in Tacitus's *History*.

11. See Ecclesiastes 1:2.

12. See Frost's "A Masque of Mercy" (1948); 31.6v, 10r; 4.32r, 35r; 22.4r, 12r; 29.9r; 33.1r, 1v; 24.32r; 21.11r; 26.12r, 13r; 19.6r.

13. See 4.21r; 29.8v; 47.

14. See 4.8v, 15r; 39.

15. See 4.13r; 31.7r, 8r, 10r, 40r, 40v; 32; 37.1r, 5v, 6v; 22.10v; 13.8r; 12.7v; 9.10r; 24.39v; 21.4r, 7r; 27.29r, 45r, 46r; 1; 5; 47; 35.13r, 16r.

16. Frost published the poem "A Minor Bird" as it appears in this notebook with some additional punctuation in 1926 in *West-Running Brook*.

17. This is an early draft of "The Times Table," first published in *The New Republic*, February 27, 1927.

18. See 22.24r; 31.8r, 43r–44v.

19. First published in booklet form as "A Cabin in the Clearing," Frost's 1951 Christmas poem.

20. Variations of this line occur on the pages that follow this one. See also 1 and 37.

21. Cf. Milton's *Lycidas,* l. 4. Variations of this line continue on the pages that follow this one.

22. Lucretius (94–55 B.C.E.), Roman poet and author of *De Rerum Natura,* didactic poem based on the thought of Greek philosopher Epicurus (341–271 B.C.E.). Cf. Frost's "Too Anxious for Rivers" (1947).

23. Cf. Shakespeare's Sonnet 29, l. 4.

NOTEBOOK 24

1. Kidney Pond Camps, in Baxter State Park, near the Penobscot River in the state of Maine began as a camp for sportsman, hunters and trappers. Roy and Laura Bradeen bought the camp in 1925 or 1926. Roy Bradeen drowned in the Kidney Pond in 1937. Laura Bradeen owned the camps until 1945. There was a road constructed to the camp from Greenville to Nesowadnehunk Field.

2. Cf. "The Strong Are Saying Nothing" (1936), 16: "But the strong are saying nothing until they see."

3. Earl H. Morris was a distinguished archeologist. Frost had an inscribed copy of *The Temple of Warriors* (1931). Frost also owned Cryus L. Lundell's *Archaelogical Discoveries in the Maya Area* (1933). However, Frost's comment about the shape of the glyphs reflects no known scholarship on the subject. Very little was known about the script in the 1930s, other than its calendrical-astronomical aspects. The script was only partly deciphered, and no one at the time knew how the system was read. The editor is grateful to Michael D. Coe of Yale University for his expertise on Mayan history and archaeology.

4. Cf. Frost's "A Masque of Mercy" (1947): "*Jonah* My name's not Joe. I don't like what she says./ It's Greenwich Village cocktail party talk—/ Big-city talk. I'm getting out of here. / I'm—bound—away. (He quotes it to the tune)." See also 4.12r; 13.12r; 11.29v.

5. Cf. "To a Thinker" (1937) (ll 1–14):

The last step taken found your heft
Decidedly upon the left.
One more would throw you on the right.
Another still—you see your plight.
You call this thinking, but it's walking.
Not even that, it's only rocking,
Or weaving like a stabled horse:
From force to matter and back to force,
From form to content and back to form,
From norm to crazy and back to norm,
From bound to free and back to bound,
From sound to sense and back to sound.
So back and forth. It almost scares
A man the way things come in pairs.

6. St. Ignatius of Loyola (1491–1556), Spanish ecclesiastic and founder of the Society of Jesus, an educational force that attempted to stem the decline of the Catholic Church in

the face of the Reformation. Many of its members became the Pope's theologians at the Council of Trent and played an important role in the Counter-Reformation.

7. Sidney Cox (1889–1952), a friend and early biographer of Frost.

8. Originally named "Smythe Isles" by Captain John Smith, who explored the area in 1614, what is now called the "Isles of Shoals" is an archipelago of nine islands off the coast of Portsmouth, New Hampshire.

9. Possibly an ironic reference to popular actor Charles Bickford's (1891–1967) play *The Cyclone Lover* about a young man who hates his hometown. It ran for several months on Broadway in 1928.

10. "Why this is Hell, nor am I out of it" is spoken by Mephistopheles in response to Dr. Faustus' question "How come it that you are out of Hell?" Christopher Marlowe, *Dr. Faustus,* I.iii, 74–75. See also Frost's poem "New Hampshire," and 22.13r.

11. Wade Van Dore (1899–1984). A close friend of Frost's whom Frost befriended early in his life. His unfinished manuscript, *The Life of the Hired Man,* was published as Wright State Univ. Monograph No. 6, rev. and ed. Thomas H. Wetmore (Dayton, Ohio: Wright State University, 1986).

12. Easton is a town about seven miles south of Franconia in New Hampshire. Frost bought a farm in Franconia in 1915. See also 10.IV; 47.

13. Thomas Ingoldsby (1788–1845), *The Ingoldsby Legends; or Mirth and Marvels* (1840).

14. *The New Republic* was first published on Nov. 7, 1914.

15. Cf. "Kitty Hawk" (1962), ll. 225–236: "Westerners inherit / A design for living / Deeper into matter—/ Not without due patter / Of a great misgiving. / All the science zest / To materialize / By on-penetration / Into earth and skies / (Don't forget the latter / Is but further matter) / Has been West Northwest."

16. Tyrus Raymond Cobb (1886–1961), a baseball player with one of the most impressive records in the history of game. Cobb was an outfielder for the Detroit Tigers (1905–1926) and the Philadelphia Athletics (1926–1927).

17. Aubrey Beardsley (1872–1898), English illustrator for works by Oscar Wilde and the literary avant-garde.

18. Cf. Frost poem, "The Lovely Shall Be Choosers" (1929).

19. See 1.1r; 47.

20. Cf. Frost's "Education by Poetry" (1935): "What I am pointing out is that unless you are at home in the metaphor, unless you have had your proper poetical education in the metaphor, you are not safe anywhere. Because you are not at ease with figurative values: you don't know the metaphor in its strength and its weakness. You don't know how far you may expect to ride it and when it may break down with you . . . All metaphor breaks down somewhere. That is the beauty of it." See also Notebooks 24.14v; 21.7r; 47; 20.16r.

21. Emily Dickinson (1830–1886), poem #536 (ca. 1862): "The Heart asks Pleasure – first – / And then – Excuse from pain – / And then – those little Anodynes / That deaden suffering – / And then – to go to sleep – / And then – if it should be / The will of its Inquisitor / The privilege to die –."

22. A possible reference to musician, painter, and prolific novelist and editor Manuel Komroff (1890–1974). Komroff was a member of the Ferrer Center, a modernist school in New York City that promulgated an aesthetics of anarchy. Man Ray, Robert Henri, George Bellows, and Max Weber were also associated with the school.

23. Chestnut blight was introduced to the United States around 1900, probably on nursery stock and wood products. It is a fungus that has wiped out chestnut species in this country. Prior to its introduction much of New England and the Alleghenies were covered by what were known as oak-chestnut forest complexes. That term is defunct; one hears of oak-beech forests now. White-pine blister rust is caused by the fungus *Cronartium ribicola.* It is co-hosted by currants and gooseberries (ribes). The spores from the latter land on the bark and needles of the pine, and gestate for 2–6 years prior to manifesting symptoms, the eponymous blisters of an orange-brown hue. The fungus consumes the cells of white pine, causing a canker which enlarges until it girdles the tree. Frost's woods would have been threatened and affected by both of these fungi. Cf. "Evil Tendencies Cancel" (1937): "Will the blight end the chestnut? / The farmers rather guess not. / It keeps smoldering at the roots / And sending up new shoots / Till another parasite / Shall come to end the blight."

24. Cf. Frost's "The Axe-Helve," in which the character Baptiste points out to the speaker of the poem "the bad axe-helve someone had sold me—/ 'Made on machine,' he said, plowing the grain / With a thick thumbnail to show how it ran / Across the handle's long drawn serpentine, / Like the two strokes across a dollar sign. / 'You give her one good crack, she's snap raght off. / Den where's your hax-ead flying t'rough de hair?'" (ll. 21–27).

25. Cf. Frost's poem "The Draft Horse," which was first published in *In the Clearing* (1962) but Frost had claimed it was written in 1920.

26. Newbury College, a Lutheran college in South Carolina.

27. Cf. Frost's "Tree at my Window" (1927).

28. A Pyrrhic victory is a victory achieved at great cost. A Parthian shot is a strategy or ruse in which one attacks while simulating flight or retreat. A Pyrrhic victory is won at too great a cost to be of use to the victor and named after Pyrrhus of Epirus, who defeated the Romans at Asculum in 279 BC but sustained heavy losses. A Parthian shot is now synonymous with *parting shot,* i.e. they both mean "a remark or glance, etc. reserved for the moment of departure." The use arose from a custom in Parthia, an ancient kingdom in western Asia: Parthian horsemen would discharge their missiles into the ranks of the enemy while in real or pretended flight. The actual connection of the terms "Parthian shot" (first recorded in 1902) and "parting shot" (1894) may have escaped the attention of readers of earlier books that were mined for the *Oxford English Dictionary.* See also 34r.

29. Publius Helvius Pertinax (126–193 A.D.), the son of a freed slave, had a long equestrian military career before being elected to the Senate by Marcus Aurelius; he distinguished himself as a general under Marcus in Raetia and under Commodus in Britain, becoming cos. II and city prefect in 192. The Praetorian Guard under its prefect Laetus proclaimed him emperor on Jan. 1, 193, following the assassination of Commodus. During his rule of eighty-seven days he attempted to restore the principles of government observed by Marcus Aurelius and revived for himself the title of *princeps senatus,* while refusing the titles of Augustus and Caesar for his wife and son. An excessive eagerness for reform, however, caused discontent in the Senate, and the sale of state offices undermined confidence in his economic policy. His strict discipline aroused the resentment of the Praetorians who now regretted the removal of Commodus, and after an abortive conspiracy to make the consul Falco emperor, Laetus urged the Praetorians to invade the Palatine. Pertinax, deserted by all his retinue except Electus, fell victim to the spear of a

Tungrian solider (Mar 28, A.D. 193) He was later deified by Septimus Severus, the successor to Didius Julianus (137–193).

Pertinax and Didius Julianus had remarkably similar later careers. Following the murder of Pertinax, his father-in-law and urban prefect, Flavius Sulpicianus, entered the praetorian camp and unsuccessfully attempted to get the troops to name him emperor. Didius Julianus allowed soldiers seeking an alternative to take him to the praetorian camp. Prevented from entering the camp, he made promises to the soldiers from outside the wall and entered into a bidding war for the empire with his rival Flavius Sulpicianus. Didius Julianus won and was proclaimed emperor. His reign, however, lasted only sixty-six days; the senate soon proclaimed Septimius Severus emperor and executed Didius Julianus on June 1, 193. Pertinax was once said to have called Didius Julianus "my colleague and successor" because they both held suffect consulships at the same time and because Didius Julianus replaced Pertinax as proconsul of Africa. The comment would later prove prophetic, as the two men not only held successive reigns as emperor but also reigned for a very short period of time. See also 31.7r; 13.16r; 35.

30. A yardarm is either end of a yard of square sail. St. Elmo's fire is a luminous discharge of electricity extending into the atmosphere from some projecting or elevated object. It is usually observed (often during a snowstorm or a dust storm) as brush-like fiery jets extending from the tips of a ship's mast or spar. The phenomenon occurs when the atmosphere becomes charged and an electrical potential strong enough to cause a discharge is created between an object and the air around it. The amount of electricity involved is not great enough to be dangerous. The appearance of St. Elmo's fire is regarded as a portent of bad weather. The phenomenon, also known as corposant, was long regarded with superstitious awe.

31. Pertinax: see note 26 above. Diocletian (245–313), Roman Emperor (284–305) who appointed three others, Maximian, Constantius I, and Galerius to rule in a tetrarchy of four large districts to repel the Germans and preserve the empire. Diocletian and Maximian were to be first-tier "Augusti" while Constantius and Galerius were to be second-tier "Caesars." Many vestiges of Republican institutions disappeared, and his attempt to restore the gold standard eventually failed. His persecution of Christians developed with his political cult of the king as a divine authority. Diocletian abdicated in 305 and retired to his castle in Salona.

32. See also 47v; 2.16r; 4; 6.22r; 8.56r; 14.17r; 15.33v; 20.11r, 16v; 21.4r, 7r; 22.49r; 28.10r; 29.14r, 23r; 31.4r, 7r, 7v, 40r; 32.7r, 10r; 34.1r, 2r, 2v; 41.7r; 47.

33. John Keats (1795–1821) in his *Hyperion* (1818–1819) depicts the Titans (Saturnians) as a race about to become overthrown and extinct. In it Oceanus makes the pronouncement, "the eternal law / That the first in beauty should be first in might" (*Hyperion* 2:228–29). Also, in a letter to Louis Untermeyer of February 17, 1935, Frost wrote, "I heard Thorpe of Anne Arbor made it out that in Hyperion Keats anticipated evolution when he had old gods go down before the new. Hell he did. Keats merely set out to show you the great revolution of form getting the better of power. But why talk about it. A. McL was wrong in thinking the object of the artist is to be untimely—not to be in fashion . . ."

34. The opening words of Horace's Book I, Ode 38: "Persicos odi, puer, apparatus / displicent nexae philyra coronae; / mitte sectari, rosa quo locorum / sera moretur. / simplici myrto nihil adlabores / sedulus, cura: neque te ministrum / dedecet myrtus neque me sub arta / vite bibentem." "Persian elegance, my lad, I hate, and take no pleasure in

garlands woven on linden bast. A truce to searching out the haunts where lingers late the rose! Strive not to add aught else to the plain myrtle! The myrtle befits both thee, the servant, and me, the master, as I drink beneath the thick-leaved vine." Trans. C. E. Bennet, *Horace: Odes and Epodes,* Loeb Classical Library (Cambridge: Harvard Univ. Press, 1968).

35. Cf. Frost's "The Demiurge's Laugh."

36. See 4.51r; 45.1r; 17.30v; 19.1r.

37. See 4.20v; 11.1r; 22.17r. "Dianner" is probably Frost's play on the pronunciation of "Diane" by a person with a New England accent. See also 11.1r.

38. Cf. Frost's "Education by Poetry" (1930): "All metaphor breaks down somewhere. That is the beauty of it. It is touch and go with a metaphor, and until you have lived with it long enough you don't know when it is going." See also 21.7r; 47; 20.16r.

39. Mary Colum (1884–1957) was an Irish author and educator whose works include *From These Roots* (1937); she and her husband, poet Padraic Colum (1881–1972), came to the United States in 1914. Mary and Padraic Colum together published *Our Friend James Joyce* (1958).

40. General William T. Sherman (1820–1891). This refers to Sherman's "March to the Sea" through Georgia and North Carolina, which began May 5th, 1864, and ended April 26, 1865, when Gen. Joseph Johnston—commander of Confederate forces in the Carolinas, Georgia, and Florida—gave his formal surrender to Sherman at Durham Station, N.C., three weeks after Lee's surrender at Appomattox. In his *Memoirs,* Sherman gives an account of the march: "The skill and success of the men in collecting forage was one of the features of this march. Each brigade commander had authority to detail a company of foragers, usually about fifty men, with one or two commissioned officers selected for their boldness and enterprise. This party would be dispatched before daylight with a knowledge of the intended day's march and camp; would proceed on foot five or six miles from the route traveled by their brigade, and then visit every plantation and farm within range. They would usually procure a wagon or family carriage, load it with bacon, corn-meal, turkeys, chickens, ducks, and every thing that could be used as food or forage, and would then regain the main road, usually in advance of their train. No doubt, many acts of pillage, robbery, and violence, were committed by these parties of foragers, for I have since heard of jewelry taken from women, and the plunder of articles that never reached the commissary; but these acts were exceptional and incidental. I never heard of any cases of murder or rape; and no army could have carried along sufficient food and forage for a march of three hundred miles; so that foraging in some shape was necessary."

Here, also, is an account by Jacob D. Cox, LL. D., Late Major-General Commanding Twenty-Third Army Corps, of the march through Georgia: "Then, the confirmed and habitual stragglers soon became numerous enough to be a nuisance upon the line of march. Here again the difference in portions of the army was very marked. In some brigades every regiment was made to keep its own rear guard to prevent straggling, and the brigade provost guard marched in rear of all, arresting any who sought to leave the ranks, and reporting the regimental commander who allowed his men to scatter. But little by little the stragglers became numerous enough to cause serious complaint, and they followed the command without joining it for days together, living on the country, and shirking the labors of their comrades. It was to these that the name 'bummer' was properly applied. This class was numerous in the Confederate as in the National Army, in proportion to its strength, and the Southern people cried out for the most summary execution of military

justice against them. Responsible persons addressed specific complaints to the Confederate War Secretary, charging robbery and pillage of the most scandalous kinds against their
own troops. Their leading newspapers demanded the cashiering and shooting of colonels
and other officers, and declared their conduct worse than the enemy's. It is perhaps vain to
hope that a great war can ever be conducted without abuses of this kind, and we may con-
gratulate ourselves that the wrongs done were almost without exception to property, and
that murders, rapes, and other heinous personal offences were nearly unknown." Though
there has been ongoing controversy, no definitive historical evidence exists to dispute these
claims. See also 25.5r.

41. Variant of line in "A Masque of Reason" (1945), ll. 194–196: "Look at how far we've
left the current science / Of Genesis behind. The wisdom there though, / Is just as good
as when I uttered it." See also 41v, 44v; 47.

42. *Boue* is French for mud, silt or sediment.

43. The Kickapoo was a North American Indian group that was eventually resettled on
reservations in Oklahoma and Kansas.

44. See 3.1r; 28.20r; 20.19v; 43.21r; 22.31r. The phrase "domestic science" also appears in
The Future of Man (unpublished version, 1959).

45. Cf. Chapter 6 of Arnold Bennett's *Literary Taste: How to Form It* (1909), titled "The
Question of Style": "When you read a book there are only three things of which you may
be conscious: (1) The significance of the words, which is inseparably bound up with the
thought. (2) The look of the printed words on the page—I do not suppose that anybody
reads any author for the visual beauty of the words on the page. (3) The sound of the
words, either actually uttered or imagined by the brain to be uttered. Now it is indubitable
that words differ in beauty of sound. To my mind one of the most beautiful words in the
English language is 'pavement.'" See also 19.4r.

46. Frost had visited Bowdoin in 1921. In May of 1925, he gave a talk on the "Vocal
Imagination." Lawrance Thompson writes: "At this stage in his career as a performing
bard, Frost increasingly enjoyed teasing and tantalizing his audiences by making bold
statements which meant much to him, and also by aiming his remarks just high enough
over the heads of his listeners to make them stretch for his meanings. He had previously
talked on Longfellow, in May of 1925, at an 'Institute of Literature' held on the campus of
Longfellow's alma mater, Bowdoin, and there he used as a topic his favorite subject, 'Vocal
Imagination.' To illustrate it, he read to his audience a passage he particularly liked: 'The
Flight into Egypt' from Longfellow's *Golden Legend*. In the discussion, afterward, one of
the Bowdoin professors had infuriated him by saying he wondered where Frost even
found that 'slight thing' which Longfellow could have written when he was an undergraduate at Bowdoin. Irritated into sarcasms, Frost had replied, 'You think it is slight, do you?
That's a very fine poem and I'll tell you how I know. I found it in an anthology compiled
by an Englishman'" (*Robert Frost: The Years of Triumph*, p. 293). See also 22.7r; 44.1r; 26.2r.

47. Lesley Frost (1899–1983), the poet's eldest daughter.

48. See 4.22r; 8.37r; 17.25r; 22.8r, 8v; 28.10r; 29; 33.5r; 35.7r; 47.

49. See *A Masque of Mercy* (1947):

Jonah. There's not the least lack of the love of God
In what I say. Don't be so silly, woman.

His very weakness for mankind's endearing.
I love and fear Him. Yes, but I fear for Him.
I don't see how it can be to His interest
This modern tendency I find in Him
To take the punishment out of all failure
To be strong, careful, thrifty, diligent,
Anything we once thought we had to be.

See also 31.6v, 10r; 4.32r, 35r; 22.4r, 12r; 29.9r; 33.1r, 1v; 24.32r; 21.11r; 26.12r, 13r; 19.6r; 23.8r, 9r.

50. William Jennings Bryan (1860–1925), Congressman, three-time presidential candidate, and Secretary of State under Woodrow Wilson. A staunch defender of small farmers and labor, Bryan worked closely with the Populist Party, a group of Midwestern and Southern farmers who suffered economically because of low prices for their crops, which they blamed on Northeastern business interests. Bryan invariably blamed private profit and big interests for the plight of farmers. In 1893, he argued that the gold standard drove down agricultural prices and advocated a silver standard instead.

51. See 1.1r, 4r; 4.1r, 12r; 12.5r; 31.39r; 33.3r.

52. Generals William Tecumseh Sherman (1820–1891) and Ulysses Simpson Grant (1822–1885). In "From Plane to Plane," Frost also mentions the origins of Sherman's middle name: "'I thought you meant to be an Indian Chief— / You said the second coming of Tecumseh. / Remember how you envied General Sherman. / William Tecumseh Sherman. Why Tecumseh? / (He tried to imitate Dick's tone of voice.) / You wished your middle name had been Tecumseh'" (in *Collected Poems*, 1949). In his *Memoirs*, Sherman wrote that his father "caught a fancy for the great chief of the Shawness" during the War of 1812 and "insisted on engrafting the name 'Tecumseh' on the usual family list."

53. A ship of English pilgrims landed at Plymouth Rock, in Plymouth, Massachusetts, on December 21, 1620.

54. See 25.6r; 11.51v; 6.27v; 26.7r.

55. See 31.31v.

56. Louis Untermeyer (1885–1977) divorced his wife, Jean Starr; he subsequently remarried and then again divorced her. Untermeyer's troubles with his wife were the cause of some concern to Frost. See also Frost's "A Star in a Stone-Boat," ll. 28–30: "Such as even poets would admit perforce / More practical than Pegasus the horse / If it could put a star back in its course."

57. A constellation that may be viewed in the eastern horizon.

58. In the later Achaemenid Persian armies and the early 5th century, Greek mercenary troops were employed in the service of Persian commanders. The term "medizing" came to describe such troops as were seen to be pro-Persian or in Persian service. "Medizing" comes from the word "Mede," which was the general term used by the Greeks to describe all Persian/Medean peoples.

59. "Over Back" is one of the subtitles of Frost's *A Witness Tree* (1932).

60. Cf. "An Answer" (1946): "But Islands of the Blessèd, bless you, son, / I never came upon a blessèd one." See also 19.1r, 9v, 2r.

61. Bertran de Born (1140–1214) was a troubadour known for his belligerent politics and

condemned in Dante's *Inferno.* Frost's playful coinage here, and used often in the note-books, was his epithet for Ezra Pound. See also 24.36v; 11.1r, 51v.

62. Cf. "The Flood," first published under variant title "Blood" (1928): "Blood has been harder to dam back than water. / Just when we think we have it impounded safe / Behind new barrier walls (and let it chafe!), / It breaks away in some new kind of slaughter. / We choose to say it is let loose by the devil; / But power of blood itself releases blood."

63. Three-time presidential candidate 1896, 1900, 1908. Gave his well-known "Cross of Gold" speech at the Democratic National Convention on July 9, 1896.

64. John Lyly (1554?–1606), Elizabethan dramatist and prose-writer. His *Euphues,* an elaborate prose romance, is comprised of two parts, *The Anatomy of Wit* (1578) and *Euphues and His England* (1580).

65. Marcus Fabius Quintilianus (ca. A.D. 30–ca. 100), Roman rhetorician. His best-known work is *Institutio Oratoria* (pre-96 A.D.).

66. Cf. Frost's "How Hard It Is to Keep from Being King When It's in You and in the Situation" from *In The Clearing* (1962).

67. Cf. "Education by Poetry" (1931): "Materialism is not the attempt to say all in terms of matter. The only materialist—be he poet, teacher, scientist, politician, or statesman—is the man who gets lost in his material without a gathering metaphor to throw it into shape and order. He is the lost soul." See also 20.17v.

68. See 22.1r, 47r; 12.10r; 37.2r; 7.3r, 4r; 33.9r; 8.58r, 58v; 1.34v; 17.41r; 19.8v; 29.23r

69. Cf. Frost's "The Black Cottage" (1914), ll. 94–95, "It was the words 'descended into Hades' / That seemed too pagan to our liberal youth." "Descended into Hades" alludes to the Apostles' Creed and refers to Christ's harrowing of hell.

70. See 4.17r, 32v; 47; 23.3r, 4r, 5r; 28.15r; 22.6r; 29.17r.

71. Cf. "West-Running Brook" (1928) and "The Master Speed" (1936).

72. See 4.13r; 31.7r, 8r, 10r, 40r, 40v; 32; 37.1r, 5v, 6v; 22.10v; 13.8r; 12.7v; 9.10r; 21.4r, 7r; 27.29r, 45r, 46r; 1; 5; 47; 23.10r; 35.13r, 16r.

73. See also 43v, 44r; 14.15r; 19.5v; 47; 27.7r; 4.32r.

74. See 19.9r.

75. Bolsheviki or bolsheviks (pl). Members of the extremist wing of the Russian Social Democratic Party in Russia that seized supreme power, and advocated violent overthrow of capitalism, during the Revolution (1917–1920).

76. Cf. Christopher Marlowe (1564–1593), *Doctor Faustus,* Scene 12, ll. 80–84:

Was this the face that launch'd a thousand ships,
And burnt the topless towers of Ilium?
Sweet Helen, make me immortal with a kiss!
Her lips suck forth my soul; see where it flies!

77. Cf. "Education by Poetry" (1931): "Greatest of all attempts to say one thing in terms of another is the philosophical attempt to say matter in terms of spirit, or spirit in terms of matter, to make the final unity. That is the greatest attempt that ever failed. We stop just short there. But it is the height of poetry, the height of all thinking, the height of all poetic thinking, that attempt to say matter in terms of spirit and spirit in terms of matter."

78. Cf. "Escapist—Never" (1962), l. 10: "His life is a pursuit of a pursuit forever."

79. Cf. "Education by Poetry" (1931):

> Let me ask you to watch a metaphor breaking down here before you. Somebody said to me a little while ago, "It is easy enough for me to think of the universe as a machine, as a mechanism."
>
> I said, "You mean the universe is like a machine?"
>
> He said, "No. I think it is one . . . Well, it is like. . ."
>
> "I think you mean the universe is like a machine."
>
> "All right. Let it go at that."
>
> I asked him, "Did you ever see a machine without a pedal for the foot, or a lever for the hand, or a button for the finger?"
>
> He said, "No—no."
>
> I said, "All right. Is the universe like that?"
>
> And he said, "No. I mean it is like a machine, only . . ."
>
> " . . . it is different from a machine," I said.
>
> He wanted to go just that far with that metaphor and no further. And so do we all. All metaphor breaks down somewhere. That is the beauty of it. It is touch and go with the metaphor, and until you have lived with it long enough you don't know when it is going. You don't know how much you can get out of it and when it will cease to yield. It is a very living thing. It is as life itself.

See also 29r.

80. "The Mixture Mechanic" is the title to part four of the poem "Kitty Hawk" from *In the Clearing* (1962). See also 26.6r; 47; 20.22r; 29.9r.

81. Frost wrote to Louis Untermeyer in an unpublished letter of 1915: "If I must be classified a poet, I might be called a Synechdochist, for I prefer the synechdoche in poetry—that figure of speech in which we use a part for the whole." See also 9.8r; 19.9r; 47; 8.36, 105.

82. See note 69.

83. "True Thomas" refers to an English ballad called "Thomas the Rhymer" by Thomas the Rhymer a.k.a. Thomas of Erceldoune (1220?–1297?), a Scottish poet reputed to have prophetic gifts. Frost commented on the poem in "Remarks on the Occasion of the Tagore Centenary." John Frederick Nims transcribed Frost's remarks from the tape and published them in *Poetry* 99 (November 1961): 106–19: "Some people think that beauty is truth. They aren't ineffable enough to know that that isn't so. Keats didn't pretend to be ineffable when he said that: 'Beauty is truth, truth beauty . . .' No. One of the poets a long time ago wrote like this: he got up a story about a fellow called True Thomas; it's in an old ballad: 'True Thomas lay on Huntley Bank, / And a wonder came riding by,' something supernatural came riding by, a beautiful lady. And he rose up from where he was, and 'louted low down,' it says, 'to his knee.' And she says: 'Rise up, Thomas! Who do you think I am?' He says: 'You're so beautiful, you must be the Queen of Heaven!' And she says: 'Oh, you couldn't make a greater mistake! I'm only the Queen of Fairyland!' You see, she was the Queen of Beauty, but not of Truth." See also 17.28v–29r; 19.10r.

84. Nathaniel Hawthorne (1804–1806), a short tale, "Rappaccini's Daughter" (1844).

85. Havelock Ellis (1859–1939), a member of the socialist Fabian Society, wrote *The Dance of Life* (1923), arguing that dance and building are the primary forms of civilization.

86. Cf. "The Strong Are Saying Nothing Until They See" (1936).

87. See 30r, 44v; 47.

88. Landaff is a small town in Grafton County, New Hampshire, near Easton and Franconia.

89. This reference continues through 44r. See also 39v; 14.15r; 19.5v; 47; 27.7r; 4.32r.

90. See 41.9m

91. Ancestor to *Homo sapiens,* the Mousterian is a Neanderthal species belonging to the Middle Paleolithic period.

92. Aurignacian is the name of a culture located in Europe and southwest Asia from the Upper Paleolithic era, dating back to 34,000–23,000 B.C.E. The name originates from the site of Aurignac in the Haute Garonne area of France. Some of the earliest cave art was produced by the Aurignacian culture. Their flint tools were more varied than those of earlier cultures, employing finer blades struck from prepared cores rather than using crude flakes, and they made pendants, bracelets and ivory beads to ornament themselves. Because of their sophistication and self-awareness, archaeologists consider the makers of Aurignacian artifacts the first modern humans in Europe. Human remains and Aurignacian artifacts originally found at Cro-Magnon in France indicate that the culture was human rather than Neanderthal.

93. Cf. Frost's "A Missive Missile," from *A Further Range* (1936), and ll. 13–15 of "To An Ancient," from *Steeple Bush* (1947): "You made the eolith, you grew the bone, / The second more peculiarly your own, / And likely to have been enough alone."

94. Ralph Waldo Emerson (1803–1882), "Uriel," *Poems* (1847): "'Line in nature is not found; / Unit and universe are round; / In vain produced, all rays return; / Evil will bless, and ice will burn.'"

95. See 7.4r; 37.9r; 4.48r; 31.7v, 9v; 14.1r, 2r, 11r; 22.8r, 12r, 17r, 18r; 15.3v; 39; 47; 19.5r, 5v, 9r. See also Frost's "The Prerequisites" (1954).

96. Possibly the Bancroft Library at the University of California Berkeley, which was founded in 1905 and contains a collection of Western Americana.

97. Cf. "A Masque of Reason" (1945), ll. 194–196: "Look at how far we've left the current science / Of Genesis behind. The wisdom there though, / Is just as good as when I uttered it." See also 30r, 41v; 47.

98. Gardner Jackson (1896–1965), journalist and friend of Frost's.

99. Leonard (Lanson) Cline (1893–1929), pseud., Alan Forsyth, journalist and short-story writer.

100. Fr. *droit de seigneur.* The right of a feudal lord to have sexual intercourse with his vassal's wife on her marriage night.

101. J. J. Lankes (1884–1960), American illustrator, with an incredible eye for detail. He provided the woodcuts for some of Frost's individual poems and for Frost's collections *New Hampshire* (1923) and *West-Running Brook* (1928). See also 26.17r.

102. See 12.10r; 31.7r; 14.4v; 47; 25.1r; 2.4v; 46.5r.

103. See also 24r; 2.16r; 4; 6.22r; 8.56r; 14.17r; 15.33v; 20.11r, 16v; 21.4r, 7r; 22.49r; 28.10r; 29.14r, 23r; 31.4r, 7r, 7v, 40r; 32.7r, 10r; 34.1r, 2r, 2v; 41.7r; 47.

104. See 5.8r; 17.40r; 32.10r; 35.19r; 41.7r.

105. See 5.8r.

106. Timothy Dwight (1752–1817), founder of Andover Theological Seminary, President

of Yale College. Frost owned a copy of the 1823 edition of Dwight's *Travels in New-England and New-York*.

NOTEBOOK 25

1. *The Amherst Student* is the Amherst College student newspaper. A version of Frost's "Letter to *The Amherst Student*," dated March 25, 1935, appears in this Notebook from 13r to 16r.

2. See 24.46v; 31.7r; 14.4v; 47; 2.4v; 46.5r; 12.10r.

3. See "The Generations of Men" from *North of Boston* (1914), ll. 82–83; "What will we come to / With all this pride of ancestry, we Yankees?" See also 29.6r, 8v; 4.21r; 22.33v; 47; 26.27r.

4. See Frost's "Build Soil" from *A Further Range* (1936), ll. 262–64: "I sent you once a song with the refrain: / Let me be the one. To do what is done—"

5. See 4.1r; 29.38r; 33.cover,3r; 1.1r; 26.27r; 28.12r.

6. General William T. Sherman (1820–1891). This refers to Sherman's "March to the Sea" through Georgia and North Carolina, which began May 5th, 1864, and ended April 26, 1865, when Gen. Joseph Johnston—commander of Confederate forces in the Carolinas, Georgia, and Florida—gave his formal surrender to Sherman at Durham Station, N.C., three weeks after Lee's surrender at Appomattox. For more details on the march and the conduct of the soldiers on it see Notebook 24, note 30.

7. Medieval romance. The earliest extant version (incomplete) was written (ca. 1185) by Thomas of Britain in Anglo-Norman French verse. About 1210, Gottfried von Strassburg wrote in German verse a version based on that of Thomas. The story, originally independent of the Arthurian legend, was later incorporated with it. In the 15th century, Sir Thomas Malory included Tristram and Isolde in his *Morte d' Arthur.* The story is mainly Irish in origin, with details from other sources. Although the many versions of the story naturally differ, the basic plot is much the same in all of them. Sir Tristram is sent to Ireland to bring Isolde the Fair back to Cornwall to be the bride of his uncle, King Mark. A potion that Tristram and Isolde unwittingly swallow binds them in eternal love. According to most versions of the story, after many trysts the lovers become estranged, and Tristram marries another Isolde, Isolde of the White Hands. Later, dying of a battle wound, Tristram sends for Isolde the Fair. Deceived into believing she is not coming, Tristram dies of despair, and Isolde, on finding her lover dead, dies of grief beside him. The names of the two chief characters appear in various forms, such as Tristran, Tristrem, or Tristan and Isolt, Yseult, or Iseult. Modern versions of the story include Matthew Arnold, *Tristram and Iseult;* A. C. Swinburne, *Tristram of Lyonesse;* Joseph Bédier, *Tristan and Iseult;* and E. A. Robinson, *Tristram.* Wagner's opera *Tristan und Isolde* is based on the version of Gottfried von Strassburg. For translation of the version by Thomas of Britain, see R. S. Loomis, *The Romance of Tristram & Ysolt* (rev. ed. 1951); for translation of the version by Gottfried von Strassburg, see A. T. Hatto, *Tristan* (1960). See also Frost's letter to Robert P. T. Coffin of February 24, 1938: "By Platonist I mean one who believes that what we have here is an imperfect copy of what is in heaven . . . Many of the world's greatest—maybe all of them—have been ranged on that romantic side. I am philosophically opposed to having one Iseult for my vocation and another for my avocation; as you may have inferred from a poem called Two Tramps in Mud Time."

8. See 24.34r; 11.51v; 6.27v; 26.7r.

9. See 29.34r; 48.11r; 21.51r; 4.25r, 27r, 22.33v.

NOTEBOOK 26

1. Cf. "An Equalizer" from *A Witness Tree* (1942). See also 4.17r; 28.7r, 47.

2. Harold Bauer (1873–1951), an influential Anglo-American pianist.

3. "Seize the Day"; cf. "Carpe Diem" (1938). The passage echoes in prose lines from the poem.

4. Mr. and Mrs. Loren E. Baily's home in Salem, N.H., where Frost, his mother and his siblings boarded, after they moved east upon the death of Frost's father.

5. See 4.9r; 5.19v.

6. See ll. 41–42 of "The Tuft of Flowers" (1906) from *A Boy's Will:* "'Men work together,' I told him from the heart, / 'Whether they work together or apart.'" See also 4.20r.

7. J. J. Lankes (1884–1960), American illustrator, with an incredible eye for detail. He provided the woodcuts for some of Frost's individual poems and for Frost's collections *New Hampshire* (1923) and *West-Running Brook* (1928). For a time, he had a studio in Gardenville, New York. See also 24.46r.

8. See Frost's poem "America Is Hard to See" from *In the Clearing* (1962). See also 12.22r; 29.9r; 5.5r; 4.21r.

9. Christopher Marlowe (1564–93) and Robert Greene (ca. 1558–93). Greene was an English poet and playwright and a literary rival of Marlowe. He later attacked Marlowe and other of his former friends, such as Peel and Nash, in his *Groatsworth of Wit* (1592). This phrase and "Plight of Pindar" are written in blue ink.

10. See 4.1r; 29.38r; 33.cover, 3r; 25.4r; 1.1r; 28.12r; 47. See also Frost's poem "The Lesson for Today," Notebook 1, note 10.

11. See 28r; 29.8v, 16r; 4.21r; 22.33v; 47.

12. See 29.6r, 8v; 4.21r; 22.33v; 25.1r; 47.

13. Mark Twain (1835–1910), "The Celebrated Jumping Frog of Calaveras County" (1865). See also 7.38r; 12.1r; 15.19v; 17.28v–29r.

14. See 4.19r; 22.22r.

15. See 4.6r, 23r; 22.19r, 34r.

16. See 27r; 29.8v, 16r; 4.21r; 22.33v; 47.

17. See 4.33v, 46r, 47v; 22.46r, 59r; 31.8r, 9r.

18. See 4.31r; 31.41v; 22.58v.

19. See 4.1r, 21r, 24r; 47; 29.8v.

20. Cf. Frost's Introduction to E. A. Robinson's *King Jasper:* "Robinson stayed content with the old-fashioned way to be new." Also, the first of Frost's lost Norton Lectures at Harvard, delivered March 4, 1936, was titled "The Old Way to Be New."

21. The seventh and last of Frost's lost Norton Lectures at Harvard, delivered April 15, 1936, was titled "Does Wisdom Signify?" See also 6r below.

22. (Harry) Sinclair Lewis (1885–1951), American novelist and first American to be awarded the Nobel prize (1930). Best known for *Main Street* (1920) and *Babbitt* (1922).

23. Ernest Christopher Dowson (1867–1900), English poet whose most famous poem is "Non Sum Qualis Eram Bonae sub Regno Cynarae," from *Cynara: A Little Book of Verse* (1907).

24. William Vaughn Moody (1869–1910), American poet and dramatist.

25. Kipling, *The White Man's Burden* (1899), a poem addressed to the U.S. on its responsibilities towards its recently acquired territory the Philippine Islands.

26. In 1936, Frost was appointed Charles Eliot Norton Professor of Poetry at Harvard and delivered seven lectures, the first on March 4, 1936, and titled "The Renewal of Words." No transcript of the lectures was ever found or produced. See also 29.40v; 38.5r.

27. See 12.2r; 22.7v; 44; 45; 13.9v; 15.13r; 47; 8.15r, 32r.

28. The fifth of Frost's lost Norton Lectures at Harvard, delivered April 1, 1936, was titled "Before the Beginning of a Poem." See also 47.

29. The sixth of Frost's lost Norton Lectures was delivered April 15, 1936, and titled "After the End of a Poem."

30. See 15.28v; 43.1r, 6r; 45.1r; 28.11r; 4.34r, 36r; 22.53r; 47.

31. The fourth of Frost's lost Norton Lectures, delivered March 25, 1936, was titled "Poetry as Prowess." See also 38.5r and Frost's "A Perfect Day—A Day of Prowess" (1956) for *Sports Illustrated*: "Prowess of course comes first, the ability to perform with success in games, in the arts and, come right down to it, in battle. The nearest of kin to the artists in performers in baseball, football and tennis." See also Frost's 1936 "Memorial Tribute to Edgar Morton Lewis," a president of the University of New Hampshire who pitched for the Boston Braves in the 1890s: " . . . So poetry to him [Lewis] was prowess from that time on, just as baseball was prowess, as running was prowess, and it was our common ground. I have always thought of poetry as prowess—something to achieve, something to win or lose."

32. The second of Frost's lost Norton Lectures at Harvard, delivered March 11, 1936, was titled "Vocal Imagination: A Merger of Form and Content." See also 22.7r; 44.1r; 24.31r.

33. See *A Masque of Reason* (1947), 105–106: "Jesse Bel. Your courage failed. The saddest thing in life / Is that the best thing in it should be courage." See also 4.19r; 52r.

34. Cf. the opening line of "The Gift Outright" (1942): "The land was ours before we were the land's / She was our land more than a hundred years / Before we were her people. She was ours / In Massachusetts, in Virginia, / But we were England's, still colonials, / Possessing what we still were unpossessed by, / Possessed by what we now no more possessed."

35. Elinor Frost (1873–1938), Frost's wife.

36. See IV above.

37. See 20.22v; 29.9r; 47; 24.41v.

38. For Yeats' attitude toward the middle class, see, among other things, "September 1913."

39. Aphasia is a loss of speech, partial or total, or loss of power to understand written or spoken language, as a result of disorder of the cerebral speech centers. Hyperphasia describes a condition of excessive talking occasioned by a want of control over the vocal organs, due to cerebral affliction. See also 24.34r; 25.6r; 11.51v; 6.27v.

40. Cf. Frost's "The Unmade Word, or Fetching and Far-Fetching." See also 8.15r; 13.2r; 47.

41. This is a non-metallic mineral that is usually lucid. Feldspar results from granite, as with the Sierra Nevada mountains. A similar type is found in Scandinavia.

42. Cf. Frost's "At Woodward's Gardens" from *A Further Range* (1936), ll. 18–21: "The al-

ready known had once more been confirmed / By psychological experiment, / And that were all the finding to announce / Had the boy not presumed too close and long."

43. *Paradise Lost*, Bk. 3. God speaks: "So without least impulse or shadow of fate, / Or aught by me immutably foreseen, / They trespass, authors to themselves in all / Both what they judge and what they choose; for so / I formed them free, and free they must remain, / Till they enthrall themselves: I else must change / Their nature, and revoke the high decree / Unchangeable, eternal, which ordained / Their freedom, they themselves ordained their fall. / The first sort by their own suggestion fell, / Self-tempted, self-depraved: man falls deceived / By the other first: man therefore shall find grace, / The other none: in mercy and justice both, / Through heaven and earth, so shall my glory excel, / But mercy first and last shall brightest shine" (ll. 120–134). This is a theme Frost picks up in a letter to Wilbert Snow dated January 2, 1938. Snow included the letter in the article "The Robert Frost I Knew" (*Texas Quarterly* 11, no. 3 [1968]: 9–48).

44. Oliver Cromwell (1599–1658), lord protector of England ([1649]1653–1658), raised a troop of men culled not from the nobility and those of landed wealth but from what he considered to be "godly men" who fought neither for pay nor for earthly glory. These men were referred to as the "Ironsides."

45. Kahlil Gibran (1883–1931), Arabic poet and illustrator. Born in Lebanon and early in life, he emigrated to America. *The Prophet* (1923) is a collection of parables on everyday life.

46. See Frost's "A Masque of Mercy" (1948); 31.6v, 10r; 4.32r, 35r; 22.4r, 12r; 29.9r; 33.1r, 1v; 24.32r; 21.11r; 19.6r; 23.8r, 9r.

47. See 5.8r; 28.19r.

NOTEBOOK 27

1. See 4.32r; 24.39v, 43v, 44r; 14.15r; 47; 19.5v.

2. See 5.3r.

3. Daughter of Priam, first wife of Aeneas, mother of Ascanius. In Virgil's *Aeneid*, her fate is left in question; on the night of Troy's fall she is perhaps "translated" into an attendant of Cybele (II, 756).

4. Moloch. A figure found in the *Old Testament* and idol of the Canaanites who demanded the sacrifice of children. Moloch also figures into book two of Milton's *Paradise Lost*.

5. The star Arrakis Draconis, in the Draco constellation, is a binary star of spectral class F7V and visual magnitude 6. It is located approximately 85 light years away and consists of two almost identical yellow-white stars in a close orbit. Arrakis is derived from an Arabic term which means "dancer."

6. See also 43r; 4.13r; 5; 31.7r, 8r, 10r, 40r, 40v; 32; 37.1r, 5v, 6v; 22.10v; 13.8r; 12.7v; 9.10r; 24.39v; 21.4r, 7r; 1; 47; 23.10r; 35.13r, 16r.

7. Cf. Frost's "Evil Tendencies Cancel" (1936).

8. Possibly Nehemiah 1:11: "For I was the king's cupbearer."

9. Edgar A. Bancroft (1857–1925), *The Chicago Strike of 1894* (1895). Horace Fletcher (1849–1919), self-taught nutritionist popular in the first part of the twentieth century and nicknamed "The Great Masticator" because of his doctrine of "Fletcherism," which advocated chewing all food until it turned to liquid before swallowing. See also 4.38r.

10. Marcelene Cox (1900–1998), columnist for *Ladies' Home Journal* and contributor to *Reader's Digest* and *Good Housekeeping,* among other publications. See also 22.19r.

11. A friend of Frost's from high school who helped develop Frost's interest in botany. Burell's legs were crushed in a box factory, an incident which contributed to the subject matter of Frost's "The Self-Seeker."

12. Plutarch (ca. A.D. 46–ca. 127), Greek biographer whose *Parallel Lives* extend comparison between the lives of eminent Greek and Roman statesmen and thinkers.

13. Frost later in life owned a border collie named Gillio and nicknamed Gillie.

14. See John 1.1.

15. See 29r; 4.13r; 5; 31.7r, 8r, 10r, 40r, 40v; 32; 37.1r, 5v, 6v; 22.10v; 13.8r; 12.7v; 9.10r; 24.39v; 21.4r, 7r; 1; 47; 23.10r; 35.13r, 16r.

NOTEBOOK 28

1. *A Further Range* (1936), which became a Book-of-the-Month selection, and for which Frost was awarded the Pulitzer Prize. Frost handwrote the dedication and table of contents to *A Further Range* over the first six pages of this notebook. There are no differences between the notebook version and the published version.

2. See 7v and the title to Frost poem, "It Is Almost the Year Two Thousand" (1946).

3. Cf. Frost's "Introduction to Sarah Cleghorn's 'Threescore'" (1936).

4. John Erskine, *The Private Life of Helen of Troy* (Indianapolis: Bobbs-Merrill, 1925). Erskine also wrote *The Memory of Certain Persons* and *The Moral Obligation to Be Intelligent.* Erskine was a professor at Amherst from 1903 to 1909.

5. See 4.11r; 22.17r; 47.

6. See 2.1r; 31.7r.

7. See 29.14r, 15r; 47.

8. See Frost's "An Equalizer" from *A Witness Tree* (1942). See also 4.17r; 26.1r; 47.

9. See 4.1r.

10. Cf. Matthew 19.24.

11. In I Kings 16:34, King Hiel loses his youngest son, Segub, when he raises the gates of Jericho; God's "curse" on the man who rebuilds the city is foretold in Joshua 6:26. See also Frost's "A Masque of Reason."

12. See 4.2r.

13. See also 2.16r; 4; 6.22r; 8.56r; 14.17r; 15.33v; 20.11r, 16v; 21.4r, 7r; 22.49r; 24.24r, 47v; 29.14r, 23r; 31.4r, 7r, 7v, 40r; 32.7r, 10r; 34.1r, 2r, 2v; 41.7r; 47.

14. See 4.22r; 8.37r; 17.25r; 22.8r, 8v; 24.31r; 29; 33.5r; 35.7r; 47.

15. See 15.28v; 43.1r, 6r; 45.1r; 47; 4.34r, 36r; 22.53r; 26.2r; 47.

16. Cf. Frost's "The Constant Symbol" (1946): "Every single poem written regular is a symbol small or great of the way the will has to pitch into commitments deeper and deeper to a rounded conclusion and then be judged for whether any original intention it had has been strongly spent or weakly lost; be it in art, politics, school, church, business, love, or marriage—in a piece of work or in a career. Strongly spent is synonymous with kept."

17. Cf. Matthew Arnold's "The Hymn of Empedocles": "Is it so small a thing to have enjoy'd the sun, / To have lived light in the spring, / To have loved, to have thought, to have done; / To have advanced true friends, and beat down baffling foes."

18. See 29.38r; 33.cover, 3r; 25.4r; 1.1r; 26.27r; 4.1r; 47. See also Frost's poem "The Lesson for Today," Notebook 1, note 10.

19. See 4.17r, 32v; 47; 23.3r, 4r, 5r; 22.6r; 29.17r; 24.39r.

20. Burr and Burton Seminary in Manchester, Vermont, which Frost visited on numerous occasions. See also note 31 in Notebook 29.

21. See 29.16v, 29v; 15.22r; 4.38r; 9.19r. See also Frost's "Kitty Hawk."

22. See 5.8r; 26.14r.

23. See 24.30r; 3.1r; 20.19v; 43.2r; 22.31r. The phrase "domestic science" also appears in *The Future of Man* (unpublished version, 1959).

NOTEBOOK 29

1. Frost's discussion on democracy continues throughout this notebook. See also 4.22r; 8.37r; 17.25r; 22.8r, 8v; 24.31r; 28.10r; 33.5r; 35.7r; 47.

2. This appears as a subtitle for the notebook. Cf. Frost's "Does No One at All Ever Feel This Way in the Least" published in *In the Clearing* (1962):

O ocean sea for all your being vast,
Your separation of us from the Old
That should have made the New World newly great
Would only disappoint us at the last
If it should not do anything foretold
To make us different in a single trait.

3. Cf. Frost's "Our Hold on the Planet" (1940): / . . . / But we forget: "Take nature altogether since time began, / Including human nature, in peace and war, / And it must be a little more in favor of man, / Say a fraction of one per cent at the very least, / Or our number living wouldn't be steadily more, / Our hold on the planet wouldn't have so increased."

4. See 31.40r.

5. At one point in his life Frost was a poultry farmer—see Notebook 2.

6. What follows is a draft of a poem first published as "Does No One But Me at All Ever Feel This Way in the Least" (1952) and later as "Does No One at All Ever Feel This Way in the Least," *In the Clearing* (1962).

7. See 32r; 47.

8. See "The Generations of Men" from *North of Boston* (1914), ll. 82–83, "What will we come to/ With all this pride of ancestry, we Yankees?" See also 4.21r; 29.8v; 22.33v; 25.1r; 47; 26.27r.

9. Alice Meynell (1847–1922), English poet and essayist who converted to Catholicism in 1872. She was friends with Meredith, Patmore, Tennyson, and Francis Thompson. Her early work was polished, refined, and Victorian. Her later work focused on the tough realities of modern existence.

10. See 4.21r; 22.33v; 47; 26.27r, 28r.

11. See 6r; 4.21r; 22.33v; 25.1r; 47; 26.27r.

12. See 4.1r, 21r, 24r; 47; 26.28r.

13. See 23.9r; 4.21r; 47.

14. This phrase recurs throughout this notebook. See also 4.24r, 24.43v.

15. See 22.20r; 47.

16. See Frost's "A Masque of Mercy" (1948); 31.6v, 10r; 4.32r, 35r; 22.4r, 12r; 33.1r, 1v; 24.32r; 21.11r; 26.12r, 13r; 19.6r; 23.8r, 9r.

17. The first line of "The Gift Outright" (1942).

18. Frost's mother was from Scottish stock. Frost sailed to Glasgow on the SS *Parisian* when he moved to England in 1912.

19. Title of Frost poem, "America Is Hard to See." First published with that title in *In the Clearing* (1962). Previously published with the variant title "And All We Call American" (1951). See also 12.22r; 26.27r; 5.5r; 4.21r.

20. "The Mixture Mechanic" is the title to part four of the poem "Kitty Hawk" from *In the Clearing* (1962). See also 26.6r; 47; 20.22r; 24.41v.

21. See 47. See also Frost's poem "Build Soil" from *A Further Range* (1936), ll. 45–48: "Many men's luck with Greatest Washington / (Who sat for Stuart's portrait, but who sat / Equally for the nation's Constitution)."

22. A possible reference to Sara Teasdale's (1884–1933) book of poems *Rivers to the Sea* (1915). Frost owned a copy of the 1915 edition inscribed to him by Teasdale as well as a copy of the 1927 edition. Cf. Frost's letter to Louis Untermeyer of August 7, 1936: "To hell with these baubles gewgaws kickshaws. I'll write 'em a poem the last night before I face the mike. I will and be damned to all the uncontrolled rivers in the country. (I've got a new slogan in for one party or the other. I hadn't broken it to you, had I?) It is the name and the theme of an eclogue I have written. This is it. No Rivers to the Sea! No water shall go back. Meanwhile, I am mowing some, chopping some, and digging a little. How could man die better?" The eclogue Frost mentions may be "Too Anxious for Rivers" (1947). See also 12v; 4.7r.

23. See 4.7r.

24. Cf. Frost's "Build Soil" from *A Further Range* (1936):

We're always too much out or too much in.
At present from a cosmical dilation
We're so much out that the odds are against
Our ever getting inside in again.
But inside in is where we've got to get.
My friends all know I'm interpersonal.
But long before I'm interpersonal
Away 'way down inside I'm personal.
Just so before we're international
We're national and act as nationals.

25. Cf. Frost's "Mending Wall" and "Choose Something Like a Star": "So when at times the mob is swayed / To carry praise or blame too far, / We may chose something like a star / To stay our minds on and be staid."

26. See 12r; 4.7r.

27. Robert Bruce (1274–1339), King Robert the Bruce of Scotland. Frost refers here to a legend about about Bruce's rise to power. In 1306, Bruce met John 't Red Comyn, his main rival, in the Greyfriars church, Dumfries. Comyn died, allegedly stabbed in front of the al-

tar by Bruce. Bruce went to Scone, where he was proclaimed King. Edward I was enraged and set his best northern general against Bruce. It took some time for Bruce to get much support, which he sought and eventually found in the Highland Clans. Bruce allegedly hid in a cave from his pursuers. As he sat in the cave, he noticed a spider trying to spin a web in the corner of the cavern. The spider could not get its web to stick to the moist surfaces, but instead of quitting, it tried again until it finally had weaved a small section, adding more web each time According to the legend, this is where Bruce conceived the idea of taking Scotland one small section at a time. Eventually, Bruce waged a successful guerilla war against the English and their Scottish allies. Frost's mother was very fond of telling the legends of Bruce's exploits to her children.

28. "Keeper" is the name of one of the speakers in Frost's "A Masque of Mercy" (1947).

29. Cf. Matthew 5:18, from Christ's Sermon on the Mount: "For assuredly, I say to you, till heaven and earth pass away, one jot or one tittle will by no means pass from the law till all is fulfilled."

30. See 32r; 22.29r; 35.7r; 47.

31. See also 23r; 2.16r; 4; 6.22r; 8.56r; 14.17r; 15.33v; 20.11r, 16v; 21.4r, 7r; 22.49r; 24.24r, 47v; 28.10r; 31.4r, 7r, 7v, 40r; 32.7r, 10r; 34.1r, 2r, 2v; 41.7r; 47.

32. H. G. Wells (1866–1946) argued for the importance of the environment in child development and for the need to be continually improving it: "The newborn child is at first no more than an animal. Indeed, it is among the lowest and most helpless of all animals, a mere vegetative lump; assimilation incarnate—wailing. It is for the first day in its life deaf, it squints blindly at the world, its limbs are beyond its control, its hands clutch drowningly at anything whatever that drifts upon this vast sea of being into which it has plunged so amazingly. And imperceptibly, subtly, so subtly that never at any time can we mark with certainty the increment of its coming, there creeps into this soft and claimant little creature a mind, a will, a personality, the beginning of all that is real and spiritual in man. In a little while there are eyes full of interest and clutching hands full of purpose, smiles and frowns, the babbling beginning of expression and affections and aversions. Before the first year is out there is obedience and rebellion, choice and self-control, speech has commenced, and the struggle of the newcomer to stand on his feet in this world of men. The process is unanalyzable; given a certain measure of care and protection, these things come spontaneously; with the merest rough encouragement of things and voices about the child, they are evoked.

"But every day the inherent impulse makes a larger demand upon the surroundings of the child, if it is to do its best and fullest. Obviously, quite apart from physical consequences, the environment of a little child may be good or bad, better or worse for it in a thousand different ways. It may be distracting or over-stimulating, it may evoke and increase fear, it may be drab and dull and depressing, it may be stupefying, it may be misleading and productive of vicious habits of mind. And our business is to find just what is the best possible environment, the one that will give the soundest and fullest growth, not only of body but of intelligence." From *Mankind in the Making* (New York: Scribner's 1904) ch. IV, "The Beginning of Mind and Language," pp. 107–108. See 17.24v.

33. Cf. Frost's "Letter to the *Amherst Student*" (1935): "Whatever progress may be taken to mean, it can't mean making the world any easier a place in which to save your soul." See also 28.7r; 47.

34. See 15.23r; 19.3v.

35. See 4.27r; 22.8v; 31.32r.

36. Frost is most likely referring to Deuteronomy 1: 9–15: "And I spake unto you at the time, saying, I am not able to bear you myself alone: The Lord your God hath multiplied you, and, behold, ye are this day as the stars of heaven for multitude. (The Lord God of your fathers make you a thousand times so many more as ye are, and bless you, as he hath promised you!) How can I myself alone bear your cumbrance, and your burden, and your strife? Take you wise men, and understanding, and known among your tribes, and I will make them rulers over you. And ye answered me, and said, The thing which thou hast spoken is good for us to do. So I took the chief of your tribes, wise men, and known, and made them heads over you, captains over thousands, and captains over hundreds, and captains over fifties, and captains over tens, and officers among your tribes."

37. Pierre Abélard (1079–1142), French philosopher and noted tutor. His teacher was William of Champeaux (ca. 1070–1121). At some point, Abélard broke with William (they were both Aristotelians) over disputes on the nature of universals. Also see the letters between Abélard and Heloise which form a tragic tale of love and misunderstanding. While tutoring Heloise (d. ca. 1164), niece of Fulbert, canon of Notre Dame, he fell in love and put her with child. He then secretly married her and sought to keep her in a convent for temporary safe-keeping. Fulbert decided that Abélard had abandoned Heloise at the abbey and had him castrated. She then retired to convent.

38. See 8v; 4.21r; 22.33v; 47; 26.27r, 28r.

39. See 29v; 4.38r; 15.22r; 28.18r; 9.19r. See also Frost's "Kitty Hawk."

40. Frost gave a talk to Amherst seniors on May 28, 1935, called "Our Darkest Concern" about the dangers of the extreme political left and right. See also "On Emerson": "I don't like obscurity and obfuscation, but I do like dark sayings I must leave the clearing of to time. And I don't want to be robbed of the pleasure of fathoming depths for myself." See also 4.17r, 32v; 47; 23.3r, 4r, 5r; 28.15r; 22.6r; 24.39r.

41. Title of Frost's Commencement Address, Oberlin College, April 8, 1937. What follows appears to be notes related to that speech.

42. See 6.24r.

43. Ford Madox Ford (1873–1939). In the typescript of his speech "What Became of New England?" Frost simply referred to him as the "distinguished critic."

44. Joseph Henry Jackson (1894–1955), *Mexican Interlude*, (New York: Macmillan, 1936).

45. Brooks and Spengler are both critics that posit the cyclical nature of history and civilization against the idea of "decline." Oswald Spengler (1880–1936), German historian and philosopher; see *The Decline of the West* (2 vols., 1918–1922; trans. 1926–1928). Brooks Adams (1847–1927), American historian and the brother of Henry Adams. His theory that civilization rose and fell according to the growth and decline of commerce was first developed in *The Law of Civilization and Decay* (1895). Adams applied it to his own capitalistic age, of which he was a militant critic, but failed to find the universal law that he persistently sought. His ideas greatly influenced his brother Henry Adams, whose essays he edited in *The Degradation of the Democratic Dogma* (1919). In *America's Economic Supremacy* (1900), Brooks claimed that Western Europe had already begun to decline and that Russia and the United States were the only potential great powers left. His other chief works include *The Emancipation of Massachusetts* (1887), *The New Empire* (1902), and *The Theory of Social Revolutions* (1913).

46. George Santayana (1863–1952), Spanish philosopher who lived in the United States

and taught philosophy at Harvard with William James and Josiah Royce. Frost took classes with him when he was a special student from 1897 to 1899. Frost's arguments with Santayana's aestheticism are indicated here and in both 15.32r and 19.7v. *The Last Puritan* (1935) is a three-volume spiritual and intellectual autobiography.

47. See note 28.

48. This discussion continues throughout this notebook. See also 4.6r; 15.19v; 19.9r; 22.33v; 24.28r.

49. Spanish-American War (1898).

50. Cf. Frost's "West-Running Brook" (1928). See also 26r.

51. William James (1842–1910), philosopher, psychologist and Harvard professor. James was on leave during the years Frost studied under Santayana, though Frost read James' *Principles of Psychology* with Hugo Munsterberg and taught his *Psychology: The Briefer Course* at the Plymouth State Normal School in 1911. Here Frost refers to the empirical and inventive quality of James's version of pragmatism in which ideas become instruments enabling a satisfactory relationship with new experience. In the published version of this essay, Frost provides a slightly different version of his objections to Santayana: "And then you can form a religion like George Santayana. He lets you see that there is nothing but illusion, and it can be just as well one kind as another. There is illusion that you are unconscious of, and there is illusion that you become conscious of later . . . But you should go on right on anyway because there is no proof." See George Santayana, *Interpretations of Poetry and Religion* (1900).

52. In Roosevelt's January 4, 1939, address to Congress, he makes his first strong references to foreign threats: "Where freedom of religion has been attacked, the attack has come from sources opposed to democracy. Where democracy has been overthrown, the spirit of free worship has disappeared. And where religion and democracy have vanished, good faith and reason in international affairs have given way to strident ambition and brute force. An ordering of society which relegates religion, democracy and good faith among nations to the background can find no place within it for the ideals of the Prince of Peace. The United States rejects such an ordering, and retains its ancient faith." Roosevelt goes on to argue for the importance of his social reforms as a means to prepare the nation against the rise of dictatorships: "Our nation's program of social and economic reform is therefore a part of defense, a part as basic as armaments themselves . . ." Frost is also probably referring to the language concluding Roosevelt's May 16, 1940 "Message to Congress: "Our ideal, yours and mine, the ideal of almost any man woman and child in the country, our objective is still peace—peace at home and abroad. Nevertheless, we stand ready not only to spend millions for defense but to give our service and even our lives for the maintenance of our American liberties. Our security is not a matter of weapons alone. The arm that *wields* them must be strong, the eye that guides them clear, the will that directs them indomitable" (emphasis mine).

53. See also 14r; 2.16r; 4; 6.22r; 8.56r; 14.17r; 15.33v; 20.11r, 16v; 21.4r, 7r; 22.49r; 24.24r, 47r; 28.10r; 31.4r, 7r, 7v, 40r; 32.7r, 10r; 34.1r, 2r, 2v; 41.7r; 47.

54. See 4.9r; 22.22r; 26.28r.

55. See 22.1r, 47r; 12.10r; 37.2r; 7.3r, 4r; 33.9r; 8.58r, 58v; 1.34v; 17.41r; 19.8v; 24.38v.

56. In 1936, with Stalin's mass-murder spree or "purges" unabated, the Soviet government produced a new constitution. Nikolai Bukharin (1888–1938), the Secretary of the committee that drafted the new document, publicly stated that the goal was to return to a

"humanist" government. The new consititution promised universal suffrage, freedom of the press, of assembly, of public protest, and of worship. Furthermore, all Soviet citizens were granted due process in matters of arrest and security of their homes and papers. With much public debate in the press, many Western intellectuals, considering whether Hitler or Stalin was worse, were taken by the promise of the USSR's new constitution. Few in the USSR believed the constitution had any practical meaning but it certainly confused outsiders.

57. Chapter I, Article 4 of the 1936 Constitution of the USSR states: "The Socialist system of economy and the socialist ownership of the means and instruments of production firmly established as a result of the abolition of the capitalist system of economy, the abrogation of private ownership of the means and instruments of production and the abolition of the exploitation of man by man, constitute the economic foundation of the U.S.S.R."

58. Chapter I, Articles 9 and 10 of the 1936 Constitution: "Alongside the socialist system of economy, which is the predominant form of economy in the U.S.S.R., the law permits the small private economy of individual peasants and handicraftsman based on their personal labor and precluding the exploitation of the labor of others." "The right of citizens to personal ownership of their incomes from work and of their savings, of their dwelling houses and subsidiary household economy, their household furniture and utensils and articles of personal use and convenience, as well as the right of inheritance of personal property of citizens, is protected by law."

59. The closest reference Yeats makes to this in print is in *A Vision* (1925), which formulates seven rotating phases of life based upon 28 psychological types.

60. Cf. Frost's "West-Running Brook" (1928). See also 21r.

61. George Santayana (1863–1952). See note 29.

62. See 54r; 62r; 4.21r; 12.4r; 12r; 22.6r.

63. Henry VII (1457–1509) reigned from 1485 to 1509. The first Tudor monarch, he was a shrewd businessman who opened up trade with Netherlands but had extortionist policies at the end of his reign for which he was resoundingly criticized.

64. See 16v; 4.38r; 15.22r; 28.18r; 9.19r.

65. Rexford G. Tugwell (1891–1979) and Raymond Charles Moley (1886–1975) were two members of a group of Franklin Roosevelt's close advisors known as the "Brain Trust," because of their academic backgrounds. They worked closely with Roosevelt when he was governor of New York State and during his first years as President.

66. Publishing house founded in 1924. Publishers of Edith Wharton, Thomas Wolfe, F. Scott Fitzgerald, Ernest Hemingway, Bertrand Russell.

67. See 4.15r, 22r.

68. See 4.17r; 44.1r.

69. See 32r; 47.

70. See 13r; 22.29r; 35.7r; 47.

71. See 48.1r; 21.5r; 4.25r, 27r; 25.14v; 22.33v.

72. The name of a genus of orchids. See also Frost's "The Self-Seeker."

73. For Moses' delegation, see Deuteronomy 1:21–25: "Behold, the LORD thy God hath set the land before thee: go up *and* possess *it,* as the LORD God of thy fathers hath said unto thee; fear not, neither be discouraged. And ye came near unto me every one of you, and said, We will send men before us, and they shall search us out the land, and bring us

word again by what way we must go up, and into what cities we shall come. And the saying pleased me well; and I took twelve men of you, one of a tribe: and they turned and went up into the mountain, and came unto the valley of Eshcol, and searched it out. And they took of the fruit of the land in their hands, and brought it down unto us, and brought us word again, and said, it is a good land which the LORD our God doth give us."

74. See 4 1r; 33.cover, 3r; 25.4r; 1.1r; 26.27r; 28.12r; 47. See also Frost's poem "The Lesson for Today," Notebook 1, note 10.

75. In 1936, Frost was appointed Charles Eliot Norton Professor of Poetry at Harvard and delivered six lectures on "The Renewal of Words." No transcript of the lectures was ever found or produced. See also 26.2r; 38.5r.

76. D. H. (David Herbert) Lawrence (1885–1930), English novelist, short-story writer, poet and essayist.

77. These are two different quotations from the *Elegies* of Albius Tibullus (ca. 60–19 B.C.): "Spes alit agricolas" (Hope nourishes farmers), *Elegies* II vi. 21. Note that Frost changes the plural ending of *"agricolas"* here to the singular *"agricolam"* as he does when he uses the line as a saying to conclude "Something for Hope": "Patience may not nourish a cow or horse, / But spes alit agricolam 'tis said." "Miles et in mensa pingere castra mero" (A soldier can draw his camp on the table with wine), *Elegies* I x. 33. The context of the phrase is the lyric poet defining himself against battle: "So I may please you: let another be brave in war, / and topple hostile generals with Mars' help, / then he can tell me his military deeds while I drink, / and draw his camp on the table with wine."

78. Albert Einstein's theory of light quanta and his later demonstration of the fluctuations of "black body" radiation raised the paradox of wave-particle duality. This paradox led to the formulation by Werner Heisenberg (1901–1976) of the "uncertainty principle" or, more precisely, the principle of complementarity by which an observer can know the position *or* the direction of a particle but not both at once.

79. See 20.19v; 15.18v.

80. Anaxagoras of Clazomenae (ca. 500–ca. 428 B.C.E.). Presocratic Greek philosopher and member of what is now often called the Ionian School of philosophy.

81. Zeno (b. 488 BCE) was born in Elea, Italy, and accompanied his teacher Parmenides to Athens. Most of what is known about him is found in Aristotle's *Physics*, VI: 9. He expounded paradoxes of multiplicity and motion that can be illustrated by the analogy of an arrow having to travel through an infinite number of positions in order move from one point to another. Movement, therefore, becomes impossible. Frost sees an analogy between the notion of complementarity in modern physics and Zeno's paradox.

82. In Plato's *Ion*, Socrates asserts that "a poet is a light and winged thing, and holy, and never able to compose until he has become inspired, and is beside himself, and reason is no longer in him" (*Ion* 534b, tr. Lane Cooper). Therefore, he argues, poetry is not an art and not informed by knowledge but only by inspiration and is dependent on emotions.

83. Aristotle discusses katharsis in his *Poetics*.

84. Cf. Joshua 6:26.

85. A national disaster that occurred in 1899 when a dam broke in the steel manufacturing town of Johnstown, Pennsylvania. The flood not only leveled the town, but killed over 2,000 people. It took five years to rebuild the town with the help of contributions from citizens and organizations from around the nation.

86. See Percy Bysshe Shelley (1792–1822), "Ode to the West Wind" (1820). "Make me thy lyre, even as the forest is: / What if my leaves are falling, like its own! / The tumult of thy mighty harmonies / Will take from both a deep, autumnal tone, / Sweet though in sadness. Be thou, Spirit fierce, / My spirit! Be thou me, impetuous one!" (ll. 57–62).

87. See 4.13r; 23.8r.

88. Walter Duranty (1884–1957) was the chief Moscow correspondent for *The New York Times* from 1922–1944 and was awarded the Pulitzer Prize in 1932 for his dispatches on Stalin's five-year plan. His journalism has become notorious for its deliberate failure to report Stalin's atrocities. The exiled Leon Trotsky began attacking Duranty's reporting publicly in 1939. An apologist for Stalin's regime, Duranty has been credited with justifying the regime with the aphorism "You can't make an omelet without breaking eggs."

89. Leon Trotsky (1879–1940), a leader of the Bolshevik revolution in Russia. Lenin's second-in-command, he fell out of favor with the Communist Party on the death of Lenin. As one of the key intellectuals of the Russian Revolution, he continued to be admired by Western intellectuals, even as they broke with the Soviet Union when they learned of Stalin's horrific genocidal policies. Stalin had him banished to the outreaches of the Soviet Union. In exile in Mexico, Trotsky was murdered with an ice-pick.

90. William Shakespeare (1564–1616), *The Passionate Pilgrim*, XII: "Crabbed age and youth cannot live together: / Youth is full of pleasure, age is full of care; / Youth like summer morn, age like winter weather; / Youth like summer brave, age like winter bare. / Youth is full of sport, age's breath is short; / Youth is nimble, age is lame; / Youth is hot and bold, age is weak and cold;/ Youth is wild, and age is tame. / Age, I do abhor thee, youth, I do adore thee; / O! my love, my love is young: / Age, I do defy thee: O! sweet shepherd, hie thee, / For methinks thou stay'st too long."

91. See note 88 above.

92. See note 40.

93. See 28v, 62r; 4.21r; 12.4r, 12r; 22.6r

94. See 28v, 54r; 4.21r; 12.4r, 12r; 22.6r.

95. Genesis 5:29: "and he called his name Noah, saying, This *same* shall comfort us concerning our work and toil of our hands, because of the ground which the LORD hath cursed."

96. A variation on a line from Kipling: "We were led by evil counselors—the Lord shall deal with them" in "A Song of the English," *The Seven Seas* (1896). A variant of "A Song of the English" appeared in the *English Illustrated Magazine* in May 1893. Kipling does not directly express this sentiment about the Boers. However, it might be construed from Kipling's works: If the Boers realized that the English were bringing technology, railways, medicine, administration and justice as well as the glory of the Empire to them, they wouldn't put up a fight but would concede that assimilation into the Empire is best for all. See Kipling's chapter on "South Africa" in his autobiography, *Something of Myself, for My Friends Known and Unknown* (1936). See also E. David Gilmour's *The Long Recessional: The Imperial Life of Rudyard Kipling* (London: John Murray, 2002), chaps. 9 and 10 ("Rhodes and Milner" and "Lessons from the Boers").

97. A reference to Santayana's famous aphorism about history in *The Life of Reason*, Vol. I, *Reason in Common Sense*, pp. 82–83: "Progress, far from consisting in change, depends on retentiveness. When change is absolute there remains no being to improve and no direction is set for possible improvement: and when an experience is not retained, as among

savages, infancy is perpetual. Those who cannot remember the past are condemned to repeat it . . . Retentiveness, we must repeat, is the condition of progress."

98. This draft of a narrative poem evokes the black child Epaminondas of the children's
story "Epaminondas and His Auntie," made famous and published as a book by Sara Cone
Bryant in 1906

99. Cf. "Provide, Provide" (1934): "The Witch that came (the withered hag) / To wash
the steps with pail and rag, / Was once the beauty Abishag // The picture pride of Hollywood."

NOTEBOOK 30

1. See 31.58r.
2. See also 4.37r; 31.33v.

NOTEBOOK 31

1. Frost was poet in residence at many American colleges and universities. He virtually
invented the office.

2. Henry Clinton Morrison (1871–1945), a graduate of Dartmouth (1895), was Superintendent of schools in Portsmouth, New Hampshire, from 1899 to 1904. Morrison had
played an important role in helping Frost climb from a teaching post at Pinkerton Academy to the faculty of the New Hampshire Normal School in Plymouth. Harold Brown
was an assistant to Morrison from 1904 to 1907.

3. Emanuel Swedenborg (1688–1772), Swedish philosopher who influenced American
thought, including that of Ralph Waldo Emerson. Frost's mother was a convert to
Swedenborgism and Frost himself was baptized in the Swedenborgian church. Frost here
may be referring to Swedenborg's idea that we continue to live by our "ruling passions,"
whether in heaven or hell. See *Heaven in Its Wonders and Hell from Things Seen and Heard*
(1758), ch. 58; "Man after Death Is as Such as His Life Has Been in the World" (Swedenborg
Society, 1953, trans. J. C. Ager).

4. Possibly Herbert Kenny (1913–2002), a journalist for *The Boston Globe* who was a long-
time friend of Frost's.

5. Søren Kierkegaard (1813–1855), *Frygt og Bæven* (1843; tr. W. Lowrie, *Fear and Trembling*,
1941): "Or perhaps he did not do at all what the story tells, if perhaps because of the local
conditions of that day it was something entirely different, then let us forget him, for what
is the value of going to the trouble of remembering that past which cannot become a
present."

6. Cf. the last stanza of Frost's poem "The Trial by Existence" from *A Boy's Will* (1913):

'Tis of the essence of life here,
   Though we choose greatly, still to lack
The lasting memory at all clear,
   That life has for us on the wrack
Nothing but what we somehow chose;

Thus are we wholly stripped of pride
In the pain that has but one close,
  Bearing it crushed and mystified.

7. Carrie Nation (1846–1911), Prohibition activist, renowned for her symbolic ax-wielding against the bottle.

8. Frost's American publisher, Henry Holt & Co., New York, New York. That year Holt hosted a dinner party at the Waldorf-Astoria in New York City for his eightieth birthday and published *Aforesaid,* a new selection of his poems, in a limited edition of 650 copies.

9. The Holy Name Society is a Catholic organization whose origins date back to the fourteenth and fifteenth centuries. One of its central objectives is to suppress blasphemy and the use of profanity, unlawful swearing, or improper language.

10. See 12.22v, 23v; 22.30v; 39.8r; 5.26r.

11. See also 7r, 7v, 40r; 2.16r; 4; 6.22r; 8.56r; 14.17r; 15.33v; 20.11r, 16v; 21.4r, 7r; 22.49r; 24.24r, 47v; 28.10r; 29.14r, 23r; 32.7r, 10r; 34.1r, 2r, 2v; 41.7r; 47.

12. William Wordsworth, "My Heart Leaps Up" (1807).

My heart leaps up when I behold
  A rainbow in the sky;
So was it when my life began;
So is it now I am a man;
So be it when I shall grow old,
  Or let me die!
The Child is the father of the Man;
And I could wish my days to be
Bound each to each by natural piety.

13. Cf. Frost's poem "Kitty Hawk" (1962), ll. 298–303: "It belonged to US, / not our friends the Russ, / to have run the event / to its full extent / and have won the crown, / or let's say the cup." See also Frost's "The Future of Man" (1959): "The standing challenge—the great challenge—is of man's originality to his law and order, to his government. And that will always be the challenge—that of man's energy and daring and originality to his law and order. That means that looking ahead into the future with my eyes shut—I see government paired with government for championship of its era—to see after whom the period will be named, in this era for instance, us or the Russ. Unfortunately, we haven't a very good name for ourselves. All my South American friends object to our calling ourselves America—we shall have to call ourselves 'us,' to rhyme with 'Russ.'"

14. Cf. Frost's "The Figure a Poem Makes" (1939): "It begins in delight, it inclines to the impulse, it assumes direction with the first line laid down, it runs a course of lucky events, and ends in a clarification of life—not necessarily a great clarification, such as sects and cults are founded on, but in a momentary stay against confusion."

15. These lines purport to be skeptical of the underlying assumptions of the Special and General Theories of Relativity that, using non-Euclidean geometry, assume the inextricable relation of space and time in *spacetime,* the curvature of space and the ability of matter

to curve space, and the absolute constancy of the speed of light. See The first two stanzas of Frost's "Skeptic" from *Steeple Bush* (1947):

Far star that tickles for me my sensitive plate
And fries a couple of ebon atoms white,
I don't believe I believe a thing you state.
I put no faith in the seeming facts of light.

I don't believe I believe you're the last in space,
I don't believe you're anywhere near the last,
I don't believe what makes you red in the face
Is after explosion going away so fast.

16. Frost here describes the process of visible refraction, whereby at a greater distance only the longer wavelengths of light are visible, causing, among other things, a change in color, which explains why the sun looks red when it is low in the sky. With regard to the "universe dissipating," Frost may be referring to the advanced stellar stage known as the Red Giant. During this stage a dying star cools off and increases considerably in volume, despite losing most of its mass, and through gaseous reactions turns bright red.

17. See Frost's "A Masque of Mercy" (1948); 10r; 4.32r, 35r; 22.4r, 12r; 29.9r; 33.1r, IV; 24.32r; 21.11r; 26.12r, 13r; 19.6r; 23.8r, 9r.

18. Publius Helvius Pertinax (126–193 A.D.), Roman emperor who ruled for 87 days in 193 AD. He was both named and assassinated by members of the Praetorian guard. See also 13.16r; 24.22r; 35.

19. See 8r, 10r, 40r, 40v; 4.13r; 32; 37.1r, 5v, 6v; 22.10v; 13.8r; 12.7v; 9.10r; 24.39v; 21.4r, 7r; 27.29r, 43r, 44r; 1; 5; 47; 23.10r; 35.13r, 16r.

20. See 2.1r; 28.6v.

21. Cf. Frost's "The Future of Man" (1959): "I want to say another thing about the god who provides the great issues. He's a god of waste, magnificent waste. And waste is another name for generosity of not always being intent on our own advantage, nor too importunate even for a better world. We pour our libation to him as a symbol of the waste we share in—participate in. Pour it on the ground and you've wasted it; pour it into yourself and you've doubly wasted it. But all in the cause of generosity and relaxation of self interest." Four separate drafts of the 1959 talk survive, including an unpublished version.

22. See 24.46v; 14.4v; 47; 25.1r; 2.4v; 46.5r; 12.10r.

23. Epimenides, a prophet of Apollo, who as a herdsman fell asleep for 56 years and awoke with the gift of prophecy.

24. This discussion continues on 7v. See also 4r, 40r; 2.16r; 4; 6.22r; 8.56r; 14.17r; 15.33v; 20.11r, 16v; 21.4r, 7r; 22.49r; 24.24r, 47v; 28.10r; 29.14r, 23r; 32.7r, 10r; 34.1r, 2r, 2v; 41.7r; 47.

25. Igdrasil, or Yggdrasil. In Norse Mythology, Yggdrasil was the "World Tree," a gigantic tree (often suggested to be an ash, an interpretation generally accepted in the modern Scandinavian mind), thought to hold all of the different worlds: such as Asgard, Midgard, Utgard and Hel. The name literally means the 'horse of Yggr', i.e. the horse of Odin, since Yggr (meaning *Dreadful*) is one of Odin's many names. Three roots supported the trunk, with one passing through Asgard, one through Midgard and one through Hel. Beneath the Asgard root lay the sacred Well of Urd, and beneath the Midgard root lay the

spring or well of Mimir. The messenger in the tree (and thus between the worlds) was the squirrel, Ratatosk. In the top of the tree was perched a giant eagle (with a hawk upon its forehead) who blew the winds over the worlds with his mighty wings. The roots of Yggdrasil were gnawed at by a dragon, Nidhogg. Heidrun, a goat, lived on top of Yggdrasil and ate its leaves. See also "The Future of Man" (1959): "I wish the young people would relieve themselves of the responsibility of attending to the future of our height. There's nothing coming beyond us. The tree Yggdrasil has reached its growth."

26. See 9v; 7.4r; 10.9r; 4.48r; 14.1r, 2r, 11r; 22.8r, 12r, 17r, 18r; 24.44r; 15.3v; 39; 47; 19.5r, 5v, 9r; 23.4r.

27. Percy Bysshe Shelley (1792–1822). See also Frost's poem "Build Soil," Notebook 37, note 5.

28. For more on "hinting" see 43r–44v; 22.24r; 23.

29. See 7r, 10r, 40r, 40v; 4.13r; 32; 37.1r, 5v, 6v; 22.10v; 13.8r; 12.7v; 9.10r; 24.39v; 21.4r, 7r; 27.29r, 43r, 44r; 1; 5; 47; 23.10r; 35.13r, 16r.

30. George Lyman Kittredge (1860–1941), Harvard professor (1888–1936) and prolific literary critic. While a special student at Harvard (1897–1899), Frost studied English poetry with Kittredge.

31. Havelock Ellis (1859–1939), English physician and writer.

32. Richard Freiherr von Krafft-Ebbing (1840–1905), theorist who published on sexual aberration. See *Psychopathia Sexualis* (1886).

33. Romulus and Remus, refugees from Troy, twin brothers and mythic founders of Rome.

34. See 9r; 4.33v, 46r, 47v; 22.46r, 59r; 26.28r.

35. A Vizier is the chief minister or administrator of a Muslim ruler, especially of the Sultan of Turkey. See also "How Hard It Is to Keep from Being When It's in You and in the Situation," ll. 118–121: "'If you had been a king of royal blood, / You'd have rewarded me for all I've done / By making me your minister-vizier, / Or giving me a nobleman's estate.'"

36. See Esther 2, 6, 10. Mordecai was cousin to Esther. Esther married the Persian King Ahasuerus (Xerxes I or II). Mordecai and Esther foiled a plot to wipe out Jews.

37. St. Thomas Aquinas maintained a traditional Christian and Augustinian understanding of man but eradicated Neoplatonic elements from Christian theology in favor of the technical language of Aristotelian logic.

38. In the *Theologico-Political Treatise,* Baruch Spinoza (1632–1677) argued against those who attempted to save the appearances of phenomena in the Old Testament by arguing for their naturalistic accuracy. However, Spinoza did argue that a great deal of Hebrew wisdom literature, particularly Solomon, "absolutely agrees" with many aspects of "natural law" (*Theologico-Political Treatise,* tr. Elwes, IV, p. 32).

39. Einstein was greatly attracted to Spinoza's pantheism. In response to a question after a talk in a New York synagogue on April 24, 1921, Einstein said "I believe in Spinoza's God who reveals himself in the orderly harmony of what exists, not a God who concerns himself with the fates and actions of human beings."

40. Cf. the Conclusion of "Education by Poetry" (1930).

41. See 4.49r; 22.1r; 22.2r; 5.1r.

42. See 8r; 4.33v, 46r, 47v; 22.46r, 59r; 26.28r.

43. Frost was likely referring to the "Court Revolution of 1937." Oliver Wendell Holmes (1841–1935) had already retired from the Supreme Court by 1932 but his version of positivism and pragmatism lived on as more liberal justices (Louis Brandeis, Benjamin Cardozo, Harlan Fiske Stone, Hugo Black, Felix Frankfurter, William Douglas, and Robert Jackson) refused to block state and federal economic regulation in the name of individual economic rights. By 1938, the old battle lines between economic reformers and conservative judges were rapidly disappearing. The court declared that in regard to economic legislation, if Congress had the power to act in a particular area—such as the control of interstate commerce—judges would not question the wisdom of the measure. The pivotal point in the transformation came in the case of the *United States v. Carolene Products Co.* (1938), in which the Supreme Court announced that Congress had the power to regulate interstate commerce and that if it chose to set minimal standards for milk quality, that was the business of the legislative and not the judicial branch. Justice Harlan Fiske Stone added by an additional and pivotal footnote that the court may also examine statutes involving rights and civil liberties. Frost may have also had in mind the pro–organized labor legislation of the late 1930s including the Wagner Act (1935), which recognized the right of collective bargaining, and the Fair Labor Standards Act (1938), which set forth unprecedented federal authority over hours and wages.

44. See 7v; 7.4r; 37.9r; 4.48r; 14.1r, 2r, 11r; 22.8r, 12r, 17r, 18r; 24.44r; 15.3v; 39; 47; 19.5r, 5v, 9r.

45. Nikolai Vasilyevich Gogol (1809–1852), Russian playwright and novelist, author of *Dead Souls* (1842)

46. Cf. Frost's Poem "Maple" (1921), ll. 105–108: "She told him of a bookmark maple leaf / In the big Bible, and all she remembered / Of the place marked with it—'Wave offering, / Something about wave offering.'" A wave offering is an offering waved before the Lord; for example, in Numbers 5, 6, 18, and 30; Leviticus 7, 8, 9, 10, 14, and 23; Exodus 29.

47. See Frost's "Introduction to Edwin Arlington Robinson's 'King Jasper'" (1936): "Grievances are a form of impatience. Griefs are a form of patience."

48. The Latin term "quid-nunc" means "what now?" and indicates a gossip. Cf. Frost's "The Milky Way in a Cowpath," ll. 1–12:

On wings too stiff to flap
We started to exult
In having left the map
On journey the penult.

But since we got nowhere,
Like small boys we got mad
And let go at the air
With everything we had.

Incorrigible Quid-nuncs,
We *would* see what could come
Of pelting heaven with chunks
Of crude uranium.

See also 22.2r.

49. See Frost's "A Masque of Mercy" (1948); 6v; 4.32r, 35r; 22.4r, 12r; 29.9r; 33.1r, IV; 24.32r; 21.11r; 26.12r, 13r; 19.6r; 23.8r, 9r.

50. A variation of a line from "Escapist—Never" (1962): "A crooked straightness yet no less a straightness." Also, from "The Constant Symbol" (1946): "The mind is a baby giant who, more provident in the cradle than he knows, has hurdled his paths in life all round ahead of him like playthings given—data so called. They are vocabulary, grammar, prosody, and diary, and it will be too bad if he can't find stepping stones of them for his feet wherever he wants to go. The way will be zigzag, but it will be a straight crookedness like the walking stick he cuts himself in the bushes for an emblem." See also 15.9v; 14.5r.

51. Abigail (1744–1818) and John Adams (1735–1826). This entry and "A Murmur of Inner Voices" are in black ink.

52. In Nehemiah 13: 15–22, the prophet describes locking the gates of Jerusalem on the Sabbath to prevent the merchants from selling their wares.

53. Frost may be evoking the legend of Lilith, Adam's first wife, who was also known as "the screech owl" and had an owl's or bird's feet.

54. Frost may be thinking of the curse in Deuteronomy 28: 53–57 because it is repeated in Leviticus 26:29: "Because of the suffering that your enemy will inflict on you during the siege, you will eat of the fruit of the womb, the flesh of the sons and daughters the Lord your God has given you . . . The most gentle and sensitive woman among you—so sensitive and gentle that she would not venture to touch the ground with the sole of her foot— will begrudge the husband she loves and her own son or daughter the afterbirth from her womb and the children she bears. For she intends to eat them secretly during the sieges and in the distress that your enemy will inflict on you in your cities."

55. A thousand-year-old tradition of binding the feet of women in Chinese society that was officially ended in 1911.

56. Alfred Kinsey (1894–1956), author of *Sexual Behaviour in the Human Male* (1947) and *Sexual Behaviour in the Human Female* (1953).

57. Plato (427–347 B.C.) distinguished between eternal forms and their physical manifestations (see especially *Parmenides*). For his student Aristotle (384–322 B.C.), forms have no existence distinguishable from matter and things (See especially *Prior* and *Posterior Analytics* and *Metaphysics*). See also 31v.

58. See 31v; 12.9v; 13.8r; 22.18r, 32v.

59. William Wordsworth (1770–1850), last line of "My Heart Leaps Up" (1807).

60. Jean-Jacques Rousseau (1712–1778).

61. See Matthew 6:28: "And why take ye thought for raiment? Consider the lilies of the field, how they grow; they toil not, neither do they spin."

62. See 12.16r.

63. The twentieth and thirty-fifth American presidents, respectively, James A. Garfield (1831–1881) and Harry S. Truman (1884–1972). Garfield was president for one year (1881) before being assassinated. Truman served two terms in office (1945–1953). Both presidents had a reputation for attacking corruption in government.

64. See Mark 4:11–12: "Unto you it is given to know the mystery of the kingdom of God; but unto them that are without, all these things are done in parables: that seeing they may see and not perceive; and hearing they may hear and not understand; lest at any time they should be converted, and their sins should be forgiven them." See also 43.4r as well as Frost's "Directive" (1947): "I have kept hidden in the instep arch / Of an old cedar at the

waterside / A broken drinking goblet like the Grail / Under a spell so the wrong ones can't find it, / so can't get saved, as Saint Mark says they mustn't."

65. See Matthew 18:3: "And verily I say unto you, except ye be converted and become as little children, ye shall not enter the kingdom of heaven."

66. See note 39.

67. This is a draft of an incomplete and unpublished narrative poem. The narrator meets a man named Rice who has just slipped on the street. Rice is known as the Gold for Christmas Man because the company at which he worked forty years as furnace stoker paid him in gold the week of Christmas.

68. This is a draft of a letter Frost apparently never sent.

69. Frost's poem "The Ax-Helve," first published in *The Atlantic,* 1917.

70. Robert Maynard Hutchins (1899–1977), American educator, was the president of the University of Chicago from 1929 to 1951. He scorned vocationalism in education and emphasized broad study of great books.

71. Frost here may be referring to an article published March 22, 1940, in the *Oakland Post Esquire.* He is quoted in the article as saying he "never works, never has worked, and never will work" in remarks after receiving a honorary degree from the University of California, Berkeley. The article went on to say Frost did not believe in working hard.

72. Small terra-cotta statuettes of well-dressed young women in various positions, usually standing or sitting, dating primarily from the 3rd century B.C. The figurines are named after the site in Boeotia, in east-central Greece, where they were found. Boeotia was the scene of the Athenian defeat by the Spartans in 457 B.C. during the first Peloponnesian War.

73. A draft of Frost's essay "The Prerequisites," the Preface to *Aforesaid,* 1954.

74. Cf. Emerson's "Brahma," ll. 9–12.

75. Cf. Frost's "The Prerequisites": "A poem is best read in the light of all the other poems ever written."

76. See 11v.

77. See 11v; 12.9v; 13.8r; 22.18r, 32v.

78. See 24.34v.

79. Thomas Jefferson (1743–1826) and John Adams (1735–1826).

80. See 43.1r, 7r; 21.2r, 5r; 6.29v; 40.23v.

81. Cf. "The Prophets Really Prophesy as Mystics, the Commentators Merely by Statistics" (1962). See also 4.27r; 22.8v; 29.15r.

82. George Meredith (1828–1909), English novelist and poet. See Sonnet L from "Modern Love":

Thus piteously Love closed what he begat:
The union of this ever-diverse pair!
These two were rapid falcons in a snare,
Condemned to do the flitting of the bat.
Lovers beneath the singing sky of May,
They wandered once; clear as the dew on flowers:
But they fed not on the advancing hours:
Their hearts held cravings for the buried day.
Then each applied to each that fatal knife,
Deep questioning, which probes to endless dole.

Ah, what a dusty answer gets the soul
When hot for certainties in this our life!—
In tragic hints here see what evermore
Moves dark as yonder midnight ocean's force,
Thundering like ramping hosts of warrior horse,
To throw that faint thin line upon the shore!

83. Irwin Edman (1896–1954), philosopher, poet, professor of Philosophy at Columbia University 1920–54. Authored several philosophical texts and edited, among other things, *The Philosophy of Santayana* (1936).

84. See 43.5r; 47; 5.25r.

85. With Gen. Dwight D. Eisenhower in the White House (and Richard M. Nixon as his Vice-President), the Republicans gained control of the Congress in 1952. Although Eisenhower was re-elected in 1956, by 1954 the Republicans had again lost control of the Congress. And Nixon lost to John F. Kennedy in 1960 by one of the narrowest margins in the history of U.S. presidential elections.

86. Adlai Stevenson (1900–1965), two-time Democratic Presidential candidate in 1952 and 1956, became Kennedy's ambassador to the United Nations. When accused of being an "egghead," he retorted with the famously brilliant, "Eggheads of the world unite, you have nothing to lose but your yolks," a play on the last line of *The Communist Manifesto* which Frost refers to in the next sentence.

87. Cf. John Milton's Sonnet XIX, "On His Blindness," the final line: "They also serve who only stand and wait."

88. Brandeis University.

89. George Borrow (1803–1881). See 15.13r, 14r, 14v, 16r, 16v.

90. Oliver Cromwell (1599–1658), English military leader and politician. As a member of the Puritan sect of Parliament and a leader of the Parliamentarian cause against the monarchy, he commanded the New Model Army, or "Roundheads," during the English Civil Wars. In 1653, after defeating the armies of Charles II, Cromwell was named Lord Protector of England, Ireland, and Scotland, a position he served until his death.

91. Cf. "The Figure a Poem Makes" (1939): "It begins in delight, it inclines to the impulse, it assumes direction with the first line laid down, it runs a course of lucky events, and ends in a clarification of life—not necessarily a great clarification, such as sects and cults are founded on, but in a momentary stay against confusion." See also 4.37r; 30.6r.

92. Calvin Coolidge (1872–1933; President 1923–1929). In his *Foundations of the Republic* (1926), Coolidge wrote: "After all, the chief business of the American people is business . . . Of course, the accumulation of wealth cannot be justified as the chief end of existence. But we are compelled to recognize it as a means to well-nigh every desirable achievement. So long as wealth is made the means and not the end we not greatly fear it." Herbert Hoover (1974–1964; President 1929–1933) said in his Inaugural address of 1929: "The dangers to a continuation of this peace today are largely the fear and suspicion which still haunt the world. No suspicion or fear can rightly be directed toward our country . . . I have no fears for the future of our country." Franklin Delano Roosevelt (1882–1945; President 1933–1945) in his first inaugural address of 1933 said, most famously, "We have nothing to fear but fear itself." In his message to Congress of January 6, 1941, Roosevelt also said that "we look for-

ward to a world founded on the four basic human freedoms": freedom of speech and religion, and freedom from want and from fear.

93. Cf. note 16.

94. Progressive education took root in the late 19th and early 20th centuries in Europe and the United States as part of a broader "Progressive Movement," and is principally associated with the American theorist John Dewey. Dewey believed that philosophy and education worked in tandem in such a way that education was a laboratory of philosophy. Society, Dewey believed, should be interpreted to the child through daily living in the classroom, which acts as a miniature society, or a microcosmic democracy. Education leads to no final end; it is something continuous, "a reconstruction of accumulated experience," which should be directed toward social efficiency. Education becomes life itself, rather than a preparation for life.

95. Cf. "Self-Reliance": "A foolish consistency is the hobgoblin of little minds."

96. See 1.1r, 4r; 4.1r, 12r; 12.5r; 24.32v; 33.3r.

97. See also 4r, 7r, 7v; 2.16r; 4; 6.22r; 8.56r; 14.17r; 15.33v; 20.11r, 16v; 21.4r, 7r; 22.49r; 24.24r, 47v; 28.10r; 29.14r, 23r; 32.7r, 10r; 34.1r, 2r, 2v; 41.7r; 47.

98. Bishop James Usher (1581–1656), the Archbishop of Armagh. Usher calculated, counting backwards from biblical evidence, that the date of the world's creation was 4004 BC. His calculations were taken by some to be truth.

99. See 39.2v.

100. See 29.2r.

101. See 7r, 8r, 10r, 40v; 4.13r; 13.8r; 32; 37.1r, 5v, 6v; 22.10v; 12.7v; 9.10r; 24.39v; 21.4r, 7r; 27.29r, 45r, 46r; 1; 5; 47; 23.10r; 35.13r, 16r.

102. Ptolemy (fl. A.D. 127–48), a Greco-Egyptian philosopher, conceived of a geocentric universe while Nicholas Copernicus (1473–1543), a Polish astronomer, posited in *De revolutionibus orbium coelestium* a heliocentric universe. This latter system is one of the principal foundations upon which our modern understanding of astronomy is built. Johannes Kepler (1571–163) and Isaac Newton (1643–1727) both built on the Copernican system.

103. John 18:37–38: "Pilate therefore said unto him, Art thou a king then? Jesus answered, Thou sayest that I am a king. To this end was I born, and for this cause came I into this world, that I should bear witness unto the truth. Every one that is of the truth heareth my voice. / Pilate saith unto him, What is truth? And when he had said this, he went out again unto the Jews and saith unto them, I find in him no fault *at all*." The someone else may be Democritus to whom is attributed the saying "Of truth we know nothing, for truth lies at the bottom of the well." The someone else may also be Job 11:7, "Canst thou by searching find out God? Canst thou find out the Almighty unto perfection?"

104. Cf. Frost's "West-Running Brook" (1928): "The universal cataract of death / That spends to nothingness—and unresisted, / Save by some strange resistance in itself, / Not just a swerving, but a throwing back, / As if regret were in it and were sacred."

105. See Emerson's "Give All to Love" (1846), ll. 43–49: "Though thou loved her as thyself, / As a self of purer clay, / Though her parting dims the day, / Stealing grace from all alive; / Heartily know, / When half-gods go, / The gods arrive." See also 26.28r; 4.31r; 22.58v.

106. Cf. Frost's "On Emerson": "Loyalty is that for the lack of which your gang will shoot you without the benefit of trial by jury. And serves you right. Be as treacherous as you must be for your ideals, but don't expect to be kissed good-bye by the idol you go back on. We don't want to look foolish, do we?" See also 4.46r; 34.6v.

107. *Grex* in Latin means "herd" or "flock" and provides the root for English words such as "gregarious," "aggregate," "segregate" and "egregious," etc. See "A Constant Symbol" (1946): "The ruling passion in man is not as Viennese as is claimed. It is rather a gregarious instinct to keep together by minding each other's business. Grex rather than sex. We *must* be preserved from becoming egregious. The beauty of socialism is that it will end the individuality that is always crying out mind your own business. Terence's answer would be all human business is my business. No more invisible means of support, no more invisible motives, no more invisible anything. The ultimate commitment is giving in to it than an outsider may see what we were up to sooner and better than we ourselves." See also 4.1r; 22.49r; 47.

108. This discussion concerning hints continues through 44v. See also 8r; 22.24r; 23.

109. Benjamin Franklin (1706–1790). Frost refers here of course to the tale of Franklin conducting electricity experiments by flying a kite out in the rain in an attempt to prove that "lightning is an electrical discharge." See "The Self-Seeker" (1923) for mention of Franklin and his kite. Franklin wrote about his experiment in an essay for *The Pennsylvania Gazette,* October 19, 1752.

110. Cf. the first of Ovid's *Heroides,* in which Penelope imagines returning Greek veterans tracing on the table in wine the topography of Troy. See also *Ars Amatoria* (2.127ff), in which Ovid describes Ulysses on the beach drawing for Calypso plans in the sand relating to the war in Troy.

111. Cf. Milton's *Comus: A Masque* (1634). When Comus first appears in the poem he is accompanied by a "rout of Monsters, headed like sundry sorts of wilde Beasts, but otherwise like Men and Women, their Apparel glistring; they come in making a riotous and unruly noise, with Torches in their hands." See also 29n.77.

112. Cf. Matthew Arnold's (1822–1888) "The Scholar-Gypsy."

113. See 30.1r.

114. See Frost's poem "November" from *A Witness Tree* (1938) (originally published as "October" in *The Old Farmer's Almanac 1939* [1938]).

115. Honus Wagner (1874–1955), shortstop for the Lousville Colonels and Pittsburgh Pirates. Wagner was one of the first five players to be inducted into the Baseball Hall of Fame in 1936, and is considered one of baseball's greatest all-around players.

116. See 1.39r.

NOTEBOOK 32

1. Emma Goldman (1869–1940), anarchist, feminist, and labor advocate. In 1936, Goldman went to Spain to support the Spanish Revolution against Franco's fascism in the Spanish Civil War.

2. See 1.3r.

3. References to "waste" continue through the remainder of this notebook. See also 1;

4.13r; 31.7r, 8r, 10r, 40r, 40v; 37 1r, 5v, 6v; 22 10v; 13 8r; 12 7v; 9 10r; 24 39v; 21.4r, 7r; 27.29r, 45r, 46r; 5; 47; 23.10r; 35.13r, 16r.

4. This is an early draft of Frost's talk entitled "The Future of Man," delivered in 1959 at the Seagram's Building in New York on the occasion of the centennial of the publication of Darwin's *On the Origin of Species.*

5. This discussion continues through 10r. See also 2 16r; 4; 6 22r; 8 56r; 14 17r; 15.33v; 20.11r, 16v; 21.4r, 7r; 22.49r; 24.24r, 47v; 28.10r; 29.14r, 23r; 31.4r, 7r, 7v, 40r; 34.1r, 2r, 2v; 41.7r; 47.

6. Thomas Henry (T. H.) Huxley (1925–1895), English biologist who was called Darwin's "bulldog" for his staunch defense of the latter's theories. Herbert Spencer (1820–1903), English philosopher who describe a theory of progressive evolution distinct from Darwin's theory on the origin of species.

7. See 5.8r; 17.40r; 24.48r; 35.19r; 41.7r.

8. Francis Galton (1822–1911) was Darwin's half-cousin. He was a geographer, a polymath, and one of the founders of modern eugenics.

NOTEBOOK 33

1. See 3r; 4.1r; 29.38r; 25.4r; 1.1r; 26.27r; 28.12r; 47. See also Frost's poem "The Lesson for Today."

2. The Hicksites were an American Quaker faction following the liberal abolitionist Elias Hicks (1748–1830).

3. Cf. Christopher Smart (1722–1771), "A Song to David." Its final couplet reads: "And now the matchless deed's achiev'd, / Determined, Dared, and Done."

4. See Frost's "A Masque of Mercy" (1948); IV; 31.6v, 10r; 4.32r, 35r; 22.4r, 12r; 29.9r; 24.32r; 21.11r; 26.12r, 13r; 19.6r; 23.8r, 9r.

5. Elihu Vedder (1836–1923), American symbolist painter. Frost may be referring to one of his best-known paintings, "Lair of the Sea Serpent" (1864), which depicts a large sea snake on the sand dune of a deserted seashore.

6. Cf. Frost's "Pod of the Milkweed: (1954):

But waste was of the essence of the scheme.
And all good they did for man or god
To all these flowers they passionately trod
Was leave as their posterity one pod
With an inheritance of restless dream.
He hangs on upside down with talon feet
In an inquisitive position odd
As any Guatemalan parakeet.

7. See Cover; 4.1r; 29.38r; 25.4r; 1.1r; 26.27r; 28.12r; 47. See also Notebook 1, note xx.

8. See 1.1r, 4r; 4.1r, 12r; 12.5r; 24.32v; 31.39r.

9. See 4.9r, 10v, 42r; 47; 31.10r; 22.15r.

10. See 4.22r; 8.37r; 17.25r; 22.8r, 8v; 24.31r; 28.10r; 29; 35.7r; 47.

11. This is a draft of "A Never Naught Song" from *In the Clearing* (1962).

12. See 22.1r, 47r; 12.10r; 37.2r; 7.3r, 4r; 8.58r, 58v; 1.34v; 17.41r; 19.8v; 24.38v; 29.23r.

NOTEBOOK 34

1. "La Noche Triste" was Frost's first published poem. It appeared in the Lawrence High School *Bulletin,* April 1890.

2. This discussion continues through 2v. See also 2.16r; 4; 6.22r; 8.56r; 14.17r; 15.33v; 20.11r, 16v; 21.4r, 7r; 22.49r; 24.24r, 47v; 28.10r; 29.14r, 23r; 31.4r, 7r, 7v, 40r; 32.7r, 10r; 41.7r; 47.

3. This is a draft of the unfinished poem "Loyalty in a Time Like This."

4. See 4.46; 31.41v.

5. Cf. T. S. Eliot's "The Hollow Men" (1925).

NOTEBOOK 35

1. Publius Helvius Pertinax (126–193 A.D.), Roman emperor who ruled for 87 days in 193 A.D. Frost continues this discussion on Pertinax and his successor, Didius Julianus, throughout this notebook. *Pertinax* is, additionally, a Latin adjective meaning "thoroughly tough" or "tenacious." Here Frost seems to be referring both to the person and to the word. See also Frost's poem "Pertinax" as well as 31.7r; 13.16r; 24.22r.

2. The Praetorians were responsible for the murder of Pertinax. Their camp also became the site of an auction for the throne of emperor in the wake of Pertinax's death as Flavius Sulpicianus and Didius Julianus attempted to outbid each other in the size of their donatives to the troops. When Didius Julianus won the throne with a bid of 5,000 sesterces, he was allowed into the camp and proclaimed emperor. How Didius Julianus seized the throne, through the "Auction of the Empire," proved to be the most memorable event in his two-month reign.

3. See 22.29r; 29.13r, 32r; 47.

4. See 4.22r; 8.37r; 17.25r; 22.8r, 8v; 24.31r; 28.10r; 29; 33.5r; 47.

5. See 16r; 4.13r; 31.7r, 8r, 10r, 40r, 40v; 32; 37.1r, 5v, 6v; 22.10v; 13.8r; 12.7v; 9.10r; 24.39v; 21.4r, 7r; 27.29r, 45r, 46r; 1; 5; 47; 23.10r; 35.13r.

6. See 4.46r.

7. See 13r; 4.13r; 31.7r, 8r, 10r, 40r, 40v; 32; 37.1r, 5v, 6v; 22.10v; 13.8r; 12.7v; 9.10r; 24.39v; 21.4r, 7r; 27.29r, 45r, 46r; 1; 5; 47; 23.10r; 35.13r.

8. See 5.8r; 17.40r; 24.48r; 32.10r; 41.7r.

9. Epicurus (341?–271 B.C.E.), Hellenistic philosopher who taught materialist metaphysics, empiricist epistemology, and hedonistic pleasure as tranquility. His work became the basis for the Roman poet Lucretius's (94–55 B.C.E.) poem *De Rerum Natura* (On the Nature of Things). Cf. Frost's poems in *Steeple Bush* (1947) "Too Anxious for Rivers" and "Lucretius Versus the Lake Poets."

10. Pelagius (ca. 354–ca. 420/440), ascetic Christian monk and reformer who denied the doctrine of original sin from Adam and was declared a heretic by the Catholic Church.

11. This appears to be a draft of "Old Gold for Christmas." See also 31.16r, 34r, 47r; 40.2r.

NOTEBOOK 36

1. Cf. Frost's "Escapist—Never" (1962), l. 10: "His life is pursuit of a pursuit forever."

NOTEBOOK 37

1. This line recurs throughout this notebook. See also 1 and 47.

2. References to "waste" continue throughout this notebook. See also 31.7r, 8r, 10r, 40r, 40v; 32; 4.13r; 22.16v; 13.8r; 12.7v; 9.10r; 24.39v; 21.4r, 7r; 27.29r, 45r, 46r; 1; 5; 47; 23.10r; 35.13r, 16r.

3. See 22.1r, 47r; 12.10r; 7.3r, 4r; 33.9r; 8.58r, 58v; 1.34v; 17.41r; 19.8v; 24.38v; 29.23r.

4. Cf. Milton's "Lycidas," l. 4. See also 23.v.

5. Cf. Frost's poem "How Hard It Is from Being King When It's in You and in the Situation" (1951), l. 194: "The only certain freedom's in departure."

6. See 47.

7. See 7.4r; 4.48r; 31.7v, 9v; 14.1r, 2r, 11r; 22.8r, 12r, 17r, 18r; 24.44r; 15.3v; 39; 47; 19.5r, 5v, 9r. See also Frost's poem "Build Soil" from *A Further Range* (1936), ll. 201–205: "We are balls, / We are round from the same source of roundness. / We are both round because the mind is round, / Because all reasoning is in a circle. / At least that's why the universe is round."

8. Cf. Frost's essay "On Emerson" (1959): "In practice, in nature, the circle becomes an oval. As a circle, it has one center—Good. As an oval, it has two centers—Good and Evil. Thence, monism and dualism."

NOTEBOOK 38

1. Cf. Frost's "New Hampshire" (1923), l. 79: Frost here refers to the mystery surrounding the origin of Cain's wife.

2. See 26.2r and 26, note 20.

3. In 1936, Frost was appointed Charles Eliot Norton Professor of Poetry at Harvard and delivered seven lectures, the first of which was titled "The Renewal of Words." No transcript of the lectures was ever found or produced. See also 26.2r; 29.40v.

4. Cf. "The Figure a Poem Makes," preface to *Collected Poems, 1939*.

NOTEBOOK 39

1. See 4.8v, 15r; 23.10r.

2. This is a draft of "Peril of Hope," a 12-line poem first published in *In the Clearing* in 1962.

3. See 7.4r; 37.9r; 4.48r; 31.7v, 9v; 14.1r, 2r, 11r; 22.8r, 12r, 17r, 18r; 24.44r; 15.3v; 47; 19.5r, 5v, 9r.

4. See 31.40r

5. This is an early draft of an unfinished poem that Frost called "Homology." It appears to have been planned for inclusion in *In the Clearing* but remained in typescript.

6. Cf. Frost's poem "The Ax-Helve" (1917).

7. See 12.22v, 23v; 22.30v; 31.4r; 5.26r.

NOTEBOOK 40

1. See 32.16r, 23r. This is a fragment of a draft of "Old Gold for Christmas," an unpublished poem.

2. Here and on 15r, 16r, 16v, and 40v appear what seem to be titles and corresponding page numbers for an edition of selected poems.

3. See 43.1r, 7r; 31.32r; 21.2r, 5r; 6.29v.

4. This is the beginning of a draft of Frost's last published poem, "The Prophets Really Prophesy as Mystics, the Commentators Merely by Statistics," published in *Poetry* (October/November 1962).

5. On October 14, 1947, the Air Force pilot Chuck Yeager (1923–) broke the sound barrier over the town of Victorville, California.

NOTEBOOK 41

1. Frost published "For John F. Kennedy His Inauguration Gift Outright of 'The Gift Outright' (With some preliminary history in rhyme)" in newspapers immediately following Kennedy's inauguration on January 20, 1961. Frost's prose preface entitled "A New England Tribute" was published in early January, prior to the inauguration, in the official program for the inaugural ceremonies. Frost's dedicatory poem of 42 lines was published in the *New York Times* on January 21, 1961, and later as a 77-line poem in a 4-page leaflet issued by El Al Airlines on March 9, 1961 (to commemorate Frost's flight to Tel Aviv). Frost did not read the prefatory poem at the inauguration and said only "The Gift Outright." The poem was also published in *In the Clearing* (1962). Nothing in the poem that follows this page ("Before the headsman takes you to the zone") was included in the published dedicatory poem.

2. See 5.8r; 17.40r; 24.48r; 32.10r; 35.19r.

3. See also 2.16r; 4; 6.22r; 8.56r; 14.17r; 15.33v; 20.11r, 16v; 21.4r, 7r; 22.49r; 24.24r, 47v; 28.10r; 29.14r, 23r; 31.4r, 7r, 7v, 40r; 32.7r, 10r; 34.1r, 2r, 2v; 47.

NOTEBOOK 42

1. This poem was first published in David A. Sohn and Richard Tyre, *Frost: The Poet and His Poetry* (New York: Holt, 1967).

2. Kay Morrison, Frost's secretary.

3. This is an early draft of "Auspex," which was first published in Elizabeth Shepley Sergeant's *Robert Frost: The Trial by Existence* (New York, 1960). The poem was written prior to December 16, 1953, the date Frost inscribed it in a copy of *Complete Poems, 1949*.

4. This poem was first published in *The Times Literary Supplement*, September 17, 1954, although Frost inscribed a copy of it into *Complete Poems, 1949* in 1952.

5. This is a draft of "The Draft Horse," which was first published in *In the Clearing* (1962). Frost told Lawrance Thompson (*Robert Frost: The Years of Triumph*, p. 673) that the poem was written about 1920.

NOTEBOOK 43

1. See 6r; 15.28v; 45.1r; 47; 28.11r; 4.34r, 36r; 22.53r; 26.2r; 47.

2. See 7r; 31.32r; 21.2r, 5r; 6.29v; 40.23v.

3. See "Education by Poetry: A Meditative Monologue" (1931): "I have been where I

came near getting up and walking out on the people who thought that they had to talk against nations, against nationalism, in order to curry favor with internationalism. Their metaphors are all mixed up. They think that because a Frenchman and an American and an Englishman can all sit down on the same platform and receive honors together, it must be that there is no such thing as nations. That kind of bad thinking springs from a source we all know. I should want to say to anyone like that: 'Look! First I want to be a person. And I want you to be a person, and then we can be as interpersonal as you please. We can pull each other's noses—do all sorts of things. But, first of all, you have got to have the personality. First of all, you have got to have the nations and then they can be as international as they please with each other.'"

4. Socrates' scolding wife.

5. See 24.30r; 3.1r; 28.20r; 20.19v; 22.31r. The phrase "domestic science" also appears in *The Future of Man* (unpublished version, 1959).

6. Cf. Frost's "Our Hold on the Planet" (1940).

7. Thales of Miletus (62?–546 B.C.), Greek natural philosopher and astronomer.

8. Plato, *Protagoras:* "The most ancient and fertile homes of philosophy among the Greeks are Crete and Sparta, where are to be found more Sophists than anywhere on earth. But they conceal their wisdom like the Sophists Protagoras spoke of, and pretend to be fools, so that their superiority over the rest of Greece may not be known to lie in wisdom, but seem to consist in fighting and courage. Their idea is that if their real excellence became known, everyone would set to work to become wise. By this disguise they have taken in the pro-Spartans in other cities, who to emulate them go about with bruised ears, bind their hands with thongs, take to physical training, and wear short cloaks, under the impression that these are the practices which have made the Spartans a great power in Greece; whereas the Spartans, when they want to resort freely to their wise men and are tired of meeting them in secret, expel all resident aliens, whether they be sympathizers with the Spartan way of life or not, and converse with the Sophists unbeknown to any foreigners . . ." (342b, translated by W. K. C. Guthrie).

9. Mark 4:11–12 : "And he said unto them, Unto you it is given to know the mystery of the kingdom of God: but unto them that are without, all these things are done in parables / That seeing they may see, and not perceive; and hearing they may hear, and not understand; lest at any time they should be converted, and their sins should be forgiven them." See also 31.14r as well as Frost's "Directive" (1947): "I have kept hidden in the instep arch / Of an old cedar at the waterside / A broken drinking goblet like the Grail / Under a spell so the wrong ones can't find it, / So can't get saved, as Saint Mark says they mustn't."

10. Also the line from Frost's "Mending Wall" (1923). It is not clear whether Frost is attributing this saying to the Spartans or mentioning it as a type of the laconic saying. The sayings of the Spartans were collected in Plutarch's *Moralia.* "Good fences make good neighbors" is nowhere attributed to the Spartans. In fact, the Spartans viewed the need for walls as a sign of weakness. However, Plato recounts a more figurative Spartan philosophy of walls: "If men must have a wall of sorts, they should construct their own dwellings from the outset in such a fashion that the town forms one unbroken wall, every dwelling house being readily defensible by the uniformity and regularity with which all face the streets. Such a town, with its resemblance to one great house, would be no unpleasing spectacle . . ." (*Laws* 779b, translated by A. E. Taylor). See also 31.32v; 47; 5.25r.

11. Lionel Johnson (1867–1902), "By the Statue of Charles at Charing Cross," stanza ix: "Brief life and hapless? Nay: / Through death, life grew sublime. / Speak after sentence? Yea: / And to the end of time."

12. See 1r; 15.28v; 45.1r; 47; 28.11r; 4.34r, 36r; 22.53r; 26.2r; 47.

13. The peace created by Britain's global domination of the 19th century.

14. See 1r; 31.32r; 21.2r, 5r; 6.29v; 40.23v.

NOTEBOOK 44

1. See 4.17r; 29.32r.

2. The second of Frost's lost Norton Lectures at Harvard was titled "Vocal Imagination—The Merger or Form and Content." See also 22.7r; 24.31r; 26.2r.

3. Discussion of "voice" and "tones of voice" continues throughout this notebook. See also 22.7v; 45; 13.9v; 12; 15.13r; 26. 2r; 47; 8.15r, 32r.

4. See 22.7r; 8.49v; 44.3v.

5. See 20.1r.

6. Milton, "Comus," ll. 78–79. Frost quotes these lines in "From Plane to Plane" (1948), 134. Line is written vertically on the left-hand side of the page, from bottom to top, in blue ink.

7. William Butler Yeats, "The Rose of the World," l. 1.

8. Cf. "Poetry and School," *Atlantic Monthly*, June 1951: "For my pleasure I had as soon write free verse as play tennis with the net down." Thompson notes: "Efforts to determine when and where RF first uttered the statement, 'I would as soon play tennis without a net as write free verse,' have not been successful, but after the initial occasion, RF repeated the remark in many of his public lectures until the end of his life."

9. Alfred, Lord Tennyson, *Ulysses* (1842). Frost's four lines present a very slight variation to the first lines of Tennyson's poem: "It little profits that an idle king, / By this still hearth, among these barren crags, / Matched with an aged wife, I mete and dole / Unequal laws unto a savage race, / That hoard, and sleep, and feed, and know not me."

10. Robert Browning, "Soliloquy in a Spanish Cloister," l. 1.

11. Browning, "Fifine at the Fair," l. 1. In talks, Frost often quoted this poem extensively from memory.

12. Rudyard Kipling, "Mandalay," l. 43.

13. Frost may be referring to John Livingston Lowes (1867–1945), the American literary scholar and critic, who became known for making intricate connections between the author's reading at a particular moment and his work. Lowes wrote extensively on Coleridge. See also 47.

14. Cf. Frost's "Snow" (1916).

15. Cf. Ezra Pound's essay "A Retrospect."

NOTEBOOK 45

1. See 4.51r; 17.30v; 24.28v; 19.1r.

2. See 15.28v; 43.1r, 6r; 47; 28.11r; 4.34r, 36r; 22.53r; 26.2r; 47.

3. See 22.8r; 26.2r; 44; 13.9v; 12; 15.13r; 47; 8.15r, 32r.

4. See 8.18v; 9.15r; 12.15v; 47.

5. Cf. Andrew Marvell (1621–1678), "The Garden."

6. Cf. Coventry Patmore (1823–1895), "Magna Est Veritas" ("Great is the truth," from the phrase "Great is the truth and it prevails"). See also 47.

7. Probably John Cournos (1881–1966), Russian-born novelist and friend of Frost's who wrote essays on Frost that Frost offered to help get published in the United States. Early exchanges of letters with Frost discuss intonation. See, for example, Frost's letter to him of July 8, 1914: "It is as simple as this: there are the very regular preestablished accent and measure of blank verse; and there are the very irregular accent and measure of speaking intonation. I am never more pleased than when I can get those into strained relation. I like to drag and break the intonation across the metre as waves first comb and then break, stumbling on the shingle."

NOTEBOOK 46

1. All challenged and irritated the Puritan community of Massachusetts in the early 17th Century. Ann Hutchinson (1591–1643) was considered dangerous because of her radical antinomianism. Thomas Morton (1579–1647) was an Anglican lawyer who outraged Puritans by erecting an 80-foot Maypole at his home at Merry Mount and staging revels to Eros. Roger Williams (1613–1683), an advocate of religious tolerance, was banished from Massachusetts for his democratic church reforms.

2. "If all the sovereigns of Europe were to set themselves to work, to emancipate the minds of their subjects from their present ignorance and prejudices, and that, as zealously as they now endeavor the contrary, a thousand years would not place them on that high ground, on which our common people are now setting out."—Thomas Jefferson to George Wythe, 1786. See also Frost's "The Black Cottage" (1928): " . . . She had seen Garrison / And Whittier, and had her story of them. / One wasn't long in learning that she thought, / Whatever else the Civil War was for, / It wasn't just to keep the States together, / Nor just to free the slaves, though it did both. / She wouldn't have believed those ends enough / To have given outright for them all she gave. / Her giving somehow touched the principle / That all men are created free and equal. / And to hear her quaint phrases—so removed / From the world's view today of all those things. / That's a hard mystery of Jefferson's. / What did he mean? Of course the easy way / Is to decide it simply isn't true. / It may not be. I heard a fellow say so. / But never mind, the Welshman got it planted / Where it will trouble us a thousand years."

3. John Curtis Marshall (1776–1835), the first Chief Justice of the U.S. Supreme Court.

4. John Churchill, first duke of Marlborough (1650–1722), perhaps among the finest of England's great soldiers and diplomats. Impoverished, though not of completely humble origin, he rose remarkably through the social and military ranks. His service was unusual in that he successfully served under four monarchs: Charles II, James II, William, and Anne.

5. See 24.46v; 31.7r; 14.4v; 47; 25.1r; 2.4v; 12.10r.

6. An Algonquin Indian word that has come to mean one who acts and thinks independently and which was initially recorded in 1663 by John Eliot for his Indian Bible. In Algonquin the word referred to a chief or other individual of high rank, but in 1884 it described a Republican who left the party by refusing to support presidential candidate James G. Blaine in favor of the Democrat Grover Cleveland.

NOTEBOOK 47

1. See 15.28v; 43.11r, 6r; 45.11r; 28.11r; 4.34r, 36r; 22.53r; 26.2r; 47.

2. See 22.8v; 26.2r; 44; 45; 13.9v; 12; 15.13r; 8.15r, 32r.

3. See 8.18v; 9.15r; 12.15v; 45.2r.

4. Upon his return to America from England in 1915, Frost bought a farm in Franconia, New Hampshire. He sold it in 1920. See also 10.1v; 24.11r.

5. See 4.16r; 15.11r.

6. A variation of this phrase appears later in this notebook. See also 4.32r; 24.39v, 43v, 44r; 14.15r; 19.5v; 27.7r.

7. Frost gave a talk to Amherst seniors on May 28, 1935, called "Our Darkest Concern" about the dangers of the extreme political left and right. See also "On Emerson": "I don't like obscurity and obfuscation, but I do like dark sayings I must leave the clearing of to time. And I don't want to be robbed of the pleasure of fathoming depths for myself." See also 4.17r, 32v; 23.3r, 4r, 5r; 28.15r; 22.6r; 29.17r; 24.39r.

8. Karl Marx (1818–1883). Edward Bellamy (1850–1898) is a novelist best known for *Looking Backward: 2000–1887* (1888). Chicopee refers to Chicopee Falls, Massachusetts, where Bellamy lived.

9. See 4.11r; 22.17r; 28.6v.

10. See 26.6r; 20.22r; 24.41v; 29.9r.

11. Cf. Frost's "Education by Poetry" (1935): "What I am pointing out is that unless you are at home in the metaphor, unless you have had your proper poetical education in the metaphor, you are not safe anywhere. Because you are not at ease with figurative values: you don't know the metaphor in its strength and its weakness. You don't know how far you may expect to ride it and when it may break down with you . . . All metaphor breaks down somewhere. That is the beauty of it." See also 24.29r; 21.7r; 20.16r.

12. Cf. "How Hard It Is to Keep from Being King When It's in You and in the Situation," *In the Clearing* (1963): "Freedom is slavery some poets tell us. / Enslave yourself to the right leader's truth, / Christ's or Karl Marx', and it will set you free. / Don't listen to their play of paradoxes. / The only certain freedom's in departure." See also 37.9r.

13. Charlotte Mary Yonge (1823–1901), *The Books of Worthies, Gathered from the Old Histories and Now Written Anew* (London, 1869). Cf. "The Future of Man," the unpublished version (1959): "And the best description of us is the humanities from of old, the book of the worthies and unworthies. The passing science of the moment may contribute its psychological bit to the book like one of the fleeting elements recently added to the chemical list. As one of the humanities itself, it is jealous for their dignity and importance."

14. See 37.9r.

15. Cf. Frost's "Kitty Hawk" (*In the Clearing*, 1963), ll. 213–224:

Pulpiteers will censure
Our instinctive venture
Into what they call
The material
When we took that fall
From the apple tree.
But God's own descent
Into flesh was meant

As a demonstration
That the supreme merit
Lay in risking spirit
In substantiation.

16. Robert Clive, Baron Clive of Plassey (1725–1774), governor of Bengal. He secured several key victories for the British that ensured the domination of the British East India Company against the Dutch and French. He is said to have fought against corruption in the Colonial and native administrations. On his return to England, he was accused of embezzlement. Cleared of the charges, he nevertheless committed suicide.

17. See 1.1r; 24.14r.

18. See 4.22r; 8.37r; 17.25r; 22.8r, 8v; 24.31r; 28.10r; 29; 33.5r; 35.7r.

19. In 1846, while living at Walden, Henry Thoreau refused to pay a poll tax for some supplies in protest for the use of tax revenues to support slavery and the U.S. war against Mexico. He was jailed for one night. Someone paid the tax for him but he insisted on remaining in jail on principle and wrote "On Civil Disobedience." See also 15.38r.

20. In Plato's *Ion*, Socrates challenges Ion to consider whether a poet *(rhapsode)* or charioteer will be a better judge of the lines about charioteers from a passage from Homer. (*Ion*, 537c). In Socrates' view, the charioteer, or the specialist, will always be the better judge. The general point is that poets and rhetoricians have no specialized knowledge of true things or things in themselves but only the ability to manipulate their audiences by inspiration (Plato, *Ion*, 537c). Elsewhere in Plato, particularly in *The Republic* (Book X), but also in the *Gorgias*, Socrates casts doubt on the poet's ability to discover eternal truths rather than to make or manipulate the beliefs of his audience (*Gorgias*, 455).

21. Robert Burns (1759–1796), Scottish poet. See the following lines from "Address to the Devil": "Then you, ye auld, snick-drawing dog! / Ye cam to Paradise incog, / An' played on a man a cursed brogue, / (Black be your fa'!) / An' gied the infant warld a shog, / 'Maist ruined a'" (1.91–96).

22. William Shakespeare, *Julius Caesar* (1623), Act II, Scene iii.

23. A long fertile plain in Attic Greece connected by a main road to Athens. The scene of two famous battles, the first in ca. 545 BC and the second in 490 BC when the Athenians, along with other Greeks, first defeated Persia.

24. Frost may be referring to Rudyard Kipling's story "The Incarnation of Krishna Mulvaney" (1899), a farcical take on the British Raj in which an Irish soldier, himself of mixed birth, crosses cultural boundaries in colonial India.

25. Cf. "Departmental," *A Further Range* (1936): "Then word goes forth in Formic: / 'Death's come to Jerry McCormic, / Our selfless forager Jerry. / Will the special Janizary / Whose office it is to bury / The dead of the commissary / Go bring him home to his people.'"

26. Palgrave entitled stanza xvi of the Third Canto of Sir Walter Scott's *Rokeby* (1813) "The Outlaw" and included it in his *Golden Treasury* (1875). Frost refers to the tradition of the outlaw ballad in Scottish literature which appears to have its written origins with Robin Ballads in the fourteenth century. Quiller-Couch in his *The Oxford Book of Ballads* (1910) included some of these outlaw ballads. Frost owned at least three editions of Percy: *Bishop Percy's Folio Manuscript, Percy Folio of Old English Ballads and Romances,* and *Reliques of Ancient Poetry.*

27. Among variants and derivations: OE Hwéol. OFris. Hwêl. In Modern French "Huile" n.f. is the equivalent of the English "oil."

28. Frost wrote to Louis Untermeyer in an unpublished letter of 1915: "If I must be classified a poet, I might be called a Synechdochist, for I prefer the synechdoche in poetry— that figure of speech in which we use a part for the whole." See also 19.9r; 24.41v; 9.8r; 8.36, 105.

29. The Levellers were English political reformers active 1645–1649 whose ideas influenced the English Bill of Rights (1689) and the United States Constitution.

30. Tiberius Sempronius Gracchus (d. 133 B.C.) and Caius Sempronius Gracchus (d. 122 B.C.), brothers, Roman statesmen, and social reformers who championed the redistribution of wealth and land.

31. The Albigenses were a neo-Manichean religious sect that flourished in southern France during the 12th century. They opposed the authority of the Catholic Church and held to the heresy that there were two mutually opposed principles of good and evil in the creation of the world. See also 4.3r.

32. John Gower (1330?–1408), a poet of three languages. His *Vox clamantis* (ca. 1382) is concerned with social justice and peasant revolt. His English work, *Confessio amantis* (1390), is an allegory of courtly and Christian love. Like Chaucer (and with whom he was friends), he helped develop English poetic style by borrowing from the French language.

33. John Bull, the English equivalent of Uncle Sam, first appeared as a character in John Arbuthnot's *The History of John Bull* (1712). He is usually depicted in cartoons as an honest farmer figure. See also 4.3r.

34. See 29.8v, 16r; 4.21r; 22.33v; 26.27r, 28r.

35. See 29.6r, 8v; 4.21r; 22.33v; 25.1r; 26.27r.

36. Cf. Frost's "An Equalizer" from *A Witness Tree* (1938).

37. See 4.1r, 21r, 24r; 29.8v; 26.28r.

38. Cf. Frost's "Our Doom to Bloom" (1962). See also elsewhere in this notebook as well as 29.6r, 32r.

39. See 23.9r; 4.21r; 29.8v.

40. See 22.29r; 29.13r, 32r; 35.7r.

41. See 4.22r.

42. See 4.33r.

43. See 29.8v; 22.20r.

44. See elsewhere in this notebook as well as 29.6r, 32r.

45. See 7.4r; 37.9r; 4.48r; 31.7v, 9v; 14.1r, 2r, 11r; 22.8r, 12r, 17r, 18r; 24.44r; 15.3v; 39; 19.5r, 5v, 9r.

46. See 29.14r, 15r; 28.7r; 4.37r.

47. Cf. title to Frost's poem "Happiness Makes Up in Height for What It Lacks in Length" from *A Witness Tree* (1942).

48. Cf. Frost's couplet, "Precaution," *A Further Range* (1936): "I never dared be radical when young / For fear it would make me conservative when old."

49. See 4.9r, 10v, 42r; 33.3v; 31.10r; 22.15r.

50. See 4.17r, 32v; 23.3r, 4r, 5r; 28.15r; 22.6r; 29.17r; 24.39r.

51. Cf. Frost's "A Masque of Reason." See also 1.11r; 4.1r; 29.38r; 33.cover, 3r; 25.4r; 26.27r; 28.12r.

52. See 4.42r; 15.24v; 19.9v; 22.6r.

53. Cf. Shakespeare's Sonnet 116, l. 8 "It is the star to every wandering bark / Whose worth's unknown, although his height be taken." Also, Frost's "Choose Something Like a Star" (1947).

54. The fifth of Frost's lost Norton Lectures at Harvard, delivered April 8, 1936, was titled "Before the Beginning of a Poem." See also 26.2r.

55. James Shirley (1596–1666), poet and playwright. "Death the Leveler" is from the *Contention of Ajax and Ulysses for the Armor of Achilles* (1659).

56. A variation of this phrase appears earlier in this notebook. See also 24.39v, 43v, 44r; 14.15r; 19.5v; 27.7r.

57. Cf. John Keats's sonnet "On First Looking into Chapman's Homer," ll. 11–14: "Or like stout Cortez, when with eagle eyes / He stared at the Pacific—and his men / Look'd at each other with a wild surmise— / Silent, upon a peak in Darien." Frost thus probably refers to Keats's uncorrected error in which he identifies Cortez as the discoverer of the Pacific, rather than Ferdinand de Balboa (1513).

58. See 31.32v; 43.5r; 5.25r.

59. Percy Bysshe Shelley (1792–1822), *Epipsychidion* (ca. 1821).

60. Vachel Lindsay (1879–1931). Perhaps from "Springfield Town Is Butterfly Town": "Here butterflies have their pony / Who can go beyond their range, / Into regions they / Consider strange. / They mount his curly / Pegasus mane / And fly past the North Pole. / Or he wings through / Smoking craters, / Emerging gay and whole. / Only a few can cling unsigned / All the way and back / From the big sun, from the far stars / On his accustomed track."

61. Cf. Frost's "Home Burial," ll. 17–19: "But at last he murmured, 'Oh,' and again, 'Oh.' / 'What is it—what?' she said. / 'Just that I see.'"

62. See elsewhere in this notebook as well as 4.42r; 15.24v; 19.9v; 22.6r.

63. Frost here seems to be paraphrasing Albert Einstein's axiom: "Great men talk about ideas; mediocre men talk about things; small men talk about other men."

64. Here Frost plays with the rhetoric of I Corinthians 13:13. See also *A Constant Symbol* (1946): "The ruling passion in man is not as Viennese as is claimed. It is rather a gregarious instinct to keep together by minding each other's business. Grex rather than sex. We *must* be preserved from becoming egregious." See 4.1r; 31.42r; 22.49r.

65. See 24.46v; 31.7r; 14.4v; 25.1r; 2.4v; 46.5r; 12.10r.

66. See 15.28v; 43.1r, 6r; 45.1r; 28.11r; 4.34r, 36r; 22.53r; 26.2r; 47.

67. See 29.10r. See also Frost's poem "Build Soil," Notebook 29, note 21.

68. Cf. Frost's lecture at the Browne and Nichols School, "The Unmade Word, or Fetching and Far-Fetching" (1918). See also 8.15r; 26.8r.

69. John Livingston Lowes (1867–1945), literary critic and Harvard professor, whose works include *The Road to Xanadu* (1927), a study of Coleridge; during a conversation with Frost, Lowes is reported to have said that poetry "is one texture of quotations" written out of all the books a poet has read, and "it is my pleasure to come after you and trace it to its sources." See Frost's uncollected poem that begins "Lowes took the obvious position" (1930). See also 44.6r

70. Cf. Matthew 22.21, in which Jesus says, "Render therefore unto Caesar the things which are Caesar's; and unto God the things that are God's."

71. Cf. "A Masque of Reason" (1945), ll. 194–196: "Look at how far we've left the current

science/ Of Genesis behind. The wisdom there though,/ Is just as good as when I uttered it." See also 24.30r, 41v, 44v.

72. See 15.28v; 43.11r, 6r; 45.11r; 28.11r; 4.34r, 36r; 22.53r; 26.2r; 47.

73. See 14.15r; 24.43v, 44r; 19.5v.

74. See also 2.16r; 4; 6.22r; 8.56r; 14.17r; 15.33v; 20.11r, 16v; 21.4r, 7r; 22.49r; 24.24r, 47v; 28.10r; 29.14r, 23r; 31.4r, 7r, 7v, 40r; 32.7r, 10r; 34.1r, 2r, 2v; 41.7r;.

75. See 4.13r; 31.7r, 8r, 10r, 40r, 40v; 32; 37.1r, 5v, 6v; 22.10v; 13.8r; 12.7v; 9.10r; 24.39v; 21.4r, 7r; 27.29r, 45r, 46r; 1; 5; 23.10r; 35.13r, 16r.

76. See 7.3v; 9.20r; 20.10r.

77. John Masefield (1878–1967), "Sea Fever" from *Saltwater Ballads.*

78. Robert Louis Stevenson (1850–1894), "Romance."

79. Bliss Carman (1861–1929), "The Joys of the Road."

80. Rudyard Kipling (1865–1936), "L'Envoi."

81. Lionel Johnson (1867–1902), "By the Statue of Charles at Charing Cross"

82. Gordon Bottomley (1874–1947), "To Iron Founders and Others" (1908).

83. Arthur William Edgar O'Shaughnessy (1844–1881), "The Fountain of Tears."

84. Margaret L. Woods (1856–1945), "The Mariners."

85. Wilfrid Scawen Blunt, "The Desolate City."

86. Algernon Charles Swinburne (1837–1909), "Hesperia."

87. Sydney Dobell (1824–1874), "Return!"

88. John Davidson (1857–1909), "A Runnable Stag."

89. "The Blessed Damozel," an oil painting by Dante Gabriel Rossetti (1828–1882).

90. William Morris (1834–1896), "The Sailing of the Sword."

91. Alfred, Lord Tennyson (1809–1892), "The Lady of Shalott."

92. Jean Ingelow (1820–1897), "The High Tide on the Coast of Lincolnshire."

93. Robert Louis Stevenson (1850–1894), "Christmas at Sea."

94. Wilfrid Wilson Gibson (1878–1962), "Flannan Isle."

95. Cf. Coventry Patmore (1823–1895), "Magna Est Veritas" ("Great is the truth," from the phrase "Great is the truth and it prevails"). See also 45.2v.

96. Frederick Locker-Lampson (1821–1895), "At Her Window."

97. Christina Rossetti (1830–1894), "Italia, Io Ti Saluto!"

98. Francis Thompson (1859–1907), "Daisy."

99. John Millington (J. M.) Synge (1871–1909), "A Question."

100. James Elroy Flecker (1884–1915), "Riouperoux."

101. William Henry Davies (1871–1940), "Leisure."

102. William Ernest Henley (1849–1903), "England, My England."

NOTEBOOK 48

1. See 25.14v; 29.34r; 21.5r; 4.25r, 27r; 22.33v.

Acknowledgments

The publishers acknowledge the libraries that own the various notebooks. For Notebooks 3 and 8: Clifton Waller Barrett Library of American Literature, Special Collections, University of Virginia Library, Papers of Robert Frost. For Notebooks 7 and 23: Paul C. Richards Collection of Robert Frost, The Harold Gotlieb Archival Research Center, Boston University. For all other notebooks: Rauner Special Collections Library, Dartmouth College Library. Library call numbers are listed with each notebook.

I am very grateful for the support of Peter Gilbert and the Estate of Robert Lee Frost in this undertaking. Philip Cronenwett of the Brundy Library at MIT, formerly of the Dartmouth College Library, was immensely helpful in navigating the complexities of the Frost archive, as was Jay Satterfield, who currently oversees the Rauner Library at Dartmouth. Sarah Hartwell, Hazen Alien, Eric Esau, and Peter Carini made working there a pleasure. I am particularly grateful to Joshua Shaw for his expertise, patience, and humor and to Morgan Campbell for her efforts under pressure. Edward Connery Lathem has been an invaluable resource and friend in tracking down files and sources. I am also indebted to Michael Plunckett of the University of Virginia and, as always, John Lancaster of Amherst College for advice and encouragement. Mariah Sakrejda-Leavitt of the Amherst College Library also provided invaluable assistance.

My colleagues Jonathan Barron, Mark Richardson, Lisa Seale, and Donald Sheehy have shared much and make studying Frost an ongoing adventure. I am also very appreciative of the pioneering work of John Ridland, who saw the importance of Frost's notebooks long before many were attentive to their richness. Robert Mezey has long known the riches of Frost's archives and generously shared his insights and resources.

I also wish to thank the National Endowment for the Humanities for a Fellowship that permitted me time to work on this project, and Claremont McKenna College for a sabbatical and other research funding. Lindsay Waters and Jennifer Snodgrass of Harvard University Press have been immensely enthusiastic and insightful in seeing this project through its many stages. I have also benefited from the sure editorial guidance of Susan Abel and the advice and assistance of Phoebe Kosman.

Over the last five years, I have been ably assisted in proofreading and research at various stages by David Mehnert, Nicholas Moschovakis, and Ivan Lincir. Nick Goodhue's sharp eye was there in the home stretch. Connie Bartling of Claremont McKenna College has been a constant help in getting so many things done. But I am especially grateful to Timothy Geaghan, who in the last year has been indispensable in every aspect of the edition's creation.

The support of friends old and new has been a rewarding part of this venture. Anne Crewe, Nick Warner, Paul Muldoon, Jean Korelitz, Charles Moore, Pia Sorenson, Anjani Thomas, Leonard Cohen, and John Farrell were there on the road and back.

Nothing would have been possible without the love and support of my family—my daughter, Tamar, and my wife, Alison, who waited long and patiently to watch the waters clear.

Index

DATE DUE